PRAISE FOR THE FIRST NEW TESTAMENT

"Jason BeDuhn . . . has produced the most generally accessible, comprehensive, and useful edition of Marcion's scriptures. Without yielding a centimeter of scholarly high ground, BeDuhn writes with considerable ease and sharp clarity as he maneuvers through the miasma of textual reconstruction. An undergraduate could read and comprehend this book. BeDuhn is so thorough and judicious that those who may wish to attempt to refute him could do so on the bases of the data and materials he has provided."
—*Review of Biblical Literature*

"In this bold undertaking, Jason BeDuhn sets forth, for the first time, a complete English translation of the Bible of Marcion. With a useful introduction to all relevant issues, a readable translation of this First New Testament, and copious notes supporting each textual decision, BeDuhn has provided a work of scholarship that is sure to be both welcomed and controversial. For historians of early Christianity, this will be a book to be reckoned with."
—Bart D. Ehrman, *University of North Carolina at Chapel Hill*

"This is an important book that fills a large gap in the resources needed for the study of second-century Christianity and Marcion in particular. It is an exhaustive examination of the relevant sources and a masterful, methodologically sensitive, treatment of Marcion's significance."
—Joseph B. Tyson, *Southern Methodist University*

"A comprehensive and impressively documented scholarly study of Marcion's original compilation of sacred scriptures . . . an essential contribution to personal and academic Christian Studies collections."
—*Midwest Book Review*

"Carefully researched and well argued, this book belongs on the shelf of any serious student of Early Christian canon formation. BeDuhn offers an English translation of Marcion's New Testament, exhaustively extracted from Early Christian writers. It should become a classic in scholarly studies and a benchmark in New Testament analysis."
—Patricia Walters, *Rockford University*

"BeDuhn's *The First New Testament* is a formidable contribution to scholarship on early Christianity. With the industry, insight, and independence characteristic of all his work, BeDuhn has collected from scattered fragments, translated, and annotated the actual text of Marcion's New Testament, enabling others the opportunity for a fresh evaluation of this pivotal second-century leader. A remarkable accomplishment."
—Luke Timothy Johnson, *Emory University*

". . . a provocative and groundbreaking contribution to the long discussion of Marcion. *The First New Testament* upends many standard 'facts' in the field of New Testament and early Christian studies, such as the long-standing claim that Marcion's Christian Bible contained texts 'mutilated' to conform to his distinctive beliefs. Anyone interested in the earliest recoverable forms of the New Testament texts needs to pay attention to this sharp and original study."
—J. Albert Harrill, *The Ohio State University*

". . . a very important book. Using text-critical tools, BeDuhn reconstructs the scope and shape of Marcion's New Testament. BeDuhn's argument that the reconstructed text of Marcion shows no evidence of an ideological redaction will prompt important conversations within the discipline. This book is a 'must have' for scholars and students of the New Testament and early Christianity."
—Perry Kea, *University of Indianapolis*

"Can we discover the first New Testament? Jason BeDuhn thinks so, and he relies upon Marcion to do it. Rather than getting bogged down in overly technical details, BeDuhn recovers Marcion's New Testament from the available evidence and teases out the implications for reconstructing early Christianity. To this end, BeDuhn recounts what we can know of Marcion's project, but, more importantly, he offers his translation of Marcion's gospel and Apostolikon of the letters of Paul, providing extensive notes on their sources. This volume provides a rich supply of evidence that will need to be seriously weighed in continuing study of the New Testament as text and canon."
—Stanley E. Porter, *McMaster Divinity College*

"*The First New Testament: Marcion's Scriptural Canon* is an outstanding high quality historical research and analysis for the sources of Marcion's theology and his New Testament canon. This book is an excellent example of how historical research should be undertaken and it is an important contribution to our understanding of early Christianity. I thoroughly recommend *The First New Testament: Marcion's Scriptural Canon* to all teachers and students of early Christianity and New Testament textual critics."
—Don Barker, *Macquarie University*

THE FIRST
NEW TESTAMENT

THE FIRST NEW TESTAMENT

MARCION'S SCRIPTURAL CANON

Jason David BeDuhn

POLEBRIDGE PRESS
Salem, Oregon

Dedicated to William R. Schoedel

Cover: P[69] (P. Oxy 2383). Image courtesy of the Egypt Exploration Society and Imaging Papyri Project, Oxford. Used by permission.

Copyright © 2013 by Jason D. BeDuhn

All rights reserved. Printed in the United States of America. No part of this book may be used or reproduced in any manner whatsoever without written permission except in the case of brief quotations embodied in critical articles and reviews. For information address Polebridge Press, Willamette University, 900 State Street, Salem, OR 97301.

Cover and interior design by Robaire Ream

Library of Congress Cataloging-in-Publication Data
BeDuhn, Jason.
  The First New Testament : Marcion's Scriptural Canon / by Jason David BeDuhn.
    pages cm
  Includes bibliographical references and index.
  ISBN 978-1-59815-195-4
  1. Bible. New Testament--Criticism, interpretation, etc.--History--Early church, ca. 30-600. 2. Marcion, of Sinope, active 2nd century. I. Title. II. Title: Marcion's Scriptural Canon.
  BS2350.B43 2013
  225.092--dc23

2013027059

Contents

Preface ix

List of Abbreviations xi

Introduction 3

Chapter 1: Marcion 11

Chapter 2: Marcion's New Testament 25

Chapter 3: The Evangelion
    Introduction 65
    The Evangelion 99
    Text Notes 128

Chapter 4: The Apostolikon
    Introduction 203
    The Apostolikon
        To Galatians 229
        To Corinthians 1 233
        To Corinthians 2 242
        To Romans 246
        To Thessalonians 1 250
        To Thessalonians 2 251
        To Laodiceans 252
        To Colossians 255
        To Philippians 258
        To Philemon 259
    Text Notes 260

Chapter Notes 321

Bibliography 363

Index 383

Preface

In my second semester as a college freshman at the University of Illinois, some thirty years ago, I took William Schoedel's course in the New Testament. One day, I was in the classroom somewhat early, when Prof. Schoedel came into the room, and eased his lanky frame into the desk beside me. He turned to me with a look of bemused curiosity, and said, "You've got it." He went on to explain that the paper I had recently handed in had all the hallmarks of competent biblical scholarship expected of a graduate student, and that once I had mastered the pertinent languages, I would be on my way in the field. It was a gesture typical of the generous character of this remarkable man, and its significance to me can be measured by my clear recollection of that day after all these years. I went on to enjoy many more classes and conversations with Prof. Schoedel. He was just as kind with regard to my bravely attempted failures as he was congratulatory of my occasional achievements. Most of all, he made me feel a part of the academic fold, comfortable enough to actually spar with him on questions of early Christian history. My audacity in doing so was enabled by his patient mentorship. In fact, I was surrounded by such generous mentors in those days: Gary Porton, Vernon Robbins, Valerie Hoffman. Their ability to make me feel part of a grand enterprise astonishes me today when I think back to how undeveloped I was as a thinker and, in many ways, as a person. I had many possible futures back then. The warmth and openness of the community of scholarship they showed me is largely responsible for my choice of this profession.

Most of my work has focused on relatively later historical subjects than those that interested Prof. Schoedel, and I sensed in a later conversation that my choice came as something of a disappointment to him. Truth be told, at the time I found biblical studies a bit crowded, and leapt all the way to the third and fourth centuries to work on the little known and less understood Manichaean tradition. My venture out into the study of radically different claims to the legacy of Jesus, such as that entailed in Manichaeism, has brought a fresh angle to my biblical research, and helped me to see how deeply buried the first Christian centuries remain beneath later orthodoxies. In fact, it now appears to me that we are at the beginning, rather than the end, of serious historical investigation of Christian, and biblical, history unfettered by entrenched assumptions that in many cases have passed into modern scholarship directly from prior theologically-motivated judgments. So when I found my research leading, by a natural progression of problems, back into Prof. Schoedel's own beloved second century and the question of the first emergence of the New Testament into history, my thoughts inevitably turned back to him and his role in inspiring me down this course. As I have worked on this project, he has been my imagined interlocutor, raising objections, cautioning against over-reaching, and intoning in my ears the dicta of Carneades, Ockham, and Sherlock Holmes. And so it is to him that I dedicate this book.

It took a decade between the inception of this project and its publication, and over that time it went through many transformations as I sought the right balance between the needs and interests of different potential readers. I wish to thank Larry Alexander, publisher of Polebridge Press, for his faith in me and his enthusiasm and support for the book. The level of meticulous detail involved here is a copy-editor's nightmare, and I am left truly astonished by, and deeply grateful to, Cassandra Farrin for her patient, temperate perfectionism. As always, I must thank the intrepid staff of Northern Arizona University's Cline Library Document Delivery Services for the many challenging requests to which I subjected them. I am particularly fortunate for the friendship I have enjoyed with my colleagues in the Religious Studies program here in Flagstaff over the last fifteen years: Arne Hassing, Bruce Sullivan, Paul Donnelly, and Lodewijk Peter van der Loo, as well as the late Wayne Mahan. Finally, and most importantly, I wish to express my gratitude to my study companion, Zsuzsanna Gulácsi, working away on her projects at her desk as I work at mine in the beautiful home we have made together in the northern Arizona forest.

Abbreviations and Sigla

Abbreviations

1,2 Chr	1,2 Chronicles
1,2 Clem	1,2 Clement
1,2 Cor	1,2 Corinthians
1,2 Thess	1,2 Thessalonians
Adam (Ad)	Adamantius, *Dialogue on the True Faith in God*
Adam* (Ad*)	Indicates either that a Marcionite gave the quotation, or that Adamantius is expressly quoting from a Marcionite text
Carmen adv. Marc. (CaM)	*Carmen adversus Marcionitas*
ClH	The Pseudo-Clementine *Homilies*
Clement, *Paed.*	Clement of Alexandria, *Paedagogus*
Clement, *Strom.* (ClS)	Clement of Alexandria, *Stromata*
Col	Colossians
CSyr	Curetonian Syriac version
Deut	Deuteronomy
DialSav	Dialogue of the Savior
Diat	Diatesseron
Did	Didache
Didy	Didymus
Dig.	*Digesta*
Diogn	Letter to Diognetus
E	Indicates pages in the English translation of a work
Elenchos (*El.*)	*Elenchos* (pl. *elenchoi*) of Epiphanius, *Panarion*

Eph	Ephesians
Ephrem, *Paul*	Ephrem Syrus, *Commentarii in Epistolas d. Pauli* (Venice: Sanctus Lazarus, 1893)
Ephrem, *Hymns* (EH)	Ephrem Syrus, *Hymns against Heretics*
Ephrem, *Marc.* (EM)	Ephrem Syrus, *Against Marcion I, II, III*, page numbers refer to Mitchell (1921)
Ephrem, *Comm. Diat.* (ED)	Ephrem Syrus, *Commentary on the Diatesseron*
Epiphanius, *Pan.* (Ep)	Epiphanius, *Panarion* (*Refutation of All Heresies*)
Exod	Exodus
Eznik, *De Deo* (Ez)	Eznik of Kolb, *De Deo* ("On God")
Gal	Galatians
Gen	Genesis
Gk	Greek
GPet	Gospel of Peter
Hab	Habakkuk
Hegemonius, *Arch* (Ar)	Hegemonius, *Acts of Archelaus* (*Acta Archelai*)
Hippolytus, *Ref.* (Hip)	Hippolytus, *Refutatio omnium haeresium* (*Refutation of All Heresies*)
Eusebius, *Hist. eccl.*	Eusebius, *Historia ecclesiastica* (*Ecclesiastical History*)
Hos	Hosea
IgnMag	Ignatius to the Magnesians
IgnPhd	Ignatius to the Philadelphians
Irenaeus, *Haer.* (Ir)	Irenaeus, *Adversus Haereses* (*Against Heresies*)
Isa	Isaiah
Jer	Jeremiah
Jerome, *Comm. Gal.* (JrG)	Jerome, *Commentarium in Epistulam ad Galatas libri III*
Jerome, *Vir. ill.*	Jerome, *De viris illustribus*
Josephus, *Ant.*	Josephus, *Jewish Antiquities*
Josephus, *J.W.*	Josephus, *Jewish War*
Justin, *1 Apol.*	Justin Martyr, *First Apology*
Justin, *Dial.*	Justin Martyr, *Dialogus cum Tryphone*
Lev	Leviticus
LXX	Septuagint (the Greek OT)

Matt	Matthew
ms(s)	manuscript(s)
NT	New Testament
OL	Old Latin version
Origen, *Cels.* (OrC)	Origen, *Contra Celsum* (*Against Celsus*)
Origen, *Comm. Jo.* (OrJ)	Origen, *Commentarium in evangelium Joannis*
Origen, *Comm. Matt.*	Origen, *Commentarium in evangelium Matthaei*
Origen, *Comm. Rom.* (OrR)	Origen, *Commentarii in Romanos*
Origen, *Fr. 1 Cor.* (Or1)	Origen, Catena Fragments on 1 Corinthians, page numbers refer to Cramer (1842)
Origen, *Fr. Luc.* (OrL)	Origen, *Fragments on Luke*, page numbers refer to Raur (1998)
Origen, *Hom. Ezech.* (OrEz)	Origen, *Homiliae in Ezechielem*
Origen, *Princ.* (OrP)	Origen, *De principiis*
OT	Old Testament
P^{69}	Papyrus 69 (POxy 2383)
Phil	Philippians
Philastrius, *Div. her.* (PhH)	Philastrius of Brescia, *Diversarum hereseon liber*
PolPhil	Polycarp to the Philippians
POxy	Oxyrhynchus Papyrus
Ps.-	pseudo-
Ps.-Clement, *Hom.* (ClH)	Pseudo-Clementine *Homilies*
Ps.-Eph A (PsE)	Pseudo-Ephrem A
Ps.-Tertullian, *Adv. haer.*	Pseudo-Tertullian, *Adversus omnes haereses*
Ps(s)	Psalm(s)
Q	*Quelle* ("source")
Rom	Romans
Scholion (Sch.)	*Scholion* (pl. *scholia*) of Epiphanius, *Panarion*
SCopt	Sahidic Coptic version
SSyr	Sinaitic Syriac version
Tertullian, *Marc.* (T)	Tertullian, *Adversus Marcionem* (*Against Marcion*)
Tertullian, *Carn. Chr.*	Tertullian, *De carne Christi* (*The Flesh of Christ*)
Tertullian, *Idol.*	Tertullian, *De idololatria* (*Idolatry*)

Tertullian, *Ieiu.*	Tertullian, *De ieiunio adversus psychicos* (*On Fasting, against the Psychics*)
Tertullian, *Praescr.*	Tertullian, *De praescriptione haereticorum* (*Prescription against Heretics*)
Tertullian, *Prax.*	Tertullian, *Adversus Praxean* (*Against Praxeas*)
Tertullian, *Pud.*	Tertullian, *De pudicitia* (*Modesty*)
Tertullian, *Paen.*	Tertullian, *De paenitentia* (*Repentance*)
Tertullian, *Res.*	Tertullian, *De resurrectione carnis* (*The Resurrection of the Flesh*)
Thom	Gospel of Thomas

Sigla

≠	Disagreement with previous reconstruction by . . .
=	Partial agreement with previous reconstruction by . . .
>	Indicates a Greek word that a Latin term translates
. . .	Additional material likely existed, but cannot be confirmed
(parentheses)	English supplied to clarify the Greek
[brackets]	Connective content necessary for the directly attested material to have coherent meaning
Italics	Indicates a variant that does not correspond with witnesses to the catholic New Testament

Photo: P[69] (P. Oxy 2383), a possible fragment of Marcion's gospel text. Image courtesy of the Egypt Exploration Society and Imaging Papyri Project, Oxford. Used by permission.

Introduction

Many modern Christians think of the New Testament as a book outside of history, something that was just suddenly there. Historians of Christianity, able to trace its gradual authorship and formation, nonetheless typically find themselves describing this development as an anonymous process, a spontaneous evolution accomplished by the nameless and faceless members of ancient communities of faith.[1] Historians often resort to this story of collective group action to provide an account of historical developments for which we do not have enough information to fix names and dates to key personal decisions, shifting individual alliances, or local revolutions. But when it comes to the origin of the New Testament, we ought to do better, and we can. We know the name of the individual responsible for the first New Testament, the circumstances of his work in compiling it, and even a date that relates to his momentous decision to establish a textual foundation for the fledgling Christian communities of his time: 144 CE. More than that, we actually know the bulk of the content of this First New Testament.

Modern New Testaments are based upon thousands of manuscripts, most copied many centuries later than the First New Testament. The oldest relatively complete New Testament manuscripts date to the first half of the fourth century CE. Incomplete portions of earlier New Testament collections survive in fragmentary papyri from about a century earlier, the early third century. With a little ingenuity, reconstructions culled from the quotations of early Christian writers can be pushed back about as far. It is largely on the basis of these sources that the modern New Testament is edited and translated. But there is an older New Testament, reconstructible to the same degree as those early third-century manuscripts and sources, but dating back another century earlier to the mid-second century, and so to within a generation or two of the original composition of the texts themselves. This earliest New Testament is contemporaneous with the oldest tiny scrap of Christian writing surviving today, but it must be recovered from the comments made about it by later writers. Nevertheless, we have it, in large part. We can expect to find no earlier New Testament in any form, for in fact it is the very first New Testament ever to have been made.

Historians of Christianity widely acknowledge that Marcion (circa 95–165 CE)[2] compiled the first authoritative collection of distinctly Christian writings from texts already known and valued by segments of the Christian movement. In doing so, he defined for the first time a biblical *canon*—that is, in the useful distinction made by Bruce Metzger, not just a "collection of authoritative books," such as a circulating set of Pauline letters, but an "authoritative collection of books," with set limits that clearly signaled a unique status for the texts included.[3] Marcion clearly intended his First New Testament to serve as the touchstone of Christian belief and practice at a time when these were still quite fluid and conveyed in a primarily oral environment. Although we cannot be sure that Marcion himself ever referred to this collection as the "New Testament" (and in fact that phrase was slow to be applied to such a collection of Christian scripture in other Christian circles), it serves as an appropriate designation for Marcion's two-volume set of authoritative texts, since it in so many ways anticipates the content and stature of the New Testament more familiar to us today.

Yet this First New Testament has never been published in English, nor for that matter in any modern language.[4] It has remained an artifact of study to a relatively small number of biblical researchers with widely varying views of its reconstructibility, significance, and place in the transmission of the texts it contains. This is all the more remarkable because, besides being in all probability the very first Christian canon, Marcion's New Testament is also the earliest extensive witness to content found in the New Testament used by Christians today. Marcion is the first known witness to explicitly identify Paul as the author of several letters now included under his name in Christian scripture, including what is known as the letters to the Ephesians (which Marcion understood to have been addressed instead to the Laodiceans) and Colossians. His New Testament provides the first certain evidence for the existence of the gospel now known as Luke (although his version was shorter, and did not bear Luke's name). The First New Testament is significant, therefore, both where it corresponds with and confirms later evidence for biblical content and where it presents fundamentally different readings than those later sources.

Moreover, as the first formalized collection of Christian scripture, it affords us an early glimpse of a Christian community defining itself by the texts it holds sacred. Even with the extensive publication in recent years of compilations of other early Christian writings, both "gnostic" and varying shades of "orthodox," the First New Testament of Marcion has remained largely neglected. This book seeks to remedy this state of affairs by offering a reconstruction of the Marcionite New Testament accessible and useful to all levels of expertise and interest.

*****

The first generations of Christians formed diverse, local groups with several distinct understandings of their experience of Jesus Christ, and divergent interpretations of the meaning of his instruction. The letters of Paul provide only momentary snapshots in an ongoing struggle over the legacy of Christ, and we have no reliable knowledge of the ultimate outcome of these conflicts in the lives of their participants. Instead we peer into a dark space of early Christian history between the more-or-less datable letters of Paul and the writings of late second-century Christians such as Irenaeus of Lyons and Clement of Alexandria. The century-and-a-half between is full of floating, disembodied voices that we can fix in time and place only tentatively, sound bites from a tumultuous period of division, debate, and self-definition. This was a time, as B. H. Streeter reminds us, in which "there was no unifying authority, no worldwide organisation, however informal, to check the independent development of the various local churches each on its own lines."[5] These local Christian communities had a complex relationship to the broader Jewish community—itself diverse—within which they first developed, and which passed through a series of violent uprisings against the Roman order in 66–70, 115–17, and 132–34 CE. With each successive wave of Jewish restiveness and anti-Jewish repression, local Christian communities were faced with fundamental questions of identity and association with respect to the Jewish roots of their faith. They fell under social and cultural pressure: from without, for their links to Jewish identity; from within, for their nonconformity to newly emerging Jewish orthodoxies.[6] In the face of such conditions, Christians could offer their own rival claim to the Jewish religious tradition or walk away from it.

Onto this scene stepped Marcion. Following what he believed to be the views of Paul, he pushed for a clean break with the Jewish religious tradition. It is quite possible that he came from a community where Christianity had reached a non-Jewish audience and from the beginning caught on in a form only tenuously connected to its Jewish heritage.[7] Marcion applied his intellectual and organizational gifts to working out a resolution of the troubled relationship between the parent religious culture and its prodigal offspring. If Paul was correct that the message of Christ ultimately transcended the boundaries of the Mosaic covenant, what role remained for the Jewish scriptures that enjoined, celebrated, and promoted that covenant? And if those scriptures were obsolete, as this line of understanding might be taken to imply, where was one to turn for authoritative guidance? What were to be the distinctly *Christian* scriptures?

This book is not about Marcion, but about the canon of Christian scriptures he introduced as the new touchstone of Christian faith. Before Marcion there was no New Testament, with him it took its first shape, and after him it gradually developed into the form we now know. Before Marcion there were Christian writings that were read and treated as, in some sense, authoritative. But they had limited, local circulation and were not incorporated into a larger Bible. Traditions about Jesus were known, recounted, and recorded. The readers of these records regarded them as accurate, informed, perhaps even inspired. But the impetus to collect them into either a distinct scripture or a supplement to the Jewish one simply had not arisen. In quite a few places, the majority of texts that would ultimately be included in the New Testament were completely unknown. For those who considered the Jewish scriptures as authoritative as ever, the growing set of new writings may have been seen as a secondary, subordinate body of literature. It was for someone with Marcion's perspective, for whom the Jewish scriptures were ideologically problematic, that the stakes were raised on this body of early Christian literature to the point of elevating it to a unique status of authority.

So it was that Marcion collected, for the first time in history, a set of authoritative Christian writings intended to be afforded a status above that of other Christian literature. We need to deal up front with the discomfort that many have with Marcion's role in this decisive event of Christian history. By later standards of orthodoxy,

Marcion's *interpretation* of the New Testament writings was "heretical." But that is a completely separate matter from the value of the New Testament text he used. This distinction often has not been appreciated, and it is one of the principal tasks of this book to demonstrate why it should be made, and how much more significant the Marcionite New Testament becomes as a consequence. Marcion was a participant in a process going on all around him of defining Christianity, organizing it, and taking the steps from a loose movement or set of movements into various institutional forms. However inevitable one imagines the formation of a distinctly Christian canon to have been, the fact remains that Marcion took the decisive initiative, and in doing so he made a permanent impact on the Christian Bible and the faith shaped by reference to it.

Marcion's New Testament consisted of two parts: the *Evangelion*, a narrative account of the teachings and deeds of Jesus related literarily to the gospel we now know as Luke, and the *Apostolikon*, a collection of ten letters of Paul—those very ten, incidentally, that modern critical scholarship has concluded have the greatest likelihood of being authentic. We have some reason to think that he adopted the latter from an existing set compiled by some unknown collector of Paul's letters. But Marcion put his distinctive stamp on all subsequent attempts to formalize a New Testament for the very reason that his particular ideology led him to elevate such a set of the letters of Paul to parity with an account of the life and teachings of Jesus himself. That decision puts Marcion's work in a direct line of continuity with later Christian New Testaments, however delayed or otherwise influenced the formation of the latter might have been; and that is why the recovery of Marcion's biblical text is a recovery of the First New Testament.

Thus, it is not only the *idea* of a New Testament that can be credited first to Marcion, but also the distinctive *structure* of that New Testament, combining a "gospel" narrative of the life of Jesus with apostolic letters, specifically, the letters of Paul. There is little to be said in favor of the claim that the formation of the New Testament followed an inevitable trajectory, and that the Christian Bible would have turned out exactly as it did even if Marcion had never lived. On the contrary, the correspondence between what Marcion did and what the New Testament ultimately became in the hands of his triumphant competitors suggests his lasting impact on the Christian Bible, and so on Christianity itself.

In order to situate this First New Testament, the introductory chapters that follow consider this distinctive contribution of Marcion to Christianity in its historical and religious setting: Marcion himself as the enigmatic figure behind the First New Testament, the sources and methods involved in the reconstruction of the text Marcion put into circulation among his communities, and the history of modern research and opinion about it. Furthermore, they consider the question of the First New Testament's relationship with the texts found in the current New Testament, and the significance and meaning of this First New Testament as the embodiment of a decisive moment in the formation of early Christianity.

Following these introductory studies, the reconstructed texts of the Evangelion and Apostolikon are presented as best as we are able given the currently available sources, along with a detailed set of text notes justifying and explaining the reconstruction verse by verse. The form these reconstructed texts take will be familiar to those who work in text-critical study of the Bible; that is, those who, over the last 150 years, have made good use of editions of the biblical text as attested in the writings of major early Christian figures, such as Justin Martyr, Irenaeus, Tertullian, Clement of Alexandria, and others.[8] One could very well call the current contribution "the Biblical Text of Marcion," building on and refining the one edited by Adolf von Harnack in 1924, and occasionally cited as "Marcion" in the textual apparatus of modern editions of the New Testament. In fact, given his dates, Marcion joins the ranks of the so-called Apostolic Fathers as a witness to the very earliest recoverable forms of New Testament texts. Yet, because he did not merely make occasional quotations from or allusions to their content as other Apostolic Fathers did, but compiled and disseminated complete editions of them, Marcion far exceeds other early witnesses in the extent of evidence he provides for the state of New Testament texts in that time.

My intention in preparing this book has been to overcome two obstacles to appreciating the importance of the First New Testament. First, study of Marcion's New Testament has for too long been held captive by debate over tiny details—a classic case of not being able to see the forest for the trees. The desire to recover the exact wording of Marcion's texts has interfered with full appreciation of what we can learn about its overall content. Those who endeavor to reconstruct an exact Greek text of Marcion's New

Testament confront major challenges, because our sources (1) are in multiple languages, not just Greek, (2) often paraphrase or allude to content, rather than quote verbatim, and (3) often give conflicting evidence regarding the exact wording of a passage. The resulting frustration and pessimism over solving these problems is understandable, and is one of the reasons that the First New Testament has not been previously translated and made generally available. I agree with my colleagues who have worked on this problem that such a word-for-word reconstruction of the original Greek text is problematic, because too many unresolved issues remain on individual points of wording. Yet, frankly, many of these issues involve such minor points of grammar as to be all but irrelevant to a basic English translation. While remaining uncertain of exact wording in many passages, we have much greater certainty on the presence or absence of whole passages of meaningful content, regardless of which preposition or verb tense may have been used at a particular point. So we are actually in a good position to read this first Christian Bible as a whole in its general sweep of themes and teachings, and in this way appreciate its distinctive message and its place in the early development of Christianity, while the challenge of pursuing the exact Greek text continues into the future.[9]

As a second obstacle, study of Marcion's New Testament has generally been subservient to investigations of Marcion as a theologian and key figure in Christian history. But Marcion did not compose these texts (even if there remains the separate question of whether he edited them to some degree); he collected them from a broader existing Christian movement, and bestowed them in their collected form back to living Christian communities. As we will see, there are good reasons to question the assumption that these texts were fundamentally altered for service only to Marcionite Christians. A number of recent studies, and the evidence compiled here, argue against a case for Marcion's editorial hand in the shape of these texts. They may well provide an unusually early, datable glimpse into what was considered most essential and significant to a wide spectrum of the Christian movement in its formative phase. Even if Marcion's Church was the primary heir of the particular form the texts took in the Evangelion and Apostolikon, that fact, in itself, would connect them with what was perhaps the dominant form of Christianity in the second century CE. It is long overdue, therefore, to consider these texts in their own right, as windows into earliest Christianity and into the lives, thoughts, and values of early Christians before Marcion, while imagining how they might have shaped those lives, thoughts, and values after Marcion, among those who accepted his First New Testament as canonical scripture.

Chapter 1

Marcion

What do we know about Marcion himself? Our sources on him are varied, each with its own agenda and place in a tradition of hostile attacks on him. They cannot always be treated as independent witnesses, because later writers may merely repeat the statements of earlier ones, and several of those earlier writings are lost, making it difficult for us to map literary interdependence.[1] We do not know nearly as much as we would like about how information circulated in late antiquity, and a late source is not automatically worthless, since it may preserve information from an earlier one we otherwise no longer have. Moreover, some writers, no matter how much closer to Marcion in time, may simply not have bothered to check their facts very closely, whereas later ones may have worked diligently with Marcion's own writings. In short, we face many challenges in sifting our sources for reliable information about Marcion.

No substantial new data on Marcion has been discovered since Adolf von Harnack made his compilation of it in 1924.[2] But the long-known materials have undergone constant reevaluation in subsequent decades. In the late 1980s, Gerhard May summarized the state of the issues. Building on the observations of his predecessors, he cautioned against conflating separate lines of tradition about Marcion's life into artificial syntheses, tempting as they are for filling out a life so poorly known.[3] Sebastian Moll has recently revisited the state of the field, with new suggestions.[4] In order to better understand the circumstances in which Marcion's creation of the First New Testament occurred, this chapter attempts to situate that creation in the very few bits of information about Marcion in which we have some confidence, contextualizing both man and text within the social, political, cultural, and religious environment of the time.

The things we think we know with some confidence about Marcion's life—leaving aside his teachings and literary activities for the moment—easily fit into this paragraph. All of them are sufficiently attested by multiple, plausibly independent witnesses, and none of them is particularly suspect as serving a polemical portrait. Marcion came from the Roman province of Pontus, on what is today the north coast of Turkey.[5] He had his profession in the sea-trade, being a shipmaster, or shipowner (*nauclerus*, ναύκληρος).[6] Eventually, he made his way to Rome, probably early in the reign of the emperor Antoninus Pius (138–61 CE).[7] His understanding of Christianity differed enough from that of leaders within the Roman Christian community that they could not retain communion with each other, and Marcion became the organizer and leader of a separate Christian community that rapidly drew in adherents from across the Roman Empire. That is all we reliably know; but it is worth reviewing some of the more interesting elaborations of this information in our various sources, being alert to their questionable worth as historical data.

The most solid date we have connected to Marcion—one remembered in the Marcionite community itself, and therefore not suspect as a polemical invention (although Tertullian manages to use it to make a polemical point)—is "115 years and 6½ months between Christ and Marcion."[8] The point of reference with Christ can scarcely be anything else than the date given in the first verse of the Evangelion: the fifteenth year of the reign of Tiberius, 29 CE. The calculation yields a date in mid-July 144 CE,[9] even if the exact event commemorated by this date is not clear. One might as well refer to it, in the witty expression of Sebastian Moll, as "Marcion-day."[10] Since the date connected to Jesus is the latter's public advent as a religious leader (not his birth), it seems reasonable that the corresponding event be some sort of advent of Marcion, either in the mundane or spiritual sense.[11] While Epiphanius nearly two centuries later gives a date approximating this one for Marcion's arrival in Rome,[12] Irenaeus of Lyons, writing much closer to the events, places Marcion's arrival in Rome slightly earlier, circa 138–42 CE;[13] and Clement of Alexandria, writing at about the same time, also seems to imply that Marcion started his religious activities already during the latter part of the reign of Hadrian (117–38 CE).[14] From all of this information, we can place the broader dates of Marcion's life at approximately 95–165 CE,[15] but will continue to use 144 CE as the one certain date connected to Marcion, and therefore to the First New Testament.

Regarding Marcion's arrival in Rome, Tertullian refers to a letter in which Marcion had expressed in some way an original solidarity with the faith of the Roman Christians,[16] as well as to a remarkable donation of 200,000 *sesterces* he contributed to their community.[17] These two acts served Tertullian's argument that Marcion fit the profile of a typical "heretic"—someone who initially adhered to an orthodoxy from which he later deviated. Tertullian's wording[18] has been taken by some as implying that Marcion became a Christian for the first time in Rome.[19] But this interpretation demands too much specific information from a very broad statement made as part of a polemical theme.[20] Marcion need not have first converted to Christianity in Rome for Tertullian's argument to hold good, and Tertullian surely would have made much of Marcion's baptism at the hands of the Roman elders if he believed such a thing had occurred.

Marcion's falling-out with members of the Roman Christian leadership may have been expressed through rival interpretations of certain sayings of Jesus, regardless of the larger ideological differences that may have stood behind the argument.[21] Our sources seem to share the impression that such exegetical conflict lit the spark of dissension. Tertullian and Philastrius of Brescia (the latter probably dependent on the former) associate the conflict with two sayings of Jesus: concerning the good and the bad tree (Luke 6.43)[22] and the old and new wineskins (Luke 5.36–37).[23] Pseudo-Tertullian mentions only the first,[24] while Epiphanius mentions only the second.[25] Both images relate to Marcion's belief that Jesus brought a fundamentally new message and way of practicing religion at odds with the Jewish religious tradition.[26]

A number of dates and references connected to Marcion's later activities turn up in our sources. He was still alive at the time Justin Martyr was writing his *First Apology*, probably in the mid-150s, and by that time had achieved remarkable success spreading his version of the Christian faith.[27] None of our sources place him in Rome in the period between his break with the local community there and Justin's reference, and the latter likewise does not suggest his presence in the city. But other sources place him back in Rome in the following decade, between 155 and 166 CE,[28] perhaps returning to edify the Marcionite community that most certainly remained in place there.

Unfortunately, the most colorful biographical anecdotes come from individual sources and cannot be checked against others for reliability.[29] Perhaps the story most worthy of credence is the one Irenaeus relates from Polycarp of Smyrna, whom he knew "in my early youth"[30] in their common homeland of the province of Asia (modern west Turkey). Polycarp had apparently rebuffed Marcion on some occasion, though whether before or after Marcion's time in Rome is unclear—just as it is unclear whether Irenaeus had learned the story directly from Polycarp when he knew him personally, or learned the story later through a third party, as he had learned other things about Polycarp's later life.[31] The rejection turns on a pun in the Greek in which the exchange occurred. When Marcion met Polycarp, he asked him if he recognized, or acknowledged (*epiginōske*), "us"—that is, the Marcionite community. With the Christian community divided, with whom would Polycarp keep communion? But since the word for acknowledgment also means to recognize or know someone personally, Polycarp played on that second meaning when he answered, "Yes, I recognize you: the firstborn of Satan!"[32] A similar story told by Philastrius of Brescia and other late sources about an encounter between Marcion and the apostle John(!) may be a distorted derivative of this episode involving Polycarp.[33] Irenaeus goes on to mention Polycarp's letter to the Christians of Philippi, without specifically pointing out that the expression "firstborn of Satan" is used in it by Polycarp to refer to an otherwise unidentified opponent within Christianity. Either this was a favorite expression of Polycarp's, or the person in question is Marcion. In the letter, Polycarp says:

> For anyone who does not confess that Jesus Christ has come in the flesh is an antichrist; and whoever does not confess the witness of the cross is from the devil; and whoever distorts (*methodeuēi*) the words of the Lord for his own passions, saying that there is neither resurrection nor judgment—this one is the firstborn of Satan.[34]

The issues Polycarp raises here overlap with positions Marcion held on the transcendent nature of Jesus and the salvation of the human soul apart from the body by a deity who does not judge.[35] Nevertheless, that Marcion is in fact the referent of the allusions in Polycarp's letter remains uncertain.[36]

These scant notices are all the direct information we have on Marcion's life aside from his biblical and theological activities. We are left to fill out the context of these latter activities from related circumstantial evidence connected to Marcion's homeland, profession, and possible religious background.

Marcion's Homeland

From surviving Christian sources, we know next to nothing about the state of Christianity in Pontus in the earlier part of Marcion's life. The book of Acts (18.2) identified Pontus as the homeland of Aquila, a colleague of Paul's that the latter mentions in some of his letters. If we could be certain of this information, we might speculate that at some point Aquila could have returned to his native land and helped spread Christianity there. The First Letter of Peter is addressed to Christians in the neighboring (and at times administratively combined) provinces of Pontus and Bithynia, among other nearby regions, presupposing established communities there at the time of its composition, which unfortunately cannot be conclusively determined. One can observe a striking correlation between the letter's stress on Christians being "aliens" in the world, and the world-view Marcion inherited or developed, even if First Peter ultimately did not find a place in his New Testament canon.

Fortunately, however, we have a rare non-Christian source of information on the state of Christianity in the region in the time when Marcion would have been a young man there, in a letter of the Roman governor Pliny to the emperor Trajan, circa 112 CE. Pliny explains his procedure in enforcing a ban on secret societies, including Christian clubs. He considered Christianity "a depraved and extravagant superstition," which apparently had been present in the area for as much as twenty years (or at least there were people brought before him who had been Christians twenty years earlier, whether locally or in some other place). He also reports that two women slaves actually held important positions in the church as *ministrae*, or deaconesses, who probably distributed the ritual meal.[37] Under interrogation, some of the Christians provided Pliny with an account of their religious observances:

> On an appointed day they had been accustomed to meet before daybreak and to recite a hymn antiphonally to Christ, as to a god, and to bind themselves by an oath, not for the commission of any crime but to abstain from theft, robbery, adultery and breach of faith, and not

to deny a deposit when it was claimed. After the conclusion of this ceremony it was their custom to depart and meet again to take food; but it was ordinary and harmless food.³⁸

Pliny's subtext in providing this description is that the secret activities of the Christians did not fit the suspicions that lay behind the ban on secret societies. This was apparently not a criminal or political organization, as other secret societies were, nor did it entail religious rites considered outright immoral by Roman standards. It was, however, having a deleterious effect on traditional religion in the province and, to Pliny's grave concern, had spread not only through the cities, but also the country towns and villages. Several modern researchers have pointed to features in common between Pliny's Christians and Marcion's brand of Christianity. These include the absence of Jewish characteristics in the service, the direct worship of Christ as something like a deity, and the relatively high position accorded women. What is missing, of course, is any reference to either the Old or New Testaments, or to any written texts, which we would have expected to catch Pliny's interest as a source of information on the secretive group.³⁹

Marcion's Profession

Marcion's profession in the sea-trade may be the most significant thing we know about him personally.⁴⁰ Pontic shipmasters played a crucial role in supplying grain to Roman armies during two major campaigns in the reign of Trajan, the Dacian and Parthian wars.⁴¹ For the latter expedition, conducted when Marcion would have been getting started in his career, Trajan reorganized the governance of the area and had new roads built across neighboring Cappadocia to expedite the shipment of grain from Pontic ports to the troops campaigning in the upper Euphrates and Tigris river valleys. Marcion would have learned of the Jewish resistance to Trajan's occupation of Mesopotamia, including attacks on supply lines, and of Trajan's brutal and ultimately futile efforts to suppress it. We can do no more than speculate about any impressions made on Marcion, or any connections he may have drawn between events under Trajan and the Bar Kokhba revolt of the Jews fifteen years later. We do know, however, that Marcion came to believe that the creator of this world favored the Jews, just as their scriptures stated, and ultimately would give them mastery of it at the hand of a messianic warrior. Conversely, he held that Christians had nothing to do with such aspirations, and were called upon by Jesus and the god he spoke for to abstain from violence of any kind. David Balás sees an ironic historical moment in this exegetical alliance between non-Christian Jews and Marcion's de-Judaizing Christianity.

> Marcion may have found a way to effect this desirable separation by using Jewish self-interpretation at several main points. For instance, by accepting the anti-Christian contention of some Jews that Jesus Christ was not the Messiah promised by the Old Testament, a Messiah the Jews rightly expected to be political and warlike, Marcion made a counter claim that Christ was in fact the self-revelation of a previously entirely unknown, all-good God. . . . Paradoxically, it was precisely by having accepted Jewish scriptures and history, at least to a large extent, in their contemporary Jewish interpretation that Marcion arrived at his radical dissociation of the two Testaments![42]

Trajan's successor, Hadrian, quelled the Bar Kokhba revolt and issued laws against the free practice of Judaism, including an order to destroy copies of the Jewish scriptures. Hadrian's orders brought to a crisis the simmering issue of Christian ties to Jewish identity. Whatever the internal developments within Christianity that prepared the way for the creation of a New Testament, it is simply impossible to dismiss the coincidence in time of Hadrian's anti-Torah campaign and Marcion's call for the establishment of a distinct and separate Christian sacred scripture. Given the political and social circumstances, it is not at all surprising that it was precisely at this time that Marcion became a major voice for the clear differentiation of "Christianity" and "Judaism."

Marcion's business enterprises are potentially significant for his role as a religious leader. Ships were the fastest and most effective means of communication and transport of goods in the Roman Empire. Through the organization of his business, Marcion would have had agents or contacts in many major ports throughout the empire, and would have visited these far-flung places for business reasons. This means that Marcion would have been unusually well-informed about regional differences in the Christian movement, and would have had access to more local Christian literature and traditions than most other Christians of his time.[43] When, later in life, he realized that the form of Christianity with which he identified faced competition from rival interpretations of the faith, he had a tremendous advantage over the latter in his ability to spread his message rapidly and organize communities on an empire-wide scale.[44] Many of those engaged in the sea trade were wealthy, prominent, well-connected people, and they formed exclusive guilds that coordinated ventures and built up solidarity in clubs. They were one of the only segments of the population to have channels of communication independent of government control. The role they may have played in spreading Christianity must remain for now mostly speculation. But it may be pertinent to note that, precisely at the time when Marcion was active, the emperors Antoninus Pius and Marcus Aurelius both found it necessary to issue laws against people not actually involved in the sea trade being admitted to membership in its professional associations,[45] suggesting that the latter were being employed for some sort of networking beyond their original purpose. Moreover, any explanation of the Christian innovation in adopting the codex instead of the scroll as the format for books must take into consideration the previous primary use of the codex as a shipmaster's almanac and businessman's account ledger.

Marcion's Religious Environment

Christian texts dating to the lifetime of Marcion vary in their conception of Christian identity in relationship to its Jewish roots. Marcion's own position, severing any connection to Jewish scripture and the kind of God it extols, put him toward one end of the spectrum of Christian identity. At the other end of that spectrum stood the Roman Christian community, or at least a large segment of it, where evidently there was considerably more discomfort with the figure of Paul than with the Jewish heritage of the faith. From the evidence of the letter of Clement to Corinth[46] and the writings of Justin Martyr, Christianity in Rome was deeply committed to its Jewish roots,[47] and, when it did not outright reject Paul,[48] it relegated him to a very minor place in Christian thought.[49] Yet Christian literature produced by others in Marcion's lifetime reveals a diverse environment in which his break with Christianity's Jewish heritage was not a unique aberration.

Some of this Christian literature contemporary with Marcion reflects a struggle between followers of Jesus and others within the broader Jewish tradition over the meaning and lasting value of the Jewish scriptures. The author of the Letter of Barnabas, for example, insists on the obsolescence of literal application of those scriptures. The typological and allegorical interpretive tradition he promotes would come to dominate non-Marcionite forms of

Christianity from that point forward and would allow the continued authority of the Jewish scriptures, primarily as repositories of symbolic imagery whose meaning was detached from Jewish religious practice.[50] Claiming to be the "true Israel," such Christians laid claim to Jewish heritage while breaking continuity with more literal ways of reading and applying Jewish sacred texts.

Somewhat later than Barnabas, the seven letters penned by Ignatius[51] display considerable concern over the still ill-defined distinction between Christian and Jewish observances.[52] Ignatius apparently was involved in debates with fellow Christians about the trustworthy foundations of the faith. His opponents refused to believe anything not explicitly supported by the *archeiois*, the Jewish scriptures,[53] while Ignatius embraced the independent authority of "the gospel," the oral instruction and interpretive tradition of the Christian communities.[54] "For Ignatius," William Schoedel concludes, "the teachings and myths of Judaism are 'old' (cf. Mag. 9.1; 10.2)—a term that he uses to describe what is opposed to God (cf. Eph. 19.3). 'Judaism,' then, is not granted even a historically limited role in the unfolding of God's plan."[55]

From the same period, the Letter to Diognetus[56] goes even further in criticizing the Jewish tradition in a manner unqualified by any claim that Christianity is a truer Judaism, repeatedly emphasizing the newness of Christianity, instead of the more typical claim that it was something ordained from of old.[57] According to the author, no one had any knowledge of God before the coming of Christ,[58] and God held back his "own wise counsel as a well-guarded mystery."[59] The author concedes that the one God is the creator, and that the Jews worship this God, but they misunderstand his character. So while the author has not taken the step—which Marcion did—of distinguishing between the creator god of the Jews and the higher god of the Christians, the Jewish depiction of God comes in for sharp criticism as unworthy of Christ's Father. Moreover, the author says, nature in no way serves to direct attention to its ultimate creator; God conceals all until revealing it exclusively to his Son. All other faiths, both Greek and Jewish, are human doctrines[60] and earthly inventions.[61] God revealed his true character, his inherent goodness and power to save, only at the end of time.[62] His followers are aliens in this world.[63] This text, then, offers an ideology closely akin to Marcion's, and suggests the existence of a wider environment from which Marcion drew inspiration.[64]

In the world Marcion knew, therefore, some strands of Christianity displayed an effort to maintain close ties to Christianity's Jewish heritage in both symbolism and practice; others appropriated the Jewish religious tradition with increasing hostility to its contemporary Jewish practitioners; still others showed themselves to be on the verge of severing all connections with the Jewish origins of Christianity.[65] On the basis of such early Christian sources, Charles Nielsen concludes, "The process of dissociating Christianity from Judaism was already well under way within certain circles in Asia Minor before Marcion. Marcion pushed the process to its bitter end, but he really did not have very far to go!"[66] David Balás sees a role in the process for pressures connected to the Jewish revolts, noting that Marcion's decision to go to Rome was made at or shortly after the time of the suppression of the Bar Kokhba revolt and anti-Jewish imperial legislation. "Politically and socially," he writes, "the Christians, especially hellenistic Christians with no national or cultural roots in Judaism, found at this time their association with Jewish history an embarrassing and dangerous liability."[67] In contrast, Gerhard May reads Marcion's situation in terms of broad questions about authority within emerging Christianity:

> During the time of Marcion's appearance, the church was on its way to a crisis. . . . It was a crisis of the foundations as well as of the content of the Christian faith, and it developed gradually. . . . The question that became more and more urgent was: How does one verify the one original truth? . . . The problem of the authoritativeness of the Old Testament—in spite of Paul, never uniformly solved—was raised anew and pointedly: It was no longer just a question of the validity of the law. Could the Bible of the Jews, as a matter of fact, be the revelatory book of the true God?[68]

Marcion's Christian Conflict

We have no way of knowing whether Marcion was raised in a Christian community already disconnected from its Jewish roots, or later joined such a community, or whether he was himself an innovator in that direction. Whether due to expulsion from the synagogues, or dissociation connected to the recurrent repression of Jews, the circumstances of the time raise a historical question: what happened when Gentile Christian dependence on a Jewish Christian core group became untenable, and Gentile Christians either willingly or unwillingly went their own way? One result was the sort of religious environment from which Marcion apparently emerged, in which the Jewish background of Christianity was minimized. Another outcome was the sort Marcion found prevalent in Rome: that is, a fresh appropriation of Jewish elements in a synthesis of formerly distinct Jewish and Gentile missions. These two different ways of responding to the same situation then came into conflict in the second century CE.

We do not know if Marcion set out for Rome with the intention of reforming the Christian community (or communities) there. He may have thought that any local difference of opinion he had experienced in the provinces came from ignorance, and that the Christians in the capital certainly would share the views he regarded as "orthodox." If so, he was in for quite a surprise. John Knox pictures such a scenario:

> Now imagine a zealous and forceful Christian of the early second century whose Christianity has been of a decidedly non-Jewish type, who has been nourished on Paul's Epistle to the Galatians and other writings of that apostle, who has found salvation in the Lord Jesus Christ and in his God and Father, who has made little use, if any, of Jewish Scripture, thinking of it as the "law" which Christ has brought to nought—imagine such a Christian suddenly finding himself in a community where the historical continuity with Judaism is prized as one of the most precious values, where ultimate authority is vested in the Jewish Scriptures, where the sharp Pauline antithesis between law and gospel, between letter and Spirit, is softened, if not effaced. Do we not have in such a situation all we need to explain what seems to have happened several years after Marcion came to Rome . . .?[69]

If Marcion arrived in Rome with any illusion that he would find a community living according to his Pauline ideal, he must have quickly discerned the divergence between his vision and local reality. He began to urge Roman Christians to reform themselves, to shed the Jewish trappings of their faith, as well as their attachment to a fleshly rather than spiritual Jesus, and the closely related hope in their own bodily resurrection, rather than an ascent of their soul to heaven. His attempt to work out a theological and metaphysical setting within which to understand the sharp divergence he perceived between Jesus' characterization of God and the image of God in Jewish scripture only would have widened the gulf between him and other Christian leaders.

We do not know whether it was Marcion or his opponents who finally forced the issue. But there was a showdown of some sort, with Marcion no doubt calling on Roman Christians to join him, and the local leaders on their side presenting Marcion with an ultimatum of conformity, perhaps taking the form of a statement of faith close in form to the Old Roman Symbol, an earlier version of the Apostles' Creed, which seems framed specifically to rule out several of Marcion's key positions.[70] Marcion rejected the proposed creed, took with him those who had been won to his side, and organized a rival communion, which he endowed with a New Testament to replace the Old Testament that alone had scriptural status for most Roman Christians at the time.[71]

Those opposed to Marcion, including groups ancestral to later Christian orthodoxy, produced a string of writings against him, his teachings, and his New Testament—more than against any other rival form of Christianity prior to the fourth-century christological and Manichaean controversies.[72] Of this extensive anti-Marcionite literature, only one is preserved in its entirety: Tertullian's *Against Marcion* (*Adversus Marcionem*). As pointed out by E. Evans, this work, written in the first decade of the third century, has the distinction of containing "the earliest surviving Christian commentary on any book of the New Testament,"[73]—namely, on the books of Marcion's New Testament; we must wait another generation for the writings of Origen for the first commentaries on books now found in the modern Christian New Testament. Many more anti-Marcionite writings, such as those mentioned by Eusebius,[74] are now lost. There were works by Justin Martyr,[75] Rhodo,[76] Dionysius of Corinth,[77] Theophilus of Antioch,[78] Hippolytus of Rome,[79] Philip of Gortyna,[80] and Modestus.[81] Irenaeus intended to write one, as he says in his surviving work,[82] but Eusebius found no trace that he ever carried through this intention.[83] All of this anti-Marcionite labor suggests the extent of Marcion's success, noted with chagrin by Justin[84] and attested in the anti-Christian polemic of the second-century writer Celsus.[85]

It is remarkable that so many of these anti-Marcionite tracts are no longer extant, and one must wonder at the reason for that. Did they perhaps go too far in some of their remarks? Gerhard May suggests that what survives of Justin and Rhodo shows that they did not recognize the scriptural status of a New Testament, since they characterize the Marcionites as lacking (scriptural) proof of their doctrines.[86] While some sought to appropriate the authority of Paul against Marcion, others apparently found it necessary to attack rather than domesticate Paul himself, and through him Marcion, under the thin disguise of the arch-heretic Simon Magus in the novelistic Pseudo-Clementine literature.[87] The early orthodox tracts against Marcion may have been considered largely worthless to later generations because they reflected views at odds with later orthodoxy, such as overt criticism of Paul, attacks on the Gospel of Luke, or a view of sacred scripture that did not recognize a place for a "new" testament.[88]

But Marcion also had his supporters, who became convinced as he did that the Law and Prophets, whose authority was severely qualified already in the ideology of Paul, could not serve as a sacred text for the Christians, and must yield its place to some set of the new Christian literature being written and circulated. He bestowed upon his community a formalized canon consisting of a single gospel (the Evangelion) and a collection of Paul's letters (the Apostolikon), perhaps deliberately modeled in this double structure as a replacement for the Law and Prophets.[89] His action appears to have served as a catalyst for discussions and debates about which Christian writings should be accorded this status. Arguments were made, new sources were sought out, and lists were drawn up[90] (including the so-called Muratorian Canon, with its explicitly anti-Marcionite concern, whenever and wherever it was actually compiled[91]). This process went on for another two hundred years before any of the proposed canons matched what modern Christians consider to be the New Testament. Any talk of a New Testament apart from Marcion's in the second and third centuries is anachronistic, and must be treated as a shorthand way to refer to individual books or subsets of texts recognized as authoritative amid an indeterminate larger set of Christian literature. Marcion, by issuing a delimited set of Christian texts considered exclusively authoritative as early as the mid-second century, was far ahead of his time.

Chapter 2

Marcion's New Testament

"The history of the development of the New Testament Canon," C. F. Evans observes in the *Cambridge History of the Bible*, "is the history of the process by which books written for the most part for other purposes and from other motives came to be given this unique status."[1] Historical hindsight all too easily creates the illusion of inevitability in this process; but we can discern a distinct before-and-after transformation of attitudes towards early Christian writings, with Marcion as the middle term. As Lee McDonald states, "Although the mid-second–century Church was gradually recognizing the usefulness of a body of *Christian* literature for its life and worship, there were as yet no fixed normative collections to which one could appeal. It was Marcion . . . who first saw the importance of a collection of authoritative Christian writings for worship and teaching in his community of churches."[2] It is important to stress here the broad modern consensus of scholars on this point. "It is denied by none," F. F. Bruce remarks about that consensus, "that Marcion played a crucial part in the formation of the New Testament canon."[3] Or, put more strongly (and perhaps more controversially) in the words of Hans von Campenhausen, the idea of a New Testament "came into existence at one stroke with Marcion and only with Marcion," and it "remains his peculiar and unique creation."[4]

In the time before Marcion we find few quotations from the books that were to be included in the New Testament. "At most," Bruce Metzger observes, "the Apostolic Fathers disclose for this or that geographical area a certain (or rather, an uncertain) amount of knowledge and use of several first-century documents that later came to be gathered into what we know as the New Testament."[5] Metzger demonstrates a clear difference in how these writers informally handled material later included in the New Testament, in contrast to their more formal, precise citation of Jewish scriptures; the two sources of instruction simply did not share the same level of sacredness and authority for these authors. Marcion's contemporary Justin Martyr, for instance, made use of a collection of stories and sayings of Jesus culled from various gospels both known and unknown to us today, with little indication that he considered it important to preserve the exact wording of anything other than Jesus' own statements.[6] As Campenhausen characterizes the situation, "In the first one and a half centuries of the Church's history there is no single Gospel writing which is directly made known, named, or in any way given prominence by quotation. Written and oral traditions run side by side or cross, enrich or distort one another, without distinction or even the possibility of distinction between them."[7] Early in the second century, Papias of Hierapolis felt free to criticize the sequence of the Gospel of Mark, and to prefer oral traditions to written ones generally.[8] The various collections of Paul's letters in circulation were only looked upon favorably in certain circles and were not yet treated as scripture.[9]

All of this changed with Marcion. He formed for the first time "a coherent canon," displaying two crucial features by which Bruce Metzger justifies this characterization: (1) it contained a fixed number of books, and (2) it was put forward in place of the Jewish scriptures, as equivalently scriptural.[10] Through these moves, Marcion "first makes Christians conscious both of the idea of a new canon of Christian literature and of the identification of certain kinds of documents as carrying greater authority than others, and hence being 'canonical.'"[11] P. Rougier points out the contrast of perspective between Papias, writing probably before 130 CE, who shows not even an inkling of a notion of a New Testament canon and explicitly critiques reliance on texts for Christian tradition, and Irenaeus of Lyons, working half a century later, who argues for the acceptance of a four-gospel proto-canon.[12] Even Irenaeus was not seeking to define a closed "canon" of Christian scripture, but reported on and justified a tradition of use for individual authoritative texts within his community.[13] Several researchers have argued that the rapid formation and dissemination of this four-gospel "canon" between the time of Justin and that of Irenaeus suggests a deliberate, conscious decision by the leaders of the non-Marcionite party in the western Roman Empire, with Marcion's activities there serving as the catalyst.[14]

But in fact the process of canonization within non-Marcionite circles appears to have been a slow one, and we must wait two hundred years to find one as formally defined as Marcion's. Harry Gamble draws attention to the resistance of the mainstream Christian communities to Marcion's innovation, casting doubt on any immediate counter-move at canonization: "The fixation of a canon by Marcion did not in fact lead to an immediate or concerted effort in the church to delimit its own authoritative literature, and the number of writings valued continued for a long time to be large and fluid."[15] John Barton has argued similarly that the long delay in formalizing a New Testament canon among the non-Marcionite mainstream speaks against a direct influence of Marcion on that process, and might even be read as a self-conscious rejection of his scriptural move.[16] Ongoing debate among biblical scholars on Marcion's exact role in the formation of the Christian Bible, therefore, does not question that Marcion compiled the First New Testament, but proposes different assessments of how much his innovation directly shaped the modern New Testament canon. Yet even if Marcion's opponents did not follow him by quickly instituting a closed canon of their own, or by seeking to "restrict the compass of acceptable Christian texts"[17] to the same degree that he did, it nevertheless is difficult to deny that his New Testament remained the elephant in the room of deliberations over sacred scripture until the question was settled for the mainstream church as well, and some of the choices he made undeniably came to be incorporated into the ultimate form taken by the New Testament.[18]

Despite a number of qualifications, therefore, we still can affirm in large part Harnack's summary of Marcion's contribution to the formation of the Christian Bible:[19]

1. Christians owe to Marcion the idea of a New Testament. It had occurred to no one before and can best be understood as originating in the context of Marcion's rejection of an Old Testament base for Christianity.[20]
2. Christians owe to Marcion the particular form of the New Testament. The equal standing of the letters of Paul with the memoirs of Christ's life is something that would not be

expected in a sacred literature from any precedent up to that time.[21]
3. Christians owe to Marcion the prominence of the voice of Paul in the New Testament, and consequently in subsequent Christian tradition. Many of Marcion's contemporaries had all but forgotten Paul, or subsumed him within the broader apostolic mass.[22]
4. Christians owe to Marcion the push towards a Christianity rooted in its own distinctive scripture, rather than in an oral tradition of interpreting Jewish scripture, or in a scriptureless system of authority and practice like most Greco-Roman religions of the time.

Wolfram Kinzig has presented a strong case that it was even Marcion who first coined the expression "New Testament" as a designation appropriate to his collection of Christian scriptures — a name whose origin otherwise has proven difficult to trace.[23] The evidence shows not only some of the earliest appearances of the expression in discussions of Marcion's views, but also the degree to which anti-Marcionite Christian leaders initially resisted the name before yielding to widespread popular usage, which can be plausibly attributed to the extensive reach of the Marcionite mission in the second and third centuries. Kinzig's case is by no means proven, however, and the expression remained throughout the early Christian centuries primarily a theological rather than textual one. Our sources speak of writings "belonging to" the old or new covenants in the character of their contents, just as Buddhists at times speak of texts being "Hinayana" or "Mahayana." It took a while for the designation to narrow its reference to a specific collection of texts.

Marcion's Role as Editor

Did Marcion merely compile and "canonize" texts he found already in use among certain Christian communities? Or did he select some, reject others, according to ideological principles? Did he go on to edit those he selected, in order to bring them into conformity with his views? Or did he faithfully transmit the texts as he found them, while simply interpreting them in line with his beliefs? From the hindsight of the later New Testament canonized by non-Marcionite Christians and in use today, it has been easy to believe the traditional polemical suspicions of Marcion's "heretical" motives and methods, in order to explain Marcion's smaller New Testament canon and shorter individual books within it. Tertullian, writing three generations after Marcion, assumed that he had taken an already existing set of Christian scriptures, universally recognized as authoritative, and had rejected some, edited others. But we are able to recognize immediately the anachronism in Tertullian's assumption. He was not aware that no such authoritative set of Christian scriptures is anywhere in evidence prior to Marcion, and that even in Tertullian's day agreement on such a set was far from universal.[24]

Multiple gospels had already been written by Marcion's time, and he almost certainly knew more than one of them. He may have commented negatively on some passages from the Gospel of Matthew in his only known composition, the *Antitheses*.[25] But we do not know whether he knew of Matthew already when he selected a different gospel for his New Testament, or only learned of it afterward. Nor do we have any evidence that he knew or commented on any other work not included in his New Testament, except, of course, the Jewish scriptures, or "Old Testament." The primary purpose of the *Antitheses* was not to debate "canonical" issues (note the anachronism involved in imagining that it would), but to compare the religious principles expressed in the Evangelion and Apostolikon with the ideas and narratives of the Jewish scriptures, in order to demonstrate the incompatibility of the two religious systems. Although Tertullian and other anti-Marcionite writers believed that Marcion had deliberately omitted Paul's "Pastoral Letters" (1 Timothy, 2 Timothy, Titus), we now know that his Pauline collection contained the same ten letters circulating among many non-Marcionite churches of his time. Since the earliest certain citation of the Pastorals occurs only a generation or two after Marcion, it may well be that he had no knowledge of them, or even that they had yet to be written (if they are, in fact, written by someone pretending to be Paul, as most modern researchers conclude). Even the priority given to Paul's letter to the Galatians in the Apostolikon, long explained as due to Marcion's particular ideological interests, has now been shown to have occurred also in the ten-letter collection of Paul's letters circulating among non-Marcionite Christians in Syria.[26] In short, we need to break free from anachronistic judgments that Marcion "omitted" or "rearranged" texts relative to a later New Testament canon that did not yet exist in his time. As the first compiler of a New Testament, Marcion was at liberty to select and arrange texts as he chose, just as were later non-Marcionite Christian leaders when they compiled their own New Testament.

Tertullian further charged that Marcion "mutilated" (*caederet*) those texts he did include in his New Testament—that is, that he altered them by excising passages that contradicted his views, or occasionally making slight changes in wording for the same purpose.[27] More than a century later, Epiphanius similarly referred to Marcion having "excised" (*parekopse*) passages. Someone with Tertullian's and Epiphanius' presuppositions about the accuracy of *their* versions of these texts, and about Marcion's motives as a "heretic," would necessarily draw such an inference from the simple fact that Marcion's texts were shorter than the versions of the works in question known to them.[28] There was a well-known tradition of correcting corrupted manuscripts of the *Iliad* and other classic works of literature by excising what the editors regarded as inauthentic additions to the text, so it was easy to imagine that someone with Marcion's concern with the "corruption" of the "gospel"—that is, the message of Jesus—would take up the editorial knife in a similar fashion. Yet Tertullian and Epiphanius found it easy—remarkably easy—to cite apparent inconsistencies in Marcion's supposed editing: passages that were to be found in his texts even though they contradicted the very views he was busy promoting on the authority of these very texts.[29] Either Marcion was an incredibly inept editor, as Tertullian sometimes suggested, or he had never undertaken such an ideological purge of these texts.[30]

The way this issue has been handled by modern biblical researchers is instructive. Despite a number of questioning voices going back to the very beginning of modern critical study of the Bible, most have simply accepted the polemical claim that Marcion edited out portions of the texts he received. When it comes to the evidence contrary to this claim, modern commentators have either embraced Tertullian's answers—that Marcion was an incompetent editor or cleverly left in passages contrary to his views to allay suspicions that he had tampered with the text—or have worked to come up with ideological motivations for Marcion's editorial decisions that went unrecognized by Tertullian and others. The common supposition has been that the polemical testimony to Marcion's editorial activity is basically reliable, and fundamental, and everything else is to be explained in accord with it. Few researchers seem to have considered the fact that writers such as Tertullian were in no position to know the state of texts in or before the time of Marcion, nor did they have any independent information that would have told them whether Marcion's or their versions of these writings were the earlier one.[31] For these reasons, the testimony of these opponents of Marcion on this question is utterly without merit. Many other critics of Marcion (e.g., Justin Martyr, Clement of Alexandria, Ephrem Syrus) say nothing about any tampering with texts.[32] Even Tertullian himself, in the heat of polemic, acknowledged that he could not actually prove the priority of his community's versions of the texts over Marcion's. Modern commentators rarely have been as careful to qualify their assertions.

In short, the acceptance by modern researchers of the claims made about Marcion's handling of the texts included in his New Testament is an example of uncritical adoption of polemic as history.[33] First, Tertullian and his associates in this charge against Marcion are working from an anti-Marcionite bias that shapes their assumptions. Second, they are writing from a position in time that makes it impossible for them to have any sure knowledge of the state of either anything like a New Testament canon or its constituent books at the time of Marcion. Third, we know for a fact that several of their assumptions are incorrect: there was no New Testament canon before Marcion, from which the latter rejected parts unsuited to him;[34] there was no larger Pauline corpus from which Marcion excised the Pastorals; there was no universal, undisputed orthodoxy from which Marcion diverged.[35] All of these are anachronisms that Marcion's later critics project back into the circumstances of his activity. In many cases, Tertullian and Epiphanius claim erroneously that the particular wording of the Evangelion or Apostolikon is Marcion's invention, when in fact we find the same wording in catholic biblical manuscripts. The almost canonical status afforded the accusations made against Marcion, therefore, shows a remarkable lack of critical historical assessment among modern researchers.

Adolf von Harnack, the great historian of Christianity whose 1924 study of Marcion is the chief reference point of all subsequent scholarship on the subject, helped to perpetuate this uncritical reading of sources hostile to Marcion, inasmuch as he sought rationales within Marcion's ideology for the differences between Marcion's texts and their catholic versions. Yet even he readily admitted, "No definite statements by Marcion exist concerning the grounds for proceeding as he does in his critique of individual passages from the Gospel or Apostle."[36] He likewise conceded that many passages were apparently in Marcion's text that worked against his theology. A growing alertness to such issues with the evidence in the research conducted since Harnack has called into question his claim to have an accurate grasp of Marcion's dogmatic principles when it came to handling the biblical text.[37] Any conclusions drawn on this question must be based on the evidence of the texts themselves, not any assumptions about Marcion and his motives. Unfortunately, we lack the basis for a truly objective comparison, since we are in no better position than Tertullian when it comes to certainty about the shape of the texts in question before the time of Marcion. Moreover, conditioned as we are by a long tradition of making sense of these texts in the longer form in which they appear in modern Bibles, it may be hard for us to step back, dismantle that sense, and consider with an open mind the possible priority of Marcion's versions.

There is nothing inherently implausible about the idea that Marcion edited his texts to make them more representative of what he valued and considered important. In fact, he lived at a time when gospels were still being actively composed, often by reworking, merging, and elaborating on earlier gospels. The problem with attributing this sort of authorship to Marcion comes from an examination of texts themselves, and can be summed up in a series of questions: Why did not he not produce a more novel set of texts, fitted exactly to his beliefs? Why do his versions of the texts contain so much material in direct conflict with his own ideas? Why are the differences in his versions relatively minor in comparison with non-Marcionite versions, with minimal impact on the overall message? Why did he leave in passages expressing the exact same views for which he supposedly removed other passages? Why did he not add anything? As such questions pile up, it becomes increasingly difficult to make a case for the notion that Marcion's New Testament contained texts "mutilated" to conform to his distinctive beliefs.

The little that we know factually is that Marcion charged that "the gospel" adhered to by members of the Christian community in Rome was not authentic, that it diverged from the true record of "the gospel" known to him.[38] We know that he presented to those who heeded him an textual embodiment of "the Gospel and Apostle" that he considered authentic, along with a systematic interpretive exposition of how the faith embodied in these authentic texts was incompatible with the teachings of the Jewish scriptures. That is all we know. We do not have a single statement of Marcion on those passages he supposedly excised from his texts as corruptions. We cannot be sure that Marcion's statements regarding a corrupt "gospel" in use in Rome even referred to a text, rather than to an oral teaching. In fact, the expression "the gospel" continued to be used in the latter sense of the religious message of Christianity in general long after Marcion, and his own innovation in titling a part of his New Testament "The Gospel" (Evangelion) may have been in pointed response to what he regarded as the instability of resting authority on an uncodified set of traditions. Even when Tertullian says that Marcion excised something from "the gospel," he often refers not to edits worked upon a specific gospel text, but to Marcion's failure to include in his New Testament all of the gospel materials accepted in Tertullian's community, including not only Luke but also Matthew, Mark, and John.[39] These remarks of Tertullian have been regularly misunderstood in modern scholarship.[40] Furthermore, as noted above, our sources frequently accuse Marcion of having changed the wording of passages, but it turns out that the "changed" wording also occurs in non-Marcionite manuscripts, so that wording once thought by researchers to be indicative of his ideology have since been found in lines of textual transmission outside the confines of his church.[41]

The reconstruction of Marcion's New Testament offered in this study, therefore, does not assume that Marcion edited the texts; neither does it accept uncritically Marcion's own implicit claims for the authenticity of the form of the texts he canonized. Rather, it makes use of the data we have on the content of Marcion's canon in a neutral way, in order simply to present the First New Testament as a historical event in its own right, and to establish a more secure base from which arguments may be made and conclusions drawn about the history of these texts both before and after this event. There is an important place for examining Marcion's collection of Christian scriptures in itself, and not primarily in terms of debatable suppositions about Marcion and Marcionism. It may be that an independent analysis of this collection of texts actually sheds light on Marcion, rather than the reverse. But, in any case, Marcion's New Testament holds its primary significance as the earliest substantial witness we have to texts ultimately incorporated into the New Testament used by Christians today, and potentially provides new insight into their literary history and the forms of Christianity they represent.

The Sources

Our ability to reconstruct the First New Testament is hampered by the nature of our sources, all of which are polemical attacks on Marcionite views written by leaders of other forms of Christianity. They make no attempt to quote every word of Marcion's text, and even when they do quote, they do not always do so exactly. Rather, they cite that which is relevant to their argument, skipping over passages that contain nothing they can use against Marcion. The three principal sources used by Harnack and relied upon in more recent studies are Tertullian's *Against Marcion* from the early third century, Epiphanius' *Medicine-Chest (Panarion)* from the second half of fourth century, and *On the Correct Faith in God (De Recta in Deum Fide)*, an anonymous dialogue of the late third to early fourth century whose main character is given the name Adamantius. A number of lesser sources provide important confirmation of readings given by the major three, or fill in gaps otherwise left by them.

A. Tertullian

Our earliest and best evidence for the content of Marcion's Evangelion and Apostolikon comes from books 4 and 5, respectively, of Tertullian's massive refutation of Marcion's teachings.[42] He undertook this work around the year 207 CE, about half a century after Marcion's death. Tertullian's intent was to show that even Marcion's own selected sacred scripture does not support the heretic's teaching. This strategy of refutation had been proposed by Irenaeus (*Haer.* 1.27.4). As far as we know, the latter never carried out this plan; but it became a favorite, employed by Tertullian, Epiphanius, Pseudo-Ephrem A, and, to a lesser degree, Adamantius. Tertullian proceeds fairly systematically through Marcion's texts, and this approach is greatly to our benefit. But comparison with our other sources shows that Tertullian does skip over passages. He passes over content that either offered nothing useful to his polemical purposes or contained elements that would actually weaken his argument. As he works through the letters of Paul, he skips over more and more material simply because (as he expressly says, *Marc.* 5.3) he considered it redundant to keep making the same arguments over and over again.[43]

Because it is evident that Tertullian had an actual copy of Marcion's New Testament in front of him as he worked, modern researchers universally rate his evidence very highly, and have turned to close readings of his quotations to reconstruct the exact wording of Marcion's text. This has proven to be problematic, however. Research since Harnack has pointed out that Tertullian, in all of his writings, quotes the Bible loosely, sometimes from memory, sometimes paraphrased. Although Tertullian is being careful in *Against Marcion* to argue against Marcion on the basis of the content of passages actually included in the Marcionite Bible, there is no reason to think that he reliably quotes these passages verbatim. He freely reorders clauses and whole verses within a particular section he is discussing according to the flow of his own argument. Often he merely uses the overall thrust of a passage as the basis of his comments. It is only when his argument hinges on particular wording, or in those few instances where he mentions a difference in wording between the Marcionite text and his own, that we can rely on Tertullian confidently as a source for a word-by-word reconstruction of Marcion's text,[44] and the reconstruction must involve comparison with how Tertullian words the passage in other writings, when quoting from his own texts of Luke and Paul.[45]

A related concern for those who would reconstruct Marcion's text from Tertullian is whether Tertullian was working from a Marcionite-approved Latin translation, or was using his own translation skills on a Greek text.[46] When the uncertainty over the answer to this question is combined with the observations on Tertullian's loose habits of quotation, one is forced to admit that supposed variances in wording between Marcion's texts and those in use among non-Marcionites must be substantiated by other sources. Tertullian's chief value as a source, therefore, comes from the fact that he provides reliable information on the presence of particular passages of content in the Evangelion and Apostolikon, whenever he alludes to them in his argumentation, even if the full extent and exact wording of the passage remains uncertain.

Although few have questioned that Tertullian had direct access to the Evangelion and Apostolikon, we cannot be absolutely sure. A couple of features of his discussion invite caution. First, he frequently comments on Marcion's interpretation and application of a particular verse, as if he is looking at Marcion's *Antitheses* and drawing scriptural quotations from it, rather than directly from the Evangelion and Apostolikon. Second, Tertullian's selective quotations from the Apostolikon possess a kind of running logic, as one quoted verse follows upon another in what has the appearance of a connected argument; yet that argument is not Tertullian's.

Rather, by selectively skipping over intervening material, a cogent Marcionite reading of Paul comes sharply into focus, which Tertullian does his best to disarticulate and refute. This impression is subjective, of course, and may be an illusion. But if Tertullian relied completely on the quotations of scripture in Marcion's *Antitheses*, and did not have direct access to the Evangelion and Apostolikon, any comment he makes about passages missing from these texts would be suspect, the result of mere supposition on his part based on Marcion's failure to quote them.

B. Epiphanius

Epiphanius, bishop of Salamis on the island of Cyprus in the later fourth century, provides a second valuable set of firsthand readings from Marcion's biblical texts, independent of that offered by Tertullian. His discussion of Marcion's New Testament, like Tertullian's, is part of a larger refutation of Marcionite teaching, which in turn constitutes only a small portion of a much larger refutation of all varieties of Christianity known to him besides his own Nicene faith.[47] This *Panarion*, or "medicine-chest," against heresy, dates to around 377 CE. Epiphanius incorporated into it an anti-Marcionite treatise he had written some years earlier, and his description of how he composed this treatise is worth quoting in full.

> Some years ago, to find what lies and silly teachings this Marcion had invented, I took up his very books which he had mutilated, that named by him *Evangelion* and that called by him *Apostolikon*. From these two books I made a series of extracts and selections of the material which was capable of refuting him, and I wrote a sort of outline for a treatise, arranging the points in order, and numbering each saying one, two, three (and so on). And in this way I went through all of the passages in which it is apparent that, like a fool, he still retains these leftover sayings of the Savior and the Apostle to his own disadvantage. For some of the sayings had been entered by him in an altered form and not matching those in the Gospel according to Luke nor the characteristic presentation of the Apostolic (section of the New Testament). But others correspond with those of both the Gospel and the Apostle—unchanged by him, and yet capable of disproving his whole case. (*Pan.* 42.10.2–5)

Epiphanius, like Tertullian, only mentions passages pertinent to his arguments, but in his case this involves a more concerted effort with regard to the Evangelion to note which passages are lacking or different in Marcion's text when compared with the version of Luke accepted in his own faith community; for some reason, however, he does not continue this sort of analysis for the letters of Paul in the Apostolikon. His testimony is valuable, therefore, in providing specific notations of textual differences down to the exact wording of Marcion's text in its original Greek, at least with respect to the Evangelion. As regards the order of Marcion's text, Epiphanius seems to follow this strictly with only a very few exceptions. Indeed, his presentation reflects the procedure he describes of taking notes from Marcion's text and recording them in a notebook as notations, or *scholia*. He has seventy-eight such notes from the Evangelion and forty from the Apostolikon (eight from Galatians, sixteen from 1 Corinthians, three from 2 Corinthians, eight from Romans, three from "Ephesians," and one each from Colossians and "Laodiceans"). Yet Epiphanius frequently abbreviates his quotes, reducing them to the key phrases, and so his evidence, just as Tertullian's, must be used cautiously. Like Tertullian, he shows much less interest in sustaining his analysis through the letters of Paul, and he quite frequently makes sweeping charges that Marcion had altered the text, without providing any specific examples.[48]

Despite potentially offering a more direct witness to the original Greek of the Evangelion and Apostolikon, Epiphanius has not enjoyed the same generally positive assessment among modern researchers as has Tertullian.[49] The striking difference between Epiphanius' handling of the Evangelion and of the Apostolikon does invite some suspicions about his access to the latter. He is able to comment very precisely on text lacking from the Evangelion in comparison to Luke, but fails to specify any similar omission in the letters of Paul (for which we have Tertullian's testimony), instead making sweeping, apparently baseless remarks about the corruption of their texts by Marcion. He also seems confused about something as basic as which letters were included in the Apostolikon, referring to both "Ephesians" and "Laodiceans," even though these are one and the same letter under its catholic and Marcionite designation, respectively. From evidence such as this, John Clabeaux concludes that, "It is clear from an examination of Epiphanius' citations from the Marcionite Apostolikon in *Panarion* 42 that he had no Marcionite Bible in his hands, despite his claim to the contrary. . . . His quotations were taken from anti-Marcionite literature that was available to him."[50] But Clabeaux has gone too far. A couple of problems in Epiphanius' handling of the Apostolikon do not force conclusions about his access to the Marcionite New Testament as a whole, particularly when he can make very precise statements about the text of the Evangelion.

Epiphanius does not claim to have a Marcionite Bible in his hands at the time he is writing the *Panarion*; rather, he explicitly states that he drew up a set of notes (*scholia*) at some time in the past when he had the opportunity to examine Marcion's Evangelion and Apostolikon. Of course, he could be lying, as Clabeaux suggests. But this hypothesis raises many more problems than it solves. Clabeaux cannot suggest a possible source from which Epiphanius acquired his quotations, as he very effectively demonstrates that it was neither Tertullian nor Adamantius, nor any common anti-Marcionite source, either.[51] Furthermore, Clabeaux's view forces us to imagine Epiphanius laboriously scouring through his sources for quotations from Marcion's canon, and then copying them out in the Marcionite order, which he somehow knows without ever having seen the Marcionite New Testament. It is much simpler to imagine him doing precisely what he said he did: reading through the Marcionite New Testament and taking notes which, looking back at them years later, confused him on a few points.[52] The location of his single note on "Laodiceans," at the very end of his set of *scholia*, suggests that it, and it alone, derived as Clabeaux suggests from some intermediate source, copied into Epiphanius' notes in the intervening years. Until a stronger case can be made against the worth of Epiphanius' testimony, he continues to merit second place among our sources.

C. Adamantius

The work passing under the name "Adamantius" is a dialogue composed in Greek by an as-yet-unidentified author sometime in the last decade of the third century or first decade of the fourth century CE.[53] "Adamantius" is the name given to the character in the dialogue who upholds "orthodoxy" from the author's viewpoint against representatives of various "heresies," including two Marcionites (in parts 1 and 2 of the treatise). As the latter speak, they offer sporadic quotations from the Marcionite New Testament, as does Adamantius in rebuttal.[54] Unlike Tertullian and Epiphanius, the author offers these quotations and allusions as the argument calls for them, not in the order in which they appeared in the

Marcionite New Testament, and he makes no attempt at systematic coverage of the entire canon. The Marcionite scriptures play no role (with one brief exception[55]) in parts 3 and 4 of the treatise, as Adamantius enters into debate with other "heretics," followers of Bardaisan and Valentinus. But as the set of debates draws to its conclusion in part 5, some passages are expressly said to be read out from the Marcionite Evangelion and Apostolikon.[56]

Most modern researchers suspect that Adamantius had his information on the Evangelion and Apostolikon secondhand, copied from earlier, now lost anti-Marcionite sources.[57] Part 1 of the dialogue, however, shows a distinctive structure involving repeated contrasts of New Testament passages to Old Testament ones,[58] suggesting the possibility that the author may have drawn on Marcion's treatise, the *Antitheses*, for some of the biblical quotations he puts into the mouth of imagined Marcionite debaters. The appearance of two different Marcionite debaters may reflect two distinct sources, while the odd momentary reappearance of one of them in books 3 and 5 perhaps signals an editorial seam, where the author has drawn on an anti-Marcionite source to address the issue at hand.

Adolf von Harnack and Ulrich Schmid represent the two extreme poles in modern assessments of the worth of *Adamantius'* evidence: Harnack accepts nearly every biblical quotation in the dialogue as informative about the Marcionite New Testament, even in parts of the dialogue where Marcionites are not involved, while Schmid considers the dialogue all but worthless, even when the text explicitly says that it is quoting from the Evangelion and Apostolikon.[59] In only a single instance is Schmid forced to acknowledge that Adamantius has accurate information matched by Tertullian on the very distinctive wording of a passage (Adam 2.19, on 1 Corinthians 15). But, from that one exception, Schmid's extreme skepticism about the value of Adamantius rapidly unravels. Adamantius never quotes a verse known from any other source to have been absent from Marcion's text, and in fact in a number of places he matches other sources on distinctive wording.[60]

Further complications in the use of Adamantius as a source stem from the fact that the manuscripts of the dialogue are medieval at the earliest, and the biblical quotations in them may have been corrupted or conformed to the catholic text familiar to later copyists. One possible safeguard against such corruption is the existence of a Latin translation made by Rufinus in the closing years of the fourth century. Rufinus' paraphrastic tendencies as a translator are notorious, however, and a close analysis of his handling of biblical passages in Adamantius has led Vinzenz Buchheit to conclude that his translation cannot be used—contra Harnack's view—to recover the wording of Marcion's New Testament texts that may have been lost in the late and corrupt Greek manuscript tradition.[61] In any case, the kind of textual corruption very likely to impact Adamantius' biblical quotations would alter the wording without necessarily distorting the record of which passages were mentioned. So Adamantius continues to serve in reconstructions of the content of the First New Testament, even if compromised as a witness to the exact wording of that content.

D. Pseudo-Ephrem A

Two Armenian manuscripts preserve two alternate editions of a work attributed to Ephrem Syrus.[62] Critical study of this work a century ago determined that it is a composite text of various and uncertain authorship.[63] The first separable component of the text has been accordingly labeled "Pseudo-Ephrem A," and is devoted to a refutation of Marcionite views based upon the analogies and parables used by Jesus in his teaching. The latter, which the author invariably refers to as quoted from "the gospel," are drawn exclusively from Luke, suggesting that the author is quoting from the Evangelion, using the same strategy employed by Tertullian and Epiphanius of refuting the Marcionites from their own accepted scripture.[64] This probability is heightened by the author's remarks at two points that the particular material he wishes to cite in his argument was not included in "the gospel" of the Marcionites (Ps.-Eph A 44, 64). Moreover, the form of expression used by the author in citing evidence from "the gospel" closely matches that apparently used by Marcion himself in his *Antitheses*, as attested by Tertullian.[65] Pseudo-Ephrem A thus offers a potentially valuable check on our other sources for the Evangelion, both as regards the inclusion or exclusion of certain passages known from Luke, and for their particular wording,[66] despite Harnack's summary rejection of it for these purposes[67] and the issues raised subsequently by George Egan,[68] both of which are methodologically problematic.[69]

Although some have wished to mine Pseudo-Ephrem A for evidence regarding the Apostolikon as well, there appears to be no good reason to think it offers any. The author quotes the letters of Paul only as part of his anti-Marcionite argument when, after citing a specific parable or analogy found in the Marcionite Evangelion, he proceeds to draw on his own set of scriptures. He does not confine himself to the limits of the Marcionite canon. The value of Pseudo-Ephrem A for the reconstruction of the Marcionite New Testament, therefore, appears limited to the Evangelion. Still unresolved is the exact provenance of the text in place and time, and whether it can be identified with any of the lost anti-Marcionite works mentioned in our sources.

E. Acts of Archelaus 44–45

The *Acts of Archelaus* (*Acta Archelai*) is a dramatized set of debates, similar to Adamantius, written by a certain Hegemonius in the early fourth century CE—against not the Marcionites but a later "heresy," Manichaeism. It is preserved in an abridged Latin version, but isolated passages of an earlier Greek version can be found quoted in Epiphanius and Cyril of Jerusalem. The Manichaeans held a view similar to Marcion's on the incompatibility of the Jewish and Christian faiths, and developed Marcion's own technique of posing antithetical contrasts of Old and New Testament texts. Harnack thought it justifiable to reconstruct some of the content of Marcion's *Antitheses* indirectly from similar Manichaean arguments, assuming some dependence of the latter on Marcion's earlier effort. But since the Manichaeans made use of the larger catholic New Testament canon for this purpose, Harnack could not claim it all for Marcion; instead, he took the questionable liberty of ascribing to Marcion any Manichaean antithesis that happened to cite a text included in Marcion's New Testament. Researchers since Harnack have been right to reject the evidence he collected on the basis of such an unsound approach. But it is now possible to refine this use of Manichaean material, with the demonstration that a specific section of the *Acts of Archelaus* (44–45) definitely limits itself to the Marcionite canon, and therefore its content can be traced back to Marcion's *Antithesis* more confidently than can other Manichaean antithetical biblical arguments.[70]

F. Papyrus 69—A Fragment of the Evangelion?

A third-century papyrus fragment from Oxyrhynchus in Egypt, housed in the Ashmolean Museum, Oxford, under the catalog number P. Oxy. 2383, and designated P^{69} within biblical textual criticism, was originally published as a fragment of canonical Luke.[71] It shows an unusual degree of divergence, however, from other manuscripts of Luke, in both length and phrasing,[72] approaching the degree of independence of parabiblical gospels. This raises the possibility that it is a remnant of Marcion's Evangelion.[73] While we have only limited allusions to this part of the Evangelion in our principal sources, the text of P^{69} agrees substantially with what little other evidence we have. If P^{69} does indeed represent a remnant of Marcion's Evangelion, it shows the degree to which Marcion's text differed from the canonical version even in minor points of narrative and vocabulary. It would also be telling that such minor divergences and idiosyncrasies in the text elicited no comment from Tertullian or Epiphanius. This would force us to be very cautious about any conclusions on exact wording within Marcion's text, a point well made by David Salter Williams.[74]

G. The Marcionite Prologues to Paul's Letters

In 1907, Donatien De Bruyne demonstrated that a set of Latin prologues to Paul's letters, found in a number of Vulgate biblical manuscripts, contained wording suggesting that they derived originally from a Marcionite context.[75] First, they have as their central unifying theme the conflict between Paul and "false apostles" who promoted the Jewish law, even for letters where this was at best a minor subject of Paul's discussion.[76] Second, of the existing prologues, the ones introducing letters not included in Marcion's Apostolikon can be shown to be secondary additions to an original set for only those letters known to Marcion.[77] Third, their wording indicates that they originally had a different sequence than the canonical order of the letters in which they currently appear in catholic Bibles, and that they relate to each other in the order of the Apostolikon. These prologues can be traced back at least to the mid-fourth century.[78]

Several researchers have cast doubt on De Bruyne's hypothesis of a Marcionite provenance for these prologues, not least because no anti-Marcionite polemicist ever refers to them. Sharing the sequence of the Apostolikon does not itself prove their Marcionite origin, since the "Marcionite" sequence of the letters (in particular, Galatians-Corinthians-Romans) is found outside of Marcionite circles, and apparently was the original order in Syria.[79] After all, why would catholic copyists include Marcionite texts in their Bibles? Yet there remain several features of the prologues that are difficult to explain if they are not Marcionite. For example, the prologue to the letter to the Colossians only makes sense within a Pauline corpus in which it followed one addressed to the Laodiceans—since it begins, "Colossians also, like Laodiceans, are Asians." Moreover, the prologues' understanding of Paul's final movements—in prison in Ephesus and transported from there to Rome—ignores or is ignorant of Acts, as would be the case with Marcion or a Marcionite writer.[80] Finally, concern with "Judaizers" is one thing, but speaking of Christians being "led astray into the Law and Prophets," as the prologue to Romans does, puts the author beyond the pale of "orthodox" Christian sentiments, and pretty squarely into a Marcionite world view.[81]

The prologues, whether Marcionite or not, provide confirmation of the sequence of Paul's letters in the Apostolikon, and help us to see its logic. The letters are not arranged by length (as they are in the catholic canon), nor geographically (while the two "Asian" cities are clustered, the "Macedonian" cities are separated), but chronologically by an assumed historical order,[82] with the "prison letters" (Colossians, Philippians, Philemon) last. Through their reference to specific content of each letter, the prologues also attest the presence of particular verses in the text known in the time and circumstances when the prologues were composed. Since I remain convinced that the prologues have a Marcionite origin, this information supplies a handful of additional passages to the reconstruction of the Apostolikon.

H. Other Sources

A number of other early Christian writers provide isolated quotations of and references to passages in the Marcionite Evangelion and Apostolikon. The larger heresiological treatises of Irenaeus (late second century) and Hippolytus (early third century) include short sections on the Marcionites, and make some allusions to scriptural passages important to the Marcionites in their own teaching. Eusebius of Caesarea occasionally cites material from other early anti-Marcionite tracts, otherwise lost.

Origen, writing in the first half of the third century, apparently wrote extensively against the Marcionites, but most of that work is lost. Fragments of a commentary on Luke preserve remarks on differences between Luke and the Evangelion, as well as points of Marcionite interpretation of their gospel, and he makes the same sort of observations with regard to the Apostolikon in his commentary on Paul's letter to the Romans. Two factors weaken Origen's value for our purposes, however. First, Origen generally does not follow the principle of arguing on the basis of scripture accepted by the Marcionites, and shows no interest in giving a close analysis of Marcion's text, so he cannot be relied upon to provide information on the Marcionite canon even when he is engaged with Marcionite Christianity in his discussion. Second, he at times appears to be dealing with Marcionites who are willing to cite Christian texts outside of Marcion's New Testament (this is true also of Adamantius), so that even material cited from Marcionites may not be pertinent to the reconstruction of the original Marcionite canon. In one case, Origen relays important testimony from another source. In his refutation of the philosopher Celsus' attack on Christianity, he quotes a passage where Celsus appears to be using Marcion's *Antitheses* to show (as Marcion argued) that the "laws" of Jesus and those of Moses were fundamentally incompatible—the "laws" of Jesus, of course, would have been drawn from the Evangelion.[83] The famous biblical translator and commentator Jerome, writing in the late fourth and early fifth century, often preserves information from Origen that is otherwise lost. But because he worked secondhand, he may have drawn incorrect inferences about the state of Marcion's text, which he had never seen himself.[84]

In the mid-fourth century, the Syrian writer Ephrem wrote against Marcion in several different compositions. In the process, he alluded to a number of passages of the Evangelion. Ephrem is also important for his commentaries on his own community's New Testament texts, providing an important point of comparison with Marcion's New Testament, and at times showing unique agreements with the latter. His commentary on the letters of Paul, for instance, not only shares readings with Marcion not found anywhere else, but also originally followed the same order of Paul's letters found in the Apostolikon. He also wrote a commentary on the Diatessaron, a gospel text composed by weaving together the contents of the gospels of Matthew, Mark, Luke, and John. Since the Diatessaron can be dated confidently to just a generation after Marcion, it offers valuable evidence on the state of those four gospels close to the time of Marcion, for comparison with the related material in the Evangelion.

The fifth-century Armenian writer Eznik of Kolb composed a treatise "On God" that includes anti-Marcionite arguments occasionally alluding to passages of the Marcionite New Testament. In several of these, his testimony confirms that found in other sources.

But for two passages (2 Cor 12.2; Phil 2.5–6) he provides important supplementary information, and for two other passages he provides unique attestation (1 Cor 8.13; Phil 1.23).

Other documents may also provide information on the content of the Marcionite New Testament, even though they do not expressly identify the source of their scriptural allusions as Marcionite. The Pseudo-Clementine *Homilies* and *Recognitions*, for example, appear to target Marcion and his teachings under the guise of the arch-heretic "Simon Magus." When the latter character occasionally cites scripture, the author of these texts may be drawing upon Marcionite or anti-Marcionite works that in turn rely on the wording of the Evangelion and Apostolikon.[85]

All of these "other sources" involve reporting the quotation and interpretation of specific biblical verses by Marcionites, and in this way suggest that the particular verse was found in the Marcionite New Testament.[86] Reports of this kind could come from actual encounters with Marcionite spokespersons, or from Marcionite literature, such a Marcion's own *Antitheses*, which quoted and commented on the Evangelion and Apostolikon. Anomalies do occur, however, such as reported citation by Marcionites of texts known not to have been included in their Bible. Discrepancies of this sort have led some modern researchers to reject all such secondhand reports of Marcionite quotations from their own scriptures. I consider this to be an overreaction. Polemicists make mistakes, and some of what they attribute to the biblical exegesis of their opponents could certainly be wrong; but to systematically exclude all such testimony is excessive. In no other case in the historical study of intra-Christian debates over biblical interpretation do researchers throw out similar such reports of what an opponent cites from scripture in defense of his or her position. Although we cannot put much stock in the exact wording of a verse in such a report, we can reasonably conclude in most cases the presence of the particular verse in some form in the Marcionite New Testament.

The early wide dissemination of Marcion's New Testament raises the possibility that other early Christian literature may depend on it as a source. Where previous scholarship has suggested that a piece of literature shows literary dependence on Luke, it may have depended on the Evangelion instead. The Gospel of Thomas, the Diatessaron, the Longer Ending of Mark, the Apocryphal Acts, and the various pieces of Gnostic literature are all potential candidates for the recovery of such material. The same holds true, of course, for the possibility that quotations from the letters of Paul have been taken from the Apostolikon.

It has been proposed in the past that Marcionite readings somehow crept into catholic manuscripts and versions of Luke and Paul.[87] While possible, this proposition needs to be tested against the alternative scenario: perhaps Marcion's Evangelion and Apostolikon preserve readings from the common stock of pre-Marcionite copies of these texts, from which the catholic copies also descend. Such agreements between catholic biblical manuscripts and testimony about Marcion's texts help to confirm that a particular phrasing is not just a source's idiosyncratic paraphrase. John J. Clabeaux's work in this regard is invaluable.[88] At the same time, the presence of the particular phrasing in Marcion's biblical texts increases the importance of rare alternative readings in the catholic biblical manuscripts that otherwise might be ignored as isolated aberrations, by proving that they go back to very early in the textual tradition, to at least the first half of the second century.

The Reconstruction

Interest in reconstructing the Marcionite New Testament has fallen into two broad camps of researchers, with two distinct projects that can be summed up as, on the one hand, interest in the *content* of Marcion's texts and, on the other hand, interest in their *wording*. The first project seeks to determine which passages were in Marcion's Bible and what ideas they conveyed, as part of understanding the redaction of these texts across time and distinct Christian communities, as different editorial interests added or removed certain episodes, themes, or other material. Confidence in the close literary relationship between the Evangelion and the Gospel of Luke, and between the Apostolikon and the catholic version of the letters of Paul, permits conclusions to be drawn about the meaningful content of passages referred to in our sources, even if caution is required about possible differences in meaning due to redactional and textual variations. The second project seeks to establish the exact word-for-word text of individual verses, as part of the textual criticism of the New Testament, in order to apply the evidence of Marcion to the history of particular major or minor textual variants in wording in the transmission of the text. The two projects cannot be completely separated, as evidence from either one is relevant to the other; but the reconstruction offered in this book aligns more closely with the first project, and is focused on recovering the meaningful content of the First New Testament despite any uncertainty over the exact wording with which that content was conveyed.

Since it may sound a bit odd on the surface to talk of reconstructing the content of a book without being able to provide its exact wording, a comparative example may be helpful. I have mentioned before the second-century gospel text known as the Diatessaron. No copies of this book survive. Modern researchers attempt to reconstruct it based on a number of sources who describe or quote it, such as a fourth-century commentary on it written by Ephrem Syrus. Because we know that the author of the Diatessaron composed it by drawing material from the gospels of Matthew, Mark, Luke, and John, even a mere allusion to a passage often can be identified as to its content, by recognizing the corresponding passage of one of those gospels. Specialists in the study of the Diatessaron have concluded that an eleventh-century Arabic gospel harmony may be of particular importance. Similarities in the sequence of passages between this text and Ephrem's commentary have persuaded them that it is indeed based upon the Diatessaron. However, the exact wording in each passage is suspect, since in many cases it differs in small details from other witnesses to the wording of the Diatessaron; it more closely resembles the later Syriac translation of the four separate gospels. Therefore, the Arabic gospel harmony is considered a reliable source for determining whether or not a specific gospel episode was present in the Diatessaron, and in what sequence the episodes appeared, but not for the exact wording in each episode. It can be used to establish the *content* of the Diatessaron, but not its *wording*. This is precisely the level of reconstruction of the Marcionite New Testament attempted here.

Most studies of Marcion's New Testament have focused individually on either the Evangelion or Apostolikon, and the history of scholarship on them generally has followed separate trajectories. Although many of the sources are the same for the two texts, the premises and issues of reconstruction have developed very differently. Adolf von Harnack's comprehensive attempt at reconstructions of both in 1924 was atypical, and marked a watershed in the effort to recover the Marcionite Bible.[89] The culmination of a lifetime of research, it involved the assessment of every potential scrap of information, rendered all previous work largely obsolete, and remains the standard against which any new proposal is measured. Harnack was guided in his work by his confidence that we are able to know a great deal about the content of Marcion's New Testament, not only from generally reliable sources and a close literary relationship to catholic versions of the Gospel of Luke and the letters of Paul, but also from understanding the ideological motives that guided Marcion's presumed editorial work. While many parts of Harnack's interpretation of Marcion have been called into question in the decades since he wrote, his conception of Marcion's editorial activity continues to be repeated in most treatments of Marcion as if established fact. In the decades following Harnack, most contributions to the subject sought merely to refine his reconstruction on individual points. Kenji Tsutsui's updated reconstruction of the Evangelion from 1992 is representative of this trajectory of scholarship, following Harnack's own approach to the material while contributing a number of corrections and new interpretations of the sources.[90]

A handful of Harnack's reviewers, however, already raised methodological objections to his reconstruction of the Marcionite canon.[91] In recent decades there has arisen a growing consensus among those who work closely with the primary sources on Marcion's biblical texts that Harnack's results are too speculative and no longer acceptable.[92] This emerging revisionist view reached a critical point in in the late 1980s and early 1990s in contributions by David Salter Williams[93] and Ulrich Schmid.[94] Both Williams and Schmid fault the overconfidence with which Harnack asserted insight into Marcion's editorial motives, and both call for a more cautious approach rooted in the evidence for texts of the Evangelion and Apostolikon themselves, apart from any assumptions about Marcion. Schmid has articulated the two principles that distinguish his approach, and that of Williams, from previous work: (1) abandoning "appeals to Marcionite tendency," that is, any presupposition of what Marcion would be expected to do, based on our presumed understanding of his motives, and (2) screening sources first for their quotation habits, theological agendas, and rhetorical strategies before drawing conclusions about the accuracy of their reports on the Marcionite text.[95] From this common viewpoint, however, Williams and Schmid develop quite different methodologies, yielding minimalist and maximalist reconstructions, respectively.

David Salter Williams attempts a reconstruction of passages from the Evangelion in which relative confidence can be placed due to confirmation from multiple sources on exact wording, yielding minimal results. Williams convincingly demonstrates that close comparison of Tertullian and Epiphanius on those passages they quote in common reveals significant differences in wording. His analysis highlights the looseness with which these authors quote or allude to Marcion's text, and hence the uncertainty involved in any effort to reconstruct Marcion's original Greek text word-for-word.[96] Consequently, his reconstruction yields a minimal text of twenty-three passages, equivalent to a mere twenty-six verses in Luke. Even these passages often show variations in wording between the sources. Based on the very limited amount of text reconstructible by his methodology, Williams proposes that (1) the Evangelion may have diverged widely from Luke; (2) we should be very cautious about filling in the gaps between content our sources directly report (by assuming either inclusion or omission); and (3) we have no firm evidence that Marcion exercised any sort of editorial work on the text.[97]

Ulrich Schmid has offered a reconstruction of the Apostolikon along maximalist lines.[98] Whereas Williams will only accept explicit, multiple testimony for *inclusion* of material in what he regards as an otherwise unknown text (in his case, the Evangelion bearing some ill-defined relationship to Luke), Schmid argues that one should rely solely on explicit testimony for *exclusion* of material from a text that he thinks we have good reason to believe is very closely related to the otherwise familiar texts of Paul's letters. Harnack had exceeded the testimony of his sources by proposing that certain passages must have been omitted because they conflicted with Marcion's ideology, even where the sources are silent on any such omission. "Arguments *e silentio*, creating positive evidence out of lack of evidence, should not be allowed," Schmid counters, "even if the alleged omission would match supposed theological preferences of Marcion."[99] Lacking any direct testimony to the contrary, he contends, we should assume all of the remaining material known from the catholic text was present.[100]

The critical stance towards Harnack's methodology that is the starting point of Williams' and Schmid's work is the one taken as well in the reconstruction offered here. I agree entirely with the caution expressed by these two researchers that we do not really know what Harnack thought we knew about Marcion's possible editorial motives. We must approach the Evangelion and Apostolikon as texts in their own right, without assuming that Marcion's interpretation of them played a role in shaping their actual content. We should look for the editorial motives behind the texts in the same way we do with any other biblical text, by looking first of all at the structure and themes of the texts themselves, and then in comparison to the alternative forms these materials take in Luke (or the gospel tradition more generally) and the Pauline letters in their catholic version, without assuming priority on either side. I further agree with Williams on the possibility that Marcion's Evangelion text may have differed from Luke even in very minor word choices and phrasing, given the fluidity of the early textual tradition shown by even the catholic manuscript evidence. For example, the Lukan fragment P^{69} displays extensive variation in phrasing from the majority of witnesses to Luke, even though most of it is insignificant in terms of the general meaning of the narrative. I likewise agree with Schmid that our sources cannot be relied upon to deal comprehensively with every verse of the Evangelion and Apostolikon; they individually skip over material that other witnesses remark upon, and so we often must forge ahead on the word of a single witness. Yet my reconstruction differs from that offered by either Williams for the Evangelion or Schmid for the Apostolikon, and I must explain why.

Williams set himself the project of determining how far one could securely go in reconstructing the original word-for-word Greek text of the Evangelion, and I agree with his conclusions about the daunting challenges facing any such attempt.[101] My own work with the sources has convinced me that, in a large number of the passages attested by more than one source, it is impossible to draw any certain conclusion about a single original wording of the text. Williams' minimal results should surprise no one, once we recognize that the attempt to recover Marcion's text word-for-word flies in the face of the character of our sources. As Ulrich Schmid has observed, a source such as Tertullian is only interested in putting passages from Marcion's New Testament to work in his own argument, and is "oriented primarily to the content, more than to the concrete wording of the text (*sich primär an Inhalten, weniger an konkreten Textlesarten orientiert*)."[102] Therefore, the problem with accepting a minimalist outcome on the narrow terms of being able to establish an exact original wording is that we (including

Williams) know that Marcion's Evangelion was much more extensive than what can be reconstructed by this approach. As Joseph Tyson observes, "if Marcion's opponents refer to a sentence that is included in his gospel, with or without variations, it is reasonable to conclude that the pericope which surrounds the sentence in Luke, or something very much like it, also appeared in Marcion's gospel. Williams' issues make us rightly dubious about determining the wording of Marcion's gospel, but we can be reasonably confident about the inclusion or exclusion of the larger discourses and narratives"[103] In most cases, there is little doubt that Tertullian or Epiphanius actually saw the passage to which they refer in the Marcionite New Testament, even if we have reason to question the accuracy of their transcription of it. In fact, the sort of differences in wording we see between our sources when they report on a verse from Marcion's Bible is not qualitatively different than the differences they have when quoting a particular verse from their own catholic Bible. In the latter instance, we do not doubt that the catholic Bible contained the verse, and we strive to understand the difference in terms of the transmission of the text over time and the general tendency toward paraphrase in ancient authors.

Likewise, we cannot limit our knowledge of the Evangelion and Apostolikon only to what can be confirmed by the holy grail of having more than one source confirm it. The same sources that prove their worth by concurring on some quotations go on to individually provide other quotations; and if we accept their testimony in the first instance, there is no good reason to dismiss it in the second. True, their exact wording cannot be checked against another witness, and this limits their value for the sort of word-for-word reconstruction in which Williams is interested. But they do confirm the presence of particular content, however much their report paraphrases its wording; and I contend that the presence or absence of particular content has significance in itself for the history of New Testament texts, apart from the more narrow concern with what are often very minor variations in wording. John Clabeaux makes a similar point in his analysis of how Marcion's biblical texts handled Abraham as a subject, noting that "the precise wording of the passages about Abraham is rarely necessary. In most cases we need only determine whether the reference to Abraham was maintained or excised."[104] David Williams himself—once he has used the standard of agreement among the sources on exact wording to select only the best attested verses—draws his more significant conclusions about the Evangelion mostly from the mere presence and semantic content of the passages he has so identified, rather than from the differences of a word here or there. The text we can recover for the "Gospel and Apostle" of the Marcionite New Testament is every bit as good as that we can recover for the catholic Bible from patristic witnesses, whose local individual copies we attempt to reconstruct from cautious analysis of their quotations and allusions in spite of their paraphrastic nature and appearance in languages other than Greek.[105] For these reasons, my reconstruction goes well beyond the goals of Williams' study in the amount of text I find reasonable to present.

While the approach offered by Williams unnecessarily minimizes our reasonably secure knowledge of the content of the First New Testament, Schmid's project overestimates the amount of content that we can confidently conclude to have been present. Just as our sources cannot be relied upon to mention every passage present in the Evangelion and Apostolikon, so we cannot count on them to note every passage lacking in those texts relative to the longer orthodox versions. Ekkehard Mühlenberg stated already in 1979, "We are not furnished with a list of omissions, so that the *argumentum e silentio* cannot be admitted."[106] Mühlenberg voiced this caution against Harnack's assumption that silence equals absence, an assumption to which Schmid likewise objects. But the exact same problem arises with Schmid's assumption that silence equals presence. Just as the anti-Marcionite writers might have had reasons to skip over passages which did not serve their purposes, and so falsely give an impression that it was missing from Marcion's text, as Schmid rightly argues, so they may also have failed to mention that content was missing when it absence did not significantly impact their argument. This holds particularly true of the very perfunctory attention Tertullian and Epiphanius give to some of Paul's letters. Tertullian simply did not take it as an important part of his task to note differences between Marcion's text and his own, though he occasionally did. Epiphanius, on the other hand, made a point of noting differences between Marcion's Evangelion and the Gospel of Luke; even so, he apparently failed to note a number of such differences.[107] He attempted nothing similar with regard to the Apostolikon, simply making sweeping charges that Marcion tampered with the text of Paul's letters, without providing a single specific example. Schmid is careful to distinguish verses specifically mentioned from all those that go unmentioned, and is even particularly rigorous about what he accepts into the first category. He is certainly right, as well, that the burden of proof falls on those who propose a difference in Marcion's text for a verse that is not mentioned by any source. Nevertheless, in the reconstruction below, I have minimized the inclusion of anything not directly attested in our sources, as the more conservative approach to take to the evidence.

Given that our sources are in Latin, Syriac, and Armenian, as well as Greek, any attempt to render their testimony back into a single underlying Greek text faces daunting challenges, is necessarily speculative, and doomed to perennial debate. The catholic textual traditions of Luke and Paul's letters even in their original Greek are replete with minor variations in wording, as well as some significant divergences of content. At times we can draw comparisons of Marcion's wording to one or another variant in these larger textual traditions. But in a large percentage of instances the language barrier or the allusiveness of our sources makes direct identification of underlying Greek wording problematic. If P^{69} is a manuscript fragment of the Evangelion, as I have suggested it may be, it serves only to confirm the potential divergence even in very minor points of wording between the Evangelion and Luke. For reasons such as these, my reconstruction does not claim to retrieve the exact Greek *wording* of the First New Testament, even though in many cases fairly reliable conclusions about that wording are drawn. But since conclusions about the exact wording of the texts cannot be resolved in many cases, I confine the reconstruction offered here to an English text, both to signal that it should be considered an approximation of the original, and to provide accessibility of the information to a broad readership, who can make use of it in a variety of constructive ways even without a word-for-word Greek text.

In my reconstruction, therefore, I use the quotations, paraphrases, and allusions in the multiple languages of our sources to identify the content of the Evangelion and Apostolikon, and present that content in English. The established literary relationship of the Evangelion to the Gospel of Luke, and of the Apostolikon to the familiar letters of Paul, makes such an identification of their content possible even from mere allusion in our sources. So, just as one may recognize when an early Christian writer paraphrases or alludes to a passage of Luke or Paul, one can recognize when they paraphrase or allude to the Evangelion or Apostolikon in a context where they explicitly refer to Marcion or Marcionites citing their own authoritative texts. Everything that a Marcionite may cite from those texts has some sort of corresponding passage in the catholic texts of Luke and Paul, and that fact aids in the effort of reconstruction. At the same time, it is essential to take account of omissions and variant wording relative to the catholic text that produce a significant difference in the meaningful content of Marcion's texts. Evidence of such differences must be sifted very carefully through a number of methodological filters, and compared with a source's own paraphrastic habits as well as with known variants in the catholic textual tradition of Luke and the letters of Paul. It is in this way that the English text of the Evangelion and Apostolikon offered here is produced directly from information from the Greek, Latin, Syriac, and Armenian sources at our disposal.

*****

The following five steps constitute the basic procedure used in reconstructing the text of the First New Testament, and also provide a key to how the text is presented:

Step 1 Include in any passage to which our sources refer, however allusively, only those elements of each passage the source explicitly mentions. Take account of any peculiarities in the way it is quoted (relative to the catholic text in all its variants) that, with good probability, reflect actual wording rather than the result of paraphrase on the part of the source. This is most securely done in those cases where our source specifically refers to Marcion's text as differing from the catholic version, or where the variation does not recur in places where our source quotes the catholic version of the same text.

Step 2 Resolve or explain any apparent contradictions in the sources, either to the inclusion of a passage or to its wording. Confirm or clarify wording by comparison with known variants in the witnesses to the catholic version of the text; any phrasing that cannot be correlated with a variant found in such witnesses is printed *in italics*, and may be distinctive to the Marcionite edition.

Step 3 Omit passages expressly stated to have been lacking in Marcion's text. In notes, identify any related omissions in the textual tradition of the catholic version of the text in order to lay the groundwork for assessing the probability that the omission is Marcionite or pre-Marcionite.

Step 4 Omit passages unattested in our sources. In notes, assess the relative probability that an omission in our sources constitutes evidence of actually missing material in Marcion's text on the basis of (a) the existence of any related omissions in the textual tradition of the catholic version of the text, and (b) the likelihood that a passage was skipped over in our sources as offering nothing pertinent to their arguments. Do not treat an omission in our sources as positive evidence of the absence of the material from Marcion's text, on the basis of any presumed ideological editorial principle of Marcion.

Step 5 Retain [in plain type in brackets] connective content necessary for the directly attested material to have coherent meaning.

In the margins of each page of the Evangelion and Apostolikon appear references to the sources justifying the inclusion of each verse. The text notes printed after each reconstruction provide more details on what those sources report and how they agree or differ, as well as any uncertainty about their reliability in a given case. All unattested material left out of the reconstructed text is identified in the text notes, with occasional discussion of the relative probability of its presence in or absence from Marcion's text. While we do not know enough about Marcion's motives to hypothesize fruitfully about the likelihood that unattested material was actually absent, we do know the motives of our anti-Marcionite sources well enough to draw reasonable conclusions about the probable absence of a passage that would have served their polemical purposes, if it had been present in Marcion's text. This is not a fool-proof line of reasoning, since one can never rule out oversight on their part, but it carries a sufficient amount of weight to merit discussion in the text notes.

There are certain kinds of material certainly present in the Evangelion and Apostolikon that our sources are prone to neglect. In the former, the beginning and ending of episodes that provide the setting of an event, report its denouement, or describe the reaction of those present held little interest for our sources, who were intent on getting to the core actions and teachings of each passage as most relevant to their argument. They often skip over names or characterizations of those interacting with Jesus as not germane to their purpose, as they do geographic references in the narrative. They tend to use their own preferred way of referring to Jesus (generally "Christ"), rather than record exactly whether a passage used his name, one of his titles, or simply "he/him." Generally speaking, our sources offer abbreviated summaries of narrative, giving exact quotations most often of the words of Jesus.[108] In discussing the letters of Paul, our sources similarly tend to skip over the beginning and ending, where Paul first greets the letter's addressees and finally gives them some practical information or instruction, often of an ephemeral character. For the most part, only the ideological core of the letters attracts comment, and even there, Paul's frequent reiteration of key themes made it unnecessary for our sources to discuss every letter in equal detail. As a result, our sources provide much less information on the Apostolikon than they do on the Evangelion.

Regarding those places where our sources report wording different than the standard catholic text, and often different from each other, the general trend of close study of the Evangelion and Apostolikon over the last two centuries has been the progressive discovery that more and more readings once thought distinctive to our reports on Marcion—and therefore either the product of his editorial innovation or the result of paraphrasing by our sources—can be found in the textual tradition of the Gospel of Luke and the catholic version of Paul's letters. It is not simply that in a given case Tertullian offers one form of a passage and Epiphanius another, but quite often Tertullian's form matches a known form in some witnesses to the catholic text and Epiphanius' matches one found in other witnesses to it. Our sources are not simply generating novel renderings through inattention and paraphrase. They quite often are carefully quoting known forms of the text. But is this Marcion's text, or have they let the form of the text more familiar to them influence how they quote it? This can be checked by comparison to how the same author quotes the same passage in other places, when not discussing Marcion's text, but presumably quoting from the catholic version of the text known to him.[109]

Given the differences among manuscripts and other witnesses to the catholic version of New Testament texts, it should come as no surprise that the First New Testament, too, circulated in copies that contained some differences in wording from each other. This is a natural and unremarkable result of the copying process by which this sacred literature was "published." But, contrary to some premature claims in the research on this subject, *such differences in what our sources report about the Marcionite New Testament never amount to disagreement over the presence or absence of particular passages as a whole*—that is, we have no case where one source says a particular episode or saying of Jesus known from the Gospel of Luke was absent from the Evangelion while another source says that it was present, and similarly with regard to testimony about passages in Paul's letters. At most they diverge on the presence or absence of a particular phrase or clause within their quotation of a passage, just as do different catholic manuscripts of Luke and Paul.[110] Nor is there any evidence that the influence of the form of a passage more familiar to them from their own Bibles went so far as to cause them to treat as present a substantial sense-unit that was absent, or vice versa. Here again, the sort of problems that must be taken into consideration when attempting to reconstruct the precise wording of the Evangelion and Apostolikon, do not form as serious of an obstacle to reconstructing their content.

In fact, the differences in what our sources report for Marcion's New Testament texts, usually treated as a hindrance to knowing more about them, actually point to a very important insight into their character and origin. Harnack proposed deliberate ongoing revision of the Evangelion and Apostolikon within the Marcionite Church to explain discrepancies among our sources.[111] But already his predecessor Theodor Zahn explained the same discrepancies by ordinary processes of textual transmission, through scribal error, clarification of grammar and syntax, stylistic improvement, and so forth, just as seen in manuscripts of the catholic New Testament.[112] More recently, John Clabeaux and Ulrich Schmid have endorsed Zahn's opinion.[113] "It is quite likely that Marcion's text, like any other text, underwent a certain amount of alteration over time," Clabeaux observes. "This might explain how Tertullian could cite a verse from Marcion one way and then, one hundred years later, the verse appears in a different form" in Epiphanius.[114] Yet, certain kinds of textual changes, such as influence from the wording of other gospels on the Evangelion, should not have taken place within the Marcionite Church, where no other gospel was used; it would more plausibly have occurred prior to its canonization in Marcion's New Testament. Evidence of such harmonization to the wording of the Gospel of Matthew in some apparently reliable reports about the Evangelion, and not in others reporting on the same passage, suggests that Marcion may have adopted the Evangelion in multiple copies with varying degrees of influence from Matthew in their pre-Marcionite transmission.[115] In other words, the evidence points to the conclusion that Marcion did *not* edit a single exemplar of the Evangelion from which all copies of the Marcionite New Testament were made. Perhaps, then, he did not edit the Evangelion at all, and possibly the same was true of the Apostolikon. Definitive conclusions about these possibilities await further research.

Significance

Dominick LaCapra has observed, "Rarely do historians see significant texts as important events in their own right."[116] But the creation of the First New Testament by Marcion must be seen as such an event in its own right. Nothing necessitates that a religion, founded by individuals and spread through personal contacts, develop a written sacred literature, or that such a literature assume an authority superior in theory to any living voice of the faith. In past ages where illiteracy predominated, a written codification of a religious community's faith would have remained directly accessible to few, and treated by the rest as a precious object that symbolized continuity with the founders and a safeguard against innovations and deviation. The earliest Christians lived in an oral society that only flirted with literacy, and transmitted the teachings of Jesus, and the exemplary stories about him, primarily by word of mouth. The written word entered their world only sporadically, and even then only as a script to be read aloud. There were always a small number of more literate followers of Jesus who sought to put his ideas into conversation with textual traditions, but they could hardly be representative of the spirit of the larger movement. Fixity and referentiality give text distinct advantages in shaping our perception of the time and place from which it comes, with the result that the writer, however idiosyncratic in his or her own time, wins out historically over the now silenced voices of illiterate contemporaries. The conscious, deliberate adoption of text as a defining feature of a religious community marks a dramatic transition in the shape of belief and the character of authority over it.

Early Christianity had a fluid oral form in which various reductions of oral material to written form came and went without defining Christian identity as a whole until Marcion stepped on the scene. When those writings that predate Marcion make reference to the teachings of Jesus, "the custom is to refer not to documents" but to freestanding sayings known and remembered in the community, "applied rather than quoted, in the strict sense of that word; and never are they explained or 'expounded' in their fixed form like a sacred text."[117] No distinction is made between sayings now known from gospel texts and so-called *agrapha*, free-floating sayings of Jesus in the oral tradition. In the face of strong disagreement over the Christian message to be distilled from such fluid resources, Marcion sought to codify and secure an authoritative body of knowledge in a written form that would serve as a reliable touchstone of faith. Thus, Marcion could have taken the step to form a distinctively Christian canon, in the words of Helmut Koester, as a "conscious protest against the still undefined and mostly oral traditions to which the churches of his day referred as their dominical and apostolic authority."[118]

Marcion made his textual move in the context of competing traditions, where authority of both an oral and written form was at issue. The always-fraught relationship between the Jesus movement and its larger Jewish heritage arrived at a crisis, and Marcion proposed a set of sacred texts that could serve in place of Jewish scriptures for a form of Christianity that did not see itself as inextricably linked to Judaism. Marcion may have come out of and represented, rather than originated, such a form of Christianity, although he developed its outlook further. He lived at a time when the ambiguities of the Christian relationship to an equally emerging "Judaism" were beginning to sort themselves out into more starkly opposed alternatives. Marcion presented himself as safeguarding an original and authentic form of Christian faith against innovations that subordinated its message to the weight of the substantial Jewish tradition, which threatened to claim a kind of "parental rights" over its prodigal religious offspring. Contrary to the image of a Christian movement that headed in a straight line away from its Jewish origins, modern research has increasingly drawn attention to how much Christianity and Judaism "co-evolved," and the degree to which "orthodox" Christianity might even be said to represent a historical "convergence" with Jewish religious views and values, in contrast to other forms of Christianity, such as Marcionite and Manichaean Christianity, where such a convergence never occurred.[119] If Marcion came from a Gentile Christian community already substantially separated from a Jewish religious background (such as the one described by Pliny in Marcion's time and place), he may have understood himself to be anchoring resistance to such a developing convergence, rather than leading a radical break from an existing religious identity. "Hence Marcion is better viewed as a conservative or traditionalist than as an innovator," suggests Harry Gamble,[120] summing up an assessment of Marcion offered by John Barton.[121] Yet this may be an unnecessary either/or. As with contemporary religious leaders who see themselves as "fundamentalists," anchoring a conservative position typically requires innovation—the creation or reformation of what will count as authoritative tradition.

Marcion's scriptural innovation can be understood as a direct consequence of his stance as a conservative or traditionalist over against ongoing developments in Christian doctrine and ethos. Much of the discussion about Marcion in contemporary scholarship involves debating his originality in raising specifically Christian texts to the status of sacred scripture. This debate gets bogged down, in my opinion, in endlessly circling the issue of what counts as handling a text as sacred scripture rather than as just an edifying piece of religious literature. It would be misguided to deny that the copying and dissemination of collections of Jesus' sayings, narrative accounts of his life, or Paul's letters suggests a heightened value of these texts on the way to an eventual recognition as sacred scripture. In this sense I agree with Geoffrey Hahneman (in turn building on a distinction made by Albert Sundberg) that, "it is entirely possible to possess scriptures without having a canon."[122] But I would like to suggest that it is precisely in closing a canon, however provisionally, that Marcion suddenly and exponentially elevated the status of particular texts, and launched them into an undeniably superior authority relative to any others, in a way no one before him had dared to do.[123] That is, he accentuated their place as scripture precisely by including them within a limited canon. In doing so, he set boundaries on what could be used as touchstones in evaluating various positions put forward as "Christian," narrowing the range of permissible variety within the Christian movement.

By rooting authority in text, Marcion displaced it from the personal and individual. This shift implied that the personal authority of Christian teachers, even Marcion himself, could no longer be self-sufficient, but should be dependent on and subordinate to an impersonal, objectified repository, on the basis of which any claim on the tradition would have to be made and assessed. Marcion's act of canon-making was simply the first of a whole set of subsequent efforts to define Christianity through rival canons. David Brakke is surely right when he says, "To speak of the history of the formation of the single Christian biblical canon may oversimplify the development and interaction of diverse forms of early Christian piety, which carried with them unique practices of scriptural collection and interpretation—that is, different kinds of canons."[124] If Barton is similarly right in his depiction of larger Christianity showing itself to be very reluctant and slow to follow Marcion's example, it suggests that many non-Marcionite Christians (for several centuries) preferred a more open-ended exploration of the possible meaning of Christianity, attentive to a greater plurality of voices that were treated as authoritative, if not as decisively so as those settled on by Marcion.

The sources on Marcion's New Testament show that it exhibited the fluidity of text typical of all early Christian literature. These writings were valued, copied, distributed, and refined, but not yet treated as "sacred." It is only when a text has been declared authoritative, and so much rests upon exactly what it says, that the concern arises to establish a fixed form of it.[125] When the Qur'an was canonized, rival versions were destroyed, and new copies made from the single sanctioned exemplar. Or so the story goes; and at least theoretically it was possible to do this just a few decades after the death of Muhammad. The evidence of the Evangelion and Apostolikon suggests that Marcion did not take such an approach; instead, he apparently identified existing texts as authoritative, which then were taken up in multiple copies full of variant readings. For all his focus on the merits of stabilizing Christianity in text, he apparently did not fully make the mental shift from the oral to the written gospel, or realize the issues regarding the proper fixity of a literary text. Much the same happened two centuries later when mainstream Christianity followed suit: the many variants in the existing manuscripts were carried over into the New Testament collections now given the status of canon. By this time, each text could have existed in hundreds of copies, and the infrastructure simply did not exist to exert textual control on this scale. Nevertheless, canonization brought with it a fundamentally new attitude towards the text, opposed to fluidity and further adaptation. In the generation after Marcion, it was still possible for Tatian to edit Matthew, Mark, Luke, and John into a new gospel, the Diatessaron, and many less successful gospel reworkings date to roughly this period. But the followers of Marcion had already shut the door on this further literary innovation, and by the end of the second-century Irenaeus put forth a similar argument against new gospels on behalf of non-Marcionite Christians. These were arguments about the ultimate resort of authority, carried out among a literate elite of Christian leadership. Most believers remained illiterate, but they could appreciate the symbolism and ceremony of their leaders' appeal to a sacred text as an unchangeable reference point of authority that transcended any individual's claim to be the arbiter of Christian truth.

Chapter 3

The Evangelion

The Evangelion

Introduction

Marcion used the term *evangelion* to describe the narrative of Jesus included in his canon. *Evangelion*[1] was a term used in both political and religious contexts to refer to a proclamation or manifesto of the actions of an individual of power, whether divine or human, that brought benefit to those hearing it. It was a term that had been adopted by the earliest Greek-speaking Christians, such as Paul and Mark, to refer to the overall message connected to the mission of Jesus. Adolf von Harnack suggested that Marcion may have been the first to transfer this abstract use of the term to the title of a specific textual account of Jesus' life,[2] and the more systematic investigation of Helmut Koester strongly supports this hypothesis.[3] Many other teachings espoused by early Christians may have merited the term *evangelion*, but Marcion fixed on a narrative account of Jesus as best claiming this designation. This was a logical choice to make, since Jesus stood as the ultimate authority of the Christian movement. By reporting core teachings given by Jesus during his lifetime, Marcion strengthened the reception of those teachings. Soon Christians of all kinds were calling such narratives of Jesus "*evangelion* according to . . ." But for Marcion, the narrative he incorporated into his New Testament was *the evangelion*, whose authority was not to be dissipated by comparison to others.

Marcion's decision to endow a text with the status of "the gospel" suggests that he was endeavoring to depersonalize authority within the Christian movement, and undercut ongoing developments within the fluid oral tradition by anchoring authority uniquely in a pure and fixed original form of the faith. By its very anonymity and disassociation from an individual's memory, the Evangelion may have carried greater authority. Consequent to Marcion's elevation of a written record of Jesus to ultimate authority, we see a shift in the invocation of authority within early Christianity. Writers before Marcion—such as James, Barnabas, Clement of Rome, and even Paul himself—certainly root their authority in the fact of Jesus, but beyond that mere fact they rarely display a recognized need to have their personal views authorized by direct citation of Jesus' own instructions or precedent. But in the century that follows Marcion, that attitude of independent authority gradually evaporates, replaced in the face of the Marcionite challenge by more careful justification of teaching by reference to specific words and deeds of Jesus. In the process, the gospel genre rose to the unique status it has enjoyed ever since, and debates over the canonicity of different gospel texts outpaced concern with any other type of Christian literature.

Marcion did not invent the textualization of Jesus traditions; but his adoption of a narrative of Jesus as part of his canon anchored the Christian memory of Jesus in text in a way that would become increasingly dominant. That may have been an inevitable trend, but Marcion represents a decisive step in that direction. His contemporaries were still referencing Jesus' authority from oral tradition, or from a constantly remolded collection of Jesus materials. Marcion "is in fact the first witness to *any* Gospel text treated as an independent and free-standing whole," Andrew Gregory reminds us.[4] And as C. H. Cosgrove has observed, Marcion leads the way towards viewing gospel texts "not only as literary guardians of the sacred tradition but as literary *guarantors* of that tradition. This is the decisive move" that Marcion took and other Christian leaders initially resisted.[5] Contemporaries such as Ignatius, Justin, Polycarp, and Tatian still worked with malleable gospel materials; but subsequent generations of non-Marcionite Christianity took up and promoted the option of preserving individual gospel texts as separate and distinct accounts, leading to the four-gospel canon found in modern New Testaments. The distinctive authorial voices preserved by this choice have both enriched and problematized the Christian memory of Jesus.

Our principal sources agree in identifying Marcion's Evangelion as a version of the same basic narrative found under the name of Luke in use among non-Marcionite Christians (only Hippolytus refers to it as a version of Mark[6]). The judgment of such sources is borne out by a comparison of their quotations from Marcion's gospel text to matching content in Luke. In Marcion's New Testament, however, the book was not attributed to Luke, or to any particular author.[7] In other words, like much of ancient religious literature, it circulated anonymously. The earliest notice of the Evangelion is that of Irenaeus, who, not insignificantly, is also our earliest witness to the existence of Luke. Irenaeus records a tradition that the "Luke" to which the gospel was ascribed was "the attendant of Paul," who "recorded in a book the gospel which Paul had declared."[8] Marcion apparently declared a similar close connection to Paul for the Evangelion, and it is noteworthy that both Marcion and his opponents agree on the Pauline connections of the gospel they shared, particularly given the difficulty modern commentators have in pointing to specifically Pauline characteristics of the kind of Christianity reflected in it.

Irenaeus goes on to indicate that the Evangelion was shorter than the text of Luke known to him, a difference he attributes to Marcion "removing all that is written [in Luke] respecting the generation of the Lord, and setting aside a great deal of the teaching of the Lord, in which the Lord is recorded as most clearly confessing that the maker of this universe is his Father."[9] Tertullian similarly refers to Marcion's text as "adulterated"[10] and "mutilated"[11] compared to Luke, but does not bother to provide much information on the differences.[12] Epiphanius likewise refers to Marcion cutting or altering (*parekopse*) the text, and supplies some of the details of these textual differences a century and a half after Tertullian, listing passages of varying length missing from Marcion's text compared to that of Luke, at least those that Epiphanius would have liked to cite against Marcion's views. None of these witnesses mention any additional material in the Evangelion that was not also found in Luke. Other anti-Marcionite writers (Justin, Clement of Alexandria, Hippolytus, Ephrem Syrus) say nothing about the differences between Marcion's version of texts and those more familiar to them, nor report anything about supposed editorial activity on his part.

Such testimony confronts us with a major question: how did Irenaeus, Tertullian, and Epiphanius *know* what they claimed to know, that Marcion had tampered with the text of Luke to produce the Evangelion? It is worthwhile to look closely at what Tertullian says on this question, particularly since neither Irenaeus nor Epiphanius address it explicitly.

> I say that mine is true: Marcion makes that claim for his. I say that Marcion's is falsified: Marcion says the same of mine. Who shall

decide between us? Only such a reckoning of dates, as will assume that authority belongs to that which is found to be older, and will prejudge as corrupt that which is convicted of having come later. . . . If that gospel which among us is ascribed to Luke . . . is the same that Marcion by his *Antitheses* accuses of having been falsified (*interpolatum*) by the upholders of Judaism with a view to its being so combined in one body with the law and prophets that they might also pretend that Christ had that origin, evidently he could only have brought accusation against something he had found there already. . . . And so, by making these corrections, he assures us of two things: that ours came first, for he is correcting what he has found there already, and that that other came later which he has put together out of his correction of ours, and so made into a new thing of his own.[13]

Tertullian's argument depends on a statement in Marcion's only known prose composition, the *Antitheses*, in which he speaks of a "falsified (*interpolatum*) gospel." What exactly did Marcion mean by this expression? Tertullian presumes that by "gospel" (*evangelion*) Marcion means a text, since Marcion himself went on to use the term as the title of a text in his own collection. But such a presumption is anachronistic, and overlooks the fact that "gospel" in Marcion's day referred primarily to a body of teaching, not a text; even Tertullian writing several generations later usually uses "gospel" in this way, and only narrows its meaning to a text at times when engaging in debate with Marcionites over the value of specific texts that communicate "the gospel." Marcion innovated in applying this abstract term to a specific text that he wished to promote as *the* authoritative source for the teachings of Jesus ("the gospel"). So when Marcion wrote his *Antitheses* to explain his theological outlook, and wrote about a "falsified gospel," he is most likely to have referred to a *form of Christian faith* corrupted "by the upholders of Judaism with a view to its being combined in one body with the Law and Prophets."

Tertullian has an interest in taking "gospel" to be a book rather than a body of teaching, and "interpolated" as textual rather than doctrinal falsification, in order to find a solution to the impasse of rival claims made by his Church and the Marcionite Church to possess more original scriptures. It is Tertullian who supplies the necessary premise of identifying the "gospel" to which Marcion refers with a specific gospel book, namely Luke: "*If* that gospel which among us is ascribed to Luke," he says, "is the same (gospel) that Marcion accuses in his *Antitheses* . . ." Marcion, then, did not name Luke in his work, nor in any way identified it by a specific comparison of textual content. Otherwise, Tertullian would not be forced to hypothesize. This detail has been overlooked by many modern researchers, who repeat Tertullian's polemical charges as if they are established historical facts.[14] In fact, there is not a shred of evidence that Marcion wrote anything comparing the text of the Evangelion to an alternate version of the same text, in other words, catholic Luke.[15] The few references from the *Antitheses* that relate to other specific Christian texts besides those of Marcion's canon are a couple of references to passages in Matthew. Whether Marcion cited the text of Matthew itself, or only knew the content of the passages from oral discussions with other Christians, we cannot say. For Marcion, some of the material found in the Gospel of Matthew reflected the corrupted views of the Roman "gospel," a kind of Christianity entangled with "the Law and the Prophets" in its outlook. In Marcion's Evangelion, as well as Luke, Jesus said that, "the Law and Prophets were (in effect) until John (the Baptist)," whereas in Matthew Jesus said "I have not come to abolish the Law, but to fulfill it." Marcion could not see how these two statements could be reconciled. One of these traditions about what Jesus believed and stood for had to be "falsified," and Marcion trusted the testimony of the text he knew as the Evangelion. Or did he have to edit Luke down into the Evangelion to bring it in line with his views? Tertullian and other of his opponents believed that he had.

But Tertullian was in no position to know the state of biblical texts in the time of Marcion. The same is true of Irenaeus, Epiphanius, and the other critics of Marcion. They assumed that the text of Luke passed on to them by their communities went back by reliable tradition to the original author, before the time of Marcion. Because they trusted in the originality and antiquity of their own Church's text of Luke, they based their charges against Marcion on the observable fact that the Evangelion was clearly related to Luke literarily and in its content, and yet was shorter than Luke by several pages. They noticed that the Evangelion lacked the birth stories found in chapters 1 and 2 of Luke, as well as the story of Jesus' baptism in chapter 3; it was missing several other episodes in Jesus' life, and several of the places in Luke where the Jewish scriptures were quoted. What else could explain why the heretic's version of the text was missing this material, other than that he had removed things that disproved his interpretation of Christianity? As logical as this conclusion seemed to them, it was at best a guess on their part, and it cannot be given any weight as history just on their word, but must be investigated and demonstrated.

The Character of the Evangelion

In the Evangelion Jesus "comes down to Capharnaum" in Galilee in the fifteenth year of the reign of Tiberius Caesar, or 29 CE. There are no birth or childhood stories, and the text leaves Jesus' origins ambiguous, just as Mark and John do. His family is mentioned only twice (8.20; 11.27), and both times treated by him as irrelevant, which was apparently taken by Marcionites as a denial of human parentage. Yet he is unambiguously Jewish, as reflected in his reference to a Samaritan as "this foreigner" (17.18), and he operates mostly in a Jewish setting. He is seen by the people as a "physician" or healer (4.23, 4.40, 5.31), or as a prophet (7.16; 9.19); and he makes healing an express part of the mission of his designated emissaries (9.2; 9.6; 10.9). Yet he chooses "pupils" like a teacher or philosopher (6.40; 6.1; 6.13; 18.18; 20.39; 21.7), and they appropriately call him "preceptor" (*epistatēs*, 8.45). The Asclepiads and other medical guilds come to mind for comparison from Hellenic culture. Jesus attributes his power to "the finger of God" (11.20), and goes beyond mere medical charisma by working nature miracles (8.22–25; 9.10–17) and giving his emissaries "the authority to trample upon snakes and scorpions, and on all hostile power," about which he adds, "Nothing will in any way hurt you" (10.19). Jesus himself manages to pass unscathed through a crowd intent on doing him bodily harm (4.29–30), but ultimately is crucified and "expires" (23.46).

Jesus never explicitly affirms the title Christ (Messiah) in the Evangelion. In the key scene where Peter makes this identification, Jesus rebukes him and "order[s] them to say this to no one" (9.21), seeming to contrast this with his identification as the "Human Being" (lit. "son of man"), "who must suffer many things and be rejected by the elders and scribes and priests, and will be staked, and after three days rise" (9.22; cf. 9.44). This is much the same as in Mark and Luke (contrast Matthew). Similarly, when asked at his hearing in the Jerusalem council-chamber whether he is the Christ, he does not directly affirm it (contrast Mark), but reverts to the self-designation "Human Being" (22.69), which those confronting him equate with being "the child of God" (22.70). In accordance with his rebuke of Peter for identifying him with the Christ, Jesus' associates rebuke and silence a blind man near Jericho who seems to make the same messianic identification by addressing Jesus as "child of David" (18.38-39). Yet Jesus does point out to "scribes" that Jewish scripture, properly interpreted, indicates that the Christ is David's master, not his son (20.41-44). He also predicts that "many will come under my name, saying, 'I am the Christ'" (21.8), although this could be read in a Marcionite fashion as a denial that he is the Jewish Messiah: "many will come under my name, saying that I am the Christ," to which he adds, "Do not follow them." Jesus consistently uses "the Human Being" as his self-designation, while daemons[16] reveal him to be "the one consecrated by God" (4.34) or "the child of God" (4.41, 8.28). While frequently referring to God as "Father" (but not uniquely *his* father, see 6.35; 11.2, 13), Jesus uses "Son" language only once in a way that could be considered self-designation (10.22), and in context this may be meant as a general analogy to father-son relationships, as it is elsewhere (11.11-13). "Lord" or "master" appears rarely in the Evangelion as a designation of Jesus (6.46; 11.1), yet appears to have been the designation used of Jesus by Marcion in the *Antitheses*.

The Evangelion repeatedly emphasizes the central importance of listening to Jesus and putting his instructions into practice, even in places where Luke points instead to God or the Jewish scriptures (8.21; 24.25). "The sky and earth will pass away, but my teachings will remain forever" (21.33). In his only appearance in the gospel, God orders people to listen to Jesus (9.35). Jesus sees his role as rescuing "that which had been lost" (19.10; cf. 15.4ff.), which does not correspond with Marcionite views of the novel and gratuitous nature of God's intervention on behalf of the people of this world. Although Jesus at times disassociates himself from the role of punisher (9.54-55), at other times his words sound threatening (e.g., 12.49, 51) in a manner not in accord with Marcionite Christology. Yet the future coming or return of "the Human Being . . . coming from the heavens with great power," means deliverance for his followers (21.27).

The Evangelion shows no reserve on Jesus' part in reaching beyond Israel to a Gentile audience, such as is seen for example in Mark and Matthew. In fact, Jesus delivers the Sermon on the Plain before a presumably Gentile audience "from the coastlands of Tyre and Sidon" (6.17), whereas in Luke the audience includes people of Judea and Jerusalem as well. He praises the trust of a Gentile as unlike any he has found "in Israel" (7.9). He sends a group of mostly Jewish lepers on to the priests, invoking the example of Elisha, who chose to heal only a Syrian (17.11ff., including 4.27); all are miraculously healed as they go, but only the Samaritan among them turns back to thank Jesus. At the same time, Jesus does much of his teaching in Jewish synagogues (4.16, 33), or in the Jewish temple in Jerusalem (20.1; 21.37).

The behavior of his followers ("eating and drinking") is contrasted with the ascetic conduct of the followers of John and the Pharisees (5.33), yet the door is left open to a future ascetic regimen (5.35), such as the Marcionites followed. Jesus breaks with conventional social relations, replacing his own family with those "who hear my words and put them into practice" (8.21), and summoning his followers to leave their families likewise (9.59–62; 14.26; cf. 21.16). He states that "those counted worthy by God of attaining that age and the awakening from among the dead neither marry nor are married" (20.35), and Marcionites similarly committed themselves to celibacy when baptized (even though in context in the Evangelion, the lack of marriage is clearly identified as a post-resurrection state, "because neither do they die anymore," 20.36). The death of the body is insignificant (12.4), but Jesus discusses the resurrection from the dead (20.35), and his own resurrection has a physical character (24.39, 41–42), in contrast to Marcionite rejection of the idea of physical resurrection. Concern with property and profit comes in for ridicule (12.13ff.), and is treated as incompatible with serving God (16.13–14), or entering his realm (18.24). Money is not among "God's things" (20.25), and should be given away to beggars (18.22). A terminological distinction appears to be made between the "entreaties" or "appeals" made to God by other religious groups (5.33), and the "invocations" made by Jesus and his followers (6.12, but cf. 11.1), although the significance of this remains unclear.

Only one God is mentioned in the Evangelion; nothing is said of a distinct demiurge responsible for this world, as found in Marcionite belief. Contrary to the latter, God plays a direct role in managing the earth. He feeds the ravens (12.24) and clothes the grass (12.28) gratuitously, and so can be relied upon to feed and clothe human beings, too. He knows people's mundane needs and will supply them without being asked; for that reason, people are free to focus on seeking the realm of God (12.29–31). Yet this realm of God appears to be just now reaching into the world. God is "Lord of the Sky" (10.21, not including "and earth" as in most witnesses to Luke) and "Father" (10.21–22; 11.2, 13; 18.19; etc.), the "approach" of whose "realm" is to be proclaimed in association with acts of healing (10.9). In fact, the centerpiece of Jesus' teaching is "proclaiming the realm of God" (4.43; 9.2), which is dealt with more as a reign or regime than as a locale (the expression "realm of the sky" appears only once synonymously, in 18.16). The realm "has approached" (10.9, 11), and Jesus says his followers should seek it (12.31) and pray for it to "come" (11.2), and Jesus' power over daemons is offered as evidence that it "has reached you" (11.20). It is characterized as something small that develops (a seed or yeast, 13.18–21). When asked specifically when it will come, Jesus denies it any external visibility, declaring that "the realm of God is within you" (17.20–21). Yet he also outlines future hardships whose occurrence will signal "that the realm of God is near" (21.31), and promises that the day of its arrival "will come in upon all those dwelling upon the face of the earth" (21.35). God has resolved to give his realm to those whom Jesus addresses (12.32), and those worthy to receive it or enter it are characterized variously as beggars (6.20), children (18.16), ethical or "upright" (13.28), and those who, having resolved on a course of action, do not look back (9.62). Jesus repeatedly presumes a judgment to which people will be subject (6.24–25; 11.4; 12.5; 12.8–10; 12.47–48; 13.27–28; 16.22ff.; 17.2; 21.34–35; 22.22), even though the Marcionites refused to associate God or Jesus with any sort of judgment.

God has a "plan" (*logos*, which must have this sense in this context) that can be put into practice by human beings (11.28), but he has apparently hidden it "from learned and intelligent people," while revealing it to "novices" (10.21). In fact, "no one has known who the Father is except the Son" (10.22), and it is in this context that Jesus says "everything has been confided to me by the Father." All of this accords with Marcionite views, but is present in Luke as well. God confirms Jesus' unique authority to others in the only statement attributed to him in the Evangelion, saying "This is my beloved child; listen to him!" (9.35). In its context this phrase may be taken to supersede listening to the Law (Moses) and the Prophets (Elijah).

God is "beneficial (even) to the ungenerous and unwell" (6.35), and compassionate (6.36), and will "vindicate his chosen ones, who cry out to him day and night" (18.7). In prayer, God is asked to supply "sustaining bread day by day," to "dismiss for us our faults," and to not "permit us to be brought to a trial" (11.3–4). He rejoices in the change of heart of a wrongdoer (15.10). The operative word in Jesus' characterization of those who are "rescued" or "saved" is trust (*pistis*: 7.9; 7.50; 8.48; 17.19). Such an attitude requires a re-orientation of thinking (*metanoia*, 15.7, 10) away from wrongdoing broadly defined. Instead, one must prioritize doing what Jesus teaches, or carrying out God's plan, over any mundane concern. Yet obeying God and Jesus entails a heroic code of nonviolent, non-retaliatory, generous and forgiving conduct (6.27ff.). God sends his "sacred spirit" in response to invocation (11.2; 11.13), and as needed in a crisis (12.12). Speaking against this sacred spirit is a more serious offense than speaking against Jesus himself (12.10). God is credited for Jesus' miraculous powers (7.16; 11.20; 17.15–17; 18.43, and implicitly in the statements of daemons identifying Jesus as "child of God" or "consecrated by God," 4.34; 4.41).

The only supernatural opposition to God and Jesus comes from easily overpowered daemonic beings. The Evangelion assumes readers' familiarity with the term "daemon," and uses it in preference to the term "spirit" in its sources, such as Mark. Since daemons were ambivalent beings in Hellenic culture (Socrates famously had a daemon that both afflicted and benefitted him), the Evangelion specifies an "impure" daemon at the first use of the term (4.33), which apparently is meant to carry over to all subsequent occurrences of it. Satan or the Devil plays a much reduced role in the Evangelion compared to any of the gospels of the catholic canon. The term "devil" (*diabolos*) occurs seven times in Luke, but not at all in the Evangelion. Satan, who is named five times in Luke, appears only twice in the Evangelion. He is said to "bind" people with illness (13.16), to be in possession of a "realm" or "kingdom" (11.18), just as God is, and apparently is identified with Beelzebub, who has command over the daemons.

In terms of human opposition, nowhere is this said to be "the Jews" (as in the Gospel of John). Instead, Jesus enters into conflict with authority figures with whom he shares Jewish identity. Above all, Jesus engages with the Pharisee movement, which the Evangelion features in an oppositional role more consistently than does Luke. He interacts with them on a number of occasions where issues of Torah law and other rules of purity come up, and ultimately condemns them as hypocrites, who put on a show of piety but inwardly are driven by base motives. Other legal authorities ("lawyers") come in for equal condemnation, although they implicitly had access to "the key of knowledge," because "you did not enter yourselves, and you hindered those who are entering" (11.52). Nevertheless, it is the captains of the temple guard who arrest and beat Jesus (22.4; 22.63–64), and he is remanded to the Roman authorities by a decision made in the Jerusalem council-chamber without any specific individual (such as the high priest) or group (such as the Sanhedrin) being explicitly named as responsible (22.66). In condemning him, Pilate "handed over Jesus to their will" (23.25), which refers to those who had accused him from among the Jerusalem authorities.

In apparent disjunction with Marcionite ideology, Jesus advocates or affirms Torah law repeatedly in the Evangelion. When asked the way to "inherit life," Jesus invokes Torah law (10.26), and specifically affirms Deut 6.5 (10.27–28). Likewise, when asked the means to obtain "eternal life," Jesus affirms the good start effected by following the core commandments of Exod 20.12–16 (or Deut 5.16–20) from one's youth, to which one need only add one thing more to "have a treasure in the sky": dispose of possessions and follow Jesus (18.20–22). This one thing more, of course, amounts to the basic demand made throughout the gospel, and possibly renders the prior affirmation of Torah commandments more rhetorical than substantive. The Marcionites apparently drew a key distinction between these two passages on the difference between what produces "life" and what yields "eternal life." In the story of the Rich Man and Lazarus (16.19ff.), "Moses and the prophets" supply sufficient guidance to avoid suffering in Hades, and those who failed to listen to them are said to be unlikely to "listen to someone returned from the dead." Jesus instructs healed lepers to "show yourself to the priest, and offer a gift for your purification just as Moses commanded, so that it may be a testimony to you" (5.14; cf. 17.14). Even though most witnesses to Luke read "a testimony to them," the Evangelion follows its Markan source in giving "a testimony to you," which is indeed the correct characterization of the purpose of the sacrifice for a healed leper: the priest's acceptance of the offering is a testimony that the offerer is truly cured. When Jesus and his followers violate Torah law, such as Sabbath restrictions, it is not presented as a denial of the validity of such restrictions, but as a qualification of them supported by precedent from elsewhere in Jewish scripture (6.3), or by a supervening principle (6.9) in typical rabbinic fashion. On one occasion, the pertinent question appears to be whether it is proper to deny "a daughter of Abraham" healing on the Sabbath (13.16). Jesus also observes Passover (22.8; 22.15). Nevertheless, Jesus declares in a rather contrastive way that "the Law and the Prophets lasted until John; since then the realm of God is proclaimed" (16.16), and he is accused before Pilate of "destroying the Law and Prophets" (23.2, missing from most, but not all, witnesses to Luke). These latter two passages align better with Marcionite opinion.

Jesus speaks positively of "the prophets" as comparable to his followers in the abuse they suffered (6.23), contrasted to "the false prophets" who received praise (6.26), and decries the hypocrisy of those who build monuments to prophets their own ancestors killed (11.47–48). Yet nothing in these passages requires the reader to understand it specifically with reference to the prophets of Jewish scripture. In accord with a Marcionite understanding of the novelty of Jesus' mission, even the prophets did not see what Jesus' followers see (10.24). John is praised as "a prophet and more than a prophet" (7.26). Jesus implies that he and John derive their authority from the same source (20.3–8), an idea sharply at odds with Marcionite views. He explicitly identifies John as the fulfillment of a prophecy in Mal 3.1 (7.27). Yet Jesus does not directly answer John's question whether he is the "coming one" (presumably the one implied in the same prophecy). And although John is "greatest among those born of women," nevertheless "the least in the realm of God is greater than he" (7.28).

Jesus confers with Moses and Elijah supernaturally (9.30, hence Peter "did not know what he was saying" in proposing to house them in tents, although more could be read into this editorial remark, and probably was by Marcion). He is imagined by some even to be Elijah (9.19). Yet Jesus disassociates himself from Elijah's violence as belonging to a different sort of spirit (9.54–55), and supersession of Moses and Elijah may be implied in the Transfiguration story, and particularly God's word at its conclusion, just as the Marcionites understood it. On the other hand, Jesus cites David's actions (6.3) and words (20.42) as authoritative, and Elisha likewise serves as an exemplar (4.27, placed between 17.14a and 17.14b in the Evangelion). Jesus also compares the coming world crisis to the situations of Noah and Lot (17.26, 28). In the story of the Rich Man and Lazarus, the latter is rewarded in death by being "carried away by angels to the lap of Abraham" (16.22) and "comforted" there (16.25), in contrast to the rich man who suffers in flame in Hades (16.23–24; cf. "Gehenna" in 12.5).

In summary: the Evangelion aligns with Marcionite theology no better and no worse than it aligns with "orthodox" theology. Nothing distinctly "Marcionite" was added to it. The "missing" material relative to Luke does not contain any concept contrary to Marcionism not found also in other passages retained in the Evangelion. A number of themes and ideas found in it flatly contradict the developed Marcionite ideology known to us. Like the catholic gospels, however, the Evangelion could be interpreted in a way to accord with the beliefs of its readers, rendering unnecessary any resort to editorial modification. The absence of Luke's birth story scarcely can be taken as indicative of a Marcionite redaction, when in this respect it is in the company of Mark and John. More tellingly, the presence in the Evangelion of clear connections to the Jewish tradition and its scriptures, of affirmations of Torah law and positive references to biblical figures, of a notion of God as directly engaged in managing the natural processes of this world, of the concepts of judgment and resurrection, point to a text that has not been redactionally tailored to Marcionite views, but nonetheless could in other respects be found to be amenable to them: in the idea of a divine order breaking into the existing natural and supernatural governance of this world, of a secret plan newly revealed exclusively through Jesus, of a supersession of the Law and Prophets, of a radical break with family and property, of a pacifist relinquishment of strict justice, and of salvation rooted in an attitude of trust toward Jesus. All these ideas accord with Marcionite emphases, and so would give this gospel value in that community. But they are scarcely unique to this text among the gospels, and its adoption by the Marcionites as *the* gospel may have been largely fortuitous rather than the result of a selection of the most "pro-Marcionite" text among choices. The evidence of the actual content of this text must be given primary importance in assessing the different possibilities of its origin, far more than any hearsay report made by those openly hostile to it as a defining text of the Christian tradition.

The Question of Priority

Which came first, the Gospel of Luke or the Evangelion? Whether Marcion edited Luke, or made use of an unaltered proto-Luke, is one of the founding debates within modern biblical studies.[17] The first scholar to raise the question independently of dogmatics was none other than Johann Salomo Semler, the founder of canon criticism, and "probably the most important biblical scholar of the eighteenth century."[18] In his *Vorrede zu Townson's Abhandlung über die vier Evangelien* (1783), he proposed that both Marcion's gospel and Luke go back independently to a common proto-Luke; he identified Marcion's text as a product of the same age of gospel formation to which the familiar canonical gospels belong, and as one among the larger set of gospels from which the Church selected the contents of its later canon.[19] Semler put forward the intriguing suggestion that the version of the gospel found in the Evangelion arose in the context of the Gentile mission, and that its relatively lesser Judaic material relative to Luke finds its explanation within the context of this intended audience. Many of the leading scholars of the time quickly agreed;[20] but others strongly opposed the idea.[21]

The emergence of the Tübingen school of religious history in the 1840s saw both a defense of Semler's idea and a development beyond it by the German biblical scholars Albert Schwegler,[22] Albrecht Ritschl,[23] and Ferdinand Christian Baur.[24] Schwegler and Ritschl argued that Luke is actually an edition produced after Marcion, correcting the Evangelion in line with the orthodox view of Jesus of the mid-second century.[25] Baur, who was usually lumped with Schwegler and Ritschl by their critics, took a more qualified position akin to Semler's. While agreeing that Marcion's Evangelion preserved the original form of the gospel that Marcion found already in existence, he saw Luke as an independent Jewish-Christian edition of the gospel unconnected to an anti-Marcionite reaction in the mid-second century.[26]

Further work on the sources for Marcion's text within Tübingen School circles began to stiffen opposition to the more radical revisioning of biblical history proposed by Schwegler and Ritschl. Gustav Volckmar[27] and Adolf Hilgenfeld[28] both argued that Marcion, in fact, did make ideological revisions of a gospel closely resembling Luke in form and content, but that his version may preserve more primitive readings in some passages that have been altered in manuscripts of Luke.[29] Ritschl was brought around to this position,[30] and this is more or less the view carried forward by Theodor Zahn[31] and Adolf von Harnack, and incorporated into modern critical editions of the New Testament as the majority position in modern biblical scholarship. Baur moved closer to this position, too, ascribing a bit more editorial action to Marcion than he previously held,[32] while still maintaining that Luke reached its final form through additions and changes beyond the text Marcion had to work with.[33] The Schwegler Hypothesis that Luke is later than the Evangelion continued to find adherents in the twentieth century in Paul-Louis Couchoud[34] and John Townsend,[35] and most recently by Matthias Klinghardt.[36] Karl Reinhold Köstlin, meanwhile, revived Semler's original thesis of the independent development of the Evangelion and Luke from a common original.[37] This middle position was taken up in the twentieth century by John Knox[38] and has been advocated more recently by Andrew Gregory,[39] and Joseph Tyson.[40]

Since we have no explicit reference to the Gospel of Luke before Marcion, and no datable evidence that proves the existence of material unique to Luke—that is, not found in Marcion's Evangelion—before Marcion,[41] but rather see both texts enter public notice more or less simultaneously in the second century, we cannot *assume* the priority of either. Both texts must be compared to each other on an even ground of assessment for their possible literary relationship. We therefore have three possible connections between the Evangelion and Luke:

1. Marcion's Evangelion derives from Luke by a process of reduction (The Patristic Hypothesis).
2. Luke derives from Marcion's Evangelion by a process of expansion (The Schwegler Hypothesis).
3. Marcion's Evangelion and Luke are both independent developments of a common proto-gospel (The Semler Hypothesis).

Both the Patristic and the Schwegler hypotheses place the editorial activity one way or another during the Marcionite/anti-Marcionite conflict in the second century: either Marcion or his opponents deliberately changed the text for ideological reasons. The Semler Hypothesis places the development of the two gospels earlier, before Marcion and the reaction to him. We shall examine each hypothesis in turn.

A. The Patristic Hypothesis

The Patristic Hypothesis can be considered the received, consensus opinion among modern biblical scholars,[42] relying primarily on the work of Zahn and Harnack, who of course incorporated that of their predecessors. This view generally assumes that Luke, more or less in its canonical form, was composed along with the book of Acts some time before the career of Marcion, and goes on to argue that the best explanation for the shorter text of the Evangelion is that Marcion cut passages from Luke that did not match Marcion's distinctive views.[43] In terms of its argumentation, this view has the luxury of being a default position, carrying forward the entrenched picture painted in anti-Marcionite patristic sources, and defended primarily by negative argument against the other two hypotheses. As discussed earlier, however, the patristic writers were not in the best position to know what they were talking about. In order to accept their testimony, one must share with them the assumption that their text of Luke went back, intact, to the first century. But the trend of biblical research has been toward a recognition of just how unstable biblical texts were before they became "biblical." Arthur Bellinzoni, for instance, states emphatically, "New Testament textual critics have been deluded by the hypothesis that the archetypes of the textual tradition which were fixed ca. 200 CE — how many archetypes for each gospel? — are (almost) identical with the autographs. *This cannot be confirmed by any external evidence.* On the contrary, whatever evidence there is indicates that not only minor, but also substantial revisions of the original texts have occurred during the first hundred years of the transmission."[44] Likewise, William Petersen argues that it "not only defies common sense, but mocks logic and our experience with the texts of other religious traditions" to presume that "in the period when the text was the *least* established, the *least* protected by canonical status, and the *most* subject to varying constituencies . . . vying for dominance within Christianity, the text was preserved in virginal purity, magically insulated from all of these tawdry motives."[45] We cannot assume continuity of the Lukan text available to our anti-Marcionite sources with one that predates Marcion. Further, there are no certain quotes of or allusions to Luke before Marcion that could not equally be attributed to the Evangelion (nor any at all to Acts[46]). Thus, there is no external evidence that can be cited in favor of the priority of Luke. Such positive arguments as are offered for this position, therefore, must be internal in character.

As regards the internal evidence of Luke, arguments have been made for consistency and continuity in language, style, themes, and interests between, on the one hand, those portions of Luke found also in the Evangelion and, on the other hand, those portions unique to Luke. Such consistency cannot be easily accounted for within the theory of a derivation of Luke from Marcion's Evangelion (the Schwegler Hypothesis), because it would require a later author in a very different ideological setting adding material to the Evangelion that duplicated the distinctive vocabulary, style, and themes of the original author. On the other hand, the same consistency is not a problem for the alternative theory of a common derivation of Luke and the Evangelion from a common proto-gospel (the Semler Hypothesis), if the development into Luke took place at the hands of the original author, or at least within the same community that initially produced the proto-gospel from which the Evangelion also derives. Nevertheless, the simplest explanation for a consistent style of expression and set of themes throughout Luke would be that the whole gospel was written by the same person. But is it true that those parts of Luke missing from the Evangelion show the same author's hand as those parts included in the Evangelion?

The most systematic attempt to demonstrate the grammatical and stylistic consistency of Luke specifically with an eye to support its priority over Marcion's Evangelion was undertaken more than a century ago by William Sanday.[47] Sanday's handling of the evidence, however, is not satisfactory,[48] and has been subjected to a devastating critique by John Knox,[49] which to date has not been answered by any fresh examination of the evidence. With the benefit of Harnack's reconstructed text of the Evangelion, Knox was able to revisit the same stylistic analysis of Luke relied upon by Sanday (that of Holtzmann), and come to very different results. Of 492 terms or phrases considered characteristic of Luke or Luke-Acts— but not Acts alone—Knox found that only 162 were present in passages known to have been included in Marcion's Evangelion,[50] and therefore useful for a comparative stylistic analysis. But when the passages containing these terms are examined in the version of the gospel Marcion actually had (based on Harnack), 87 do not to appear, leaving only 75 overlapping terms (in 110 appearances) for comparison. Moreover, another 13 of these (in 17 appearances) match the wording of Matthew and Mark, and so are not peculiarly Lukan in these passages. This leaves 67 words in 93 appearances as supposedly common vocabulary proving the common authorship of both portions of Luke—that present also in the Evangelion and that absent from it. Yet Harnack's reconstructed text of the Evangelion has problems of its own that artificially inflate even these greatly reduced numbers. Recall Harnack's assumption that Marcion was editing Luke. Forty-eight terms out of the 67 (in 64 out of 93 appearances) are based on Tertullian's Latin, retro-translated by Harnack in line with canonical Luke's vocabulary. These retro-translations cannot be relied upon; terms are considered peculiarly Lukan precisely because there are, in many cases, other Greek words which convey the same sense and could equally stand behind Tertullian's Latin.[51] In fact, Harnack reconstructs whole passages in line with canonical Luke's text when Tertullian no more than alludes to them. Even assuming that some percentage of this material did indeed read the same in both Luke and the Evangelion and contained some of the characteristic phrasing, the amount of such grammatical and stylistic overlap would be reduced to a level where it no longer has much significance.[52] Henry Cadbury has expressed additional reservations about the value of the sort of exercise Sanday attempted, given the small amount of data about an author's characteristic style available from a single text, and the commonly shared expressions of the time, the subject, and specifically the traditions about the life of Jesus.[53] Such stylistic analyses, he maintains, can only reach conclusions about the final editor of a text, who is able to put his own distinctive linguistic and stylistic varnish over the entire work, "whatever the underlying sources or development" of earlier editions.[54]

Lacking any conclusive proof from the supposed author-related consistencies between those parts of Luke that are also found in the Evangelion and those parts that are not, the Patristic Hypothesis depends mostly on making a convincing case for Marcionite ideological motives for the absence of the latter from the Evangelion. Imagining such motives has been a recurring exercise, with researchers drawing up lists of things Marcion presumably could not tolerate in his biblical texts; and these explanations have proven so compelling that they have been repeated in the face of rather obvious and strong contrary evidence. For example, when omissions or variant readings once explained by Marcionite ideology were discovered to be present in non-Marcionite, catholic biblical manuscripts, Harnack proposed that Marcion's edition had somehow influenced the catholic textual tradition[55]—and he was far from alone in making such a proposition.[56] While such a textual influence is not impossible (particularly if formerly Marcionite communities were absorbed into Nicene Christianity at a later date), a far simpler explanation of such parallels would be that the readings should not be attributed to Marcion's editorial activities, but regarded as variants already present in the textual tradition before Marcion. Even though we can imagine possible ideological motives for them, such an explanation simply is not called for if they are found in non-Marcionite texts as well, and we should take the latter evidence as a cautionary reminder that speculation of this sort can be very circular.

Regardless of what one thinks about the possibility that the catholic textual tradition has been influenced by the Marcionite New Testament, the thesis that Marcion created the Evangelion by removing passages contrary to his ideology from Luke runs up against a seemingly insurmountable problem: the Evangelion contains dozens of passages contrary to the very Marcionite ideological positions cited as explanations for the differences between the Evangelion and Luke. In other words, proponents of the Patristic Hypothesis have identified an ideological motive for the omission of a particular Luke passage from the Evangelion, but have not bothered to check to see if other Lukan passages, *not* omitted from the Evangelion, violate the same Marcionite position, so that Marcion's failure to omit them too shows either arbitrary inconsistency or an acute attention deficit on Marcion's part. In fact, for every single motive cited for why a passage was omitted, one can find a passage of equivalent content that was not.[57] Against Marcion's disparagement of the Jewish scriptures and its heroes, we have a number of passages where these scriptures are cited as authoritative and their heroes taken as exemplary; against Marcion's distinction of the creator from the God of Jesus, we find a number of passages where God's management of creation is noted and praised; against Marcion's supposedly docetic views of Jesus, we read a very conventional account of Jesus' death and resurrection, along with references made by

Jesus himself to his death, his body and blood, his suffering, and so on. In short, the content of the Evangelion simply does not line up with the editorial principles supposed in the Patristic Hypothesis.[58]

The entire exercise of identifying ideological motives for why the Evangelion has less text than Luke rests upon the hidden assumption that the Evangelion is the secondary text that needs explaining, rather than Luke. R. M. Grant, for instance, sums up his survey of Marcion's presumed omissions with the statement that "It is difficult to believe that all these changes were not motivated solely by theological factors"[59] — revealing the circularity of an analysis that *starts* with the premise that textual differences between the two gospels involve "changes" on the Marcionite side, rather than considering the possibility that it is the text of Luke that shows "changes" that might involve "theological factors." Many differences between the Evangelion and Luke are of a kind that would normally be considered evidence that Luke is the secondary text, such as when Luke's wording duplicates that of Matthew (in the "minor agreements") or John (in the Passion narrative) when the Evangelion does not,[60] or when one of Luke's "additional" passages show substantial differences in vocabulary, style, and outlook from the rest of the gospel, as has been noted by many researchers regarding the first two chapters of the gospel.[61] A number of very serious problems, therefore, beset the Patristic Hypothesis, and it survives only to the degree that either of the other two alternatives fail to establish themselves.

B. The Schwegler Hypothesis

At the opposite end of the spectrum of opinion from the Patristic Hypothesis stands the second theory about the relationship between the Evangelion and canonical Luke, namely, the Schwegler Hypothesis, according to which Luke derives from the Evangelion as a post-Marcion editorial reaction. This is the position taken in the twentieth century by Paul-Louis Couchoud[62] and John Townsend,[63] and in the current century by Matthias Klinghardt.[64] In addition to pointing out weaknesses in the Patristic Hypothesis, all three build their positive case on isolated signs of secondary redaction in Luke. These signs include: (1) the greater length of Luke, in the context of the general tendency of ancient redactors to expand earlier texts, (2) chapters 1–2 of Luke, which explicitly copy the vocabulary and style of the Greek Old Testament (the Septuagint) in contrast to anything found in the rest of the gospel,[65] (3) other inconsistencies between these chapters and the rest of the gospel, including the depictions and importance of Mary and John the Baptist, (4) indications of narrative disruption in chapter 4 of Luke compared to the Evangelion, including the notorious anachronism of Jesus referring to deeds he had done in Capharnaum at a point in the narrative before he has gone to Capharnaum,[66] and (5) evidence in Luke but not in the Evangelion suggesting a relatively late place in the development of gospel literature.[67]

John Knox has brought forward further arguments on the last point, even though he is not an unqualified proponent of the Schwegler Hypothesis. He notes that while both Luke and the Evangelion have a close literary relationship to the other two Synoptic gospels (50 percent and 61 percent, respectively, of their content shared with Matthew and/or Mark), Luke diverges from that relationship in the content unique to it that is not found in the Evangelion: of the 283 additional verses of Luke not found in the Evangelion, 225 verses, or 80 percent, have no parallel in the other Synoptic gospels. Knox believes this striking statistic points to Luke being a later expansion of an earlier, more "synoptic" gospel closer in its scope to the Evangelion.[68]

One objection to the Schwegler Hypothesis is how late it makes the final edition of Luke—making it, in fact, one of the latest writings in the New Testament. How did this supposedly mid-second century edition manage to get such wide circulation and acceptance so quickly on a par with earlier gospels like Mark and Matthew?[69] The earlier we place the redaction that produces Luke from the Evangelion, the less problematic the scenario becomes; but even a few decades earlier would make it less likely to be a post- and anti-Marcion edition.

A second, more substantial objection to the Schwegler Hypothesis is the problem why the supposed additions to Luke are not more clearly anti-Marcionite in intent. Since other pseudonymous writings of the period, while avoiding anachronistically naming Marcion, direct more or less transparent attacks upon him, why would a mid-second-century redaction of Luke not similarly offer prophetic criticism of future heretics who will deny that God is the creator or that Christ had a physical resurrection? It is true that adding more quotes of the Old Testament, and certain elements of the resurrection narrative, may subtly work in this direction; but subtlety was not a hallmark of most second-century Christian literature.

While neither of these objections to the Schwegler Hypothesis is decisive, a third appears to be fatal. Already Volckmar noted several places where the wording of the Evangelion, but not that of Luke, appears to have been brought into harmony with the wording of Matthew where the same story is being told.[70] Harnack's reconstruction expanded the evidence for such *harmonizations* of the text of the Evangelion to that of Matthew,[71] and my own reconstruction appears to further support their presence. Unless these harmonizations are dismissed as errors committed by our sources in quoting the Evangelion, it is impossible within the Schwegler Hypothesis to account for Luke not sharing these readings with its presumed source, the Evangelion.[72] Since, by the accepted principles of text-criticism, unharmonized readings should be more original than harmonized ones, how can Luke have more original readings in those passages where the Evangelion shows the effects of secondary harmonization, if Luke depends on the Evangelion? Any further consideration of the Schwegler Hypothesis probably stands or falls on the resolution of this problem.[73] In the opinion of John Knox, the evidence of different exposures of Luke and the Evangelion to harmonizing textual influence means that the derivation of either text directly from the other seems to be ruled out on strictly text-critical grounds—in other words, both the Patristic Hypothesis and the Schwegler Hypothesis are historically impossible.[74]

C. The Semler Hypothesis

The third possible model of the relation of Marcion's Evangelion to canonical Luke is the Semler Hypothesis, according to which the Evangelion and Luke are both pre-Marcionite versions going back to a common original. It starts from the observation that anti-Marcionite sources, despite their charge that Marcion edited Luke ideologically, are apparently unable to cite any explicit claim on his part to have done so, that is, to have "restored" a text from corruption. At most, they cite his judgment that the form of "the gospel" he found in Rome differed from that which he already considered legitimate. Whether Marcion's comments about "the gospel" referred to an actual text, as Semler assumed, or merely to teaching content, as seems more likely, the scenario imagined in the Semler Hypothesis requires neither the Evangelion nor Luke to be a direct ideological "fix" of the other, but to be two alternate editions coexisting in Marcion's time, reflecting two independent trajectories of dissemination and history of use. This scenario accords with the consensus opinion that Luke must have been composed by the time of Marcion's youth at the latest, and not as a "correction" of Marcion's Evangelion in the mid-second century. At the same time, it accounts for characteristics of the Evangelion that do not fit a presumed Marcionite ideological redaction of Luke.

The relative ease with which Tertullian demolishes Marcion's interpretation of Jesus from the words of the Evangelion effectively demonstrates that the latter was not, as Marcion's critics charged, adapted to his beliefs. Tertullian rarely needs to resort to extraordinarily imaginative exegesis to accomplish this. He himself expresses amazement that Marcion "left intact" so many passages whose obvious meaning and context contradict Marcion's views. Tertullian gratuitously offers that Marcion may have left in passages that are difficult for him in order to claim that he has not tampered with the text, or that Marcion simply was incompetent as an editor. Once we step away from Tertullian's polemical context, a much more plausible scenario immediately suggests itself: that Marcion did not, in fact, do any substantial editing, but that he sanctioned the use of a gospel text already in existence in the form it was incorporated into the Marcionite canon. It may have been only upon coming to Rome that he became aware of divergent "gospel" texts. If his criticism of the "interpolated gospel" of the Roman Christians referred to such a gospel text (and not simply the form of Christian doctrine found there), then it reflected his encounter with a gospel text at variance with one *he already had*. Anyone who has studied the fluidity of the gospel text tradition in the second century, including the many noncanonical gospels that bear various relationships to the canonical ones, recognizes that variant texts were the norm, rather than the exception at the time. Given this context, Marcion's position loses all of the dubiousness it appears to have from the later position of a relatively stable and accepted gospel text.

What, then, of the Evangelion's "omissions"? Tertullian admits that such charges as he and Marcion might exchange over each other's biblical text could not be resolved by any objective means then available. For that reason, he did not undertake the kind of critique of Marcion's supposed "cuts" that we find in Epiphanius. But the chief argument that has been made against the Semler Hypothesis has followed Epiphanius in maintaining that the Evangelion's omissions relative to Luke correlate with established Marcionite beliefs. This argument depends, however, upon demonstrating not just that the Evangelion lacks content found in Luke that offends one of these beliefs, but that it does so *consistently*. Notwithstanding the remarkable ingenuity of those who have attempted this demonstration, it simply fails in the face of the data. For every single Marcionite belief by which "omissions" are explained, obvious contrary examples can be cited that rule out any consistent purging of the text of such content.

We must consider, therefore, the distinct possibility that Marcion's "omissions" actually were "non-interpolations"; that is, the text known to him lacked material found in the alternative version of the gospel that came to be known as Luke. In part, this is a text-critical question and, indeed, several of Marcion's minor "non-interpolations" are precisely the same as those found within the Western text tradition of Luke that prompted the coining of this expression. Other, larger non-interpolations based on the "omissions" of the Evangelion can be identified only tenuously without confirming support from surviving manuscripts of Luke. While the patristic explanation for the supposed omissions of the Evangelion can be shown to be indefensible, it is an altogether different proposition to prove that Luke's longer text involves interpolations that formed no part of the original.

Setting aside the difficult issue of omissions versus interpolations, what about the remaining content that Luke and the Evangelion have in common? It is here that perhaps decisive evidence comes forward. The Evangelion and Luke often switch places when it comes to harmonization to other gospels. Sometimes Luke appears to have a more independent text, while the Evangelion's has been conformed to Matthew's wording; at other times, the situation is reversed, and the Evangelion has the more independent text, and Luke's shows harmonization to Matthew. This surprising evidence suggests that both texts were equally and *independently* subjected to harmonizing influence.[75] It cannot be shown that either duplicates the secondary harmonizations of the other. In fact, from the evidence of the Evangelion we actually can identify harmonizations in Luke that we did not know before were harmonizations, because they are found in *all* of the surviving manuscripts of Luke—such as the "minor agreements" with Matthew, which some researchers guessed might be explained by textual harmonization, but could not prove it before now. So Marcion's gospel text goes back to a period before most of the "minor agreements" got into the manuscript tradition of Luke. It might be argued that the different set of harmonizations found in the Evangelion simply goes back to the condition of the one manuscript of Luke used by Marcion to make his pared-down edition; and this would be plausible if the copies of the Evangelion known to Tertullian in third-century North Africa and to Epiphanius in fourth-century Cyprus had the same set of harmonizations derived from that single-source manuscript of Luke. But they do not.

The testimony of Tertullian and Epiphanius to Marcion's Evangelion conflicts in several verses where harmonization is a factor, showing that the Evangelion, like Luke, was influenced differently in distinct lines of transmission. This should not be so, if the standard patristic understanding of Marcion's editorial activity were true. Harmonizing influence from other gospels on Marcion's Evangelion is extremely unlikely after the establishment of a separate Marcionite Christian community which rejected all other gospels. Harmonization between gospels happens because scribes are exposed to another gospel text over and over again, and inadvertently (or sometimes deliberately) modify the text they are working on by their familiarity with the other one. It cannot happen when Marcionite scribes are copying the single gospel of their canon, away from all contact with the gospels of other kinds of Christians. So any harmonization to Matthew had to happen *before* Marcion made his edition. Then, if Marcion issued a definitive edition of his Evangelion by making significant editorial changes to a manuscript of Luke, any harmonization that had occurred in the transmission of the gospel up to that point would have been frozen in his edition, and this single set of harmonizations would have been passed on in copies made of it in an environment where it was not being read alongside of other gospels. In that scenario, even with other kinds of textual variation due to conscious or unconscious scribal changes, we should not see any variation in harmonization between the text known to Tertullian in the third century, and that known to Epiphanius in the fourth century. But we do.[76]

Previous researchers have suggested that Tertullian and Epiphanius must have introduced different harmonizations of the wording of the Evangelion unconsciously by their own familiarity with Matthew, rather than reliably recording what was in the Marcionite text in front of them.[77] Yet where we can compare how Tertullian or Epiphanius quote the same verse elsewhere, we do not find the same particular harmonizations. Therefore, it cannot be demonstrated that they are responsible for the different wording they give ostensibly from the Marcionite text, and the latter's varied readings begin to look more and more like the differences found between any two biblical manuscripts. But if different harmonizations were introduced into different manuscripts of the Evangelion, and if harmonizations can only have been introduced in a pre-Marcion environment where manuscripts of the gospel were still being copied by scribes familiar with other gospels, then Marcion *could not* have produced an original edition of the Evangelion from a single manuscript of Luke with a single set of harmonizations. He must have adopted an existing gospel text in multiple copies, or instructed his followers to acquire copies of the particular gospel he identified as authoritative.

These points of textual evidence and historical circumstance, therefore, suggest that Marcion may not have produced a definitive edition of the Evangelion after all, but rather took up a gospel already in circulation in multiple copies that had seen varying degrees of harmonization to other gospels in their transmission up to that point in time. The process of canonizing this gospel for the Marcionite community involved simply giving it a stamp of approval, acquiring copies already in circulation, and making more copies from these multiple exemplars, so that their varying degrees of harmonization passed into the Marcionite textual tradition of the Evangelion. They continued to circulate in these slightly variant forms within that community, plucked from there in different manuscripts at different times by Tertullian and Epiphanius (as well as other polemicists). This conclusion from the textual evidence lends strong support to the Semler Hypothesis.[78]

In the mid-twentieth century, John Knox introduced a variation on the Semler Hypothesis that combined it with elements of the other two hypotheses.[79] His position has been further developed recently by Joseph Tyson.[80] Both scholars approach the issue from research on the book of Acts, especially the evidence for its second-century date and its interest in domesticating Paul. Both find an anti-Marcionite intent behind the handling of Paul in Acts. Given the arguments for the common authorship of Luke and Acts, at least in their final form, Knox and Tyson examine the case for dating Luke as well to the second century, and the possibility that it, too, has an anti-Marcionite agenda. The results of that investigation have obvious ramifications for the relation of Luke to the Evangelion.[81] They think it likely that both Marcion and the redactor of Luke made changes to a common source, with Marcion's Evangelion produced mostly by deletions and Luke mostly by additions.[82] They consider Marcion responsible for removing passages deeply rooted in the Synoptic tradition common to Matthew, Mark, and Luke (for example, the baptism of Jesus by John the Baptist and the Temptation), whose absence from a prior edition of the gospel would be hard to explain within the accepted view of Luke's literary relationships with those other gospels.[83] "The relation between Marcion's Gospel and the canonical Gospel of Luke," Knox sums up, "is not accurately described either by the simple statement that Marcion abridged Luke or by the assertion that Luke enlarged Marcion. The position would rather be that a primitive Gospel, containing approximately the same Markan and Matthean elements which our Luke contains and some of its peculiar materials, was somewhat shortened by Marcion or some predecessor and rather considerably enlarged by the writer of our Gospel, who was also the maker of Luke-Acts."[84]

The synthetic hypothesis of Knox and Tyson runs into difficulties by abandoning the strengths of the Semler Hypothesis, while not disentangling itself from the weakness of the Patristic and Schwegler hypotheses. Efforts to demonstrate either consistent editorial principles for Marcion's supposed removal of passages or clear responses to Marcion in the supposed additions of Luke have proven futile. Tyson does make a strong case for Luke 1–2 representing a late addition to Luke aimed at anchoring both Jesus' physicality and his close connection to Jewish traditions, as well as for an intent in certain isolated passages to affirm the authority of Jewish scriptures. But ascribing this material to an anti-Marcionite editor removes the bulk of what otherwise would be attributed to Marcion's edits, so that what remains of the latter do not have clear ideological motives, and might just as well represent a text untouched by Marcion.[85]

On the whole, the differences between Luke and the Evangelion resist explanation on ideological grounds, and point instead toward Semler's original suggestion 250 years ago: the two gospels could be alternative versions adapted for primarily Jewish and primarily Gentile readers, respectively. In other words, the differences served practical, mission-related purposes rather than ideological, sectarian ones. Under such a scenario, the Evangelion would be transmitted within exactly the wing of emerging Christianity in which we can best situate Marcion's own religious background.

Behind the event of Marcion's creation of the First New Testament, therefore, as significant as that is in itself, there is the high likelihood that there stands an earlier significant event: the composition of the Evangelion, by an unknown author, at an uncertain time, in an undetermined location. Some internal evidence helps us to narrow the possibilities of these questions; its accessibility to Marcion largely supports such internal evidence. It appears most likely that the Evangelion was composed in the region of modern Turkey, probably in the heavily Hellenized western portion of that region, sometime in the last third of the first century, and so contemporaneously with the other narratives of Jesus that would eventually be incorporated into the larger *second* New Testament familiar to modern Christians. We will probably never know the identity of the author, but we can say a great deal about the kind of Christianity he or she represented, and reasonably propose that it was a kind not unique to the author, but shared by a particular community or segment of the early Christian religious movement. Now that a reconsideration of the Evangelion gives us good reason to trust its original independence from Marcion and his movement, we will be in a position to elucidate the Christianity of the Evangelion in its own right alongside of other Christian writings from the first Christian century as a witness to the faith in its diverse formative period.[86]

Implications for Biblical Studies

Once the Evangelion is taken seriously as a possible independent witness to gospel traditions within the first century of Christian literature, we are in a position to assess how its evidence might inform modern attempts to understand the relationships among the gospels. The prevailing theory of those relationships can be summed up as (1) the synoptic relationship between the gospels of Matthew, Mark, and Luke, (2) the two-source hypothesis accounting for the synoptic relationship, entailing (3) Markan priority among the three, and (4) the dependence of Matthew and Luke, independent of one another, on Mark and a second common source ("Q"). A number of complications of this fourfold theory have emerged over the years, including two that involve Luke, and so the Evangelion, directly.

One challenge to the prevailing theory is the argument that Luke shows signs of dependence on Matthew, in the form of "minor agreements" between the two against Mark in passages for which they otherwise depend on Mark. In fact, the minor agreements pose the single greatest point of criticism of the two-source hypothesis.[87] Upholders of the prevailing theory attribute these "minor agreements" either to an overlap of content between Mark and Q, or to scribal harmonization subsequent to the original composition of the two works. The evidence of the Evangelion favors the latter suggestion. *The Evangelion has substantially fewer (one third) of the "minor agreements" accepted in the current critical text of Luke,*[88] drastically reducing the significance of this sort of textual evidence for the literary relationship among the gospels. At the same time, the fact that it contains other, different harmonizations to Matthew suggests that all such "minor agreements" have the same origin, as secondary scribal harmonizations that have no bearing on the relationship among the original compositions.[89] Even if one does not accept the priority of the Evangelion to Luke, nor the independent derivation of the two from a common original, and if one adheres to the Patristic Hypothesis of Marcion redacting Luke, the consequence is the same for the minor agreements: the absence of the bulk of the minor agreements from Marcion's text would suggest they were absent from his exemplar, and so they are most likely to have been introduced into the textual tradition of Luke at a later date, rather than being significant clues to the compositional relationship of the Synoptic gospels.

A second challenge to the prevailing theory is the suggestion that a proto-Luke can be reconstructed by removing all of the Markan material from Luke; what remains after this excision is a coherent gospel narrative, following its own sequence and logic, within which the Markan additions can be seen to have a minor place.[90] The existence of such a proto-Luke eliminates the need for a "Q" document, since Matthew could just as well depend on proto-Luke for the material the two gospels share independently of Mark.[91] This hypothesis deserves further study.[92] But the Evangelion is not such a proto-Luke; it contains so-called "Q" material integrated with Markan material. It therefore would represent a stage beyond this hypothetical proto-Luke, in that it has already incorporated most, if not all, of the material from Mark found in canonical Luke, and so offers no greater—and actually somewhat less—plausibility as a source for Matthew than does Luke itself.

On the other hand, either "Q" or "proto-Luke" would look different if the Evangelion is taken as the closer witness to them than Luke. Some of the material now included in both of these hypothetical works could turn out to be later expansions of Luke derived from Matthew, *after* the text had reached the form in which Marcion knew it, although not necessarily after Marcion in time if Marcion's text escaped developments that already had occurred in other lines of transmission. Whether the evidence of the Evangelion undermines the proto-Luke hypothesis itself, by so reducing the supposed freestanding narrative as to make it implausible, remains to be assessed. Similarly, Q becomes correspondingly reduced in scope once the evidence of the Evangelion is factored in. But far from undermining the Q hypothesis, this reduction in the scope of Q actually strengthens it.

The Q hypothesis proposes that Matthew and Luke made use of a written source—a sayings collection similar, for example, to the Gospel of Thomas. This source apparently possessed no narrative structure that could offer a substantial alternative to dependence on Mark for the sequence of events, which is why both Matthew and Luke follow Mark's sequence with little variation, each adding sayings material from Q at different points in Mark's narrative. The chief anomaly in the currently accepted reconstruction of Q lies in the opening passages of the reconstruction, where the evidence of Matthew and Luke suggests some sort of sequential narrative introduction involving John the Baptist, his baptism of Jesus, and the latter's temptation by the devil. Matthew and Luke share details in these episodes not found in Mark. One is then forced to assume that the sequence Baptist/Jesus/Temptation was so well established in the oral tradition that it was duplicated in Mark and Q (or else resort to a more elaborate hypothesis entailing Mark's knowledge of Q). Yet it is striking that, following this reconstructed narrative introduction, Q does not seem to have contained any narrative holding its individual statements of Jesus together, nor for that matter even a single narrative element other than brief circumstantial information setting up one of Jesus' utterances. Only two more passages outside of the introduction involve any sort of action: the healing of the centurion's servant and the Beelzebul controversy. Both are classical *chreias*, self-contained episodes creating the conditions for a statement or action of the hero, that do not change the character of Q as a sayings collection. In fact, we have no other example of a hybrid text of the sort Q is imagined to be, with a narrative introduction yielding to a sayings collection. The anomalous introductory narrative therefore presents a problem for the Q hypothesis which has been taken by some as evidence against it.

The evidence of the Evangelion suggests a more localized problem in the reconstruction of Q's opening that, once resolved, leaves the basic hypothesis intact. The Evangelion lacked all of the introductory narrative hypothesized in the current reconstruction of Q: it contained no mention of John the Baptist here, nor of Jesus' baptism and temptation.[93] The idea that Q began with some sort of introduction of John and his baptizing activity is based on additional content of John's preaching found in both Matthew and Luke, but not Mark. The fact that this material (Q 3:7–9) is lacking in the Evangelion draws attention to its word-for-word correspondence in Matthew and Luke; such precise duplication of wording is actually quite unusual in the Q material, where Matthew and Luke typically show the same basic semantic content, but with considerable variation in exact wording. We may be dealing, therefore, with a secondary dependence of Luke on Matthew here, rather than Q material. Similarly, the only transition from John to Jesus currently attributed to Q is the expansion of John's prediction of the one coming after him, where we again find a nearly word-for-word match between Matthew and Luke (Q 3:17), as well as a very rare identical editorial splice with material from Mark by both authors. The problems are much the same for the Temptation in Q: a presumed identical decision on Matthew and Luke's part about splicing Q with Mark, and a degree of word-for-word correspondence well outside the norm for Q. The Temptation passage is full of vocabulary atypical of Q: *anagō, deiknumi, oikoumenē, hieron, katō, diaphulassō, proskuneō, hupsēlos, pterugion* (vs. *pterugas* in Luke 13:34 and Matt 23:37), and *diabolos*. Moreover, it contains a density of scriptural quotation unique for Q (which quotes scripture only rarely: 7:27, 10:15, 13:27, 13:35, 19:33). Of course, no actual statements of Jesus appear in any of this material; the preaching of John and scriptural quotations fill that role.[94]

If the Evangelion, rather than Luke, is taken as the point of comparison with Matthew to establish the text of Q, all of these problems evaporate at a stroke. Q would open with the Sermon on the Mount/Plain material.[95] The only prior word that might be traceable to Q would be the anomalous reference to *Nazara* (Matt

4:13, Luke 4:16), the hometown of Jesus which otherwise goes unmentioned in Q and is referred to as Nazareth throughout the rest of Matthew and Luke. From this one word, *Nazara*, a reconstruction of Q based on the Evangelion and Matthew would go straight into the Sermon on the Mount or Plain. We might surmise, therefore, that the reference to Nazara originally occurred in an identification of the speaker of the Sermon, as well as of all the content of Q: "The words of Jesus of Nazara. He said . . ." The evidence of the Evangelion, therefore, points to a Q that more consistently takes the familiar form of a sayings collection than does the text of Q reconstructed on the basis of Luke.

Another way in which the reconstruction of the Evangelion might impact biblical studies lies in the area of research on the Gospel of Thomas. Debate rages on whether Thomas represents a fundamentally independent sayings gospel drawing on oral tradition, or whether it has a literary dependence on other gospels. The bulk of its material has parallels in the canonical gospels, nineteen passages with a strong relationship to material in Luke.[96] But it is worthy of note that none of these nineteen passages would have to have come from Luke rather than the Evangelion. That is, none of them derives from sections of Luke known to have been absent in the Evangelion. In fact, only four of the nineteen have content unattested for the Evangelion;[97] and given the selective character of our sources, even these four could have been present in the Evangelion's text. It therefore remains a possibility that the author/editor of Thomas worked with the Evangelion, rather than Luke, as a source.

A reconstruction of the Evangelion, and an acceptance of it as a significant witness to gospel development, may not revolutionize New Testament studies, therefore, but it does present the possibility of clarifying and even solving certain long-standing questions, and opens a number of interesting lines of investigation worth pursuing. The reconstructions of Q and of "proto-Luke" need to be reconsidered, as does the analysis of the possible sources of Thomas. More complex processes of borrowing back and forth between gospel texts as they developed need to be explored. The value of the "minor agreements" for source and redaction criticism, rather than text-criticism, needs to be reexamined. The material unique to Luke needs to be evaluated in terms of its possible origin in two separate phases of story collection/composition. And, of course, any reconstruction of the communities and ideologies that might stand behind or around the respective gospel texts must be adjusted to deal with discrete phases of development that the Evangelion may permit us to distinguish for the first time. Perhaps the most intriguing aspect of the latter point is the conclusion that the community and ideology of the Evangelion is not necessarily Marcionite, but possibly reflects a particularly early Asian "Gentile" form of Christianity not yet subject to the developments of the second and later centuries.

The Evangelion

3 ¹In the fifteenth year of Tiberius Caesar, when Pilate was governing Judea, 4 ³¹Jesus came down to Capharnaum, a city of Galilee. And he was teaching them *in the synagogue;* ³²and they were amazed at his teaching, because his speech was (delivered) authoritatively.

³³And in the synagogue there was a man who had a spirit, an impure daemon, and he cried out with a loud voice, ³⁴"What is there between us and you, Jesus? Did you come to destroy us? I know who you are: the one consecrated by God!" ³⁵And Jesus rebuked it . . .

¹⁶And he came to Nazara, where he was in the synagogue, in accord with the custom on the sabbath days. ²³And he said to them, "No doubt you will say to me this analogy, 'Physician, cure yourself—[the things that we heard happened in Capharnaum do here as well].' . . ."

²⁹And standing up, they threw him out of the city, and they led him to the edge of the mountain upon which their city had been built, in order to hurl him down. ³⁰But he, after passing among them, went away.

⁴⁰[. . . people sick with various diseases . . .] . . . And by placing his hands upon each one of them he was curing them. ⁴¹Daemons also were coming out of many, crying out and saying, "You are the child of God!" And by rebuking them he would not permit them to speak.

⁴²Now when it had become day, he departed and went to a deserted place. And the crowds were looking for him and caught up to him and were detaining him from departing from them. ⁴³But he said to them, "I must proclaim the realm of God to other cities also . . ."

3.1 Ep 42.11.5; T 1.19.2; 4.7.1; Ir 1.27.2; Ad* 2.3, 19; PsE 1; Hip 7.31.5
4.31 T 4.7.1, 5–6; Ad* 2.19; Hip 7.31.5
4.32 T 4.7.7
4.33 T 4.7.9
4.34 T 4.7.9, 12–14; 5.6.7
4.35 T 4.7.13
4.16, 23 T 4.8.2
4.29–30 T 4.8.2–3
4.40 T 4.8.4
4.41 T 4.8.5–6
4.42–43 T 4.8.9

Verse numbers are those of the Gospel of Luke.

5.2-3, 6, 8-11 T 4.9.1-2	
5.12 T 4.9.3	
5.13 T 4.9.4-7	
5.14 Ep *Sch* 1; T 4.9.9-10	
5.18-19 T 4.10.1	
5.20 T 4.10.2, 4	
5.21 T 4.10.1, 13	
5.22, 24 Ep *Sch* 2; T 4.10.6, 8, 13; Ar 44	
5.25 T 4.10.1	
5.27, 31 T 4.11.1	
5.33 T 4.11.4-5	
5.34-35 T 4.11.6; PsE 64	
5.37-38 Ep 42.2.1; T 4.11.9-12; Ad* 2.16; PsE 9; PhH 45	

5 [2]... fishermen... [3]... Simon... [6]... they enclosed a great abundance of fish... [8]... Peter... [9]For astonishment seized him... [10]and likewise... Zebedee's sons....

And Jesus said to Simon, "Do not be afraid. From now on you will catch people alive." [11]So... the boats... abandoning... they followed him.

[12]... a leprous man...

[13]And... he (Jesus) touched him, saying, "Be purified." And the leprosy left him at once. [14]And he instructed him to tell no one, "But go off and show yourself to the priest, and offer for your purification just as Moses commanded, so that it may be a testimony to you."

[18]... a man who was paralyzed... [19]... the crowd... in the middle (of the crowd) in front of Jesus. [20]... [... he said,] "Your misdeeds have been dismissed for you."

[21]And... saying, "Who can dismiss misdeeds except God alone?"

[22][But Jesus... said... in reply,] "... [24]Now in order that you might know that the Human Being has the right to dismiss misdeeds on the earth" [—he said to the paralyzed man—] "... Get up and pick up your cot..." [25]And instantly he rose up before them...

[27]... a toll collector... And he said to him, "Follow me. [31]... Not those who are healthy, but those who are ill have need of a physician."

[33]But they said to him, "Why are the pupils of John... fasting frequently and making supplications, but yours are eating and drinking?"

[34]But Jesus said to them, "The children of the bridal chamber cannot fast while the bridegroom is with them, can they? [35]... When the bridegroom might be taken away from them, then they will fast...."

[37]"No one pours new wine into old bags; and if one does, then the new wine will burst the bags, and it will be spilled out. [38]But new wine must be poured into fresh bags, and both are preserved.

³⁶"And no one puts an unshrunk patch on an old cloak; but if one does, then both the full fabric tears away and the old (cloak) does not hold together, for a greater tear occurs."

6 ¹Now it happened on a sabbath . . . that his pupils were plucking the heads of grain, rubbing (them) in their hands. ²Now some of the Pharisees said, "Why are you doing that which is not permitted on the sabbaths?" ³And in reply Jesus said to them, "Do you not recognize that this is what David did when he himself and those with him got hungry? ⁴How he entered into the house of God *on the sabbath* and, having taken the loaves of offering, he ate and gave to those with him?"

⁶Now it happened on another sabbath . . . that there was a person there and his right hand was shriveled. ⁷And the Pharisees were watching him closely (to see) whether he cures on the sabbath, in order to find (a way) to accuse him. ⁸Now he knew their intentions. . . . ⁹ Then Jesus said to them, "I ask you, is it permitted on the sabbath to do good or to do harm, to preserve a life or to destroy (it)?" ¹⁰And after looking around at all of them, he said to him, "Extend your hand." And he did so, and his hand was restored. ⁵And he said to them, "The Human Being is master even of the sabbath."

¹². . . When he went out to the mountain to invoke, he spent the whole night in invocation. . . . ¹³. . . He summoned his pupils and chose from among them twelve, whom he also designated as emissaries: ¹⁴Simon, whom he also named Peter [and Andreas his brother, and Jacob and John his brother, and Philip and Bartholomai, ¹⁵and Matthai and Thoma, and Jacob (the son) of Alphai, and Simon who is called 'the zealot,' ¹⁶and Judah (the son) of Jacob], and Judah Iskariotes, who became a traitor. ¹⁷And after he came down *among* them, . . . a great multitude of people from all of the coastlands of Tyre and Sidon. ¹⁹And the whole crowd was trying to touch him. . . .

5.36 Ep 42.2.1; T 4.11.9–10; Ad* 2.16; Ps-E 15, 18
6.1–2 T 4.12.1, 5; Ar 44
6.3–4 Ep *Sch* 21; T 4.12.5
6.6 T 4.12.14; EM III 141
6.7 T 4.12.9
6.8 Adam 1.16*
6.9 T 4.12.10, 15
6.10 T 4.12.14; EM III 141
6.5 Ep *Sch* 3; T 4.12.11
6.12 T 4.13.1–2
6.13 T 4.13.3–4
6.14–16 Ep *Sch* 4; T 4.13.5; 2.28.2; 5.1.1; Ad* 1.5
6.17 Ep *Sch* 4; T 4.13.6
6.19 Ep *Sch* 5

²⁰And he raised his eyes . . . and began to say:

The beggars are fortunate, because the realm of God is theirs. ²¹Those who are hungry are fortunate, because they will be full. Those who are weeping are fortunate, because they will laugh. ²²You will be fortunate whenever people will hate you, and reproach you, and reject your name as bad due to the Human Being; ²³your ancestors acted in the same ways toward the prophets.

²⁴However, woe for you rich people, because you are fully receiving your consolation. ²⁵Woe for you who are completely filled, because you will be hungry. Woe for you who are laughing now, because you will grieve. ²⁶Woe whenever people may speak well of you; this is the manner their ancestors also treated the false prophets.

²⁷But I say to you, you who are listening: love those hostile to you, [act well towards] those who hate you, ²⁸bless those who curse you, and invoke on behalf of those who insult you. ²⁹If someone strikes you on the right jaw, offer to him also the other (side); and if someone takes your tunic, present to him also your cloak. ³⁰Give to everyone who asks you, and do not ask back from the one who takes. ³¹And just as you wish that people would do for you, you do similarly for them. ³⁴And if you lend to those from whom you hope to receive, what sort of generosity on your part is that? . . . ³⁵However, you are to . . . lend without despairing . . . and you will be children of *God*, because he is beneficial to the ungenerous and unwell.

³⁶Become compassionate, just as your Father who is compassionate for you. ³⁷Do not accuse, so that you will not be accused; do not condemn, so that you will not be condemned. Acquit, and you will be acquitted. ³⁸Give, and you will be given to—they will give into your bundles a fine, overflowing measure that has been pressed down. With the measure that you measure, it will be measured to you in return.

³⁹Then he also told them an analogy: "Can a blind person guide a blind person? Won't both fall into a pit?

⁴⁰A pupil is not above the teacher. . . . ⁴²How can you say to your brother, 'Brother, allow me to extract the splinter that is in your eye,' while you yourself are not seeing the post in your eye? You hypocrite! First extract the post from your eye, and then you will see clearly to extract the splinter that is in your brother's eye.

⁴³"For a fit tree cannot produce unfit fruit; nor, conversely, does an unfit tree produce fit fruit. ⁴⁵The good person brings forth the good from the good deposit of one's heart, and the unwell person brings forth the unwell from one's unwell (deposit). . . .

⁴⁶"So why do you call me 'Master, Master' and not do the things I say? ⁴⁷Everyone who comes to me and hears my words and does them . . . ⁴⁸. . . is like a wise person building a house, who dug and deepened and placed a foundation upon the bedrock. . . ."

6.43 T 4.17.11; Ad* 1.28; Hip 10.19.3; PhH 45; OrP 2.5.4
6.45 T 4.17.12
6.46 T 4.17.12–13
6.47–48 Ps-E 7
7.9 Ep *Sch* 7; T 4.18.1
7.12, 14–16 T 4.18.2–3
7.17–18 T 4.18.4; Ad* 1.26
7.19–20 T 4.18.6; Ad* 1.26; EM I 82
7.21 Ad* 1.20; Ad 1.26
7.22 T 4.18.6; Ad 1.26

7 ⁷[. . . ". . . But say a word, and let my boy be healed. ⁸ . . ."]

⁹Now when Jesus heard these (words), he was amazed at him, and after turning to the crowd following him he said, "I am telling you, I have not found such trust in Israel."

¹². . . Someone who had died was being carried out, an only son of his mother, and she was a widow. . . . ¹⁴. . . And he said, "Young man, I say to you, be awoken." ¹⁵And the dead one sat up. . . .

¹⁶Now . . . everyone . . . began to praise God, saying, "A great prophet has arisen among us," and, "God has visited his people." ¹⁷And this idea about him spread . . . ¹⁹. . . as far as John the Washer *in prison*, who when he had summoned . . . his pupils, said, "Go and ask him, 'Are you the Coming One, or are we to expect a different one?'"

²⁰[When they came up to him, the men said, "John the Washer dispatched us to you saying, 'Are you the Coming One, or are we to expect another?'"]

²¹Now in the same hour he cured many . . . and he made blind people see. ²²And responding, he said to

Marginalia	
7.23	Ep *Sch* 8; Ad 1.26; EM I 86
7.24	T 4.18.8; EM I 81–82
7.26	T 4.18.7
7.27	Ep *Sch* 9; T 4.18.7; Ad* 2.18
7.28	Ep *Sch* 8; T 4.18.8; EM II 107–8
7.36–38	Ep *Sch* 10; T 4.18.9
7.44–45	Ep *Sch* 11
7.48	T 4.18.9
7.50	T 4.18.9; Ps-E 34
8.2–3	T 4.19.1
8.4	T 4.19.2
8.5–8a	Ps-E 22
8.8b	T 4.19.2

them, "Go tell John . . . that the blind are seeing again, the lame are walking, and the deaf are hearing, the dead are being awoken, ²³and whoever is not scandalized by me is fortunate."

²⁴. . . He began to speak to the crowds about John: "What did you go out into the wilderness to look at? A reed being swayed by the wind? ²⁶. . . A prophet? Yes, I am telling you, and far more than a prophet. ²⁷This is the one about whom it has been written, 'Look! I am sending my messenger ahead of you, who will prepare your road.' ²⁸I am telling you, no one is greater among those born of women than John; but the one who is less in the realm of God is greater than he."

³⁶[. . . One of the Pharisees asked him to eat with him.] So when he had entered into the Pharisee's house, he reclined (for the meal). ³⁷And, look! there was a woman . . . who was a wrongdoer . . . ³⁸and she positioned herself behind (him) at his feet. She began to wet his feet with her tears and was wiping them off with the hair of her head, and was smothering his feet with kisses and oiling them. . . . ⁴⁴[. . . he said:] "She has wet my feet with her tears and has wiped them off with her hair. ⁴⁵. . . She has not stopped smothering my feet with kisses." ⁴⁸Then he said to her: "Your misdeeds have been dismissed. ⁵⁰. . . Your trust has rescued you."

8 ². . . And certain women . . . ³. . . the wife of . . . Herod's quartermaster . . . were rendering service to him from their property. ⁴. . . He spoke by means of an analogy:

> ⁵The planter went out to plant his seed. And, as he was planting, some fell along the road and was trampled upon, and the birds consumed it. ⁶And other (seed) landed upon the bedrock, and, after sprouting, it withered because of having no moisture. ⁷And other (seed) fell amid the thorn bushes, and when they grew together the thorn bushes choked it. ⁸And other (seed) fell into the good soil and, after sprouting, it produced fruit. . . . The one who has ears . . . listen!

¹⁶No one, after lighting a lamp, covers it with a pot or puts it under a bed, but puts it on the lampstand, so that those who walk in may see the light. ¹⁷For there is no hidden thing that will not become visible, nor a concealed thing that will never be known or come to be visible. ¹⁸Pay attention to how you listen. . . . Whoever may have, to such a person it will be given, but whoever may not have, from such a person even that which one seems to have will be taken away.

²⁰Now, it was reported to him, "Your mother and your brothers have stood outside wanting to see you." ²¹But in reply he said to them, "*Who are* my mother and my brothers? These are, who hear *my words* and put *them* into practice."

²²Now it happened . . . [that he and his pupils boarded a boat. . . .] ²³[And] as they were sailing he fell asleep. [And a violent storm descended. . . .] ²⁴[. . . They woke him. . . .] But he, having been awoken, rebuked the wind and the sea, and they subsided, and it became calm. ²⁵. . . They were astonished, saying to one another, "Who then is this, who orders the winds and the sea?"

²⁷. . . He encountered a certain man from the city who had daemons. . . . ²⁸Now when he saw Jesus, . . . he said, ". . . Jesus, child of God. . . ." ³⁰But Jesus asked him, "What is your name?" And he said "Legion," because many daemons had entered into him. ³¹And they were appealing to him that he not order them to go away into the abyss. ³²Now a sizable herd of pigs was feeding there on the mountain; so they appealed to him that he permit them to enter into those. And he permitted them (to do so).

⁴². . . And it happened that, as *they* were moving along, the crowds were smothering him. ⁴³And a certain woman, living with a flow of blood for twelve years . . . , ⁴⁴having approached . . . , touched him, and . . . her flow of blood stopped. ⁴⁵So Jesus said, "Who touched me?" Now since they were all denying (it), the pupils said, "The crowds

8.16–17 T 4.19.5
8.18 T 4.19.3–4; 2.2.6
8.20–21 Ep *Sch* 12; T 4.19.6–7, 10–11; 4.36.9
8.22–23 Ep *Sch* 13
8.24 Ep *Sch* 13; T 4.20.3
8.25 T 4.20.1
8.27–28 T 4.20.4–5
8.30–31 T 4.20.4–5; Ad* 1.17
8.32 T 4.20.7
8.42b–44 Ep *Sch* 14; T 4.20.8, 10, 12–13
8.45–46 Ep *Sch* 14; T 4.20.8

8.47–48 T 4.20.9
9.1–3 T 4.21.1; Ad* 1.10; 2.12
9.5–6 T 4.21.1; Ad* 2.12
9.7–8 T 4.21.2
9.10–11 T 4.21.3–4
9.12–14 Ep *Sch* 15; T 4.21.3–4
9.16–17 Ep *Sch* 15; T 4.21.3–4; Ad 2.20.
9.18–22 Ep *Sch* 16; T 4.21.6–7; 4.22.6; 4.34.16; Ad 2.13 (vv. 18–20); Ps-E 6

are surrounding you, Preceptor, and crushing (you)." ⁴⁶But he said, "Someone touched me, for I perceived that power went out of me." ⁴⁷[. . . She came. . . . ⁴⁸. . . He said, . . .] "Daughter, your trust has rescued you."

9 ¹Then, after he called together the Twelve, he gave them power and authority over all the daemons and to cure sicknesses. ²And he sent them out to announce the realm of God and to heal, ³and he said to them: "Take nothing on the road, . . . neither bread nor money; nor have two tunics. ⁵And however many may not welcome you, upon leaving that city shake the dust off from your feet as testimony." ⁶Then, after departing, they traveled from city to city and village to village, proclaiming and curing everywhere. ⁷Now Herod [the quadrant ruler] heard . . . it being said by some that John had been awoken from the dead, ⁸yet by some (others) that Elia had appeared, but by others that a certain prophet from the ancient ones had risen (from the dead).

¹⁰[. . . a deserted place. ¹¹. . . crowds . . . ¹². . .] And, having approached, the Twelve said to him: "Dismiss the crowd, so that when they go into the surrounding villages and fields, they might disperse and find provisions, because here we are in a deserted place." ¹³But he said to them: "Give them (something) to eat yourselves." And they said: "We have no more than five loaves and two fish. . . ." ¹⁴For they were about five thousand men. . . .

¹⁶Then, when he had taken the five loaves and the two fish, as he looked up into the sky, he said a blessing on them, and he broke off and was giving (pieces) to the pupils to serve to the crowd. ¹⁷So they ate and all were satisfied, and the surplus was carried off by them. . . .

¹⁸. . . The pupils gathered around him, and he questioned them, saying, "Whom are the crowds saying that I, the Human Being, am?"

¹⁹And in reply they said "John the Washer; but others, Elia; and others, that a certain prophet from the ancient ones had awoken (from the dead)."

²⁰Then he said to them: "But you, though, whom are you saying I am?"

And Peter said in reply, "You are the Christos."

²¹But, rebuking them, he ordered them to say this to no one, ²²saying that the Human Being must suffer many things and be rejected by the elders and scribes and priests, and will be *staked*, and after three days awaken. ²⁴"Whoever wants to preserve one's life will lose it; but whoever loses it on account of me will preserve it. ²⁶Whoever may be ashamed of me, I also will be ashamed of this one."

²⁸. . . Taking along Peter and Jacob and John, he went up onto the mountain. . . . ²⁹And it happened . . . his clothing was gleaming white. ³⁰And look! Two men were speaking with him, who were Elia and Moses, ³¹who were visible in his splendor. . . . ³². . . They saw his splendor and the two men who had been standing with him. ³³. . . Peter said to Jesus, "It is a good thing that we are here, that we may make three tents: one for you, and one for Moses, and one for Elia," not knowing what he was saying. ³⁴But as he was saying these things a cloud formed and was overshadowing them, ³⁵and a voice from the cloud: "This is my beloved child. Listen to him!"

³⁷[. . . They had come down from the mountain. . . .] ³⁸. . . a man . . . saying, ". . . ³⁹[. . . a spirit . . .] ⁴⁰I begged your pupils that they might expel it, but they were not able to."

⁴¹But . . . Jesus said *to them*: "O mistrustful generation, how long will I continue with you? How long will I put up with you? ⁴⁴. . . Put these words into your ears, for the Human Being is about to be handed over into people's hands."

⁴⁷Jesus . . . after reaching for a child, stood it beside himself, ⁴⁸and said to them, "Whoever might welcome this child on the basis of my name is welcoming me. . . ."

⁵². . . They entered into a village of Samaritans. . . . ⁵³Yet they did not welcome him. ⁵⁴Now when the pupils

9.24 T 4.21.8–9; Ir 3.18.4
9.26 T 4.21.10
9.28–31 Ep *Sch* 17; T 4.22.1–16; EM I 87–88, 91
9.32–35 Ep *Sch* 18; T 4.22.1–16; 4.34.15; EM I 93–94
9.37–41 Ep *Sch* 19; T 4.23.1–2
9.44 Ep *Sch* 20
9.47–48 T 4.23.4; Ad* 1.17
9.52–55 T 4.23.8; 4.29.12

9.57–62 T 4.23.9–11; CIS 3.4.25.1–3	Jacob and John saw (this), they said, "Do you want us to tell fire to come down from the sky and destroy them as also Elia did?" ⁵⁵But turning around, he rebuked them and said, "You do not know of what sort of spirit you are. . . ."

9.57–62 T
4.23.9–11; CIS
3.4.25.1–3

10.1 T 4.24.1;
Ad* 1.5; 2.12;
EM I 89

10.2–5 T
4.24.1–4; Ad*
1.10; Ps-E 52

10.7–11 T
4.24.4–7, 12;
Ps-E 76 (Codex B only)

10.16 T 4.24.8

10.19 T
4.24.9–12

⁵⁷. . . Someone said to him, "I will follow you wherever you may be off to." [⁵⁸ And Jesus said to him, "The foxes have dens and the birds nests, but the Human Being does not have (a place) where he may lay his head."]

⁵⁹Then he said to another, "Follow me."

And the person said, "Permit me first to go away to hold a funeral for my father."

⁶⁰But he said to him, "Leave the dead alone to hold funerals for their own dead, but you, when you go away, declare the realm of God."

⁶¹And yet another one said, "I will follow you, but first permit me to say goodbye to those in my house."

⁶²But Jesus said to him, "No one who has placed one's hand upon a plow and looks at the things behind [is suitable for the realm of God.]"

10 ¹. . . He designated also seventy others and sent them out . . . into every city and place where he himself was soon to come. ²And he was saying to them, ". . . ³Look, I am sending you out as lambs among wolves. ⁴Do not carry a money pouch, nor a satchel, nor sandals, and greet no one along the road. ⁵And into whatever house you may enter, say . . . , 'Peace to this house.' ⁷So stay in this house, eating . . . the things (given) by them, for the worker deserves pay.

⁸"And into whatever city you may enter and they welcome you, . . . ⁹cure the sick ones in it, and tell them, 'The realm of God has approached.' ¹⁰But into whatever city you may enter and they do not welcome you, when you go out into its streets say, ¹¹'Even the dust that has stuck to our feet from your city we are wiping off against you. Nevertheless, know this, that the realm of God has approached.'

¹⁶The one who listens to you listens to me. And the one who rejects you rejects me. Moreover, the one who rejects me rejects the one who sent me. ¹⁹Look, I have given you

the authority to trample upon snakes and scorpions, and on all hostile power, and nothing will in any way hurt you."

²¹. . . He said: "I *thank you* and praise you, Lord of the celestial sphere, because these things which were hidden from learned and intelligent people you have revealed to novices. Yes, Father, because to do thus became gratifying to you. ²²Everything has been confided to me by the Father, and no one has known who the Father is except the Son, nor *recognizes* who the Son is except the Father, and the one to whom the Son discloses (it)." ²³[And turning to the pupils . . . he said,] "The eyes that see the things you are seeing are fortunate. ²⁴For I am telling you that prophets did not look upon the things you are seeing. . . ."

²⁵. . . A certain lawyer stood up, testing him out, saying, "By doing what shall I inherit life?"
²⁶And he said to him, "What has been written in the Law?"
²⁷. . . "You will love your lord, God, with your whole heart and with your whole life and with your whole strength. . . ."
²⁸Then he said to him, "You answered correctly. Do this and you will live."

11¹. . . When he was in a certain place invoking, when he stopped, a certain one of his pupils said to him, "Teach us to invoke, Master, just as John also taught his pupils."
²Then he said to them, "Whenever you may invoke, say, 'Father, let your sacred spirit come upon us. . . . Let your realm come. ³Give us *your* sustaining bread day by day. ⁴And dismiss for us our misdeeds. And do not *permit us to be brought* to a trial.'"
⁵And he said, "Who among you will have a friend and will go to him at midnight and say to him, 'Loan me three loaves, ⁶. . .' ⁷[And that one from inside in reply would say] '. . . (my) children are with me in bed . . .' ⁸. . . even if he will not get up and give to him because of being his friend, yet awoken because of his audacity, he will give him as much as he needs.

10.21–22 Ep *Sch* 22; T 4.25.1, 7, 10, 12; 4.26.6; 2.27.4; Ad* 1.23; Ir 4.6.1; ClH 17.4–5; 18.4, 15; EM I 72; OrC 7.18

10.23–24 T 4.25.12

10.25 Ep *Sch* 23; T 4.25.14; 4.19.7; OrL 166

10.26–27 Ep *Sch* 23; T 4.25.14; 4.19.7; 5.8.10; OrL166

10.28 Ep *Sch* 23; T 4.25.14; 4.19.7; OrL 166

11.1–4 T 4.26.1–5; OrL 180

11.5–8 Ep *Sch* 24; T 4.26.6–9

11.9 Ep *Sch* 24;
T 4.26.5–7

11.11–13 Ep *Sch* 24; T 4.26.9–10; Ad 2.20

11.14–15, 17–22 T 4.26.10–12; 4.28.2; 5.6.7

11.27–28 T 4.26.13

11.29 Ep *Sch* 25; T 4.27.1

11.33 T 4.27.1

11.37–41 T 4.27.2–3, 6

⁹"So I am telling you, ask, and it will be given to you; seek, and you will find; knock, and it will be opened to you. ¹¹Is there, then, any father among you of whom his son will ask (for) a fish, and instead of a fish he will give him a snake? ¹²Or else he will ask (for) an egg, (and) he will give him a scorpion? ¹³If you, therefore, although being unwell, know to give good gifts to your children, how much more so will your *supercelestial* Father give a sacred spirit. . . ."

¹⁴Now he was expelling a mute daemon. And it happened, after the daemon came out, the mute person spoke. . . . ¹⁵But some among them said, "He is expelling the daemons by means of Beelzebub. . . ."

¹⁷But he said to them, ". . .¹⁸. . . If even the Satan was divided against himself, how will his realm stand . . . ? ¹⁹Now if I expel the daemons by means of Beelzebub, by whom are your sons expelling them? ²⁰But if I expel the daemons by means of God's finger, then the realm of God has reached you. ²¹Whenever the strong person, who has been well armed, might guard one's own home, that person's property is in peace. ²²But whenever a stronger person, having attacked, may conquer the first, the stronger removes the other person's armament in which the latter had trusted, and distributes the latter's booty."

²⁷. . . A certain woman who raised a voice from the crowd said to him, "The womb that carried you and the breasts that you sucked are fortunate!"

²⁸But he said, "On the contrary, the fortunate are those who hear the plan of God and do it!"

²⁹Now as the crowds were swelling, he began to say, "This generation [is an unwell generation; it seeks an omen, yet] an omen will not be given to it. ³³No one places a lit lamp into a hiding place . . . , but upon the lampstand, *so that everything is illuminated*."

³⁷. . . a Pharisee requested that he might take the midday meal with him [. . . and] he reclined (at the table).

³⁸But the Pharisee began to question within himself to say, 'Why does he not first be washed . . . ?' ³⁹But Jesus said to him,

> As it is, you Pharisees purify the outside of the cup and the dish, but your inside is full of plunder and pathology. ⁴⁰Did not the one who made the outside also make the inside? ⁴¹Give the things that you possess as alms and, look, all things will be pure for you. ⁴²But woe to you Pharisees, because you give the tenth of the mint and the rue and of every (other) vegetable, yet you disregard the *invitation* and the love of God! ⁴³Woe to you Pharisees, because you love the front bench in the synagogues and the salutations in the marketplaces!

⁴⁶Then he said,

> Woe also to you lawyers, because you load the people with intolerable loads, yet yourselves do not touch the loads even with a finger! ⁴⁷Woe to you, because you build the tombs of the prophets, but your ancestors killed them! ⁴⁸Do you testify to the deeds of your ancestors without agreeing with them? Because they killed them, but you build (their tombs). ⁵²Woe to you lawyers, because you carried off the key of knowledge; you did not enter yourselves, and you hindered those who are entering!

12 ¹. . . He began to say to his pupils,

> Be on your guard against the yeast of the Pharisees, which is hypocrisy. ²But nothing is concealed that will not be uncovered, and nothing hidden that will not become known. ³Consequently, whatever you spoke in the darkness will be heard in the light, and that which you uttered in someone's ear in the storerooms will be announced on the roofs.
>
> ⁴Now I am telling you, my friends, do not be afraid of those who kill the body and after this *have no further authority over you*. ⁵But I will indicate to you of whom to be afraid: Be afraid of the one who, after the killing, has authority to throw (you) into Gehenna. Yes, I am telling you, be afraid of this one.

11.42–43 Ep *Sch* 26; T 4.27.4–6
11.46–48 Ep *Sch* 27; T 4.27.1, 6–8
11.52 T 4.27.9
12.1–5 Ep *Sch* 29; T 4.28.1–3

12.8 Ep *Sch* 30; T 4.28.4

12.9 T 4.28.4; Ad 2.5

12.10 T 4.28.6

12.11–12 T 4.28.7

12.13–14 T 4.28.9–10

12.16–20 T 4.28.11

12.22–24 T 4.29.1; 4.21.1; OrC 7.18

12.27–28 T 4.29.1–3; 4.21.1; OrC 7.18

12.29–30 Ep *Sch* 32; T 4.29.3

12.31–32 Ep *Sch* 33, 34; T 4.29.5; 3.24.8; Ps-E 52

⁸For I am telling you, everyone who affirms me in front of people, I also will affirm that person in front of God. ⁹But the one who renounces me in front of people will be disowned in front of God. ¹⁰And the one who speaks against the Human Being, it will be dismissed for him; but the one who speaks against the sacred spirit, it will not be dismissed.

¹¹But whenever they might bring you in to the assemblies and the officials and the authorities, do not worry about how you will defend yourself or what you will say; ¹²for the sacred spirit will teach you in that very hour what must be said.

¹³. . . A certain person . . . said to him, "Tell my brother to divide the inheritance with me."

¹⁴But he (Jesus) said to him, "Who appointed me a judge over you?" ¹⁶Then he told an analogy to them, saying,

> The land of a certain rich man produced well. ¹⁷So he was considering within himself, saying, ". . . ¹⁸ . . . ¹⁹ . . . you have many goods, celebrate!" ²⁰But God said to him, "Fool, this (very) night they are demanding back your life. For whom, then, will be the things you prepared?"

²²". . . I am telling you, do not worry about life, what you might eat, nor about your bodies, what you might wear. ²³For life is more than food and the body (more) than clothing. ²⁴Observe the ravens, that they neither plant nor reap, nor do they gather into storehouses, yet God feeds them. By how much do you surpass the birds? ²⁷Observe the lilies, how they neither spin nor weave. But I am telling you, not even Solomon in all his splendor was wrapped up like one of these. ²⁸Now if God so clothes the grass . . . how much more (will he clothe) you, who trust feebly? ²⁹Do not seek what you might eat and what you might drink, and do not be anxious. ³⁰For the peoples of the world pursue these things, but your Father knows that you need these things. ³¹Nevertheless, seek the realm of God, and all these things will be given to you as well.

³²Do not be afraid, little flock, because the Father resolved to give you the realm.

³⁵"Let your waist be aproned and your lamps burning, ³⁶and yourselves like people waiting for their own master whenever he might return from the wedding festivities. ³⁷[Those] slaves [are fortunate whom the master, when he comes, will find alert. . . .] ³⁸Even if he might come in the evening watch and might find them thus, they are fortunate. ³⁹But know this, that if the householder had known at what hour the thief would come, he would not have allowed his house to be broken into. ⁴⁰You also become prepared, because the Human Being will come at an hour that you do not expect."

⁴¹Then Peter said, "Are you speaking this analogy to us, or also to everyone?"

⁴²And Jesus said: "Who really is the trustworthy steward, the good one whom the master will appoint over his staff to give the rations at the scheduled time? ⁴³That slave is fortunate, whose master finds (him) doing so when he comes. ⁴⁴I am telling you truthfully that he (the master) will appoint him over all his possessions. ⁴⁵But if ever that slave might say in his heart, 'My master delays to come,' and might begin to beat the menservants and the maidservants, to both eat and drink and to get drunk, ⁴⁶the master of that slave will come on a day that he is not expecting and in an hour that he does not know, and he will dismiss him and assign him a part with the untrustworthy ones. ⁴⁷For the slave who knew yet did not act will be flogged many times. ⁴⁸But the one who did not know but did things that deserve strokes will be flogged a few times.

⁴⁹"I came to throw a fire upon the earth, and I wish that it were already kindled. ⁵⁰I have a baptism with which to be baptized, and *what (more) do I wish if already I have accomplished it? I have a cup to drink, and what (more) do I wish if already I shall have filled it?* ⁵¹Do you suppose that I arrived to throw peace on the earth? Not at all, I am telling you, but division. ⁵³They will be divided, a father against a son and a son against a father, a mother against a daughter and a daughter against her mother, a mother-

---

12.35–36, 38–40
Ep *Sch* 35; T 4.29.6–7

12.41–48 Ep *Sch* 36; Ad 2.21; T 4.29.9–10

12.49 T 4.29.12; Ps-E 19

12.50 Ep 42.3.10

12.51 T 4.29.13–14

12.53 T 4.29.13–14

12.56–57 T 4.29.15	
12.58–59 Ep *Sch* 37; T 4.29.16	
13.10–16 Ep *Sch* 39; T 4.30.1	
13.18–19 T 4.30.1; Ad* 2.20; Ps-E 28	
13.20–21 T 4.30.3; Ad* 2.20; Ps-E 28	
13.25 T 4.30.4	
13.26–28 Ep *Sch* 40, *El* 56; T 4.30.2, 4–5; Ad 1.12, 23.	

in-law against a daughter-in-law and a daughter-in-law against a mother-in-law."

⁵⁶. . . "Hypocrites! Do you examine the face of the celestial sphere and earth, but do not examine this moment? ⁵⁷And do you not judge also for yourselves what is right? ⁵⁸For example, as you are proceeding with your legal adversary to an official, on the way make an effort to be settled with the other, so that the latter may not sometime drag you to the judge, and the judge deliver you to the court officer, and the court officer throw you into a prison. ⁵⁹I am telling you, you would certainly not come out from there until you would surrender even your last quarter."

13 ¹⁰. . . on the sabbaths. ¹¹. . . a woman . . . ¹². . . ¹³. . . restored to health . . .

¹⁴But in response . . . was saying ". . . not on the sabbath day!"

¹⁵But Jesus answered and said, "Does not each one of you untie his mule or his bull from its stall on the sabbaths and lead it away to give it a drink? ¹⁶But must this person, who is a daughter of Abraham, whom the Satan bound . . . not be untied from this bond on the sabbath day?"

¹⁸. . . ". . . The realm of God . . . ¹⁹is like a grain of mustard, which a person took and *planted* in the person's own garden, and it grew and developed into a tree, and the birds of the sky nested in its branches.

²⁰". . . The realm of God . . . ²¹is like yeast, which a woman had taken and infused into three bushels of flour until the whole (quantity) was leavened. . . .

²⁵". . . From the time when the householder might arise and shut the door, and . . . might begin . . . to knock . . . in reply he will say . . . 'I do not know where you are from.' ²⁶Then . . . will begin to say, 'We ate and drank in your presence, and you taught in our streets.' ²⁷Yet he will speak, saying, '. . . Get away from me, all you workers of unlawfulness!' ²⁸There is where the weeping and the grinding of teeth will be, when you see *all the ethical* coming into the realm of God, but yourselves *kept* outside."

14 ¹². . . "[Whenever you may make] a midday meal or a dinner, do not call . . . so that it not happen that sometime they might also invite you in return. . . . ¹³But . . . invite beggars . . . ¹⁴. . . since they have nothing with which to reward you, because it will be rewarded to you in the awakening. . . ."

¹⁶. . . A certain person was making a dinner, and invited many. [And he sent out his slave . . . to those who were invited . . .] ¹⁸Yet they all alike began to decline. . . . "I bought a field. . . ." ¹⁹. . . "I bought . . . cattle. . . ." ²⁰. . . "I just took a wife. . . ." ²¹So [. . . the slave] reported these things to his master.

Then the householder, becoming *disturbed*, said . . . , "Go out . . . into the streets and the lanes of the city . . . ."

²²[And the slave said,] ". . . That which you ordered has been done, and yet there is space.'

²³[And the master said . . . ,] "Go out into the roads and the hedges. . . ."

²⁶. . . "If someone does not leave one's own father and mother and brothers and wife and children . . . such a person is not worthy to be my pupil. ³³. . . Anyone who does not give up all . . . property is unable to be my pupil."

15 ⁴. . . "What person among you who has a hundred sheep and, upon losing one of them, does not leave behind the ninety-nine in the mountains in the wilderness and go out to search for the one that has been lost until you might find it? ⁵. . . celebrating. ⁷. . . There will be such joy for one wrongdoer who has a change of heart. . . .

⁸". . . who has . . . silver coins, and having lost one, does not . . . search . . . until . . . might find it? ¹⁰. . . Such joy occurs in the presence of God for one wrongdoer who has a change of heart."

16 ¹. . . [Jesus said . . .]

There was a . . . person who had a steward . . . ². . . he said to him, ". . . Deliver the account of your stewardship, for you can no longer be steward."

³Then the steward said to himself, ". . . ⁴I know what I shall do, so that, whenever I may be removed from

14.12–14 T 4.31.1
14.16–23 T 4.31.1–8
14.26 Ep *El* 70; T 4.19.12
14.33 Ar 44
15.4–5, 7–8, 10 T 4.32.1–2; Ps-E 52
16.1–7, 9 T 4.33.1

16.11–12 T 4.33.4

16.13 T 4.33.1; Ad* 1.28

16.14–15 T 4.33.2, 6

16.16–17 Ep *Sch* 43; T 4.33.7, 9; 5.2.1; 5.8.5; Ar 45

16.18 T 4.34.1

16.19–31 Ep *Sch* 44, 45, 46, *El* 56, 59; T 4.34.10–17; 3.24; Ad* 2.10

the stewardship, people will welcome me into their own homes."

⁵So when he had summoned each one of the debtors of his own master, he was saying to the first, "How much do you owe my master?"

⁶And that one said, "A hundred. . . ."

But he said to that one, "Take your accounts and . . . write fifty."

⁷Next, he said to another one, "Now you, how much do you owe?"

And that one said, "A hundred. . . ."

He said to that one, "Take your accounts and write eighty."

⁹"And I am telling you, make friends for yourselves from the profit of misdeeds. . . . ¹¹Therefore, if you have not become trustworthy with regard to ill-gotten profit, who will entrust to you the genuine (profit)? ¹²And if you are not trustworthy with regard to that which is another's, who will give to you that which is mine? ¹³No one is able to serve two masters, because the person will disregard one and adhere to the other. You cannot serve God and profit."

¹⁴Now the Pharisees, who are money lovers, were listening to these things, and they were ridiculing him. ¹⁵So he said to them, "You are those who present yourselves as ethical in the presence of people, but God knows your hearts, because that which is highly regarded among people is disgusting in the presence of God. ¹⁶The Law and the Prophets (lasted) until John; from then the realm of God is being proclaimed, and everyone is pressing into it. ¹⁷But it is easier for the celestial sphere and the earth to pass away than for a single stroke of *my words* to fall. ¹⁸*The one who* releases his wife and marries another commits adultery, and the one who marries someone who has been released *is like an adulterer.*"

¹⁹Now there was a certain rich person, and he dressed in purple cloth and fine linen, enjoying himself day by day magnificently. ²⁰But a certain beggar named Lazarus had been left diseased near his gate, ²¹wanting

to be fed from what fell from the rich man's table. But even the dogs who came were licking his sores. ²²It happened that the beggar died, and was carried away by angels to the lap of Abraham. Now the rich man also died and was buried ²³in Hades. And when he lifted up his eyes while he was being tortured, he saw Abraham from a distance, and Lazarus in his lap. ²⁴So calling out, he said, "Father Abraham, pity me and send Lazarus so that he might dip the tip of his finger in water and cool my tongue, because I am suffering in this flame."

²⁵But Abraham said, "Child, remember that you received the good things in your lifetime, and Lazarus likewise the bad things. But now he is being comforted here, but you are suffering. ²⁶And besides all these things, a great chasm has been established between you and us, so that they are unable to cross over from here to you, neither may they cross over from there to here."

²⁷... "Then I ask you, father, that you send him to the house of my father, ²⁸because I have five brothers there, so that he might intervene with them that they might not also come into this place of torture."

²⁹But he (Abraham) said, "They have there Moses and the prophets; let them listen to them."

³⁰Then he said, "Nay, father, but if someone from among the dead might go to them they would have a change of heart."

³¹But he said to him, "If they did not listen to Moses and the prophets, neither would they listen to someone returned from the dead."

17 ¹Then he said to his pupils, "... [snares ... come.] ... Woe to the one through whom they come. ²It would be better for that person to have never been born or to have had a millstone hung around the neck and been hurled into the sea, rather than to have snared one of these little ones. ³... "If your colleague ever might do wrong, rebuke the person, [and if that one has a change of heart, forgive the person]. ⁴Even if this one might do

17.1–2 T 4.35.1; Ad 2.15; 1.16
17.3–4 T 4.35.2–3

17.11–12 Ep *Sch* 48; T 4.35.4, 9	
17.14a; 4.27; 17.14b Ep *Sch* 48; T 4.35.4, 6–7	
17.15–19 T 4.35.7, 9, 11	
17.20–21 T 4.35.12; EM II 114	
17.22 Ep *Sch* 49	
17.25 T 4.35.14	
17.26, 28, 32 T 4.35.15	
18.1–7 T 4.36.1	

wrong seven times . . . [and . . . seven times . . . have a change of heart . . .] you should forgive the person."

¹¹And it happened . . . that he was passing through the midst of Samaria. ¹²And as he was entering into a certain village ten leprous men met him. . . . ¹⁴ᵃAnd *he sent them away, saying,* "Go, show yourselves to the priests. ⁴·²⁷There were also many lepers in Israel in the time of Elissai the prophet, yet not one of them was cleansed, except Naaman the Syrian."

¹⁴ᵇAnd it happened that, as they went away, they were purified. ¹⁵One of them, when he saw that he was healed, turned back, praising God with a loud voice. ¹⁶And he fell on his face at Jesus' feet, thanking him. And he was a Samaritan.

¹⁷And in reply Jesus said, ". . . ¹⁸Were not (any) found turned back to give praise to God except this foreigner?" ¹⁹And he said to him, ". . . Your trust has rescued you."

²⁰Now when he was asked by the Pharisees when the realm of God was coming, he answered them and said, "The realm of God is not coming together with observation. ²¹Nor do they say, 'Look here!' or 'There!' For, look, the realm of God is within you. ²². . . Days will come when you will desire to see one of the days of the Human Being . . . ²⁵But first it is necessary that he suffer many things and be rejected. . . . ²⁶And just as it happened in the days of Noah, so it will be also in the days of the Human Being. ²⁸Likewise, just as it happened in the days of Lot. . . . ³²Remember Lot's wife."

18 ¹Then he was telling them an analogy for the necessity that they always invoke and not to neglect (it),

². . . In a certain city there was a certain judge. . . . ³And there was a widow in that city . . . saying, "Pass judgment in my favor against my legal adversary."

⁴. . . He said to himself, ". . . ⁵Because this widow causes me trouble, I will pass judgment in her favor, so that she may not come to harass me forever."

⁶"Did you hear what the . . . judge said? ⁷Is it possible then that God would not make the judgment in favor of his chosen ones, who cry out to him day and night . . . ?

⁹[Then he told . . . this analogy . . .]

¹⁰Two people [went up] into the temple to invoke, one a Pharisee and the other a toll collector. ¹¹The Pharisee, having stood, was invoking these things to himself, "God, I thank you because I am not the same as the rest of people, thieves, lawbreakers, adulterers, or even like this toll collector. ¹²I fast twice a week, I give a tenth of all that I acquire."

¹³But the toll collector, who had stood at a distance, did not want even to raise his eyes toward the celestial sphere, but was striking his chest, saying, "God, be merciful to me the wrongdoer." ¹⁴I am telling you that the latter went down to his home rectified more than the former, because those who exalt themselves will be abased, but those who abase themselves will be exalted.

¹⁶. . . "Permit the children to come to me. . . . For the realm of the celestial sphere belongs to such as these."

¹⁸And a certain person said to him, "Good teacher, by doing what shall I obtain eternal life?"
¹⁹But he (answered), "Why do you call me good? No one is good, except one: the Father."
²⁰*Now the other* said, "*I* know the ordinances: Do not murder, do not commit adultery, do not steal, do not testify falsely, honor your father and mother." ²¹And he said, "All these I have kept from my youth."
²²Now when Jesus heard that, he said to him, "There is still one thing missing in you. Sell all of whatever you have and distribute (it) to beggars, and you will have a treasure in the celestial sphere; then come on, follow me! . . . ²⁴. . . With such difficulty do those who have money go into the realm of God!"

18.9–14 T 4.36.1–2
18.16 Ad* 1.16
18.18–19 Ep *Sch* 50; T 4.36.3–4; Ad* 1.1, 2.17; Hip 7.31.6
18.20–21 Ep *Sch* 50; T 4.36.4, 7; Ad 2.17
18.22 T 4.36.4, 7; Ad 2.17
18.24 OrC 7.18

18.35–37 Ep Sch 51; T 4.36.9; Ad* 5.14	
18.38–39 Ep Sch 51; T 4.36.9; 4.39.10; Ad* 5.14; EM II 106	
18.40–43 Ep Sch 51; T 4.36.10–14; 4.37.1; 4.39.10; Ad* 5.14; EM II 106; EM III 123.	
19.2, 6 T 4.37.1	
19.8–10 T 4.37.1–2	
19.11–13 T 4.37.4; 4.39.11; Ps-E 32, 36, 38	
19.15–19 T 4.37.4; Ps-E 42	

[35]Now it happened, as he was approaching Jericho, a certain blind person was sitting beside the road begging. [36]And when he heard a crowd passing through, he was inquiring what this might be. [37]And people reported to him, "Jesus is passing by!" [38]So he cried out, saying, "Jesus, child of David, pity me!" [39]And those who were going in front were rebuking him that he should be silent. . . .

[40]So stopping, Jesus ordered that he be led (to him). And when he approached, he asked him, [41]"What do you want me to do for you?"

So he said, "Master, that I might see again."

[42]And, answering, he said to him, "See again; your trust has rescued you." [43]And instantly he saw again. . . . And when all the people saw (it), they gave acclaim to God.

19 [2]. . . There was a man called by the name Zacchaeus. . . . [6]He . . . happily received him (as a guest). [8]. . . Zacchaeus said . . . "Look! Half of my property I give to the beggars, and if I extorted something from someone I repay (it) fourfold."

[9]So Jesus said to him, "A rescue has occurred in this house today. [10]Because the Human Being came to rescue that which had been lost."

[11]. . . He told an analogy:

[12]A person of noble birth traveled to a distant land to secure a kingship for himself and return. [13]And, calling ten of his . . . slaves, he gave them each a mina and told them, "Do business until I come."

[15]And it happened when he returned . . . that he said to summon to him these slaves to whom he had given the silver, so that he might know what they achieved in business.

[16]Now the first one arrived, saying, "Master, your mina earned ten mina."

[17]So he said to him, ". . . Take authority over ten cities.'

[18]And the second came, saying, "Your mina, Master, made five mina."

¹⁹Then he said to this one also, "So you be over five cities."

²⁰. . . The other one came, saying, "Look. . . your mina. . . . ²¹For I was afraid of you, because you are a stingy person; you take what you did not deposit, and you harvest what you did not plant."

²²He said to him, "Out of your own mouth I judge you, unreliable slave! You had known that I am a stingy person, taking what I did not deposit and harvesting what I did not plant. ²³So why did you not place my silver with a bank? Then when I came I would have collected it with interest." ²⁴So to those standing by he said, "Take the mina from this one and give it to the one who has ten mina."

²⁶. . . From the one that does not have, even what this one seems to have will be taken.

20 ¹. . . And it happened on one of the days when he was teaching . . . in the temple . . . the *Pharisees* . . . . ². . . ³And . . . he said to them, ". . . You tell me: ⁴was the washing of John derived from the *celestial spheres* or from human beings?"

⁵Then they calculated among themselves, saying, "If we would say, 'From the *celestial spheres*,' he will say, 'Why did you not trust him?' ⁶But if we would say, 'From human beings,' all the people will stone us. . . ." ⁷So they replied that they did not know from where (it derived).

⁸And Jesus said to them, "Neither am I telling you by what sort of authority I am doing these things."

¹⁹And *they* sought to lay their hands on him . . . yet they were afraid of the people.

²¹*And there came to him Pharisees, testing him,* saying, ". . . ²²Is it permitted for us to pay a tribute to Caesar or not?"

²³[. . . He said to them, ²⁴"Show me] a denarius. [Whose] image and *likeness* [does it have?"

And they said, "Caesar's."]

²⁵So he said to them, "Return Caesar's things to Caesar, and God's things to God."

19.20–24 T 4.37.4; Ps-E 36, 42
19.26 T 4.37.4
20.1–8 Ep *El* 53; T 4.38.1–2
20.19 Ep *Sch* 54, *El* 53
20.21–25 T 4.38.3; 4.19.7

20.27–31, 33 T
4.38.4

20.34 T 4.38.5, 8

20.35 T 4.38.5–7; 4.39.11

20.36 T 4.38.5; 4.39.11; 3.9.4

20.39 T 4.38.9

20.41–42, 44 T 4.38.10; EM II 104–5.

21.7–11 T 4.39.1–3, 12–13, 17; 5.1.3

21.12–13 T 4.39.4

21.14–15 T 4.39.6

²⁷... The Sadducees, those who say there is no awakening (of the dead), ... questioned him, ²⁸saying, "Teacher, Moses wrote for us, 'If someone's brother who has a wife should die, and he be childless, his brother should take the wife and draw forth a seed for his brother.' ²⁹Suppose, then, there were seven brothers; and the first, after taking a wife, died childless. ³⁰... ³¹... So likewise the seven also did not leave behind children, and died. ³³In the awakening, therefore, the wife becomes the wife of which of them? For the seven had her as their wife."

³⁴And ... Jesus said, "The children of this age marry and are married; ³⁵but those counted worthy *by God* of that age and the awakening from among the dead neither marry nor are married, ³⁶because neither do they die anymore; for they will be like angels, because they are children of God and of the awakening."

³⁹In response some of the scribes said, "Teacher, you spoke well."

⁴¹Then he said to them, "How do they say that the Christos is David's child? ⁴²Because David himself [says ... 'The Lord said to my master, Sit at my right.' ⁴⁴David, then,] calls him a master; so how is he his child?"

21 ⁷Then the pupils questioned him, saying, "Teacher, when, then, will these things be, and what will be the sign when these things may be about to happen?"

⁸And he said,

> ... Many will come under my name, saying, 'I am the Christos....' Do not follow them. ⁹But whenever you might hear of wars and disorders, you should not be frightened, because it is necessary that these things occur, ¹⁰because a people will be stirred up against a people, and a realm against a realm; ¹¹and there will be both great earthquakes and, in place after place, epidemics and famines; and there will be fearful sights and great signs from the celestial sphere.
>
> ¹²But before all these things people will lay their hands upon you and persecute (you).... ¹³But it will turn out to be a testimony *and rescue* for you. ¹⁴Therefore settle (it) in your hearts not to rehearse being defended,

¹⁵because I will give you a mouth and a wisdom that all your adversaries will not be able to resist. ¹⁶And you will be handed over even by parents and siblings and relatives and friends . . . ¹⁷and you will be objects of hatred to everyone because of my name. ¹⁹By your endurance you will *preserve yourselves.*

²⁰But whenever you may see Jerusalem being encircled by military camps, then know that her desolation has approached. ²⁵And there will be signs in the sun and moon and stars, and on the earth anguish and perplexity of nations, roaring and agitation of the sea, ²⁶while people faint from fear and expectation of the things coming upon civilization; for the powers of the celestial spheres will be destabilized. ²⁷And then they will see the Human Being coming *from the celestial spheres* with much power. ²⁸But *when these things occur*, you will look up and lift your heads, because your liberation has arrived.

²⁹Then he told an analogy to them: "Look at the fig tree and all the (other) trees. ³⁰When they produce their fruit, by seeing it people know that the summer is near.

³¹"Thus you also, whenever you might see these things happening, know that the realm of God is near. ³². . . The celestial sphere *and the earth* in no way may pass away until everything may happen. ³³The celestial sphere and the earth will pass away, but my teachings will *remain forever*. ³⁴But watch yourselves that your hearts not at some time be burdened by hangover and drunkenness and life's anxieties, and that day might surprise you unexpectedly ³⁵as a snare. For it will come in upon all those dwelling upon the face of all the earth."

³⁷So by day he was teaching in the temple, but by night, departing, he was lodging on the mountain called (the Mount) of Olives. ³⁸And all the people were coming before dawn to him in the temple to listen to him. . . .

22 ¹Now the festival of the unleavened (bread), the one called Pascha, was approaching. ³But Judah, the one called Iskariotes, who was among the number of the

21.16–17, 19 T 4.39.8
21.20 T 4.39.9
21.25–26 T 4.39.9
21.27–28 T 4.39.10
21.29–31 T 4.39.10–11, 13, 16–17
21.32–35 T 4.39.18; 4.33.9
21.37–38 T 4.39.19
22.1 T 4.40.1
22.3 T 4.40.2; 5.6.7

22.4	Ep *Sch* 60
22.5	T 4.40.2
22.8	Ep *Sch* 61
22.14–15	Ep *Sch* 62, *El* 61; T 4.40.1, 3
22.19–20	T 4.40.3; 3.19.4; Ep *El* 61; Ad 2.20
22.22	T 4.41.1
22.33–34	T 4.41.2
22.41	Ep *Sch* 65; P[69]
22.45–46	P[69]
22.47–48	Ep *Sch* 66; T 4.41.2; P[69]
22.54, 56–61	P[69]

twelve, ⁴having departed, talked with the captains (of the temple guard) about how he might hand him over to them. ⁵And they were delighted and agreed to give him silver.

⁸. . . and he (Jesus) sent Peter and [John], having said, "When you have gone, prepare the Pascha for us so that we may eat (it)."

¹⁴And when the hour arrived, he reclined (at the table), and the twelve emissaries with him. ¹⁵And he said, "I desired very much to eat this Pascha with you before I suffer."

¹⁹And *after they had dined*, taking a piece of bread, when he had given thanks, he broke it, and gave (it) to them, saying, "This is my body which is being given on your behalf. . . ."

²⁰And (he took) the cup likewise, saying, "This cup is the contract in my blood. . . . ²². . . Woe to that one through whom the Human Being is handed over!"

³³. . . Then Peter said to him, "I [am ready to go] with you, [both into prison and into death]."

³⁴But he (Jesus) said, "[I am telling you, Peter, a rooster will not call out today until] you will have [three times] denied [to have known] me."

⁴¹Then he himself drew away from them about (the distance of) a stone's throw, and having bent his knees, he was invoking. ⁴⁵[And arising from] the [invocation, he came to the] pupils slee[ping from] grief, ⁴⁶and [he said to them] "Why are you lying down? [Get up,] invoke [so that you may not enter into] trial." ⁴⁷[Now while he was still speaking,] look! [a crowd, and the one called] Judah, [one of the Twelve, was going before] them; and he approached Jesus to kiss him.

⁴⁸And (Jesus) said [to him, "Judah, do you] hand over [the Human Being] with a kiss?"

⁵⁴[. . . Peter . . . ⁵⁶. . . (A person) saw him . . . said, "This one also was with him." ⁵⁷But he denied (it), saying,

"I do not know him...." ⁵⁸... Another person who saw] him said, ["You also are one of them."] But he said, ["Sir, I am not." ⁵⁹And after] standing about [an hour some other] was insisting, saying, "This one [absolutely] was with [him; for] he is [also] a Galilaean!" ⁶⁰[But Peter said] "Sir, I do not know [what you are talking about." And instantly,] while he was still speaking, [a rooster] called out. ⁶¹[And] turning, Peter [looked at] it. Then [Peter remembered] the statement [of Jesus when he said] to him, "Be[fore a rooster calls out to]d[ay you will disown me....]"

22.63–64 Ep *Sch* 68
22.66–67 T 4.41.2–3
22.69–70 T 4.41.4–5
23.1–3 Ep *Sch* 69–70; T 4.42.1
23.6–9 T 4.42.2–3
23.18, 25 T 4.42.4

⁶³Then the men who were holding him (Jesus) were mocking him, thrashing ⁶⁴and striking him, saying, "Prophesy! Who is the one that hit you?" ⁶⁶... They brought him for charges into their council-chamber, saying, ⁶⁷"If you are the Christos, tell us."

But he said to them, "If I should tell you, you would in no way trust (it). ⁶⁹But from now on the Human Being will be sitting to the right of God's power."

⁷⁰Then they all said, "Are you, therefore, the child of God?" And he said to them, "You are the ones that are saying (it)."

23 ¹And arising, they led him to Pilate. ²Then they started to accuse him, saying, "We found this person subverting the nation, and destroying the Law and Prophets, and forbidding the paying of taxes, *and turning away women and children,* and calling himself a consecrated king."

³So Pilate questioned him, saying, "Are you *the Christos?"* And in reply to him he said, "You are the one saying (it)."

⁶Now ... Pilate ... ⁷... sent him on to Herod.... ⁸So when Herod saw Jesus he was very happy ... ⁹... but he answered nothing to him.

¹⁸[... they cried out "... release] ... Barrabas ..." ²⁵... So he released the one who had been thrown into prison for riot and murder, whom they were demanding, but he handed over Jesus to their will.

23.32–33 Ep *Sch* 71; T 4.42.4	
23.34 Ep *Sch* 71	
23.44–45 T 4.42.5–6; Ep *Sch* 71 (vv. 44b–45); ED 21.3; Ez 358	
23.46 Ep *Sch* 73; T 4.42.6; Ad 5.12	
23.50 Ep *Sch* 74; T 4.42.7–8; Ad 5.12	
23.51–52 T 4.42.7–8	
23.53 Ep *Sch* 74; T 4.42.7–8; Ad 5.12	
23.55–56 Ep *Sch* 75	
24.1 T 4.43.1	
24.3 T 4.43.2	
24.4–7 Ep *Sch* 76; T 4.43.2, 5	
24.9, 11 T 4.43.2–3, 5	
24.13 T 4.43.3	
24.15–16 Ep *Sch* 77; T 4.43.3	
24.17–19 Ep *Sch* 77; T 4.43.3	

³²Now two other wrongdoers were also being led with him to be executed. ³³And when they came to the place called Skull, they staked him and the wrongdoers, one at (his) right and one at (his) left. ³⁴. . . [Then Jesus] said: "Father, forgive them, because they do not know what they are doing." And . . . they distributed his garments. . . . ⁴⁴Now it was already about the sixth hour, and a darkness fell over the whole earth . . . , ⁴⁵since the sun was eclipsed. Then the curtain of the sanctuary ripped down the middle. ⁴⁶And crying out in a loud voice, Jesus said, "Father, I entrust my spirit into your hands!" And when he had said this, he expired.

⁵⁰And, look, a man named Joseph . . . ⁵¹who had not agreed with the council and their action. ⁵²This one . . . asked Pilate for the body. ⁵³And when he had taken it down, he wrapped (it) up in linen, and he placed (it) in a quarried tomb.

⁵⁵Now the women who had come with him from Galilee followed after and viewed the tomb and how his body was placed. ⁵⁶And when they returned, they prepared aromatics and perfumes. And yet they rested the sabbath in accordance with the *Law*.

24 ¹Now on the first (day) of the week they went well before dawn to the tomb, carrying the aromatics they had prepared. ³But when they entered they did not find the body. ⁴And . . . look, two men in shining clothing . . . ⁵. . . said to them, "Why are you looking for the living one among the dead? ⁶He was awoken. Remember what he spoke to you in Galilee, ⁷saying that it is necessary that the Human Being be handed over, and be staked, and awaken on the third day."

⁹And when they returned from the tomb, they reported all these things to the pupils. ¹¹Yet . . . they distrusted them.

¹³. . . two of them were traveling . . . ¹⁵. . . Jesus himself, having come up to them, also was traveling with them; ¹⁶but . . . they did not recognize him. ¹⁷And he said . . . , "What are these matters . . . ?"

¹⁸. . . Kleopas said to him, "Do you . . . not know the things that have occurred . . . ?"
¹⁹And he said to them, "What sort of things?"
[. . . said to him,] ". . . ²¹But we supposed him to be the *ransomer* of Israel."
²⁵So he said to them, "O senseless people and slow in heart to trust in all the things *he* spoke *to you*—²⁶that it was necessary for the Christos to suffer these things."
³⁰. . . When he had taken the bread . . . , and when he had broken (it), . . . ³¹their eyes were opened and they recognized him.

³⁷. . . They thought they were seeing a phantom. ³⁸So he said to them, "Why are you troubled, and why are doubts arising in your heart? ³⁹Look at my hands and my feet, that it is I myself; because a spirit does not have bones just as you see that I have."
⁴¹But while they were still distrusting, he said to them, "Do you have something there to eat?" ⁴²And they handed him a piece of broiled fish. ⁴³And when he had taken it, he ate it in their presence. . . . ⁴⁴Then he said to them . . . ⁴⁷. . . "*Go and proclaim* . . . *to all the peoples*. . . ."

24.21 T 4.43.3
24.25 Ep *Sch* 77; T 4.43.4; Ad 5.12
24.26 Ep *Sch* 77; Ad 5.12
24.30–31 Ep *Sch* 77
24.37 T 4.43.6; Ad 5.12
24.38–39 Ep *Sch* 78; T 4.43.6–8; Ad 5.12
24.41–43 T 4.43.8; Ez 407
24.44a, 47 T 4.43.9

TEXT NOTES

Omission: Luke 1.1–2.52 Our sources unanimously report that the Evangelion opened with wording corresponding to 3.1 in Luke, and lacked any of the content found in Luke 1.1–2.52; e.g., Epiphanius writes,

> At the very beginning he excised all of Luke's original discussion—his "Inasmuch as many have taken in hand," and so forth—and the material about Elizabeth and the angel's annunciation to the virgin Mary, John and Zacharias and the birth at Bethlehem, the genealogy and the subject of the baptism. (*Pan.* 42.11.4)

Cf. also the Manichaean Faustus, quoted in Augustine, *Contra Faustum* 32.7, who appears to be drawing on a Marcionite source in alluding to the same set of passages as secondary. On an apparent testimony of Ephrem Syrus to a version of Luke that likewise lacked 1.1 (or 1.5)–2.52, see Conybeare, "Ein Zeugnis Ephräms." For an argument that 1.1–4 is actually composed with knowledge of, and in response to, Papias, see Annand, "Papias and the Four Gospels," 48–53.

3.1 Epiphanius, *Pan.* 42.11.5; Tertullian, *Marc.* 1.19.2, 4.7.1; Irenaeus, *Haer.* 1.27.2; Adam* 2.3, 19; Ps.-Eph A 1; Hippolytus, *Ref.* 7.31.5. Irenaeus and Adamantius attest a text reading "now in the fifteenth year of Tiberius Caesar, at the time of Pilate" (*en etei de pentekaidekatō Tiberiou Kaisaros epi tōn xronōn Pilatou*). Tertullian ends the quote after "Tiberius," omitting "Caesar" and the reference to Pilate. Epiphanius also omits the reference to Pilate, and opens the passage with different wording for the date (*en tō pentekaidekatō etei* in place of *en etei de pentekaidekatō*). Hippolytus' wording on the date is similar to that of Epiphanius, and characterizes it as the "year *of the hegemony* of Tiberius Caesar" (*etei pentekaidekatō tēs hēgemonias Tiberiou Kaisaros*). Pseudo-Ephrem A (1) gives only the wording "in the years of Pontius Pilate." We have no testimony to the presence of v. 1b–2a. Since Herod is mentioned at two other points in the Evangelion as if a known character, we may surmise that the introduction of him in v. 1b as "ruling the quadrant of Galilee" was perhaps present in the Evangelion. The same cannot be said of the reference to "Annas and Caiaphas" in Luke v. 2a, however, since these two figures go unmentioned in the rest of the Evangelion; indeed, the appearance of the two names together is a strikingly Johannine combination.

Omission: Luke 3.2–4.15 was absent from the Evangelion, according to Tertullian, *Marc.* 4.7.1, who remarks on its abrupt beginning, "From heaven straightway into the synagogue." Likewise, in connection with the first mention of John the Baptist in 5.31, Tertullian remarks, "From what direction does John make his appearance? Christ unexpected: John also unexpected. With Marcion all things are like that" (*Marc.* 4.11.4). Here again, Faustus provides indirect testimony to the lack of this material: Augustine, *Contra Faustum* 32.7. Luke 3.23–31 (Jesus' genealogy) is absent also from Gk mss W and 579.

Order: 4.31–35 precedes 4.16ff. Tertullian, *Marc.* 4.7.1, 5–6; Adam* 2.19; Hippolytus, *Ref.* 7.31.5. The order of these two episodes is reversed in the Evangelion's text relative to Luke, and evidence suggests that the Evangelion's order is more original. The most important of these is the expectation of the people of Nazara that Jesus would perform healings there as he had in Capharnaum (4.23) — before Jesus has ever been to Capharnaum in the narrative (4.31). It does no good to argue, as some have, that this narrative displacement is caused by Luke's editorial decision to move the visit to Nazara to an earlier place in the activities of Jesus than where it stands in Mark (and Matthew), jumping it ahead of Capharnaum material. The offending phrase "what you did in Capharnaum do also here" is not found in Mark, but is unique to Luke, and presumably also found in the Evangelion. Why would Luke introduce a clause that contradicts his ordering of events? The identification of Capharnaum as "a city of Galilee" also suggests that this episode originally stood first, and is redundant in Luke, where Jesus' presence in Galilee was already noted, and where his visit to the town of Nazara was not similarly qualified as "of Galilee." Schürmann, *Das Lukasevangelium*, vol. 1, 246–47, sees this as evidence that the Capharnaum episode preceded that of Nazara in a stage of the material prior to Luke (which he takes to be Q). A possible motive for a redactional reordering from Luke's sequence to the Evangelion's is not particularly obvious, unless it be to solve the problem of the phrase "what you did in Capharnaum." Elements in favor of the order of Luke include the expression "came down to Capharnaum," which suits a transition from Nazara in the hill country to Capharnaum in the valley of Lake Gennesar, and the continuity between activity in Capharnaum and the episode along the shore of Lake Gennesar that follows (but see the intervening 4.43, where Jesus says he is going away). But precisely such a logic might have induced reversing the order of the two episodes in a redaction from the Evangelion to Luke.

4.31 Tertullian, *Marc.* 4.7.1, 5–6; Adam* 2.19; Hippolytus, *Ref.* 7.31.5. Tertullian mocks the Evangelion's abrupt beginning: "From heaven straightway into the synagogue." Hippolytus concurs on the reading "teach(ing) . . . in the synagogue" although he has the plural "synagogues." Luke reads "on the sabbaths," and the Evangelion either had the two phrases side by side, as they are found in Mark 1.21, or the one phrase in place of the other. The Evangelion necessarily had the name Jesus here, as many Greek manuscripts of Luke do.

4.32 Tertullian, *Marc.* 4.7.7.

4.33 Tertullian, *Marc.* 4.7.9. Tertullian refers loosely to a *spiritus daemonis*, which I have taken as supporting the reading now found in most manuscripts of Luke.

4.34 Tertullian, *Marc.* 4.7.9, 12–14; 5.6.7. The Evangelion lacks "Nazarene" after Jesus, which is found in Luke and in the parallel episode in Mark. It also is missing the exclamation "ah!" (a classicizing touch) at the beginning of the daemon's remark; the same is true of Gk mss D and 33, SSyr, and OL.

4.35 Tertullian, *Marc.* 4.7.13. Tertullian only says that Jesus rebuked the daemon, and offers no more details from the episode after that.

Luke 4.36–37 is unattested.

Luke 4.38–39 The healing of Simon's mother-in-law is unattested. Harnack thinks it probably was present; Knox thinks its presence there uncertain, and Tsutsui concurs. But one must note that it is one of the anomalies of Luke that the statement in 4.38, "he entered into Simon's house," comes before the calling of Simon as a disciple in 5.1–11, indeed before any mention of Simon at all, and it therefore belongs with other indications of textual disruption of Luke relative to the Evangelion in this part of the text. It is based on Mark 1.29–31.

4.16 Tertullian, *Marc.* 4.8.2. The original reading here (found in Gk mss ℵ, B, and 33, among others) is "Nazara," but it has been corrected in many manuscripts of Luke to conform to the more usual forms "Nazaret" or "Nazareth," found in Matt 2.23; 21.11; Mark 1.9; and John 1.45, 46. It is noteworthy that "Nazareth" is also used (without known variants in the manuscripts) in Luke 1.26; 2.4, 39, 51—none of which were present in the Evangelion—and Acts 10.38. This inconsistency within Luke supports the idea that its first three chapters are a later addition deriving from a separate line of tradition. See Walker Jr., "'Nazareth': A Clue to Synoptic Relationships?" who notes the use of "Nazara" likewise in Matt 4.13, and suggests that both authors are dependent on a common source, such as Q, for this anomalous reference. Walker does not explain the failure of the authors to harmonize the reference in composing their texts, and does not consider the evidence of Marcion's text. The fact that the latter contained only Luke 4.16, the one passage with "Nazara," and lacked the passages with "Nazareth" can scarcely be mere coincidence. The Evangelion reads "where he was in the synagogue," in agreement with Gk ms D (corrected by a later scribe), instead of "where he was *raised*" found in other manuscripts of Luke. It also reads "in accord with the custom," in agreement with D and several OL manuscripts, instead of "in accord with *his* custom" found in other manuscripts of Luke. See Harris, "New Points of View."

Omission: Luke 4.16b–22 was absent from the Evangelion, according to Tertullian, *Marc.* 4.7.4: "[Jesus] makes it clear on his first appearance that he is come not to destroy the Law and the Prophets, but rather to fulfill them"—cf. 4.21—"[but] Marcion has deleted (*erasit*) this as an interpolation." Notice the incongruity between Jesus' remark in

Luke 4.23, assuming a hostile audience, and 4.22 (not present in the Evangelion) where the crowd is described as viewing Jesus positively at the conclusion of his declaration of the fulfilment of prophecy. Luke 4.16b is omitted in many Greek manuscripts; 4.22 is also missing in the Greek manuscript Family 13.

4.23 Tertullian, *Marc.* 4.8.2. Tertullian says that Jesus was thrown out of Nazara "for one single proverb," but does not quote the proverb itself. Note the reference to prior deeds in Capharnaum, which does not fit the order of Luke, where there is no previous scene in Capharnaum by this point of the narrative. Although none of our sources for the Evangelion directly quote the clause "the things that we heard happened in Capharnaum do here as well," the whole logic of the sequence unique to the Evangelion here depends on the presence of these words.

Luke 4.24 is unattested for the Evangelion, and probably could not have been passed over in silence by Tertullian and Epiphanius if it had been present in Marcion's text, since it clearly identifies Jesus' connection to this town, and to him having a human past, both of which these authors sought to argue against the Marcionites. Notice that the statement is a reply to the question of the audience in v. 22, as it is in Mark and Matthew where the answer follows directly on the question; in Luke, v. 23 seems to intrude, and indeed has no logical relation to what comes before or immediately after in the text, but rather sets up what follows in vv. 25ff. Thus Luke has the appearance of a composite text. Gk ms 1241 and OL e read "but he said <to them,> 'Amen I say to you,'" leading directly into the main clause of 4.25, omitting the rest of v. 24. Usually treated as a case of haplography caused by the repetition of the phrase *legō humin*, this reading may reflect the wording of the Evangelion (which is not to say that an early haplography could not stand behind the Evangelion's text).

Luke 4.25–26 is unattested. It has been assumed in previous scholarship that this reference to Elias (Elijah) was absent from Marcion's Evangelion, because he supposedly could not let stand an affirmation of the actions of a Jewish prophet. But we know that the content of 4.27, which does exactly that, was found in Marcion's Evangelion (in a different location: Luke 17.14), and once we drop the assumption that Marcion sought to expunge such material from the Evangelion (because in fact much material of this kind remained in his text), the assurance of the prior conclusion collapses. None of our witnesses refers to the passage, either as present or as missing. But since the episode shows a prophet refusing to aid Jews while helping a non-Jew, its citation may have been passed over as unhelpful to the argument of Marcion's critics. In fact, a passage such as this may be necessary to set up or otherwise contextualize the violent reaction of the people of Nazara.

Luke 4.28 is unattested.
4.29–30 Tertullian, *Marc.* 4.8.2–3.
4.40 Tertullian, *Marc.* 4.8.4 (≠Tsutsui).

4.41 Tertullian, *Marc.* 4.8.5–6. In Luke, "he would not permit them to speak" is followed by the explanation "because they knew him to be the Christ" (*christos*, i.e., messiah), but this was absent from the Evangelion; cf. Mark 1.34 "because they knew him."

4.42–43 Tertullian, *Marc.* 4.8.9. Tertullian does not mention the final clause in Luke 4.43: "because I was sent for this (purpose)," which derives from Mark 1.38; it is lacking also in SSyr. Word order and vocabulary in 43a seem to correspond most closely to that of Gk ms D, OL d, e.

Luke 4.44–5.1 is unattested.

5.2–3, 6, 8–11 Tertullian, *Marc.* 4.9.1–2 (=Harnack vv. 3, 9–11; Tsutsui vv. 3, 10–11, although he presumes the presence of vv. 1–10). Tertullian alludes to several details of the story while quoting verbatim only the statement of Jesus in 5.10. Although Tertullian alternates betwen "Simon" and "Peter" in his allusions to this passage, there is some uncertainty in the manuscript tradition regarding the appearance of both names. "Peter" is omitted by Gk mss D, W, and Family 13, by many OL manuscripts, and by SSyr. The combination "Simon Peter," though common in John, and particularly in the story in chapter 21 parallel to ours, does not otherwise appear in Luke except in 6.14, where "Peter" seems to be introduced to the reader for the first time. Its presence here, then, in the combined form Simon Peter, may reflect a peculiarity of the common source of John 21 and Luke 5.1–11. The Evangelion does not appear to agree with Gk ms D in the latter's idiosyncratic version of vv. 10–11.

5.12 Tertullian, *Marc.* 4.9.3. The Evangelion reads "a leprous man" with Gk ms D, the Diatessaron, and in agreement with Mark 1.40//Matt 8.2, instead of "a man full of leprosy" found in other manuscripts of Luke, the latter being a "typically Lukan" construction. "Master" (*kyrie*) is not directly attested for the Evangelion; it is one of the "minor agreements" between Matthew and Luke against Mark in this verse.

5.13 Tertullian, *Marc.* 4.9.4–7.

5.14 Epiphanius, *Scholion* 1, *Elenchos* 1; Tertullian, *Marc.* 4.9.9–10. Tertullian reads the imperative "go" (=*apelthe*) found in Gk ms D, the OL version, Vulgate (cf. Matthew's *hypage*), instead of "when you go" (*apelthōn*) found in Epiphanius and other witnesses to Luke. Tertullian reports the wording "offer a gift" (*offer munus*) found in some manuscripts and versions of Luke (and Matt 8.4), instead of "offer for your purification" found in most witnesses to Luke (and Mark 1.44). However, while Epiphanius has "offer a gift" in his own text of Luke (*Pan.* 66.57.2), when he quotes Marcion's Evangelion he attests the reading "for your purification" and expressly notes the absence of "a gift" (*Elenchos* 1). Such variations in the text of the Evangelion show it to have been transmitted in multiple variant text forms, as was Luke, as part of the fluid interchange of gospel texts in early Christianity before becoming isolated within Marcion's church. The Evangelion read "that it may be" with Gk ms D, and OL, not found in other manuscripts and versions of Luke. It also had "a testimony for *you* (pl.)," attested by both Tertullian and Epiphanius, with the latter explicitly noting that Marcion's text differed from his own, in agreement with D, the OL, and Ambrose, instead of "a testimony for *them*" found in other mansucripts and versions of Luke in agreement with Mark and Matthew. Both text variants noted in this verse by Epiphanius and attributed by him to Marcion's editorial tampering in fact are found in the non-Marcionite textual tradition of Luke, and at least one of them is considered more original by modern text criticism.

Luke 5.15 is unattested.

Luke 5.16 is unattested. It fits its context in Luke poorly, since it speaks of Jesus departing for a deserted place, while both the previous and following verses depict him in an urban setting. The intrusion appears to derive from Mark 1.45b, where however the transition back to an urban setting is expressed in 2.1.

Luke 5.17 is not directly mentioned by our sources, but some such introductory setting to the episode must have been present. The *Acts of Archelaus* (44), referring to this episode, says that it occurred on a sabbath; that detail is not attested by any other witness to this verse in Luke. Greek manuscript Family 13 says Jesus was teaching "in one of the synagogues."

5.18 Tertullian, *Marc.* 4.10.1. Here and in the following verses the Evangelion apparently read "cot" (Latin *grabatum* > Gk *krabatton*) with Gk ms D, several OL manuscripts, and Mark, instead of "bed" and "little bed," respectively, in most witnesses to Luke, which appears to be influenced by Matthew and constitutes one of the "minor agreements" absent from the Evangelion.

5.19 Tertullian, *Marc.* 4.10.1 (≠Harnack, Tsutsui). Tertullian alludes only to the crowd.

5.20 Tertullian, *Marc.* 4.10.2, 4 (≠Harnack, Tsutsui).

5.21 Tertullian, *Marc.* 4.10.1, 13.

Luke 5.22–23 is unattested, but something like v. 22a is necessary.

5.24 Epiphanius, *Scholion* 2; Tertullian, *Marc.* 4.10.6, 8, 13; Hegemonius, *Arch.* 44. The phrase "on the earth" is attested here by Epiphanius, but Tertullian lacks it (as does Gk ms D). This is another example of minor variations in the text of the Evangelion that may have arisen through influence from other Christian gospels; Mark and Matthew both have the phrase.

5.25 is implied by Tertullian, *Marc.* 4.10.1 (≠Harnack, Tsutsui). "Cot" is probable, in agreement with previous verses and with OL mss d and e. Gk ms D oddly switches over to "bed" only in this verse.

Luke 5.26 is unattested; but Burkitt, "The Exordium of Marcion's Antitheses," suggested an allusion to "ecstasy" in this verse in the opening words of Marcion's treatise. D and many other Greek manuscripts, as well as OL d, e, omit the first half of the verse ("Then an ecstasy seized everyone, and they were praising God"). It contrasts somewhat with the second half of the verse, where the people are said to be "filled with fear." Conversely, SSyr, retaining the first part of the verse, omits the part about being "filled with fear." These variations can be seen as attempts to smooth out the apparent contradiction of the two parts of the verse.

5.27 Tertullian, *Marc.* 4.11.1.

Luke 5.28–30 is unattested; POxy 1224 provides a very close, slightly abbreviated parallel to Luke 5.29–31.

5.31 Tertullian, *Marc.* 4.11.1.

Luke 5.32 is unattested.

5.33 Tertullian, *Marc.* 4.11.4–5. Tertullian notes that this is the first appearance of John in the Evangelion. This verse probably should be read as a question, as in Gk ms D, many other Greek manuscripts, the OL, the Vulgate, and other versions, as well as Mark 2.18. But here the Evangelion agrees with the majority of manuscripts in reading "but yours are eating and drinking" against D's "but your pupils do none of these things."

5.34–35 Tertullian, *Marc.* 4.11.6; Ps.-Eph A 64. By Tertullian's evidence, the Evangelion, along with Gk ms D, the majority of OL manuscripts, and Mark 2.19, has the "children of the bridal chamber" as the main actors of the situation ("The children of the bridal chamber cannot fast . . ."), instead of being the passive recipients of compulsion, as found in other witnesses ("You cannot make the children of the bridal chamber fast . . ."); but Pseudo-Ephrem A has the latter reading. Note also "while they have the bridegroom with them" (D, OL e) in place of "while the bridegroom is with them" (here, too, Pseudo-Ephrem A has the more standard text). Cf. Thomas 104.

Order: 5.37–38 precedes 5.36 Adam* 2.16; Epiphanius, *Pan.* 42.2.1; Tertullian, *Marc.* 4.11.9–12; Ps.-Eph A 9, 15, 18. That Marcion's text had the two parables of 5.36–38 in an order the reverse of that found in Mark, Matthew, and Luke is one of the best attested facts we have about the text, demonstrated by the order they are discussed in Tertullian, Epiphanius, Adamantius, and the anti-Marcionite tract Pseudo-Ephrem A. Particularly noteworthy is the fact that both Thomas 47 and the Diatessaron follow the order of the Evangelion. This would suggest that the order now found in Luke may be a late conformation of the text to Matthew and Mark (apparently already so in Tertullian's copy of Luke, see *Marc.* 3.15.5).

5.37–38 Adam* 2.16; Epiphanius, *Pan.* 42.2.1; Tertullian, *Marc.* 4.11.9–12; Ps.-Eph A 9; Philastrius, *Div. her.* 45. Based on the preponderance of witnesses, the Evangelion (as OL ms e) in v. 38 reads "must be poured," in agreement with the wording in v. 37 and the parallel in Matt 9.17, and not "must be cast" as in almost all witnesses to Luke. Pseudo-Ephrem A appears to attest the "minor agreement" between Matthew and Luke here ("the wine is spilled out"). Harnack concluded that the Evangelion probably lacked "and the bags will be ruined" (*Marcion*, E37), but this, too, is attested by Pseudo-Ephrem A. It appears to have had the additional clause "and both are preserved" at the end of the verse (Adam* 2.16), which is a harmonization to Matt 9.17, and is attested as well in several Greek manuscripts, the Old Latin (OL), and other versions of Luke; but in this case Pseudo-

Ephrem A lacks the clause. Such variants among the witnesses attest typical textual variation in circulating copies of the Evangelion, carrying forward variants that had already been introduced into the transmission of the Evangelion before it became isolated within the Marcionite community.

Luke 5.39 is unattested for the Evangelion and absent from Gk ms D, the OL, and the texts of Luke known to Irenaeus and Eusebius. It is one of the "Western non-interpolations" of Westcott and Hort. This aphorism is lacking in the parallel passages in Matthew and Mark, and is otherwise attested only in Thomas 47. Harnack (*Marcion*, 53) and Blackman (*Marcion and His Influence*, 46) assume that Marcion deleted it; and Metzger, *Textual Commentary*, 139, attributes its absence in some witnesses of Luke to Marcion's influence. On the other hand, Schmid has pointed out that there is no direct testimony to its omission, and all arguments for such an omission are based on assumptions about Marcion's editorial principles ("How Can We Access Second-Century Gospel Texts?" 142–43). In fact, the verse can be read in a way that agrees with Marcion's position on the advantages of separating the "new" from the "old."

5.36 Epiphanius, *Pan*. 42.2.1; Adam* 2.16; Tertullian, *Marc*. 4.11.9–10; Ps.-Eph A 15 (Codex B), 18 (Codex A). Epiphanius supplies the most complete text of this verse from the Evangelion, supported in part by the other witnesses. This version of the passage seems to be strongly influenced by Mark and Matthew, although elements found only in Luke also appear (*ou ballousin . . . epiblēma rakous agnaphou epi himatiōi palaiōi, ei de mē ge kai to plērōma airei kai tōi palaiōi ou sumphōnēsei, meizon gar schisma genēsetai*). The reading of the two manuscripts of Pseudo-Ephrem A differ, with one (Codex B, at 15) agreeing with our other witnesses to the Evangelion, while the other (Codex A, at 18) matches the reading of the current critical text of Luke.

6.1–2 Tertullian, *Marc*. 4.12.1, 5; Hegemonius, *Arch*. 44. Tertullian, *Marc*. 4.12.5, alludes to the disciples being hungry, an element of this story found only in Matt 12.1. Was Tertullian working from memory, or did the Evangelion's text contain this element, along with several other harmonizations to Matthew found in the Evangelion? However, Tertullian does not expressly refer to the disciples eating, one of the "minor agreements" of Matthew and Luke against Mark.

6.3–4 Epiphanius, *Scholion* 21; Tertullian, *Marc*. 4.12.5. Epiphanius cites this passage between citations of Luke 9.44 and 10.21; it is the only case where he appears to have jumbled the order of the material in the text before him. Tertullian specifies that David entered "on the sabbath," an addition to this passage otherwise unknown, and not part of the original story in 1 Sam 21.1–9; but this detail was part of the rabbinic tradition (Strack and Billerbeck, *Kommentar zum Neuen Testament*, vol. 1, 618f.; Kittel and Friedrich, *Theological Dictionary of the New Testament*, vol. 7, 22). It may be intended to bring the example of David into closer connection with the situation of Jesus and his disciples. It is noteworthy that the Evangelion contained both a favorable citation of the example of David and an express reference to "the house of God," which would seem to identify Jesus' God with the Jewish deity.

Order: 6.5 follows 6.10 Tertullian's citation of Luke 6.5 suggests that it followed v. 10 in the Evangelion, just as it does in Gk ms D. Harnack accepts the correspondence with D for the this placement of v. 5, while Delobel, "Extra-Canonical Sayings of Jesus," 107–8, rejects it, and argues that Tertullian's citation of v. 5 after v. 10 is only coincidental with D's peculiar order.

Addition following 6.4? Harnack rejects on ideological grounds the possibility that the Evangelion contained the passage found between 6.4 and 6.6 in Greek ms D in place of the relocated v. 5, despite the Evangelion's apparent agreement with D on the placement of v. 5. D's passage on Jesus' encounter with a man working on the sabbath is not explicitly cited from Marcion's text by any witness. Its presence in the Evangelion was hypothesized, however, by Vogels, *Evangelium Palatinum*, 97. The question finally comes down to whether Tertullian or other witnesses would have passed over the passage in silence, and this in turn depends on whether Jesus' blessing or cursing of the man in connection with sabbath violation was seen as the main point of his statement. It can be argued that the passage was read as too supportive of Marcion's views: if one knows the redemptive message of the good God, one is freed from the hegemony of the god of this world; otherwise one remains bound to follow the latter god's regime or face the consequences. For this reason, it would not be a good candidate for use in the arguments of Tertullian and other critics of Marcion.

6.6 Tertullian, *Marc.* 4.12.14; Ephrem, *Marc. III* (Mitchell) 141.

6.7 Tertullian, *Marc.* 4.12.9.

6.8 Adam* 1.16 (≠Harnack, Tsutsui). According to the Marcionite claim made in Adamantius, Jesus knew men's thoughts—a reference to 6.8, 9.47, and/or 11.17.

6.9 Tertullian, *Marc.* 4.12.10, 15.

6.10 Tertullian, *Marc.* 4.12.14; Ephrem, *Marc. III* (Mitchell) 141 (≠Harnack, Tsutsui). The Evangelion lacked "healthy as the other" following "restored," in agreement with many Greek manuscripts and versions.

6.5 Epiphanius, *Scholion* 3; Tertullian, *Marc.* 4.12.11. Placement is dependent on Tertullian's testimony, and one might assume that he simply is citing this verse out of order, were it not that it is found following v. 10 also in Gk ms D and its corresponding OL ms d. The Evangelion read "master *even* (Gk: *kai*) of the sabbath" in agreement with Gk mss A, D, and many others, OL, and Mark. For the Marcionite interpretation of this saying, see Tertullian, *Marc.* 4.12.1–2, discussed in Harnack, *Marcion*, 88, 91, 298*; Jackson, "The Setting and Sectarian Provenance," 286–87.

Luke 6.11 is unattested.

6.12 Tertullian, *Marc.* 4.13.1–2.

6.13 Tertullian, *Marc.* 4.13.3–4. Reading "designated" (*ōnomase*) or possibly "selected" (*ekalese*) as in Gk ms D, by assimilation to Synoptic parallels (Latin *elegit*).

6.14–16 Epiphanius, *Scholion* 4; Tertullian, *Marc.* 4.13.5 (cf. 2.28.2; 5.1.1); Adam* 1.5. In Adamantius, the names of the twelve emissaries are said to be read out from the Evangelion, but the names are not given. Likewise Tertullian alludes to "the list of the apostles in the Gospel" at *Marc.* 5.1.1 in order to make a polemical point against Marcionite exaltation of Paul, whose name does not appear in the list. Thus we cannot be sure if Marcion's text followed Mark's order or Matthew's; Luke corresponds with the latter in one of the "minor agreements." Epiphanius mentions only "Judas Iscariot, who became a traitor"; he has *Iskariōtēs*, which is a Hellenized form found in most manuscripts of Luke (but not Gk ms D or many OL manuscripts, which have *Skariōth*) instead of the form *Iskariōth* closer to the original Aramaic or Hebrew term. Tertullian refers merely to Simon's name being changed to Peter. The reading of Gk ms D ("*first* Simon, whom he also *renamed* Petros") might stand behind Tertullian's "*mutat et Petro nomen de Simone.*" This is the last (only?) use of "Simon" in the Evangelion, which from here on uses "Peter"; Luke has reappearances of "Simon" in 22.31 and 24.34.
6.17 Epiphanius, *Scholion* 4; Tertullian, *Marc.* 4.13.6. According to Epiphanius, Marcion's text read "among (*en*) them" rather than "with (*meta*) them" as in Luke and Mark 3.7. Luke has "Judea and Jerusalem and" before the references to Tyre and Sidon, but this is clearly lacking in the Evangelion, since Tertullian comments on the Gentile composition of the crowd (and so the Evangelion does not agree here with Gk ms D, which omits specific reference to Tyre and Sidon). The inclusion of these additional locales in Luke appears to be due to further assimilation to Mark 3.7–10, which actually has Jesus on the opposite, east, side of Galilee from the setting of the story in Luke and the Evangelion (cf. Matt 4.25). Only one lectionary (1761) supports the omission of "Judea and Jerusalem" found in the Evangelion.
Luke 6.18 is unattested.
6.19 Epiphanius, *Scholion* 5. Epiphanius skips the final clause in quoting this section of the Evangelion, and goes on immediately to quote the first part of 6.20. Harnack (*Marcion*, 191*) and Tsutsui ("Das Evangelium Marcions," 82) are cautious about treating that fact as evidence against the presence of v. 19b in Marcion's text, since Epiphanius often gives abbreviated quotes.
6.20 Epiphanius, *Scholion* 5; Tertullian, *Marc.* 4.14.1, 13; Eznik, *De Deo* 405; Hegemonius, *Arch.* 44; Ps.-Eph A 62. The Evangelion had the first three blessings in the third person, a reading shared by Gk ms W, the SSyr, and a few other witnesses to Luke, rather than the second person found in the majority of witnesses to Luke (although several of the latter shift to third person after the first blessing). The first blessing ("The beggars are fortunate") has been altered in Codex A of Pseudo-Ephrem A to conform to Matthew, but is given in Codex B in accord with our other witnesses to the Evangelion. Cf. PolPhil 2.3; Thomas 54.
6.21 Tertullian, *Marc.* 4.14.9, 11, 13. Luke has "now" at the end of the first clauses of the two sentences in this verse ("those who are hungry

now," "those who are weeping *now*"); the Evangelion lacks them, as does the text known to Origen and Eusebius of Caesarea; cf. Thom 69.2; Exegesis of the Soul 135.15–19; Thomas the Contender 145.5–6.

6.22 Tertullian, *Marc.* 4.14.14; Ps.-Eph A 62. The Evangelion apparently used the future tense in this verse (Tertullian and Codex A of Pseudo-Ephrem A agree), which is found also in various Greek and OL manuscripts, the Vulgate, and others. Codex B of Pseudo-Ephrem A has the present. Tertullian gives "hate, reproach, reject," omitting "exclude" with Gk ms 2542; Codex A of Pseudo-Ephrem gives "reproach, say evil," the latter phrase harmonized to Matt 5.11. Codex B has "persecute, reproach, say evil," even more harmonized to Matthew. Cf. Thom 68.1; Thomas the Contender 145.3–5.

6.23 Epiphanius, *Scholion* 6; Tertullian, *Marc.* 4.15.1. The first clause of this verse in Luke ("Rejoice in that day and leap, for look! Your reward is great in heaven") is unattested for the Evangelion. Harnack considers it to have been absent, and Tsutsui concurs. The Evangelion apparently also lacked the "for" (*gar*) of the following clause in Luke; it is also missing in D and other Greek manuscripts, as well as some manuscripts of OL. In all these differences, Luke shows harmonization to the parallel passage in Matt 5.12. The Evangelion had "your ancestors" according to Epiphanius, agreeing with a handful of Greek manuscripts (and apparently Epiphanius' own text of Luke; see *Pan.* 66.42.9, which calls the value of his testimony into question); Tertullian has "their ancestors," like the majority of manuscripts, matching a similar construction in v. 26.

6.24 Tertullian, *Marc.* 4.15.3, 6–7, 9; Hegemonius, *Arch.* 44. *However* (*plēn*) is not explicitly attested for the Evangelion. It is often pointed to as a "characteristic" word of Lukan style.

6.25 Tertullian, *Marc.* 4.15.13. "You, who are completely filled," omits a final "now" with Gk mss A, D, and many others, as well as OL; but includes "now" with "you who are laughing," as the same manuscripts do. Tertullian does not include the final phrase "and weep"; it is missing as well from a few Greek manuscripts.

6.26 Tertullian, *Marc.* 4.16.14–15; Origen, *Cels.* 7.18. "People" appears rather than "all people," with D and many other Greek manuscripts, OL ms d, the SSyr, and so on. "For" is also missing as a link between the first and second clauses, as in D, the OL, and the Vulgate. "Also" is found here in the Evangelion as well as Irenaeus and a few OL manuscripts.

6.27–28 Tertullian, *Marc.* 4.16.1, 6 (cf. 1.23.3; 4.27.1); cf. Adam* 1.12. Tertullian initially gives this in a compressed form that may or may not accurately represent the Evangelion's text: "love your enemies, and bless those which hate you, and pray for them that speak ill of you." This conflates "those who hate you" from the second clause of v. 27 with the command to "bless" from the first clause of v. 28, omitting the verb "act well" from the prior and "those who curse you" from the latter. The same conflation is found in the early Syrian Christian

Aphraates. Similar compressions were common (e.g., Clement, *Paed.* 3.12.92; *Strom.* 4.14.95; Justin, *1 Apol.* 15.9; Did 1.3). But a few lines later Tertullian refers to "those who are our enemies, who hate us *and curse us* and speak evil of us," which takes account of the full form of the passage. Likewise, in 4.27.1, he says "he forbids the return of cursing for cursing." Has he reverted to the text of Luke for these comments? Adamantius, in a context where we would expect quotation of the Evangelion, has "love your enemies and pray for those who persecute you" from Matt 5.44.

6.29 Tertullian, *Marc.* 4.16.2, 5–6; Adam* 1.15, 18; Ps.-Eph A 14; Hegemonius, *Arch.* 44; Origen, *Cels.* 7.18. Both Adamantius and Tertullian allude to the content of Matt 5.38 ("an eye for an eye and a tooth for a tooth") here. But since they presumably had Marcion's *Antitheses* in front of them as well, they could be drawing the reference from there, quoted from Exod 21.24f., Lev 24.20, or Deut 19.21. Marcion certainly did emphasize the contrast between Jesus' instruction here and the *lex talionis* of the Jewish Law, and both Tertullian and Adamantius would have been aware that that was his reading of this passage. As for more certain textual variants, the Evangelion apparently used a conditional structure for both clauses: "if someone strikes you . . ." instead of "to the one who strikes you . . ." (with a different, synonymous word for "strike"), and "if someone takes your" instead of "from the one who takes your . . ."; these variants are also attested by Did 1.4. The Evangelion agreed with several witnesses to Luke in reading "on the *right* jaw/cheek," a harmonization to Matt 5.39; and it agreed with Gk ms D and the OL in reading "offer *to him.*" Adamantius gives *parathes* as the verb of offering the other cheek, instead of Luke's *pareche*. Based on Tertullian, the Evangelion followed Matt 5.40 in having *chiton* (tunic) before *himation* (cloak); Adamantius (1.18) and Pseudo-Ephrem A, however, both have the order cloak, tunic, in agreement with Luke and the Didache. Adamantius also indicates that the Evangelion had "present to him also your . . ." (as found in Matthew) instead of "do not withhold your . . ." (as found in Luke and Justin, *1 Apol.* 16.1). The variation between our witnesses on these details adds further evidence against a single redaction of the Evangelion by Marcion.

6.30 Tertullian, *Marc.* 4.16.8, 10; cf. 4.27.1; Ps.-Eph A 14. Tertullian quotes only the first of the two instructions found in this verse in Luke; but Pseudo-Ephrem A includes both, with some variation in phrasing ("he who asks from you, do not withhold from him, and he who takes, do not ask from him").

6.31 Tertullian, *Marc.* 4.16.13. "You do" with the second person plural pronoun explicit for emphasis, follows the majority of witnesses to Luke, including Gk ms D, OL mss c, d, f, Vulgate, and others, apparently by assimilation to Matt 7.12. The Evangelion differs from Gk ms D in having "similarly" in common with the vast majority of witnesses to Luke. Cf. 1 Clem 13.2.

Luke 6.32–33 is unattested.

6:34 Tertullian, *Marc.* 4.17.1. Tertullian quotes only the first half of the verse. The second half is unattested for the Evangelion; Gk ms D, the OL, and the SSyr omit "an equal return" from this second half of the verse. Cf. Thomas 95.

6.35 Tertullian, *Marc.* 4.17.4, 6. Tertullian has "children of God" in place of Luke's "children of the Most High One." The title "Most High" for God occurs several times in Luke, but apparently never in the Evangelion. Inscriptional evidence shows it to have been the favored designation for God within a monotheistic movement of Asia Minor in this time (see Nock, "The Gild of Zeus Hypsistos"), but it is also a commonly used expression in the Septuagint. Tertullian, *Marc.* 4.17.6, alludes to terms found in Matt 5.45, a passage closely related in thought to Luke 6.35, and says that Marcion has "cleverly deprived" God of these characteristics; this is typical of Tertullian's assertions that Marcion has removed things from "the gospel," by which Tertullian always means Marcion's rejection of material found in other gospels accepted within Tertullian's church. There is a slight possibility that Tertullian is bearing witness to a Synoptic tradition that combined Luke 6.36 with Matt 5.45 also known to Justin Martyr (*1 Apol.* 15.13; *Dial.* 96.3a); see Bellinzoni, "The Gospel of Luke in the Apostolic Fathers," 8–14.

6.36 Tertullian, *Marc.* 4.17.8. The Evangelion lacked "therefore" and "also" with many other Greek and Latin manuscripts and other early witnesses to Luke, and read "just as your Father who is compassionate for you," rather than the simpler "just as your Father is compassionate," in agreement with OL ms c, Cyprian, and a few other witnesses to Luke.

6.37–38 Tertullian, *Marc.* 4.17.9; Adam 2.5. Adamantius quotes only "with the meaure that you measure, it will be measured to you in return" from v. 38. Tertullian quotes the entire passage. It is also alluded to by PolPhil 2.3, and 1 Clem 13.2. The Evangelion apparently read *"so that you will not be,"* along with A, D, W, and other Greek manuscripts, many OL manuscripts, and the SSyr, in agreement with Matt 7.1. It lacked "and shaken together" as one of the characterizations of the measure one will receive; a few other Greek and Latin manuscripts of Luke do likewise. It also lacked the connecting "for" before "the measure you give will be the measure you get," with P^{45}, other Greek and Latin manuscripts and witnesses to Luke.

6.39 Tertullian, *Marc.* 4.17.11. Cf. Thomas 34.

6.40 Tertullian, *Marc.* 4.17.11. Only the first half of the verse is quoted. The second clause of the verse is missing in a few Greek manuscripts, but apparently only as a scribal error. The Evangelion apparently lacked "his" with "teacher," as do many Greek manuscripts, the OL, and Vulgate of Luke. Cf. DialSav 53.

6.41–42 Tertullian, *Marc.* 4.17.11 (=Tsutsui v. 42 only). Tertullian alludes to the key terms of the passage without quoting verbatim. All of his allusions could be derived from the wording of v. 42 alone, although the presence of the full form of the saying is quite probable. Cf. Thomas 26.

6.43 Tertullian, *Marc.* 4.17.11 (cf. 1.2.1); Adam* 1.28; Hippolytus, *Ref.* 10.19.3; Origen, *Princ.* 2.5.4; Philastrius, *Div. her.* 45. Harnack argues that the order "fit tree ... unfit tree" was reversed in Marcion's text, basing himself upon Adamantius (*Marcion*, 195*); the same reversal is found in a single Greek manuscript. But Tsutsui (85) rejects this idea on the combined evidence of Tertullian, Hippolytus, and Origen, who all cite the verse in its usual order.

Luke 6.44 is unattested; cf. Thom 45.1.

6.45 Tertullian, *Marc.* 4.17.12. Tertullian merely alludes to Jesus making "an allegory referring to men"; cf. Thom 45.2. Thomas seems to support the sequence and content of the Evangelion and of Luke throughout this section. The last clause of the verse in Luke ("for one's mouth speaks from an overflow of [one's] heart"), unattested for the Evangelion, may be a harmonization to Matt 12.34b, although it is also found in Thom 45.2.

6.46 Tertullian, *Marc.* 4.17.12–13. Tertullian quotes the verse verbatim.

6.47–48a Ps.-Eph A 7 (≠Harnack, Tsutsui). Harnack considers vv. 47–49 unattested but probably present in the Evangelion; Tsutsui and Knox consider their presence uncertain. But the evidence of the anti-Marcionite work Pseudo-Ephrem A, which confines itself to debating the meaning of parables found in Marcion's gospel, would seem to confirm the presence of at least the basic analogy given in v. 48a. The passage is closely paralleled by Matt 7.24–27, and Pseudo-Ephrem A reads "a wise person" in place of "a person" (as does Gk ms 28 and OL ms r1) in harmony with Matthew.

Luke 6.48b–49 is unattested.

Luke 7.1–8 is not directly attested, but see the note on 7.9 below.

7.9 Epiphanius, *Scholion* 7; Tertullian, *Marc.* 4.18.1. The presence of the episode of the commander's slave (Luke 7.1–10) is attested only by the citation of Jesus' remark in 7.9 given by Epiphanius and Tertullian. The exact form of the story in the Evangelion, therefore, remains uncertain. The essential narrative elements must have been present in some form, but its exact details cannot be fixed with any certainty. Assuming that the Evangelion included the minimum elements from the source it shares with Matthew (whose 8.10 uniquely parallels the statement of Jesus given here), we can probably infer the setting in Capharnaum (cf. John 4.46), the identity of the figure as a military commander, and the problem being an ill member of the household (Matthew's *pais*, "child," is a term used of both children of the family and of household servants; Luke has the less ambiguous *doulos*, "slave, servant," three times, but retains the probable original *pais* in v. 7). The indirect request through Jewish elders and their praise of the commander to Jesus as the sponsor of the synagogue are unique to Luke, and we would expect the latter in particular to be mentioned by one or another of our sources in their polemic had it been present. The word order of the last clause of v. 9 as given by Epiphanius diverges somewhat from

Luke. He also has *euron* instead of *euron*. Tertullian attests the reading *toiautēn* in place of Luke's *tosautēn*.

Luke 7.10 is unattested.

Luke 7.11, which provides the setting in the town of Nain for the following episode, is unattested.

7.12, 14–16 Tertullian, *Marc.* 4.18.2–3. Tertullian alludes just to the most salient points of the story; only v. 16 is quoted verbatim.

7.17–18 Tertullian, *Marc.* 4.18.4; Adam* 1.26. The Marcionite spokesperson in Adamantius says,

> John did not recognize him. . . . Now when he had heard in prison the works of Christ, he sent his disciples to him saying, "Are you the one who is to come, or should we look for another?"

This reading is close to that found in Gk ms D and OL ms e of Luke, matching in its construction more closely the parallel account in Matt 11.2 ("Now when John heard in prison about the deeds of Jesus"), whereas most manuscripts of Luke read, "The disciples of John told him of all these things." Tertullian agrees that the Evangelion included a reference to John being in prison, which otherwise is found only in Matthew. In Luke the mention of John's imprisonment here is unnecessary, because his arrest on the orders of Herod Antipas had already been reported in 3.19–20—a passage that the Evangelion did not have.

7.19 Tertullian, *Marc.* 4.18.6; Adam* 1.26; Ephrem, *Marc. I* (Mitchell) 82. The Evangelion's text appears to be reflected in Gk ms D and OL ms e.

7.20 is unattested; but some such content is necessary to set up v. 21.

7.21 Adam* 1.20, Adam 1.26 (≠Harnack, Tsutsui). Adamantius refers to giving sight to the blind, and in 1.26 he says that after the arrival of John's pupils, Jesus "proceeded to perform his works."

7.22 Tertullian, *Marc.* 4.18.6; Adam 1.26 (≠Harnack, Tsutsui). Tertullian says, "the Lord returned answer to John that it was by those same works that he ought to be recognized." Adamantius quotes more explicitly: "the blind are seeing again, the deaf are hearing, and the lame are walking, the dead are being raised up." This lacks two clauses found in Luke and the parallel passage in Matt 11.5: "lepers are purified" and "beggars are proclaimed." The latter phrase derives from Isa 61.1, quoted at length in Luke 4.18, which was not part of the Evangelion, and is also lacking in Clement, *Paed.* 1.10.90's allusion to this passage.

7.23 Epiphanius, *Scholion* 8; Adam 1.26; Ephrem, *Marc. I* (Mitchell) 86. Adamantius quotes the verse verbatim, just as it is found in Luke. But Epiphanius, after quoting the verse in the same words as Adamantius, insists that the wording was somehow altered, "for he had it as though in reference to John." Similarly, Tertullian says, "John is offended when he hears of Christ's miracles" (*Marc.* 4.18.4; cf. 4.18.8). Perhaps Epiphanius and Tertullian are reporting Marcion's interpretation of this episode, rather than a variation in the text. Burkitt conjectures (in Mitchell, *Against Marcion*, vol. 2, xxxix n. 1) that Marcion's text lacked *hos* ("whoever"), and so read "Happy is he, if he [i.e., John] is not scandalized by me." Such a form of the saying would have a good case for being more original, subsequently generalized to "whoever" in the tradition.

7.24 Tertullian, *Marc.* 4.18.8; Ephrem, *Marc. I* (Mitchell) 81–82. Tertullian quotes only the first part of the question, "What did you go out into the wilderness to look at?" Ephrem supplies "a reed being swayed by the wind." Cf. Thomas 78.

Luke 7.25 is unattested; cf. Thomas 78.

7.26 Tertullian, *Marc.* 4.18.7.

Order: 7.28 before 7.27? Epiphanius, *Scholion* 8, quotes v. 28 before v. 27 (*Scholion* 9), and the same order is found in Gk ms D. On the other hand, Tertullian cites the two verses in the order found in all other witnesses to Luke. This difference between our two primary sources can best be explained by variants in the manuscript tradition of the Evangelion found also in the manuscript tradition of Luke.

7.27 Epiphanius, *Scholion* 9; Tertullian, *Marc.* 4.18.7; Adam* 2.18. All three sources agree verbatim on the Evangelion's text matching that of Luke in this verse, each quoting just a bit more than the other (Epiphanius the least, Tertullian a little more, Adamantius the most). "He is" appears rather than "this is" according to Epiphanius, who also omits the emphatic *egō* from the quote with many manuscripts of Luke (but Tertullian attests it). The final phrase "before you" is absent in D and the OL, as it is in Mark 1.2, and both Epiphanius and Tertullian end their quotes before reaching it (Epiphanius lacks the entire clause "who will prepare your road before you"); but Adam* 2.18 attests it, making this one of the few "minor agreements" between Luke and Matthew against Mark that is also found in the Evangelion. The presence of an explicit quote from the Jewish scriptures in Marcion's text appears to belie the assumption that he edited out such material. He could hardly have missed the formula of quotation here.

7.28 Epiphanius, *Scholion* 8; Tertullian, *Marc.* 4.18.8; Ephrem, *Marc. II* (Mitchell) 107–8. Tertullian says variously, "Greater indeed is he than all that are born of women, but . . . he is less than the least in the kingdom of God" and "John . . . is greater than men born of women." Epiphanius paraphrases, "whom he had ranked as the greatest of those born of women" and quotes, "The one that is less in the kingdom is greater than he." So although the first clause is missing from Gk ms D, it was clearly present in the Evangelion, despite its high praise of a prophet representing the Jewish covenant. By saying "than all born of women" rather than "than all prophets born of women," all three of our witnesses suggest that the Evangelion has a widely shared reading, including by P^{75} and many other Greek manuscripts, Origen, and OL. Cf. Thomas 46.

Luke 7.29–35 is unattested. Harnack considered 7.31–35 as probably lacking in Marcion's text, because it has some ideas contrary to Marcion's ideology. Would not Tertullian or Epiphanius have made much of Marcion's bodiless Jesus eating and drinking? But Knox and Tsutsui are more cautious, noting only the uncertainty of its presence in the text.

7.36–38 Epiphanius, *Scholion* 10; Tertullian, *Marc.* 4.18.9. The testimonies of Tertullian and Epiphanius nicely complement each other in this passage. Both are abbreviating as they refer to the key elements of the story while skipping inessential detail. Epiphanius omits any reference to the act of wiping Jesus' feet with her hair, but Tertullian includes it. But is it only coincidence that neither mentions the alabaster container of ointment so central to the story of the anointing at Bethany found in Matthew and Mark, while both refer to the woman oiling Jesus' feet? Likewise the reference back to the perfumed oil in v. 46 is unattested for the Evangelion. It has long been remarked by biblical researchers how different in setting and meaning Luke's story is from its Synoptic parallels. The version found in the Evangelion seems to be even more remote from those parallels, while Luke may have been colored to a degree by them. See also the similar story in John 12.1–8, which parallels Matthew and Mark in being set in Bethany (although in a different home), yet parallels Luke in having Jesus' feet, rather than his head, oiled, and includes the detail of them being wiped with the woman's hair. The Evangelion apparently lacked the explicit verb "weeping" in v. 38, a feature shared with the OL and Vulgate.

Luke 7.39–43 is not directly attested. None of the exchange between Jesus and his host is explicitly quoted by our sources. The sudden introduction of the name "Simon" for the Pharisee in this verse of Luke 7.40 (repeated in Luke 7.43–44, but not mentioned by either Epiphanius or Tertullian) shows the influence of Mark 14.3–9, where the anointing of Jesus by the woman takes place in the home of Simon the Leper. But it is clearly an intrusion into the form of the story in Luke, perhaps added naively by a scribe to help sort out the confusing "he"-"him" references back and forth between Jesus and the Pharisee.

7.44–45 Epiphanius, *Scholion* 11 (=Harnack v. 44 only; Tsutsui vv. 44–46). Epiphanius abbreviates, and does not explicitly quote any contrast of the woman's behavior with that of the host. Therefore we cannot be certain that such a contrast was featured in the Evangelion.

Luke 7.46–47 is unattested; but see the note on 7.48.

7.48 Tertullian, *Marc.* 4.18.9 (≠Harnack, Tsutsui). Tertullian refers only to "a sinful woman's repentance won for her pardon," an allusion to Jesus' comment in 7.47 and/or 7.48. Gk ms D omits the second and third clauses of v. 47 ("because she loved much; but the one for whom little is dismissed, loves little"), which are not directly attested for the Evangelion.

Luke 7.49 is unattested.

7.50 Tertullian, *Marc.* 4.18.9; Ps.-Eph A 34. Both witnesses quote only the first part of Jesus' statement to the woman as it is known in Luke, and lack "go in peace."

Luke 8.1 is unattested.

8.2–3 Tertullian, *Marc.* 4.19.1. Presumably, the Evangelion listed the other women mentioned in Luke beside "the wife of . . . Herod's quartermaster," but Tertullian passes over them as not germane to his argument. The Evangelion read "rendering service *to him*," with many manuscripts (but not D) and versions of Luke, against "to them." It is uncertain whether the Evangelion contained the reference to the twelve traveling with Jesus found in Luke 8.1.

8.4 Tertullian, *Marc.* 4.19.2. Tertullian merely alludes to Jesus speaking parables at this point, then jumps to the content of Luke 8.8b, followed by that of 8.16–18. So either the analogy of the planter was not a part of the text known to him, or he could see nothing in it worth using in his anti-Marcionite arguments. The analogy is included in Pseudo-Ephrem A, however, which supposedly only discusses the parabolic imagery contained in the Evangelion.

8.5–8a Ps.-Eph A 22 (≠Harnack, Tsutsui). Codex B says only, "the teaching of our Lord is likened to seeds, and because us he likened to the ground which receives the seeds." Codex A provides a more direct quote, which lacks "of the sky" with "birds," as in Gk mss D, W, most OL manuscripts, and both the SSyr and CSyr (cf. Matt 13.4 and Mark 4.4). The addition of "of the sky" to "birds" is characteristic of Luke (see Luke 9.58; 13.19; Acts 10.12; 11.6). The amount of fruit produced ("a hundred times as much" in most witnesses to Luke 8.8) is not directly given.

8.8b Tertullian, *Marc.* 4.19.2. The Evangelion has only "ears" in agreement with a single Greek manuscript of Luke and Matt 13.9, instead of "ears *to hear*" found in most witnesses to Luke and Mark 4.9.

Luke 8.9–15, the interpretation of the analogy of the planter derived from Mark 4.10ff., may or may not have been included in the Evangelion. Irenaeus, *Haer.* 4.29.1, expressly notes the absence from the Evangelion of vv. 9–10, but says nothing about the presence or absence of the interpretation which follows; and his own quotation of the interpretation appears to derive from Matt 13.10–16 rather than Luke 8.11–15 (but with several minor differences from either text). Pseudo-Ephrem A 22 quotes material equivalent to Luke 8.12–15 or its Synoptic parallels, but does so as part of his anti-Marcionite exegesis of the planter analogy, just as he supplies such exegesis of all the analogies found in the Evangelion. The author makes no claim that this exegesis is present even in the Evangelion itself, and may be quoting from his own gospel text, although in that case we might expect him to remark about the shift, as he does in Ps.-Eph A 44.

8.16–17 Tertullian, *Marc.* 4.19.5.

8.18 Tertullian, *Marc.* 4.19.3–4; cf. 2.2.6. Tertullian quotes v. 18 before verses 16–17; Tsutsui ("Das Evangelium Marcions," 88) considers this their probable order in Marcion's text. Confirmation from another source would be welcome. The Evangelion apparently lacked "therefore" following "pay attention," as does the SSyr, the OL, and several Greek manuscripts of Luke. The Evangelion may have lacked "for" at the beginning of the second clause.

Omission: Luke 8.19 was absent from the Evangelion, according to Epiphanius, *Scholion* 12. The manner in which Tertullian discusses the following verses (*Marc.* 4.19.6–7, cf. 3.11.3–4) shows that it was missing in his text of the Evangelion as well (and perhaps from his own codex of Luke), since he would have cinched his argument just by quoting it. The absence of this verse could be seen as a Marcionite deletion to remove an explicit narrative statement that Jesus had a mother and brothers. Alternatively, it could be seen as a scribal addition to clear up an ambiguity in the text as to whether the people announced are indeed Jesus' mother and brothers. Such an explicit identification by the narrator that the people in question were who people said they were is found in the parallel accounts in Matt 12.46 and Mark 3.31. But it is missing in Thomas 99 and G Ebi5 (in Epiphanius, *Pan.* 30.14.5).

8.20–21 Epiphanius, *Scholion* 12; Tertullian, *Marc.* 4.19.6–7, 10–11; cf. 4.36.9. Both Epiphanius and Tertullian attest the presence of Jesus' rhetorical question "who are my mother and brothers?" similar to that found in the parallel accounts in Matt 12.48 and Mark 3.33. There is no such question in most witnesses to Luke; but Tertullian, *Carn. Chr.* 7 presumably quotes it from his own text of Luke. In the Evangelion, Jesus refers to those "who hear my words and put them into practice" (*Marc.* 4.19.11) rather than Luke's "who hear the word of God and put it into practice." The Synoptic parallels, Thomas 99, and Gospel of the Ebionites (in Epiphanius, *Pan.* 30.14.5) have "whoever does the will of my Father/God." Volckmar, "Über das Lukas-Evangelium," 208, regards the wording of the Evangelion as more original than Luke.

8.22–23 Epiphanius, *Scholion* 13. Epiphanius ends his quote halfway through v. 23, but something equivalent to the second half is necessary to set up the crisis to which Jesus responds in v. 24.

8.24 Epiphanius, *Scholion* 13; Tertullian, *Marc.* 4.20.3. Tertullian alludes to the miracle of this story while providing almost no details; in his remarks he seems to confuse this episode with that of Jesus walking on the water from Matt 14.24–33/Mark 6.47–52, an episode not found in Luke. The cry of the pupils to Jesus in v. 24 and Jesus' reply in v. 25 are not explicitly attested for the Evangelion. The second half of the verse is quoted by Epiphanius. Jesus rebukes "the wind *and the sea*" rather than "the wind and the raging of the water," with some points of agreement with Gk ms D and SSyr (see the note on 8.25).

8.25 Tertullian, *Marc.* 4.20.1. There are several minor agreements between the Evangelion and OL. The reaction of the pupils can be translated as "who then is this?" or "what manner of man is this?" They say he "orders the winds and sea," in agreement with the parallel accounts in Matt 8.27 and Mark 4.41, instead of "the winds and water" in Luke. The last clause of this verse in Luke, "and they obey him," is unattested for the Evangelion, and is absent also from Gk mss P[75], B, and others.

Luke 8.26, which shifts the scene to the area of Gerasa, is unattested, but note the reference to "the city" in v. 27.

8.27–28 Tertullian, *Marc.* 4.20.4–5. Tertullian merely alludes to Jesus encountering a man filled with many daemons, but the Evangelion must have provided some setting for this encounter. How much detail was given is unclear. Our incomplete witness to the Evangelion offers us no help on the question of the town's name—Gadara, Gerasa, and Gergesa are all found in manuscripts of the three Synoptics, but Gerasa is favored in P^{75}, D, and OL. Tertullian says that the man addressed Jesus as "child of God." Here, as elsewhere, the Evangelion lacked "most high" as an epithet of God (D and other Greek manuscripts read "son of the Most High," with other manuscripts conflating "God" and "Most High"), despite its apparent suitability to Marcion's doctrines.

Luke 8.29 is unattested; Tsutsui ("Das Evangelium Marcions," 89) considers it to have been present.

8.30–31 Tertullian, *Marc.* 4.20.4–5, 7; Adam* 1.17. Tertullian mentions the "legion" of daemons involved in this encounter, presumably from the self-identification made at the command of Jesus in v. 30. Adamantius also has an allusion to the "legion" and goes on to note their appeal not to be sent into the abyss in v.31, implied as well in Tertullian's reference to "their request" (Tertullian, *Marc.* 4.20.7).

8.32 Tertullian, *Marc.* 4.20.7. The presence of this verse is implied when Tertullian says the daemons obtained their request. There is no hint in this remark that it turned out badly for them.

Luke 8.33–40 is unattested; but Tsutsui assumes the whole episode of daemon-possession was present through v. 39.

Luke 8.41–42a is unattested. Since neither Tertullian nor Epiphanius mention the healing of Jairus' daughter (Luke 8.40–42a, 49–56), an episode well-suited to their critique, it is likely that it was not found in the Evangelion (Epiphanius, *Elenchos* 2 and 37 on Ephesians, mentions the episode, but this probably is not taken from the Evangelion). Harnack, Knox, and Tsutsui are all noncommital.

8.42b–44 Epiphanius, *Scholion* 14; Tertullian, *Marc.* 4.20.8, 10, 12–13. The Evangelion read, "and it happened that, as . . ." in agreement with a substantial number of manuscripts and versions of Luke, including D and the OL. Epiphanius gives the reading "as *they* went," without saying that it constituted a difference from the text of Luke, which it does ("as he went"). The final part of v. 43, elaborating the failure of the woman to have found a cure, is not explicitly attested for the Evangelion. Epiphanius says merely that she touched "him"; Tertullian adds the detail that what she touched was his cloak (*Marc.* 4.20.13), agreeing with Gk ms D, OL mss a, d, ff2, l, r1, and Mark against "the fringe of his cloak" found in other manuscripts of Luke and in Matthew. The latter is considered to be one of the "minor agreements" between Matthew and Luke against Mark; it is significant that it was not present in the Evangelion.

8.45–46 Epiphanius, *Scholion* 14; Tertullian, *Marc.* 4.20.8. The Evangelion seems to agree in the form of the question (both times it is repeated in v. 45) with Mark 5.30, Gk ms D, OL mss a, c, q, Origen (and more, including the SSyr and CSyr, in the second occurrence), against the majority of witnesses to Luke ("who is the one who touched me?"); but it apparently lacked Mark's "the garment" (See Williams, "Reconsidering Marcion's Gospel," 483). It read "the pupils," agreeing with Mark 5.30 against Luke's "Peter." "For I perceived that power went out of me": this form of Jesus' statement is given by all three witnesses to the Evangelion. Harnack cites Adam 5.6, but the Evangelion is not being quoted there.

8.47–48 Tertullian, *Marc.* 4.20.9. Although v. 47 is not directly attested, some sort of action bringing the woman to Jesus is required to set up his remark in v. 48. Tertullian quotes the latter remark of Jesus without mentioning the second clause ("go in peace"; cf. 7.50), which is found in Luke and Mark 5.34.

Luke 8.49–56 is unattested; see comment to 8.41–42a above.

9.1–3 Tertullian, *Marc.* 4.21.1; Adam* 1.10, 2.12. The Evangelion apparently lacked an object ("the sick") for the verb "cure" in v. 2, in agreement with Gk ms B and the SSyr and CSyr against most other witnesses to Luke. For v. 3, Tertullian alludes broadly to a ban on taking food or clothing on the mission (corresponding to two of the five prohibitions known from Luke). Adam* 1.10 could be a reference to either this passage or 10.4 (or, for that matter, Matt 10.9), and mentions bans on shoes, a knapsack, two tunics, or "gold in one's belt"; the latter is known only from Mark 6.8, while the first is attested for this passage only in the OL manuscripts.

Luke 9.4 is unattested.

9.5–6 Tertullian, *Marc.* 4.21.1; Adam* 2.12. Based on Tertullian, the Evangelion lacked "as testimony *against them*" in v. 5. The mention of cities in v. 6 is found also in Gk ms D, as well as OL and SSyr and CSyr.

9.7–8 Tertullian, *Marc.* 4.21.2. Although a more logical narrative would have 9.1–6 lead into v. 10ff., and 9.7–8 lead into v. 18ff., the order of Tertullian's discussion indicates that the Evangelion followed the same interlacing of the two topics as is found in Luke.

Luke 9.9 is unattested; but Tsutsui ("Das Evangelium Marcions," 90) assumes it to have been present.

9.10–11 is unattested; but something equivalent to vv. 10–11 must have been present to set the scene (the twelve, the crowds) for the events that follow. The setting in "a deserted place" (Tertullian refers to *in solitudine*) matches that of Gk ms א and a few others, and the CSyr, as well as Mark 6.30–34 and Matt 14.13–14, and seems better matched to the story. P75, D, and many other Greek manuscripts, however, place the story in the city of Bethsaida; other manuscripts combine the two readings in various ways.

9.12–14a Epiphanius, *Scholion* 15; Tertullian, *Marc.* 4.21.3–4.

Luke 9.14b–15 is unattested.

9.16–17 Epiphanius, *Scholion* 15; Tertullian, *Marc.* 4.21.3–4; Adam 2.20. "Said a blessing on them" rather than "blessed them" appears in v. 16 according to Epiphanius, with Gk ms D, the OL and SSyr and CSyr; but Adamantius has "gave thanks" (*eucharistei*). The amount of surplus is not specified in our sources.

9.18–22 Epiphanius, *Scholion* 16; Tertullian, *Marc.* 4.21.6–7; 4.22.6; cf. 4.34.16; Adam 2.13 (vv.18–20); Ps.-Eph A 6 (Harnack cites Adam 5.12, but it cannot be shown that the Evangelion is used there). Jesus' identification of himself with the Human Being in v. 18 (Adamantius) is found in the Matthean parallel, but not in Luke. The Evangelion possibly read "the pupils said" in v. 19 (Adamantius), rather than "and in reply they said," as does the SSyr and CSyr. In v. 20 the Evangelion apparently read "But whom are you saying I am," omitting "that" before "I am" (a reading found in only one other Greek manuscript); likewise, it had "You are the Christos" without the additional qualification "of God" (Tertullian, *Marc.* 4.21.6; 4.22.6; 4.34.16; Adamantius), as do also the SSyr and CSyr and OL ms a, in line with the text of Mark 8.29, and so lacking another of the "minor agreements" with Matthew found in most witnesses to Luke. I have given the order of the groups listed in v. 22 in accord with Tertullian (so also the CSyr): elders, scribes, priests (not "chief-priests" as in Luke); Pseudo-Ephrem A lists elders and scribes, without mentioning priests. Epiphanius omits the whole clause ("and be rejected by the elders and scribes and head priests"), probably simply abbreviating. Apparently, the Evangelion read "and will be staked" instead of "and will be killed" (Tertullian; Adam 5.12 has the same reading, suggesting it was found in his manuscript of Luke). It had "after three days" in agreement with Gk ms D, OL, and Mark 8.31, against "on the third day" found in most manuscripts of Luke and Matt 16.21—the latter being one of the "minor agreements" of Luke and Matthew against Mark, missing from the Evangelion. It seems to have had "awaken" (*anastēnai*) with Mark and many manuscripts of Luke (Tertullian, *Marc.* 4.21.7; here again, Adam 5.12 shows this reading for Luke) against "be awoken" (*egerthēnai*) in Matthew and other manuscripts of Luke (but Epiphanius has the latter). Gundry considers "on the third day" and "be raised" to be examples of "subsidiary influence of Matthew on Luke" ("Matthean Foreign Bodies").

Luke 9.23 is unattested. Tsutsui ("Das Evangelium Marcions," 92) argues that this verse was lacking since (1) it is unattested, and (2) the "for" (*gar*) was definitely missing from the beginning of v. 24, suggesting that it was not a continuation of a previous statement. Harnack (*Marcion*, E37) is uncertain.

9.24 Tertullian, *Marc.* 4.21.8–9; Irenaeus, *Haer.* 3.18.4. The "for" (*gar*) at the beginning of this verse in Luke was apparently absent from the Evangelion. Based on Irenaeus, it possibly read "and whoever ruins *it* for my sake" with OL ms e, and "will preserve it," omitting the explicit subject "this one," in agreement with the SSyr and CSyr and OL.

Luke 9.25 is unattested; Tsutsui thinks it was absent, while Harnack is uncertain (*Marcion*, E37).

9.26 Tertullian, *Marc.* 4.21.10. As in v. 24, so also here the "for" (*gar*) found in Luke was apparently absent. The Evangelion shows considerable deviation from Luke and its source in Mark 8.38: "ashamed of me" instead of "ashamed of me and my words"; but Ambrose reads the same, while Gk ms D, OL mss a, d, e, l, CSyr, and Origen read "of me and mine." The Evangelion had "I also will be ashamed" instead of "the Human Being will be ashamed" in Luke and Mark. The final clause of this verse in Luke ("when he arrives in his glory and that of the Father and of the holy angels"), also from Mark, is not attested for the Evangelion.

Luke 9.27 is unattested; Harnack and Tsutsui consider it to have been absent.

9.28–31 Epiphanius, *Scholion* 17; Tertullian, *Marc.* 4.22.1–16; Ephrem, *Marc. I* (Mitchell) 87–88, 91. The Evangelion possibly had the three pupils in v. 28 in the order Peter, Jacob, John, as do P[45], D, and many other Greek manuscripts, the SSyr and CSyr, and several manuscripts of the OL (cf. 9.54). "In *his* splendor" would seem to be required in v. 31 not only by Tertullian's paraphrase, "in the splendor of the first (mentioned)" (Tsutsui, "Das Evangelium Marcions," 93), but by his consistent reference to "his splendor" nearly a dozen times in his discussion (similarly Epiphanius, "he brought both Elias and Moses with him in his own splendor"; implied as well in Ephrem); cf. "his splendor" in v. 32. A few Greek manuscripts have *en tē doxē*, which contextually indeed means "in his splendor," and a number of other Greek manuscripts, along with the Ethiopic version, read "speaking about his *splendor (doxan)*" rather than "about his departure *(exodon)*." On the basis of a remark of Tertullian ("For even if Marcion has refused to have him shown conversing with the Lord, but only standing there," *Marc.* 4.22.16), Harnack argues for "standing with," rather than Luke's "conversing with" in v. 30 as a tendentious emendation by Marcion to avoid the appearance that Jesus consulted with Jewish prophets (*Marcion*, 202*–203*). But Epiphanius, *Scholion* 17, reads "speaking with" *(sunelaloun)* and in fact Tertullian, *Marc.* 4.22.1–3, 16 refers to *cum illis loqui* (as noted by Tsutsui, "Das Evangelium Marcions," 93f.). In his previous remark, Tertullian's eye seems to have momentarily slipped to v. 32, where the pupils awake to see Moses and Elias *standing* with Jesus. Harnack likewise thinks the second half of Luke v. 31 ("discussing his departure which was about to be completed in Jerusalem"), for which there is nothing comparable in Mark or Matthew's account of this episode, was likely to have been stricken out by Marcion due to its emphasis on the role of Elias and Moses as prophets, discussing with Jesus his fulfilment of prophecy in Jerusalem (Harnack, *Marcion*, 203*; cf. E37); and Knox and Tsutsui concur that it was missing. But Drijvers, "Christ as Warrior and Merchant," has argued that part of the Marcionite christology depends upon the continuation of v. 31. Analyzing Ephrem Syrus' critique of Marcionite use of the transfiguration story, Drijvers concludes, "The implication of this polemic is that Marcion undoubtedly included Luk. 9,30–31 in his Gospel text" (76). Moreover, Ephrem indicates that, according to Marcionite interpretation, "the confrontation between Moses, Elijah, and Jesus certainly ended with a pact," since Ephrem refers to "the perverse tale of Marcion" dealing with "this pact that Moses, etc., agreed on with the Stranger on the mountain" involving the purchase of human souls at the price of Jesus, and so enthralled by his glory, "they made a bargain with him, because they loved him" (78, citing *Prose Refutations* [Mitchell, ed.] II, xli–xlii). This interpretation, along with the alternative one also mentioned by Ephrem of some sort of "battle" or "struggle" between Jesus and Moses and Elias, are both based on some sort of discussion, bargaining, or debate that presupposes text equivalent to Luke v. 31. However, whether it depended specifically on the details of v. 31b remains an open question, since already in v. 30 Moses and Elias are said to be speaking with Jesus.

9:32–35 Epiphanius, *Scholion* 18; Tertullian, *Marc.* 4.22.1–16; cf. 4.34.15; Ephrem, *Marc. I* (Mitchell) 93–94. Luke has an additional clause at the end of v. 34 for which there is no parallel in other gospels and which is unattested for the Evangelion: "As they entered into the cloud, they became fearful." But this may have formed part of the Evangelion's text on which the idea of a cosmic battle was built in Marcionite interpretation (see the previous note). Nevertheless, our sources give the impression that in the Evangelion v. 35 appears to have followed directly on the first clause of v. 34: "a cloud formed and overshadowed them, and a voice from the cloud" leading directly into the quote of the voice. The wording "beloved child" is attested by Epiphanius and Ephrem for v. 35, agreeing with the parallel passages in Mark 9.7 and Matt 17.5 as well as with many witnesses to Luke against the variant, "my son, the one who has been chosen," preferred by modern text critics for Luke. Williams, "Reconsidering Marcion's Gospel," 486 and 481 n. 13, suggests that the latter was in fact read in Marcion's text by Tertullian, based on the reading *delictus* in the 1954 edition of *Adversus Marcionem* (4.22.10). But the 1960 edition reads *dilectus*, which is also the reading in Tertullian, *Prax.* 19, and the uncertainty between these two readings is understandable in the manuscript tradition. So Epiphanius is to be preferred as a more certain witness here.

Luke 9.36 is unattested; Harnack is uncertain about its presence (*Marcion*, E37), but Tsutsui assumes it to have been included ("Das Evangelium Marcions," 93).

9:37–41 Epiphanius, *Scholion* 19; Tertullian, *Marc.* 4.23.1–2. Only vv. 40–41 are quoted verbatim, and the description of the boy's affliction is not detailed in our sources. But the manuscript tradition of Luke shows considerable contamination from the parallel account of Mk 9.14ff., showing how a source used in writing the gospel can secondarily supply harmonized readings in the gospel's transmission. Epiphanius apparently regarded the whole of v. 41 as a Marcionite addition; but no other known witness to Luke lacks it. The Evangelion read "In response Jesus said *to them*" in v. 41—so explicitly in Epiphanius, and suggested as well by Tertullian's *personam discipulorum, in quos insiliit* (*Marc.* 4.23.2) and *nec ille eos insilisset* (4.23.4); only the Georgian version shares this textual variant, derived from the wording of Mark 9.19. Our sources seem unanimous that the additional phrase "mistrustful *and twisted*" found in v. 41 of Luke and Matt 17.17, was absent from the Evangelion, as it is from OL mss a and e, and from the parallel in Mark 9.19; thus another of the "minor agreements" between Matthew and Luke against Mark evaporates. Tertullian attests the separate articulation of two questions ("How long will I continue with you? How long will I put up with you?"), agreeing with Mark 9.19// Matt 17.17, and found also in many manuscripts of Luke, while other manuscripts compress the two questions into a single compound question; Epiphanius skips the first question and only attests "How long will I put up with you?"

Luke 9.42–43 is unattested.

9.44 Epiphanius, *Scholion* 20. Tertullian perhaps skips this passage as not useful to his argument.

Luke 9.45–46 is unattested. If something like v. 46 is needed to set up Jesus' action and statement in vv. 47–48 (Harnack and Tsutsui think so), it might be suggested that the debate among the disciples in v. 46 followed immediately upon Jesus' prediction of his fate in v. 44, as a depiction of an argument over succession. But other possible contexts would give a different meaning to vv. 47–48.

9.47–48 Tertullian, *Marc.* 4.23.4. Tertullian only alludes to the passage, and seems to draw most of his observation not from the Evangelion itself, but from Marcion's *Antitheses*, where Jesus' love for children in this episode was contrasted to Elissai's curse of the children who taunted him, resulting in their deaths. Adamantius (1.17) possibly alludes to v. 47 when it is stated "Christ knew even men's thoughts" (cf. 6.8; 11.17).

Luke 9:49–51 is unattested; cf. POxy 1224.

9.52–55 Tertullian, *Marc.* 4.23.8, 4.29.12. In v. 53 Luke has an additional clause, unattested for the Evangelion: "because his face was set for going to Jerusalem." Tertullian's testimony clearly indicates that the Evangelion contained references to "Elia" and "spirit," and this makes it certain that it contained the alternate text of vv. 54–55 widely attested in the majority of manuscripts and versions, but considered secondary by modern textual criticism of Luke (which prefers: "'and destroy them?' But he turned and rebuked them, and they traveled to another village"). Harnack proposes that the majority text derives from Marcion's Evangelion. Delobel, "Extra-Canonical Sayings of Jesus," 113, follows Blass, *Philology of the Gospels*, 94, in speculating that the shorter text (as preferred by modern text critics for Luke) is actually an orthodox emendation of the original reading (as found in the Evangelion and in the majority of witnesses to Luke) to avoid too sharp of a contrast with the OT.

Luke 9.56 is unattested (≠Harnack and Tsutsui). Delobel, "Extra-Canonical Sayings of Jesus," 112–16, has rightly cautioned that our evidence for the presence in the Evangelion of the alternate text of vv. 54–55 does not extend to the extra material for v. 56 seen in this same alternate tradition of Luke ("For the Human Being came not to destroy people's lives, but to rescue them"). Gk ms D, for instance, follows the alternate text in vv. 54–55, but does not have the continuation in v. 56.

9.57–62 Tertullian, *Marc.* 4.23.9–11; Clement, *Strom.* 3.4.25.1–3. Jesus' answer in v. 58 ("Foxes have dens . . .") is not reported by Tertullian, but given the pattern of the whole passage, it almost certainly was present in the Evangelion (probably reading, as elsewhere, "birds" instead of "birds of the sky" (although Clement, *Strom.* 1.3.23.2, quotes this passage, presumably from Luke, without the entire "birds" clause). Clement of Alexandria says the Marcionites cite the episode in vv. 59–60, which he gives in reverse order, with Jesus' request to follow him following rather than preceding the advice to leave the dead to bury the dead. But Tertullian seems rather to confirm the same order as found in Luke, and Clement may have paraphrased. Clement identifies Jesus' interlocutor in this exchange as Philip, but it is unclear if this identification was made in the Evangelion or is part of the legendary material that Clement sometimes draws on to fill out gospel episodes and characters. Tertullian neglects to complete the thought of Jesus' statement in v. 62, which in Luke reads "is suitable for the realm of God." The Lukan manuscript tradition shows a secondary introduction of "master" into the address to Jesus made by each of the three interlocutors in this passage. It is inconsistently found in manuscripts for two of the three cases, and Irenaeus, *Haer.* 1.8.3, our earliest witness to this passage, lacks it in the third case as well.

10.1 Tertullian, *Marc.* 4.24.1; Adam* 1.5; 2.12; Ephrem, *Marc. I* (Mitchell) 89. The Evangelion, with Gk ms D, reads *apedeixen*, rather than the majority reading *anedeixen* (synonymous terms for designating or appointing). It apparently omitted "the master" as the subject of the verb, along with a few Greek manuscripts (including D), OL, SSyr, and CSyr; the Diatessaron and some other witnesses have "Jesus" here. The Evangelion apparently read "designated *also*" in reference to the prior appointment of the Twelve, in agreement with the majority of manuscripts and many versions and patristic witnesses to Luke. Tertullian refers to "seventy" while Adamantius and Ephrem refer to "seventy-two"; the same variation is found in the manuscript tradition of Luke. Among supporters of "seventy-two" are P^{75}, D and several other Greek manuscripts, the Diatessaron, and the older versions (including the Syriac, Coptic, and Armenian). The correspondence in this case between variants in the reports of the Evangelion with variants in the manuscript tradition of Luke supports the hypothesis that other variants in our sources on the Evangelion are to be explained by similar processes of textual transmission. Because such variants exist in both the Marcionite transmission of the Evangelion and the non-Marcionite transmission of Luke, they are most likely to have originated before the separation of the Evangelion and Luke as distinct texts transmitted within separate communities. Tsutsui ("Das Evangelium Marcions," 95) argues on the basis of Tertullian's wording (*adlegit et alios septuaginta apostolos*) that the text read "seventy other *apostles*"; but the possibility that Tertullian is paraphrasing based on the presence in the text of the verb "sent out" must be considered.

10.2–3 Ps.-Eph A 52 (≠Harnack, Tsutsui). Luke 10.2b ("The harvest, indeed, is abundant, but the workers are few") is unattested (cf. Matt 9.37–38, Thomas 73).

10.4–5 Tertullian, *Marc.* 4.24.1–4; Adam* 1.10. Our sources show some conflation of this passage with the parallel charge to the Twelve in 9.3. Tertullian mentions that those sent out are to carry no staff, a detail found in 9.3 in Luke, but attested for Luke 10.4 only in Didymus and Epiphanius. Adamantius, who could be alluding to either passage, has the prohibition of a satchel common to both passages, with the ban on two tunics known from 9.3, the order against shoes seen in Luke 10.4, as well as the forbidding of "gold in one's belts" seen only in Mark 6.8 (on the whole, this list most closely approximates Matt 10.9). The word "first" in "say *first*" was apparently lacking from the Evangelion in v. 5, as it is in Gk ms D and its corresponding Latin ms d, and a few other witnesses; cf. Matt 10.13.

Luke 10.6 is unattested.

10.7–11 Tertullian, *Marc.* 4.24.4–7, 12; Ps.-Eph A 76 (Codex B only). In v. 7, Pseudo-Ephrem A reads only "eating" and omits "and drinking," as does Gk ms W (Tertullian is silent on this clause). Whereas Tertullian reads "deserves pay," Pseudo-Ephrem A has "deserves food," the alternative form of this saying found in the CSyr and some manuscripts of the Bohairic Coptic version of Luke, as well as Matt 10.10. Luke has an additional clause in v. 7 ("Do not be transferring from house to house"), unattested for the Evangelion. In v. 9, the Evangelion apparently read "the realm of God has approached," rather than "approached *you*," in agreement with a half-dozen Greek manuscripts (but Tertullian has the same shorter wording in his own text of Luke in *Res.* 33). Perhaps it read "we wipe off *as a testimony* against you" in v. 11 (*Marc.* 4.24.7 reads: *Sic et pulverem iubet excuti in illos in testificationem*), wording found in the mission charge in 9.5, and again apparently "approached" rather than "approached *you*," agreeing in this latter case with a wide sweep of Greek manuscripts as well as the SSyr and CSyr.

Luke 10.12–15 is unattested. Since the woes upon the cities of Galilee and Judea were well suited to Tertullian's and Epiphanius' critiques of Marcion's interpretation of the teachings of Jesus (cf. their use of the woes from 6.24ff.), and yet go unmentioned by them, they almost certainly were absent from the Evangelion (so Harnack and Tsutsui). For 10.12, cf. Matt 10.15, 11.24; for 10.13–15 cf. Matt 11.21–23.

10.16 Tertullian, *Marc.* 4.24.8.

Luke 10.17–18 is unattested. Tsutsui, "Das Evangelium Marcions," 96, however, conjectures that 10.17 was present. 10.18 was certainly present in Tertullian's own text of Luke (*De spectaculis* 16; *Marc.* 2.10.3; *De anima* 17), and this saying of Jesus appears to have been known to Papias (in Andrew of Caesarea [Armenian text]; Fragment 24 in Lightfoot et al., *Apostolic Fathers*, 326–7), who was a contemporary of Marcion. It is possible that in the Evangelion the subsequent remarks in 10.19 follow directly on 10.16, and form part of the initial instruction to the seventy.

10.19 Tertullian, *Marc.* 4.24.9–12.

Luke 10.20 is not directly attested for the Evangelion in the sequential part of Tertullian's survey (Tsutsui, "Das Evangelium Marcions," 96).

Tertullian does quote its content, however, in *Marc.* 4.7.13–14 ("for it was he who would have his disciples rejoice not because the spirits were subject to them but because of their election to salvation"). But he may be recollecting the wording of Luke here.

10.21–22 Epiphanius, *Scholion* 22; Tertullian, *Marc.* 4.25.1, 7, 10, 12 (cf. 4.26.6; 2.27.4); Adam* 1.23; Ephrem, *Marc. I* (Mitchell) 72; Origen, *Cels.* 7.18; Irenaeus, *Haer.* 4.6.1. The first part of Luke 10.21 is unattested. Tertullian (*Marc.* 4.25.1) and Epiphanius both attest "I thank you" (similarly in Gospel of the Nazarenes 9; Eusebius, *De ecclesiastica theologia*) in v. 21—alone in Epiphanius, but in addition to "I praise you" in Tertullian (when citing this passage from Luke in *Prax.* 26, Tertullian does not include "I thank you"), perhaps reflecting a conflation of the two alternative readings. In a passage in the Clementine *Homilies* where the Marcionite tradition may be engaged, the wording is "I praise you" (17.5; 18.15). Both Tertullian and Epiphanius read "Lord of the sky" in place of "Father, Lord of the celestial sphere and the earth" (when citing this passage from Luke in *Prax.* 26, Tertullian reads "Father," without "Lord of the celestial sphere"). The omission of "Father" among witnesses to Luke is attested only in Athanasius, but the omission of "and the earth" is found also in P[45], and Gk ms 27. Both "Father" and "and of earth" are found in the same context in Matt 11.25, and Luke could have been brought into conformity with it (so Williams, "Reconsidering Marcion's Gospel," 491; Klijn, "Matthew 11:25//Luke 10:21," 13–14). The possibly Marcionite passages in Ps.-Clement, *Hom.* 17.5 and 18.15, however, read "master of the celestial sphere and earth." In Luke, God is said to have hidden things from the wise and smart (Tertullian, *Prax.* 26: *quod absconderis haec a sapientibus*) in contrast to the Evangelion's use of a passive construct that eliminates God as the subject (Tertullian, *Marc.* 4.25.1: *quod ea quae erant abscondita sapientibus*); and in Ps.-Clement, *Hom.* 18.15, Peter corrects "Simon's" (i.e., Marcion's) quote on this very point. Many Greek manuscripts add a transition between the prayer in v. 21 and Jesus' statement that follows in v. 22; but the oldest manuscripts and versions lack it. The Evangelion reads "confided to me by *the* Father" in v. 22, rather than "my father," agreeing with Gk ms D, several OL manuscripts, the SSyr, Justin, Irenaeus, and Eusebius; for "my father" cf. Matt 11.27. The Evangelion has the alternative order father-son (rather than son-father) found in some Greek manuscripts of Luke (and Matthew), OL ms b, and some of the church fathers (e.g., Irenaeus, Eusebius; see Tsutsui, "Das Evangelium Marcions," 97). Whereas most witnesses to Luke give only one verb of knowing (*epiginōskei*) referring syntactically to both Father and Son, the Evangelion gives two verbal forms, differentiated from each other as well as from that in Luke: "No one has known (*egnō*, in agreement with Justin, the Diatessaron, Clement of Alexandria, Irenaeus, Origen, and Eusebius) who the Father is . . . nor recognizes (*ginōskei*) who the Son is." Tertullian gives the reading "to whom the Son discloses it" (agreeing with Justin, *1 Apol.* 63.3; Clement of Alexandria; Origen; Athanasius; and Irenaeus, *Haer.* 1.20.3); but

Irenaeus, *Haer.* 4.6.1, reports the wording "to whom the Son wishes to disclose it" for Marcion's text, which matches the preferred reading of both Luke and Matt 11.27. This would seem to be another example of different readings transmitted in copies of the Evangelion.

10.23–24 Tertullian, *Marc.* 4.25.12. The Evangelion's reading "prophets" in v. 24 differs from the preferred reading in Luke, "prophets *and kings*," but agrees with Gk ms D and many OL manuscripts, as well as Methodius (compare Matt 13.17, "prophets and righteous ones"). "Many" before "prophets" is also unattested for the Evangelion (and lacking in Gk ms 1241, but found in Matt 13.17). Most crucially, the Evangelion appears not to have said anything about prophets having "desired to see" (or desired to hear), but simply having not seen (and not heard). Tertullian certainly would have made much of language of (the OT) prophets desiring to see what Jesus reveals if it had been in Marcion's text (so Harnack; Tsutsui, "Das Evangelium Marcions," 97). Either Marcion tendentiously omitted such language to heighten discontinuity between the prophets and Jesus' message, or a redactor of Luke added it to emphasize continuity between them, copying from Matthew. The clause regarding "hearing" is not expressly attested for the Evangelion, and indeed even Luke's v. 23 sets up only a discussion of seeing, whereas Matt 13.16–17 contains a seeing/hearing parallelism throughout.

10.25 Epiphanius, *Scholion* 23; Tertullian, *Marc.* 4.25.14 (cf. 4.19.7); Origen, *Fr. Luc.* (Rauer) 166. The detail that the man was "testing" Jesus is not mentioned in Tertullian, *Marc.* 4.25.14, but is made a point of Tertullian's argument in 4.19.7, and so presumably with reference to the Evangelion. In most manuscripts and versions of Luke (as well as Mark 10.17; Matt 19.16; 22.36), the man addresses Jesus as "teacher"; but this is lacking in the Evangelion, as it is in Gk ms D. The man asks about inheriting life, rather than "eternal" life as found in Luke— Tertullian, *Marc.* 4.25.14, draws attention to this difference and concludes his analysis of the passage's meaning with the surprising rhetorical remark, "It is by now no matter if our people have added 'eternal'" (4.25.18). Given the citation of Lev 18.5 in v. 28 ("Do this, and you will live"), it could be argued that the Evangelion has the more original wording, with the addition of "eternal" in the manuscript tradition of Luke explained as a harmonization with the later parallel passage in Luke 18.18. Origen appears to assume the wording "eternal life" in his comment on the Marcionite use of this passage. Cf. Theophilus of Antioch, *To Autolycus* 2.36.

10.26–27 Epiphanius, *Scholion* 23; Tertullian, *Marc.* 4.25.14 (cf. 4.19.7; 5.8.10); Origen, *Fr. Luc.* (Rauer) 166. Tertullian appears to have had before him a text in which v. 26b and 27a is missing, and the citation of the greatest commandment is made by Jesus himself, rather than by the man in response to a question from Jesus, as it now stands in Luke v. 26b. See the discussion of this problem in Harnack, *Marcion*, 206–7* and Tsutsui, "Das Evangelium Marcions," 98. Tsutsui maintains that the allusion to "in lege" in Tertullian, *Marc.* 4.25.14, indicates that the full exchange was present, and so supports Harnack's suggestion that Tertullian paraphrased. Epiphanius expressly quotes v. 26 as Jesus' question, and implies that the citation of the Law that followed in v. 27 was made by the man. Origen likewise expressly states that it is the young man who speaks in v. 27 in Marcion's Evangelion. An additional complication in this testimony is that the two stories from Mark used by our author here and in 18.18ff. both have Jesus as the speaker of this material, rather than the man who asked the question. Our apparently conflicting witnesses therefore may attest two divergent texts from the Evangelion, one of which shows a version closer to the Markan sources, and the other a version developed more independently. Luke has an additional clause in v. 26 ("How do you read?") unattested for the Evangelion. The latter read "with (*ex*) your whole life," rather than "in (*en*) your whole life"—a widely attested stylistic variant in parallel with the previous "with (*ex*) your whole heart," with no substantial difference in meaning. Most manuscripts of Luke have an additional phrase after "with your whole strength" ("and with your whole mind") that appears to be a secondary harmonization to Matthew and Mark (who both have heart/life/mind instead of the LXX reading of Deut 6.5 heart/life/power); the additional phrase is lacking in Gk ms D, the OL, and several patristic witnesses to Luke. Origen appears to attest it for Marcion's text, but he may be reverting to the wording of Luke. Tertullian, *Marc.* 5.8.10, is the only attestation of the presence of the second commandment to love one's neighbor as oneself, if he is citing the Evangelion and not Luke there (this quotation also varies the order of the previous clause: heart, strength, life).

10.28 Epiphanius, *Scholion* 23; Tertullian, *Marc.* 4.25.14 (cf. 4.19.7); Origen, *Fr. Luc.* (Rauer) 166. Harnack and Tsutsui do not credit the evidence of Tertullian. All questions of detail aside, the presence of this passage in Marcion's gospel directly contradicts assumptions of redaction on his part. Epiphanius and Origen cite it as contradicting Marcion's teachings, and the Marcionite interpretation of it reported by Tertullian shows a community dealing with problematic texts by interpretation rather than excision.

Luke 10.29–37 The parable of the Good Samaritan is unattested for the Evangelion. It goes unmentioned by any of the witnesses to Marcion's text, most tellingly by Pseudo-Ephrem A, which gives orthodox interpretations of the parables found in Marcion's gospel. The story is first attested in Clement of Alexandria and P[45] in the early third century.

Luke 10.38–42 is unattested. Although not mentioned by any of our sources for the Evangelion, this episode may simply have offered no material for criticism of Marcion's system.

11.1 Tertullian, *Marc.* 4.26.1–5; Origen, *Fr. Luc.* (Rauer) 180.

11.2 Tertullian, *Marc.* 4.26.1–5; Origen, *Fr. Luc.* (Rauer) 180. The Evangelion is one of a handful of witnesses to what are generally regarded as original and better readings within this passage, while also showing some rare readings whose standing in the textual tradition is actively debated. The most likely reconstruction of the Evangelion's text of the prayer has a clear pattern: a pair of couplets with repeated verbs in the primary position (*elthetō* + *elthetō*; *aphes* + *aphes*) framing a middle clause with the verb following its object phrase (this pattern is missed by Delobel, "Extra-Canonical Sayings of Jesus," 296 and Amphoux, "Les premières editions de Luc," 110, both cited below). The Evangelion read simply "Father," lacking "our . . . who is in heaven," in agreement with P[75], several other key Greek manuscripts (including ms 700), the SSyr, and Origen; the longer text derives from Matt 6.9–10 (and is given in this form in the Diatessaron). Based on Tertullian's reference, the Evangelion lacked "Hallowed be thy name," and instead had a request concerning "your spirit" as the first petition, followed by the request for God's realm to come. This reading seems to be related, but not identical, to that found (in slightly varying forms) in the Gk mss 700 (eleventh century) and 162 (twelfth century), Gregory of Nyssa, *De oratione dominica*, 3.737f. (PG 44, col. 1157C) (fourth century), and Maximus the Confessor, *Expositio orationis dominicae* 1.350 (PG 110, col. 884B) (seventh century), all of which have a petition for the spirit *following* "Hallowed be thy name" and *instead of* a request for the God's realm to come. Delobel is correct to fault citing Marcion as a witness to this latter reading without further qualification ("The Lord's Prayer in the Textual Tradition," 296–98). Gregory comments: "Luke . . . when he desires the Kingdom to come, implores the help of the Holy Spirit. For so he says in his Gospel; instead of 'Thy Kingdom come' it reads 'May thy Holy Spirit come upon us and purify us.' . . . What Luke calls the Holy Spirit, Matthew calls the Kingdom" (Graef, *St. Gregory of Nyssa*, 52–53). The additional wording found in these witnesses, "and purify us," is not specifically attested for the Evangelion. Internal evidence that the earliest form of our gospel contained a petition for receiving the spirit in 11.2 is supported by the reference to such a request in 11.13, as pointed out by Wilson, *Marcion: A Study of a Second-Century Heretic*, 142. Moreover, Gk ms D adds to the traditional text an anomalous "upon us" ("Hallowed be thy name upon us") which is best explained as a fragment of the original "May your sacred spirit come upon us" (see Parker, *The Living Text of the Gospels*, 66–68). S. Carruth and A. Garsky list eighteen modern researchers who have published favorably on the petition for the spirit as original ("The Database of the International Q Project"), among whom, see Schneider, "Die Bitte um das Kommen"; Freudenberger, "Zum Text der zweiten Vaterunaserbitte"; Magne, "La réception de la variante"; Leaney, "The Lucan Text of the Lord's Prayer." A completely novel text for the Evangelion here has been proposed by Amphoux, "La révision marcionite": "Hallowed be thy spirit." Amphoux argues that Tertullian's use of two distinct Latin verbs for the first and second petitions in his summary is unlikely to derive from a repeated use of *elthetō* in the Evangelion. But the immediately following clause in Tertullian ("of whom not even a mundane spirit is offered") only makes sense if the preceding clause is read contrary to Amphoux;

and Tertullian does in fact use distinct Latin verbs for the final two petitions (*dimittet, sinet*), which in the original Greek employ the same verb (*aphes*). The Evangelion also has the shorter, more original text at the end of v. 2, lacking "may your will be done on the earth as in the sky"; this shorter text, which can easily be rationalized as a Marcionite edit, is in fact found also in P^{75}, many other Greek manuscripts, the SSyr and CSyr, and Origen, demonstrating the danger of assuming an ideological intent behind readings of the Evangelion. The longer text is a secondary harmonization to Matthew in the manuscript tradition of Luke.

11.3 Tertullian, *Marc.* 4.26.1–5; Origen, *Fr. Luc.* (Rauer) 180. The Evangelion read "your . . . bread" rather than "our bread" according to Origen; the SSyr and CSyr have simply "the bread," which may be the reading Tertullian had before him.

11.4 Tertullian, *Marc.* 4.26.1–5; Origen, *Fr. Luc.* (Rauer) 180. The justifying clause, "for we ourselves also forgive everyone that is in debt to us," is unattested for the Evangelion. It also had the probably more original shorter text omitting "but deliver us from evil" found in many manuscripts of Luke borrowed from Matthew; likewise P^{75}, Sinaiticus, 700, and other Greek manuscripts, SyriacS, the Coptic and Armenian versions, and Origen. Harnack reconstructed the wording "Do not permit us to be brought," which would be a pious emendation from the more original "do not bring us" attested as early as PolPhil 7.2. But Schmid, "How Can We Access Second Century Gospel Texts?" 143–44, argues against this reconstruction, maintaining that Tertullian's rephrasing of the text into a rhetorical question masks the original wording, and brings it into line with his own pious exegesis of this phrase of Luke elsewhere in his writings. While Schmid's observations are perfectly valid, it cannot be ruled out that both Tertullian and the redactor of the Evangelion embraced a widespread avoidance of directly attributing testing to God (all the more so if Marcion was that redactor, but I do not assume that). The clear parallelism of structure with the repeated use of *aphes* matching the prior repetition of *elthetō*, inclines me to follow Harnack's reconstruction.

11.5–8 Epiphanius, *Scholion* 24; Tertullian, *Marc.* 4.26.6–9. Epiphanius only directly quotes v. 5, reading "and will go to him at midnight *requesting* three loaves" instead of "and will go to him at midnight and say to him, 'Friend, loan me three loaves.'" The explanation for the request given in v. 6 is not attested for the Evangelion. Tertullian, *Marc.* 4.26.6 refers to knocking again at the door from which one has been driven away, apparently alluding to v. 7; likewise his reference to *instantiae* (persistence) in knocking seems to allude to v. 8 (Tertullian may have had the combination *laboris et instantiae* in the text before him, since he repeats this phrasing three times). More details from v. 7–8 follow in *Marc.* 4.26.7–9. The Evangelion apparently read "the children," rather than "my children," with some Greek manuscripts (including ms 700), the majority of OL manuscripts, and the SSyr and CSyr.

11.9 Epiphanius, *Scholion* 24; Tertullian, *Marc.* 4.26.5–7. Epiphanius quotes only the first clause of v. 9, "Ask and it will be given" and goes directly on to v. 11, no doubt abbreviating.

Luke 11.10 is unattested.

11.11–13 Epiphanius, *Scholion* 24, *Elenchos* 24; Tertullian, *Marc.* 4.26.9–10; Adam 2.20. It is uncertain that, when Adamantius says here that he will quote from "the Gospel," he means the Marcionite Evangelion. Most witnesses of Luke harmonize this passage with Matthew, and add a "bread and stone" clause. The testimony of Epiphanius and Tertullian clearly aligns the Evangelion with P^{45}, P^{75}, B, and other Greek manuscripts, some OL manuscripts, the SSyr, SCopt, and Armenian versions of Luke, and Origen in having what is considered by modern textual criticism the original shorter text without such a clause. But Adam 2.20 has the harmonized text, perhaps evidence that the Evangelion circulated with variant texts. Adamantius has "is there any among you," omitting "father" (as do one Greek manuscript, one OL manuscript, and the SSyr and CSyr); but Epiphanius includes "father." For v. 13 Epiphanius, *Scholion* 24, ends his quote with "how much more the Father"; but in *Elenchos* 24 he completes the quote with a unique reading "how much more your supercelestial Father" (*ho patēr humōn epouranois*). Among all the variants here, the original reading of Luke is likely to be *ho patēr ex ouranou dōsei*, with *ex ouranou* to be read with the verb rather than with the subject: "give from the celestial sphere." Epiphanius does not mention spirit as what the Father gives, and could be read in line with Gk ms D, the OL, SSyr, and Armenian versions of Luke, which have instead "goods" or "good gifts," harmonized to Matt 7.11; but Tertullian expressly refers to the Father giving sacred spirit, showing the Evangelion in agreement with what is considered the original text of Luke.

11.14—22 Tertullian, *Marc.* 4.26.10–12; 4.28.2; 5.6.7. Gk ms D and the OL render v. 14 very freely, and Tertullian is too loose to allow us to know whether or not this free rendering resembles that found in the Evangelion. The reading "Beelzebub" found in Tertullian is shared by the SSyr and CSyr and some witnesses to the Diatessaron and the OL. The expression "ruler of the daemons" is not specifically mentioned by Tertullian. All of v. 16 and the first part of v. 17 is unattested for the Evangelion ("But others, testing, were seeking a sign from the sky by him. Knowing their thoughts . . ."). Tsutsui, "Das Evangelium Marcions," 100, assumes this material to have been included. In Adam 1.16 a Marcionite spokesperson refers to Jesus knowing people's thoughts (cf. 6.8; 9.47). Other than that Jesus began to respond, the rest of v. 17 ("a realm divided against itself . . .") also cannot be confirmed from Tertullian's testimony (cf. Matt 12.25). The Evangelion probably also lacked the second half of v. 18, which is also lacking in Gk ms 2643. The last clause of v. 19 ("because of this they will judge you") also is uncertain for the Evangelion, and may be a harmonization of Luke to Matt 12.27. For the Marcionite interpretation of 11.21–22, see Tertullian, *Marc.* 4.26.12; 5.6.7; Harnack, *Marcion*, 120, 129, 208*–9*, 275*, 301*; Jackson, "The Setting and Sectarian Provenance," 284–86.

Luke 11.23–26 is unattested.

11.27–28 Tertullian, *Marc.* 4.26.13. The Evangelion apparently read "and do it" (*faciunt*) rather than "and keep/guard it," as also found in some Greek, OL, and Armenian manuscripts of Luke (cf. the same verb used in parallel sayings in 6.47 and 8.21).

11.29a Epiphanius, *Scholion* 25; Tertullian, *Marc.* 4.27.1. The Evangelion may have read simply "No omen will be given to this generation," rather than "This generation is an unwell generation; it seeks an omen, and no omen will be given to it." A handful of manuscripts omit one part or another of the longer text. On the other hand, both of our witnesses may give abbreviated paraphrases.

Omission: Luke 11.29b–32 Epiphanius says "The saying about Jonah the prophet has been deleted; Marcion had 'This generation, no sign shall be given it.' But he did not have the passages about Nineveh, the queen of the south, and Solomon." Gk ms D (and its Latin counterpart d) lacks v. 32; otherwise, no manuscript evidence agrees with the shorter text of the Evangelion. 1 Clem 7.7 alludes to Jonah and the Ninevites but does not explicitly cite a particular gospel; no other early patristic source refers to this passage, including Tertullian. Its earliest witness in the text of Luke is P^{45} (early third century). While it may be tempting to assume that this material derives from Matt 12.39–42, it is more developed there than in Luke in explicitly connecting the experience of Jonah to Jesus' death and resurrection. Cf. Matt 16.4.

11.33 Tertullian, *Marc.* 4.27.1. "Nor under the measuring basket" is uncertain for the Evangelion; this phrase is found in Matt 5.15 and Mark 4.21, but for Luke is missing in P^{45}, P^{75}, many other Greek manuscripts (incl. ms 700), the SSyr, SCopt, and Armenian versions, and Origen (cf. Thomas 33b; Matt 5.14). Tertullian says that the lamp is put on the lampstand, "so that everything is illuminated" (*ut omnibus luceat*). This could represent a text conformed to Matt 5.15 (and found in Gk ms 579 of Luke), "and it illuminates everyone"; the standard text of Luke has "so that those entering may see the light."

Luke 11.34–36 is unattested. Gk ms D, the majority of OL manuscripts, and the CSyr lack v. 36; cf. Matt 6.22–23.

11:37–41 Tertullian, *Marc.* 4.27.2–3, 6. The Evangelion, several Greek manuscripts, the OL, and the CSyr share a reading of v. 38 involving the Pharisee questioning Jesus' conduct within himself, rather than the more common reading of Luke, in which the Pharisee is amazed. "Jesus" instead of "the master" appears in v. 39 — as consistently in the narration of the Evangelion — in agreement with several Greek manuscripts, the SSyr and CSyr, and a few other witnesses to Luke. Previous researchers, up to and including Tsutsui, "Das Evangelium Marcions," 101, have mistakenly cited Tertullian, *Marc.* 4.27.2 for the reading "but you do not cleanse your inward part," instead of "but your inside is full of plunder and pathology"; but this is an interpretive paraphrase by Tertullian, who a few lines before has alluded to the language of "plunder and pathology." Luke's "give as alms the inside things" in v. 41 is somewhat obscure, although possibly original; the Evangelion's reading is clearer, and agrees with the SSyr and CSyr. It apparently lacks "look" with some witnesses to Luke; and reads "will be pure" rather than "is pure," in agreement with P[45], D, and many other Greek manuscripts.

11:42–43 Epiphanius, *Scholion* 26; Tertullian, *Marc.* 4.27.4–6. Both Epiphanius and Tertullian agree that the Evangelion read *klēsin* ("call, invitation") instead of canonical Luke's *krisin* ("judgment"; cf. Matt 23.23); this reading is not attested in any other source. Tertullian, *Marc.* 4.27.3, appears to refer to a mention of "mercy" as well (cf. Matt 23.23): "Even if it is possible for that other god to have commanded mercy, yet he cannot have done it before he became known." But without a clearer indication of how it might have appeared in Marcion's text, it must remain an uncertain piece of evidence. The additional clause in Luke 11.42 — "These things you were under obligation to do, but those other things not to omit" — is unattested for the Evangelion, and was probably lacking, as in Gk ms D and its associated Latin ms d. The United Bible Societies (UBS) text committee considers its absence in D as due to Marcionite influence (Metzger, *Textual Commentary*, 159), but its presence in the majority of witnesses to Luke is just as likely to be a harmonization to Matthew.

Luke 11.44–45 is unattested; Tsutsui assumes v. 45 to have been present ("Das Evangelium Marcions," 101).

11.46–48 Epiphanius, *Scholion* 27; Tertullian, *Marc.* 4.27.1, 6–8. The Evangelion probably had v. 48 as a question, with Gk ms D and several OL manuscripts.

Omission: Luke 11.49–51 was absent from the Evangelion, according to Epiphanius, *Scholion* 28. The reference to the murder of Zechariah in the temple is derived from 2 Chr 24.20–21, and the allusion to punishment coming upon this generation parallels Matt 23.34–36.

11.52 Tertullian, *Marc.* 4.27.9. Tsutsui ("Das Evangelium Marcions," 102) considers Tertullian's use of *agnitio* in v. 52 to be unusual as a translation of Greek *gnosis*, and another underlying Greek word may be indicated, although no alternative is found in any of the witnesses to this verse in Luke. Cf. Thomas 39.

Luke 11.53–54 is unattested. The transition between this episode and the next shows a great deal of textual variation, representing at least two distinct redactions blended in various ways in the witnesses, trying to solve problems about the location and audience for Jesus' remarks.

12.1–5 Epiphanius, *Scholion* 29; Tertullian, *Marc.* 4.28.1–3. The setting of these remarks in the Evangelion is not reported. For the beginning of v. 4 ("Now I am telling you, my friends"), Tertullian, *Marc.* 4.28.3 attests the "you," but not "my" (*dico autem vobis amicis*; a handful of Greek manuscripts similarly omit "my"); Epiphanius attests "my," but not "you" (*legō de tois philas mou*). Textual variants, or loose citation? In either case, Harnack's assumption that both "you" and "my" were lacking is not supported by this evidence, and there is no reason to resort to the hypothesis that Marcion edited out the two words "to remove any identification of Jesus' disciples as the friends of Jesus"

(*Marcion*, E38). Epiphanius quotes a conflated text of the first part of v. 4 and the second part of v. 5—"Do not be afraid of them that kill the body. . . . Fear him who, after he has killed, has authority to throw (you) into Gehenna"—but Tertullian quotes the full wording of both verses. Tertullian's quote suggests the reading "kill you (pl.)," omitting "the body"; but Epiphanius attests "kill the body" in agreement with nearly all witnesses to Luke. The reading of the last clause of v. 4 as "have no further authority over you" instead of "are not able to do anything more," is from Tertullian, *Marc.* 4.28.3 (Epiphanius skips this clause), and shows parallelism to the wording of the following verse; but it is not found in any witness to Luke, and Tertullian may be paraphrasing. Ps.-Clement, *Hom.* 17.5, in a presumably Marcionite context, gives a reading corresponding to Matt 10.28.

Omission: Luke 12.6–7 was absent from the Evangelion. Epiphanius, *Scholion* 29, explicitly notes the omission of 12.6. Both Epiphanius and Tertullian pass over 12.7 in silence, despite its serviceability for their argument, and for this reason it, too, almost certainly was absent from the Evangelion. Volckmar, "Über das Lukas-Evangelium," 191–92, regards the two verses as secondary additions to Luke. Clement, *Paed.* 3.3.17's apparent quote of 12.7a would be the earliest witness to this passage, but could just as well come from Matt 10.30. The general content of these two verses is found in Matt 10.29–31.

12.8 Epiphanius, *Scholion* 30; Tertullian, *Marc.* 4.28.4. The Evangelion read "for" at beginning of this passage, in continuity with the end of v. 5; the SSyr version also has "for." Epiphanius gives *enōpion* ("before, in front of") in this verse, forming a parallelism with the wording of v. 9, while Luke uses the synonymous *emprosthen* (cf. Matt 10.32). According to Tertullian, the Evangelion has Jesus say "I will affirm" (in agreement with Matt 10.32, and found also in a few Greek manuscripts and other witnesses to Luke), instead of "the Human Being will affirm"; but Epiphanius' abbreviated quotation reads "he will affirm," suggesting the standard Lukan reading (see Williams, "Reconsidering Marcion's Gospel," 488). This is another example where the texts known respectively to Tertullian and Epiphanius differed on points of harmonization to another gospel. They agree that the Evangelion read "in front of God," rather than Luke's "in front of the angels of God"; the Evangelion here agrees with Gk ms ℵ (later corrected) and Matt 10.32. The assumption that the absence of "angels" in Marcion's text here and 15.10 is a tendentious omission is belied by the presence of "angels" in the most positive sense in 20.36 (their role in 16.22 is more ambiguous, and they could be construed as minions of the creator god there).

12.9 Tertullian, *Marc.* 4.28.4; Adam 2.5. Although Adamantius expressly quotes from the Apostolikon in this section, it is less certain that he draws his gospel quotations from the Evangelion. It is noteworthy that this verse is absent from the oldest manuscript of Luke, P[45], as well as the SSyr. It coincides in content with Matt 10.33, and may be a harmonization to the latter in the Evangelion as well as later witnesses to Luke. Adamantius, in fact, gives a reading identical to Matthew: "Whoever denies me before men, him will I also deny before my Father *who is in the celestial spheres*"; Tertullian, however, lacks "who is in the celestial spheres" in agreement with most manuscripts of Luke that have this verse. Cf. Shepherd of Hermas 6.8.

12.10 Tertullian, *Marc.* 4.28.6. In the first clause, the Evangelion read "speaks against" rather than "speaks a word against" found in Luke, with the latter closer to Matt 12.32. In the second clause, the Evangelion read "speaks against" rather than "blasphemes" found in most manuscripts of Luke (Gk ms D and OL mss d and e being exceptions), with the former closer to Matt 12.32. Thus the Evangelion and Luke trade places of greater harmonization to Matthew. See Shepherd of Hermas 6.8; Heracleon, Fragments (Voelker) 85–86.

12.11–12 Tertullian, *Marc.* 4.28.7. The majority manuscript tradition of Luke appears to conflate two distinct readings in v. 11: "how you will defend" and "what you will defend." The same conflation occurs in Matt 10.19, but there are key witnesses to Luke with just one or the other of these alternatives. Tertullian's allusion is too vague to determine how the Evangelion read here. In v. 12, the SSyr, some OL manuscripts, and Heracleon have "what must be said," which seems to be the Evangelion's reading (*quid*), whereas most witnesses to Luke have "the things (that) must be said."

12.13–14 Tertullian, *Marc.* 4.28.9–10. As usual, the Evangelion seems to have only one alternative phrase found paired with another in the majority of manuscripts of Luke. Here, in v. 14, it lacks "or apportioner/divider" following "judge," as do Gk mss D and 28, several OL manuscripts, and the SSyr and CSyr (Thomas 72, conversely, reads "divider" without "judge").

Luke 12.15 is unattested. It is notable that Thomas 72 and 63 cover the material in this section of canonical Luke with the exception of v. 15 and 21, and so may indirectly support the Evangelion's shorter text.

12.16–20 Tertullian, *Marc.* 4.28.11. Tertullian passes over many of the details of the parable. None of the person's reflections in vv. 17–18 are directly attested, but some of his planning must have been included based on the reference to his preparations in v. 20. Verse 19 may have lacked, following "many goods," the additional wording "laid up for many years; take your ease, eat, drink," which are also lacking from Gk ms D and the OL. This is one of Westcott and Hort's "Western non-interpolations." In v. 20, it seems to have read "demanding back your life" (with a variety of witnesses to Luke) instead of "demanding back your life *from you*" found in most witnesses to Luke.

Luke 12.21 is unattested; it is omitted from Gk ms D and several OL manuscripts, and is one of Westcott and Hort's "Western non-interpolations."

12.22–24 Tertullian, *Marc.* 4.29.1; cf. 4.21.1; Origen, *Cels.* 7.18. The Evangelion differs from its usual associates, Gk ms D and the OL, by reading "ravens" rather than the harmonization to Matthew, "the birds of the sky." But it appears to be harmonized in turn to Matthew (as are a couple of Greek manuscripts of Luke) in reading "neither do they gather into storehouses" rather than "they do not have storerooms or storehouses." The clear statement that "God feeds them" (attested by Tertullian's wording *et tamen aluntur ab ipso*) belies the notion that Marcion's text had been purged of content directly contradicting his theology. For Marcion's exegesis of v. 22, see Harnack, *Marcion*, 127 n. 2.

Luke 12.25–26 is unattested.

12.27–28 Tertullian, *Marc.* 4.29.1–3; cf. 4.21.1; Origen, *Cels.* 7.18. The Evangelion apparently lacked "how they grow" (found in Matt 6.28), as do Gk ms D, OL mss a and d, the SSyr and CSyr, and Clement; and Tertullian appears to give the reading "they neither spin nor weave" (*non texunt nec nent*), in agreement with the same set of witnesses, against "they neither toil nor spin" found in most other manuscripts of Luke (the latter being closer to Matt 6.28). But a few lines later he refers to "toil," perhaps from memory of the Matthean form of the saying or his text of Luke. Epiphanius, *Scholion* 31, expressly states that Marcion's text did not have "God clothes the grass" in v. 28, and this absence was accepted by Harnack; but Tertullian, *Marc.* 4.29.1, has a clear allusion to it (*foenum . . . vestiuntur ab ipso*, likewise 4.21.1), as noted by Tsutsui, "Das Evangelium Marcions," 104. This contradictory testimony cannot be harmonized (See Williams, "Reconsidering Marcion's Gospel," 480 n. 10), and suggests a complex transmission history for the Evangelion.

12.29–30 Epiphanius, *Scholion* 32; Tertullian, *Marc.* 4.29.3. In v. 30, Tertullian gives the reading "the peoples of the world," rather than "*all* the peoples of the world," in agreement with the OL. Epiphanius attests the reading "your Father" with Gk ms D, the OL, and Clement (found in Matt 6.32), whereas Tertullian has before him the reading "the Father" generally supported by witnesses to Luke. Williams, "Reconsidering Marcion's Gospel," 489, mistakenly includes in the testimony to the text of the Evangelion Epiphanius' gloss on the phrase "these things" ("meaning, of the flesh").

12.31–32 Tertullian, *Marc.* 4.29.5; 3.24.8; Epiphanius, *Scholion* 33, 34; Ps.-Eph A 52. Tertullian, *Marc.* 3.24.8, claiming to be quoting from the Evangelion, has "seek *first*" in v. 31, a reading found in several Greek manuscripts and apparently a harmonization to Matt 6.33 (see Williams, "Reconsidering Marcion's Gospel," 492). But at 4.29.5, he does not have "first," just as Epiphanius does not. The difference between these two quotations reflects the different exegetical applications Tertullian makes of the verse in the two contexts, showing the paraphrastic liberties he takes with the text. Epiphanius reads "*all* these things" in v. 31, in agreement with Gk ms ℵ's first corrector, as well as D and a number of other Greek manuscripts, OL Luke, and Matt 6.33; but Tertullian, *Marc.* 3.24.8 and 4.29.5 read simply "these things" in agreement with P^{45}, P^{75}, many other Greek manuscripts, the SSyr, and others. Epiphanius expressly states that the Evangelion read "the Father" instead of "your Father" in v. 32, a reading also found in a few Greek manuscripts and several patristic witnesses to Luke. Pseudo-Ephrem A quotes the words "Do not be afraid, little flock" from v. 32.

Luke 12.33–34 is unattested.

12.35–40 Epiphanius, *Scholion* 35; Tertullian, *Marc.* 4.29.6–7. On v. 35, cf. Did 16.1. Verse 36b of canonical Luke ("so that at his arriving and knocking they may at once open to him") is unattested, as is v. 37, and the Evangelion may have gone directly from 36a to 38. Several Greek and OL witnesses have v. 37 following v. 38, conflating the repeated clause "fortunate are those (slaves)." In v. 38, instead of "second or third watch," Epiphanius reports that the Evangelion had "evening watch," a reading also preserved in combination with the alternative in Irenaeus and a number of other Greek and OL witnesses to Luke. In v. 39, the Evangelion and a few other witnesses (P^{75}, ℵ, some OL manuscripts, the SSyr and CSyr, etc.) give what is regarded as the original, shorter text here; others add "would have kept awake and" from Matt 24.43. In v. 40, Tertullian gives the reading "will come" (*adveniet*), found also in the OL, SSyr, and CSyr, instead of "is coming."

12.41–48 Epiphanius, *Scholion* 36; Tertullian, *Marc.* 4.29.9–10; Adam 2.21. It is not certain that Adamantius uses the Evangelion here. Tertullian's paraphrase of the initial exchange in vv. 41–42 gives no hint of the word "master" (*kurios*) either in Peter's address to Jesus or in the narration introducing the latter's response, as is found in many witnesses to Luke. In fact, there is no evidence that the narration in the Evangelion ever referred to Jesus by the title "master." The omission of "master" from Peter's question in v. 41 is seen also in a number of Greek manuscripts; and "Jesus" is used instead of "the master" in the same set of Greek manuscripts plus the SSyr and CSyr. The reading "the good one" in v. 42 is preserved as a doublet alongside the standard reading of Luke ("the discerning one") in Irenaeus, Ephrem, a few Greek manuscripts (including D), several OL manuscripts, and the CSyr, and is conjecturally given here for the Evangelion ("discerning" is the wording of Matt 24.45). Adamantius seems to read "the bad slave" in v. 46, which would be a logical contrast, and a number of Greek manuscripts have "the bad slave" in v. 45 (a harmonization to Matt 24.48); but Epiphanius has the more usual reading "*that* slave" in v. 46. On the basis of remarks of Tertullian, Harnack speculates about possible Marcionite revision of v. 46 to soften the punishment indicated here; but Tertullian's remarks are about Marcionite interpretation, not the wording of the text, and the following verses—with even more lurid descriptions of punishment—were clearly retained in the Evangelion. In v. 47, Adamantius attests the shorter reading that omits in two places the phrase "the will of his master" (following "the slave who knew" and "did not act," respectively), found in several other patristic witnesses to Luke. Adamantius gives the reading "and did not act," found also in a few Greek manuscripts (including D), Origen, Irenaeus, and others; another line of transmission of this verse (in many Greek manuscripts, the OL, the SSyr and CSyr) has "and did not prepare," while the majority of witnesses have a conflated text: "and did not prepare nor act." In v. 48, none of our sources report the second half of the verse ("Indeed, everyone to whom much was given, much will be demanded of him; and the one whom people put in charge of much, they will demand more than usual of him"). Tsutsui ("Das Evangelium Marcions," 106) believes there is an allusion to this in Tertullian, *Marc.* 4.29.11 (*prout commiset illis ita et exigentem ab eis*), but the correspondence is insufficient, and in part achieved by taking the Latin clause out of its context.

12.49 Tertullian, *Marc.* 4.29.12; Ps.-Eph A 19 (=Harnack, Tsutsui v. 49a, who do not credit the evidence of Pseudo-Ephrem A). Tertullian gives only the first half of the verse, and Tsutsui ("Das Evangelium Marcions," 106) regards the second half as absent, as it is from OL ms e. But the second half of the verse is quoted in Ps.-Eph A 19 in the form given here, which is found in a variety of patristic witnesses to Luke and the Diatessaron; cf. Thomas 10.

12.50 Epiphanius, *Pan.* 42.3.10 (≠Harnack, Tsutsui). Epiphanius cites Marcion—apparently from the *Antitheses*—quoting two sayings of Jesus, one of which is related to the wording of Luke in this verse: *baptisma echō baptisthēnai, kai ti thelō ei ēdē teteleka auto*. This agrees with Luke in the first half of the saying, but diverges in the second half, showing closer parallelism to v. 49. Intriguingly, Epiphanius says Marcion made the point that Jesus said this to his disciples "after the Lord's baptism by John," presumably in order to prove that John's baptism was meaningless. This would mean, then, that Marcion knew about and did not deny that Jesus was baptized by John (as stated in Matthew and Mark, as well as Luke), even though this episode does not appear in the Evangelion. Therefore, his supposed ideological motive for removing the episode evaporates. Lacking any other obvious place where the second saying of Jesus quoted by Marcion might have been in the Evangelion, I have placed it here due to its close parallelism to vv. 49–50: *potērion echō piein, kai ti thelō ei ēdē plērōsō auto*; cf. Matt 20.22–23; Mark 10.38–39; John 18.11.

12.51 Tertullian, *Marc.* 4.29.13–14. The Evangelion read "cast/throw upon" (rather than "give to") in parallel with v. 49, and agreeing with the SSyr, a couple of Greek manuscripts, and a number of OL manuscripts of Luke, as well as Matt 10.34 and Thomas 16a. In agreement with nearly all manuscripts of Luke, Jesus has come to cast "division." Tertullian, *Marc.* 4.29.14, in one of his few remarks on textual issues, says "The book says 'a sword,' but Marcion corrects it"—in fact, it is Matt 10.34 which has "a sword," and Tertullian either is remembering the text of Luke incorrectly or else his text of Luke had been harmonized to Matthew here. This is a perfect example of where a critic alleges an ideological alteration of a passage by Marcion that in fact can be found in a line of textual transmission independent of Marcion, and the critic may actually have the minority reading. Adam 2.5 quotes two variants side by side ("I came not to bring peace but a sword" and "I came not to bring peace but fire") in a context where we would expect him to be quoting from the Evangelion, but other quotes in the same series appear to derive from Matthew.

Luke 12.52 is unattested.

12.53 Tertullian, *Marc.* 4.29.13–14.

Luke 12.54–55 is unattested.

12.56–57 Tertullian, *Marc.* 4.29.15. The Evangelion apparently read "Do you examine . . . ?" instead of Luke's "Do you know how to examine?" (the latter a possible harmonization to Matt 16.3). This difference might be taken as evidence that the Evangelion lacked v. 54–55, since its form of the question does not presuppose an affirmation of predictive ability on the part of Jesus' audience. The Evangelion read "the face of the celestial sphere and earth," as do a great many witnesses to Luke, including the oldest Greek manuscripts (including D), the OL, the SSyr and CSyr, Coptic, and Armenian versions of Luke, as well as Thomas 91; others have the reverse order "earth and sky." For the final question of v. 56, it seems to have had "do (you) not examine?" instead of *"how* do you not examine?" in agreement with Gk ms D, OL, the SSyr, and CSyr. The fact that Tertullian uses *probantes* for "examine" in the first clause, and *dinoscentes* in the second might suggest a different Greek verb than "examine" (*dokimazete*) in the latter, but this is not certain. In v. 57, the Evangelion probably read "Do you not judge?" also given by Gk ms D, a couple of OL manuscripts, and the CSyr; others read "Why do you not judge?" (as does Tertullian when quoting Luke in *De corona militis* 4).

12.58–59 Epiphanius, *Scholion* 37; Tertullian, *Marc.* 4.29.16. The Evangelion apparently read "last quarter" (*quadrante* > Gk *kodrantēn*, a Roman unit of coinage) with Irenaeus, Gk ms D, and OL, as an apparent harmonization to Matt 5.26, instead of the Greek *lepton* (a Greek coin of even smaller value).

Omission: Luke 13.1–9 was absent from the Evangelion, as reported by Epiphanius, *Scholion* 38; neither does Tertullian, Adamantius, nor Pseudo-Ephrem A allude to any of the material from this section. The report on the Galilaeans whom Pilate slaughtered (13.1–3) is derived from Josephus; the collapse of the tower of Siloam (13.4–5) is an otherwise unknown story. Both Hilgenfeld, *Kritische Untersuchungen*, 469–71, and Volckmar, "Über das Lukas-Evangelium," 187, consider these five verses to be secondary additions to Luke. The following passage (13.6–9), a moral lesson on patience, is likewise considered secondary by Volckmar. This material was present in the Diatessaron, however.

13.10–16 Epiphanius, *Scholion* 39; Tertullian, *Marc.* 4.30.1. Only vv. 10, 15–16 are explicitly quoted by our sources. Tertullian only provides the basic scenario of a sabbath healing to which an objection was raised, and the first part of Jesus' response. Epiphanius reports only the wording of v. 16a. Undoubtedly, the Evangelion had *Jesus* instead of "the Lord" in v. 15, as do many Greek manuscripts and the SSyr and CSyr. It also apparently read "on the sabbath*s*" rather than "on the sabbath" in v. 15, and in the same verse shared with Gk ms 69 the order "mule . . . bull" rather than the reverse.

Luke 13.17 is unattested.

13.18–19 Tertullian, *Marc.* 4.30.1; Adam 2.20; Ps.-Eph A 28. It is not certain that Adamantius is quoting the Evangelion here. Burkitt, "The Exordium of Marcion's Antitheses," suggested that the verb "compare" in vv. 18 and 20 is alluded to in the opening of Marcion's treatise. Tertullian reads "realm of God," while Pseudo-Ephrem A has "realm of the celestial sphere," harmonized to Matthew. Tertullian and Pseudo-Ephrem A agree that the Evangelion read "planted" (Gk *espeiren*) in agreement with Matt 13.31, instead of "threw" (Gk *ebalen*) in Luke.

13.20–21 Tertullian, *Marc.* 4.30.3; Adam 2.20; Ps.-Eph A 28. It is not certain that Adamantius is quoting the Evangelion here. Pseudo-Ephrem A supplies the whole analogy, with Codex B more likely to retain the original reading; cf. Thomas 96. Tertullian only alludes to a "second analogy" involving "yeast"; Adamantius adds nothing more, but goes on to add, as a third analogy, a drag-net, which is not attested for Luke, but is found in Matt 13.47–50.

Luke 13.22–24 is not attested for Marcion's text, and absent, too, from Ephrem, *Comm. Diat.* Tsutsui ("Das Evangelium Marcions," 108) assumes it was present; Harnack is uncertain. Is v. 24 needed to set up v. 25?

13.25 Tertullian, *Marc.* 4.30.4. The Evangelion apparently read "When the householder might *arise*" in agreement with most witnesses to Luke, against "come in" in Gk ms D and OL. Tertullian's wording suggests that it agreed with D and a few other Greek manuscripts, and several OL manuscripts, in omitting "the door" following "knock." Tertullian speaks of those seeking entrance and the dialogue with the householder in the third person, rather than the second person used in all witnesses to Luke; but this is likely to be due to paraphrase.

13.26–28 Epiphanius, *Scholion* 40; *Elenchos* 56; Tertullian, *Marc.* 4.30.2, 4–5; Adam 1.12, 23. It is not certain that Adamantius is quoting from the Evangelion. Tertullian does not mention the repetitive second occurrence of "I do not know where you are from" in v. 27. The Evangelion apparently read "workers of *unlawfulness*" (Gk *anomias*, Adamantius; cf. Tertullian's *operarii iniquitatis*) instead of "workers of injustice," in agreement with a few Greek manuscripts (incl. D), 2 Clement, Justin, and several other patristic witnesses to Luke, as a harmonization to Matt 7.23. Adamantius (1.23) adds the words "I never knew you" (cf. Matt 7.23), but unlike Matthew places them after "get away from me, all you workers of unlawfulness!" Tertullian and Epiphanius agree on the reading "the ethical" (Tertullian) or "all the ethical" (Epiphanius) instead of canonical Luke's "Abraham, Isaac, Jacob, and all the prophets"; this alternative reading is otherwise only known from Ambrose, *Commentary on Luke* 5.21. Tertullian has "coming into" with the majority of OL manuscripts and (once again) Ambrose; but Epiphanius agrees with other witnesses to Luke in reading simply "in." Tertullian and Epiphanius again agree that Marcion's text had "kept outside," rather than "thrown outside"—a reading otherwise unattested, but more consistent with the analogy of having the door shut in one's face.

Omission: Luke 13.29–35 was absent from the Evangelion, according to Epiphanius, *Scholion* 41 ("He deleted this in its entirety"), and it is not cited by any other witness to the Evangelion. The thirteenth-century Gk ms 544 also lacks this material (in fact, all of 13.25–14.1), but at least v. 33–34 was in the Diatessaron (in Ephrem, *Comm. Diat*). Verses 13.34–35 match nearly verbatim Matt 23.37–39.

Luke 14.1–11 is unattested, although Epiphanius makes no mention of the section being omitted. These verses also go unmentioned in Ephrem, *Comm. Diat.* Verse 14.1 (lacking from Gk ms 544) sets up vv. 7–11, while the events of vv. 2–6 seem to intrude. Moreover, Tertullian's remarks on 14.12ff. do not include a reference to a setting at a meal for Jesus' instruction that would suggest the sort of continuation of the setting of v. 1 and vv. 7ff. found in Luke (similarly omitting this reference to a meal setting in v. 12a are the Diatessaron, Gk ms 1071, and one manuscript of SCopt). There is an even stronger reason to conclude that 14.2–6 was absent from the Evangelion, since the latter passage involves Jesus appearing to justify his healing on the sabbath as in accordance with the Law, and yet none of our witnesses cite it against Marcion.

14.12–14 Tertullian, *Marc.* 4.31.1. Luke has Jesus address these words "to the one who had invited him," referring back to the setting of 14.1ff.; but this phrase is missing from the Evangelion, as it is from the Diatessaron, Gk ms 1071, and one manuscript of SCopt. Tertullian does not report who should not be invited in v. 12. In v. 13 Tertullian does not include the clause, "whenever you make a party"; Irenaeus likewise omits this clause when quoting this verse of Luke.

Luke 14.15 is unattested; it is lacking in Gk ms 544 (which also omits vv. 12b–14), and is not mentioned in Ephrem, *Comm. Diat.*

14.16–23 Tertullian, *Marc.* 4.31.1–8. Tertullian quotes this as a continuation of Jesus' remarks in vv. 12–14, without noting any interruption. Gk mss 544, 348, and ℵ similarly lack "Then he said to him" at the beginning of v. 16, while several Greek manuscripts (incl. D) and several OL manuscripts lack just the "to him" that connects this passage to an exchange with an interlocutor probably lacking in the Evangelion. The text seems to have lacked the adjective "big" before "dinner" in v. 16. It possibly read *"took* a wife" (Tertullian has *uxorem duxi*) rather than "married a wife" in v. 20, as in Gk ms D, and the SSyr and CSyr. Tertullian appears to attest the reading "becoming disturbed" (*motus*) in v. 21, rather than Luke's "becoming angry."

Luke 14.24–25 is unattested (≠Harnack, *Marcion,* 219*; Tsutsui, "Das Evangelium Marcions," 109).

14.26 Epiphanius, *Elenchos* 70; Tertullian, *Marc.* 4.19.12 (≠Harnack, Tsustui). Tertullian alludes to this verse not in the sequence of his exposition, but in another context, as shedding light on 8.20–21: "giving in himself an example of his own teaching, that he who should put father or mother or brethren before the word of God was not a worthy disciple." Epiphanius similarly does not cite v. 26 in his catalog of Marcionite readings, but in a concessive remark in another context, commenting on 23.2. Nonetheless, it is probable that he is citing Marcion's own intertextual exegesis of 23.2 by 14.26. In the opening condition "if someone does not" (*ean mē tis*) the reading follows some patristic witnesses (e.g., Athanasius, John Chrysostom, but not Epiphanius' own text of Luke, see *Pan.* 61.6.2: *hos mē*). It read "leave" (*kataleipsēi*) rather than "hate" (in agreement with the Diatessaronic Persian Harmony, and apparently Epiphanius' own text of Luke, see *Pan.* 61.6.2: *katalipēi*), had "brothers" before "wife and children" (in agreement with the SSyr, CSyr, Arabic Diatessaron, and Persian Harmony), and apparently did not include an explicit "and sisters" (in agreement with the original reading of Gk ms 229, with John Chrysostom, and a few other witnesses). The clause "and even one's own life" is unattested for the Evangelion. Epiphanius gives the final clause as "is not my pupil" (*ouk esti mou mathētēs*), and this appears to be the reading of his text of Luke also (*Pan.* 61.6.2); but Tertullian attests "is not worthy to be my pupil" found in the Persian Harmony and a few other witnesses, while most witnesses to Luke read "is unable to be my pupil," which parallels the wording in 14.33 as attested by the *Acts of Archelaus*.

Luke 14.27–32 is unattested; cf. Matt 10.37–38. The statement in v. 27 is a doublet with 9.23b, whose presence in the Evangelion is equally uncertain, and is omitted in several Greek manuscripts (including 544), the SSyr, and the Vulgate. Tertullian knows v. 27 from Luke (*De fuga in persecutione* 7; *Scorpiace* 11), but does not mention it in in connection with the Evangelion. The two analogies in v. 28–32 go unmentioned in Ephrem, *Comm. Diat.* The martial elements of v. 31–32 probably would have been cited against Marcion by Tertullian or Epiphanius if they had found it in his text.

14.33 Hegemonius, *Arch.* 44 (=Harnack; ≠Tsutsui). Harnack accepts the testimony of the *Acts of Archelaus* provisionally, and the identification of sections 44–45 as a Marcionite source has been strengthened by further research.

Luke 14.34–35 is unattested. This material offers nothing for Marcion's opponents to cite against him; in fact, it probably would be in the interests of Tertullian and Epiphanius to pass over this passage in silence.

Luke 15.1–3, which provides a context for Jesus' remarks in vv. 4ff., is unattested for the Evangelion, but Tsutsui, "Das Evangelium Marcions," 110, notes Tertullian's use of *parabola* in connection with the following passage (see v. 3).

15.4–5, 7–8, 10 Tertullian, *Marc.* 4.32.1–2; Ps.-Eph A 52. Pseudo-Ephrem A reads "leaves behind . . . *in the mountains* in the wilderness," adding the alternative location from Matt 18.12; several OL manuscripts do likewise. The same witness has "go out *to search* for the one that was lost," as do the SSyr, CSyr, and Coptic versions, as well as several OL manuscripts, and other witnesses to Luke; this, too, is a harmonization to Matthew. Verses 15.6 and 15.9 are not directed attested.

Omission: Luke 15.11–32, the fable of the Prodigal Son, was absent from the Evangelion, according to Epiphanius, *Scholion* 42; other sources make no mention of it. The earliest record of the story's existence comes from a cluster of late second- and early third-century writers (Clement of Alexandria, Irenaeus, and Tertullian), but it apparently was already in the Diatessaron (Ephrem, *Comm. Diat*).

Order: Tertullian's wording might be taken to suggest that 16.13 preceded 16.1ff. in the Evangelion. It is noteworthy that Gk ms 544 omits 16.1b–12, and goes immediately from v. 1a to v. 13, which works perfectly well in terms of continuity of meaning, for which 16.1b–12 is superfluous. But without further confirmation, I have retained the order found in Luke.

16.1–7, 9 Tertullian, *Marc.* 4.33.1.

Luke 16.9b–10 is unattested.

16.11–12 Tertullian, *Marc.* 4.33.4. For v. 11 Tertullian once quotes the words as "what is true" (*quod verum*, i.e., genuine) and once as "what is more true" (*quod verius*), but the latter should be taken as an interpretive gloss in his part, softening the starkness of the contrast. In v. 12 the Evangelion apparently read "what is *mine*" instead of "what is *yours*," a reading found also in Gk ms 157, and three OL manuscripts (e, i, and l).

16.13 Tertullian, *Marc.* 4.33.1; Adam* 1.28. Adamantius reads "no one" as in the Matthean parallel (6.24) and a number of witnesses to Luke, instead of "no house servant." Both Tertullian and Adamantius agree that the Evangelion lacked the clause "he will hate the one and love the other," and had only the parallel clause "he will disregard one and adhere to the other." In this case, Luke matches the Matthean parallel, while the Evangelion diverges.

16.14–15 Tertullian, *Marc.* 4.33.2, 6. Tsutsui ("Das Evangelium Marcions," 111) corrects Harnack (*Marcion*, 220*) on the presence of 15b, as attested by Tertullian, *Marc.* 4.33.6.

16.16–17 Epiphanius, *Scholion* 43; Tertullian, *Marc.* 4.33.7, 9; cf. 5.2.1; 5.8.5; Hegemonius, *Arch.* 45. In the second clause of v. 16 Tertullian gives the wording "from which" (*ex quo*) for the Greek "from then" (*apo tote*), but this probably does not signify a textual difference, since the OL of Luke translates the same way (Epiphanius and Archelaus skip this clause). Only Epiphanius attests the clause "and everyone is pressing into it." In v. 17, the Evangelion read "one stroke of *my words* to fall" (Tertullian, *Marc.* 4.33.9); the witnesses to Luke consistently have, "one stroke of *the Law* to fall." The latter reading seems to contradict the immediately preceding verse, where it is said that the Law was in effect only until John, while the former reading has a close parallel in 21.33.

16.18 Tertullian, *Marc.* 4.34.1. In both main clauses, the Evangelion had "the one who," instead of "everyone who"; many witnesses to Luke share this variant only in the second clause. The Evangelion apparently read "is like an adulterer" (*aeque adulter est*) instead of "commits adultery."

16.19–31 Epiphanius, *Scholia* 44, 45, 46; *Elenchoi* 56, 59; Tertullian, *Marc.* 4.34.10–17; cf. 3.24; Adam 2.10. Adamantius, who may not be quoting from the Evangelion, provides the entire passage verbatim. A number of minor textual variants shared by the Evangelion and witnesses to Luke throughout the passage do not alter the sense appreciably. The Evangelion read "he was buried in Hades," in agreement with Gk ms ℵ, the OL, and several patristic witnesses to Luke, against the reading "he was buried; and in Hades" found in the majority of witnesses to Luke. In v. 25 the Evangelion read "good things" instead of "your good things," in agreement with a handful of other witnesses to Luke. In v. 26, it had "between you and us," instead of "between us and you"; this reversed order is found in a number of witnesses to Luke. It read "they are unable to cross over" with several patristic witnesses to Luke, instead of "those who to wish to cross over cannot" in most manuscripts of Luke. The Evangelion read "for I have five brothers *there*" instead of "for I have five brothers" in v. 28, as does the Armenian version and a few patristic witnesses to Luke. The Evangelion read "But he said" at the beginning of v. 29, instead of "Abraham said to him"; cf. v. 30. According to Tertullian, it had "they have *there* Moses" in agreement with several Greek manuscripts and a few patristic witnesses to Luke, instead of "they have Moses"; but Adamantius and Epiphanius do not have this reading. The Evangelion had, in agreement with a few Greek manuscripts of Luke, "Nay, father" in v. 30, instead of "Nay, father Abraham." The Evangelion maintained the subjunctive in the verb "would have a change of heart" for the conditional construction of v. 30, as do a large number of Greek manuscripts of Luke, which is more proper literary form than (and so probably secondary to) the use of the future indicative found in the majority of witnesses to Luke. In v. 31, the Evangelion read "if they *did* not listen" instead of "if they *do* not listen," a reading also found in a handful of manuscripts and patristic witnesses to Luke. It apparently had "listen to," found in the SCopt and a handful of patristic witnesses to Luke, instead of "be persuaded by" or "believe." Our sources agree that the Evangelion did not have "if someone rises from among the dead," but they disagree on what it had in place of that wording. According to Epiphanius, it read "listen to one awakened from among the dead"; but according to Adamantius, it read "listen to one who returns from among the dead." The former reading is shared with Gk mss P[75] and 579; the latter with Gk ms W, and compounded with the common reading in Irenaeus, Ambrose, Gk ms D and OL mss d and r1. The story Jesus tells in this passage closely resembles an Egyptian tale preserved on a Demotic papyrus dating to a decade or two after Jesus (see Gressmann, *Vom Reichen Mann*, 63–68).

17.1–2 Tertullian, *Marc.* 4.35.1; Adam 2.15, 1.16. Adamantius may not be using the Evangelion in either section. In v. 1, Adamantius attests the reading "that one through whom the snare comes," found also in OL, rather than "the one through whom they come" in other witnesses to Luke, whose plural is reflected in the testimony of Tertullian. In v. 2, Adamantius (1.16) quotes what appears to be Matt 26.24, but then continues with wording in line with Tertullian, both witnesses agreeing on the additional clause "that person to have never been born" (otherwise found in Matt 26.24) combined with the "a millstone" and so on, from the more widely attested text of Luke (note the telltale "or" signaling a conflation of two alternative textual traditions). The same combined reading is found in the OL, and is attested as early as 1 Clem 46.8. Volckmar, *Das Evangelium Marcions*, 256–57, regards this combined reading as more original; Green, "Matthew, Clement and Luke," has argued that our gospel actually is dependent on Clement here. Integrating the betrayal theme — from which the warning develops in Adam 1.16 — with the stumbling theme — from which it develops in Adam 2.15 — remains problematic.

17.3–4 Tertullian, *Marc.* 4.35.2–3.

Luke 17.5–9 is unattested; Tsutsui ("Das Evangelium Marcions," 114) regards vv. 7–9 as absent. See below on Epiphanius' reference to missing material in v. 10.

Omission: Luke 17.10 was at least partially absent from the Evangelion. Epiphanius, *Scholion* 47, remarks, "He deleted 'say, we are unprofitable servants: we have done that which was our duty to do.'" The Nestle-Aland edition of Luke interprets this to mean that Marcion's text omitted only the words of v. 10b directly cited by Epiphanius, but retained v. 10a: "so you also, when you have done all the things assigned to you," and Knox thinks along similar lines. Harnack thinks that perhaps even more of the verse was present, finishing off the thought of 10a, and only omitting the clause "we are unprofitable servants" (but he also considers possible the omission of all of vv. 7–10; *Marcion*, 223*). Tsutsui regards the entire verse as absent, and I concur. Epiphanius commented only on missing material that had some polemical usefulness to him. Ephrem, *Comm. Diat.*, does not mention the content of this verse.

17.11–12 Epiphanius, *Scholion* 48; Tertullian, *Marc.* 4.35.4, 9. Tertullian says "the act took place in the parts of Samaria"; most witnesses to Luke have the addition of "and Galilee."

Luke 17.13 is unattested.

17.14a; 4.27; 17.14b Epiphanius, *Scholion* 48; Tertullian, *Marc.* 4.35.4, 6–7. Epiphanius quotes the beginning of v. 14 as "he sent them away, saying," instead of Luke's, "and seeing them, he said"; Tertullian's testimony is not explicit enough to confirm or disconfirm this reading. Epiphanius reports Jesus' initial instructions as "show yourselves," while Tertullian has "go, show yourselves" in agreement with Luke. Most importantly, both witnesses attest the presence of material between 14a and 14b not found there in Luke. Epiphanius says that Marcion "excised much" and also "put (some words) in place of others" somewhere after Jesus' instructions for the lepers to go show themselves to a priest, proceeding to quote the wording of Luke 4.27.

Tertullian, *Marc.* 4.35.5–6 talks about the healing of the ten lepers as they are on their way to the priest (v. 14b), and then adds that "he said before" (*etsi praefatus*) the content found in Luke 4.27. The combination of these testimonies makes it certain that the Evangelion had the material found in Luke 4.27 here, between 17.14a and 17.14b. As to what was supposedly "excised" or displaced by the substitution of 4.27, Epiphanius appears to exaggerate, since Tertullian cites nearly everything found in Luke here for the Evangelion.

17.15–19 Tertullian, *Marc.* 4.35.7, 9, 11. Tertullian quotes only "your trust has rescued you" without mentioning the words "rise, go"; the SSyr and CSyr omit "rise."

17.20–21 Tertullian, *Marc.* 4.35.12; Ephrem, *Marc. II* (Mitchell) 114. Tertullian's rendering of v. 21 suggests the reading "nor do they say," rather than "nor will they say"; the same reading is found in a few manuscripts of the OL.

17.22 Epiphanius, *Scholion* 49. That these words were addressed to the pupils, as well as the presence of the clause "but you will not see (it)," is not explicitly attested.

Luke 17.23 is unattested, and missing from Gk ms 7 (later corrected), but loosely paraphrased in Ephrem, *Comm. Diat.*

Luke 17.24 goes unmentioned by Epiphanius or Tertullian. Adamantius (1.25) quotes from "the Gospel" the form of this saying found in Matt 24.27 rather than the different version of it found in Luke. Adamantius may be quoting from the Evangelion here, but it is possible he is actually quoting Matthew or the Diatessaron. The inclusion of this verse is therefore uncertain.

17.25 Tertullian, *Marc.* 4.35.14. The phrase "and be rejected *by this generation*" is not directly quoted by Tertullian.

17.26 Tertullian, *Marc.* 4.35.15.

Luke 17.27 is unattested, although some elaboration of the analogy of Noah is likely.

17.28 Tertullian, *Marc.* 4.35.15.

Luke 17.29 is unattested, although some elaboration of the analogy of Lot is likely.

Luke 17.30–31 is unattested.

17.32 Tertullian, *Marc.* 4.35.15.

Luke 17.33–37 is unattested. A few Greek manuscripts omit v. 35, but probably due to haplography; v. 36 is omitted from two surviving fragments of the Akhmimic Coptic version of Luke, see Lefort, "Fragments de S. Luc en akhmimique," and Lefort, "Fragments bibliques en dialecte akhmimique," 26.

18.1–7 Tertullian, *Marc.* 4.36.1. Tertullian does not include any express allusion to the negative characterization of the judge in the analogy; but he may be avoiding that element because of the heightened equation of the judge with God in his interpretation. In a Marcionite context in Ps.-Clement, *Hom.* 17.5, this passage is somewhat paraphrased: "If then the unjust judge does thus . . . how much more will the Father cause the vindication of those who call to him day and night, that is, through his delay in judging them, because he does not do it? Indeed, I tell you he will do it, and speedily." The last clause of v. 7 ("even though he is dilatory towards them") is not attested.

Luke 18.8a is unattested for the Evangelion, unless one has confidence that Ps.-Clement, *Hom.* 17.5 quotes a Marcionite source. Verse 18.8b is likewise unattested.

18.9–14 Tertullian, *Marc.* 4.36.1–2 (=Harnack, Tsutsui vv. 10, 14). Harnack and Tsutsui neglect explicit wording from vv. 11 and 13. Tertullian does not mention that this analogy was addressed to a specific audience. He does not give the wording of the respective prayers verbatim, but only characterizes them as, on the one hand, prideful, and, on the other, humble. He speaks in terms of the Pharisee being "rejected," which is stronger than the wording found in Luke, but this may be paraphrase.

Luke 18.15 is unattested.

18.16 Adam* 1.16. The Evangelion may have lacked a reference to Jesus summoning the pupils, as do the SSyr and CSyr. The clause "and do not hinder them" appears to have been absent, as it is from a few Greek manuscripts of Luke and from Origen. The wording "realm of the celestial sphere" rather than "realm of God" agrees with several Greek and OL manuscripts, the SSyr and CSyr, Origen and other patristic witnesses to Luke, and Matt 19.14.

Luke 18.17 is unattested.

18.18–19 Epiphanius, *Scholion* 50; Tertullian, *Marc.* 4.36.3–4; Adam* 1.1 (cf. 2.17); Hippolytus, *Ref.* 7.31.6. In v. 18, the Evangelion had Jesus questioned by "a certain person" rather than "a certain ruler," in agreement with Justin, *Dial.* 101.2; *1 Apol.* 16.7) and most manuscripts of OL (Volckmar, *Das Evangelium Marcions*, 256–57, regarded this as the original wording of Luke). For v. 19, our witnesses offer conflicting testimony (see Williams, "Reconsidering Marcion's Gospel," 494). For Jesus' initial rhetorical question, Adamantius and Hippolytus have "Why do you call me good?" matching Mark 10.18 (cf. Justin, *1 Apol.* 16.7; Clement, *Paed.* 1.8). Epiphanius (along with the possible evidence for the wording of the Evangelion in Ps.-Clement, *Hom.* 17.4 and 18.1) attests an imperative rather than a question: "Do not call me good." Jesus' next words are "None is good, except one" (Adamantius) in agreement with Mark 10.18, or "One is good" (Epiphanius; Hippolytus; Ps.-Clement, *Hom.* 17.4; 18.1), in agreement with Matt 19.17 (cf. Justin, *Dial.* 101.2; Clement, *Strom.* 2.20; Irenaeus, *Haer.* 1.13.2). Who is this one? Epiphanius explicitly says that Marcion "added" the words "the Father." Does he mean that Marcion added "the Father" after "God," or in place of "God"? The answer becomes clear when we compare Adam 1.1, quoted by a Marcionite, to Adam 2.17, quoted from a catholic text: the Marcionite reading is "None is good, except one—the Father" (cf. Ps.-Clement, *Hom.* 18.1; Justin, *Dial.* 101.2; Irenaeus, *Haer.* 1.13.2; Clement, *Paed.* 1.8; *Strom.* 5.10.63), while the catholic one is "None is good, except one—God." A widely attested textual variant of Luke gives in place of "God" the reading "the Father who is in the celestial spheres" (Hippolytus, *Ref.* 5.7.25; Clement, *Hom.* 16.3.4; Ephrem, *Comm. Diat.* 15.9; Irenaeus, *Haer.* 1.20.2), while Origen, OL ms d, and some manuscripts of the Armenian version of Luke combine both readings: "God the Father." Tertullian is too paraphrastic to help resolve all the uncertainties: "Who is supremely good except one, God?" (*sed quis optimus nisi unus, deus*).

18.20–21 Epiphanius, *Scholion* 50; Tertullian, *Marc.* 4.36.4, 7; Adam 2.17. Tertullian refers in one place to Jesus inquiring whether the man knew the commandments, but in another place quotes the indicative wording "You know the commandments" generally attested for Luke. Yet Epiphanius and Adamantius agree that the wording found in the Evangelion as known to them was "*I* know the commandments" rather than "you know the commandments." They are not as clear on who utters these words as one might wish, however. Epiphanius, *Elenchos* 50 theorizes on Marcion's motives for this reading, and his remarks might be taken to imply that Jesus speaks the words. Adamantius, who gives the most verbatim report but may not be using the Evangelion, has "But he said (*ho de ephē*), 'I know the commandments . . .' And he said (*kai phēsin*), 'All these . . .'" This wording suggests a new speaker with *de*, and therefore it is Jesus' interlocutor who says, "I know"; the *kai* would then be resumptive, with the same person continuing to be the speaker for "all these." In other words, the man, rather than Jesus, says all this. Gk ms 461 (later corrected) similarly has "all these" continue directly on the listing of the commandments, with no indication of a new speaker. Tertullian and Adamantius agree on the order "murder . . . adultery," found also in a few Greek manuscripts, the OL and the SSyr and CSyr, and a number of patristic witnesses to Luke, as well as Matthew and Mark, against the order "adultery . . . murder" more widely attested for Luke.

18.22 Tertullian, *Marc.* 4.36.4, 7; Adam 2.17. Tertullian supplies the entire statement of Jesus verbatim; Adamantius, the reaction of Jesus and his statement except for the final clause, "then come on, follow me."

Luke 18.23, containing the man's negative reaction in answer to Jesus' instruction, is unattested for the Evangelion.

18.24 Origen, *Cels.* 7.18 (≠Harnack, Tsutsui). Origen quotes Celsus, who in turn is apparently citing from Marcion's *Antitheses* the information that the "laws" of Jesus teach that "a man cannot come forward to the Father if he is rich."

Luke 18.25–30 is unattested. Verse 18.25 is lacking in a handful of witnesses to Luke. Adamantius cites 18.27 in a context that probably is not taken from the Evangelion (5.18). Verses 18.28–30 would have been prime material for the arguments of Tertullian and Epiphanius, and so the latter's silence makes it probable that these verses were absent from the Evangelion. They also go unmentioned in Ephrem, *Comm. Diat.*

Omission: Luke 18.31–34 was absent from the Evangelion, according to Epiphanius, *Scholion* 52; no other witness cites anything from this material for the Evangelion; but it was present in the Diatessaron

(Ephrem, *Comm. Diat*). Harnack and Tsutsui think that Epiphanius' note of omission only extends as far as v. 33, and that v. 34 is unattested.

18.35–37 Epiphanius, *Scholion* 51; Tertullian, *Marc.* 4.36.9; Adam* 5.14. Adamantius quotes the passage verbatim, expressly said to be read from the Evangelion, while Tertullian and Epiphanius note certain elements only. The Evangelion apparently had "Jesus" without the epithet "the Nazorean" (most Greek manuscripts) or "the Nazarene" (D, OL).

18.38–39 Epiphanius, *Scholion* 51; Tertullian, *Marc.* 4.36.9, 4.39.10; Adam* 5.14; Ephrem, *Marc. II* (Mitchell) 106. Adamantius, who gives the appearance of quoting the entire passage verbatim, omits v. 39, as do a number of Greek manuscripts; but Tertullian clearly alludes to at least the first part of it. The difference is due either to Adamantius abbreviating or textual variation between the two exemplars used by our sources.

18.40–43 Epiphanius, *Scholion* 51; Tertullian, *Marc.* 4.36.10–14, 4.37.1, 4.39.10; Adam* 5.14; Ephrem, *Marc. II* (Mitchell) 106; *Marc III* (Mitchell) 123. In v. 42, the Evangelion, along with a couple of Greek manuscripts (including D), many OL manuscripts and Origen, has the additional "answering." The man's interest in following Jesus in v. 43 is not directly attested for the Evangelion.

Luke 19.1 is unattested, although the setting in Jericho is logical following the approach to Jericho in the previous episode.

19.2, 6 Tertullian, *Marc.* 4.37.1. Tertullian only provides the name "Zacchaeus" and the fact that he received Jesus as a guest in his home.

Luke 19.7 is unattested.

19.8–10 Tertullian, *Marc.* 4.37.1–2. The additional explanatory clause found in v. 9b of canonical Luke ("because he also is a son of Abraham") is unattested for the Evangelion and goes unused by Marcion's opponents; in fact, Tertullian's remark about Zacchaeus, "though a foreigner" (*etsi allophylus*), demonstrates that this clause was unknown to him in his own text of Luke. The Evangelion, in agreement with a few Greek manuscripts of Luke, read "came to rescue," rather than "came *to seek and* to rescue."

19.11–13 Tertullian, *Marc.* 4.37.4, 4.39.11; Ps.-Eph A 32, 36, 38. Our two witnesses offer minimal help in identifying which details of this long passage were actually found in the Evangelion. The additional clause found in Luke 19:11b ("because he was near Jerusalem and they were imagining that the kingdom of God was going to display itself instantly") is unattested for the Evangelion.

Luke 19.14 is not mentioned in connection with the Evangelion. This material has been introduced somehow into the analogy from the account of Archelaus, son of Herod, in Josephus, *J.W.* 2.1ff. or *Ant.* 17.206ff.

19.15–19 Tertullian, *Marc.* 4.37.4; Ps.-Eph A 42 (≠Harnack, Tsutsui). The latter gives substantial quotation, somewhat paraphrastically, while Tertullian says broadly, "the servants . . . are judged variously according as they account for their master's money entrusted to them."

19.20–23 Tertullian, *Marc.* 4.37.4; Ps.-Eph A 36, 42 (≠Harnack; =Tsutsui v. 21). The Evangelion apparently read "unreliable (*apiste*) slave," as do most OL manuscripts, the SSyr, and the Armenian version of Luke, while most other witnesses to Luke attest "wicked slave"; the two readings are combined in some OL manuscripts, the CSyr, and the Arabic Diatessaron.

Luke 19.24–25 is unattested; several Greek and OL manuscripts, as well as the SSyr, CSyr, and Bohairic Coptic versions of Luke, omit v. 25.

19.26 Tertullian, *Marc.* 4.37.4. Tertullian does not refer to the first clause of this verse as found in Luke ("I am telling you that to everyone that has, it will be given, but . . ."). He attests the reading "*seems to* have" in agreement with several Greek manuscripts, the CSyr, Origen, and Ephrem (cf. Luke 8.18); other witnesses to Luke read "has."

Luke 19.27 is not attested for the Evangelion. Origen, *Comm. Matt.* 14.13, cites it against the Marcionites, but in a context where it cannot be assumed that he was being careful to cite only material contained in the Evangelion. As in the case of v. 14, it is an addition to the parable based upon Josephus' account of Archelaus' struggle to be king after the death of his father Herod.

Luke 19.28 is unattested, but some transition to a setting in Jerusalem is required.

Omission: 19.29–35, [19.36–40], 19.41–46 Epiphanius, *Scholion* 53, states that Marcion's text lacked content equivalent to Luke's 19.29–35 ("the section about the ass and Bethphage"), 19.41–44 ("and the one about the city"), and 19.45–46 ("and temple"), but he says nothing directly about 19.36–40. Of this material, vv. 29–38 parallels Mark 11.1–10, closely at first, but more remotely in the later verses; vv. 39–44 is a narrative continuation of this episode unique to Luke (containing a very clear reference to the siege of Jerusalem, whose details appear to derive from Josephus, *J.W.* 5.491ff. and 6.413ff., a work which began to circulate before 80 CE); and vv. 45–46 is a much abbreviated parallel to Mark 11.15–17. None of this material is mentioned by any other source on the Evangelion. It would have been consistent with Tertullian's line of argument to at least mention v. 40, where the stones of this world crying out in praise of the coming of Jesus would support his connection to the creator, rather than Marcion's supercelestial deity. Luke 19.33–34 is lacking in Gk mss G, 063 and 477 (v. 33 alone in D), and 19.35 in Gk mss F and V. None of these omissions has an evident cause. Verse 19.38a (the first half of what the crowd was shouting) is absent from Ephrem and OL mss e and l, and should be compared to the strikingly similar John 12.13.

Luke 19.47–48 is unattested.

20.1–8 Epiphanius, *Elenchos* 53; Tertullian, *Marc.* 4.38.1–2. Epiphanius, making a point about a previous omission in Marcion's text, quotes the opening clauses of v. 1, but gives a text that runs from v. 1 directly to v. 19b. Tertullian identifies Jesus' opponents in this episode of the Evangelion as "the Pharisees"; all witnesses to Luke have "chief priests and the scribes with the elders" in agreement with the parallels in Mark and Matthew. Verse 20.2 is not directly attested, but some action or objection of the Pharisees is necessary to set up Jesus' response to them. In vv. 4–5 the Evangelion apparently had the plural "celestial spheres" (*ouranois*) rather than the singular "celestial sphere" (*ouranos*) found in Luke.

Omission: Luke 20.9–18 was absent from the Evangelion, according to Epiphanius, *Scholion* 55, and he tellingly cites 20.19 (*Scholion* 54) before he realizes that some material found in canonical Luke has been skipped over. The additional material found in Luke is parallel to Mark 12.1–12a and Matt 21.33–45, and the part of it Ephrem quotes from the Diatessaron appears to derive from Matthew. Pseudo-Ephrem A (44) refers to this passage in association with John 15.2 and 5, and then says, "this is hidden from the Gospel which the strange Marcionites read." The wording is ambiguous whether the passage of Luke is meant to be included in this remark, in which case it agrees with Epiphanius' testimony (this is how it is understood by Schäfers, *Eine altsyrische antimarkionistische Erklärung*, 174, and Bundy, "Marcion and the Marcionites," 27), or only the passage of John, in which case mentioning the Lukan parable suggests its presence in the Evangelion in contradiction to Epiphanius.

20.19 Epiphanius, *Scholion* 54. Here, too, the Evangelion lacked the "scribes and chief priests" of Luke, and the "they" subject inherent in the verb is read in continuity with the subject of the preceding passage (the Pharisees). The Evangelion apparently lacked "seize him *in that very hour*," as does OL ms e. It also lacked v. 19b ("for they perceived that he spoke this analogy with them in mind"), also lacking in the SSyr. The analogy (Luke 20.9–16) was itself lacking from the Evangelion.

Luke 20.20 is unattested.

20.21–25 Tertullian, *Marc.* 4.38.3; 4.19.7. Tertullian, *Marc.* 4.38.3, gives only the famous reply of Jesus in v. 25, along with a reference to the fact that it was a reply to a question, and that it concerned an "image and likeness" impressed upon the object in question. In 4.19.7 he refers to "that question about tribute money" and then quotes "And there came to him Pharisees, testing him." This wording is not found in any witness to Luke or any of the Synoptic parallels; but cf. Papyrus Egerton 2: "And they, coming to test him, said . . ."

Luke 20.26 is unattested.

20.27–33 Tertullian, *Marc.* 4.38.4. The content of Luke vv. 30–31a ("So the second, and the third.") is not attested for the Evangelion and is lacking or highly abbreviated in many witnesses to Luke. Likewise, the content of Luke 20.32 ("Lastly, the woman also died"), although present in some form in most witnesses to Luke, is unattested for the Evangelion.

20.34 Tertullian, *Marc.* 4.38.5, 8. Tertullian does not mention the additional words "procreate and are procreated" before "marry and are married," seen in some of the Evangelion's usual textual associates:

Gk mss D, the OL, SSyr and CSyr. These words would very much suit Marcion's ideological position, so it would be noteworthy if the Evangelion did not have them. On the other hand, Tertullian may have passed over them as serving against rather than in favor of his position.

20.35 Tertullian, *Marc.* 4.38.5–7; 4.39.11. Tertullian offers rare remarks on a textual variant of the Evangelion in connection with its Marcionite interpretation. It is certain from Tertullian's comments that the text had "God" between "found worthy" and "of that age," either as the nominative subject of an active form of the verb (Tsutsui, "Das Evangelium Marcions," 120), or in the genitive of agency with the passive form of the verb (*hoi de kataxiōthentes tou theou tou aiōnos ekeinou*). I favor the latter possibility as requiring less speculative reconstruction of the text, and corresponding quite well to Tertullian's wording: *Quos vero dignatus sit deus illius aevi possessione*. The underlying Greek would normally be read "found worthy by God of that age" and presents a certain ambiguity of interpretation: should it be understood as "*found worthy of that age* by God" or "found worthy by *the God of that age*"? Marcion apparently favored the latter interpretation, and Tertullian disputes it, not by questioning the validity of the Evangelion's text (i.e., including "God," attested by no witness to Luke known to us), but by questioning the syntax by which a proper reading of the text should be obtained. Such an ambiguity in the original text may have prompted an emendation that removed the possibility of Marcion's interpretation by removing the explicit reference to God; and this is a more plausible direction of emendation than the introduction of a reference to God in an ambiguous position in the text. This possibly could be a case, therefore, where the text of a passage found in all surviving witnesses to Luke is secondary to that found in the Evangelion.

20.36 Tertullian, *Marc.* 4.38.5; 4.39.11 (cf. 3.9.4). The Evangelion apparently read "because they are children of God and of the awakening," in agreement with Gk ms D and most OL manuscripts, instead of "and they are children of God, because they are children of the awakening."

Omission: Luke 20.37–38 was absent from the Evangelion, according to Epiphanius, *Scholia* 56 and 57. They go unmentioned in Ephrem, *Comm. Diat.* Parallel material is found in Mark 12.26–27 and Matt 22.31–32. Yet Origen, in a fragment on 20.38 preserved in exegetical catenae, says, "the followers of Marcion and Valentinus still struggle against this passage and apply the saying to souls. For, they say that these souls live, and that the Lord said of them that God was the God of these souls." This remark would support the inclusion of v. 38 in some form in the Evangelion.

20.39 Tertullian, *Marc.* 4.38.9.

Luke 20.40 is unattested; it is not mentioned in Ephrem, *Comm. Diat.*

20.41, 44 Tertullian, *Marc.* 4.38.10; Ephrem, *Marc. II* (Mitchell) 104–5. Harnack credited the additional evidence of Adam 5.13; but in that particular context of the dialogue, the "gospel" from which the passage is read is probably the Diatessaron, rather than the Evangelion used by the Marcionites, and the text matches Matt 22.41–44 rather than the form found in Luke.

Luke 20.42–43, the direct quote of Ps 110.1 alluded to by Jesus in v. 44, is not directly attested.

Luke 20.45–47 is unattested; it is not mentioned in Ephrem, *Comm. Diat.* (cf. Mark 12.38–40).

Luke 21.1–4 (the episode of the widow's penny) and **21.5–6** (predictions of doom for Jerusalem) are unattested. The former are not mentioned in Ephrem, *Comm. Diat.* (cf. Mark 12.41–44). Verses 5–6 are unique to Luke, and are mentioned in Ephrem, *Comm. Diat.* Both passages are likely to have been mentioned by Tertullian or Epiphanius as cases where Jesus commends support for the Jewish temple and indicates his concern for the center of Jewish identity, respectively. If one leaves out all of the unattested and uncertain material from this section of the Evangelion, the narrative goes directly from the quote concerning the Messiah being enthroned at the right hand of God to the pupils asking when "these things" will occur (21.7), which Jesus answers first with a warning about false Messiahs—a logical sequence for the original text.

21.7–11 Tertullian, *Marc.* 4.39.1–3, 12–13, 17; cf. 5.1.3. The Evangelion specifies "the pupils" as the speakers in v. 7, in agreement with Gk mss D and 122, and the parallels in Mark and Matthew; other witnesses to Luke do not specify the speakers. In v. 8, the Evangelion read "I am the Christos," in agreement with Gk ms 157 and the OL (cf. Tertullian, *Marc.* 5.1.3); this appears to represent a harmonization to Matt 25.4, while most witnesses to Luke have "I am he" in accordance with Mark 13.6. It may have lacked "the moment has approached," as does Gk ms 230. The Evangelion seems to have read "it is necessary for these things to occur" in v. 9, rather than "to occur *first*," in agreement with a few Greek manuscripts and the parallels in Mark and Matthew. It possibly lacked "but it is not immediately the end" at the end of the verse as well, and continued straight on to v. 10. The Evangelion probably lacked the resumptive "then he said to them" found at the beginning of v. 10 in Luke, and instead had a connective "because," as in some Greek manuscripts (including D), the OL and the SSyr and CSyr. Tertullian gives some of the pairs of signs in v. 10–11 in reversed sequence, but this is paralleled for only one of the pairs in some witnesses to Luke. The Evangelion clearly joins most witnesses to Luke in reading "fearful sights and great signs from the celestial sphere" instead of "fearful sights from the celestial sphere and great signs" found in Gk ms D, the OL, SSyr, CSyr and Origen.

21.12–13 Tertullian, *Marc.* 4.39.4. The Evangelion apparently read "testimony *and rescue*" in v. 13, whereas Luke reads simply "testimony."

21.14–15 Tertullian, *Marc.* 4.39.6. The Evangelion evidently read "not able to resist" with Gk ms D, many OL manuscripts, and the SSyr and CSyr, against the more common reading of witnesses to Luke, "not able to *dispute or* resist," which appears to combine two textual variants.

21.16–17 Tertullian, *Marc.* 4.39.8.

Omission: Luke 21.18 was absent from the Evangelion, according to Epiphanius, *Scholion* 58. It is also absent from the CSyr, as well as from the gospel's probable source in Mark; it is not mentioned in Ephrem, *Comm. Diat.* Volckmar ("Über das Lukas-Evangelium") and Hilgenfeld (*Kritische Untersuchungen* and "Das Marcionitische Evangelium") both regard this verse as a later addition to Luke.

21.19 Tertullian, *Marc.* 4.39.8. The Evangelion read "by endurance," rather than "by *your* endurance," in agreement with several patristic testimonies to the text of Luke. It read "preserve yourselves" (*salvos facietis vosmetipsos*), instead of Luke's "acquire your lives"; cf. Mark 13.13b: "But the one who endures to the end will be preserved."

21.20 Tertullian, *Marc.* 4.39.9. The presence in the Evangelion of this clear reference to the siege of Jerusalem shows that it can be dated no earlier than the mid-70s CE, and may in fact depend on the account of Josephus, as Luke probably does.

Omission: Luke 21.21–22 was absent from the Evangelion, according to Epiphanius, *Scholion* 59. Tertullian appears to read directly from 21.20 to 21.25; elsewhere, he shows that he knows some of the intervening content from Luke (*Res.* 22). It is not mentioned in Ephrem, *Comm. Diat.*

Luke 21.23–24 is unattested. This reference to Jerusalem's destruction, probably derived from Josephus, *J.W.* 7.1ff., is not mentioned by Ephrem, *Comm. Diat.*

21.25–26 Tertullian, *Marc.* 4.39.9.

21.27–28 Tertullian, *Marc.* 4.39.10. Tertullian's report here can be compared with his citation of this same passage from Luke in *Res.* 22. The Evangelion read "coming from the celestial spheres," in place of Luke's "coming in a cloud." It read "with much power," while most witnesses to Luke have "with power and much splendor." It had "when these things occur" in v. 28, instead of Luke's "when these things *start to* occur." "You will look up and lift your heads" appears in the future indicative, rather than the aorist imperative, in agreement with several OL manuscripts; "has arrived" appears instead of "is arriving," with several Greek manuscripts, a few OL manuscripts, and a handful of patristic witnesses to Luke.

21.29–31 Tertullian, *Marc.* 4.39.10–11, 13, 16–17. The Evangelion apparently read "produce/put forth *fruit*" in v. 30, in agreement with several Greek manuscripts (including D, 157), some OL manuscripts, and the SSyr and CSyr; other witnesses read "produce/put forth" with the object undefined, which would be taken to mean budding. Verse 30 had "people know that summer is near," instead of "you yourselves know that summer is already near"; it shares the generic subject of the verb with several Greek manuscripts (including D and W) and the lack of "already" with a large number of Greek manuscripts (only a couple of which agree on the generic subject), as well as the OL, SSyr and CSyr.

21.32–35 Tertullian, *Marc.* 4.39.18 (cf. 4.33.9). The Evangelion had "*celestial sphere* and earth will not pass away" in v. 32, instead of "this generation will not pass away," supported by only OL ms e: "this celestial sphere will not pass way." This reading probably represents a secondary harmonization to the following verse, but it has the effect of resolving the problematic promise of the end coming within a single generation. This would be a possible piece of evidence for later redaction of the Evangelion rather than of Luke. Tertullian's report suggests the wording "will remain forever" in v. 33, instead of "will not pass away" in Luke, although this may be a case of paraphrase. The Evangelion apparently read "surprise you unexpectedly as a snare. For it will come," in agreement with a few Greek manuscripts (e.g., ℵ, 157, 0179) and most OL manuscripts; other witnesses to canonical Luke have "surprise you unexpectedly. For it will come as a snare." The inclusion of the rest of v. 35 is posited here based on a possible allusion in the wording of Tertullian: *utique oblitis deum ex plenitudine et cogitatione mundi* (≠Harnack, Tsutsui).

Luke 21.36 is not clearly attested for the Evangelion. It may be alluded to by Tertullian, *Marc.* 4.39.14: *filium hominis . . . vota sanctorum*.

21.37-38 Tertullian, *Marc.* 4.39.19.

Addition following 21.38? The members of Greek manuscript Family 13 (consisting of mss 13, 69, 124, 346, 543, 788, 826, 983) add here the episode of the woman caught in adultery more commonly known from many manuscripts of canonical John 7.53–8.11. The version found in the Family 13 manuscripts of Luke differs from the version found in manuscripts of John at several points, most of them minor. Its presence is not directly attested for the Evangelion, but it could have been skipped over by our sources as offering no polemical point to make against Marcion. As demonstrated by Ehrman, "Jesus and the Adultress," the story circulated in at least two versions, and patristic testimony to it does not all refer to the same version in either its content or its textual home. A number of researchers (e.g. Cadbury, "A Possible Case of Lukan Authorship"; McLachlan, *St. Luke Evangelist and Historian*, 94–126; Salvoni, "Textual Authority for John 7:53–8:11") have argued similarities of language, style, and theme make it a good match both to Luke generally, and to this point of the narrative in particular. Parker speaks for this set of opinions when he says, "In all, a better case can be made for this having been an authentic piece of Luke which dropped out than for its having been original to John" (Parker, *The Living Text of the Gospels*). Parker, however, does not think the case sufficient to warrant its inclusion in NT editions, either in Luke or John. Similarly, the case cannot yet be made that it appeared in the Evangelion.

22.1 Tertullian, *Marc.* 4.40.1

Luke 22.2 is unattested; cf. Luke 19.47b–48 (also unattested).

22.3 Tertullian, *Marc.* 4.40.2; cf. 5.6.7. Tertullian merely alludes to Jesus' betrayer being no stranger, but further along he provides the name Judas. Tertullian, *Marc.* 5.6.7 implies the absence from the Evangelion of the statement that "Satan entered into" him ("for in the gospel as I have it, it is written that Satan entered into Judas"). While this verse is present in most witnesses to Luke and John 13.27, it is not in the gospel's probable source text for this passage, Mark 14.10.

22.4 Epiphanius, *Scholion* 60. The Evangelion evidently did not mention "chief priests" along with the "captains" (i.e., of the temple guard), whereas Gk ms D mentions the chief priests, but not the captains. The SSyr, CSyr, and OL replace the captains with scribes.

22.5 Tertullian, *Marc.* 4.40.2.

Luke 22.6–7 is unattested.

22.8 Epiphanius, *Scholion* 61. Epiphanius mentions only "Peter and the rest," not naming the other pupil sent as John, but he may be paraphrasing.

Luke 22.9–13 is unattested for the Evangelion. It matches almost verbatim Mark 14.12b–16, and is passed over in silence in Ephrem, *Comm. Diat.*

22.14–15 Epiphanius, *Scholion* 62; *Elenchos* 61; Tertullian, *Marc.* 4.40.1, 3. The Evangelion read "the twelve emissaries," rather than simply "the emissaries" in v. 14, in agreement with many Gk manuscripts (but not P75, D, 157, nor the OL, SSyr and CSyr); cf. Mark 14.17 and Matt 26.20, both of which have "the twelve." Verse 15 apparently read "and he said" rather than "and he said *to them*." Epiphanius gives the reading "this Pascha," while Tertullian has "the Pascha"; the latter reading is supported by the SSyr and CSyr, Gk mss 27 and 71, and a few patristic witnesses to Luke, the former by most other witnesses to Luke. The retention of repeated references to the meal as the (non-vegetarian) Jewish Pascha runs directly contrary to Marcionite values, and is another indication that the text has not been ideologically redacted.

Omission: Luke 22.16 was absent from the Evangelion, according to Epiphanius, *Scholion* 63. See the note on Luke 22:28–30 below.

Luke 22.17–18 is unattested for the Evangelion, and v. 18 is structurely related to the certainly absent v. 16. Adamantius (2.20) appears to confirm the absence of vv. 17–18 by referring to "the bread and the cup," in the order these two items would have in the episode of the last supper without vv. 17–18 (yet it is not certain that Adamantius is using the Evangelion here). A manuscript of the Bohairic Coptic version of Luke omits vv. 16–18, while the Peshitta Syriac (fourth/fifth century), two SCopt manuscripts, and Greek lectionary 32 lack vv. 17–18. Thus, the Evangelion and these miscellaneous textual associates diverge from the textual tradition found in Gk ms D and several OL manuscripts, which have vv. 16–19a but lack vv. 19b–20, and so have the sequence cup-bread found in Did 9.2–3 and 1 Cor 10.16 (Ehrman, *Orthodox Corruption of Scripture*, 197–209, argues for this as the original reading of Luke).

22.19–20 Epiphanius, *Elenchos* 61; Tertullian, *Marc.* 4.40.3 (cf. 3.19.4); Adam 2.20. The expression "when he had given thanks" is not directly attested by Tertullian or Epiphanius, but it is in Adamantius, whose text appears to conflate this passage with 9.16 ("looking up to the sky, the master gave thanks"); cf. 1 Cor 11.24. The inclusion of "given on your behalf" in the text of the Evangelion is based on Tertullian's reference to Jesus' body being *tradere pro nobis* (Tsutsui, "Das Evangelium

Marcions," 123). It is lacking in Gk ms D and most OL manuscripts. The instruction in v. 19b, "Do this as my memorial," is not mentioned in Tertullian's report, and is lacking in Gk ms D and most OL manuscripts; this wording parallels 1 Cor 11.24. The wording "after they had dined" (cf. 1 Cor 11.25) in v. 20 is apparently attested by Epiphanius; but he seems to read this phrase at the beginning of v. 19, before both the bread and the wine, and his anti-Marcionite argument depends on such a position. The Evangelion apparently read simply "contract" rather than "*new* contract," a reading found also in one manuscript of the Peshitta Syriac; the same textual alternatives are found in the witnesses to the parallel passage in Mark 14.24 and Matt 26.28, where the reading without "new" is generally considered more original (see Williams, "Reconsidering Marcion's Gospel," 482–83); for "new contract," cf. 1 Cor 11.25.

Luke 22.21 is unattested. In fact, our sources fail to attest any explicit reference to the theme of Jesus' betrayer being at the table with him at the Pascha, including both this verse and v. 23, even though it would seem to be implicit in the reference to the "twelve" emissaries in v. 14.

22.22 Tertullian, *Marc.* 4.41.1. The first part of the verse ("The Human Being is going as has been ordained") is not directly attested; Tsutsui ("Das Evangelium Marcions," 123–24) proposes its absence, based on its suitablility to Tertullian's and Epiphanius' arguments if it had been present ("ordained" by Jewish prophecy). But it is perhaps too broad and vague of a statement to have caught their attention for polemical use. The Evangelion read "to that one through whom he is handed over," rather than "to the/that man by whom" (the reading found in the majority of witnesses to Luke, as well as in Mark 14.21); either "the one" or "that one" is attested in various witnesses to Luke. The Evangelion shares the explicit reference to "the Human Being" with several Greek manuscripts, one OL manuscript, and Irenaeus, as well as with the parallel in Mark 14.21; other witnesses to Luke have simply the implied "he" of the verb, referring back to the prior mention of the Human Being in the first half of the verse (whose presence is uncertain for the Evangelion).

Luke 22.23 is unattested; see the note on 22.21 above.

Luke 22.24–27 is unattested for the Evangelion by our best sources. It may be alluded to by Celsus, as quoted in Origen, *Cels.* 7.18, who lists among Jesus' "laws" that "a man cannot come forward to the Father if he . . . loves power." There is a certain logic in the text going straight from v. 22 to v. 33, and none of our other sources mentions any material in between. But at least vv. 24–27 offer nothing useful for the polemical arguments of Tertullian and Epiphanius, and so may have been passed over for that reason.

Luke 22.28–30 is unattested for the Evangelion, and certainly would have been mentioned by Tertullian or Epiphanius if they had found it in the text, with its reference to feasting in the kingdom of God, its identification between Jesus' pupils and the twelve tribes of Israel (cf. Matt 19.28), and its theme of judgment. Epiphanius, *Elenchos* 63, does quote

v. 30, but in a way that does not make clear whether it was present or not in the Evangelion: "Marcion excised this [22.16] and tampered with it to avoid putting food or drink in the Kingdom of God, if you please. The oaf was unaware that spiritual, heavenly things are capable of corresponding with things on earth, and can be partaken of in ways we do not know. For the Savior testifies in turn, 'You shall sit at my table, eating and drinking in the kingdom of the celestial spheres' (*kathēsesthe epi tēs trapezēs mou, esthiontes kai pinontes en tēi basileiai tōn ouranōn*)." Epiphanius quotes the saying twice in other contexts (66.38.3 and 77.37.6), both times with the wording "the table of my father" rather than "my table."

Luke 22.31–32 is unattested. Some elements of its content, including the reversion to "Simon" and the prediction of his role as caretaker of the others are reminiscent of John 21.15–17.

22.33–34 Tertullian, *Marc.* 4.41.2. Tertullian merely refers to "when Peter has made a rash utterance, and he turns him rather in the direction of denial." The Evangelion, therefore, along with the OL, had "Peter," whereas other witnesses to Luke have "he," relying on the reference to Simon in v. 31 that was probably absent from the Evangelion. The direct address "master" is not expressly mentioned by Tertullian, and is lacking in some Greek manuscripts. Cf. Mark 14.29–30; Matt 26.33–34; John 13.36–38.

Omission: Luke 22.35–37 was absent from the Evangelion, according to Epiphanius, *Scholion* 64.

Luke 22.38–40 is unattested. As a continuation of the certainly absent vv. 35–37, v. 38 probably was also absent, particularly since armed disciples would have been useful to cite against Marcion's pacifism. The Evangelion apparently lacked any of the "upper room" material, and so the setting of the Pascha meal remains unclear. A transition from an indoor meal to the outdoor location of Jesus' prayer and arrest seems likely on analogy to the account in the canonical gospels, but whether it took the same form as v. 39 remains uncertain. Could the "Fayum Fragment," in Finegan, *Hidden Records of the Life of Jesus*, 210–12, preserve this portion of the Evangelion? It reads:

> [As] he led them out, he said: "[All you in this] night will be offend[ed, as] it is written: I will smite the [shepherd, and the] sheep will be scattered." [When] Peter [said]: "Even if all, [not I," Jesus said]: "Before the cock crows twice, [three times will you] de[ny me today."]

This wording sufficiently matches Tertullian's allusion to the exchange between Peter and Jesus; and the fact that the passage cites Jewish scripture cannot be taken as an objection, since Jesus does this several times in the Evangelion. However, it may be questioned whether Tertullian would have passed over the opportunity to note such a citation.

22.41 Epiphanius, *Scholion* 65; P^{69}. The editors of P^{69} have proposed the last two words of v. 40 to fill the missing beginning of the first preserved line of the manuscript, but this conjecture is based on the assumption that the manuscript has the standard text of Luke, and it could just as well have contained the last words of v. 34.

Luke 22.42–44 is unattested for the Evangelion and appears to have been absent from P⁶⁹. Verses 22.43–44 would have been useful for Epiphanius or Tertullian in making a point of Jesus' physicality. They are lacking in many Greek manuscripts, including P⁷⁵, along with the SSyr, the SCopt, OL ms f, and were stricken out by the first corrector of the Gk ms ℵ. But no other witness to Luke lacks v. 42 except P⁶⁹, which may be crucial in identifying it as a fragment of the Evangelion.

22.45–46 P⁶⁹ (≠Harnack, Tsutsui). The reading of this manuscript compresses the wording relative to other witnesses to Luke.

22.47–48 Epiphanius, *Scholion* 66; Tertullian, *Marc.* 4.41.2; P⁶⁹. In v. 47, P⁶⁹ joins the OL, SSyr and CSyr in reading "approaching, he kissed Jesus" (harmonized to the other Synoptics in stating that Judas actually kissed Jesus) rather than "he approached (Jesus) to kiss him" (i.e., with the intent, but not expressly carried out); but the latter is the reading attested for the Evangelion by Epiphanius, who actually gives an anomalous reading in these verses: "And Judas approached to kiss him and said . . ." (*Kai ēggise kataphilēsai auton Ioudas kai eipen*). The placement of 'Judas' at the end of the first clause might be taken as a copying mistake by Epiphanius himself or in the transmission of the *Panarion*, since many witnesses to Luke read *auton Iēsous de eipen*. On the other hand, Epiphanius' text brings to mind Matt 26.49, where Judas says to Jesus "Greetings, rabbi," and Mark 14.45, where he says merely "rabbi." The fact that the verb used for "kiss" has also been harmonized to Matthew and Mark may suggest that the Evangelion did indeed have a statement of greeting from Judas to Jesus here, as in the other Synoptics but unlike other witnesses to Luke. For v. 48, Tertullian reports Jesus' remark about being betrayed with a kiss.

Omission: Luke 22.49–51, the attempted violent defense of Jesus by his pupils, was absent from the Evangelion, according to Epiphanius, *Scholion* 67. The direct evidence of P⁶⁹ resumes only with v. 58, but there is insufficient space on the reconstructed page size to have included all of the material found in Luke in 22.49–57. This episode is otherwise attested in various forms in the other three canonical gospels, with John 18.10 alone sharing the Lukan detail that it was the person's right ear that was cut off, and John 18.11 alone Jesus' express order that his pupils desist.

Luke 22.52–54a is unattested; v. 54 shows close verbal affinities with the parallel account in John 18.12, and strikingly "Johannine" terminology has been noted as well for v. 53 (cf. John 5.27; 13.1; see Matson, *In Dialogue with Another Gospel?* 127; Fitzmyer, *The Gospel according to Luke*, 1452).

22.54b–61 P⁶⁹ (≠Harnack, Tsutsui). Verses 22.54b and 22.56–57 are not directly attested. That some of the content of these verses was present is demonstrated by the continuation of the story where the evidence of P⁶⁹ resumes in v. 58. This reconstruction depends, of course, on the proposed identification of P⁶⁹ as a fragment of the Evangelion. Where our other sources resume their report of the Evangelion, in v. 63, Epiphanius gives the reading, "Then the men who were holding *him*" (the same wording is found in a number of witnesses to Luke); this pronoun refers all the way back to the last mention of Jesus in v. 54a at the closest (in v. 48 for the last mention of him attested by our sources for the Evangelion), as if no intervening episode involving Peter occurred. Nevertheless, Harnack argues that vv. 54ff. must have been present in the Evangelion to fulfill Jesus' prediction in vv. 33–34. In v. 58, P^{69} reads "But he said," rather than "But Peter said" (together with Gk ms D, several OL manuscripts, and the SSyr). In v. 61, P^{69} reads "and turning, Peter looked at him/it," while most manuscripts of Luke read: "And turning, the Master looked at Peter." Both readings can be explained by an ambiguous original: "And turning, he looked at him/it." Gk ms 544 omits this clause altogether. P^{69} breaks off in the middle of v. 61.

Luke 22.62 is unattested; it is lacking in the majority of OL manuscripts, and is one of Westcott and Hort's "Western non-interpolations."

22.63–64 Epiphanius, *Scholion* 68. The Evangelion apparently read "holding *him*" rather than "holding Jesus," a reading widely shared among early witnesses to Luke (and one that would seem to follow directly on v. 54a, since it refers to Jesus, not Peter—hence the clarification made in a number of later manuscripts, replacing "him" with "Jesus"). This passage seems to have been considerably shorter in the Evangelion (unless Epiphanius abbreviated), lacking any reference to covering Jesus (also lacking in OL ms b), or his face as the target of their blows (also lacking in Gk mss 348 and 2542 and several OL manuscripts), and not including the clause "questioning him" (also lacking in Gk mss 348 and D, OL mss d and q, and the SSyr and CSyr). These textual variants show harmonization to Matt 26.67–68, as does the inclusion of the question "Who is the one that hit you?" The latter is one of the few "minor agreements" between Luke and Matthew against Mark found in the Evangelion.

Luke 22.65 is unattested.

22.66–67 Tertullian, *Marc.* 4.41.2–3. Tertullian reads simply "they"; but he is probably paraphrasing the fuller text found in Luke, since the passage requires some specified shift from the "captains" and "the men who were holding him" to the elders, etc., who question him. For the specific request, "If you are the Christos, tell us," and Jesus' dismissal of giving an answer due to their mistrust, cf. John 10.24–25.

Luke 22.68 is unattested for the Evangelion, and is also absent from OL ms e.

22.69–70 Tertullian, *Marc.* 4.41.4–5. Tertullian may allude to a gesture made by Jesus before speaking of the Human Being, stretching forth his hand (*manum porrigens*), but it could just be a figure of speech by which Tertullian characterizes Jesus' effort to reach out to his opponents. In v. 70, the Evangelion has Jesus respond "You are . . . saying it," a reading found also in OL ms i, rather than "You are saying *that I am he*" as found in other witnesses to Luke.

Luke 22.71 is not directly quoted in our sources, but it may be intended as the referent of Tertullian's remark, "he likewise answers in the affirmative . . . and so clearly was this his meaning that they continued in the impression which his statement indicated."

23.1–3 Tertullian, *Marc.* 4.42.1; Epiphanius, *Scholion* 69–70. In v. 1, the Evangelion seems to have had the simpler text found also in Gk ms D and OL ms d: "And arising, they led him to Pilate," rather than "And arising, the entire multitude led him to Pilate"; v. 2 had "subverting *the* nation" rather than "subverting *our* nation," in agreement with about half of the Greek manuscripts of Luke. Epiphanius accuses Marcion of adding "and destroying the Law and the Prophets" in v. 2, but the same reading is found in the majority of OL manuscripts, and was even carried over into the Vulgate, and it passes without comment in Tertullian; cf. Acts of Pilate 2. The Evangelion appears to have lacked "to Caesar" as the object of "pay taxes"; it also is missing in one Greek lectionary and one OL manuscript. The additional charge of "turning away women and children" is found here in v. 2 only in the Evangelion, but appears in the second round of charges in v. 5 in OL mss c and e. In v. 3, the Evangelion read "the Christ" (*ho christos*), rather than Luke's "the king of the Jews" (the latter is found in Mark 15.2).

Luke 23.4–5 is not directly attested for the Evangelion. Tsutsui ("Das Evangelium Marcions," 125) makes the case that the Tertullian, *Marc.* 4.42.2, reference to *summi sacerdotes* alludes to v. 4. The content of v. 5 would be necessary to introduce the question of Jesus' status as a Galilaean, which in Luke forms the justification for Pilate to send him on to Herod. For Pilate's threefold declaration that he finds no grounds for condemning Jesus (23.4, 14, and 22, none of which are directly attested for the Evangelion), cf. John 18.38; 19.4, 6.

23.6–9 Tertullian, *Marc.* 4.42.2–3.

Luke 23.10–12 is unattested, and SSyr lacks these verses. But if the Evangelion lacked v. 11, the narrative would be left without any mention of Jesus being sent back to Pilate, and in fact neither Epiphanius nor Tertullian refer to Pilate again until v. 52 where he is asked to release Jesus' dead body for burial (in Tertullian, but not Epiphanius). The SSyr resumes abruptly in v. 13 with Jesus again in Pilate's custody. But it would be rash to propose that Herod manages the rest of the trial in the Evangelion narrative, due to the failure of any of our sources to comment on so dramatic of a divergence from the standard account.

Luke 23.13–17 is unattested. Verse 23.17 is missing from P[75] and many other Greek manuscripts. It turns up between vv. 19 and 20 in Gk ms D, OL ms d, and the SSyr and CSyr. This evidence together suggests a complex history of collating different versions of this passage. For Pilate's threefold expression of his desire to release Jesus (23.16, 20, 22, all unattested for the Evangelion); cf. John 19.12.

23.18 Tertullian, *Marc.* 4.42.4. Tertullian refers to the name Barrabas either from v. 18 or from a widely attested variant text of v. 25. The spelling of Barrabas differs from all variants preserved in the manuscripts and versions of Luke, and suggests an original name bar-Rab rather than bar-Abba (these two options being respective literary rationalizations of a name originally transmitted orally). The shout at Pilate to "take away" (*aire*) Jesus to execution is not directly attested for the Evangelion; cf. John 19.15.

Luke 23.19–24 is unattested. Some of this material probably was present, since it is implied in "the one . . . whom they were demanding" in v. 25. For the chanted repetition, "Stake! Stake!" in v. 21, cf. John 19.6.

23.25 Tertullian, *Marc.* 4.42.4.

Luke 23.26–31 is unattested. Taylor, "Narrative of the Crucifixion," 333–34, refers to v. 26 as a Markan insertion into what is otherwise a passage unique to Luke.

23.32–33 Epiphanius, *Scholion* 71; Tertullian, *Marc.* 4.42.4. Epiphanius omits the phrase "one on the right and one on the left" in v. 33; but he is probably abbreviating, since the phrase is implied in Tertullian's *circumfiguntur*.

23.34 Epiphanius, *Scholion* 71; Tertullian, *Marc.* 4.42.4; Ephrem, *Comm. Diat.* 21.3. The first part of this verse ("Father, forgive them, for they do not know what they are doing") is not directly attested for the Evangelion by our main sources. Harnack, *Marcion*, 236*, and Tsutsui, "Das Evangelium Marcions," 125, consider it to have been present, based upon Ephrem, *Comm. Diat.* 21.3, where he seems to be responding to Marcionite exegesis of the Passion. Wilson, *Marcion: A Study of a Second-Century Heretic*, 147, speculates that Marcion's text is actually the source of the famous passage, found in many Greek manuscript and versions of Luke, but absent from a number of others (including P^{75}, D, and the SSyr) and considered secondary by most modern textual critics (and possibly derived from a tradition of the last words of James, the brother of Jesus; see Hegesippus in Eusebius, *Hist. eccl.* 2.23.13–16). Epiphanius appears intent in his review of this section of the narrative primarily on culling examples of fulfillment of prophecy, so this sentence would not interest him. Tertullian similarly might pass over it because he wishes to emphasize the associations of Jesus and God with judgment against Marcion's conception of a pacifistic deity. Luke 23.34a is attested as early as Irenaeus, *Haer.* 3.18.5, and apparently also was in the Diatessaron. The Evangelion, while mentioning the division of Jesus' clothes, lacked a reference to "casting lots" for them, as Tertullian, *Marc.* 4.42.4 expressly says in one of the only instances where he identifies an omission in the Evangelion's text in comparison to Luke. In past scholarship on the subject, Tertullian's testimony has been treated as contradictory to that of Epiphanius. But in fact, the latter only refers to the distribution of the garments, and says nothing about casting of lots for them. So there is no contradiction between these two witnesses in this passage (≠Harnack, *Marcion*, 236*, and many who have followed him). Cf. GPet 4.12.

Luke 23.35–42 is unattested. Tsutsui ("Das Evangelium Marcions," 125) regards this whole passage as absent from the Evangelion. The idea that a sizable omission occurred here in the Evangelion is based upon Epiphanius, *Scholion* 71, which goes directly from v. 34b to v. 44b. While Epiphanius can pass over large chunks of text *between* his *scholia*, it is quite rare for him to jump over so much text *within* a single notation. Yet the evidence of Tertullian shows v. 44a at least to have been present, despite Epiphanius passing over it. In fact, the thrust of Tertullian's criticism of the omission of the short clause about casting lots from v. 34 is that Marcion should have cut out "the whole of what follows" (*totus . . . exitus*) in order to avoid fulfillment of Psalm 22, whose details include gathering of opponents, verbal abuse, and calling for God to deliver him if his claims be valid. So it is quite probable that the Evangelion had much of this content, and it is likely that *Scholion* 71 is merely a string of elements of the narrative on which Epiphanius wished to comment, rather than a verbatim copying of the text. Note the absence of v. 35a and v. 37 in a manuscript of the Bohairic Coptic version. For v. 38, cf. GPet 4.11. For the detail that the inscription posted on the stake was in "Hebrew, Greek, and Roman," cf. John 19.20. For vv. 39–41, cf. GPet 4.13.

Omission: Luke 23.43 was absent from the Evangelion, according to Epiphanius, *Scholion* 72.

23.44–45 Tertullian, *Marc.* 4.42.5–6; Epiphanius, *Scholion* 71 (vv.44b–45); Ephrem, *Comm. Diat.* 21.3; Eznik, *De Deo* 358. Ephrem engages with imagined Marcionite opponents over the significance of the eclipse and darkness, while Eznik reports Marcionite exegesis of the darkness, the eclipse, and the torn sanctuary curtain (but also apparently the tearing of the high priest's robe, which is not in Luke; on the possibility that the Marcionite exegesis known to Eznik was based on the Diatessaron rather than the Evangelion, see Casey, "The Armenian Marcionites and the Diatessaron"). Gk ms D places the tearing of the temple curtain after Jesus dies, as a harmonization to the accounts in Mark and Matthew; but Tertullian's discussion suggests the same order as found in other manuscripts of Luke, with the temple curtain tearing before Jesus dies. For this passage, cf. GPet 5.15, 20.

23.46 Epiphanius, *Scholion* 73; Tertullian, *Marc.* 4.42.6; Adam 5.12. Adamantius must be used with caution, since his testimony does not come from the anti-Marcionite section of his work, and he may be quoting the Diatessaron. The Greek manuscripts of Adamantius have "and Jesus, crying with a loud voice, said, 'Father, I will entrust my spirit into your hands.' And he expired." The future tense conforms to the wording of Ps 31.6 in the LXX and is found in many other witnesses to Luke. Adamantius' final clause lacks "when he had said this," as in the SSyr and CSyr, and OL ms a, but Tertullian includes the clause. Epiphanius reads: "And calling out in a loud voice, he expired," with no statement by Jesus and no transitional clause (cf. *Pan.* 69.49.5 and 74.6.8, where he does quote Jesus' statement from the cross from his own text of Luke). Cf. GPet 5.19; Protevangelium of James 23.3.

Luke 23.47–49 is unattested. Adam 5.12 appears to have a text that goes directly from v. 46 to v. 50, which seems supported by the resumption of reporting at v. 50 by both Epiphanius and Tertullian; but this may be a coincidence, since it is uncertain that the Evangelion is being used in this part of Adamantius. Cf. GPet 7.25; 8.28. Some of the details of this passage were included in the Diatessaron (Ephrem, *Comm. Diat*).

23.50–52 Epiphanius, *Scholion* 74; Tertullian, *Marc.* 4.42.7–8; Adam 5.12. Adamantius attests a text that lacked v. 50b–52a, reading "and look! a man named Joseph requested the body," while Epiphanius does not mention any of vv. 50b–52. But it is not certain that Adamantius is using the Evangelion in this section, and he may be abbreviating the passage. Tertullian alludes to 51a (not agreeing to the actions) and 52a (requested from Pilate). The Evangelion is likely to have lacked at least v. 51b (from Arimathea) and 51c (awaiting the kingdom), attested by none of our sources. The same two clauses are missing in OL ms c, while Gk ms 713 and the Peshitta Syriac lack 51b, and Gk ms 1215 and OL ms gat lack 51c. Verse 52 is lacking in Gk ms 0211. Gk mss 213 and 1143, as well as the CSyr, omit mention of Pilate as the recipient of Joseph's request, as the texts known to Adamantius and Epiphanius may have also. The Evangelion seems not to have specified "the body *of Jesus*," the latter detail perhaps added in the textual tradition of Luke as an editorial clarification.

23.53 Epiphanius, *Scholion* 74; Tertullian, *Marc.* 4.42.7–8; Adam 5.12. Epiphanius gives "a quarried [lit. hewn in stone] tomb," agreeing generally with most witnesses to Luke (and also its probable source, Mark 15.46), while Tertullian and Adamantius have "a new tomb," possibly a harmonization to Matthew. OL ms r1 gives a conflation of these two readings. None of our sources on the Evangelion attests the wording "in which no man had yet lain," found in most witnesses to Luke, which is a detail otherwise found only in John 19.41. For this passage, cf. GPet 6.24.

Luke 23.54 is unattested.

23.55–56 Epiphanius, *Scholion* 75. Only v. 56 is directly cited, but v. 55 is necessary to its meaning. Epiphanius omits "they prepared aromatics and perfumes," but probably he is abbreviating. He has "in accordance with *the Law*" in v. 56 rather than "with the commandment"; Gk ms D (and OL d) lacks the phrase in either form. It is possible that Epiphanius is generalizing from "commandment" to "Law" to make his point.

24.1 Tertullian, *Marc.* 4.43.1. Cf. GPet 12.50–51.

Luke 24.2 is unattested for the Evangelion, and it should be noted that a stone sealing the tomb has not been mentioned previously even in Luke. Several witnesses to Luke make various additions to the text to catch the reader up on the presence of the stone, as found in Matthew and Mark, but this verse appears to derive from a scribal harmonization to those other gospels. Cf. GPet 8.31–3; 9.37; 12.53–4.

24.3 Tertullian, *Marc.* 4.43.2. The Evangelion evidently read "the body," without the clarifying phrase "of the master Jesus" found in many manuscripts of Luke. It shares this certainly more original reading (agreeing with one of Westcott and Hort's "Western Non-interpolations") with Gk ms D and the majority of OL manuscripts. Tyson, *Marcion and Luke-Acts*, 102, points out that the combined expression *kyrios Iēsous* is otherwise unknown in Luke, but used repeatedly in Acts (1.21; 4.33; 8.16; 9.17; 11.20; 15.11; 16.31; 19.5; 19.13; 19.17; 20.21; 20.24; 20.35; 21.13; and with the additional element *christos* in 11.17; 15.26; 28.31). Several Greek manuscripts, the Diatessaron, the SSyr and CSyr, and a manuscript of the Bohairic Coptic attest an earlier expansion, adding only "of Jesus" without "the master."

24.4–7 Epiphanius, *Scholion* 76; *Elenchos* 76; Tertullian, *Marc.* 4.43.2, 5. Harnack suggests that Tertullian's reference to "angels" in v. 4 (cf. John 20.12: "two angels in white") is probably an interpretive gloss on his part, and that the Evangelion read, with Luke, "men"; Epiphanius' discussion of whether or not they were angels presupposes ambiguity in the original, as the form of his quotation attests (*hoi en estheti lampra*). Luke 24.23, in mentioning this encounter, does refer to "angels," but this verse was almost certainly absent from the Evangelion. The "minor agreement" between Matthew and Luke in the characterization of their shining cloaks (*astrapē/astraptousē*) was not present in the Evangelion (*lampra* is used instead). In v. 6 the Evangelion apparently read "he was awoken" (Epiphanius) in agreement with Mark, rather than "he is not here, but was awoken" in agreement with Matthew, found in many manuscripts and witnesses to Luke (including *Pan.* 56.2.8). Gk ms D and the majority of OL manuscripts lack both clauses; it is a "Western non-interpolation" often regarded as a secondary harmonization to Matthew (but see Epiphanius: "he is risen; he is not here"). The rest of the verse is given in very different forms by Epiphanius and Tertullian. The former has "remember how he spoke while he was still with you." The latter has "remember what he said to you in Galilee." In v. 7, Epiphanius may be paraphrasing, reading "it is necessary for the Human Being to suffer and be handed over"; Tertullian supplies the more complete text known from Luke. Epiphanius and Tertullian agree on the absence of "into the hands of wrongdoing men," also lacking in OL ms a; some other manuscripts omit "men," others omit "wrongdoing." Epiphanius also omits "and be staked," in agreement with OL ms a, but Tertullian has it.

Luke 24.8 is unattested, and lacking in a couple of Greek manuscripts of Luke.

24.9, 11 Tertullian, *Marc.* 4.43.2–3, 5. Although Gk ms D, the OL and Armenian versions omit "from the tomb," the Evangelion apparently had it, unless Tertullian is supplying it in paraphrase. Tertullian says that the women reported to "the pupils." Most witnesses to Luke have "the eleven and to all the rest"; but OL ms e reads "the eleven pupils and all the rest," while the SSyr and CSyr read "the eleven and the rest of the pupils." There is no explicit citation from the Evangelion of the initial part of v. 11 as found in canonical Luke ("their/these statements appeared as nonsense to them and . . .").

Luke 24.10 is not directly attested for the Evangelion.

Luke 24.12 is unattested, generally thought to be secondary in Luke. It is one of Westcott and Hort's "Western non-interpolations," missing from Gk ms D and most OL manuscripts. It is paralleled by John 20.3–8, with some striking verbal similarities (*parakupsas, othonia, blepei* in historical present).

24.13 Tertullian, *Marc.* 4.43.3 (≠Harnack). Tertullian says only that two of the pupils were traveling. The same scene is implied in Epiphanius, *Scholion* 77, as well (see note on 24.15–16 below). For an early second century witness to this scene, see Mark 16.12, a later addition to that gospel.

Luke 24.14 is unattested.

24.15–16 Epiphanius, *Scholion* 77; Tertullian, *Marc.* 4.43.3 (≠Harnack). Tertullian says, "The Master had joined himself with them, while it did not appear that it was he himself." Epiphanius refers broadly to Jesus meeting the two men.

24.17–19a Epiphanius, *Scholion* 77; Tertullian, *Marc.* 4.43.3 (=Harnack, Tsutsui v. 18 only). Tertullian says, "He even pretended not to be aware of the things that had happened." Epiphanius refers to "Kleopas and the other."

Luke 24.19b–20 is unattested.

24.21a Tertullian, *Marc.* 4.43.3. The Evangelion apparently read "thinking" or "supposing" (Tertullian has *putabamus*), in agreement with some witnesses to the Diatessaron, instead of "hoping" found in other witnesses to Luke. Tertullian has "the ransomer of Israel" (*redemptorem Israelis*), which is quite a departure from the verbal expression found in Luke: "the one who was going to liberate Israel."

Luke 24.21b–24 is unattested. It contains a somewhat redundant review of the immediately preceding events, including, in v. 24, an allusion to Peter's visit to the empty tomb in Luke 24.12, which as noted above is unattested for the Evangelion and absent from many manuscripts of Luke (note also the plural "pupils" said to have gone to the tomb, in line with John 20.3ff., rather than Peter alone as in Luke 24.12). Similarly problematic, it refers to "angels" at the tomb rather than "men." Overall, this passage appears to be a summary of John 20.1–10 rather than of the Lukan narrative. The entire passage goes unmentioned in Ephrem, *Comm. Diat.*

24.25 Epiphanius, *Scholion* 77; Tertullian, *Marc.* 4.43.4; Adam 5.12. Tertullian and Adamantius have "slow of heart," whereas Epiphanius reads simply "slow." Epiphanius may be abbreviating his quote. "All the things that *he* spoke" according to Tertullian, but "that *I* spoke" according to Epiphanius and Adamantius—in either case differing from Luke's "that the prophets said." Tertullian's text is more logical in context, while the other reading anticipates Jesus' self-revelation. All agree on the final words, "to you," not found in witnesses to Luke. Adamantius' agreement here with distinctive readings attested for the Evangelion complicates the assumption that he would be using his own text of Luke in this part of the dialogue (where he is not debating a Marcionite).

24.26 Epiphanius, *Scholion* 77; Adam 5.12. Adamantius has "that it was necessary for the Christos to suffer these things," agreeing with Gk ms D, OL ms d, the Diatessaron, and several patristic witnesses to Luke, whereas Epiphanius gives "Was it not necessary for him to suffer these things?" along with most witnesses to Luke.

Luke 24.27–29 is unattested. Verse 27 would surely have been commented upon by Tertullian or Epiphanius if they found it in Marcion's text. It is somewhat surprising that Epiphanius does not note the textual variance. The same verse is likewise lacking in Gk ms 1313 (possibly due to haplography), and goes unmentioned in Ephrem, *Comm. Diat.* Some of the content of vv. 28–29 was probably present, since it is needed to advance the narrative to a meal setting.

24.30–31 Epiphanius, *Scholion* 77. Epiphanius does not quote the last clause of v. 31, which completes the encounter with the two on the road, and does not resume with the Evangelion's text until 24.38. Nor do our other sources for the Evangelion report anything until 24.37b. Theoretically, then, the Evangelion could have read directly from v. 31 to 37b, and the further dialogue following v. 37 would in that case be part of the encounter with the two on the road, rather than a second encounter with "the eleven" as found in Luke. Nonetheless, we would expect Epiphanius to comment on such a radical departure from the narrative familiar to him from Luke.

Luke 24.32 is unattested for the Evangelion. It is coordinated to v. 27, also unattested for the Evangelion, and would certainly have been cited by our sources if it appeared. It is not mentioned in Ephrem, *Comm. Diat.*

Luke 24.33–36 is unattested. Some of the material in vv. 33–36 must have been present for the narrative to continue, unless the rest of the narrative takes place in the presence of only the two pupils on the road to Emmaus. This possibility cannot be altogether ruled out, since Tertullian, Epiphanius, and Adamantius all quote the Emmaus material, go on to the rest of Jesus' resurrection appearance with no notation of a change of scene or audience, and do not include anything that demands a new setting. But assuming that the Evangelion did not depart so radically from the text known to us in Luke, an early second-century witness to this scene change is Mark 16.13, a later addition to that gospel. Verse 34 was almost certainly absent from the Evangelion, as were the other two references to Peter visiting the empty tomb found in Luke (note the use of the name "Simon" in this material; the Evangelion consistently refers to "Peter" after the first introduction of the figure as Simon Peter). Jesus saying, "May you have peace" in v. 35 is one of Westcott and Hort's "Western non-interpolations," missing from Gk ms D and the OL; it is paralleled in the resurrection account of John 20.19, which also shares the image of Jesus suddenly appearing, "standing in their midst."

24.37 Tertullian, *Marc.* 4.43.6; Adam 5.12. The Evangelion read "phantom" or "apparition" (Gk *phantasma*) in agreement with Gk ms D and OL ms d, instead of "spirit" found in most manuscripts of Luke.

24.38–39 Epiphanius, *Scholion* 78; Tertullian, *Marc.* 4.43.6–8; Adam 5.12. Adamantius must be used with caution because he may be quoting the Diatessaron. Epiphanius omits "and why are thoughts/doubts arising in your hearts" in v. 38, but Tertullian and Adamantius both attest it — the first with the wording "thoughts" (*cogitationes* > *logismoi*) found in a few Greek manuscripts of Luke, the second with "doubts" (*dialogismoi*) found in the majority of witnesses to Luke. In v. 39, Epiphanius omits the clause "that it is I" (as do a few Greek manuscripts), but Tertullian and Adamantius both attest it. All three witnesses agree that the Evangelion lacked a clause found in Luke, "feel me and see"; the latter seems to be related to a tradition recorded in Ignatius to the Smyrneans 3.2 ("Take hold, handle me, and see that I am not a bodiless daemon"). Tertullian and Epiphanius agree on the reading "does not have bones," found also in Athanasius, whereas Adamantius has "flesh and bones" in agreement with other witnesses to Luke (including Epiphanius, *Pan.* 64.64.7, when he quotes his own text of Luke). Interestingly, Tertullian (*Carn. Chr.* 5) and Ephrem (*Against Bardaisan* 147 [XIV]) both quote Jesus' statement without "flesh and" in contexts in which we would not be expecting them to be quoting from the Evangelion; in Ephrem's case, in a text not in any way directed against the Marcionites. On the possibility that *daimonion asōmaton* is the original wording, more consistent with the terminology of Luke (and the Evangelion), later replaced with *pneuma*, see Petersen, "What Text Can New Testament Textual Criticism Ultimately Reach?" 144–5. Epiphanius, *Pan.* 64.64.7, shows several other differences in v. 39 between the Evangelion's text (*kathōs eme theōreite echontai*) and his text of Luke (*hōs orate me echontai*); the latter quote also omits "my hands and my feet" and the object of "look."

Luke 24.40 is unattested, and one of Westcott and Hort's "Western non-interpolations," missing in Gk ms D, the OL, SSyr, and CSyr, and not mentioned in Ephrem, *Comm. Diat.*; cf. John 20.19.

24.41–44a Tertullian, *Marc.* 4.43.8; Eznik, *De Deo* 407. The clarification "distrusting *from joy and in amazement*" is unattested for the Evangelion, and evidently is a gloss meant to explain "distrusting" in a positive way. The SSyr and CSyr preserve what may be the original wording, "from their fear" in addition to the phrasing found in other witnesses to Luke. Eznik reports Marcionites basing their distinctive views on the significance of eating fish upon the fact that Jesus, "after his resurrection ate the fish which he found among the fishermen." This certainly refers to our passage here, but the reference to finding the fish "among the fishermen" is odd, given that in Luke this encounter takes place in Jerusalem. But in John 21.12–12, this sharing of a meal of fish after the resurrection takes place after the pupils have returned to their life as fishermen in Galilee. This story seems to have been appended to John as a secondary addition, and does not fit well with the previous resurrection appearance narrative in John 20, set in Jerusalem like that in Luke. The story in John 21 has some oral or literary relation to the story of the miraculous catch of fish in Luke 5, likewise set in Galilee, but early in Jesus' career (and so not a resurrection story in Luke or the Evangelion). Interestingly, the terse account of a resurrection appearance to the pupils in Matthew is also set in Galilee, and the same is implied in Mark 16.7. Exactly where the resurrection appearance to the pupils occurred in the Evangelion, then, remains uncertain. The inclusion of "and taking what was left he gave it to them" (found in some witnesses to Luke in v. 43) in the Evangelion, while not expressly attested, is suggested by the same notation of Eznik regarding the significance Marcionites attribute to eating fish.

Luke 24.44b–46 is unattested, and likely to have been cited by Tertullian or Epiphanius if present. It goes unmentioned in Ephrem, *Comm. Diat.*

24.47 Tertullian, *Marc.* 4.43.9. Tertullian's wording suggests that the Evangelion gave this as direct speech (as it is in Gk ms 33 and SSyr), and so a continuation of the direct speech introduced at v. 44a. Luke has an additional phrase at the end of v. 47, "starting out from Jerusalem," unattested for the Evangelion and absent from the Diatessaron. For possible evidence regarding how the Evangelion ended, see the Excursus.

Excursus: The Ending of the Evangelion

The ending of Marcion's text is not explicitly cited by Tertullian or Epiphanius, and must be reconstructed by conjecture; for an attempt to do this on the basis of Marcion's ideology, see Vinzent, "Der Schluß des Lukasevangeliums bei Marcion." Harnack thinks that nothing followed verse 24.47 (cf. the ending of Matthew), and Vinzent supports this conclusion with arguments based on Marcion's theological outlook. But the question needs to be reexamined without the assumption that Marcion made ideological edits of the text before him.

There is considerable textual disruption in the manuscripts for the ending of canonical Luke. Ephrem Syrus, in his commentary on the Diatessaron, cites nothing found in canonical Luke after 24.49; this verse is unattested for the Evangelion, and is suspect as an addition at the time the gospel was joined to Acts as a two-volume work. Luke 24:50–51a ("Now he led them towards Bethany, and when he had lifted his hands, he blessed them. And it happened that, while he was blessing them, he parted from them.") would serve the purpose of an ending for the Evangelion if we could be sure that the previous events took place in Jerusalem in our text. The additional clause in canonical Luke 24:51b ("and began to be borne up to heaven") is missing in Gk mss ℵ and D, as well as in the OL and SSyr (it is one of Westcott and Hort's "Western non-interpolations"). "Worshipping him" is absent from v. 52 in Gk ms D and OL a, b, d, e, ff2, l, as well as the SSyr (another "Western non-interpolation").

Acts may retain some traces of the ending of Luke in an earlier edition, before Acts was added as a second volume. Such literary expansions typically rework the ending of the original to accommodate the continuation of the second volume. Ehrman, *Orthodox Corruption of Scripture,* 227–32, points out major discrepancies between the end of Luke and Acts 1. This sort of discordance suggests that one or the other of these passages represents an episode not completely adapted to Luke's two-volume narrative. If the last verses of Luke are in various ways ill-fitted to the Evangelion, Acts 1.8b–11 could be a remnant of the original ending of the gospel, since it follows, in Acts 1.8b, a doublet with Luke 24.48: "And you will be witnesses." One might compare the wording of Acts 1.8b, "to the most distant parts of the earth," to the words of Tertullian, *Marc.* 4.43.9: "when sending forth his emissaries to preach to all the nations, he fulfilled the psalm by his instruction that their sound must go out into all the world and their words unto the ends of the earth" (cf. Ps 19.4, which is quoted in Rom 10.18). It is noteworthy that Justin Martyr, who clearly knows Lukan material in some form, but whose knowledge of Acts is not otherwise obvious, gives a set of narrative allusions in *1 Apol* 50.12 that combines Luke 23.49a, 24.24, 24.44–45, and Acts 1.8.

Another possible source on the ending of the Evangelion is the Longer Ending of Mark, a second-century text that clearly relies on either the Evangelion or Luke for some of its content. One notes the following parallels:

Verse	**Probable Source**	**Content**
Mark 16.10–11	Luke 24.9, 11	The women report to the pupils, who do not believe.
Mark 16.11	Luke 24.5b, 23	Jesus is characterized as "alive."
Mark 16.12–13	Luke 24.13–33, 35	Jesus appears to two "of them," who likewise report "to the rest."
Mark 16.14	Luke 24.33, 36, 38, 41–43	Jesus appears to "the eleven" while at a meal, reproaching their lack of faith.

Other elements of the Longer Ending also depend on the Evangelion or Luke (cf. Mark 16.9 to Luke 8.2; Mark 16.18 to Luke 10.19). From Mark 16.15a//Luke 24.44a ("and he said to them . . ."). The Longer Ending of Mark diverges from the text of Luke, and up until this point it has not repeated anything certainly absent from the Evangelion. Does it possibly retain anything else from the ending of the Evangelion? Mark 16.15b reads, "Go into all the world and preach (*kēruxate*) the *evangelion* to all of creation," which parallels Luke 24.47 on the verb and the use of "all" — that is, on precisely those points that we know the Evangelion also overlapped with Luke 24.47 from the testimony of Tertullian, *Marc.* 4.43.9 ("sending forth his emissaries to preach to all the nations"; cf. Matt 28.19: "Go and make disciples of all the nations") as well as an additional correlation to Tertullian's allusion to Ps 19.4 ("go into all the world").

I propose for future consideration, therefore, the possibility that the Evangelion's text here included the direct commission (already supposed from Tertullian's allusion to direct rather than reported speech) as found in Mark 16.15b, but that the content of commanded preaching was not Luke's "repentance and forgiveness," but Mark 16.15b's "good news" (*euangelion*). This proposal correlates well with Marcion's identification of this text as the "Evangelion." Furthermore, Tertullian may allude to this very wording when, concluding his commentary a few lines after his last recognized allusion to a reading of Marcion's text, he says, "Even in your Evangelion Christ Jesus is mine" (*Christus enim Iesus in euangelio tuo meus est*). Compare also the apparent original conclusion of Pseudo-Ephrem A's exposition of the analogies of the Evangelion, at 76 (Codex B): "In like manner also in the time when our Lord sent the twelve apostles in order *to preach the gospel (euangelion) to every man*." The passage goes on to give an apparent quote of Evangelion/Luke 10.7, which is from the sending out of the seventy, not the twelve (9.1ff.); but one notes the particular phrasing I have highlighted, not found in either earlier commission, but parallel to that used by what I have identified as other possible sources for the end of the Evangelion. We can likewise compare the remark of Eutropius in Adam 2.13: "what is read in the Gospel (*euangelion*), that Christ sent out the Twelve to preach the gospel (*euangelion*)."

I have not wished to push speculation further in the reconstruction here. But it is worth noting a couple further observations. The Longer Ending of Mark goes on to material paralleling Luke 10.19, which in the latter setting is likewise connected to a commissioning of missionaries; could this parallelism have been employed at the end of the Evangelion? One might compare *Sophia of Jesus Christ* 119.4–15:

> "I have given you authority over all things as children of light, that you may tread upon their power with [your] feet." These are the things [the] blessed savior [said, and he disappeared from] that day on. [And his disciples] began to preach [the] *euangelion* of God.

We could also note verbal parallels between Mark 16.19 and Acts 1.9–11. In both cases, we have the conclusion of Jesus' resurrection speech, followed by an ascent. This includes a very closely matching reference to Jesus being taken up to the celestial spheres (Mark: *Iēsous . . . anelēmphthē eis ton ouranon*; Acts: *Iēsous . . . analēmphtheis . . . eis ton ouranon*). As an ending, one could scarcely imagine something more fitting, and it corresponds with what we know was Marcion's interpretation of the gospel narrative: that Jesus "came down" from the sky at the beginning and "returned" to the sky at the end. A reference to Jesus being borne up to the sky is found in many manuscripts at Luke 24.51. This or any other proposal for the ending of the Evangelion remains uncertain at this stage of research, awaiting further direct testimony.

Chapter 4

The Apostolikon

The Apostolikon

Introduction

Marcion placed greater importance on the authority of Paul than did any other Christian leader of his time. According to one of his early opponents, Irenaeus, Marcion taught that "only Paul, to whom the mystery has been given by revelation, knew the truth" (*Haer.* 3.13.1). A later writer, Eznik of Kolb, records a Marcionite tradition that makes Jesus' revelation to Paul an essential completion of the former's mission on earth, reporting to Paul the "purchase" of humanity, at the price of Jesus' death, from the god of this world.[1] The question naturally follows: how large of a role did Marcion play in elevating Paul to the central and determinative place the latter now has, both in the Christian biblical canon and in Christian doctrine?

It would not be at all surprising if those who see Paul as an essential part of Christian orthodoxy would be predisposed against crediting any role to Marcion in rescuing the apostle from obscurity. Yet the evidence is poor for widespread and sustained attention to Paul across the spectrum of early Christianity from his lifetime to the end of the second century.[2] Many writers of the period between Paul and Marcion (and well beyond) show no knowledge of Paul or his letters.[3] The exceptions acknowledge his stature in some way, while dealing with him as a problem: difficult to understand (2 Peter), in need of subordination and harmonization to other Christian authority figures (Acts), or in need of correction (James).[4] Of other writers before Marcion, only Clement explicitly cites and endorses statements by Paul—but notably in a letter to the Corinthian community Paul had founded, where it would be difficult to avoid his local authority.[5] Clement's testimony makes it clear that some of Paul's letters were circulating beyond the places to which they had been sent; but it is not enough to prove that there existed a collection—a Pauline *corpus*—in which a set of letters had been edited together as a text of Christian instruction. The first clear evidence of such a Pauline corpus is the Apostolikon of Marcion.[6]

If Marcion was unique in his time for the amount of authority he vested in Paul, perhaps he was the one who first collected some of Paul's most important letters into a corpus. Adolf von Harnack explored this possibility in his classic study of Marcion, and others have endorsed it.[7] Accepting this hypothesis would require imagining that Marcion's opponents found it expedient to co-opt the authority of Paul, rather than throw out the Pauline baby with the Marcionite bathwater, and to adopt the Pauline corpus in a modified form more accommodated to "orthodoxy." If one assumes that Marcion's collection contained the original form of Paul's letters, then the additional material found in the catholic version of the letters would be second-century non-Pauline inventions, meant to "correct" the letters in a non-Marcionite direction.[8] Alternatively, if one assumes that Marcion had edited the letters to suit his own purposes, then it could be that his opponents retrieved pre-Marcionite copies of the letters (and even additional letters) in their original form for their own rival collection.

Harnack adopts the latter scenario of a post-Marcion revival of interest and retrieval of Paul's original letters; such a circumstance was the only way he could account for the appearance, in catholic copies of the letters, of readings he considered to be the product of Marcion's editorial hand, while still maintaining that the fuller catholic text reflected Paul's original compositions. He imagined that a Latin translation of the Marcionite Apostolikon had preceded a Latin translation of the catholic form of the letters, and that the former had profoundly influenced the latter. Perhaps even copies of the Apostolikon had been appropriated by catholic users, and had their omissions filled in by comparison to a catholic exemplar, saving labor by only making new Latin translations of the missing passages found in a Greek exemplar. Yet Harnack found the distinctive readings of the Apostolikon he attributed to Marcion not only in the Old Latin version of Paul's letters, but also in a set of Greek manuscripts as well as in the Syriac textual tradition. The work of others since Harnack, culminating in the study of John Clabeaux, has only increased the number of such identified parallels. Should we imagine, then, that the Apostolikon not only pioneered the text of Paul in the Latin West and the Syriac East, but also worked its way into certain strands of the Greek textual tradition? If so, then we would have good reason to credit Marcion with rescuing Paul from obscurity and giving him the centrality he subsequently enjoyed throughout the Christian world.

Nevertheless, a number of researchers have expressed doubts that this is the best way to account for the evidence.[9] They argue that Harnack's scenario is too complex, and suggest a simpler explanation of why some of the distinctive readings of the Apostolikon turn up in various parts of the catholic textual tradition. According to this view, the variant readings found in some Greek, Syriac, or Latin manuscripts that agree with the Apostolikon against most other witnesses to the catholic text are not the product of Marcion's editorial hand, but come from the common textual tradition that Marcion shared with the ancestors of the catholic text. The very fact that these variant readings are found in catholic manuscripts, they argue, proves that Marcion is not responsible for them. Just because we *can* imagine ideological motives for any meaningful textual variant in New Testament texts does not mean that we *should*—if other, non-ideological reasons for the variant can be identified. Nor should we presume that only Marcion was capable of introducing ideologically-motivated changes into the biblical text; Marcion himself could have been on the receiving end of such prior "correction" of the text.

A great deal of study in recent decades has been devoted to reconstructing the origin of the Pauline corpus.[10] "The early history of the Pauline letters is a continuing enigma in New Testament scholarship," Harry Gamble acknowledges. "Despite a great expenditure of effort over the past century, we are able today to claim very few assured conclusions and cannot describe with any confidence the process by which the individual letters of the Apostle were gathered into a collection and came to form a substantial part of the New Testament canon."[11] Nevertheless, a few key pieces of evidence do appear to support the conclusion that "Marcion's Pauline corpus is derivative in both content and structure from another early edition of the letters."[12] Based upon the recent studies of Clabeaux and Schmid, Gamble observes that

> the large majority of peculiar readings attested for Marcion can otherwise be closely paralleled in the larger textual tradition of Paul's letters, especially the so-called Western text and some parts of the

Syrian tradition. This means that Marcion is not to be credited with extensive tendentious emendations, and that his text of the epistles belonged to a common pre-Marcionite form of the Pauline text that was already current around the beginning of the second century.[13]

This would mean not only that Marcion did not create the first collection of Paul's letters, but also that he did not rescue Paul from complete obscurity, since others before him cared enough about what Paul had written to collect and circulate his letters. Both the Apostolikon and the catholic Pauline corpus go back to a common collection ancestral to both. "Consequently," Gamble concludes, "Marcion's importance for the history of Pauline texts has been substantially diminished."[14]

On the one hand, Gamble's conclusion of Marcion's diminished importance follows reasonably on what has been discovered about the Apostolikon's dependence on a preexisting Pauline corpus. The supposed role of Marcion's editorial hand in *shaping* the history of Pauline texts has been diminished. "The role of Marcion in all of this recedes further and further into the background," John Clabeaux concludes. "The text-type he used could have already enjoyed a fairly broad circulation."[15] On the other hand, the very same demonstration that Marcion faithfully transmitted a text of Paul already in place before him, unmarred by ideologically tendentious alterations (possible omissions aside), vastly *increases* his importance as a *witness* to the state of the text in the early second century, by providing a text "appreciably older than the text represented in P^{46}," the oldest manuscript of the catholic Pauline corpus.[16] A smaller role in making history results in a larger role for Marcion as a source for our knowledge of that history, by providing information about the content and wording of Paul's letters more than half a century earlier than our next source with a comparable amount of information. The Apostolikon ceases to be a sectarian byway and dead-end in the history of the transmission of Paul's letters, and becomes, quite simply, the earliest witness to their general transmission, and hence the first substantial source on their content prior to any possible further revision in the second century before the manuscript evidence appears.[17] "If we were speaking of a papyrus fragment from the first half of the second century," Clabeaux observes, "then even a few pages would be accepted as highly significant."[18]

Regardless of various hypotheses about the early formation of a Pauline corpus, therefore, it remains true that Marcion's Apostolikon is "the only second-century edition of Paul about whose shape we have fairly detailed information."[19] We know which letters of Paul Marcion included, and the order in which they appeared in the collection. The manuscript P^{46}, from about three generations after Marcion, is the oldest surviving set of the letters in their catholic form, and in an order that begins to approximate the later canonical one, based on the length of each letter, from longest to shortest.[20] The order of Paul's collected letters remained in flux throughout the first several Christian centuries; but the relatively unusual order in the Apostolikon, with Galatians first, was long considered to have been ideologically motivated. This sequence, clearly reported by both Tertullian and Epiphanius, was thought to be Marcion's conscious attempt to prioritize the content of Galatians, in which Paul dealt with "Judaizers" who were distorting the Christian message, much as Marcion saw in his own time.[21] This explanation remained plausible only so long as the placement of Galatians at the beginning of the collection could not be accounted for by anything other than ideological reasons.

The discovery of non-Marcionite collections of Paul with Galatians first has presented an opportunity to look into other possible reasons for the "Marcionite" order. With regard at least to the first several letters, we find the same order in a list of New Testament books preserved in a book from the Monastery of St. Catherine on Mount Sinai, the so-called *Catalogus Sinaiticus* (also referred to as the *Kanon Sinaiticus*),[22] as well as in the original sequence of a commentary on Paul's letters written in the fourth century by Ephrem Syrus.[23] A third example comes from a set of prologues to Paul's letters found in catholic Latin manuscripts, whose wording reveals an original order identical to the Apostolikon; for that reason, some researchers have proposed that they actually derive from the Apostolikon itself, and are referred to as the "Marcionite Prologues."[24] Prompted by this evidence of a wider circulation of a Galatians-first Pauline corpus, researchers have convincingly argued that such a sequence represents an attempt to arrange the letters in chronological order.[25] Marcion's imagined ideological motives for the sequence of the Apostolikon therefore evaporate, and it begins to appear that he simply received and transmitted an order already in place before him.[26]

Previous attempts to reconstruct the Apostolikon of Marcion have been made by Adolf Hilgenfeld,[27] Theodore Zahn,[28] and Adolf von Harnack.[29] The text of Galatians has attracted special efforts at reconstruction by Hilgenfeld,[30] W. C. van Manen,[31] and K. Schäfer;[32] and Hermann Raschke produced a similar focused study on the text of Romans.[33] The latest attempt at a reconstruction of the Apostolikon has been provided by Ulrich Schmid,[34] who thoroughly revisits the principal sources used in all previous studies. He attempts to reconstruct both *content*, where mere allusion suffices, and *wording*, where more exact quotations in the sources provide an opportunity to recover the original Greek phrasing. Schmid displays relatively greater restraint than Harnack in positing omissions not explicitly identified by the sources, and finds them only in Galatians, Romans, and one brief passage in Colossians. Yet, because he *does* presuppose the traditional model of Marcion as redactor, he relies on his sense of what Marcion would find ideologically problematic and suggests exactly which verses were omitted even when sources (principally Tertullian) refer to omissions in quite vague terms. Nevertheless, he follows the example of Clabeaux in explaining features of the text by ideological redaction only when no other explanation can be found, and entertains the possibility of "mechanical" scribal errors for textual variants in a number of cases where others have found ideological motives.[35]

Schmid's main methodological advance lies in checking the testimony of Tertullian and Epiphanius to particular readings of Marcion's text against their quotation of the same biblical passage elsewhere, where they can be assumed to be using their own catholic text. This comparison allows Schmid to assess how certain we can be that a particular reading belongs to the Apostolikon and not to the paraphrastic habits of the person discussing it, unconsciously influenced by the form of the passage more familiar to him.[36] But Schmid's rejection of the evidence of Adamantius, and his general neglect of other sources, shows that he has allowed the criteria necessary for establishing exact wording to intrude into his criteria for use of sources to establish content—that is, the presence of particular passages, however uncertain their wording.

The Character of the Apostolikon

A characterization of the content of the Apostolikon will not differ all that much from a summary of Paul's thought based on the catholic form of his letters (without the Pastorals and Hebrews). As far as we can tell, the Marcionites read identical versions of 1 and 2 Corinthians, 1 and 2 Thessalonians, Ephesians ("Laodiceans"), Philippians, and Philemon, while very minor differences affected their reading of Galatians and Colossians. Only Romans would make a substantially different impression. Arguably, nothing that deserves mention in a brief overview of Paul's core ideas would be left out if it were based on the Apostolikon.

Paul presents himself as a man of Jewish ancestry and heritage (Gal 1.13; Phil 3.4–5), called directly by "Jesus Christos" in a dramatic ascent through the celestial spheres that surround the earth (2 Cor 12.2–4), and commissioned to be Christ's emissary to the Gentiles (Gal 1.1, 11–12). The latter were formerly "the nations in flesh, those called 'uncircumcision' . . . without Christ, alienated from the citizenship of Israel and strangers to their contracts and promises, having no hope and without a god in the world" (Laod 2.11–12). In fact, God chose "the low-born, the least, the despised" deliberately, in order to invert the world's valuation of things (1 Cor 1.28). God was not truly known to the wisdom of this world (1 Cor 1.21)—indeed even to the Jews (Rom 10.3)—at least in part because "the god of this aeon" blinds the minds of those who do not open themselves up to trust (2 Cor 4.4), but also because God hid his plans from the aeons (Laod 3.9). God reaches out to the Gentiles, according to Paul, not by extending Torah Law over them and incorporating them into the "old contract" based on specified commandments, but by establishing a "new contract" based on trust. By invoking trust, Paul draws on the legal discourse of his time, building on a distinction between criminal and family law. Torah Law functions like criminal law, he suggests, forming the basis of judgment, condemnation, and punishment (Gal 3.10, 22; 2 Cor 3.6; Rom 7.8; 8.1–2). By contrast, the "new contract" functions like a bequest given to adopted children, an image Paul employs repeatedly (Gal 3.26; 4.5–6; Rom 8.14–19; Laod 1.5). Not only are Christians adopted as God's children, but they gain that status from a previous life as slaves—slaves to "the ordering forces of the cosmos" (Gal 4.3; Col 2.8), "those who by nature are not gods" (Gal 4.8), "the rulers of this aeon" (1 Cor 2.6), or "the ruler of the authority of the air" (Laod 2.2). Paul can also characterize people as slaves to wrongdoing itself, by a kind of built-in compulsion to do even what one knows is wrong (Rom 6.19–20; 7.23–25). But Christians are purchased from this former owner by God at the price of Jesus' life (Gal 2.20; 4.5; 1 Cor 5.7; 6.20; Rom 5.6), and for this reason owe Jesus and God their obedience like a dutiful slave (1 Cor 3.23; 6.19–20), with the promise that at the reading of God's last will and testament, so to speak, they will be freed and adopted as God's own children and heirs. All of this, of course, is analogy and metaphor—Paul's way of getting across a mind-boggling dramatic change in status in terms of more familiar experience.

In an apparently more literal way, he teaches belief in a future "awakening" of the dead, in which the spiritual, incorruptible, "supercelestial" body will be altogether different than the animate, corruptible, flesh-and-blood, "soily" body of this life (1 Cor 15.35–50; cf. 2 Cor 4.7–5.4; 7.1; Phil 3.21). Indeed, "in my flesh good does not dwell" (Rom 7.14). Even though Jesus came "in the likeness of a human being" (Phil 2.7) and "in the likeness of wrongdoing flesh" (Rom 8.3), he still provides the visible image of the invisible God (2 Cor 4.4, 6; Col 1.15; Phil 2.6), and therefore serves as a model through whose emulation the Christian can be transformed into a Christ-like child of God (2 Cor 3.18). He is the culmination and fulfillment of human nature, the anti-Adam who initiates a new kind of humanity (1 Cor 15.1–26; 2 Cor 5.17; Laod 2.10), and whose awakening from death foreshadows the same destiny for all (15.22). That destiny involves a future, dramatic descent of Jesus from the celestial spheres, and a meeting with him "in the air" by all the awakened dead (1 Thess 4.16–17; 2 Thess 2.7).

In many of his letters, Paul speaks of conflict with other interpreters of the message of Jesus, who in various ways drew Christians to practices that Paul considered inessential or even detrimental to the faith: circumcision (Gal 2.3–4), keeping kosher in food (Gal 2.11–14; Col 2.16), Sabbath and new moon observance (Col 2.16). These issues relate in an obvious way to Paul's core message that the Gentiles are brought into God's grace apart from Torah Law—"for Christ is an end of law" (Rom 10.4), and "abolished the Law" (Laod 2.15). Paul connects the religious observance of "days and months and seasons and years"—including such things as Sabbaths and holy days—with obedience to those "ordering forces" from whom God has purchased and freed the Christian (Gal 4.9–10; Col 2.16), or with the "commands and teachings of (mere) human beings" (Col 2.21–22). The slavery that characterizes life before God's grace included slavery to "Mount Sinai"—the Torah Law itself (Gal 4.5, 24; 5.1; 2.3–4; Rom 7.4–6). For Christians, the "entire Law" is fulfilled in the single commandment of "Love your neighbor as yourself" (Gal 5.14; cf. Rom 13.8–10), and carried out through spiritual guidance which naturally produces good actions as its fruit (Gal 5.22–23). Yet the Torah Law remains valid and binding for those who choose to adhere to it and gain the reward of what it promises (Gal 5.3; Rom 2.12–13, 25; 7.12). Paul criticizes those who claim to follow the Law but fail to live up to its demands (Gal 6.13; Rom 2.21–24). He can occasionally cite the Torah as authoritative, at least symbolically (Gal 1; Cor 9.9; 10.1–11; Laod 6.2); but he can, in the same way, cite "pagan" Greek literature (1 Cor 15.33).

Despite the contrast of the relation of trust to the "Law of commandments," Paul still expects Christians to adhere to certain principles of good conduct—guided either by the spirit or by ways of thinking about themselves. Besides conceiving of themselves as purchased slaves who owe obedience to their master, Christians should think of their community or their individual body as the temple of God (1 Cor 3.16), as the body of Christ (1 Cor 6.15; 1 Cor 12.12–27; Col 1.24), or as the bride of Christ (Laod 5.21–32). Paul refers to the goal and outcome of this good conduct by a set of words built on the Greek root *dikē*, meaning something that is right, straight, in-line. Traditional translations of these terms include "righteous/righteousness" and "justify/justification." But within the context of the social and legal use of these terms in Paul's time, the sense may be better captured by expressions such as "rectify," "rectitude," "upright," "ethical" in the sense of adhering to a community's approved ethos, or "moral" in the sense of following a particular set of mores. Paul also describes a vibrant set of religious practices in Christian assemblies: baptizing (including surrogate baptism on behalf of those who are already dead, 1 Cor 15.29), a ritual meal symbolizing Christ's body and blood through which people were purchased from the masters of this world (1 Cor 10.16; 11.23–25), along with more spontaneous, inspired acts of prayer, prophecy, singing, healing, instruction, and uttering of unknown languages (1 Cor 11.4–5; 12.8–10; Laod 5.19, 6.18).

Marcionites and non-Marcionites alike could find confirmation of their views and ways of life in this material. But have these texts been custom-tailored to Marcion's positions, or were those positions determined by careful (selective?) attention to these texts? In previous scholarship, the main "proof" of Marcion's hand in editing the texts has been the omission of quotations from the Jewish scriptures, in accord with his well-attested rejection of the value and authority of those scriptures. Is not the absence of the biblical quotations of Gal 3.6–9, and of Romans 9–11 and 15, proof that a

Marcionite agenda shaped the Apostolikon? If it is, what are we to make of the many, many more biblical quotations left in place, including:

Gal 3.10 (Deut 27.26)
Gal 3.11 (Hab 2.4)
Gal 3.13 (Deut 21.23)
Gal 4.22 (Gen 16.15, 21.2)
Gal 5.14 (Lev 19.18; cf. Luke 10.27)
1 Cor 1.19 (Isa 29.14)
1 Cor 1.31 (Jer 9.23)
1 Cor 2.16 (Isa 40.13)
1 Cor 3.19 (Job 5.13)
1 Cor 3.20 (Ps 94.11)
1 Cor 6.16 (Gen 2.24)
1 Cor 9.9 (Deut 25.4)
1 Cor 14.21 (Isa 28.11–12)
1 Cor 15.32 (Isa 22.13)
1 Cor 15.45 (Gen 2.7)
1 Cor 15.54–55 (Hos 3.14; Isa 25.8)
2 Cor 13.1 (Deut 19.15)
Rom 2.24 (Isa 52.5)
Rom 11.34–35 (Isa 40.13–14)
Rom 12.17 (Lev 19.18)
Rom 12.19 (Deut 32.35)
Laod 4.8 (Ps 68.18; cf. Col 2.15)
Laod 5.14 (Isa 26.19, 60.1)
Laod 5.31 (Gen 2.24)
Laod 6.2 (Exod 20.12)

Not only do all these biblical quotations remain in place in Marcion's text, but not once is either a quotation or its context altered in order to treat the text critically or negatively. Marcion apparently left intact the extensive review of the experience of Moses and Israel from Exodus and Numbers in 1 Cor 10.1–10, including its identification of Christ with the rock that traveled with them. Likewise, he let stand the description of Christ in 1 Cor 5.7 as the Passover sacrifice. He did not omit the characterization of God as creator of all things in 1 Cor 8.6, or as fashioner of the human body in 1 Cor 12.24, and of animal and plant bodies in 1 Cor 15.38. The God of Genesis is the same God who shines in the hearts of believers in 2 Cor 4.6. Marcion did not alter Paul's description of his cooperation with the Jerusalem leadership, and their partnership in a dual mission to Jews and Gentiles, in Gal 2.1–10. He did not remove references to believers as true Jews (Rom 2.28–29) or as needing to join Israel to be reconciled with God (Laod 2.11ff.). He allowed Paul to justify his positions on the basis of the Law in 1 Cor 14.37. Indeed, the Law is sacred, spiritual, just *and* good in Rom 6.12–14. The Ten Commandments are cited not once, but twice (Rom 13.19; Laod 6.2). Christ, on the other hand, brings retribution in 2 Thess 1.8, and God sends error, misleading people so that they might be judged in 2 Thess 2.11. If there were readings of these passages consistent with Marcionite views, they involved interpretation, not textual emendation. In light of such evidence, it simply is not plausible to propose ideological motives for the differences between the Apostolikon and the catholic text of Paul's letters.

The Question of Priority

As we have seen, very few of the differences between the Evangelion and Luke have an obvious ideological motive, leading to the strong likelihood that the two versions of the gospel arose out of non-ideological literary causes, probably before the time of Marcion. In the case of the Apostolikon, it is somewhat easier to understand why many have been convinced that ideological edits play a role, since certain specific themes appear to be missing from Marcion's text in comparison to the catholic one. Because of Marcion's close identification with Paul, it has been common to look at his Pauline texts first, and the impression they make has then carried over into assumptions about his gospel text. But now that we have allowed the Evangelion to stand apart from the Apostolikon in our consideration, we need to revisit the latter with fresh eyes, perhaps even illuminated by the possibility that it, too, might represent a form of the text that arose independently of Marcion's ideology.

Alongside the question of the authenticity of all of the Pauline letters now included in the New Testament canon, the integrity of the letters of Paul in their current form has been a matter of debate throughout modern biblical studies. "It has been a strong and growing conviction among many critics," Harry Gamble reports, "that the transmitted texts of at least some of the letters of Paul do not correspond in form to the letters actually written by Paul, but are to be regarded as 'editorial products' in which originally independent pieces of Paul's correspondence are conflated."[37] Textual evidence, in the strict sense, has played a decidedly secondary role in that debate. Most proposals for composite or interpolated letters rely almost entirely on subjective judgments regarding tensions and contradictions in the content. For those making such proposals, the manuscript evidence from the third and following centuries comes too late to be of much assistance, as it derives from already composite and interpolated exemplars. The evidence of the Apostolikon rarely enters into consideration, due to the prevailing assumption that Marcion himself is responsible for its textual differences. Yet it offers the only means for checking whether various proposed combinations of letters or interpolations were already in place in the mid-second century, and in this way takes some of the subjectivity out of the proposals. "Whatever position may be taken on the integrity of any individual letter," Gamble observes, "it is generally granted as a firm critical principle that the form of the transmitted text of any letter should not be assumed, without further ado, to represent the original form of the Pauline correspondence."[38]

In point of fact, in the Apostolikon we are dealing with only a very few explicitly noted omissions relative to the catholic text. The sweeping redaction Marcion supposedly carried out to purge positive references to Jewish scriptures and to bring the text into harmony with his doctrines fails to materialize. Marcion's critics have no difficulty finding quotations of Jewish scriptures, clear references to Jesus' flesh and blood and the physical resurrection, characterizations of God as creator of the world and of humanity, and other such ideas to cite against Marcion's interpretation of his own scriptures. In short, an *ideological* redaction is quite difficult to substantiate, since the supposedly objectionable content of missing passages is found in other passages left in place. If there are some differences of content, therefore, we must seek a different sort of circumstance to account for them. Three possibilities present themselves:

1. Marcion's Pauline corpus derives from an "ecumenicizing" redaction that removed from the letters what were considered local issues or ephemeral details specific in time and place, in order to produce a body of instruction for general use.
2. Marcion's Pauline corpus derives from alternative editions of specific letters produced by Paul or his colleagues for

various reasons, such as versions addressed to different audiences (Gentile, Jewish), or versions actually sent versus versions recorded and later modified or expanded among Paul's papers.
3. Marcion's Pauline corpus is a product of the unregulated circulation of copies of Paul's letters, in which many modifications of the text freely occurred, prior to a settling and standardization of the texts where differences in the source copies were harmonized in various ways, generally tending towards inclusiveness (hence greater length).

The free-for-all nature of the last possibility would make it very hard to trace any consistent tendency in our source material, and amounts to a default hypothesis if the other two possibilities prove untenable. These other two scenarios both amount to some sort of "two editions" theory of the origin of the Pauline corpus; so we will consider the evidence for and plausibility of such a theory.

The idea that Paul's letters circulated in an alternative "ecumenical" version is supported by places in the manuscript tradition where the specific addressees of the letters are omitted, for example, in a number of manuscripts of Ephesians (at 1.2), and in some manuscripts of Romans (at 1.7 and 1.15)[39] and 1 Corinthians (at 1.2).[40] Some would attribute these ecumenicizing edits to Marcion, as part of his purpose of turning highly circumstantial letters into doctrinal resources.[41] But there is no evidence that the addressees were omitted in the Apostolikon; on the contrary, Marcion's version of Paul's letters quite clearly included the specific references to Rome, to Corinth, and to "Laodicea" in place of Ephesus. Harry Gamble looks instead to a "Pauline school" descending from the circle of Paul's co-workers, which at some point assembled the ten-letter collection found in the Apostolikon as an ideal set addressed to seven churches "symbolizing universality."[42]

Removing specific addressees would not have been the only, or even a necessary, modification in order to make the letters more "ecumenical." Paul's letters contained sections devoted to ephemeral matters, such as travel plans, arrangements for collecting funds, commendations of individuals, and so forth, which an editor likely would remove. The nature of Tertullian's and Epiphanius' remarks about the Apostolikon may provide evidence that the latter contained such "ecumenically" redacted versions of the letters. Both writers make repeated critical remarks about Marcion mutilating and shortening Paul's letters, but neither cites very many specific passages that he supposedly omitted. This is in sharp contrast to their handling of the Evangelion, in which Epiphanius in particular regularly notes specific passages of Luke that would support his argument, if Marcion had not omitted them from his text. If we presume any kind of consistent purpose and plan of argument in Epiphanius' work, and at the same time credit his claim that the letters were lacking passages, then we would be led to conclude that these omitted passages had little relevance for the core doctrinal differences at issue between Epiphanius and Marcion. Neither Tertullian nor Epiphanius refer to any of the passages of ephemeral content in Paul's letters, that is, those passages where Paul discusses his past movements, his personal associates, or his future plans. Could it be that these sections were removed from the "ecumenical" redaction of the letters, for which such material had no purpose? On the other hand, precisely because such material offered little of use to their polemic, Tertullian and Epiphanius may have simply passed it by in silence.

As an alternative to the scenario of longer original letters, corresponding to those now found in the Christian canon, later shortened into "ecumenical" versions, it may be that Paul's original letters were shorter, and the longer canonical versions have been supplemented with expansions Paul or his followers added later.[43] The length of Romans and 1 Corinthians has in itself induced some researchers to propose that they represent either composites of several letters or that their original texts have been supplemented beyond the bonds of a letter. Others have pointed to apparent inconsistencies in the sort of audience presupposed in different parts of Paul's letters. For instance, in his letter to the Galatians, Paul introduces elaborate arguments based in the Jewish scriptures; this material not only would be indecipherable to the Gentile Galatians, but would undercut Paul's whole point in the letter to dissuade them from deepening their engagement with Jewish teachings. Did he develop a scriptural argument for a separate version of the letter meant for his Judaizing opponents, or in his own notebooks in preparation for further debate? Much the same can be said regarding Romans: an elaborate and scripturally dense discussion of the status of Jews in relation to God, understandable only to those deeply versed in the Jewish scriptures, occupies a strange place in a letter explicitly addressed to first-generation Gentile converts to Christianity. Not that the additional material is completely irrelevant to the themes of either letter. One could view them not as letters, but as theological treatises comprehensively dealing with a particular line of inquiry. Interpolations usually have a logic to their placement. But as parts of letters addressed to specific audiences, the passages would have been confusing, to say the least. Subjective observations such as these have always had their place in modern biblical studies, but they gain real traction when supported by concrete textual evidence that alternative versions of the letters, lacking the problematic passages, circulated in the earliest period of the Christian movement.

Our habits of reading the catholic versions of these letters predispose us to think that every section is a necessary part of a grand argument running through the entire letter. But this situation is much like our sense of Shakespeare's plays as "canonical" compositions with every scene, every line a necessary part of a great whole, despite the fact that Shakespeare himself apparently lengthened and shortened them as circumstances, or his own whim, dictated. Nor can the fact that Paul's compositions were letters sent out to specific locations undercut this comparison, as if at that moment the text was permanently fixed. We still must account for the collection of these letters, and for that we must abandon the romantic scenario of some lone devotee traveling from church to church collecting the autographs. Either the Pauline corpus was assembled from Paul's own recorded copies, which he could have revised and expanded at odds with the versions actually sent, or it grew gradually from the loose and unsupervised production of multiple copies circulating throughout the Mediterranean. Undoubtedly our current Pauline corpus goes back in some way to both sorts of sources, and that would mean that there was, for a time, competing copies in circulation.

Marcion's canon-forming activity occurred within this unregulated period. The very question of the "canonical" form of the letters had not arisen prior to Marcion. We cannot even speak very safely of "better" or "worse" copies of Paul. We cannot be sure that the longer catholic versions represent the full extent of what he wrote, versus some abbreviated version in Marcion's hands, since expansions may have been introduced not by Paul, but by later hands, as many scholars suggest. This possibility comes quite close to Marcion's own suspicion, that the teachings of Jesus and Paul had been enveloped by a Judaizing development in the movement. What if Marcion was right? What if Paul's letters circulated in different versions, some of which contained greater engagement with Jewish tradition than others? These could have been the product of Paul's own efforts to persuade the Jewish leadership of the Christian movement that his views were right. Or they could be the result of such efforts instigated by Paul's successors in the Gentile mission, touching up his texts to develop his positions. Or it could have happened as part of a "domestication" of Paul, incorporating his ideas and authority into a wing of the Christian movement that did not entirely agree with some of his more radical positions. I do not pretend to know which of these scenarios actually played out historically; I merely wish to point out that we have no idea how these texts actually took shape, or any real sense of the vicissitudes to which they were subject in their early circulation in multiple copies prior to textual stabilization from the second to the fifth centuries. We can address the question of priority, therefore, only on a case-by-case basis, comparing the evidence of the Apostolikon to each individual corresponding letter in the catholic canon.

A. Galatians

The version of Galatians included in the Apostolikon lacked a set of verses found in the catholic version of the letter. Does this material represent a later addition to the text, or something edited out from the original?[44] The set of verses involved belongs to a passage that is "one of the most difficult in the Pauline corpus."[45] "There is agreement among the exegetes that Paul's argument in this section is extremely difficult to follow."[46] Paul appears to interweave two themes without successfully joining them. The first theme deals with reception of the spirit through trust, not through the Law (3.2–5, 10–13, 14b); the second theme, absent from Marcion's text, declares all those who trust to be like Abraham, and therefore his spiritual descendants as part of the blessing of the nations through him promised in Genesis (3.6–9, 14a; cf. Gen 12:3; 18:18).[47] This second theme then gets developed in 3.15–21, where God's promise in Genesis to bless the nations through Abraham's "seed" (in the singular) is interpreted as referring to Jesus, culminating in the idea that Christians, through Jesus, count as Abraham's "seed" and heirs (3.29). Meanwhile, the first theme resumes with an exploration of the tension between trust and the Law, and of the believer's union with Christ through the spirit, and culminates in the idea that the Christian, through Christ, is a child of God (3.21–4.7). An inescapable contradiction exists between the respective conclusions of the two themes: are Christians children of Abraham or children of God?

Modern commentators labor to connect the two themes of the passage in ways Paul never explicitly offers to his readers. True, both themes evoke the contrast of trust and Law; yet that connection could explain an interpolation as much as it could signal an original interweaving of the themes. The central role of the spirit in the first finds no parallel in the second, and its line of argument needs nothing from the Abraham motif. Most significantly, Paul makes the adoption of Christians as children of God a central concept of his message,[48] whereas the idea of Christian descent from Abraham is found nowhere else in Paul (but is found in a closely parallel passage in Acts 3.25). Hans Dieter Betz has pointed out just how odd it is for Paul to base his argument on passages from Genesis that would have been the centerpieces of his opponents' teaching,[49] in which the blessing and promise given to Abraham and his "seed" is signified by circumcision. This very passage must certainly have been part of the argument made by Paul's opponents for circumcision of the Galatians, in order to bring them into the covenant and make them heirs of Abraham. The best that can be said for Paul taking up this very material, is that he is bravely appropriating and counter-interpreting the proof texts of his opponents, accepting the application of the passage to the situation, while insisting that something other than circumcision signifies entry into the covenant and inheritance. But his argument that the covenant with Abraham predates Torah, and so cannot entail Torah observance, achieves nothing with regard to his chief concern—circumcision—which is explicitly stipulated for Abraham in the very section of Genesis he invokes. If Paul's Galatian readers received the letter in its catholic form, they would have been baffled by just what Paul meant. That does not mean that Paul could not have written the baffling passages; but even Paul rarely writes at such dramatic cross-purposes.

B. 1 Corinthians

None of our sources point out any omissions or significant variants in the text of 1 Corinthians found in the Apostolikon. In fact nearly every section of the letter finds mention, and the sequence of Tertullian's remarks prove that Marcion's text had the same order as the catholic one. Therefore, the evidence of the Apostolikon does not support any hypothesis that the letter is a composite, or originally had a different order, or has substantive interpolations.[50]

Of course that does not rule out the possibility that compilation, reorganization, or interpolation had occurred prior to Marcion, or even that Marcion himself had compiled the letter out of previous pieces. Nevertheless, 1 Corinthians was in its current form by the time it was included in the First New Testament.

C. 2 Corinthians

The inclusion of 2 Corinthians in the Apostolikon represents the earliest known existence of this letter.[51] Epiphanius notes only one minor omission in this letter in the Apostolikon (4.13b). But the silence of all our witnesses on a large part of the middle of the letter raises questions related to various theories about the composite nature of 2 Corinthians. In sharp contrast to his detailed treatment of 1 Corinthians and Romans, before and after his discussion of 2 Corinthians, Tertullian makes no comment on much of the latter, passing over in silence several passages suited to his favorite anti-Marcionite themes (e.g., quotations from the OT, God characterized as material provider, close relations between Paul and the Jerusalem "saints"). He appears to be just as detailed as before up to 2 Cor 5.17, but at that point he leaps to 7.1b followed immediately by 11.2 (indeed, reading the latter in direct continuity with the former). At that point, his fairly detailed scrutiny resumes to the end of the letter. Our other sources do little to fill this gap: Adamantius offers two references in parts of his treatise where the Apostolikon may not be being used, while Epiphanius provides nothing.

We cannot ignore the coincidence of this evidence with propositions that 2 Cor 6.14–7.1 and 8.1–9.15 represent textual fragments that came to be embedded in a composite compilation now called 2 Corinthians.[52] The close connection of subject matter between chapters 8 and 9 and Romans 15,[53] known to have been absent from the Apostolikon's text of Romans, is also suggestive. Thus, what is known about the Apostolikon allows for some of these hypotheses about the composite nature of 2 Corinthians, without offering any definitive proof. At the same time, our sources otherwise follow the order of 2 Corinthians. This means an inversion of sequence between chapters 1ff. and chapters 10ff., as widely proposed to explain anomalies in the content, would have to have occurred prior to Marcion (or have been the result of his own compilation efforts, if one wishes to attribute to him such a large editorial role in compiling the Pauline corpus).

D. Romans

Despite the weaknesses of various subjective theories of the composite nature of Romans, fairly strong evidence exists that Romans once circulated in two, three, or four alternative forms.[54] Our sources make it clear that the version in the Apostolikon lacked chapters 15 and 16; but a version lacking the same two chapters once circulated outside of Marcionite circles, a fact established by multiple strands of evidence.[55] It appears that even Tertullian knew the letter in this form, since in all of his extensive writings he never cites anything from the last two chapters of the letter, and that may explain why he says nothing about Marcion omitting these chapters. J. B. Lightfoot suggested that Paul himself produced the shorter fourteen-chapter edition of Romans in order to "divest it of all personal matter, and to make it available as a circular letter or general treatise," and that Marcion made use of this abridged edition.[56] On the other hand, Harry Gamble notes the alternative possibility: "That the fourteen-chapter text was the letter sent to Rome has been urged on occasion," but goes on to remark "this view has never secured a firm footing in the internal evidence or any scholarly approbation."[57]

The main objection to the priority of the shorter letter has been the apparent artificiality of its termination at 14.23, since the same topic appears to continue in 15.1–13, and the shorter letter has no proper conclusion. Yet already a century ago, William Benjamin Smith demonstrated the circularity of arguing for the continuity between chapter 14 and 15.1–13: it only holds if you start by *assuming* the presence of 15.1–13, in which case the removal of the latter verses appears to arbitrarily interrupt a topic; but nothing prevents a later addition continuing a topic that originally terminated with 14.23.[58] Kirsopp Lake endorsed Smith's point that a break at 14.23 can only be original, since once 15.1–13 was present in the letter, it would make no sense to make an edit at 15.1 rather than after 15.13.[59] Lake proposed that Paul composed a shorter, general letter first, and later adapted it for Rome when he anticipated going there en route to Spain. Lake's hypothesis was adopted and developed by John Knox.[60] Knox observes that Paul usually writes in lieu of a visit, rather than in preparation for one, Romans being the one exception. Knox proposes, therefore, that the letter was originally written "not to announce a visit but to take the place of a visit which was having to be postponed" to Gentile communities with which he wished to make contact, and perhaps assert his authority, "to validate and interpret his role as apostle to the Gentiles." He subsequently adapted the letter specifically for Rome.[61] The existence of some sort of general version of the letter is made certain from the textual evidence for a generic address in 1.7 and 1.15. But researchers have been too hasty to equate this general or ecumenicized form of the letter with Marcion's, when in fact he clearly had a version addressed to the Romans. As for the lack of a proper farewell at the end of the letter, we depend entirely on Origen's word that *nothing* followed 14.23 in Marcion's text of the letter. He may have meant that nothing substantive followed. D. De Bruyne discovered in four Latin manuscripts an apparent closing salutation that he speculated may be the conclusion the letter had in the Apostolikon.[62]

The version of Romans in the Apostolikon differed from even the more widely-circulating fourteen-chapter version, however, since it had a shortened text in other sections of the letter as well. It apparently lacked much, if not all, of chapter 9, and the bulk of chapter 11. Many commentators have seen chapters 9–11 of Romans as a separate essay, not well-integrated with the rest of the letter, regardless of whether it was original to the letter or a later addition. C. H. Dodd, for example, states that these chapters "form a unity in themselves. They can be read and understood independently, and equally without them the epistle could be read through without any sense of a gap in the sequence of thought."[63] Reaching the end of chapter 8, Paul has prepared his readers for an exposition of Christian ethics, pointing forward to it multiple times, and so the "immediate sequel" to 8.31–39 is 12.1ff., not chapters 9–11. Dodd goes on to surmise that Paul may have composed the latter piece separately, as a sermon, and incorporated it at the time he composed the letter.[64] "The sermon (if we may call it so) starts abruptly, with no connection with what has preceded," even if Dodd refuses to consider it "a mere interpolation."[65] François Refoulé has taken the next step of considering the possibility that it is an interpolation, either an authentic composition of Paul added secondarily to the letter, or a non-Pauline intrusion.[66]

Tertullian makes vague reference to another omission earlier in the letter, towards the end of chapter 1 or beginning of chapter 2; but without further specification, little can be said about how the evidence of the Apostolikon may support proposals for interpolations in this part of the letter. Our sources appear to miss a golden opportunity to cite the content of chapter 4 against Marcion, raising the suspicion that it did not appear in his text. This chapter occupies a central place in debates over the intended audience of the letter. Although the rest of Romans directs its remarks to a Gentile readership, Paul speaks at 4.1 of "Abraham, our forefather according to the flesh." Paul does not use Abraham here in the same way he does in Galatians 3, where Christians descend from Abraham spiritually through Christ; rather he clearly means to address fellow Jews here, and continues to do so throughout the chapter. Paul may have addressed the letter to a congregation that included both Jews and Gentiles, or it may be a letter intended to circulate to the larger Christian world to believers of both backgrounds, or it could be a composite of materials addressed to distinct audiences. In assessing the merits of each of these possibilities, the Apostolikon's form of the letter offers the only solid textual evidence from the second century.

E. First and Second Thessalonians

The Apostolikon provides the earliest identification of these two letters as compositions of Paul, including the controversial Second Thessalonians, which a number of modern researchers have declared inauthentic.[67] Given the largely parallel content of the two letters, with the exception of a few key differences in eschatological teachings, they appear to many to be rival claimants to the identity of Paul's authentic letter to Thessalonika, with Second Thessalonians explicitly addressing the possibility of forgery (2.2 and 3.17), while at the same time acknowledging another letter to the same community (2.15). Harnack suggested that Paul addressed the two letters to separate Christian communities in Thessalonika, the first Gentile, the second Jewish,[68] while E. Earle Ellis proposed that the first was a public letter, the second a private letter for the leaders of the community.[69] In either hypothesis, for some reason the two letters were not edited together, as may have occurred in other instances.

A number of researchers have argued against the integrity of the letters, and for the presence of later interpolations.[70] The remarks of 1 Thess 2.13–16 offer the most compelling example of a problem for which interpolation provides an attractive solution.[71] Our sources do not specifically refer to an omission in the Apostolikon in this part of the letter (although Epiphanius implies some omissions), but only directly attest 2.14–15a, failing to mention the most problematic material in 2.15b–16, which may have been absent from the Marcionite version.

F. Laodiceans

The Apostolikon contained the letter known in modern Bibles as "Ephesians" under the name "Laodiceans," and by its inclusion Marcion was the first to identify this letter, under any name, as a composition of Paul's.[72] That ascription of the letter to Paul has been a matter of considerable controversy in modern biblical research, with a number of scholars deciding that the letter cannot have been written by Paul.[73] In the words of Markus Barth, the character of the letter forces a difficult interpretive choice: "If Paul himself wrote this epistle, then it could hardly have been addressed to Ephesus. Or if it was really written for the Ephesians, then Paul was most likely not its author."[74] Despite the well-documented association of Paul with Ephesus, he speaks to the recipients of this letter as a community not known to him personally (1.15, 3.2–3, 4.21). He does not greet anyone by name and does not mention any specific past or present circumstances of the community. For that reason, those who still credit Paul's authorship tend to identify it as some kind of general letter sent out in multiple copies to many communities, pointing to the strong textual evidence for the omission of "in Ephesus" in early copies of the letter.[75]

A number of modern researchers have accepted Marcion's identification of the letter as the one Paul wrote to the Laodiceans and mentions in his letter to the Colossians.[76] At the very least, with no obvious ideological motive for the identification,[77] and pre-dating any other testimony by half a century, the evidence of the Apostolikon deserves serious consideration.[78] Of course, Marcion simply could have supplied the identity of the recipients to fill in the blank, so to speak, attested by several other early witnesses to the text, based on the same reference in Col 4.16 that inspired a later forger to stitch together a pathetic "Laodiceans" from passages culled from other letters of Paul. But the obvious similarities of content between Ephesians and Colossians suggest the same sort of close association of time, place, and subject matter Paul indicates for the Colossian and Laodicean letters.

G. Colossians

The Apostolikon provides the earliest documented identification of this letter as a genuine composition of Paul. Many modern researchers do not accept its authenticity.[79] Through a series of rhetorical questions, Tertullian implies that Marcion's text lacked the phrases found in Colossians 1.15b–16, which form part of a poetic passage often referred to as the "Colossians Hymn." Precisely these phrases, lacking from Marcion's text, have caused a great deal of comment and consternation in modern scholarship. Paul nowhere else refers to Christ in these terms as creator of the universe, or as the goal or end of creation, a role he elsewhere ascribes to the Father (e.g., Rom 11.36; 1 Cor 8.6). This tension between the Colossians Hymn and Paul's other letters has contributed significantly to doubts that Paul could have written Colossians, or to the alternative theory that Paul incorporated here a hymn composed by someone else despite its different christology. No one, to my knowledge, has taken into consideration the evidence of the Apostolikon in a possible solution to the problem. The version of the hymn reported for Marcion's text conforms to the christological views Paul expresses elsewhere, and from that perspective the longer version found in the catholic text has the appearance of containing interpolated phrases.

H. Philippians

The Apostolikon provides the earliest documented identification of this letter as a genuine composition of Paul. Many modern researchers point to a number of disjunctions in Paul's train of thought as evidence that the letter is a composite of two or three letters. But, based on the testimony of Tertullian, it already appeared in the Apostolikon in the same general form it has in the catholic textual tradition. None of our sources mention any omissions.

I. Philemon

The Apostolikon provides the earliest testimony to the existence of this letter. As in the case of 1 and 2 Thessalonians, so with Philemon, Epiphanius says, "I likewise make no selections from it, since in Marcion it is distorted" (*Pan.* 42.12.1). No weight should be given to this claim. Tertullian, in contrast, says, "This epistle alone has so profited by its brevity as to escape Marcion's falsifying hands" (*Marc.* 5.21.1).

*****

Many uncertainties shadow our knowledge of the origins, initial circulation, and compilation of Paul's letters. This brief survey has demonstrated that no objective evidence exists by which to settle the priority of one version of a letter over another, and different judgments rest largely on subjective impressions and relative plausibility. Once we set aside the deeply ingrained familiarity of the catholic text, the shorter Marcionite text cannot be simply dismissed as an ideological edit. In nearly every case, the omitted material represents unique ideas appearing in single passages, which Paul repeats nowhere else. Therefore we cannot easily conclude that some significant component of Paul's thought has been systematically excised. In several cases, the omissions fall in places where contemporary commentators find particular difficulties and obscurities in what Paul says, or unusual challenges in understanding how Paul progresses from one point to another. Interpolation therefore presents itself as a possible explanation, or alternatively the formation of a composite text in which originally distinct discussions were interwoven at the cost of succinct clarity. In one case—the end of Romans—the substantially shorter text is attested outside of the Apostolikon, and so can be attributed to Marcion's editorial hand only if we are prepared to credit him with bestowing Paul's letter on non-Marcionite Christians who had no previous knowledge of it.

But what about the impression that all of the omissions fall into the category of things to which Marcion would object, raising the suspicion of an ideological edit? After all, in Galatians Abraham is (almost) removed from Paul's discussion, along with the idea that Christians are "children of Abraham." Similarly, in Romans, Paul's reflections on Christians as branches grafted onto the tree of Israel disappears. Yet, in the Apostolikon's Galatians, Christians remain, in a vivid allegory, the spiritual children of Abraham (4.22–31). In Romans, Paul's characterization of Christians as true Jews, circumcised in their hearts, stands intact in the Marcionite text; while in Laodiceans, he speaks of reconciling Jew and Gentile in one body, remedying the latter's alienation from citizenship in Israel, and bringing them into the household of God (Laod 2.11–19). The list of ways in which the Apostolikon defies what would be expected of a Marcionite purge of the text can be easily multiplied.

Arguments in favor of the priority of Marcion's texts of Paul's letters are at least as good as those against it. The Apostolikon attests with certainty a form of the letters in existence in the early second century, while the same cannot be said of the catholic form. The time has come, then, for a fresh approach to the history of the transmission of Paul's letters that fully incorporates the data of the Apostolikon on the same level as any other textual evidence, be it from a manuscript or the testimony of an Apostolic Father of the same era.

Implications for Biblical Studies

If we have grounds to stop consigning the Apostolikon to a heretical byway, and give it a place alongside of other early evidence for the state of Paul's letters, a number of important implications for biblical studies follows. First, the evidence of the Apostolikon corresponds with the consensus judgment of modern biblical research that the Pastoral letters (1 and 2 Timothy and Titus) are not authentic compositions of Paul, but are instead late (second-century?) efforts to "domesticate" Paul within the larger Christian movement. Biblical researchers reached this current opinion without any reference to the evidence of the Apostolikon, so the coincidence of the latter's evidence with that opinion is all the more striking. The same can be said of the relative certainty that Paul did not compose Hebrews, and its absence from Marcion's canon. On the other hand, many researchers would go even further, and question Paul's authorship of Ephesians, Colossians, and 2 Thessalonians. For all three of these disputed texts, Marcion is the earliest known person to identify them as letters of Paul. If that attribution is a mistake, we may very well have Marcion to blame for it, and for whatever ramifications have followed from their inclusion in the New Testament. The evidence of the Apostolikon allows us to say that they were already accepted among Paul's letters by the mid-second century.

Yet some of Marcion's copies of Paul's letters did have differences from the versions of them later accepted among non-Marcionite Christians. Those differences confirm the picture that has been developing in recent decades of research of a quite fluid phase of textual formation in early Christian literature. Any hand Marcion may have had in shaping these texts would be similar in kind to the many major or minor changes worked by countless anonymous redactors and copyists, and so there is no reason to set aside his collection as uniquely irrelevant to efforts to recover the history of the transmission of Paul's writings. Researchers have attempted to explain certain difficulties in the received form of these texts by various hypotheses that individual letters are composites of several letters, or that certain passages are interpolations by someone other than Paul. These hypotheses only rarely have any basis in textual variants; usually they are based on subjective judgments about the coherence and integrity of the content. The Apostolikon provides a datable reference point by which we can check these proposals (see the Apostolikon Text Notes). Most of them fail this test. Nearly all of the rearrangement and interpolation of the letters that has been proposed would have to have occurred before Marcion, since they are in place in his texts. The few exceptions include: the last two chapters of Romans (with a broad consensus of researchers considering chapter 16 an originally separate letter); possibly the midsection of 2 Corinthians (distributed by some among three distinct documents that have been inserted between possibly two originally separate letters to Corinth); and possibly 1 Thess 2.15b–16.

Finally, identifying the heart of Paul's message has been a perennial issue in biblical studies. Among all the things he talks about, what stands at the core of his teachings, and what should be relegated to the periphery? In particular, a great deal of recent discussion has focused on exactly how he conceived of the coexistence of the "new contract" of Gentile Christianity with the "old contract" of Judaism, and perhaps of Jewish Christianity. In the past, Marcion had importance in these discussions as an interpreter of Paul, who in some ways may have been—in Harnack's famous characterization—the only one to understand Paul, and yet misunderstood him. But the possibility that the Apostolikon was the source rather than the product of Marcion's understanding of Paul resets the terms of this discussion. How might we redefine core and periphery in Paul based on these slightly different editions of his writings? Does the shift of perspective they provide clarify anything that was previously ambiguous? Does it bring to the foreground a different set of cultural reference points at the heart of Paul's thinking? Does it compel us to think of Paul in closer relation to elements of Marcionite and Gnostic Christianity than we previously recognized, particularly in the sharp contrast between the natural and supernatural governing forces of this world and the unknown God who kept his own counsel until he suddenly revealed himself through Christ? The answers to these questions await further research and reflection.

The Apostolikon

To Galatians

Galatians are Greeks. These accepted the true teaching first from the Emissary, but after his departure were tempted by false emissaries to turn to the Law and to circumcision. The Emissary recalls these people to the trust of truth, writing to them from Ephesus.

1 ¹Paul, an emissary, not from human beings nor through a human being, but through Jesus Christos . . . ²[. . . to the assemblies of Galatia—]

³(May there be) favor and peace for you from God our Father and Master Jesus. . . .

⁶I am amazed that you are deserting so quickly from the one who called you with favor (over) to a different proclamation. ⁷*There* is no other *in accord with my proclamation*, except there are certain people who are disturbing you and wishing to change (it) *into a different* proclamation of the Christos. ⁸But even if we or an angel from (the) celestial sphere were to proclaim to you (something) else than what we have proclaimed to you, may that one be damned. ⁹. . . If one of you proclaims (something) else than [that which you received, may that one be damned.]

[¹¹For I inform you, (my) colleagues, that the proclamation which was proclaimed by me is not according to a human being; ¹²for neither did I receive it at the hands of a human being, nor was I taught (it), except through a revelation from Jesus Christos. ¹³For you heard about my conduct formerly in Judaism, that I excessively] persecuted [the assembly of God and sought to destroy it, ¹⁴and I was exceeding in Judaism many of my peers among my people, being overly zealous for the traditions of my ancestors.

1.1 T 5.1.3, 6
1.3 T 5.5.1–2
1.6 T 5.2.4; Ad* 1.6
1.7 T 5.2.5 (v. 7a); 4.3.2 (v. 7b); Ad* 1.6
1.8–9 T 5.2.5–6 (v. 8); Ad* 1.6
1.13–17 T 5.2.7; 5.3.5 (v. 17)

Verse numbers are those of the catholic text of Paul

2.1–2 T 5.3.1, 4	
2.3–5 T 5.3.2–3	
2.9b–10a T 5.3.5–6; cf. 4.3.3.	
2.11–12 T 5.3.7	
2.14a T 5.3.7	
2.16a T 5.3.8	
2.18 T 5.3.8; Ar 45	
2.20b Ad* 5.22	

¹⁵But when God, who had separated me from my mother's womb and called (me) through his favor, thought (it) good ¹⁶to reveal his child in me, so that I might proclaim him among the nations, I did not present myself immediately to flesh and blood, ¹⁷neither did I go up into Jerusalem to] those who were emissaries before me, [but . . .

2 ¹. . .] after fourteen years I went up to Jerusalem . . . ². . . [And I laid before them the proclamation that I am declaring among the nations . . .], in order that I not somehow run or have run pointlessly. ³But not even Titus, who was with me, although he was Greek, was compelled to be circumcised ⁴because of the false colleagues brought in quietly, who snuck in to spy upon our freedom which we have in Christos, that they might completely enslave us. ⁵We did not yield even for an hour to submission. . . . ⁹[And when they came to know the favor that was given me], Peter and Jacob and John . . . gave me the right hand [of partnership], so that we (were assigned) to the nations, while they (were assigned) to those who are circumcised—¹⁰(with) only (the condition) that we should keep the poor in mind. . . .

¹¹[But, when] Peter [came to Antioch], I resisted him face to face, [because] he was culpable. ¹²For [before the arrival of certain persons . . .] he used to eat with (people) from the nations; but [when they arrived,] he withdrew and separated himself, in fear of those from circumcision. ¹³[And the others . . . joined him in hypocrisy. . . . ¹⁴But . . .] they were not walking straight according to the truth of the proclamation. . . . ¹⁶. . . A person is rectified, not by lawful conduct, but only through trust [. . . and we have trusted in Christos Jesus, so that we might be rectified on the basis of Christly trust, and not on the basis of lawful conduct. . . .] ¹⁸[For if] I build up again the very things that I once tore down, [I prove myself to be a defector.] . . . ²⁰. . . But what I now live in flesh I live entrusted to the child of God who *purchased* me. . . .

3 ¹[O senseless Galatians! Who has cast a spell on you, to whom Jesus Christos was portrayed staked before (your) eyes? ²I want to learn from you only this: did you

receive the spirit based on lawful conduct or based on trust in what you heard? . . . ⁵Does the one who supplies you with the spirit and operates power among you, therefore, (do so) based on lawful conduct or based on trust in what you heard? . . .] ¹⁰For whoever is *under* law is under a curse; for it is written: "Accursed is every one that does not continue in all the things written in the scroll of the Law in order to do them."

¹¹[Moreover, (it is) evident that by law no one is rectified with God.] *Learn therefore* that "the ethical person will live based on trust." ¹²[But the Law is not (observed) based on trust,] but "the one who does them shall live by them." ¹³Christos has purchased us from the curse of the Law by becoming a curse on our behalf—[because it is written:] "Accursed is everyone hanged upon a tree"— ¹⁴. . . so that we might receive the blessing of the spirit through that trust. . . .

²²[But] the *Law* imprisoned all things under wrongdoing [so that the promise based on Christly trust might be given to those who trust. . . .] ²⁶For you are all children through trust. . . .

¹⁵I still speak in a human fashion. 4 ³When we were infants, we were enslaved by the ordering forces of the world. ⁴But when the completion of the time arrived, God sent forth his child . . . ⁵so that he might purchase those under law, so that we might receive adoption. ⁶So, because you are God's children, he has sent forth his spirit into our hearts, crying out: "Abba, Father!" ⁷[Thus, you are no longer a slave but a child; and if a child, also an heir through God. ⁸But then, when you did not know God,] you slaved for those who by nature are not gods. ⁹[And now that you have come to know God, or rather now that you have come to be known by God, how is it that] you are turning back to the weak and impoverished ordering forces, to which you wish to enslave yourselves again? ¹⁰You scrupulously observe days and months and seasons and years. . . .

¹⁹My children, with whom I am in labor again [until Christos is formed in you. . . . ²¹Tell me, you who want to be under law, do you not heed the Law? ²²For it has been

3.10–12 Ep *sch* 1; T 5.3.8–10 (v. 11b); JrG 3.13a (v. 10)
3.13–14 Ep *sch* 2 (v. 13b); Ep 42.8.1; Ad* 1.27 (v. 13a); T 5.3.9–11; JrG 3.13a; cf. Deut 21.23
3.22 T 5.14.11
3.26 T 5.3.11
3.15 T 5.4.1
4.3 T 5.4.1
4.4–5 T 5.4.2–3; 5.8.7; Ad* 2.19 (v. 5); JrG 4.4–5
4.6 T 5.4.4
4.8b T 5.4.5
4.9b T 5.4.5
4.10 T 5.4.6
4.19 T 5.8.6

4.22b–24 T 5.4.8; Ep *sch* 2 (v. 23b); JrG 4.25–26 (v. 24a)	
Eph 1.21 T. 5.4.8	
4.26b T 5.4.8	
4.31 T 5.4.8	
5.1 T 5.4.9	
5.3 Ep *sch* 3	
5.6 T 5.4.10–11	
5.9 Ep *sch* 4	
5.10 T 5.4.12; Ad* 2.5, 15	
5.14 Ep *sch* 5; T 5.4.12	
5.19–21 Ep *sch* 6; T 5.10.11	
5.24 Ep *sch* 7	

written that] Abraham had two sons, one from the servant girl and one from the free woman. ²³But the one from the servant girl was conceived in the manner of flesh, while the one from the free woman through a promise, ²⁴which things are allegorized: for these (women) represent two contracts, the one from Mount Sinai, which gives birth into the *synagogue* of the Jews in accordance with the Law, into slavery, *the other one giving birth* ᴱᵖʰ ¹·²¹above all autocracy, authority, and power, and (above) every name that is named, not only in this world but also in that (world) which is coming. ²⁶For she is our mother, that sacred assembly to which we have promised ourselves. . . . ³¹Therefore, (my) colleagues, we are children, not of a servant girl, but of a free woman.

5 ¹Christos set us free for freedom. . . . Do not let yourselves be confined again in a yoke of slavery, *which is the Law*. . . . ³I testify again that a circumcised person is obligated to fulfill the whole Law. . . . ⁶[But] in Christos neither circumcision has any effect, nor (does) uncircumcision, but (only) trust operating through love. ⁹A little yeast spoils the whole batch. ¹⁰. . . But the one who is causing you trouble will bear the sentence. . . . ¹⁴For the entire Law has been fulfilled in you. "You must love your neighbor as yourself."

¹⁶[But I say, walk in spirit and you in no way will arrive at fleshly desire. ¹⁷Because the flesh desires contrary to the spirit, and the spirit contrary to the flesh, since these (two) are at odds with one another, so that you cannot do whichever of these you want. ¹⁸But if you are led by spirit, you are not under law.] ¹⁹Now the works of the flesh are clear, namely, sexual misconduct, impurity, lack of self-control, ²⁰idolatry, poisoning, enmities, conflicts, rivalries, rages, contentions, divisions, partisanships, ²¹envies, drunken binges, wild parties, [and things like these,] about which I am forewarning you, just as I said before, that those who do such things will not inherit (the) realm of God. ²²[But the fruit of the spirit is love, joy, peace, patience, kindness, goodness, faith, ²³mildness, self-control. There is no law against such things. ²⁴And] those who belong to the Christos have staked the flesh together with (its) passions and (its) desires. . . .

6 ²Carry one another's burdens, and thus fulfill the law of the Christos. . . . ⁶. . . Let the one who is instructed share in all good things with the one who instructs. ⁷*You are* misled; a god is not flouted. For whatever a person may plant, this also the person will harvest; ⁸[because the one who plants for one's own flesh] will harvest corruption [from the flesh, but the one who plants for the spirit] will harvest . . . life [from the spirit.] ⁹So let us do what is fine, [let us not neglect (it),] for at an opportune time we shall harvest if we do not tire out. ¹⁰[Really, then,] as long as we may have opportunity, let us perform the good.

¹²[Those who wish to make a good appearance in flesh are requiring you to be circumcised only] so that the stake of the Christos Jesus might be persecuted. ¹³For not even those who are circumcised are themselves observing the Law. . . . ¹⁴. . . The world has been staked to me and I to the world. ¹⁶[And (may there be) peace and mercy upon whoever] will walk orderly by this standard. ¹⁷. . . I carry on my body the brand marks of the Christos. . . .

6.2 T 5.4.13
6.6 JrG 6.6
6.7–8 T 5.4.14; Ad* 2.5 (v. 7b)
6.9–10 T 5.4.14
6.12 T 5.4.15
6.13a Ep *sch* 8
6.14b T 5.4.15
6.16 T 4.5.1
6.17 T 5.4.15 (v. 17b); Ad* 5.22

To Corinthians 1

Corinthians are Achaeans. These also likewise heard the true teaching from the Emissary and were perverted by various false emissaries, some by the wordy eloquence of philosophy, others led on by the sect of the Jewish Law. The Emissary recalls these people to the true and evangelical wisdom, writing to them from Ephesus.

1 ¹Paul, [called to be] an emissary of Jesus Christos [through God's will . . . ²to the assembly of God that is in Corinth—]

³May you have favor and peace from God our Father and Master Jesus. . . .

¹⁷. . . The stake of the Christos . . . ¹⁸is foolishness to those who are perishing, but to those who are being rescued, it is God's power *and wisdom*. ¹⁹For it has been written: "I will destroy the wisdom of the wise, and I will dismiss the intelligence of the intelligent." ²⁰. . . Did not God make the wisdom of the world foolish? ²¹Since, by God's wisdom, the world through its wisdom did not

1.1 Ad* 2.12
1.3 T 5.5.1–2
1.17–19 Ep *sch* 9 (v. 19); T 5.5.5
1.20b–21 T 5.5.7

1.22	T 5.5.8
1.23a	T 5.5.9
1.25	T 5.5.9
1.27–28	T 5.5.9
1.29–31	T 5.5.10 (vv. 29a, 31); Ad 1.22; Ep *sch* 10 (v. 31)
2.6–7	Ep *sch* 11 (v. 6c); T 5.6.1–4 (vv. 6a, 7)
2.8	T 5.6.5
2.16	T 5.6.9
3.9–11	T 5.6.10
3.12–15	T 5.6.11
3.16–17	T 5.6.11–12

know God, God thought well of rescuing those who trust through the foolishness of the declaration.

^{22}For the Judeans ask for signs and the Greeks look for wisdom; ^{23}[but] we declare Christos [staked]—to the Judeans a pitfall [and to the nations foolishness.] ^{25}Because a foolish thing of God is wiser than human beings, and a weak thing of God is stronger than human beings. ^{26}[As you see, colleagues, your calling (involved) not many (who are) wise in fleshly terms, not many (who are) powerful, not many (who are) well-born.] ^{27}God chose the foolish of the world, that he might put the wise to shame; and God chose the weak of the world, that he might put the strong to shame; ^{28}and God chose the low-born, the least, the despised—the nothings, so that he might nullify the somethings, ^{29}in order that no flesh might boast [in his presence. ^{30}But it is from him that you are in Christos Jesus, who has become for us wisdom from God, as well as rectification and sanctification and indemnification;] ^{31}so that (it may be) just as it is written: "The one who boasts, let that person boast in the Master."

2 . . . ^{6}Now we speak wisdom among those who are perfect, [but not the wisdom of this aeon nor that] of the rulers of this aeon, who are being nullified. ^{7}[But] we speak God's hidden wisdom in an initiation, which God premeditated before the aeons for our glory, ^{8}which none of the rulers of this aeon knew; for if they had known, they would never have staked the glorious Master. . . . ^{16}For "who knew (the) Master's mind, and who became its counselor?"

3 . . . ^{9}. . . [You are God's] building. ^{10}. . . As a wise construction manager, I laid a foundation, . . . ^{11}which is Christos. ^{12}Now if anyone builds on the foundation . . . ^{13}each one's work will become manifest [. . . it will be revealed] by fire, [and . . . ^{14}if . . . it remains,] (the builder) will receive a reward; ^{15}[if someone's work burns down, the person will suffer loss, but will themselves be rescued, but as if] through fire. ^{16}Do you not know that you are God's temple, and that the spirit of God dwells in you? ^{17}If someone destroys the temple of God, *he will be destroyed*. . . .

¹⁸[If someone among you thinks oneself (to be) wise in this aeon,] let that person become a fool, so that the person may become wise. ¹⁹For the wisdom of this world is foolishness compared with God; for it is written: "He catches the wise in their own cunning." ²⁰And again: "The Master knows that the contemplations of the wise are futile." ²¹Hence let no one among human beings boast. [Sure,] all things are yours²² —whether Paul or Apollos or Kephas or the world or life or death or present things or future things—all things (are) yours; ²³but you (belong) to Christos, and Christos (belongs) to God.

4 ⁵[Hence do not judge anything before the due time, until the Master comes, who] will bring the secret things of darkness to light [and make the counsels of hearts manifest, and then] the praise for each one will come to be from God. . . . ⁹. . . We [emissaries . . .] have become a show to the world, and to angels, and to humanity. . . . ¹⁵. . . I gave birth to you by the proclamation. . . . ¹⁷[. . . I sent Timothy to you . . .]

5 ¹[. . . It is reported among you . . . that] someone possesses his father's wife. ²[. . . The one who has done this deed should be removed from among you.] ³For I, *thus* absent in (my) body but present in (my) spirit, have already judged, as though present, the one who has carried this out this way, ⁴in the name of our Master Jesus *Christos* drawing together your and my spirit with the energy of our Master Jesus, ⁵to hand over such a person . . . for the destruction of (his) flesh, so that (his) spirit may be rescued on the day of the Master. ⁶[. . . Do you not know that a little yeast spoils the whole batch?] ⁷Clean out the old yeast, so that you may be a new batch, since you are unleavened. For, indeed, our Pascha was sacrificed: Christos. . . . ¹³. . . Remove the wicked from yourselves.

6 . . . ¹³. . . The body (is) not for sexual misconduct, but for the Master; and the Master (is) for the body, *as the temple is for God and God for the temple*. ¹⁴God both awakened the Master and will awaken us. . . . ¹⁵Do you not know that your bodies are limbs of Christos? Shall I, then, take the limbs of the Christos and make them a prostitute's limbs? May it not be! ¹⁶For do you not know that

---

3.18c–20 T 5.6.12; Ep *sch* 12 (vv. 19b–20)

3.21–23 T 5.6.13 (v. 21a); 5.7.9 (vv. 21b–22); Ad 2.19

4.5 T 5.7.1

4.9b T 5.7.1

4.15b T 5.7.2; 5.8.6

5.1 T 5.7.2

5.3–5 Ad* 2.5, 8 (v. 5); Ad 2.21 (v. 5); T 5.7.2 (vv. 3, 5)

5.7 Ep *sch* 13 (v. 7b); T 5.7.3; Ad* 2.18 (v. 7b)

5.13b T 5.7.2

6.13–14 T 5.7.4

6.15 T 5.7.4 (v. 15a); 4.34.5 (v. 15b); Ad* 5.22

6.16 Ep *sch* 14; Ad* 5.23

6.18–19 T 5.7.4–5	
6.20 T 5.7.4–5	
7.1–2 T 5.7.6	
7.6–7a T 5.7.6	
7.7b Or1	
7.10–11 T 5.7.6	
7.29b T 5.7.8	
7.39 T 5.7.8	
8.4–6 T 5.7.9	
8.13 Ez 408	

the one joined to a prostitute is a single body? For, it says, "The two will be one in flesh." . . . [18]Flee from sexual misconduct. . . . [19]. . . You do not belong to yourselves, [20]for you were purchased with a price. Glorify *and exalt* God in your bodies.

7 [1]. . . It is well for a man not to touch a woman; [2]yet, [because of prevalence of sexual misconduct,] let each man have his own woman and each woman have her own man. [3][Let the man render to the woman her due; but let the woman also do likewise to the man. [4]The woman does not exercise authority over her own body, but the man does; likewise, also, the man does not exercise authority over his own body, but the woman does. [5]Do not be depriving each other, except by mutual consent for an appointed time, that you may devote time to invocation and may come together again . . .]. [6]I say this by way of concession, not in the way of a command. [7]I wish that everyone was as I myself am. But each one has one's own gift from God, one this way, one that way. [8][Now I say to the unmarried persons and the widows, it is well for them that they remain even as I am. [9]But if they do not have self-control, let them marry. . . .] [10]To those who have married, I instruct—not I, but the Master—a wife not to separate from a husband; [11]but if she does separate, let her remain unmarried or be reconciled to (her) husband; and (I instruct) a husband not to send away a wife. . . . [29][But this I say, colleagues,] the moment is fast approaching. [Henceforth let those who have wives be as though they had none. . . . [38]. . . The one that gives his virgin in marriage does well, but he that does not give her in marriage will do] better. [39]A woman . . . is [free] to be married [to whomever she wants,] only in the Master.

8 [4]Concerning eating idol-offerings, we know that an idol is nothing . . . [5]even though there are those who are called "gods," whether in the *celestial spheres* or on earth, . . . [6]but there is for us (only) one god, the Father, from whom (comes) all things. . . . [7][Nevertheless, there is not this knowledge in all persons. . . . [13]Therefore, if food trips up my colleague,] I will absolutely not eat flesh forever, that I may not trip up my colleague.

9 . . . ⁷Who is it that ever serves as a soldier [at his own expense]? Who cultivates a vineyard [and does not eat of its fruit? Or] who shepherds a flock and does not eat from the milk? ⁸[I am not speaking these things in a human way,] even if the Law does not say these things (explicitly). ⁹For in the Law of Moses it is written: "You will not muzzle a threshing bull." Is it for bulls that God cares? ¹⁰Or (is it) entirely regarding us (that) he speaks? It was written regarding us, because the one who plows ought to plow with hope [and the one who threshes with hope of partaking (of the grain). . . . ¹⁴In this way, too, the Master assigned for those announcing the proclamation] to live by means of the proclamation. ¹⁵But I have not made use [of a single one of these (rights) . . .] (so that) no one (can) negate my boast. . . . ¹⁸ . . . [So that while declaring the proclamation I may furnish the proclamation] without cost. . . .

10 ¹For I do not want you to be ignorant, colleagues, that our ancestors were under the cloud, and all passed through the sea, ²and all got washed for Moses by the cloud and by the sea; ³and all ate the same spiritual food, ⁴and all drank the same spiritual drink. For they drank from the spiritual rock that followed (them). Now the rock was the Christos. ⁵But he did not think well of most of them . . . in the wilderness. ⁶Now these things occurred as examples for us, for us not to desire wicked things, as they desired them. ⁷Neither should you become idolaters, as some of them (did), as it is written: "The people sat down to eat and drink, and they arose to play." ⁸[Neither let us practice sexual misconduct, as some of them committed sexual misconduct, only to fall, twenty-three thousand in one day.] ⁹Neither let us put the Christos to the test, as some of them put (him) to the test, only to perish by the serpents. ¹⁰Neither be murmurers, just as some of them murmured, only to perish by the destroyer.

¹¹Now these things befell them as examples, and it was written down for us as something to reflect upon, for whom the ends of the aeons have arrived. . . . ¹⁴[Therefore, my beloved ones, flee from idolatry. ¹⁵I speak as to people with discernment: judge for yourselves what I say.] ¹⁶The

9.7–10 T 5.7.10–11 (vv. 7, 9–10a); Ep sch 15–16 (vv. 8–9), el 15 (vv. 8–10a); Ad 1.22 (vv. 7c–10b)
9.14 T 5.7.11 (v. 14b); Ad 1.6
9.15 T 5.7.11
9.18 T 5.7.11
10.1–7 Ep sch 17 (vv. 1, 3–5a, 6–7); T 5.7.12 (vv. 4c, 5b–6a); Ad* 2.18 (vv. 1b–4); Ad 2.20 (v. 4c)
10.8–11 Ep sch 17; el 17 (vv. 9a, 11a); T 5.7.13–14 (vv. 8–10, 11); Ad* 2.18 (v. 11)
10.16 Ad 2.20

Marginalia	
10.19–20 Ep *sch* 18	
10.25 T 5.7.14	
11.3 T 5.8.1	
11.5 T 5.8.11	
11.7 Ep *sch* 19; T 5.8.1; Ad* 5.23 (v. 7a)	
11.8–9 T 5.8.2	
11.10 T 5.8.2	
11.19 T 5.8.3	
11.23–25 T 5.8.3	
11.29, 31–32 T 5.8.3	

cup of blessing [that we bless—is it not] a sharing of the blood of the Master? The loaf of bread that we break, [is it not] a sharing of the body of the Master? . . . ¹⁹What, then, am I to say? That a *sacrifice* is anything, or an idol offering is anything? ²⁰But (I do say) that what they offer (they offer) to daemons, and not to God; [and I do not want you to become sharers with the daemons. ²¹You cannot be drinking the cup of the Master and the cup of daemons; you cannot be partaking of the table of the Master and the table of daemons. . . .] ²⁵Eat everything that is sold in a meat market, [making no inquiry on account of your conscience. . . .]

11 ³[I want you to know that] the head of a man is the Christos, [and a woman's head (is) the man, and the head of the Christos (is) God. ⁴Every man that invokes or prophesies having something on his head shames his head; ⁵but] every woman that [invokes or] prophesies with her head uncovered [shames her head]. . . . ⁷For a man ought not to have his head covered, as he is God's image and glory; [but the woman is man's glory. ⁸For man is not out of woman, but] woman out of man ⁹and . . . because of the man. ¹⁰[That is why] the woman ought to possess authority over her head, because of the angels.

¹⁸[. . . I hear divisions exist among you. . . . ¹⁹For there must be] sects [among you, that the persons] approved [may also become manifest among you. ²⁰Therefore, when you come together to the same (place), it is not to eat the Master's dinner, ²¹since each one starts by eating one's own meal, and so one is hungry, and another is drunk. ²². . . Do you despise the assembly of God and cast shame upon those who have nothing? . . . In this I do not commend you. ²³For I received from the Master that which I also handed on to you, that] the Master [Jesus in the night in which he was going to be handed over took] a loaf of bread ²⁴[and, after giving thanks, he broke it and said: "This (represents)] my body [which substitutes for you. Do this in remembrance of me." ²⁵In the same way also (he took) the cup after the dinner, saying: "This cup (represents) the new contract in] my blood. [Do this, as often as you drink it, in remembrance of me." . . . ²⁹The one who eats and drinks, eats and drinks] a sentence [upon

oneself if one does not discern the body. . . . ³¹But if we would discern what we ourselves are, we would not be sentenced. ³²However, when] we are sentenced, [we are disciplined by the Master, that we may not become condemned with the world. . . .]

12 ¹. . . Concerning the spiritual phenomena . . . ⁸. . . to one there is given through the spirit wise speech, to another knowledgeable speech [thanks to the same spirit], ⁹to another trust by the same spirit, to another a bestowal of healing . . . , ¹⁰to yet another powerful operations, to another prophesying, to another a discernment of spirits, to another different languages, and to another interpretation of languages. ¹¹[But one and the same spirit performs all these operations, making a distribution to each one respectively just as it wills. ¹²For] just as the body is one but has many limbs, and all the limbs of that body, although being many, are one body, [so also is the Christos. ¹⁴For the body, indeed, is not one limb, but many. . . .

²⁴. . .] But God compounded the body, giving more abundant honor to that which is inferior, ²⁵[so that there may not be a division the body, but rather the limbs might have the same care for one another. ²⁶And if one limb suffers, all the limbs suffer with (it); if a limb is honored, all the limbs celebrate together. ²⁷Now you are Christos' body, and individually (its) limbs. ²⁸And] the Master has set . . . in the assembly, first, emissaries; second, prophets. . . .

³¹[. . . And yet I show you] a preeminent way: 13 ¹[If I could speak in human and angelic languages, but do not have] love, [I have become a banging bell or a clanging cymbal. ²And if I could gain a prophecy and could know all of the initiations and all (their) knowledge, and if I could possess all of the trust (needed) to move mountains, but do not have love, I am nothing. . . . ⁸. . . But as for prophecies, they will become obsolete; as for languages, they will cease; as for knowledge, it will become obsolete. . . . ¹³. . . trust, hope, love remain; but] the greatest of these is love.

14 ¹⁴For if I am invoking in (another) language, it is my spirit that is invoking, but my mind is unfruitful. . . . ¹⁸[. . . I speak in more languages than all of you do.] ¹⁹Nevertheless, in an assembly I would rather speak five

12.1 T 5.8.4
12.8–10 T 5.8.8
12.11–12 T 5.8.9
12.24 Ep *sch* 20 (v. 24b); Ad 2.19 (v. 24b–c)
12.28 T 5.17.16
12.31–13.2 T 5.8.10
14.14 T 5.8.12
14.19 Ep *sch* 21

14.21	Ep *sch* 22; T 5.8.10
14.24–25	T 5.8.12
14.26	T 5.8.12
14.34–35a	Ep *sch* 23 (v. 34); T 5.8.11; Ad* 2.18 (v. 34)
15.1a	Ep *sch* 24
15.3b–4	Ep *sch* 24, el 24; T 3.8.5
15.11	Ep *sch* 24
15.12	T 5.9.2
15.13–14 [or 16–17]	Ep *sch* 24 (v. 14), el 24 (vv. 13–14)
15.21–22	T 5.9.5
15.25	T 5.9.6
15.29	T 5.10.1; Ad* 5.23; Ez 427, 432
15.30–34	Ad* 5.23

words *regarding the Law* with my mind, [so that I might also instruct others, than ten thousand words in (another) language. . . .] ²¹In the Law it is written: "With other tongues and with other lips I will speak to this people, [and yet not even then will they give heed to me, says the Master." . . . ²⁴But if you are all] prophesying [and any unbeliever or individual comes in, that one is reproved by them all, is closely examined by all;] ²⁵the secrets of that person's heart become manifest, [so that the person will fall upon one's face and worship God, declaring: "God is really among you."]

²⁶[. . . When you come together,] one has a psalm, [another has a teaching,] another has a revelation, another has a language, another has an interpretation. . . . ³⁴The wives should keep silent in an assembly, for it has not been permitted for them to speak, but let them keep themselves under control, even as the Law says, ³⁵if they want to learn something. . . .

15 ¹Now I remind you, (my) colleagues, the proclamation that I proclaimed to you. . . . ³. . . that Christos died . . . ⁴and [that he] was entombed, and [that he] has been awoken on the third day . . . ¹¹. . . so we declare and so you believed. ¹²[Now . . . how is it that] some among you say there is no awakening of (the) dead? ¹³If *(the) dead are not awoken*, neither has Christos been awoken. ¹⁴And if Christos has not been awoken, our declaration (is) *useless*. . . . ²¹[For] since death is through a human being, awakening [of the dead] is also through a human being. ²²[For] just as in Adam all die, so also in the Christos all will be made alive. . . . ²⁵For it is necessary that he rule until he has put (his) enemies under his feet, ²⁶[death (being) the last enemy to be abolished. . . . ²⁹Otherwise,] what will they do who are being washed as surrogates for the dead? If the dead are not to be awakened at all, why are they being washed as their surrogates? ³⁰Why also are we in danger every hour? ³¹Daily I am dying, I swear— your boast, (my) colleagues, which I have in Christos Jesus our Master. ³²If humanly I have fought wild beasts at Ephesus, of what benefit (is it) to me? If (the) dead are not being awakened, "let us eat and drink, for tomorrow we die." ³³Do not be misled: "beneficial habits are spoiled

by bad associations." ³⁴Sober yourselves rightly and do not do wrong, for some are ignorant of God. I am speaking for your embarrassment.

³⁵But someone will say: "How are the dead awakened? And with what sort of body do they come?" ³⁶Nonsense! What you plant is not made alive unless *first* it dies; ³⁷and what you plant, you plant not the body that it is going to become, but a naked grain, whether it should happen to be of wheat or any of the other (grains). ³⁸But God gives it a body just as he wishes, and each of the seeds *receives* its own body. ³⁹Not every flesh is the same flesh: (there is) one *flesh* of human beings, and another flesh of land animals, and another flesh of birds, and another of fish, ⁴⁰also supercelestial bodies, and earthly bodies. Moreover, the glory of the supercelestial ones is of one sort, while that of the earthly ones is a different sort: ⁴¹the glory of (the) sun is of one sort, and the glory of (the) moon is of another, and the glory of stars is another, for one star differs from another star in glory.

⁴²So also is the awakening of the dead. It is planted in corruption, it is awakened in incorruption. ⁴³It is planted in dishonor, it is awakened in glory. It is planted in weakness, it is awakened in power. ⁴⁴It is planted an animate body, it is awakened a spiritual body. . . . ⁴⁵[It is even so written:] "The first human being, Adam, became a living soul." The last *Master* (became) a life-giving spirit. ⁴⁶The spiritual is not first, [but that which is animate (is first), afterward (comes) that which is spiritual.] ⁴⁷The first human being is from the earth, soily; the second is *the Master* from (the) celestial sphere. ⁴⁸As the soily one is, so also (are) the soily ones; and as the supercelestial one is, so also (are) the supercelestial ones. ⁴⁹Just as we have borne the image of the soily one, we should bear also the image of the supercelestial one. ⁵⁰[For] this I say, (my) colleagues, that flesh and blood do not inherit God's realm, neither (does) corruption (inherit) incorruption.

⁵¹Pay attention! I am reciting an initiation to you: While not all of us will fall asleep (in death), not all of us will be changed—⁵²in a moment, in the blink of an eye, at the last trumpet. For it will blare and the dead will be awakened incorruptible, and we shall be changed. ⁵³For it is

15.35–36 Ad* 5.23; T 5.10.2–3 (v. 35)

15.37–41 T 5.10.4; cf. 5.20.17; Ad* 5.23

15.42–44 T 5.10.4–5; Ad* 5.23 (v. 42a); Ad 5.25 (vv. 42b, 44a)

15.45–46 T 5.10.6–7; Ad* 2.19

15.47 T 5.10.9; Ad* 2.19

15.48 T 5.10.10

15.49 T 5.10.10

15.50a T 5.10.11, 15; 5.14.4; Ad* 5.22; Ad 5.26; Ez 420, 424; Ar 45

15.51 Ad* 5.23; Ad 5.26

15.52–53 Ad* 5.23; T 5.10.14; 5.12.2–3; Ep *el* 24 (vv. 52–53)

15.54–55 Ep *sch* 24 (v. 54); T 5.10.16 (vv. 54b–55); Ad* 2.18 (vv. 54b–55a); Ad 5.27 (v. 54a)	necessary that this corruptible thing put on incorruption, and this mortal thing put on deathlessness. ⁵⁴But when this mortal thing puts on deathlessness, then will occur the saying that is written: "Death is swallowed down in victory." ⁵⁵"Death, where is your victory? Death, where
15.57 T 5.10.16	is your sting?" ⁵⁶[Now the sting of death is wrongdoing, but the power of wrongdoing is the Law.] ⁵⁷But thanks to God, who gives the victory to us. . . .

16 [¹. . . just as I gave orders to the assemblies of Galatia. . . . ⁸But I am remaining in Ephesus. . . .]

To Corinthians 2

1.1 Ad* 2.12	1 ¹Paul, an emissary of Christos Jesus [. . . to the as-
1.2 T 5.5.1–2	sembly of God that is in Corinth. . . .]
1.3 T 5.11.1	²May you have favor and peace from God our Father
1.20 Ep *sch* 25; Ad* 2.18	and Master Jesus.
2.14–17 Ad 2.20, Didy (v. 17)	³(May) the God [and Father] of our Master Jesus Christos, the Father of mercies be praised! . . . ¹⁸[God is reliable (to ensure) that our word to you is not 'Yes' and
3.3 T 5.11.4; Ad* 5.27	'No.' ¹⁹Because the child of God, Christos Jesus, the one declared among you by us . . . did not become 'Yes' and
3.6–11 T 5.11.4–5 (vv. 6–7, 10–11); Ad* 5.27 (v. 11); Ar 45	'No.'] ²⁰For whatever promises of God (there are), (they have their) 'Yes' in him. Therefore [also] through him is the 'Amen' (given) to God. . . .

2 . . . ¹⁴(May there be) thanks to God, who always leads us triumphant in the Christos and manifests the scent of his knowledge through us in every place! ¹⁵Since we are an aroma of Christos among those who are being rescued and among those who are perishing; ¹⁶to the latter a scent from death to death, to the former a scent from life to life. . . . ¹⁷[For we are] not like the rest [peddling the message of God . . . but] as from God in God's presence we speak by Christos.

3 . . . ³. . . You are a letter of Christos delivered by us, inscribed not with ink but by a spirit of a living god; not on stone tablets, but on fleshy tablets of the heart. ⁴[Yet we possess such confidence toward God through the Christos. ⁵Not that we are competent in our own right to credit anything as (coming) from ourselves; rather, our competency (comes) from] God, ⁶by whom we (were

made) competent servants of a new contract, not textual, but spiritual — for the text kills, but the spirit makes alive. ⁷Now if the service of death which was carved in letters on stones came about in a glory, so that the children of Israel could not gaze at the face of Moses because of the glory of his face, which is being nullified, ⁸why should not the service of the spirit be with much more glory? ⁹For if the service of condemnation was a glory, much more does the service of rectification abound with glory. ¹⁰For even that which was once glorious has not been glorious in this respect, on account of the glory that surpasses (it). ¹¹For if that which is being nullified was through glory, much more that which remains (in effect) is in glory *and is not being nullified*.

¹²[Therefore, as we have such a hope, we are using an abundance of outspokenness, ¹³and not doing as when] Moses would put a veil upon his face, that the children of Israel might not gaze upon (its) ultimate obsolescence. ¹⁴But the thoughts *of the world* were dulled. [For] to this present day the same veil [remains unlifted at the reading of the old contract, because it is nullified by Christos. ¹⁵But until today whenever Moses is read, a veil] covers their heart. ¹⁶But when there is a turning to God, the veil is lifted away. ¹⁷[Now the Master is the spirit; and where the Master's spirit is, (there is) freedom. ¹⁸And,] while viewing *Christos* with unveiled faces, we are transforming our own image from (the) glory *of the Master* to glory, as though by the Master of *spirits*.

4 . . . [³So even if our proclamation is veiled, it is veiled among those who are perishing,] ⁴among whom the god of this aeon has blinded the minds of the untrusting, that the illumination of the glorious proclamation [about the] Christos, who is the image of God, might not shine through. ⁵For we are declaring not ourselves, but Christos Jesus (as) Master, and ourselves as your slaves by Jesus, ⁶since the God who said "May the light shine out of darkness" has shone in our hearts for (the) illumination of the recognition of his glory in the face of Christos.

⁷We have [this] treasure in earthen vessels, so that the preeminence of power may be God's and not from ourselves. ⁸[We are pressed in every way; . . . we are

3.13–16 T 5.11.5–6
3.18 T 5.11.8
4.4 T 5.11.9, 12; 5.17.9; Ad* 2.21
4.5–6 Ep *sch* 26 (vv. 5–6a); T 5.11.11 (v. 6); Ad* 2.19 (v. 6)
4.7 T 5.11.14; Ad* 5.27
4.8–10 T 5.11.15–16

4.11 Ad* 5.27
4.13 Ep *sch* 27
4.16, 18 T 5.11.16
5.1–3 T 5.12.1
5.4 T 5.12.1, 3; Ad* 5.27
5.5–6, 8 T 5.12.4
5.10 T 5.12.4; Ad 1.16

perplexed; . . . ⁹we are persecuted; . . . we are thrown down. . . .] ¹⁰We carry around the dying of *Christos* in the body, so that also the life of *Christos* might be displayed in our body. ¹¹For we the living are handed over to death . . . so that also the life of *Christos* might be displayed in our mortal flesh. . . . ¹³And since we have the same spirit of trust, and we trust, therefore also we speak. . . .

¹⁶[Therefore] we do not give up, [but even if] our outer human is wasting away, nevertheless our inner *human* is being renewed from day to day. . . . ¹⁸[while] we keep our eyes, not on the things seen, but on the things unseen. For the things seen are temporary, but the things unseen are everlasting.

5 ¹[For we know that] whenever our house upon the earth may be dissolved, we have a house not made with hands, everlasting in the celestial spheres. ²[For even] in this dwelling *of an earthly body* we are groaning, longing to put on the one from (the) celestial sphere, ³if indeed even *unclothed*, we shall not find ourselves naked. ⁴For even we who are in this tent *of the body* groan, being weighed down; because we want, not to strip off, but to put on, so that what is mortal may be swallowed down by life.

⁵[Now he that produced us for this very thing is] God [who gave us the down-payment of the spirit. ⁶[We therefore always have courage and know that] while we are in the *flesh*, we are absent from the Master. [⁷Because we carry on by trust, not by what is seen.] ⁸But we think well rather of being absent from the body and present to the Master. ⁹[Therefore we are also making it our aim that, whether being present with him or being absent from him, we may be acceptable to him.] ¹⁰For we must all be presented before the judgment seat of the Christos, so that each one may receive what one did through the body, whether good or foul. . . .

¹⁴[For the Christos' love encompasses us, since we have come to the conclusion that one (person) died in place of all. Hence everyone died. ¹⁵And he died in place of all so that those who live might no more live in their own right, but rather in the one who died in their place and was awoken. ¹⁶Thus from now on we know no one in

terms of flesh; and if we have known Christos in terms of flesh, now rather we no longer know him (in those terms). ¹⁷Thus,] if anyone is in Christos, (that one is) a new creation. The old things have passed away; take note! *All things* have become new.

7 ¹. . . Let us cleanse ourselves of all pollution of flesh and *blood, for these do not attain the realm of God.* . . .

11 ²[I am jealous over you with a godly jealousy, for I personally promised you in marriage to one husband], that I might present you as a chaste virgin to the Christos. ³[But I am afraid that somehow . . . your minds might be corrupted away from the sincerity and the chastity that are due the Christos. ⁴For, as it is, if someone comes and declares a Jesus other than the one we declared, or you receive a spirit other than what you received, or a proclamation other than what you accepted, you easily put up (with it). . . . ¹³Such (people) are] false emissaries, deceitful workers, transforming themselves [into emissaries of Christos. ¹⁴And no wonder, since] Satan [himself] transforms himself into an angel of light.

12 ²[I know] a person [. . . who, fourteen years ago—whether in the body I do not know, or out of the body I do not know, God knows—]was snatched away to the third celestial sphere. ³[Indeed, I know such a person—whether in the body or apart from the body, I do not know, God knows—⁴that he was snatched away] into paradise [and] heard unutterable words [which it is not possible for a human being to speak. ⁵On behalf of such a person I will boast; but on behalf of myself I will not boast, except in (my) weaknesses. ⁶For if I ever wished to boast, I will not be foolish, because I will tell (the) truth. But I refrain, (so that) someone might not credit me with more than one sees in me or hears from me. ⁷And because of the preeminence of (my) revelations, in order that I might not feel overly exalted,] there was given me [a thorn in the flesh,] an angel of Satan, to slap me around, [so that I might not be overly exalted. ⁸About this] I entreated the Master three times that it might depart from me; ⁹yet he has said to me: "[My favor is sufficient for you; for] power is perfected in weakness."

5.17 T 5.12.6; Ad* 2.16
7.1b T 5.12.6
11.2 T 5.12.6
11.13–14 T 5.12.6–7
12.2–4 T 5.12.8; Ez 362, 379
12.7–9 T 5.12.8

13.1 T 5.12.9; Ad* 2.18	
13.2, 10 T 5.12.9	

13 ¹This (is) the third (time) I am coming to you. "At the mouth of two or three witnesses every testimony must be established." ². . . Those who have done wrong . . . I will not spare. . . . ¹⁰[Because of this, I write these things while absent, so that] when present, I may [not] act with severity according to the authority that the Master gave me, [to build up and not to tear down].

To Romans

Romans are in the region of Italy. These were reached beforehand by false emissaries and under the name of our lord Jesus Christos had been led on to the Law and the Prophets. The Emissary recalls these people to the true and evangelical faith, writing to them from Athens.

1.7b T 5.5.1–2	
1.16–17 T 5.13.2	
1.18 T 5.13.2	
2.2 T 5.13.3	
2.12–13 Ep sch 28	
2.14, 16 T 5.13.4–5, Ad* 1.6; 2.5 (v. 16), OrJ 5.7	

1 ¹[Paul, a slave of Jesus Christos, called (to be) an emissary ⁵among all the nations on behalf of his name . . . ⁷to those who are in Rome . . . —]

May you have favor and peace from God our Father and Master Jesus. . . .

¹⁶For I am not ashamed of the proclamation; for it is God's power for rescue for everyone who trusts, for the Judean and for the Greek. ¹⁷For in it God's rectitude is being revealed from trust to trust, [just as . . .] ¹⁸God's wrath is being revealed from (the) celestial sphere against all impiety and injustice of people who are suppressing the truth by injustice. . . .

2 ²Now we know that the sentence of God is in accord with truth. . . . ¹²[For] whoever did wrong lawlessly will also perish lawlessly, while whoever did wrong by law will be judged through law. ¹³For it is not those who hear the Law who are upright before God, but those who do the Law who will be rectified. ¹⁴[For] whenever those [of the nations] that do not have law do the things of the Law naturally, [these people, although not having law, are a law to themselves, ¹⁵who demonstrate the work of the Law written in their hearts, while their conscience is bearing witness with them, and (their) thoughts among each other are accusing or else defending ¹⁶on the day when] God judges the secrets of human beings, according to my proclamation through Jesus Christos.

¹⁷[But if you are called a Judean and rest upon law and take pride in God, ¹⁸and you know (his) will . . . because you are instructed from the Law, ¹⁹and you have convinced yourself that you are a guide of (the) blind, a light of those in darkness ²⁰an instructor of fools, a teacher of infants,] possessing the appearance of the knowledge and truth by the Law—²¹[(you), then, who teach others, do you not teach yourself?] (You) who *teach* "Do not steal," do you steal? . . . ²³[(You) who take pride in law, you are dishonoring God through the transgression of the Law. ²⁴. . .] "The name of God is being defamed on account of you. . . ." ²⁵For circumcision benefits (you) if you carry out law; but if you are a transgressor of law, your circumcision has become uncircumcision. . . . ²⁸[For] a Judean is not (one) in the visible way, nor is circumcision in the visible way in flesh. ²⁹But a Judean is (one) in the hidden way, and circumcision is of the heart—by spirit, not (by) text. . . .

3 . . . ¹⁹[We know that all the things the Law says it speaks to those under the Law], so that every mouth may be stopped and all the world may become liable [to God] for punishment. ²⁰[Therefore by deeds of law no flesh will be rectified in his eyes, for] by law (comes) familiarity with wrongdoing.

²¹But] now . . . (the) rectitude [of God has been made manifest . . . ²². . .] through Christos' trust [for all those having trust.] *What* is the distinction? ²³[For all have done wrong and fall short of the glory of God. ²⁴Since we are rectified as a gift by his favor through the indemnity (paid) by Christos Jesus, ²⁷where then is our boasting? It is excluded.] . . . 4 ²For if Abraham was rectified on the basis of deeds, he has a boast, but not toward God.

5 ¹[Therefore,] now that we have been rectified on the basis of *Christos' trust, not on the basis of the Law*, let us have peace toward God [through our Master Jesus Christos, ²through whom also we have acquired progress by trust toward this favor in which we now stand], . . . ⁶For while we were yet weak, Christos died as a substitute for impious people at an opportune time. . . . ²⁰The Law came in additionally for the multiplication of violations, *so that* favor abounded still more. ²¹. . . So that, just as wrongdoing

2.20b Ep *sch* 30
2.21 T 5.13.6
2.24 T 5.13.7
2.25 Ep *sch* 29; Ad 2.20; OrR 2.13.27
2.28–29 T 5.13.7; Ar 45 (v. 28)
3.19 T 5.13.11
3.20–22 T 5.13.8; Ar 45 (v. 20)
4.2 Ar 45
5.1 T 5.13.9
5.6 Ep *sch* 31
5.20–21 T 5.13.10; OrR 5.6.2

6.14 Ad* 1.27	
6.19 Ad 3.7	
6.20 Ad 1.27	
7.4–5 T 5.13.12	
7.7a T 5.13.13; cf. 1.27.5	
7.8 T 5.13.14	
7.11 T 5.13.14	
7.12 Ep *sch* 32; T 5.13.14; Ad 2.20	
7.13b Ad 2.20	
7.14a T 5.13.15	
7.18 ClS 3.11.76	
7.23 T 5.14.1; Ar 45	
7.25 Ad* 5.27; T 5.14.1	
8.1–2 Ad* 5.27	
8.3 T 5.14.1	

ruled in death, likewise also favor might rule *in* rectitude *in* everlasting life through Jesus Christos.

6 . . . ¹⁴Because wrongdoing will no *longer* master *us*, [since *we* are not under law, but under favor. ¹⁹. . .] For just as you supplied *injustice* and impurity with your limbs as slaves for lawlessness, so supply God with (your) limbs as slaves to rectitude. ²⁰[For] when you were slaves of wrongdoing, you were free in relation to rectitude. . . .

7 [¹Or do you not know, (my) colleagues—since I am talking to people who know law—that the Law is master of a person (only) for as much time as the person lives? ⁴. . . You were made dead to the Law through the body of Christos, [that you might become (wed) to another, to the one who was] awakened from the dead, [that we should bear fruit to God. ⁵For when we were in] the flesh, [the drives for wrongdoing that were excited by] the Law [were at work in our limbs for the fruit-bearing to] death. ⁶[But now we have been discharged from the Law, because we have died to that by which we were being oppressed, that we might be slaves in a newness of spirit, and not in the oldness of text.]

⁷What, then, shall we say? Is the Law (itself) wrongdoing? May it not be (said)! But I would not have known wrongdoing if not through the Law. . . . ⁸But wrongdoing, getting a start through the commandment . . . ¹¹ . . . seduced [me and killed me through (the commandment).] ¹²Thus the Law is sacred, and (its) commandment is sacred and just and good. ¹³. . . [But] wrongdoing, in order that it might be exposed as wrongdoing, achieved death for me through the good (thing). . . . ¹⁴[For we know that] the Law is spiritual [but I am fleshy. . . . ¹⁸I know that in me, that is,] in my flesh, good does not dwell. . . . ²³[I look upon] another law in my limbs, warring against the law of my mind . . . the law of wrongdoing that is in my limbs. . . . ²⁵. . . For truly, I myself serve with (my) mind the law of God, but with (my) flesh a law of wrongdoing.

8 ¹But now there is no condemnation at all for those in Christos Jesus. ²For the law of the spirit of life in Christos Jesus has freed us from the law of wrongdoing and of death. ³. . . God, sending *Christos* in the likeness of faulty

flesh . . . ⁴so that the decree of the Law might be fulfilled among us [who conduct (ourselves) not in accord with the flesh, but in accord with the spirit. . . .] ⁹. . . You are not in flesh, [but in spirit]. . . . ¹⁰. . . The body indeed is dead on account of wrongdoing, but the spirit is life through rectification.

¹¹. . . The one who awakened Christos [Jesus] from the dead will also make your mortal bodies alive [through his spirit that dwells among you. . . . ¹⁴For whoever is led by the spirit of God, these are children of God. ¹⁵For *we* did not receive a spirit of slavery again into fear, but] *we* received [a spirit of] adoption, [by which we cry out "Abba! Father!" ¹⁶The spirit itself testifies together with our spirit that we are children of God. ¹⁷But if children, also heirs— heirs indeed of God, but joint heirs of Christos. . . .]

¹⁹For the eager expectation of the creation awaits the unveiling of the children of God [²⁰—for the creation was subjected to uselessness, not willingly, but through the one who subjected (it)—on the hope ²¹that also the same creation will be freed from the slavery of corruption, to the freedom of the glory of the children of God. ²²For we know that all of the creation groans together and suffers together until now. ²³And not only (that), but also we ourselves, even though we possess the firstfruits of the spirit, also ourselves groan within ourselves, as we await adoption. . . .]

9 ¹[I am telling you (the) truth in Christos, not lying. My conscience testifies together with me by sacred spirit, ²that there is great grief for me and relentless pain in my heart. ³For I could wish that I myself be damned apart from the Christos on behalf of my brethren, my kinsfolk in the flesh. . . .]

10 . . . ²For I bear Israel witness that they have a zeal for God; but not according to experience. ³Since, ignorant of God, and seeking to establish (their) own rectitude, they did not subject themselves to the rectitude of God. ⁴For Christos is an end of law for rectification for everyone who trusts. . . .

11 . . . ³³O the depth of God's riches and wisdom [and knowledge]! How unsearchable [are his judgments and

8.4a Ep *sch* 33
8.9a, 10 T 5.14.4
8.11 T 5.14.5
8.15b Ad* 2.19
8.19 OrEz 1.7.2
10.2–4 T 5.14.6; Ep *sch* 34 (v. 4)
11.33 T 5.14.9

11.34–35 T
5.14.10

12.9–10, 12, 14
T 5.14.11

12.16 T 5.14.12

12.17–19 T
5.14.12–13

13.8b Ep *sch* 35

13.9–10 T
5.14.13 (v. 9b);
Ad 2.17

14.5a Ad* 2.5

14.10 T 5.14.14

14.21 Ez 408

14.23 OrR
10.43.2

untraceable] are his ways! ³⁴For "who knew the Master's mind, or who became its counselor? ³⁵Who has first given to him, so that it must be repaid to him?"

12 ⁹. . . Abhor what is pathological, cling to what is good. ¹⁰Have tender affection for one another in sibling love. . . . ¹²Rejoice in hope. Endure affliction. . . . ¹⁴. . . Praise, and do not curse. . . . ¹⁶. . . Do not ponder lofty things, but associate with the lowly things. Do not become witty in your own eyes. ¹⁷Do not return wrong for wrong to anyone, *and do not remember your fellow's bad behavior.* . . . ¹⁸. . . Be peaceable with all. ¹⁹Do not pass judgment yourselves . . . for [it is written:] "Judgment is mine; I will repay, says the Master." . . .

13 . . . ⁸. . . The one who loves (one's) neighbor has fulfilled law. ⁹For the "You shall not murder, you shall not commit adultery, you shall not steal," and whatever other commandment there is, is summed up in this aphorism, in the "You must love your neighbor as yourself." ¹⁰Love toward the neighbor does not commit a wrong; love therefore is fulfillment of law. . . .

14 . . . ⁵Someone distinguishes one day over another; someone appraises every day (the same). . . . ¹⁰[But why do you pick out your colleague, or why do you treat your colleague with contempt?] For we shall all stand before the tribunal of *Christos*. . . . ¹⁹[So, then, let us pursue the things of peace and the things of edification for one another. ²⁰Do not destroy the work of God on account of food. . . .] ²¹It is well not to eat meat or to drink wine or (do anything) by which your colleague stumbles. . . . ²³[If the one who has doubts should ever eat (it), that one stands condemned, because (it) was not based on trust.] Everything that is not based on trust is wrongdoing.

To Thessalonians 1

Thessalonians are Macedonians, who having accepted the true teaching, persevered in the faith even under persecution from their own citizens; and moreover they did not accept what was said by false emissaries. The Emissary congratulates these people, writing to them from Athens.

1 ¹ [Paul . . . to the assembly of the Thessalonians . . . —]

May you have favor and peace from God our Father and Master Jesus. . . .

2 . . . ¹⁴[You became imitators, (my) colleagues, of the assemblies of God that are in Judea in Christos Jesus; because you also began suffering at the hands of your own countrymen the same things as they also are suffering at the hands of] the Judeans, ¹⁵who killed both the Master [Jesus] and their own prophets. . . .

3 [¹. . . We saw good to be left alone in Athens, ²and we sent Timothy, our colleague and God's servant in the proclamation of the Christos, in order to make you firm and offer support for your trust.] . . .

4 . . . ³. . . Abstain from sexual misconduct. ⁴Each of you should know how to acquire one's own vessel with . . . honor, ⁵not with lust such as the nations (do). . . .

¹⁵[This is what we tell you by the Master's word, that . . . ¹⁶. . .] by a command *of God*, with an archangel's voice and with *the last* trumpet, *the Master* will descend from (the) celestial sphere, and those who are dead in Christos will awaken first. ¹⁷Then we *also* who remain *for the presence of Christos*, together with them, will be snatched away in clouds to a meeting with the Master in the air. . . .

5 . . . ¹⁹Do not extinguish the spirit. ²⁰Do not treat prophecies with contempt. . . . ²³. . . May your spirit and body and soul be preserved without complaint in the presence of our Master *and Rescuer*, Christos.

1.1 T 5.5.1-2
2.14–15a T 5.15.1
4.3–5 T 5.15.3
4.16–17 T 5.15.4; 5.20.7 (v. 17); Ad 1.25 (vv. 16–17)
5.19–20 T 5.15.5
5.23 T 5.15.7-8

To Thessalonians 2

1 ¹[Paul . . . to the assembly of the Thessalonians . . . —]

²May you have favor and peace from God our Father and Master Jesus.

⁶. . . It is right for (the) *Master* to repay affliction to those who afflict you, ⁷and relief to those afflicted with us, in the revelation of the Master Jesus, when he comes from (the) celestial sphere with his powerful angels, ⁸as he brings retribution upon those who do not know God and

1.2 T 5.5.1–2
1.6–7 T 5.16.1; Ad* 2.5–6
1.8 T 5.16.1

	those who do not obey the proclamation. . . . ⁹those who
1.9 T 5.16.2	will pay the punishment of everlasting destruction from
2.1–4 T 5.16.4	the Master's face and from the glory of his strength. . . .
2.9 T 5.16.4, 6; 5.13.10	2 ¹[However, (my) colleagues, regarding] the pres-
2.10–12 T 5.16.5	ence of [our] Master, . . . ³. . . it will not come unless . . .
3.10 T 5.16.7	

those who do not obey the proclamation. . . . ⁹those who will pay the punishment of everlasting destruction from the Master's face and from the glory of his strength. . . .

2 ¹[However, (my) colleagues, regarding] the presence of [our] Master, . . . ³. . . it will not come unless . . . first . . . the person of wrongdoing gets revealed, the child of destruction ⁴. . . exalting himself over everyone who is called "god" and is an object of reverence, . . . to sit down in the temple of God, presenting himself as a god . . . ⁹[. . . whose] presence is according to the operation of Satan with every power and signs and false portents, ¹⁰[and with every unjust deception for those who are perishing,] because they did not accept the love of the truth that they might be rescued. ¹¹So that is why God sends to them a force of error, [that they may trust in the lie,] ¹²so that all who did not trust the truth, but were pleased with injustice, may be distinguished. . . .

3 ¹⁰. . . If anyone does not want to work, neither let them eat.

To Laodiceans

Laodiceans are of Asia. They had been reached beforehand by false emissaries, and the Emissary himself does not come to them; but he corrects them by a letter . . . writing to them from Ephesus.

Title Tert 5.11.12; 5.17.1; Ep 42

1.1 Ad* 2.12
1.2 T 5.5.1–2
1.5 Ad* 2.19
1.9–10 T 5.17.1
1.12 T 5.17.3
1.13 T 5.17.4

1 ¹Paul, an emissary of Jesus Christos [. . . to . . . in Laodicea—]

²May you have favor and peace from God our Father and Master Jesus.

³[(May) the God and Father be praised! . . . ⁵for he foreordained us] for adoption [as his own through Jesus Christos. . . . ⁹[. . . He made known to us] the initiation about his will, according to the pleasing thought that he strategized [in himself] ¹⁰for implementation of the completion of the opportune times, to sum up everything in the Christos, the things in the celestial spheres and on the earth . . . ¹²that we should exist for the praise of glory, we who have previously hoped in the Christos, ¹³in whom you also, when you heard the true teaching—the procla-

mation—and when you trusted in it, you were sealed by the sacred spirit of *his* promise. . . .

¹⁷. . . May the Father of glory give you a spirit of wisdom [and revelation by experience of him], ¹⁸when the eyes of your heart have been illuminated, [that you may know what is the hope to which he called you, what are the glorious] riches of his inheritance among the sacred ones, ¹⁹[and what is the superlative] greatness of his power [for we who trust . . . ²⁰with] which he has operated in the Christos when he awakened him from the dead and seated him at his right hand [among the supercelestials. ²²And he] subjected all things [under his feet. . . .] . . .

2 ¹. . . You were dead in (your) misdeeds, ²in which you [once] walked according to the aeon of this world, according to the ruler of the authority of the air, [the spirit] that now operates in the children of distrust, ³in which also we all [once] behaved with *misdeeds and* the lusts of (our) flesh, . . . we were naturally children of wrath just like the rest.

⁴[But God . . . ⁵made us alive together with the Christos, even when we were dead in trespasses . . . ⁶and he awakened (us) together and seated (us) together among the supercelestials in Christos Jesus . . . ⁸For by this favor you have been rescued through trust . . . ⁹not on the basis of deeds,] in order that no one may boast.

¹⁰For we are his product, created in Christos . . . ¹¹. . . remembering that formerly you were the nations in flesh—those called "uncircumcision" by that which is called "circumcision" in hand-made flesh—¹²that you were in that time without Christos, alienated from the citizenship of Israel and strangers to (their) contracts and promises, having no hope and without a god in the world. ¹³But now in Christos you who were [once] far off have come to be near by his blood. ¹⁴For he is our peace, the one who made the two one (and) destroyed the intervening wall of the enmity in the flesh, ¹⁵abolishing the Law of commandments by decrees, so that he might create the two in himself into one new human being practicing peace, ¹⁶and that he might fully reconcile both to God in one body when he had slain the enmity in

1.17–22a T
5.17.5–6

2.1–2 T 5.17.7

2.3 T 5.17.9–10

2.10 T 5.17.11

2.11–14a
Ep *sch* 36; T
5.17.12–14;
5.11.13 (v. 12);
Ad* 2.18 (vv. 11–13)

2.14b–16 T
5.17.14–15

2.17–20 T	
5.17.16; 4.39.6; Ad 2.19 (vv. 17–18)	
3.8–9 T 5.18.1; Ad 2.20	
3.10 T 5.18.2	
4.5–6 Ep *sch* 40	
4.8 T 5.18.5	
4.25–26 T 5.18.6; Ad* 1.13 (v. 26b)	
5.2 EH 36.3	
5.11 T 5.18.6	
5.14 Ep *sch* 37	
5.18 T 5.18.7	
5.19 T 5.18.7	
5.21–23 T 5.18.8	

it through the stake. [17]He [came and] proclaimed peace to those far off, and to those near, [18]because through him we both have access to the Father by one spirit. [19][Certainly, therefore,] you are no longer strangers and alien residents, but you are fellow citizens of the sacred ones and are members of the household of God, [20]built up upon the foundation of the emissaries, while Christos is its chief cornerstone. . . .

3 . . . [8]To me, the least of all sacred ones, this favor was given, to proclaim among the nations the unfathomable riches of the Christos, [9]and illuminate somewhat for all the implementation of the initiation that has been hidden from the aeons by God, who created everything, [10]so that the very profuse wisdom of God might be made known [now] through the assembly to the leaders and the authorities among the supercelestials. . . .

4 . . . [5]One Master, one trust, one washing, [6]one God and Father of all, who is over all and through all and in all. . . . [8][Therefore he says: "When he ascended into (the) height,] he captured captivity. . . ." [9][But the "he ascended"—what does it mean except that he also descended into the lower parts of the earth? [10]The one who descended, he is also the one that ascended far above all of the celestial spheres, so that he might complete everything. . . .]

[25][Therefore,] putting away falsehood, each of you speak truth with your neighbor. . . . [26]Be angry yet not doing wrong; let the sun not set upon your perturbedness. . . . 5 [2][And conduct yourself with love, just as also] the Christos [loved you, and as a substitute for you handed himself over] as an offering and a sacrifice to God. . . . [11]Quit participating in the fruitless works of the darkness. . . . [14]Therefore he says: "Awake, O sleeper, and arise from among the dead, and the Christos will shine upon you." . . . [18][And do not] become drunk with wine, [in which there is dissipation, but keep getting filled with spirit,] [19]singing [among yourselves] with psalms and hymns to God [and spiritual songs. . . .]

[21]Subject yourselves [to one another . . .], [22]wives to their own husbands . . . [23]because a husband is head

of (his) wife as also the Christos is head of the community. . . . ²⁸[Thus husbands ought to love their wives as their own bodies.] He loves his own *flesh* who loves his own wife, ²⁹[for] no one ever hates his own flesh; but feeds and cherishes it, as also the Christos (does) the assembly, ³⁰[because we are limbs of his body.] ³¹"For this reason a person will leave (one's) father and mother [and will be joined] and the two will become one flesh." ³²This is a great initiation, for I am speaking about Christos and the assembly.

6 ¹Children, obey your parents. . . . ²"Honor your father and mother." . . . ⁴And parents, nourish your children with instruction and admonition from the Master. . . . ¹¹Put on the armor [of God] that you may be able to stand against the strategies of the Devil; ¹²[because] the combat for us is [not against blood and flesh, but . . .] against the authorities, against the world rulers of this darkness, against the spirit forces of wickedness among the supercelestials. ¹³[For this reason,] *put on* God's suit of armor. . . . ¹⁴[Stand firm, therefore, with your waist wrapped with truth, and wearing the breastplate of rectitude, ¹⁵and wearing readiness for the proclamation of peace on (your) feet. ¹⁶. . . Take up the shield of trust,] *in order to be able* to extinguish the flaming darts of the wicked one. ¹⁷[And accept the helmet of protection, and the sword of the spirit, which is a saying of God, ¹⁸through every invocation and] supplication [when you invoke on every occasion by spirit . . .] ¹⁹on my behalf, so that speech may be given to me by opening my mouth in outspokenness to make known the initiation [of the proclamation, ²⁰for which I am acting as an emissary] in chains. . . .

5.28–29 T
5.18.8–9
5.31–32 Ep *sch* 38 (v. 31); T
5.18.9–10
6.1–2, 4 T
5.18.11
6.11–12
5.18.12–14
6.13, 16 Ad*
1.19
6.18–20 T
5.18.14

To Colossians

Colossians also, like the Laodiceans, are of Asia. They, too, had been reached beforehand by false emissaries, and the Emissary himself does not come to them; but he corrects them also by a letter. For they had heard his word from Archippus, who also accepted a service to them. So the Emissary, already in bonds, writes to them from Ephesus.

1.1 Ad* 2.12	
1.2 T 5.5.1–2	
1.5–6a T 5.19.1	
1.15a T 5.19.3; 5.20.4	
1.17 T 5.19.4	
1.19–20 T 5.19.5	
1.21–22, 24 T 5.19.6	
2.4, 8 T 5.19.7	
2.13 T 5.19.9	
2.16–17 Ep *sch* 39; T 5.19.9	

1 ¹Paul, an emissary of Christos Jesus [... ²to ... Colossae—]

May you have favor and peace from God our Father and Master Jesus. ...

³[We thank God ... ⁵because of] the hope reserved [for you] in the celestial spheres, about which you heard in the true teaching of the proclamation ⁶available for you, just as (it) is in all the world ... ¹²[as we thank the Father who called us to the allotted class of the sacred ones in the light, ¹³who delivered us from the authority of the darkness and transferred us into the realm of the child of his love, ¹⁴by whom we have the indemnity, the discharge of (our) misdeeds,] ¹⁵who is an image of the unseen God; ¹⁷and he is before all [and everything coexists in him; ¹⁸and he is the head of the body of the assembly, who is the primary, firstborn from the dead, so that he might become first in everything, ¹⁹because] he thought well of all the fullness dwelling in himself, ²⁰[and through him] to reconcile everything to himself by making peace through the blood of his stake. ... ²¹[Even] you, who once were alienated and enemies in (your) thought by (your) bad deeds, ²²[now] he has reconciled in his body through (his) death. ...

²⁴[I rejoice now in (my) sufferings on your behalf, and] I am filling up what is lacking of the afflictions of the Christos in (my) flesh in place of his body, which is the assembly. ...

2 ¹[For I want you to realize how great a struggle I am having on behalf of you and of those at Laodicea and of all those who have not seen my face in the flesh. ... ⁴I am saying this] so that no one [may mislead] you with persuasive speech ... ⁸... through philosophy, empty fallacies according to human tradition, in accord with the ordering forces of the world [and not in accord with Christos. ... ¹³...] He made you alive together with him, kindly disregarding in us all (our) trespasses, ¹⁴[having erased the warrant by decrees against us. ...] ¹⁶[Therefore] let no one judge you in eating and drinking or in respect of a festival or of a new moon or of a sabbath, ¹⁷which are a shadow of the things to come; but the body (of the things

to come) belongs to the Christos. ¹⁸[Let no one deprive you of the prize who] wishes to get involved in servility and *visions* of the angels . . . ¹⁹. . . who does not hold firmly to the head, [from whom all the body, furnished and joined together by its joints and ligaments, grows the growth of God. ²⁰If you died together with Christos to the ordering forces of the world, why do you, as if living in the world, subject yourselves to decrees—] ²¹"Do not handle, nor taste . . ." —²²[regarding things that are all destined to destruction . . .] in accord with the commands and teachings of human beings? . . .

3 . . . [⁵Mortify, therefore, (your) limbs which are upon the earth: sexual misconduct, impurity, emotion, bad desire, and the greediness which is (a kind of) idolatry . . . ⁷in which also you behaved once when you lived by such things. ⁸But now you should put away everything from your mouth: wrath, anger, badness, blasphemy, foul language. ⁹Do not lie to one another, as] you strip off the old humanity [with its practices], ¹⁰and clothe yourselves with the new. . . . ¹²[Clothe yourselves, therefore, as God's chosen ones, sacred and loved, (with) compassionate feelings, kindness, humility, mildness, patience . . . ¹⁴but above all these things, (with) love, which is the ligament of perfection. . . .]

4 . . . ¹⁰Aristarchos my fellow captive greets you, and (so does) Markos the cousin of Barnabas—about whom you have received instructions *that* he might come to you; *therefore* welcome him—¹¹and Jesus who is called Justus. Although they come from circumcision, they alone are my coworkers for the realm of God who became a comfort to me. . . . ¹⁴Lukas greets you, and (so does) Demas. ¹⁵[Give my greetings to the colleagues at Laodicea and to Nympha and to the community at her house. ¹⁶And when this letter has been read among you, arrange that it also be read in the assembly of the Laodiceans and that you also read the one from Laodicea. ¹⁷And tell Archippus: "Watch the service which you received in (the) Master so that you may fulfill it." ¹⁸Remember my shackles. . . .]

2.18–22 T
5.19.10–11
3.9–10 T
5.19.11; *CaM*
5.20
4.10–11, 14 Ad*
1.5

To Philippians

Philippians are Macedonians. These, having accepted the true teaching, persevered in the faith and they did not receive false emissaries. The Emissary congratulates these people, writing to them from prison at Rome by Epaphroditus.

1.2 T 5.5.1-2
1.14–18 T 5.20.1
1.23 Ez 420
2.5–8 T
5.20.3–5; Ez 375
(v. 5, 7)
3.4–9 T 5.20.6
3.20–21 T 5.20.7

1 ¹[Paul . . . to . . . Philippi . . . —]
²May you have favor and peace from God our Father and Master Jesus. . . .
¹⁴[. . . Most], emboldened by my shackles, are increasingly daring in speaking the message [of God,] ¹⁵. . . some through envy and discord, but some also through goodwill—¹⁶the latter out of love . . . ¹⁷but the former out of contentiousness, are publicizing the Christos. . . . ¹⁸[Regardless], whether in pretense or in truth, Christos is being publicized. . . . ²³. . . I have the desire to be released *from the flesh* and to be with Christos. . . .

2 . . . ⁵[Think this about yourselves (what you think) also about] Christos Jesus, ⁶who, although he existed in God's form, did not consider a seizure of equality to God, ⁷but emptied himself, taking a slave's form, becoming in the likeness of a human being; ⁸and being found in an appearance as a human being, [he humbled himself and became] obedient as far as death, even a death by staking. . . .

²⁵[I have considered it necessary to send to you Epaphroditus, my colleague and fellow worker and fellow soldier, but your emissary and commissioner for my needs. . . .]

3 ⁴[If anyone else seems] to be confident in the flesh, [I (have) more (confidence):] ⁵circumcised . . . of the tribe of Benjamin, a Hebrew (born) from Hebrews, . . . a Pharisee. . . . ⁷[But] what were gains to me, these I have considered loss . . . ⁸. . . on account of the superiority of the knowledge of Christos . . . I consider them as dung . . . ⁹. . . since I do not have my rectitude on the basis of law, but through *him* on the basis of God. . . . ²⁰[For] our citizenship is in the celestial spheres, [from which place also we are eagerly waiting for a rescuer, the Master

Jesus] Christos, [21][who] will transform our abased body to conformity with his glorious body.

To Philemon

To Philemon he composes a private letter by Onesimus his slave. He writes to him from Rome out of prison.

[1][Paul, a prisoner of Christos Jesus . . . to Philemon . . . —]   1.3 T 5.5.1–2

[3]May you have favor and peace from God our Father and Master Jesus. . . .

[[10] . . . Onesimus . . . [12]whom I have sent back to you . . .]

Text Notes

Order of the Letters Tertullian's discussion of the Apostolikon in book 5 of *Adversus Marcionem* gives a clear indication of the order of Paul's letters in Marcion's edition, and is supported by Epiphanius' explicit notation of the order of the letters in *Pan.* 42.9.4 as well as the order in which he reviews selected passages in the *elenchoi* of *Pan.* 42.11.17. The *scholia* of *Pan.* 42.11.5 present the letters in the catholic canonical order, but with a dual numbering system that counts the cited passages both in the catholic order and in the order of Marcion's Apostolikon. Tertullian and Epiphanius disagree only on whether Philemon follows (Tertullian) or precedes (Epiphanius) Philippians. Epiphanius also calls Laodiceans "Ephesians," while commenting, "He also has parts of the so-called Epistle to the Laodiceans," from which he cites a single verse, corresponding to catholic Eph 4.5–6. The wording of the so-called "Marcionite Prologues" to Paul's letters suggests that they were composed for the same sequence (e.g., the Galatians "heard the word of truth," and the Corinthians "*also* heard the word of truth"; cf. Schmid, *Marcion und sein Apostolos*, 236). The non-Marcionite Syriac stichometry known as the *Kanon Sinaiticus* (Syriac ms 10 of St. Catherine's monastery; see Lewis, *Studia Sinaitica*, 11–14) has a similar sequence in the first part of the corpus (Galatians, Corinthians, Romans), but differs in the rest (Colossians, Ephesians, Philippians, Thessalonians, Philemon; also adding Hebrews after Romans, and 2 Timothy and Titus before Philemon, but omitting 1 Timothy; cf. Schmid, *Marcion und sein Apostolos*, 288). The original order of Ephrem Syrus' commentary on the Pauline letters shows a similar sequence.

To Galatians

Prologue *Galatae sunt Graeci. Hi verbum veritatis primum ab apostolo acceperunt, sed post discessum eius temptati sunt a falsis apostolis, ut in legem et circumcisionem verterentur. Hos apostolus revocat ad fidem veritatis scribens eis ab Epheso.* Cf. Marius Victorinus, *Commentary on Galatians* PL 8, 1146 D: *Paulus scribit hanc epistolam eos volens corrigere et a iudaismo revocare, ut fidem tantum in Christum servent.* There is nothing in the content of Galatians to identify Ephesus as the place where Paul composed it. On the priority of Galatians to the Corinthian correspondence, see the reference in 1 Cor 16.1 to prior instructions given to the Galatians.

1.1 Tertullian, *Marc.* 5.1.3, 6. Harnack includes "who raised him from the dead," while omitting the previous "and through God the Father." This apparently nonsensical reading is based upon the testimony of Jerome, *Comm. Gal.* 1.1 (presumably derived from Origen's lost commentary):

> One should know that in the *Apostle* of Marcion the words "and through God the Father" have not been written, because he wanted to stress his point that Christ has not been raised by God the Father, but arose spontaneously through his own strength.

T. Baarda, "Marcion's Text of Gal. 1:1," challenges the value of Jerome's testimony, arguing that either Jerome or Origen (Baarda inclines to the latter) drew an erroneous inference about the state of Marcion's text. In any case, the idea that God raised Jesus from the dead is found in at least three other passages included in the Apostolikon (1 Cor 6.14 [*Marc.* 5.7.4]; Rom 8.11 [*Marc.* 5.14.5]; Laod 1.20 [*Marc.* 5.17.6]). Baarda concludes (251) that we have no firm basis to assert that Marcion's text differed at all from canonical Galatians in this verse. Clabeaux (*A Lost Edition of the Letters of Paul*, 162) is equally noncommittal on any variant here.

Gal 1.2 is unattested.

1.3 Tertullian, *Marc.* 5.5.1–2 (≠Schmid). Tertullian retroactively discusses this verse in his treatment of the superscription of 1 Corinthians.

Gal 1.4–5 is unattested.

1.6 Tertullian, *Marc.* 5.2.4; Adam* 1.6 (Latin only; Schmid erroneously cites Tertullian, *Marc.* 5.1.4, and does not accept the evidence of Adamantius). Rufinus' Latin translation of Adamantius alone supplies v. 6, omitting "from the one who called you in (the) favor [of Christ]" before "to a different proclamation," while the Greek gives only v. 7, which is the relevant part of the quotation for the argument being made. Tertullian's quotation of v. 6 includes most of the words omitted in Adamantius and omits only "of Christ," also omitted in *Praescr.* 27.3 and Gk mss P^{46}, F, G, some witnesses to the OL, and by Ephrem Syrus, and considered by Clabeaux, *A Lost Edition of the Letters of Paul*, 83–84, to be the original reading of the verse.

1.7 Tertullian, *Marc.* 5.2.5 (v. 7a), 4.3.2 (v. 7b); Adam* 1.6 (=Schmid v. 7a only, not crediting the evidence of *Marc.* 4.3.2 or Adamantius). Tertullian's wording (*nam et adiciens quod aliud evangelium omnino non esset*: "when he also adds that there is no possible other gospel") suggests that Marcion's text lacked the relative pronoun *ho* at the beginning of the verse (cf. Ephrem Syrus); on the other hand, it suits Tertullian's subsequent argument to read it this way, rather than with *ho* (Schmid assumes the presence of *ho*). The verse is alluded to in Adam* 1.6 first with the words, "The Apostle says that there is only one proclamation," and again, "The Apostle did not say 'according to my proclamations,' but 'according to my proclamation.'" Then the verse is quoted verbatim, with additional words as indicated: "There is no other *in accord with my proclamation (kata to euaggelion mou*, cf.

Rom 2.16), except that there are certain people who are disturbing you and wishing to change (it) *into a different* proclamation of the Christos (*metastrepsai eis heteron euaggelion tou christou*)." *Eis heteron* is apparently drawn from v. 6; most witnesses to the catholic text read "wishing to misrepresent the proclamation of the Christ (*metastrepsai to euaggelion tou christou*)," and this is what Tertullian, *Marc.* 4.3.2, attests (*pervertentes evangelium Christi*).

1.8–9 Tertullian, *Marc.* 5.2.5–6 (v. 8); Adam* 1.6 (=Schmid v. 8 only, not crediting the evidence of Adamantius). In Adamantius, the Marcionite Megethius quotes these verses in reverse order: "If someone among you proclaims (something) other than what we *proclaimed* to you, may that one be damned" (=v. 9b, with "proclaimed" instead of "delivered" in agreement with Gk ms Ψ). A few lines later, Adamantius quotes v. 8, leaving off the final "may that one be damned." At first, Tertullian has: "Even if an angel from (the) celestial sphere were to proclaim differently, may he be damned," omitting "we or" before "an angel," and "than what we have proclaimed to you" following "differently"; but when he repeats the quotation, he has the missing "we or."

1.10–12 is not directly attested, but vv. 11–12 are central to the image of Paul held within the Marcionite Church, and provide an implicit foundation of its view of Paul's role.

1.13–17 Tertullian, *Marc.* 5.2.7, 5.3.5 (v. 17). In 5.2.7, Tertullian refers vaguely to this section of the letter: "After that, as he briefly describes the course of his conversion from persecutor to apostle, he confirms what is written in the Acts of the Apostles." The quotation of v. 17 in Tertullian, *Marc.*, 5.3.5 is more exact.

Gal 1.18–24 is unattested.

2.1–2 Tertullian, *Marc.* 5.3.1, 4.

2.3–5 Tertullian, *Marc.* 5.3.2–3. Lacking *Iesou* following *Christou* in v. 4, as in Ephrem Syrus and some OL witnesses. Because Tertullian, *Marc.* 5.3.3, says that Marcion's "falsification of scripture (*vitiatio scripturae*) will become evident" in analyzing this passage, Schmid (*Marcion und sein Apostolos*, 105–6) looks for some textual variant in what is quoted, even though Tertullian himself does not draw explicit attention to anything. The one possible difference is perhaps the omission of "and/but" (*de*) in v. 4, so that the role of the false brethren in the attempt to circumcise Titus is more explicit. But the meaning of the passage scarcely changes, and in fact the absence of *de* helps to resolve awkward syntax. In any case, the sense with which Tertullian uses "falsification" here remains ambiguous, since his argument is wholly on interpretation of the passage. In v. 5, Tertullian attests the reading "*not* for an hour" with the major Greek manuscripts the Syriac, Bohairic Coptic, and Armenian versions, and the Vulgate, against Tertullian's own text (shared by Gk ms D, Irenaeus, and some OL manuscripts): "for an hour" (Clabeaux, *A Lost Edition of the Letters of Paul*, 84–85, considers Marcion's text the original reading of the verse). But Marcion's text appears to break with most other witnesses in omitting "to whom" at the beginning of the verse (Clabeaux, 84–85). Harnack includes v. 5b, although it is not directly attested.

Gal 2.6–9a is unattested. Harnack insists on an omission here in Marcion's text on an ideological basis (*Marcion*, 71*); but only vv. 7b–8 present any sort of problem for Marcion's views, as they are currently understood. Barnikol, "The Non-Pauline Origin of the Parallelism," has argued that vv. 7–8 are an interpolation into the catholic text. His argument, originally published in German in 1929, has not won wide acceptance (see Betz, *Galatians*, 96–97). Dinkler, *Signum Crucis*, 279ff., maintains that the non-Pauline features and inserted quality of vv. 7–8 pointed to by Barnikol can be better explained if the passage represents a quotation or paraphrase of a formal statement issued by the "pillars" in Jerusalem validating Paul's mission. While Dinkler attributes the insertion to Paul himself, it may represent a later addition of documentary support to Paul's original argument.

2.9b–10a Tertullian, *Marc.* 5.3.5–6 (cf. 4.3.3). Tertullian has the names Peter ... Jacob ... John in that order (cf. Peter, John, Jacob in 4.3.3, as well as in *Praescr.* 15.2 and *Prax.* 15.8). Most manuscripts have Jacob, Kephas, John; but Gk mss D, F, G, and some witnesses to the OL, as well as Ephrem Syrus, have the same names and order given by Tertullian (P[46] has "Peter," but in the second place). Schmid, *Marcion und sein Apostolos*, 101, notes that the three are listed together also in the Synoptic gospels in the episode of the transfiguration (see Luke 8.51 and 9.28), where Peter appears first, but witnesses vary on the order of the other two. The Aramaic equivalent of Peter—Kephas—found in most witnesses to Gal 2.9 (cf. 1 Cor 3.22), is found outside of Paul's letters only in John 1.42. Is the form "Peter" and the order an influence of the "Western" text on Marcion's edition (so Quispel, "Marcion and the Text of the New Testament," 352)? Or has Tertullian changed the wording and order in line with his own preference and that of the Western textual tradition? Tertullian makes no mention of Barnabas in v. 9b, and writes as though Paul is mentioned alone.

2.11–12 Tertullian, *Marc.* 5.3.7. Tertullian alludes to the gist of v. 12 while directly quoting only the last portion. He consistently refers to "Peter" (as do D, F, G, and many other Greek manuscripts, and Ephrem Syrus) rather than Kephas in this passage; but we cannot be sure he is exactly recording Marcion's text, or simply substituting Peter as the more familiar name for the figure.

Gal 2.13 is unattested.

2.14a Tertullian, *Marc.* 5.3.7.

Gal 2.14b–15 is unattested.

2.16a Tertullian, *Marc.* 5.3.8.

Gal 2.16b–17 is unattested.

2.18 Tertullian, *Marc.* 5.3.8; Hegemonius, *Arch.* 45 (Beeson, *Hegemonius: Acta Archelai*, 66.13–14).

Gal 2.19–20a is unattested, but Harnack considers the verses included.

2.20b Adam* 5.22 (≠Schmid). Rufinus' Latin translation of Adamantius has "redeemed/purchased" (*redemit* > Gk *agorasantos*) instead of "loved" (*agapēsantos*), but the Greek text of Adamantius has the latter. As Clabeaux, *A Lost Edition of the Letters of Paul*, 169, points out, the variant can be understood as a mistake made by the visual similarity of the two words, and he is inclined not to accept the variant as the actual reading of Marcion's text, but a change made either by Rufinus in looking at the Greek text, or by the copyist of the Greek manuscript Rufinus had at his disposal. On the other hand, the concept of Christ's "purchase" of humanity was central to Marcionite theology; cf. Gal 3.13; 1 Cor 6.20; 7.23.

Gal 2.20c–21 is unattested, but Harnack considers the verses included.

Gal 3.1–5 is unattested. The sharp contrast of Law to trust did not offer Marcion's critics anything to use against him, and in fact seemed to support him. Hence, they probably skipped over it. In any case, some of the passage must have been present for what followed to make sense. At this point of his commentary on Galatians, Jerome says, "Let us here inquire of Marcion, the repudiator of the prophets, how he would interpret what follows below (*Interrogemus ergo hoc loco Marcionem, qui prophetas repudiat, quemodo interpretur id quod sequitur*)." But this is a purely hypothetical question, and does not indicate anything about Marcion's text.

Omission: Gal 3.6–9 Both Harnack (*Marcion*, 72*) and Schmid (*Marcion und sein Apostolos*, 106) conclude that Marcion's text lacked Gal 3.6–9. Jerome, *Comm. Gal.* 3.6, says, "In this passage all the way to where it is written 'who from faith are blessed together with the faithful Abraham,' Marcion erased from his *Apostle*" (*Ab hoc loco usque ad eum, ubi scribitur 'qui ex fide sunt benedicentur cum fideli Abraham,' Marcion de suo apostolo erasit*). Tertullian, who jumps from Gal 2.18 to 3.10 in his comments without saying anything about an omission, goes back to note one when he comes to comment on Gal 3.26, contending that the logic of the latter verse is ruined by the absence of the connection to the faith of Abraham:

> And again when he adds, "For you are all the sons of faith," it becomes evident how much before this the heretic's diligence has erased (*eraserit*), the reference, I mean, to Abraham, in which the apostle affirms that we are by faith the sons of Abraham (Gal 3.7), and in accordance with that reference he (i.e. Paul) here (Gal 3.26) also has marked us off as sons of faith. (*Marc.* 5.3.11)

Later (5.4.8), he seems to suggest that Marcion's text of Galatians lacked any mention of Abraham except Gal 4.22.

3.10–12 Epiphanius, *Scholion* 1; Tertullian, *Marc.* 5.3.8–10 (v. 11b); Jerome, *Comm. Gal.* 3.13a (v. 10). Epiphanius gives these verses in the order 11b, 10a, 12b:

> *Learn* therefore that the vindicated will live by trust [=11b]. For whoever is under a law is under a curse [=10a]. But the one who does them will live by them [=12b].

In v. 10b the catholic text has: "for whoever is by works of law is under a curse," but cf. Gal 3.23 and Jerome's comment below. Tertullian gives the quotation of Hab 2.4 in v. 11b. Jerome quotes v. 10 according to the catholic text, commenting, "If he (Marcion) wanted to bind us to this testimony of the Apostle . . . and if he wanted to assert that everyone *under* law had been cursed," appearing to confirm the alternate wording reported by Epiphanius. No witness attests vv. 11a or 12a. Whether we should think that Marcion's text had the order Epiphanius seems to give it remains uncertain, but it could be argued that it follows more smoothly from 3.5.

3.13–14 Epiphanius, *Scholion* 2 (v. 13b); cf. *Pan.* 42.8.1 (Holl, *Panarion*, 103.25–28); Adam* 1.27 (v. 13a); Tertullian, *Marc.* 5.3.9–11. Cf. Deut 21.23. In Adamantius, the Marcionite Megethius quotes just the clause "Christ has purchased us (*christos hēmas exēgorase*)" from v. 13, which appears to have been a central *theologoumenon* of the Marcionite faith (cf. Eznik). Tertullian says in regard to v. 14, "So we have received, he says, a spiritual blessing by trust (*accepimus igitur benedictionem spiritalem per fidem*)," which appears to attest the reading "blessing" (*eulogian*) in v. 14b, in agreement with Gk mss P^{46}, D*, F, G, and others, as well as some OL manuscripts and Ephrem Syrus, instead of "promise" (*epaggelian*) found in other witnesses to the text (cf. "the blessing of Abraham" in v. 14a, unattested for the Apostolikon; Gk ms 1245 reads "blessing of God"). Although it would be possible to imagine an ideological reason for Marcion to make such an alteration in wording, its presence in the non-Marcionite textual tradition rules out such a scenario. The phrase "promise of spirit" as found in most witnesses to the catholic text is something of a non-sequiter here. Metzger, *Textual Commentary on the Greek New Testament*, 594, represents a widespread opinion in assuming that the variant "blessing" in v. 14b has occurred under the influence of v. 14a. On the other hand, an original "blessing" could have been changed to "promise" under the influence of the dominance of that term in the subsequent verses. The visual and phonetic similarity of the two terms helps to account for influence either way. Jerome, *Comm. Gal.* 3.13a, criticizes Marcion for having "twisted the plain word of scripture in such a way as to condemn his own teaching" by not understanding the difference between "procure" (*emere*) and "redeem" (*redimere*), the first meaning that one "gets something that does not belong to him" (as the Marcionite good God does in his acquisition of human souls), while the second more properly expresses the idea that one "gets back what once was his" (as God does in Jerome's view). But this is a comment on Marcion not understanding the words of the text, rather than altering them, since Jerome refers specifically to Marcion's "claiming that we have been redeemed by Christ (*asserens nos redemptos esse per Christum*)."

3.15a See discussion below on 4.3.

Omission: Gal 3.15b–16 Tertullian, *Marc.* 5.4.1–2, comments on the transposition of 3.15a to 4.3, "and yet the sequence of thought shows him wrong. . . . This is not an illustration but the truth." He then quotes 3.15b–16 as the proper context for what Paul says in 3.15a, before adding, "Let Marcion's eraser be ashamed of itself! Except it is superfluous for me to discuss the passages he has left out, since my case is stronger if he is shown wrong by those he has retained." Both Harnack and Schmid, however, assume the omission to have extended beyond vv. 15b–16: Harnack extends it through v. 25, Schmid through v. 18, in both cases implicitly based on Tertullian's remark in 5.4.8 implying that Gal 4.22 was the only mention of Abraham in Marcion's text of the letter.

Gal 3.17–18 is unattested. Harnack and Schmid regard the verses as omitted. Gk mss 056 and 0176 show how the phrase mentioning Abraham could be omitted from v. 18 and leave a passage that makes perfect sense, by omitting *tōi de Abraam epaggelias* by homeoteleuton with the *epaggelias* at the end of the previous phrase.

Gal 3.19–21 is unattested. Harnack regards the verses as omitted. Most of the same witnesses that agree with Marcion in reading "blessing" in v. 14 (P^{46}, F, G, d and g of the OL, Ambrosiaster), along with others, read "because of deeds" (*praxeōn*) in v. 19 rather than "because of transgressions."

3.22 Tertullian, *Marc.* 5.14.11 (≠Harnack, Schmid). Commenting on Rom 12.9–14, Tertullian asks, "Had the creator's law for this reason concluded all things under sin. . .?" This appears to be an allusion to Gal 3.22, unless this same wording was found interpolated into Marcion's text of Romans. Tertullian's wording suggests that Marcion's text had "Law" instead of "scripture" here—an otherwise unknown textual variant.

Gal 3.23–25 is unattested. Harnack regards the verses as omitted.

3.26 Tertullian, *Marc.* 5.3.11. "For you are all are children of trust" or "through trust" (*omnes enim filii estis fidei*), in agreement with Hilary ("children of trust," *Commentary on Psalms* 91; Clabeaux, *A Lost Edition of the Letters of Paul*, 126) or Gk ms 1175 ("children through trust"), instead of "For all are children of God through trust" found in most witnesses to the catholic text (Clement of Alexandria has "children through trust of God"; P^{46} reads "children of God through trust of Christ Jesus"). We cannot be sure if, following "trust," the Apostolikon had "of God," "of Christ Jesus," "in Christ Jesus" (as the majority of witnesses to the catholic text do), or nothing. But it had "children of God" in Gal 4.6. Harnack's attempt to explain this variant by accidental omission by Tertullian or his copyist (*Marcion*, 73*) is elaborate and unconvincing. Clearly, Tertullian did not see "of God" in this verse, since he assumes that Abraham is the symbolic parent meant here. In fact, Tertullian's entire argument, that "children of trust" here depends on "children of Abraham" in 3.7 for its meaning, requires that v. 26 read "children of trust" rather than "children of God through trust." A probable allusion to this phrase in Tertullian's own text of Paul in *Prax.* 13.4, however, does give "children of God through trust (*per fidem filio Dei*)."

Gal 3.27–29 is unattested. Harnack and Schmid think the mention of Abraham in v. 29 must have been omitted—Harnack on ideological grounds, Schmid on the basis of Tertullian's apparent indication that Abraham was absent from Marcion's text of the letter except for 4.22.

Gal 4.1–2 is unattested. Harnack, *Marcion*, 74*, suggests that the verses probably were present as the referent of 3.15a, which was transposed to the beginning of 4.3. But Tertullian complains that 3.15a makes no sense because what follows in 4.3ff. is not an analogy from human practice, but a statement of actual spiritual fact; this criticism would lose its cogency if 4.1–2, with its analogy from human practice, immediately preceded, in which case 3.15a would be taken to refer back to it, just as Harnack supposes.

4.3 (+ 3.15a) Tertullian, *Marc.* 5.4.1. Tertullian attests a transposition of 3.15a, adding "still" ("I *still* speak," Latin *adhuc* > Gk *eti*), to the beginning of this verse and omitting 4.3a "thus also you" in agreement with Clement of Alexandria. Ephrem Syrus omits the clause at 3.15, but does not place it at 4.3.

4.4–5 Tertullian, *Marc.* 5.4.2–3; 5.8.7; Adam* 2.19 (v. 5; Schmid does not credit the evidence of Adamantius). In v. 4 Tertullian does not include the words "born from a woman" (nor "born under law"); but Jerome, *Comm. Gal.* 4.4–5, appears to attribute "born through a woman (*factum per mulierum*)" to Marcion's text, when he says "Please note that he (Paul) did not say 'born through a woman'—phrasing opted for by Marcion and other heresies which pretend that the flesh of Christ was imaginary—but 'born of a woman.'" Harnack, who usually credits Jerome's testimony as based on Origen, rejects it here because he assumes Marcion's views about Jesus preclude him allowing the words to remain in the text. Such an ideologically-based argument is unacceptable. A more sound reason for questioning Jerome's testimony comes from a quotation of the original words of Origen on which Jerome probably based his remark. These are preserved by Pamphilus, *Apology for Origen* 113: "We need not give a hearing to those who say that Christ was born through Mary and not of Mary, because the Apostle, in his foresight, said in anticipation of this," quoting Gal 4.4, followed by, "You see why he did not say 'born through a woman,' but rather 'born of a woman.'" It appears, then, that Origen offers a hypothetical textual variant, rather than attributing it—or v. 4b in any form—to Marcion's text. It therefore remains unattested. Adamantius gives at best merely an allusion to v. 5: "We have been received into adoption (*eis huiothesian elēphthēmen*)"; cf. Rom 8.15, Laod (Eph) 1.5.

4.6 Tertullian, *Marc.* 5.4.4. Marcion's text shows some differences with most witnesses to the catholic text: "you are God's children," instead of "you are children," in agreement with Gk mss D, F, G; "he has sent" rather than "God has sent," in agreement with Gk mss B and 1739; "his spirit" (*to pneuma autou*) in place of "the spirit of his son" (*to pneuma tou hiou autou*), in agreement with P[46], 1734, and 1738; "into *our* hearts," rather than "into *your* hearts" (most early manuscripts agree). Harnack considers Tertullian to be loosely paraphrasing, and so reserves judgment on any of these variants. But Tertullian's supposed paraphrasing matches known textual variants, and the ambiguity of "he has sent" and "his spirit" suggests an earlier text, which the other textual variants clarify. Unfortunately, Tertullian does not quote the verse elsewhere for comparison.

Gal 4.7–8a, 9a is unattested.

4.8b, 9b Tertullian, *Marc.* 5.4.5. Tertullian may be paraphrasing, giving "if therefore you serve" (*si ergo his . . . servitis*) instead of "but then, when you did not know God, you served." The verb "you served/slaved" occurs at the end of v. 8, following "gods," as in Gk mss D, F, G, and some witnesses of the OL. Harnack (Marcion, 46, 75*) drew attention to variant wording in Tertullian's quote of v. 8: "who in/by nature are gods" (*qui in natura sunt dei*), instead of "who are not by nature gods" (*qui non natura sunt dei*), and concluded that Marcion's text must have read *tois en tēi phusei ousi theois* instead of the two variants attested in the catholic textual tradition: *tois phusei mē ousi theois* or *tois mē phusei ousi theois*. Drijvers, "Marcion's reading of Gal. 4,8," developed a Marcionite ideological analysis around this reading. But caution is called for, since the variant may be no more than a scribal error in the transmission of Tertullian's treatise, mistakenly writing *in* for *non*, and is so treated in the Evans (1960) edition. Tertullian's comments on the passage presuppose that he wrote *non*, and make Evans' judgment all but certain. If the variant was in the copy of the Apostolikon used by Tertullian, it scarcely represents the widely divergent wording proposed by Harnack, but would be the result of a simple omission of "not" (*mē*), as occurs in Gk mss 440 and 1243.

4.10 Tertullian, *Marc.* 5.4.6. Schmid, *Marcion und sein Apostolos*, 102, observes that Tertullian elsewhere (*Ieiu.* 14.1–2, cf. 2.6) repeatedly quotes this verse in a form that differs from the majority of Greek manuscripts, but here reads a text in line with the latter. Note that it is Tertullian in his comment, not Marcion's text, that adds "sabbaths," etc. to expand the reference to cover all ritual observances of the Jewish Law (cf. Col 2.16).

Gal 4.11–18 is unattested.

4.19 Tertullian, *Marc.* 5.8.6 (≠Schmid). Tertullian is reviewing Paul's rhetoric of giving birth to his followers from various places in his letters. Was Tertullian sticking strictly to the Marcionite text in developing this theme?

Gal 4.20–22a is unattested. Harnack suggests v. 21–22a may have been present as the start of the following passage.

4.22b–24 Tertullian, *Marc.* 5.4.8; Epiphanius, *Scholion* 2 (v. 23b); Jerome, *Comm. Gal.* 4.25–26 (v. 24a) (Schmid does not credit the evidence of Epiphanius or Jerome). Epiphanius simply adds his note on v. 23b to the same *scholion* as that for Gal 3.13; we should not read anything into that about the intervening verses. His reading of v. 23 reverses the phrases relative to their order in the typical catholic text: "But the one from the promise through the free woman" instead of "but the one from the free woman through promise"; but Tertullian's rendering reflects the catholic text. Referring to v. 24a, Jerome comments, "Marcion and Mani did not want to omit from their versions of the Bible Paul's statement 'these things are allegorical.'" In v. 24, Tertullian gives the familiar catholic reading "two contracts," but then comments, "or two revelations, as I see they have interpreted it (*sive duae ostensiones, sicut invenimus interpretatum*)." Does he mean to refer to a textual variant? Or to a Latin translation of the Apostolikon? Or does he simply mean that this is how the Marcionites understand "contracts"? Schmid opts for the latter; others have proposed the other two choices. I follow Schmid, with reservations.

Tertullian also attests the addition of "into the synagogue of the Judeans according to the Law"; Ephrem has similar additional elements, though lacking the reference to "synagogue": *Hae vero fuerunt symbola duorum testamentorum. Una populi* Judaeorum, *secundum legem in servitute generans ad similitudinem ejusdem Agar. Agar enim ipsa est mons Sina in Arabia; est autem illa similitudo hujus Jerusalem, quia in subjectione est, et una cum filiis suis servit Romanis.*

Eph 1.21 Tertullian, *Marc.* 5.4.8. Tertullian seems to signal the inclusion here (in place of catholic v. 25?) of text paralleling catholic Eph 1.21: *aliud super omnem principatum generans, vim, dominationem, et omne nomen quod nominatur, non tantum in hoc aevo sed et in futuro, quae est mater nostra, in quam repromisimus sanctam ecclesiam* (as in codex Montepessulanus; *Adversus Marcionem* [1954 ed.], 673, prefers the reading that reverses the order of the last two clauses, but see the evidence of Ephrem Syrus below). Harnack (*Marcion*, 76*) attributes this addition to Marcion's editorial hand. But a portion of the same combined reading is found in Ephrem Syrus' commentary on the letters of Paul (135), as first noted by Harris (*Four Lectures*, 19; cf. Zahn, *Der Brief des Paulus*, 298; Clabeaux, *A Lost Edition of the Letters of Paul*, 3, 118–19): *Superior autem Jerusalem libera est, sicut Sara; et eminet supra omnes potestates ac principatus. Ipsa est Mater nostra, Ecclesia sancta, quam confessi sumus.* Harris explains the difference between Ephrem's *confessi* and Tertullian's *repromisimus* by a commonly found uncertainty about how to render the original Greek *hōmologēkamen*.

With regard to this allegory based on the story of Abraham and the mothers of his two principal children in Genesis, Tertullian remarks, "Now it does happen to thieves that something let fall from their booty turns to evidence against them: and so I think Marcion has left behind him this final reference to Abraham—though none had more need of removal—even if he has changed it a little." Does this mean that all previous verses mentioning Abraham were absent from Marcion's text? This would mean the omission of 3.6–9, 14, 16–18, 29. Harnack and Schmid conclude that this is indeed the case; but can Tertullian's polemical remark be read safely in such a precise manner?

Gal 4.25 is unattested.

4.26b Tertullian, *Marc.* 5.4.8. The Apostolikon may have had the shorter text "mother of us" rather than "mother of us all," in agreement with a great many early witnesses to the catholic text, and considered to be the original wording; but Tertullian himself has the shorter reading when he quotes the verse from his own text (e.g., *Marc*. 3.24.3).

Gal 4.27–30 is unattested.

4.31 Tertullian, *Marc*. 5.4.8.

5.1 Tertullian, *Marc*. 5.4.9. Even though several Greek manuscripts read "Christ *purchased* us for freedom," which accords with the prominent Marcionite theme, Tertullian attests the more common reading "freed us for freedom" here for the Apostolikon. At the end of the phrase "the yoke of slavery" Tertullian adds, "which is the Law." Could these additional words have been in Marcion's text? Harnack, *Marcion*, 77*, thinks not. But some of the capitulation notations for this verse in Greek manuscripts explicitly refer to "the Law" here, and Ephrem Syrus similarly has *sub jugo servitutis legis intremus*.

Gal 5.2 is unattested.

5.3 Epiphanius, *Scholion* 3. Epiphanius provides a text with two key differences from the catholic text: "a circumcised person" instead of "every circumcised person" (this involves more than just the omission of *panti*, but also giving "circumcised person" in a different case); "is obligated to fulfill" (*plērōsai*) instead of "to do" (*poiēsai*), in agreement with several Greek manuscripts and Ephrem Syrus. Unfortunately, Epiphanius does not quote this verse elsewhere for comparison.

Gal 5.4–5 is unattested.

5.6 Tertullian, *Marc*. 5.4.10–11.

Gal 5.7–8 is unattested.

5.9 Epiphanius, *Scholion* 4. Epiphanius states that, in place of the verb "leavens" (*zumoi*) Marcion's text reads "spoils" (*doloi*); but far from being a tendentious alteration, "spoils" appears also in Gk ms D*, some witnesses to the OL and Vulgate (also in 1 Cor 5.6, unattested for the Apostolikon), and some church fathers. Clabeaux (*A Lost Edition of the Letters of Paul*, 86) considers this reading probably the original wording of the verse (in agreement with Zuntz, *The Text of the Epistles*, 114, 236).

5.10 Tertullian, *Marc*. 5.4.12; Adam* 2.5, 15 (Schmid does not credit the evidence of Adamantius). Adam* 2.15 has "causing *us* trouble" instead of "causing *you* trouble"; but Adam* 2.5 has the standard catholic text.

Gal 5.11–13 is unattested. Jerome, *Comm. Gal*. 5.12, asks, "On what grounds do Marcion and Valentinus here excuse (Paul) as the apostle of the good God," referring to Paul's wish that those promoting circumcision would be castrated. But this is just a hypothetical question, and there is no guarantee that Jerome (or Origen) confirmed the presence of the verse in Marcion's text (≠Harnack, *Marcion*, 78*).

5.14 Epiphanius, *Scholion* 5; Tertullian, *Marc*. 5.4.12. Tertullian and Epiphanius agree in reading "the Law has been fulfilled in you," rather than "the Law is fulfilled in one saying" found in many witnesses to the catholic text. Neither comments or in any way indicates that the reading represents an altered text, even though it is not found in any other witness to this verse. However, Gk mss D, F, G, some manuscripts of the OL, and the Gothic version, all have a text that conflates Marcion's text with the catholic one: "in you in one saying."

Moreover, the same set of witnesses (except the Gothic version) agree with Marcion's text in skipping over "in the" before the quotation of "love your neighbor as yourself," seemingly breaking the connection between the two halves of the verse, where in the catholic text the quotation is the "one saying" that fulfills the Law. Clabeaux, *A Lost Edition of the Letters of Paul*, 115–16, explores the issues of how Marcion's text may have arisen and its possible meaning; see also Schmid, *Marcion und sein Apostolos*, 130–31, 182, 261 n. 55, 281. As it stands, this reading requires a full stop at the end of v. 14a, and taking v. 14b as a distinct sense unit.

Gal 5.15–18 is unattested.

5.19–21 Epiphanius, *Scholion* 6; cf. Tertullian, *Marc.* 5.10.11. Tertullian, commenting on 1 Cor 15.50, cites this parallel passage; speaking of "those works of flesh *and blood* which, when writing to the Galatians, he said could not inherit the kingdom of God." But since Epiphanius has simply "works of flesh" in agreement with the catholic text, it is likely that Tertullian was conflating this with the Corinthians passage. In v. 20, Epiphanius gives plural forms of "conflicts" and "rivalries," bringing them in line with the other plural forms in the series; many witnesses to the catholic text have the same reading, although singular forms for these two terms is generally considered the original wording of the verse. At the end of the list in v. 21, Epiphanius omits "and things like these."

Gal 5.22–23 is unattested.

5.24 Epiphanius, *Scholion* 7. Epiphanius omits "Jesus" with "Christos" (a recurring pattern in Tertullian's quotes as well). Does this indicate a tendency of Marcion's text, or of patristic preference for the title Christ rather than the name Jesus? The omission of Jesus here is generally considered to be the original wording, and is found in P^{46}, D, F, G, and many other Greek manuscripts.

Gal 6.1 is unattested.

6.2 Tertullian, *Marc.* 5.4.13.

Gal 6.3–5 is unattested.

6.6 Jerome, *Comm. Gal.* 6.6. Jerome reports that, "Marcion interpreted this verse to mean that catechumens and the faithful ought to pray at the same time and that the master must share in prayer with his disciples. He got especially carried away by the phrase 'all good things.'"

6.7–8 Tertullian, *Marc.* 5.4.14; Adam* 2.5 (v. 7b) (Schmid does not credit the evidence of Adamantius). Tertullian appears to read "you are misled" rather than "do not be misled," involving the absence of the negative particle *mē*. Adamantius does not quote this part of the verse, and P^{46} has a lacuna here. Adamantius reads "the things a person may plant . . . these" rather than "whatever a person may plant . . . this," in agreement with P^{46} and no other witness to the text; but Tertullian appears to support the more common text.

6.9–10 Tertullian, *Marc.* 5.4.14. Tertullian quotes v. 9a, then jumps to the end of the verse ("if we do not tire out") as if it read continuously. Only later does he go back and quote part of what falls between. This does not indicate, as some have proposed, that Tertullian first quotes Marcion's text exactly, and then comments based on his own text; rather, with Marcion's text before him, he quotes selectively and in a sequence that suits his rhetorical argument.

Gal 6.11 is unattested.

6.12 Tertullian, *Marc.* 5.4.15 (≠Harnack, Schmid). Tertullian indicates that somewhere near the end of the letter, Paul "calls them persecutors of Christ." The only verse that has "persecute" and "Christ" is this one. Although most witnesses to the catholic text say that those who require circumcision do so "only so that they might *not* be persecuted for the stake of Christos" or "only so that the stake of Christos might *not* be persecuted," Gk ms 1837, by dropping the negative particle *mē*, reads "only so that the stake of Christos might be persecuted." Apparently, the copy of the Apostolikon available to Tertullian had the same variant.

6.13a Epiphanius, *Scholion* 8.

Gal 6.13b–14a is unattested.

6.14b Tertullian, *Marc.* 5.4.15.

6.16 Tertullian, *Marc.* 4.5.1 (≠Harnack, Schmid). Although given in the context of discussing the Evangelion, Tertullian's allusion to this verse belongs to a programmatic statement that seems to have the Marcionite canon self-consciously in mind.

6.17 Tertullian, *Marc.* 5.4.15 (v. 17b); Adam* 5.22 (Schmid does not credit the evidence of Adamantius). The Greek text of Adamantius reads *tōn d'allōn eikē* instead of *tou loipou* (but Rufinus' *de cetero* reflects the latter), and *parechesthō* instead of *parechetō*. Tertullian reads "Christ" rather than "Jesus," in agreement with several Greek manuscripts; but Adamantius has "Jesus."

Gal 6.18 is unattested.

To Corinthians 1

Prologue *Corinthi sunt Achaici* [/*Achaei* AP]. *Et hi similiter ab apostolis* [pl.] *audierunt verbum veritatis et subversi multifarie a falsis apostolis, quidam a philosophiae verbosa eloquentia, alii a secta legis Iudaicae inducti* [*sunt* RM]. *Hos revocat* [*apostolus* not in mss *apud* Corssen] *ad veram et evangelicam sapientiam scribens eis ab Epheso per Timotheum*. The information that the letter was written close in time to Galatians comes from 1 Cor 16.1; that it was written from Ephesus depends on 1 Cor 15.32 (which is attested for the Apostolikon) and 16.8; that it came through Timothy, on 1 Cor 4.17. Harnack, *Marcion*, 128*, regards "through Timothy" to be a secondary addition to the original Prologue, and I have tentatively followed his judgment. Note the plural: the Corinthians had received the word of truth from *apostles*. Dahl, "The Origin of the Earliest Prologues," 259, takes this as evidence that the prologues are not Marcionite, because Paul does not have exclusive status as the true apostle. Yet Paul's mention of the other apostles Peter and Apollos is attested for the Marcionite text.

1.1 Adam* 2.12 (≠Schmid).
1 Cor 1.2 is unattested.
1.3 Tertullian, *Marc.* 5.5.1–2.
1 Cor 1.4–16 is unattested. Adam 1.8 quotes vv. 11–13, and Harnack accepts this testimony, but the Apostolikon may not yet be involved in the dialogue. The quotation shows many variants from the standard text: In v. 11, instead of "for I was informed about you, my colleagues," Adamantius reads "I heard (*ēkoustai moi*)" (but Rufinus' Latin translation reflects the catholic reading, except for "my colleagues"). In v. 12, in place of "Now I say this, that each of you is saying," he has "For one of you says (*hos men gar humōn legei*; cf. Rufinus: *et alius dicit*)." "I am of Christ" at the end of v. 12 is omitted, as it apparently is in 1 Clement 47. In Rufinus' Latin translation, v. 13b is omitted (as it is in Gk ms 1573), but it is present in the Greek text of Adamantius.
1.17–19 Tertullian, *Marc.* 5.5.5; Epiphanius, *Scholion* 9 (v. 19). It is unclear whether Tertullian takes "the stake of the Christos" from v. 17, or Marcion's text of v. 18 had "of the Christos" in addition to "the stake." He has "those who are being rescued" instead of "we who are being rescued," in agreement with Gk mss F, G, 6, 2147, and some witnesses to the OL (Zuntz, *The Text of the Epistles*, 220 and 236, regards this as the original text). Tertullian reads "power *and wisdom*" (repeated in 5.5.6) instead of simply "power" (cf. 1 Cor 1.24). The quotation in v. 19 is from Isa 29.14; note that Marcion's text retains it, despite the clear indication of quotation.
1 Cor 1.20a is unattested.
1.20b–21 Tertullian, *Marc.* 5.5.7. Schmid, *Marcion und sein Apostolos*, 102, notes that Tertullian elsewhere (*Idol.* 9.7) has "this world," a variant found in a number of Greek manuscripts and versions, but here reads "the world" in agreement with P^{46}, Sinaiticus, A, B, D*, etc. A textual variant in *Adversus Marcionem* makes it uncertain whether v. 21 should be read "did not know God (*deum*)" or "did not know the Master (*dominum*)"; the latter is the reading Tertullian uses from his own Bible elsewhere (e.g., Tertullian, *Marc.* 2.2), and both variants are attested in the Latin textual tradition for this verse.
1.22 Tertullian, *Marc.* 5.5.8. Marcion's text appears to omit "both" in the construction "both the Jews . . . and the Greeks," as do Gk mss P^{46}, F, G, 323, the Peshitta Syriac version, and some witnesses to the OL. Clabeaux considers this to be the original wording of the verse (*A Lost Edition of the Letters of Paul*, 86, following Zuntz, *The Text of the Epistles*, 200, 237).
1.23a Tertullian, *Marc.* 5.5.9.
1 Cor 1.23b–24 is unattested.
1.25 Tertullian, *Marc.* 5.5.9.
1 Cor 1.26 is unattested.
1.27–28 Tertullian, *Marc.* 5.5.9. In v. 28, Tertullian appears to have an additional attribute, "small/least," alongside of "low-born," "despised," and "nothings" (twice second in the series, and once first), as does Aphrahat. Handling "the nothings" as an appositive to the previous

series, rather than another term in the series, is found in a number of Greek manuscripts: P⁴⁶, ℵ*, A, D*, F, G, 33, 1739.

1.29–31 Tertullian, *Marc.* 5.5.10 (vv. 29a, 31); Adam 1.22; Epiphanius, *Scholion* 10 (v. 31; neither Harnack nor Schmid credit the evidence of Adamantius, and indeed the Apostolikon may not be used here). Tertullian omits v. 30, reading directly from v. 29 to v. 31, and both Harnack and Schmid follow this reading (Adamantius quotes the whole passage). In v. 29, Tertullian ends with "that no one may boast" (=Harnack and Schmid), while Adamantius continues with "in his presence," a reading found in a number of Greek manuscripts, while most witnesses to the catholic text read "in God's presence." The quotation in v. 31 is from Jer 9.23; note again the presence of an unmistakable quote from Jewish scripture.

1 Cor 2.1–5 is unattested.

2.6–7 Tertullian, *Marc.* 5.6.1–4 (vv. 6a, 7); Epiphanius, *Scholion* 11 (v. 6c). Our sources are complementary, with Epiphanius supplying one of two clauses that Tertullian skips over. The other ("but not the wisdom of this aeon, nor") is unattested. Without it, the sense of the passage would be: "We speak wisdom among those who are perfect about the rulers of this aeon who are being nullified." The proposition that 1 Cor 2.6–16 is a non-Pauline interpolation (Widmann, "1 Kor 2.6–16"; Walker Jr., "1 Corinthians 2.6–16") is not supported by the evidence of the Apostolikon.

2.8 Tertullian, *Marc.* 5.6.5. Tertullian's wording may reflect the reading "by no means" or "never" (*oudepote*) instead of "not" (*ouk*), in agreement with Ephrem Syrus and some witnesses to the OL (see Clabeaux, *A Lost Edition of the Letters of Paul*, 116–17).

1 Cor 2.9–15 is unattested.

2.16 Tertullian, *Marc.* 5.6.9. The quotation is from Isa 40.13, whose original wording in the LXX is *tis egnō noun kuriou, kai tis autou sumboulos egeneto, hos sumbibai auton*. Most witnesses to the catholic text here skip over the second clause. But Tertullian clearly attests a reading that has the second clause, and omits the third: "For who has known the Lord's mind, and who has been its counselor?" (*quis enim cognovit sensum domini, et quis illi consiliarius fuit*). This matches the form quoted in Rom 11.34 in the catholic text.

1 Cor 3.1–9a is unattested. Harnack accepts with reservation vv. 2–4 on the basis of Adam 5.22; but this quotation falls before Adamantius takes quotations from the Apostolikon. Adam 1.9 likewise quotes vv. 2–3a, but may not be employing the Apostolikon either.

3.10–15 Tertullian, *Marc.* 5.6.10–11.

3.12–15 Tertullian, *Marc.* 5.6.11.

3.16–17 Tertullian, *Marc.* 5.6.11–12. Tertullian gives the second clause of v. 17 in a pious passive, as "will be destroyed," rather than as "God will destroy" found in most witnesses to the catholic version. He then comments to clarify that, implicitly, it is the God of the temple who would do the destroying. So possibly, the pious passive is found in Marcion's text (Harnack believes so); elsewhere Tertullian quotes this verse as "God will destroy" (e.g., *Pud.* 16.2).

3.18c–20 Tertullian, *Marc.* 5.6.12; Epiphanius, *Scholion* 12 (vv. 19b–20). The scripture quotations, clearly identified as quotations, are taken from Job 5.13 and Ps 94.11. Epiphanius reads for the latter "contemplations of human beings" (found also in a number of Greek manuscripts), while Tertullian and most witnesses to the catholic text have "contemplations of the wise"; Epiphanius, *Pan.* 76.20.14, quotes directly from Ps 94.11 to read "thoughts of the wise."

3.21–23 Tertullian, *Marc.* 5.6.13 (v. 21a); 5.7.9 (vv. 21b–22); Adam 2.19 (=Schmid vv. 21–22a only, not accepting the evidence of either *Marc.* 5.7.9 or Adamantius, who may not be using the Apostolikon here). Tertullian, *Res.* 59.2, reads "whether future or present" from the catholic text of 3.22, but here gives Marcion's text in the usually attested order "whether present or future" (see Schmid, *Marcion und sein Apostolos*, 102). In v. 22, Adamantius omits "or Apollos," probably by homeoarcton; Tertullian attests the words.

1 Cor 4.1–4 is unattested.

4.5 Tertullian, *Marc.* 5.7.1.

1 Cor 4.6–9a is unattested.

4.9b Tertullian, *Marc.* 5.7.1.

1 Cor 4.10–15a is unattested.

4.15b Tertullian, *Marc.* 5.7.2; 5.8.6.

1 Cor 4.16–21 is unattested.

5.1 Tertullian, *Marc.* 5.7.2.

1 Cor 5.2 is unattested.

5.3–5 Adam* 2.5, 8 (v. 5); Adam 2.21 (v. 5); Tertullian, *Marc.* 5.7.2 (vv. 3, 5) (=Schmid v. 5 only, despite the implicit reference to v. 3 in Tertullian's *displicuisse* and *iudicarit*, and not crediting the evidence of Adamantius). In reference to v. 3, Tertullian says that Paul "disapproved" of the man, and "has spoken as a judge." Adamantius quotes verbatim, with "*thus (hōs)* absent in my body" (a reading widely shared in the Greek manuscript tradition). Adamantius has "our master Jesus *Christos*," following "in the name of" (agreeing with Gk mss P[46], F, G, and many others, as well as nearly all versions), but simply "our master Jesus" following "with the energy of" (shared by Gk mss P[46], ℵ, A, B, D*, Sahidic Coptic, and several others, but not F or G). Clabeaux (*A Lost Edition of the Letters of Paul*, 87–89) considers Marcion's text to retain the original wording of this verse in these instances. Adam 2.5 ends the quote at v. 5a with "for destruction"; but Tertullian's testimony picks up there, providing "for destruction of the flesh, so that (his) spirit may be rescued on the day of the Master" (Marcion's text agrees with Gk mss P[46], B, and a few others in not adding "Jesus," "Jesus Christos," or "our Master Jesus Christos" as found in many other witnesses). In Adam 2.8, reading *paredōka* rather than *paradounai*, and omitting "to Satan," Adamantius continues the quote with "so that (his) spirit may be rescued." Adam 2.21, where the Apostolikon may not be the source, again has *paredōka* rather than *paradounai*, but here "to Satan" is included, concluding as in 2.5 with "for destruction."

1 Cor 5.6 is unattested.

5.7 Epiphanius, *Scholion* 13 (v. 7b); Tertullian, *Marc.* 5.7.3; Adam* 2.18 (v. 7b).

1 Cor 5.8–13a is unattested.

5.13b Tertullian, *Marc.* 5.7.2 (≠Schmid, who apparently overlooks Tert's *et auferri iubens malum de medio*). The quotation here of Deut 21.21 may have gone unrecognized by most readers. When Tertullian quotes it directly in a set of examples of OT passages quoted by Paul (5.18.6), the wording is different: *auferte malum de medio vestrum*.

1 Cor 6.1–12 is unattested. Harnack cites Tertullian, *Marc.* 2.9.7, for "judging angels" in v. 3, and Adam* 5.22 for v. 11; but neither of these can be assumed to be quotations from Marcion's text. Our sources may have skipped over Paul's discussion of lawsuits because it offered no point of critique to use against Marcion. Or it may have been lacking in Marcion's text, as an intrusion into an otherwise consistent discussion of sexual issues. Or Tertullian may have been relying on some mediating source (such as Marcion's *Antitheses*) that itself drew only upon Paul's discussion of sexual issues, and bypassed the subject of lawsuits. Gk ms A omits vv. 3–6; F and G omit vv. 7–14; 2344 omits vv. 9–10.

6.13–14 Tertullian, *Marc.* 5.7.4. Tertullian's wording suggests the inclusion, at the end of v. 13, of "as the temple is for God and God for the temple" (*ut templum deo et deus templo*); the clause does not appear when Tertullian quotes this verse elsewhere from the catholic text (*Pud.* 16.6). Tertullian's text of v. 14 diverges from most witnesses to the catholic version of this verse: he uses the same verb twice for "awaken" (*suscito* > Gk *egeirō*), whereas most use a distinct verb for "and will rouse (*exegerei*) us" (but Gk mss 460, 618, and 1738 share this divergence). He also has "he who awakened the Master" instead of "now God both awakened the Master." Schnelle, "1 Kor 6:14," 217–19, has suggested that v. 14 is a non-Pauline gloss.

6.15 Tertullian, *Marc.* 5.7.4 (v. 15a); 4.34.5 (v. 15b); Adam* 5.22 (=Schmid v. 15a only, accepting the evidence of neither Tertullian, *Marc.* 4.34.5, or Adamantius, who quotes the entire verse). In discussing the import of Jesus' teaching on divorce in the Evangelion, Tertullian comments, "But, you know, your own apostle does not permit the members of Christ to be joined to a prostitute" (4.34.5). How careful was Tertullian that the words were actually in the Apostolikon? The evidence of Adamantius confirms that they were.

6.16 Epiphanius, *Scholion* 14; Adam* 5.23 (Schmid does not credit the evidence of Adamantius, while Harnack mistakenly cites it as Adam 2.23). Adamantius has "for" (*gar*) instead of "or" (*ē*) at the beginning of the verse. This verse quotes Gen 2.24.

1 Cor 6.17 is unattested.

6.18–19 Tertullian, *Marc.* 5.7.4–5 (≠Harnack, Schmid). Harnack and Schmid apparently overlook Tertullian's allusions to both v. 18 (*avertens . . . a fornicatione* = *pheugete tēn porneian*) and v. 19 (*non nostra* = *ouk este heautōn*).

6.20 Tertullian, *Marc.* 5.7.4–5. Tertullian appears to attest a second verb: "glorify *and exalt*" (*tollemus* > Gk *arate*). Harnack (*Marcion*, 85*) suggests that Tertullian's wording (*in corpore perituro*) indicates a reading of "in (your) *mortal* (*thnētōi*) bodies."

7.1–2 Tertullian, *Marc.* 5.7.6 (≠Schmid). Tertullian attests the presence of the entire chapter, with a few more specific references to individual verses. Harnack (*Marcion*, 85*) finds evidence of vv. 1–3, 7, 10–11, 29b, 39; of these, Schmid does not see direct citation of vv. 1–3. For vv. 1–2, Tertullian paraphrases loosely: *Etenim apostolus, etsi bonum continentiae praefert, tamen coniugium et contrahi permittit et usui esse.*

1 Cor 7.3–5 is not directly attested, unless it be by Tertullian's remark that Paul permits the "use" (*usui*) of marriage.

7.6–7a Tertullian, *Marc.* 5.7.6 (≠Schmid; =Harnack v. 7a only). These verses are alluded to by *continentiae praefert, tamen coniugium . . . permittit.*

7.7b Origen, *Fr. 1 Cor* (Cramer, *Catenae Graecorum*, 125,5f.14). See Harnack, *Marcion*, 86*; Schmid, *Marcion und sein Apostolos*, 323 n. 31.

1 Cor 7.8–9 is not directly attested.

7.10–11 Tertullian, *Marc.* 5.7.6. Tertullian paraphrases: *Et magis retineri quam disiungi suadet. Plane Christus vetat divortium.*

7.12–29a is not directly attested.

7.29b Tertullian, *Marc.* 5.7.8.

1 Cor 7.29c–38 is not directly attested. Verse 38 is omitted in Gk mss F, G, 323, 614, 630, 1319, 1352, 1837, 2147, 2412.

7.39 Tertullian, *Marc.* 5.7.8.

1 Cor 7.40–8.3 is unattested.

8.4–6 Tertullian, *Marc.* 5.7.9. In v. 5, Marcion's text apparently had the plural "celestial spheres" (*in caelis* > Gk *ouranois*) instead of the singular "celestial sphere" (*ouranōi*); Tertullian's own text of Paul agrees with the latter (e.g., *Marc.* 3.15.2).

1 Cor 8.7–12 is unattested.

8.13 Eznik, *De Deo* 408 (≠Schmid). According to Eznik, this verse provided the justification for Marcionite vegetarianism.

1 Cor 9.1–6 is unattested.

9.7–10 Tertullian, *Marc.* 5.7.10–11 (vv. 7, 9–10a); Epiphanius, *Scholion* 15, 16 (vv. 8–9); *Elenchos* 15 (vv. 8–10a); Adam 1.22 (vv. 7c–10b) (Schmid does not credit the evidence of Adamantius, who may not be using the Apostolikon, and so does not include v. 8a). Tertullian inverts the sequence of examples in v. 7, reading "soldiers and shepherds and cultivators" instead of "soldier . . . cultivator . . . shepherd." The latter is supported by Adamantius and is the order found in most witnesses to the catholic text. In the last clause of v. 7, Tertullian and Adamantius agree in reading "does not eat from the milk" instead of "does not eat from the milk *of the sheep*" or "*their* milk" found in nearly all other witnesses to the text; P[46] is the only Greek manuscript to agree with this shorter text. In vv. 8–9, mss V and M of Epiphanius (accepted as the valid text by Schmid, *Marcion und sein Apostolos*, 323 n. 38, in place of the critical text of Holl, *Panarion*, 121.15–17), Scholion 15 reads: "Altered (*metēllagmenōs*), for in place of 'does not the Law also say these things?' (v. 8), he says this: 'even if the Law of Moses does not say these things'." This suggests two variants in Marcion's text of v. 8: (1) the addition of the conditional "if" (*ei*), effectively reversing the sense of the clause in comparison with the catholic text, and (2) the addition of "of Moses," which in the catholic text is found with "the Law" in v. 9, but not in v. 8. But Epiphanius does not say quite the same thing when he repeats his quotation of these verses before his commentary on them in *Elenchos* 15. There, he says, "Altered, for in place of 'in the Law' (v. 9), he says 'in the Law of Moses'; and he says before this, 'even if the Law does not say these things' (v. 8)." This second report confirms the addition of the conditional "if" in v. 8, (which is also found in Gk ms 1875, and evidence for it in the conflated reading of mss F and G), but shifts the supposed addition of "of Moses" from v. 8 (as he appeared to say in *Scholion* 15) to v. 9. As they stand, these two reports suggest that Epiphanius was confused by his own notes as to where the "of Moses" stood in Marcion's text—either in v. 8, where it would differ from the catholic reading (but not significantly affect the sense), or in v. 9, where it would agree with many witnesses to the catholic text, but apparently not Epiphanius' text (nor that of P[46] and some witnesses to the OL). The latter is almost certainly what Epiphanius originally saw in the Apostolikon. The evidence of Epiphanius is to be preferred here to that of Adamantius, whose Greek text matches the majority text of later Greek manuscripts, while Rufinus' Latin translation has *an et lex haec dicit*, a variant found in several witnesses to the catholic text that omits the rhetorical negative. The quotation in v. 9 is from Deut 25.4, and it is noteworthy that Marcion did not excise (as his critics would expect) a direct quote of the Law of Moses, which Paul cites authoritatively, attributes to God, and interprets allegorically—all of which would appear to be diametrically opposed to the views of Marcion as our sources (and modern scholarship) represent them. When Epiphanius includes v. 10a in his comments in *Elenchos* 15, he may be quoting his own text of Paul rather than Marcion's.

1 Cor 9.11–13 is unattested.

9.14 Tertullian, *Marc.* 5.7.11 (v. 14b); Adam 1.6 (Latin only; ≠Schmid). Tertullian alludes to the second part of this verse, with the words *de evangelio viventibus patrocinantum*. Only Rufinus' Latin translation of Adamantius quotes the verse: *ita et dominus his qui evangelium annuntiant, ut de evangelio vivant*.

9.15 Tertullian, *Marc.* 5.7.11 (Schmid credits only v. 15c, apparently overlooking the allusion to v. 15a: *sed noluit uti legis potestate*).

1 Cor 9.16–17 is unattested.

9.18 Tertullian, *Marc.* 5.7.11 (≠Harnack, Schmid, both apparently overlooking the allusion to this verse: *quia maluit gratis laborare*).

1 Cor 9.19–27 is unattested. Tertullian quotes 9.20 and 9.22 earlier in his discussion (*Marc.* 5.3.5), but in a context and manner—including citations from Acts—that cast doubt on his use of the Apostolikon there. P^{46} omits v. 20a ("and I became to the Jews like a Jew, that I might gain Jews").

10.1–7 Epiphanius, *Scholion* 17 (vv. 1, 3–5a, 6–7); Tertullian, *Marc.* 5.7.12 (vv. 4c, 5b–6a), cf. 5.5.9; Adam* 2.18 (vv. 1b–4); Adam 2.20 (v. 4c) (Schmid does not credit the evidence of Adamantius, and therefore does not include v. 2; by a typographic error, he fails to identify his source for vv. 1, 3–4a, which is Epiphanius). Epiphanius lacks "all" with "our ancestors" in v. 1 (but Adamantius has it), though he has "and all passed through the sea." Epiphanius omits v. 2, but Adamantius has it (reading *ebaptisthēsan* instead of *ebaptisanto*; Clabeaux, *A Lost Edition of the Letters of Paul*, 89–90, considers this the original reading of the verse, based on agreement in a number of Greek manuscripts). In addition to quoting v. 4c in the regular sequence of his exposition, Tertullian also comments on it at 5.5.9: "'And the rock was Christ.' Even Marcion has kept that!" Epiphanius omits v. 5b ("for they were scattered in the wilderness") and quotes it nowhere else; Tertullian mentions "in the wilderness," but does not quote "for they were scattered." Epiphanius lacks the explicit subject "God" for the verb in v. 5a ("did not think well"), and understands the subject of the verb to be Christ (*Elenchos* 17); the omission of "God" is shared by Clement, Irenaeus, and Gk mss 257 and 1610 (see Zuntz, *The Text of the Epistles*, 232, who regards this reading as original, with Christ the implied subject of the verb). In v. 6 Epiphanius has the syntactically synonymous *pros* for the *eis* ("for") of the catholic text. Schmid, *Marcion und sein Apostolos*, 103, discusses a minor textual variant given here by Tertullian that diverges from his typical way of quoting the verse, corresponding to *hēmin* ("for us") instead of *hēmōn* ("of us"), but Epiphanius has the latter.

10.8–11 Epiphanius, *Scholion* 17; *Elenchos* 17 (vv. 9a, 11a); Tertullian, *Marc.* 5.7.13 (vv. 8–10); 5.7.14 (v. 11); Adam* 2.18 (v. 11). Epiphanius omits v. 8 (and quotes it nowhere else). For v. 9, he explicitly notes in *Elenchos* 17 that Marcion's text read "neither let us put Christos to the test," rather than "neither let us put the Master to the test"; but Marcion's text is found also in Gk mss P^{46}, D, F, G, and a great many others, plus several versions and early witnesses such as Irenaeus, Clement, Origen, and Ephrem Syrus (hence Clabeaux, *A Lost Edition of the Letters of Paul*, 90–91, following Zuntz, *The Text of the Epistles*, 126, 232, 237, considers it the original reading of the verse). Tertullian alludes broadly to the "fears" induced by the stories of vv. 8–10, asking, "If I now commit the same sins as Israel committed, shall I receive the same treatment, or shall I not? If not the same, vainly does he set before me terrors I am not going to experience." Epiphanius indicates the presence of vv.

9b–10, without quoting them. In v. 11, he reads "it was written for us" and stops quoting at this point, but suggesting the rest of v. 11 with "and so on"; but he adds the missing words in *Elenchos* 17 (*egraphē de hēmin eis nouthesian* instead of *egraphē de pros nouthesian hēmōn*). Tertullian quotes all of v. 11, diverging somewhat in the first part of the verse: "Now in whatsoever way these things happened to them (*haec autem quemadmodum evenerunt illis*)" instead of "Now these things befell them." In Adam* 2.18, the Marcionite Markus claims that the verse reads "without an example" (*atypōs*); Harnack, *Marcion*, 87*–88*, accepts this isolated testimony, while Zuntz, *The Text of the Epistles*, 233, conjectures that the claim is based upon uncertain word separation in the letters *tautatypōs*. In any case, this entire passage is at odds with Marcion's ideology as it has been traditionally understood, saying as it does that Christ accompanied the Israelites out of Egypt, and punished them for wrongdoing, and that these incidents, as reported in Jewish scripture, serve as examples for Christians. Either our understanding of Marcion's beliefs is totally wrong, or Marcion did not touch a passage even as problematic for him as this one is, and found some way to interpret it away. The proposal of Cope, "First Corinthians 8–10," that 10.1–22 constitutes an interpolation, is not supported by the evidence of the Apostolikon.

1 Cor 10.12–15 is unattested.

10.16 Adam 2.20 (≠Schmid). The paraphrastic quotation compresses two clauses into one: "When he says: 'The cup of blessing, the bread that we break, is a sharing of the blood and the body of the Master.'" For "Master" instead of "Christ" in both clauses, see Gk ms 1735; in the second clause only, see D*, G, F; in the first clause only, see Ψ. It is not certain that Adamantius is quoting from the Marcionite Apostolikon in this section.

1 Cor 10.17–18 is unattested.

10.19–20 Epiphanius, *Scholion* 18. Epiphanius reads: "What, then, am I to say? That a sacrifice (*hierothuton*) is anything, or an idol offering (*eidōlothuton*) is anything?" and then adds: "But Marcion added the 'sacrifice.'" Indeed, P⁴⁶ ℵ*, A, C, and several others read simply "that an idol offering is anything"; most other witnesses to the catholic text read: "that an idol offering is anything, or that an idol is anything" (or the same two clauses in reverse order). The term *hierothuton* appears in the catholic text just a few verses later, at 10.28. Zuntz, *The Text of the Epistles*, 229, observes that many witnesses to the catholic text alter the latter to conform to v. 19's *eidōlothuton*, and proposes the reverse harmonization behind Marcion's text in v. 19. Epiphanius does not comment on the omission of "the nations" as the subject of the verb "they offer," which is missing in both Marcion's text and his own, as well as in Gk mss B, D, F, G, and some witnesses to the OL, and considered the original reading of the verse by Clabeaux, *A Lost Edition of the Letters of Paul*, 91–92, and Zuntz, *The Text of the Epistles*, 102, 237.

1 Cor 10.21–24 is unattested.

10.25 Tertullian, *Marc.* 5.7.14 (≠Schmid). Tertullian almost certainly refers to v. 25 when he says with irony, "It is a great argument for that other god, this permission to use meats contrary to the Law!" The presence of this verse in the canon of the vegetarian Marcionites would seem to rule out the theory that they redacted the text ideologically.

1 Cor 10.26–11.2 is unattested. Gk mss 323, 618, 1242, 1738 omit 10.27–28.

11.3 Tertullian, *Marc.* 5.8.1. Tertullian reads "the head of a man is the Christos" (*caput viri Christus est*), and Ephrem Syrus appears to support this reading, while most witnesses to the catholic text have "the head of every man is the Christos." The evidence of the Apostolikon does not support the proposition that 11.3–16 is a non-Pauline interpolation, interrupting Paul's discussion of food and food-ritual (see Walker Jr., "1 Corinthians 11:2–16 and Paul's Views regarding Women" and "The Vocabulary of 1 Corinthians 11:3–16"; Cope, "1 Cor 11:2–16: One Step Further," 435–36; Trompf, "On Attitudes toward Women in Paul and Paulinist Literature").

1 Cor 11.4 is unattested.

11.5 Tertullian, *Marc.* 5.8.11 (≠Schmid). Tertullian refers back to this passage to acknowledge the seeming contradiction with the command for women's silence in the assembly in 14.34–35.

1 Cor 11.6 is unattested.

11.7 Epiphanius, *Scholion* 19; Tertullian, *Marc.* 5.8.1; Adam* 5.23 (v. 7a, Greek only; Schmid credits the evidence of neither Epiphanius nor Adamantius). At the beginning of the verse, Epiphanius omits *men gar*, while Tertullian attests the *gar*, and Adamantius has the catholic text. Epiphanius reads, somewhat ungrammatically, "a man ought not (to have) long hair (*koman*)," and quotes it the same way from his own text of Paul (*Pan.* 70.3.7; 80.6.6), harmonizing the wording of this verse with the references to long hair in vv. 14–15. But Tertullian and Adamantius have the catholic text, reading "ought not to have his head covered." Tertullian has only "God's image"; but Epiphanius has "God's glory and image" having both terms found in the catholic text, but in reverse order; Adamantius has them in the catholic order, as does Epiphanius when quoting from his own text of Paul (*Pan.* 70.3.7; 80.6.6). These differences are difficult to reconcile into a single reading for Marcion's text.

11.8–9 Tertullian, *Marc.* 5.8.2.

11.10 Tertullian, *Marc.* 5.8.2.

1 Cor 11.11–18 is unattested, but vv. 17–18 were probably present as the context of v. 19.

11.19 Tertullian, *Marc.* 5.8.3. Tertullian alludes to this passage when he says, "I have already observed several times that by the apostle sects (*haereses*) are set down as an evil thing . . . and that those persons are to be understood as meeting with approval who flee from sects as an evil thing."

1 Cor 11.20–22 is unattested. Harnack considers all of vv. 20–34 to be present, based on Tertullian's reference to the meal as the body and blood of Christ (cf. vv. 20, 23–25, 27), as well as to "judgment" (cf. vv. 29, 31–32), while Schmid credits the presence only of vv. 23–33.

11.23–25 Tertullian, *Marc.* 5.8.3. Tertullian alludes at a minimum to these verses, excusing his failure to comment further upon the subject: "I have already, in discussing the Evangelion, by the sacrament of the bread and the cup, given proof of the verity of our Lord's body and blood." Thus, the argument of J. Magne, "Les paroles sur la coupe," 485–90, that this passage constitutes an interpolation, is not supported by the evidence of the Apostolikon.

1 Cor 11.26–28, 30 is not directly attested.

11.29, 31–32 Tertullian, *Marc.* 5.8.3. Tertullian says, as he continues to mention topics he has already discussed sufficiently, "Also that every mention of judgement has reference to the creator as the god who is a judge, has been discussed almost everywhere in this work."

1 Cor 11.33–34 is unattested.

12.1 Tertullian, *Marc.* 5.8.4.

1 Cor 12.2–7 is unattested.

12.8–10 Tertullian, *Marc.* 5.8.8. Tertullian appears to attest singular constructions ("a bestowal of healings" rather than "bestowals of healings," and "a discernment of spirits" rather than "discernments of spirits"), found also in various witnesses to the catholic text of these verses.

12.11–12 Tertullian, *Marc.* 5.8.9 (=Harnack, Schmid v. 12 only; but Tertullian alludes to v. 11 in saying, "he has brought the unity of our body, in its many diverse limbs, *into comparison with the compact structure of the various spiritual gifts*").

1 Cor 12.13–21 is not directly attested, but Harnack considers it included in Tertullian's reference to the "many diverse limbs," and I concur.

1 Cor 12.22–24a is not directly attested, but would seem necessary for the following verses.

12.24b–c Epiphanius, *Scholion* 20 (v. 24b); Adam 2.19 (v. 24b–c) (Schmid does not credit the evidence of Adamantius, who may not be using the Apostolikon here). Adamantius reads *hysterounti* instead of *hysteroumenōi*, in agreement with Gk mss P^{46}, D, F. G, and a number of others, as well as Origen (Epiphanius' testimony does not extend to that part of the verse); Clabeaux considers it the original wording of the verse (*A Lost Edition of the Letters of Paul*, 92–93, following Zuntz, *The Text of the Epistles*, 128, 237).

1 Cor 12.25–27 is unattested.

12.28 Tertullian, *Marc.* 5.17.16 (≠Schmid). Tertullian refers to this passage when he comments on the omission of "prophets" in Laod 2.20: "The heretic has taken away 'and prophets,' forgetting that the Master has set in the church prophets as well as apostles." He apparently read *kurios* ("the Master") instead of *theos* ("God") found in most witnesses to the catholic text.

1 Cor 12.29–30 is unattested.

12.31–13.2 Tertullian, *Marc.* 5.8.10. Tertullian alludes broadly to this passage, when he says, "love must be more highly regarded than all spiritual gifts." This testimony perhaps encompasses 13.8 and 13.13 as well, and undercuts any effort to use the silence of our other witnesses in support of the proposition that 12.31b–14.1a is a non-Pauline interpolation (see Titus, "Did Paul Write I Corinthians 13?" 299–302; Walker Jr., "Is First Corinthians 13 a Non-Pauline Interpolation?" 484–99), although there remains the possibility that the love poem proper of 13.4–7 was lacking.

1 Cor 13.3–14.13 is unattested. Harnack's evidence for including 14.2 is insufficient.

14.14 Tertullian, *Marc.* 5.8.12 (≠Harnack, Schmid). Tertullian refers to this verse in the context of the list of gifts brought to the assembly in 14.26. Whether this suggests any displacement in the text of the Apostolikon relative to the catholic text cannot be proven.

1 Cor 14.15–18 is unattested.

14.19 Epiphanius, *Scholion* 21. Epiphanius states that, after "Nevertheless in an assembly I would rather speak five words with my mind," Marcion's text adds "regarding the Law" (*dia ton nomon*); yet he has some difficulty articulating its supposed negative implication for the Law. Frank Williams makes a gallant effort to construe it in his translation, proposing that Epiphanius understood the words to mean "I wish to speak (no more than) five words in church on the Law's account" (*The Panarion of Epiphanius of Salamis*, 325). According to Zuntz, this reading (*pente logous tōi noi mou lalēsai dia ton nomon*) is found in some texts of the Vulgate (D, Z: *quinque verbis loqui in ecclesiis in sensu meo per legem*) and appears to be a conflation of two variants of an original *dia tou noos mou*: (1) *dia ton nomon* (cf. Ambrosiaster, Paulinus of Nola), (2) *tōi noi mou* (cf. Zuntz, *The Text of the Epistles*, 230; Harnack, *Marcion*, 90*). In any case, it is clear that the reading was found outside of the Marcionite Church, and therefore cannot be attributed to Marcion.

1 Cor 14.20 is unattested.

14.21 Epiphanius, *Scholion* 22; Tertullian, *Marc.* 5.8.10. Note the explicit favorable citation of the Law (although the words are a paraphrase of Isa 28.11). Epiphanius attests "other lips" (*cheilesin heterois*), seemingly supported by Tertullian (*aliis labiis*), in agreement with Gk mss P^{46}, F, G, and a large number of other manuscripts, as well as the OL and other versions, and Origen, rather than "lips of others" (*cheilesin heterōn*) found in other witnesses to the verse. Epiphanius also has a different construction of "speak to this people" than most other witnesses to the verse (*pros ton laon touton* rather than *tōi laōi toutōi*). Unfortunately, he does not quote the verse elsewhere.

1 Cor 14.22–23 is unattested.

14.24–25 Tertullian, *Marc.* 5.8.12 (=Harnack, Schmid v. 25 only). Tertullian speaks of "prophets . . . who have made manifest the secrets of the heart" (*prophetas . . . qui . . . cordis occulta traduxerint*), thus alluding to v. 24 as well as v. 25.

14.26 Tertullian, *Marc.* 5.8.12 (≠Schmid). Tertullian lists several items in this series of gifts, with the addition of prayer (cf. 14.14) and omission of teaching (omitted also by several Greek manuscripts, probably by homeoteleuton; Tertullian could have made the same mistake, or wanted to limit the list to gifts that are clearly miraculous).

1 Cor 14.27–33 is unattested. Tertullian alludes to vv. 32–33a in his commentary on Marcion's Evangelion (*Marc.* 4.4.5), where we cannot be certain that he is careful to quote it from Marcion's text of Paul, rather than from his own. His wording suggests "spirits" as the subject of v. 33a, rather than "God" (*et spiritus prophetarum prophetis erunt subditi, non enim eversionis sunt, sed pacis*), as also found in Ambrosiaster. Harnack, *Marcion*, 90*, and Zuntz, *The Text of the Epistles*, 231, 236 regard this reading as Paul's original wording.

14.34–35a Epiphanius, *Scholion* 23 (v. 34); Tertullian, *Marc.* 5.8.11; Adam* 2.18 (v. 34) (=Schmid v. 34 only). Tertullian, Epiphanius, and Adamantius all attest the reading "in an assembly" (*en ekklēsia*), rather than "in the assemblies" (*en tais ekklēsiais*) found in most witnesses to the catholic text (but Gk mss 119, 330, 2400, the Syriac, Coptic, and Ethiopic versions have "in the assembly"). Epiphanius and Adamantius have "has been permitted" (*epitetraptai*) instead of "is permitted" (*epitrepetai*), (a reading also found in several Greek manuscripts); Tertullian's testimony is too paraphrastic to compare. Adamantius has *hypotassesthai* instead of *hypotassesthōsan*, but Epiphanius reads the latter (both readings are found in Greek manuscripts). Tertullian explicitly notes that Marcion's text included the whole of v. 34, including the citation of the authority of the Law. Schmid apparently overlooks Tertullian's reference to v. 35a: *ne quid discendi duntaxat gratia loquantur*. This is taken by Tertullian as a qualification of the prohibition; women are not to speak to learn something, though they can speak in service of the spiritual gifts. Thus the Apostolikon contained this controversial passage thought by many to be a non-Pauline interpolation (see, e.g., Fitzer, *Das Weib schweige in der Gemeinde*; Murphy-O'Connor, "Interpolations in 1 Corinthians," 90–92; Fee, *The First Epistle to the Corinthians*, 699–708). But it remains uncertain where it appeared in this section of the letter. Catholic witnesses provide two options, with Gk mss D, F, G, and 88 placing it after 14.40. Tertullian cites it following a discussion of 14.21, and before mentioning 14.24ff.; Epiphanius' testimony places it anywhere between 14.21 and 15.1.

15.1a Epiphanius, *Scholion* 24. Harnack accepts the evidence of Adam 5.6 for the presence of vv. 1–4; but there is no good reason to think that Marcion's text is being used by Adamantius in this portion of the work.

1 Cor 15.1b–3a is unattested (≠Harnack). Epiphanius quotes the last part of v. 2 in *Elenchos* 24, in a very free reworking of this section of Paul's letter. But we cannot be sure he is relying on Marcion's text there. Clabeaux, following Harnack (*Marcion*, 91*) and Blackman (44 and 168), claims that Marcion's text omitted "that which I received" (*ho kai parelabon*) in v. 3a (*A Lost Edition of the Letters of Paul*, 111), and cites several church fathers with the same omission (111, 119–20). Birdsall, in his review of Clabeaux, 633, corrected him on some of these citations; nevertheless Eusebius, Adamantius (using his own biblical text in 5.6), and some OL manuscripts still show that the omission was found outside of the Marcionite church, and therefore cannot be shown to be an ideological edit. In fact, even the claim that the words were omitted in Marcion's text cannot be confirmed; but see the evidence of Epiphanius in the next note.

15.3b–4 Epiphanius, *Scholion* 24 (vv. 3b–4), cf. *Elenchos* 24. Epiphanius is compressing a string of clauses into a neat rhetorical proof of Christ's physical resurrection, so his omissions should be viewed cautiously. His order does not follow that of the catholic text; he quotes the verses in the order 1, 14 (or 17), 11, 3–4. In both the *scholion* and the *elenchos*, he gives an abbreviated and conflated text: "So we are declaring and so you have trusted (=v. 11b), that Christos died and was entombed and rose on the third day" (=vv. 3b, 4a). He omits v. 3a, quoting only v. 3b ("that Christos died"), and then skips over "on behalf of our misdeeds in accord with the scriptures"; in *Elenchos* 24, this same text appears alongside of a fuller quotation, in which he quotes the missing words "on behalf of our misdeeds in accord with the scriptures" without any comment on the discrepancy or about any omissions in Marcion's text. Harnack found supporting evidence for the omission of "according to the scriptures" in the agreement of Tertullian, *Marc.* 3.8.5, and Adam 5.6; but neither passage can be assumed to be quoted from the Apostolikon. Epiphanius' fuller quotation does have two anomalous readings: (1) it begins *"For I proclaimed to you* that Christos died," perhaps confirming the conflation of v. 1 and v. 3 without an intervening v. 2; (2) it omits "he was entombed," in contrast to the wording in his *scholion*. Epiphanius' construct of "on the third day" reflects a widely attested variant (*tēi tritēi hēmerai* instead of *tēi hēmerai tēi tritēi*). It is clear that the evidence of the Apostolikon does not support the suggestion that 15.3–11 is an interpolation, put forward by Price, "Apocryphal Apparitions."

1 Cor 15.5–10 is unattested. Harnack considers the verses to have been present, but his case specifically for v. 9 is insufficient.

15.11 Epiphanius, *Scholion* 24. Epiphanius quotes this verse following v. 14 (or 17) and before vv. 3–4; but he may be reordering the verses to construct a tidy rhetorical package for his point.

15.12 Tertullian, *Marc.* 5.9.2.

15.13–14 [or 16–17] Epiphanius, *Scholion* 24 (v. 14), *Elenchos* 24 (vv. 13–14). Both Harnack and Schmid credit only v. 14/17, not v. 13/16. In *Scholion* 24, Epiphanius quotes either v. 14 or 17: *ei christos ouk egēgertai, mataion*, after which he adds, "and the rest"; cf. v. 14 *ei de christos ouk egēgertai, kenon* and v. 17 *ei de christos ouk egēgertai, mataia*. Although the final term used matches v. 17, the neuter form suggests that it belongs to v. 14, where it modifies *to kērugma*. This conflation plays out in *Elenchos* 24, where Epiphanius provides a fuller quote: "If the dead are not awoken, neither has Christos been awoken (=v. 16, with close parallel to v. 13, which reads *ei de anastasis nekrōn ouk estin, oude christos* *egēgertai*), and if Christ has not been awoken, our declaration is vain" (=v. 14, with close parallel to 17, which reads "your trust is useless" instead of "our declaration is useless").

1 Cor 15.15, 18–20 is not directly attested, but probably implied in Epiphanius' "and the rest" following his quote of 15.14 or 15.17 in *Scholion* 24. Harnack cites Adam 5.6–7, 11 in support of v. 20–23; but it cannot be shown that Marcion's text is being quoted in that portion of the work.

15.21–22 Tertullian, *Marc.* 5.9.5.

1 Cor 15.23–24 is unattested. Harnack includes 24b, but with insufficient evidence.

15.25 Tertullian, *Marc.* 5.9.6. Tertullian reads, "until he has placed (his) enemies under his feet" instead of "all enemies"; the same reading is found in Gk mss Ψ and 1424, and Ephrem Syrus.

1 Cor 15.26–28 is unattested.

15.29 Tertullian, *Marc.* 5.10.1; Adam* 5.23; Eznik, *De Deo* 427, 432. Adamantius, Tertullian, and Eznik all agree in omitting "since" (*epei*) at the beginning of the verse, as does P^{46}—although, as Clabeaux (*A Lost Edition of the Letters of Paul*, 170) points out, such connecting words are likely to be dropped when verses are quoted in isolation. Adamantius omits "and" (*kai*) in the last clause, as do several Greek manuscripts; Eznik inverts the order of the first and second clauses. Eznik explicitly says that the Marcionites practiced baptism of the dead; Tertullian himself is critical of the practice, but excuses Paul for using it as a reinforcement of faith.

15.30–34 Adam* 5.23 (≠Schmid). In v. 31, Adamantius has *apothnēskontes*, in agreement with several Greek manuscripts, instead of *apothnēskō*. Verse 32 quotes Isa 22.13 (cf. Luke 12.19) and v. 33 quotes the Greek poet Menander. Dennis R. MacDonald has proposed an interpolation in 15.31c ("A Conjectural Emendation of 1 Cor 15:31–32").

15.35–36 Adam* 5.23; Tertullian, *Marc.* 5.10.2–3 (v. 35) (=Schmid v. 35 only, not crediting the evidence of Adamantius). In v. 36, Adamantius reads *aphron* ("nonsense"), in agreement with several Greek manuscripts, instead of *aphrōn* ("senseless one"), and "unless *first* it dies" instead of "unless it dies," in agreement with Gk mss D, F, G, 1175, Origen, etc.

15.37–41 Tertullian, *Marc.* 5.10.4 (cf. 5.20.7 for v. 41b, omitted in 5.10.4); Adam* 5.23. In v. 38, the Greek text of Adamantius has *ēthelesin, hekaston de tōn spermatōn to idion sōma apolambanei* instead of *ēthelēsen kai hekastōi tōn spermatōn to idion sōma*; but Rufinus' Latin translation reflects the latter wording (Tertullian is too paraphrastic to compare usefully). In v. 39, the Greek of Adamantius omits "flesh of birds"; but Rufinus' Latin translation and Tertullian both attest the reference to birds (*volucrum* > Gk *ptēnōn*), while Rufinus omits "flesh of animals" instead, and Tertullian omits "flesh of fish." In v. 41, Adamantius omits "and" before "another glory of stars," but Tertullian seems to have it.

15.42–44 Tertullian, *Marc.* 5.10.4–5; Adam* 5.23 (v. 42a); Adam 5.25 (vv. 42b, 44a). In v. 44a, Tertullian twice omits "body" in the clause, "it is planted an animate thing (*animale*), it is raised a spiritual thing (*spiritale*)," but then in commenting introduces it again: *corpus animale, corpus spiritale*; Adamantius has "body" in each case.

15.45–46 Tertullian, *Marc.* 5.10.6–7; Adam* 2.19. Tertullian draws attention to a variant in Marcion's text, reading "last Master" rather than "last Adam," which Adamantius confirms. P[46] likewise omits "Adam" in this clause, but does not have "Master" instead. Cf. 15.47 for a parallelism in phraseology.

15.47 Tertullian, *Marc.* 5.10.9; Adam* 2.19. Tertullian (along with Adamantius) reads without dispute, "the second is the Master from (the) celestial sphere" (the same reading is found in Gk mss 630, 1912, 2200). Tertullian still insists that "human being" is understood with the term "second," and a number of Greek manuscripts, while retaining "Master" have made this understood "human being" explicit, while some have "human being" but omit "Master." These textual variants feature explicitly in Adamantius. When Adamantius responds to the quotation of this verse by the Marcionite Markus, he reads simply "the second" with neither "Master" nor "human being"; when the pagan moderator Eutropius quotes the verse yet again, he repeats the Marcionite reading, with the comment *kath' hymas*, that is, "according to you (Marcionites)" (Rufinus' Latin translation does not have this comment). Finally, Adamantius directly comments on the textual difference:

> Observe now this impious audacity, how they have corrupted the Scripture. Wishing to expunge the teaching about the birth of Christ in the flesh, they changed the words "the second man" (*ho deuteros anthrōpos*), and made it read "the second master" (*ho deuteros kyrios*).

15.48 Tertullian, *Marc.* 5.10.10. Tertullian appears to be paraphrastic: "As is the one who is from the earth . . . so also are the earthy . . . as is the human being from (the) celestial sphere, so also are the human beings from (the) celestial sphere."

15.49 Tertullian, *Marc.* 5.10.10. Note "we should bear" (subjunctive) rather than "we will bear" (future): this is a moral imperative of imitation of Christ, rather than a promise of a future state. Tertullian expressly comments on this distinction, and the Greek manuscripts' evidence is divided between these two readings. But Schmid (*Marcion und sein Apostolos*, 109) concludes that Tertullian's remarks are not a comment on a variant reading in Marcion's text.

15.50a Tertullian, *Marc.* 5.10.11; 5.10.15; 5.14.4; Adam* 5.22, 26; Eznik, *De Deo* 420, 424; Hegemonius, *Arch.* 45 (Beeson, *Hegemonius: Acta Archelai*, 66.11–12). Schmid, *Marcion und sein Apostolos*, 103, demonstrates that Tertullian's wording differs from his quotation of this verse in *Res.* 48.1 and 49.9 (*non possidebunt* or *non consequentur* instead of *hereditati possidere non possunt*), suggesting that Marcion's text agreed with Gk mss F and G (as well as Irenaeus, the Bohairic Coptic version and some witnesses to the OL) in reading *ou klēronomēsousin* (cf. 1 Cor 6.9–10; Gal 5.21) against the majority of manuscripts and versions of this verse, which have *klēronomēsai ou dunatai*; Rufinus's Latin translation of Adam* 5.26 (where the Greek text is lacking) and Eznik concur (Tertullian, *Marc.* 5.14.4, seems to conflate Marcion's text and his more familiar one, giving *consequi non possunt*). The same verse is quoted earlier in Adamantius where the Greek text is preserved, and there the more common wording is used; but Rufinus has the alternative wording in this place, too. The *Acts of Archelaus* also reflects the more common catholic text, reading *possidere non posse*.

15.51 Adam* 5.23; Adam 5.26 (Latin only; ≠Schmid). This verse appears in four variations in the catholic textual tradition: (1) "We will not all fall asleep, but we will all be changed"; (2) "We will all fall asleep, but we will not all be changed," as in ℵ, C, 0243*, 33, 1739; (3) "We will not all fall asleep, but we will not all be changed," as in P^{46}, Origen; (4) "We will all arise, but we will not all be changed," as in D*, OL, Vulgate. The Greek manuscripts of Adam* 5.23 all have the third form, in agreement with P^{46}, but in two of the manuscripts the "not" of the second clause is erased to conform to the first form of the text found in the majority of catholic witnesses. Yet Rufinus in his translation of Adamantius follows the fourth form (repeating it again, with *surgemus* instead of *resurgemus*, in 5.26 where the Greek text is missing), and Harnack believed that Rufinus preserved the original wording of Adamantius, while the Greek text had been conformed to the Byzantine text. But Bakhuyzen, *Der Dialog des Adamantius*, 226, suggested that Rufinus had simply ignored the Greek text in front of him and gave the form of the verse more familiar to him. The other three forms of the text attempt to create coherence from the *lectio difficilior* offered in P^{46} (and the original Greek text of Adamantius); but the latter might in turn have been an early corruption of one of the readings guessed at by the later corrections.

15.52–53 Adam* 5.23; Tertullian, *Marc.* 5.10.14; 5.12.2–3; Epiphanius, *Elenchos* 24 (vv. 52–53; Schmid does not credit the evidence of Adamantius). In v. 52, Tertullian inverts the order of phrases, reading "in a moment, in the blink of an eye" after "the dead will be awakened incorruptible, and we shall be changed." He omits any mention of the "last trumpet" sounding. Epiphanius inverts the order of v. 53, reading "this mortal thing must put on deathlessness" before "this corruptible thing must put on incorruption" (but not when quoting his own text of the verse: *Pan.* 56.2.10; 64.68.3; 77.8.8; 77.27.6). Adamantius shows the same inversion of clauses; but Tertullian has the more usual order.

15.54–55 Epiphanius, *Scholion* 24 (v. 54); Tertullian, *Marc.* 5.10.16 (vv. 54b–55); Adam* 2.18 (vv. 54b–55a); 5.27 (v. 54a). Epiphanius attests the whole of v. 54 (omitting the article before "deathlessness"), with its quote from Hos 3.14. In 2.18 Adamantius begins at 54b, gives the quotation from Hosea, and then the first clause of the quote of Isa 25.8 in 55a (the latter, however, is omitted in Rufinus' Latin translation); but in 5.27, where the Apostolikon may not be used, Adamantius gives v. 54a in a form that has been conflated with the wording of 54b: "But when the mortal is swallowed down by the deathless" (*hotan de katapothēi to* *thnēton hupo tēs athanasias*). Tertullian likewise begins at 54b with the words introducing a quote, but then skips over the quote of Hosea in v. 54c, going directly on to the quote of Isaiah in v. 55. He subtly remarks on a slight difference of reading, interrupting his quote at the word "victory" (*victoria* > Gk *nikos*) and adding "or, strife" (*aculeus* > Gk *neikos*), before continuing with the quotation, and in *Res.* 47.13, 51.6, and 54.5 he always has the latter reading (see Schmid, *Marcion und sein Apostolos*, 98–100). The two variants are found throughout the manuscript tradition for this verse.

1 Cor 15.56 is unattested. It is possible that our sources pass over this verse in silence, since it seems to support Marcion's position ("the power of wrongdoing is the Law"). On the other hand, Horn, "1 Korinther 15,56," argues that the verse is an interpolation.

15.57 Tertullian, *Marc.* 5.10.16.

1 Cor 15.58 is unattested. Harnack includes it based on the Pseudo-Pauline Laodiceans.

1 Cor 16.1–24 is unattested. It is possible that Marcion's text represented a generalized version that did not include the ephemeral content of this last section of the letter. On the other hand, nothing in this chapter had any use for the arguments of Tertullian, Epiphanius, or Adamantius. The Prologue implies the presence of vv. 1 and 8.

To Corinthians 2

1.1 Adam* 2.12 (≠Harnack, Schmid). Adamantius has "Jesus Christos" rather than "Christos Jesus," in agreement with the majority of catholic manuscripts; cf. 1 Cor 1.1.

1.2 Tertullian, *Marc.* 5.5.1–2 (≠Harnack, Schmid). Tertullian reports that Paul uses the same greeting in all of his letters: "favor and peace from God the Father and Master Jesus."

1.3 Tertullian, *Marc.* 5.11.1. Tertullian reads "the God of our Master" rather than "the God and Father of our Master," a unique reading.

2 Cor 1.4–19 is unattested; nothing in this passage offered relevant material for Marcion's critics; on the other hand it supplies a key part of the Marcionite self-image as persecuted on earth. Gk mss 618 and 1738 omit vv. 6–7 for no obvious scribal cause.

1.20 Epiphanius, *Scholion* 25; Adam* 2.18 (Schmid does not credit the evidence of Adamantius). Epiphanius omits "for glory through us" at the end of the verse. Adamantius quotes only the first clause of the verse.

2 Cor 1.21–2.13 is unattested; nothing in this passage offered relevant material for Marcion's critics.

2.14–17 Adam 2.20 (vv. 14–16b); Didymus (v. 17: Mai, *Novae Patrum* vol. 4.2, 122) (≠Schmid). In v. 15, Adamantius reads "we are an aroma of Christos among those being rescued," instead of "we are an aroma of Christos *to God* among those being rescued," a reading shared with Gk ms K. He does not quote the last clause of v. 16. In v. 17 he has "like the rest (*hoi lopoi*)," in agreement with Gk mss P^{46}, D, F, G, etc., instead of "like the many (*hoi polloi*)." It is not certain that Adamantius is quoting from the Apostolikon in this section.

2 Cor 3.1–2 is unattested.

3.3 Tertullian, *Marc.* 5.11.4; Adam* 5.27 (Schmid does not credit the evidence of Adamantius). Adamantius reads "fleshy tablets of the heart," rather than "fleshy heart tablets," in agreement with a small variety of witnesses to the catholic text (Tertullian does not quote this part of the verse).

2 Cor 3.4–5 is unattested.

3.6–11 Tertullian, *Marc.* 5.11.4–5 (vv. 6–7, 10–11); Adam* 5.27 (v. 11); Hegemonius, *Arch.* 45 (Beeson, *Hegemonius: Acta Archelai*, 65.31–66.8) (=Schmid vv. 6–7 and 11 only, since he credits the evidence of neither Adamantius nor the *The Acts of Archelaus*). In v. 6, the *Acts of Archelaus* reads "by which/whom" rather than "which/whom" (and makes the verb explicit, as the OL and Vulgate do). Adamantius has an additional clause at the end of v. 11: "and is not being nullified," which may be a Marcionite gloss on the text completing the contrast, rather than part of the Apostolikon's text.

2 Cor 3.12 is unattested.

3.13–16 Tertullian, *Marc.* 5.11.5–7. In v. 14, Tertullian gives a significantly different text: "But the thoughts of the world were dulled" (*Sed obtunsi sunt sensus mundi*), instead of "But their thoughts were dulled" found in the catholic text; cf. 2 Cor 4.4. He has a compressed text of vv. 14b–15, reading "Until this present day the same veil" from v. 14b, continuing with "covers their heart" from v. 15b. This reading can be explained, of course, by homeoteleuton, passing from the first "veil" in v. 14 to the second in v. 15. Yet in his comment on the passage, Tertullian refers again to Moses, perhaps implying the fuller text: "He indicates that the veil of the face of Moses was a figure of the veil of the heart of that people, because among them even now Moses is not clearly seen with the heart, just as then he was not clearly seen by the face." For v. 16 Tertullian has "God" instead of "the Master" found in the catholic text.

2 Cor 3.17 is unattested.

3.18 Tertullian, *Marc.* 5.11.8. Instead of "reflecting as a mirror (Gk *katoptrizomenoi*) the glory of the Master" found in most catholic witnesses, Tertullian has "viewing Christos" (*contemplantes Christum*), probably rendering a variant in the verb found also in Gk mss F and G (*apoptrizomenoi* vs. the more widely attested *katoptrizomenoi*). He has "master of spirits" rather than "master of spirit." Instead of "from glory to glory," he has "from glory of the Master (*domini*) to glory."

2 Cor 4.1–3 is unattested.

4.4 Tertullian, *Marc.* 5.11.9, 5.11.12, 5.17.9; Adam 2.21* (Schmid does not credit the evidence of Adamantius). Instead of *eis to mē augasai ton photismon*, the Greek text of Adamantius reads *pros to mē diaugasai autōn ton photismon*, sharing some features with other variant readings in the Greek manuscripts, but agreeing exactly with none (but Rufinus' Latin text reflects the more common text: *ut non fulgeat illuminatio*). Tertullian refers to this verse again in *Marc.* 5.17.9: "And this must be the devil, whom again in another place—if at least they wish to read the apostle in this way (*si tamen ita et apostolum legi volunt*)—we shall recognize as the god of this aeon." He says this because he challenges (in 5.11.9–12) reading it thus as "the god of this aeon," suggesting that "of this aeon" should be read with "untrusting (people)" rather than with "the god." Adamantius makes much the same argument in his response to this verse being quoted by the Marcionite Markus. Neither of them are remarking on a different wording in Marcion's text, but a different interpretation of Paul's ambiguous wording.

4.5–6 Epiphanius, *Scholion* 26 (vv. 5–6a); Tertullian, *Marc.* 5.11.11 (v. 6); Adam* 2.19 (v. 6; Schmid does not credit the evidence of Adamantius). In v. 5, Epiphanius has the genitive "by Jesus" (*dia Iēsou*) rather than the accusative "for Jesus" (*dia Iēsoun*), in agreement with Gk mss P^{46}, ℵ*, A*, C, and a number of others. In v. 6, Adamantius has *lampsai* instead of *lampsei*, and this appears to be Tertullian's reading as well, along with the majority of Greek manuscripts; Adamantius also has "your hearts" rather than "our hearts" (but Tertullian agrees with the latter, and both readings are widely attested). Tertullian reads "recognition of him" (*agnitionis suae*; cf. Gk ms 33: "recognition of God"). Schmid accepts an emendation of Tertullian adding *gloriae*, which matches the reading ("recognition of his glory") in Adamantius, as well as P^{46}, C*, D*, F, G, 326, 1837, and some witnesses to the OL (and Tertullian's own text of Paul, *Res.* 44.2), in place of "recognition of the glory of God" found in most witnesses to the catholic text (Epiphanius' testimony does not reach this part of v. 6). Note the favorable quotation of Gen 1.3, and the identification of that God with the God of Jesus.

4.7 Tertullian, *Marc.* 5.11.14; Adam* 5.27 (Schmid does not credit the evidence of Adamantius; Harnack mistakenly cites Adam 2.27). Adamantius has "we have therefore" (*echomen oun*) rather than "but we have" (*echomen de*) at the beginning of the verse, and "not of us" (*ouch hēmōn*) rather than "not from us" (*mē ex hēmōn*) at the end, both unique readings.

4.8–10 Tertullian, *Marc.* 5.11.15–16. Tertullian alludes to "the earthen vessels in which he says we suffer so many things," referring to vv. 7–9, before adding "in which also we carry around the death of Christos. . . . For he sets down the reason, 'That the life also of Christos may be made manifest in our body,' that is, just as his death too is carried around in the body." Tertullian has in both instances "Christos," in agreement in the first instance with Gk mss D, F, G (rather than "Jesus"), but in the second instance D, F, G have "Jesus Christos."

4.11 Adam* 5.27 (≠Schmid). Adamantius omits "on account of Jesus" in the first clause. He has "Christos" rather than "Jesus" in the second clause (although Rufinus' Latin translation has the latter), in agreement with Gk ms C.

2 Cor 4.12 is unattested.

4.13 Epiphanius, *Scholion* 27. Epiphanius reads "And since we have the same spirit of trust, and (*kai*) we trust, therefore also we speak," a text which skips over, as he duly notes, v. 13b: "according to (*kata*) what has been written, 'I trusted, therefore I spoke.'" This shortened reading might be explained by a scribal error (homeoarcton), slipping from *kata* to *kai* (harder to explain is the omission of just the words of the quotation by Gk mss 618 and 1738). Epiphanius suspects deliberate excision ("he excised," *exekopsen*) of a quote from Jewish scriptures.

2 Cor 4.14–15 is unattested.

4.16 Tertullian, *Marc.* 5.11.16. Tertullian quotes the two expressions in exact parallel (*exteriorem . . . hominen nostrum . . . interiorem hominem nostrum*), suggesting an explicit *anthropos* in both not otherwise attested in the catholic text (he has it explicit in the first, not the second clause in *Res.* 40.2).

2 Cor 4.17 is unattested.

4.18 Tertullian, *Marc.* 5.11.16.

5.1 Tertullian, *Marc.* 5.12.1. Tertullian omits the appositive "this tent" following "house upon the earth" (but not when he quotes from his own text of Paul, *Res.* 41.1) and reads "we have a house not made with hands," instead of "we have a building from God, a house not made with hands" (but also in his own text, *Res.* 41.1).

5.2 Tertullian, *Marc.* 5.12.1. Tertullian omits "our," reading "this dwelling" rather than "this our dwelling" (but has it in his own text of Paul, *Res.* 41.5), and specifies a dwelling "of an earthly body," which might suggest a textual variant here, and/or the influence of the wording of 5.4.

5.3 Tertullian, *Marc.* 5.12.1. Tertullian has *"unclothed"* (*despoliati* > Gk *ekdusamenoi*) in agreement with Gk ms D (as well as F and G, with the emendation a scribal error), some witnesses to the OL, Aphrahat, and Ephrem Syrus, instead of "clothed" found in other witnesses to the catholic text.

5.4 Tertullian, *Marc.* 5.12.1, 3; Adam* 5.27. Tertullian appears to attest the use of demonstrative pronouns with both *"this tent"* and *"this mortal (thing),"* differing from his own text of the verse in *Res.* 42.2; both are found in Gk mss F and G, while the first alone is found in several Greek manuscripts, the OL, SSyr and CSyr, and Ephrem Syrus (see Schmid, *Marcion und sein Apostolos*, 101). He also has "tent *of the body*" (some OL witnesses have "this body" instead of "this tent"). Adamantius gives a paraphrase of the last clause: "but when (*hotan de* instead of *hoti*) the mortal thing may be swallowed down by deathlessness" (*athanasias* instead of *zōēs*, but Rufinus reflects the latter, as does Tertullian).

5.5–6 Tertullian, *Marc.* 5.12.4. For v. 6 Tertullian reads, "while we are in the flesh" (*quamdiu in carne sumus*) instead of "while present in the body," which is Tertullian's own text of this verse (*Res.* 43.1); the different verbal sense probably reflects a variant found in Gk mss D*, F, and G, while "flesh" for "body" is otherwise unattested.

2 Cor 5.7 is unattested.

5.8 Tertullian, *Marc.* 5.12.4.

2 Cor 5.9 is unattested.

5.10 Tertullian, *Marc.* 5.12.4; Adam 1.16 (Schmid does not credit the evidence of Adamantius, who may not be using the Apostolikon here). Schmid, *Marcion und sein Apostolos*, 100–101, notes differences in how Tertullian quotes this verse here and in *Res.* 43.6 and suggests that Marcion's text agreed with Gk mss D*, F, G, etc., in reading *ha dia tou sōmatos epraxen* instead of *ta dia tou sōmatos pros ha epraxen*. Instead of "each may receive that for which they acted through the body, either good or bad," Adamantius reads, "each receives from Christos either good or bad" — probably a paraphrase.

2 Cor 5.11–16 is unattested. Critics of Marcion such as Tertullian had good reason to skip over v. 16, which lends support to Marcionite positions.

5.17 Tertullian, *Marc.* 5.12.6; Adam 2.16* (Schmid does not credit the evidence of Adamantius). Both Tertullian and Adamantius read *"all things have become new,"* a widely found variant for "(it) has become new" (Tertullian usually has the latter, 4.1.6; 4.11.9). Cf. Isa 43.19.

2 Cor 5.18–7.1a is unattested. Tertullian might be expected to comment on "all things are from God" in 5.18 or the several quotations from Jewish scripture in this section. Otherwise, it contains little that would be relevant to Marcion's critics. Adam 2.20 cites 6.14c, but it is doubtful that it is taken from the Apostolikon. Note how 7.1b follows quite logically on 5.16–17.

7.1b Tertullian, *Marc.* 5.12.6. Tertullian reads "flesh and blood," whereas the catholic text has "flesh and spirit," and he appears to attest a continuation of this verse along the lines of "for these do not attain the realm of God" (*non . . . capere regnum dei*; cf. 1 Cor 15.50), instead of "perfecting holiness in fear of God." When he quotes from his own text of Paul, *Pud.* 15.8, he follows the standard catholic text.

2 Cor 7.2–11.1 is unattested. Tertullian says nothing about a large gap occurring here in Marcion's version of the letter, in comparison to the catholic version. But it should be noted that in his works Tertullian has an unusual absence of quotations from this very part of the letter. For most of Paul's letters, he quotes several passages from each chapter, but he shows a conspicuous void here, with no quotations or allusions to anything between 7.10 (*Paen.* 2.3) and 10.2 (*Res.* 49.11). It is a striking anomaly that stands out in any index of his scriptural references. Could it be that Marcion and Tertullian shared a text of this letter that lacked a sizable section found here in what is now the canonical form of the letter? Several scholars have proposed that chapters 8 and 9 constitute originally separate letters (see Furnish, *II Corinthians*, 30–41, and the literature cited there). Although their content is largely ephemeral, and therefore not very usable to later Christian commentators, it would be highly relevant to Marcion's critics as testimony to Paul's close ties to the Jerusalem church and the apostles there, on which Tertullian comments frequently, as well as for the scriptural quote and comment on God as supplier of natural goods in 9.9–10. Adam 2.12 quotes 10.18, but it is doubtful that the Apostolikon is involved in this section.

11.2 Tertullian, *Marc.* 5.12.6. Harnack (*Marcion*, 101*) notes that Tertullian seems to have a continuous quote that runs from 7.1 directly to 11.2, and indeed there is good continuity of sense running from 5.16–17 to 7.1b to 11.2. Does this reflect the text of the Apostolikon, or perhaps the selective citation of an argument Marcion presented in his *Proevangelion*?

2 Cor 11.3–12 is unattested. Would not Tertullian comment on the reference to Genesis 3 in v. 3?

11.13–14 Tertullian, *Marc.* 5.12.6–7. Some of the immediately preceding text must have been present for this passage to make sense.

2 Cor 11.15–12.1 is unattested.

12.2–4 Tertullian, *Marc.* 5.12.8; Eznik, *De Deo* 362, 379. Eznik quotes Marcionites citing this passage in argument: "But Paul, they say, 'was snatched into the third celestial sphere, and he 'heard' these 'unutterable words' which we proclaim here." Tertullian says merely, "Concerning paradise there is a separate work of mine touching on every question suggested by it." He goes on to mention a similar case of "lifting a man up to heaven" in the OT.

2 Cor 12.5–6 is unattested.

12.7–9 Tertullian, *Marc.* 5.12.8. In v. 7, Tertullian omits "a thorn in the flesh"; in v. 9 he does not give the exact wording of the first clause of the response to Paul.

2 Cor 12.10–21 is unattested.

13.1 Tertullian, *Marc.* 5.12.9; Adam* 2.18 (Schmid does not credit the evidence of Adamantius). Adamantius quotes verbatim; Tertullian says simply "in three witnesses every word shall be established." Adamantius reads "at the mouth of two or three witnesses," while most witnesses to the catholic text have "at the mouth of two witnesses and three." The verse quotes Deut 19.15.

13.2 Tertullian, *Marc.* 5.12.9.

2 Cor 13.3–9 is unattested. Harnack includes vv. 3–4 based on Adam 5.6 and 5.12, but it cannot be shown that Adamantius quotes from the Apostolikon in these instances.

13.10 Tertullian, *Marc.* 5.12.9.

2 Cor 13.11–14 is unattested.

To Romans

Prologue *Romani sunt in partibus Italiae. Hi praeventi sunt a falsis apostolis et sub nomine domini nostri Iesu Christi in legem et prophetas erant inducti. Hos revocat apostolus ad veram evangelicam fidem scribens eis ab Athenis* [var.: *a Corintho*]. Dahl, "The Origin of the Earliest Prologues," 259–60, argues against reading this prologue to say that the Romans first received false apostles. He contends that it says nothing about how they first received the gospel, but presupposes the standard pattern of the other prologues, with an originally correct teaching being overtaken (this is how he reads *praeventi*, but cf. the Colossian prologue) by false apostles. He believes his reading mitigates the otherwise strong case this prologue makes for a Marcionite provenance. But he does not deal with the most telling part: the negative reference to "the Law and the

Prophets." He goes on, 260, to make a quite circular argument about this: The author of the prologue

> must have inferred what he says about the activity of the false apostles from those parts of Romans in which Paul explains how the law and the prophets are properly to be understood. But precisely these parts of the letter (Rom 1:17b, 3:31–4:25, most of 9–11) are not attested for Marcion, who is likely to have deleted them (Harnack, 1924: 102*–111*).

Therefore, Dahl concludes, the author of the prologue could not have had the Marcionite text in front of him. "He was a staunch anti-Judaizer but no Marcionite." Not only should we be cautious about uncritically accepting Harnack's conclusions about what Marcion must have deleted, but chapters 9–11 (where Tertullian does attest significant textual omissions in Marcion's text) is scarcely where Paul combats upholders of the "law and prophets"; the latter issue is at the center in 1–7. Dahl himself acknowledges that his proposed handling of the prologue "may not be entirely satisfactory."

On what basis was it thought that the letter had been written in either Athens or Corinth? Manuscripts containing the prologue differ on this point; see Harnack, *Marcion*, 128*. The previous letter, Corinthians 2, speaks of Paul's plan to visit that city (12.14; 13.1). The next letter, Thessalonians 1, implies that Paul is in Athens (3.1).

Rom 1.1–7a is unattested. There must have been something equivalent to v. 1. We would certainly expect Tertullian and Epiphanius to cite vv. 2–3 against Marcion had they been present in the Apostolikon; yet why do they not explicitly note an omission? They would have had the opportunity to do so either here or elsewhere where they discuss Paul's attribution of Davidic ancestry to Jesus (cf. Tertullian, *Carn. Chr.* 22.2; *Prax.* 27.11). Origen, *Comm. Jo.* 10.21–4, when discussing various heretical responses to this passage, likewise fails to say that Marcion's text lacked the reference to David, remarking only that Marcion omitted the birth story from his gospel text because he "rejects [Jesus'] birth from Mary *so far as his divine nature is concerned*." The latter statement could be construed as implying that Marcion had no objection to this passage, since it makes a clear distinction between Jesus' Davidic ancestry "according to the flesh" and his divine status as "son of God," which the birth stories do not. Note that Origen appears to distinguish Marcion's views from those of docetists, who would reject any human ancestry for Jesus. Perhaps some reconsideration of Marcion's christology is needed. The evidence of Gk ms G is suggestive, reading directly from v. 1a to 5b in an apparently coherent redaction: "Paul, a slave of Jesus Christ, called (to be) an emissary / among the nations on behalf of his name."

1.7b Tertullian, *Marc.* 5.5.1–2 (≠Harnack, Schmid). The notion that Marcion is responsible for the omission of the address to "Romans" in this verse and v. 15, found in Gk ms G and known already by Origen, cannot be substantiated. On the one hand, it is clearly attested outside of Marcionite circles, and on the other hand it is not certain that it occurred in Marcion's text. It is clear from our sources, and quite explicit in both Tertullian and Epiphanius, that the Apostolikon contained a letter "to Romans," so there was no attempt on Marcion's part to deny that this letter was addressed to Rome, as some have imagined (e.g., Manson, "St. Paul's Letter to the Romans—and Others," 7).

Rom 1.8–15 is unattested.

1.16–17 Tertullian, *Marc.* 5.13.2. Tertullian seems to lack "first" in the phrase "to the Jew *first*," as do Gk mss B and G; it is unattested in Ephrem's commentary.

1.18 Tertullian, *Marc.* 5.13.2. Although in his initial quotation Tertullian omits "of God" following "wrath," he immediately asks, "Which god's wrath?" (*cuius dei ira*), suggesting that the text before him actually did read "God's wrath." Therefore the supposition that Marcion excised "of God" to avoid ascribing wrath to God (Harnack, *Marcion*, 103*) is not solidly grounded (Gk ms 47 does omit "of God"). W. O. Walker Jr.'s proposal that 1.18–2.29 constitutes an interpolation ("Romans 1.18–2.29: A Non-Pauline Interpolation?") is not supported by the evidence of the Apostolikon, at least as far as including this verse. Harnack (*Marcion*, 103*) believed that Tertullian read continuously from 1.18 directly to 2.2.

Rom 1.19–2.1 is unattested. P. N. Harrison has argued that 1.19–2.1 constitutes an interpolation, and that the Apostolikon preserves the original reading of the letter, passing directly from 1.18 to 2.2 (*Paulines and Pastorals*, 79–85). Yet Tertullian, *Marc.* 4.25.10, appears to allude to this passage when he says that the Marcionites and "other heretics" argue that the nations knew about the creator from nature. Origen, *Comm. Rom.* 1.18.2, rhetorically asks how the Marcionites deal with 1.24 in light of their theology. But there is no guarantee that Origen has been careful to cite something actually in the Marcionite Bible; in fact, based on his conduct of this sort of argument, e.g., *On First Principles* 2.5, he does not take care to cite only passages accepted by the Marcionites.

2.2 Tertullian, *Marc.* 5.13.3.

Omission: 1.19–2.1 or 2.3–11? After quoting 2.2, and before alluding to 2.14ff., Tertullian remarks, "But how many ditches Marcion has dug, especially in this epistle, by removing all that he would, will become evident from the complete text of my copy. I myself need do no more than accept, as the result of his carelessness and blindness, those passages which he did not see he had equally good reason to excise." But did the omission to which he refers occur before or after 2.2? Harnack (*Marcion*, 103*) interprets it as referring to an omission of 1.19–2.1, and hence as a comment on how in Marcion's text the two separate passages of 1.18 and 2.2 were read together. Schmid (*Marcion und sein Apostolos*, 85–87, 110) thinks that Tertullian means to refer to an omission following the verse he has just quoted, 2.2, and before the verse he next quotes, 2.14. Unfortunately, Tertullian says nothing specific enough to settle the question. Both 1.19–2.1 and 2.3–11 contain comments that Tertullian would be likely to cite against Marcion. Yet Tertullian has just said (5.13.1) that he will not repeat points already sufficiently raised before, including the theme of God as judge, which features prominently in 2.3–11.

Rom 2.3–11 is unattested.

2.12–13 Epiphanius, *Scholion* 28. Note the affirmation of the validity of the law in v. 13; Marcion almost certainly took this whole section of Romans as Paul's description of the existing order of this world, under the creator god, whose law had full force for all those who did not avail themselves of the grace of the higher God through Jesus.

2.14, 16 Tertullian, *Marc.* 5.13.4–5; Adam* 1.6 (v. 16); 2.5* (v. 16); Origen, *Comm. Jo.* 5.7. In Adam* 1.6, a Marcionite quotes "according to my proclamation" from v. 16; in Adam 2.5, Adamantius quotes the bulk of the verse, concluding with "through Jesus Christos," while Tertullian has "of Christos," and Origen has "in Christos Jesus" (most witnesses to the catholic text have "through Christos Jesus"). R. Bultmann's suggestion that 2.16 constitutes an interpolation ("Glossen im Römerbrief," 200–201) is not supported by the evidence of the Apostolikon.

Rom 2.15–20a is unattested.

2.20b Epiphanius, *Scholion* 30.

2.21 Tertullian, *Marc.* 5.13.6. Perhaps reading "teaching" (*docentes*) instead of "preaching" not to steal, influenced by the first clause of the verse.

Rom 2.22–23 is unattested.

2.24 Tertullian, *Marc.* 5.13.7. The saying quoted here is from Isa 52.5.

2.25 Epiphanius, *Scholion* 29; Adam 2.20; Origen, *Comm. Rom.* 2.13.27 (Schmid does not credit the evidence of Adamantius, who may not be using the Apostolikon here). Epiphanius probably cites this verse out of order because it is a logical development of 2.12–13. Origen states that Marcion is at a loss to explain Paul's words "circumcision benefits."

Rom 2.26 is unattested.

2.28–29 Tertullian, *Marc.* 5.13.7; Hegemonius, *Arch.* 45 (v. 28, Beeson, *Hegemonius: Acta Archelai*, 66.15–16).

Rom 3.1–8 is unattested. Tertullian or Epiphanius would be expected to cite v. 2 against Marcion. But Tertullian does not refer to it in any of his works.

Rom 3.9–18 is unattested. Given the presence of 3.19ff., and the argument it entails, there is good reason to think that 3.9–18 was present in the Apostolikon. But then why would our sources not mention this extensive set of OT quotations?

3.19 Tertullian, *Marc.* 5.13.11 (≠Schmid). In a summarizing string of citations from several of Paul's letters on the outcome of the Law, Tertullian says, "and brought the whole world under accusation, and stopped every mouth." This would appear to be a paraphrase, with the two clauses inverted, of this verse. The context of argument makes it clear that he is quoting from the Apostolikon.

3.20–22 Tertullian, *Marc.* 5.13.8 (vv. 21–22 only); Hegemonius, *Arch.* 45 (v. 20 only: *tantummodo agnitionem peccati per legem fieri*, Beeson,

Hegemonius: Acta Archelai, 66.18) (=Schmid vv. 21–22 only). Tertullian summarizes some previous verse or verses with *tunc lex*, "then (there was) the law," before going on to paraphrase 3.21–22. His reference could be to 3.2, or 3.19 (see *Marc.* 5.13.11), or 3.20. But Harnack (*Marcion*, 104*), noting that Tertullian quotes this exact wording twice, and comments directly on it, suggests that it is a direct quote of a variant text. Accordingly, Harnack reconstructs the text as "Then law, now vindication" (*tunc lex, nunc iustitia* > Gk *tote nomos, nuni dikaiosunē*). Yet the *Acts of Archelaus* attests the standard reading of v. 20b for Marcion's text, and in this way casts doubt on taking Tertullian's wording as an exact quotation of the text. Harnack cites Origen, *Comm. Rom.* 3.6.9, for v. 20b (*per legem agnitio peccati*); yet Origen does not explicitly attribute a comment on this verse to the Marcionites, but simply equates a possible misunderstanding of it with the Marcionite idea that the Law is bad. Tertullian does not quote v. 21b, with its reference to "the Law and the Prophets," which might suggest that it was absent from the Apostolikon. In v. 22 he appears to have read "what is (*quae est* > Gk *ti estin*) the distinction?" rather than "there is no (*ou estin*) distinction," and omits "Jesus" with "Christos" in agreement with Gk ms B.

Rom 3.23–4.1 is unattested. Talbert, "A Non-Pauline Fragment at Romans 3:24–26?" presents a persuasive argument that 3.25–26 constitutes an interpolation.

4.2 Hegemonius, *Arch.* 45 (Beeson, *Hegemonius: Acta Archelai*, 66.17–18; ≠Harnack, Schmid). The section of the *Acts of Archelaus* that appears to be based upon a Marcionite source quotes the words "Abraham has glory, but not in God's eyes" (*Abraham habet gloriam, sed non apud deum*). Our other sources may have skipped mentioning this verse, because it would be difficult wrestle it into an anti-Marcionite argument.

Rom 4.3–4.25 is unattested. Harnack considers these verses to have been omitted. Neither Tertullian nor Epiphanius say anything about an omission in Marcion's text here, but we would expect them to cite some of the content against Marcion. Various proposals for small interpolations in this section of the letter have been made.

5.1 Tertullian, *Marc.* 5.13.9. Tertullian writes, "He enjoins us who are rectified by trust *of Christos, not on the basis of the Law,* to have peace towards God." Do the italicized words indicate additional phrasing in the Apostolikon? Harnack (*Marcion*, 104*) thinks so. Tertullian's understanding of the verse requires significant restructuring of, and some omission from, the catholic text, in which "we have peace toward God through our Master Jesus" falls between "trust" and "of Christos."

Rom 5.2–5 is unattested. It offered nothing to Marcion's critics, and likely was present in the Apostolikon.

5.6 Epiphanius, *Scholion* 31. Epiphanius has *eti gar* instead of *ei ge* at the beginning, a widely attested variant. Keck, "The Post-Pauline Interpretation of Jesus' Death in Rom 5,6–7," argues that this verse is part of an interpolation; but the evidence of the Apostolikon does not support this proposal.

Rom 5.7–19 is unattested. Harnack includes vv. 8–9 based on Adam 5.12; but Marcion's text is not being used there.

5.20–21 Tertullian, *Marc.* 5.13.10; Origen, *Comm. Rom.* 5.6.2. Tertullian joins the two clauses of v. 20 with "so that," rather than "But where wrongdoing abounded," but this may be mere paraphrase (cf. *Res.* 47.14 where the standard wording appears). Origen says that Marcion and other heretics "want to accuse the Law based on these words of the apostle." Following this passage, Tertullian alludes to the content of Gal 3.22, Rom 3.19, and perhaps one or more other verse (Laod 2.9?):

> Had the creator's law for this reason concluded all things under wrongdoing, and brought the whole world under accusation, and stopped every mouth, so that no man might glory because of it, but that grace might be reserved for the glory of Christos?

Tertullian's wording for v. 21 (*in mortem . . . in iustitia in vitam*) appears to suggest the same repeated preposition, rather than the three different ones found in the catholic text (*en . . . dia . . . eis*; *Res.* 47.12 has *in . . . per . . . in*).

Rom 6.1–13 is unattested. Harnack (*Marcion*, 105*) argues for inclusion of vv. 1–2 based on Tertullian's reference at 1.27.5 to a Pauline *absit*, which Harnack thinks can only come from this passage, apparently overlooking the *absit* of Rom 7.7. Harnack also includes vv. 3, 9–10 on the basis of parts of Adamantius where it cannot be shown that Marcion's text is being quoted (3.7, 5.11–12). None of the content of book 6 offered anything for Tertullian or Epiphanius to use against Marcion; their failure to mention it is therefore neither surprising nor significant.

6.14 Adam* 1.27 (Latin only; ≠Schmid). As first argued by Bakhuyzen, *Der Dialog des Adamantius*, 56–57, Rufinus is likely to preserve the original wording of Adamantius here, while the Greek manuscripts are defective (cf. Pretty, *Adamantius*, 73 n. 186). It shows two variants from the familiar catholic text: "us" (*nobis* > Gk *hēmōn*) rather than "you," not paralleled in catholic witnesses; and "no longer" (*ultra non* > Gk *ouketi*) rather than "not," found in a few Greek manuscripts.

Rom 6.15–18 is unattested.

6.19 Adam 3.7 (≠Schmid). It is uncertain if Adamantius is reading from the Apostolikon here. In this section of the work, he has been debating a Bardaisanite, but suddenly the Marcionite Megethius interrupts, and quotes from the Evangelion, to which Adamantius replies in part with this quote. Possibly, then, the author has dropped in a passage from an anti-Marcionite source; but that does not mean that the source has been careful to quote only from the Apostolikon. In place of "to impurity and lawlessness" (*tē akatharsia kai tē anomia*), he has "to injustice and impurity" (*tē adikia kai tē akatharsia*), perhaps under the influence of 6.13. In the second clause, he omits "now" (with Gk ms 69), the explicit "your" with "limbs" (implied in the article), and "for holiness" at the end, and adds "God" as the indirect object of the verb "supply" alongside of "rectitude." Hagen, "Two Deutero-Pauline Glosses in Romans 6," 364–67, argues that 6.13 and 6.19 are interpolations.

6.20 Adam 1.27 (≠Schmid). It is uncertain if Adamantius is reading from the Apostolikon here.

Rom 6.21–7.3 is unattested. It probably was present in the Apostolikon.

7.4–5 Tertullian, *Marc.* 5.13.12 (=Schmid v. 4a only, apparently overlooking Tertullian's reference to "awakened from the dead" in the second part of v. 4, as well as to v. 5 with the words *carnis in quam lex mortis est dicta*). Harnack also cites Adam 5.22 for v. 5, but this quote falls before Adamantius turns to Marcion's text in that part of his work.

Rom 7.6 is unattested.

7.7a Tertullian, *Marc.* 5.13.13 (cf. 1.27.5).

7.8, 11 Tertullian, *Marc.* 5.13.14 (=Schmid v. 11 only). Tertullian could be referring to nearly identical wording in either verse.

Rom 7.9–10 is unattested.

7.12 Epiphanius, *Scholion* 32; Tertullian, *Marc.* 5.13.14; Adam 2.20. Tertullian has "the Law is sacred, and its commandment is just and good," lacking the repeated "sacred" in the latter series of characterizations (as does Gk ms 1836); but Epiphanius and Adamantius have the full catholic text (quoting this verse from his own text of Paul elsewhere, Epiphanius has "and the commandment *of God* is holy, etc.," *Pan.* 64.56.6). The presence of this positive affirmation of the Law in Marcion's text is noteworthy. It is not certain that Adamantius is quoting from the Marcionite Apostolikon in this section.

7.13b Adam 2.20 (≠Schmid). It is not certain that Adamantius is quoting from the Apostolikon in this section.

7.14a Tertullian, *Marc.* 5.13.15.

Rom 7.15–17 is unattested.

7.18 Clement, *Strom.* 3.11.76 (≠Schmid). Clement says the Marcionites cite the words of Paul, "in flesh good does not dwell."

Rom 7.19–22 is unattested.

7.23 Tertullian, *Marc.* 5.14.1; Hegemonius, *Arch.* 45 (Beeson, *Hegemonius: Acta Archelai*, 66.19–20). The *Acts of Archelaus* makes a loose allusion to this verse (*lex ipsa peccatum sit*).

Rom 7.24 is unattested. Harnack includes it based on Adam 5.21; but this is not a section of the work where Adamantius uses Marcion's text.

7.25 Adam* 5.27; Tertullian, *Marc.* 5.14.1 (≠Schmid). Tertullian may allude to this verse when he says that Paul "attributed fault to the flesh." Adamantius has *ara gar* rather than *ara oun*, and *tōi nomōi tou theou* instead of *nomōi theou*. R. Bultmann's proposal that 7.25b is an interpolation ("Glossen in Römerbrief," 198–99) is not supported by the evidence of the Apostolikon.

8.1–2 Adam* 5.27 (≠Schmid). Adamantius reads "freed *us*" in v. 2, rather than "freed me" or "freed you"; all three readings are attested in the catholic textual tradition. R. Bultmann's proposal that 8.1 is an interpolation ("Glossen in Römerbrief," *TLZ* 7 [1947] 199) is not supported by the evidence of the Apostolikon.

8.3 Tertullian, *Marc.* 5.14.1. Tertullian has "the Father sent Christos" rather than "God sent his own child"; is this unparalleled variant Tertullian's paraphrase or the reading of the Apostolikon?
8.4a Epiphanius, *Scholion* 33.
Rom 8.4b–8 is unattested (≠Harnack, Schmid). Harnack includes vv. 4–6 on the basis of Adam 5.22, but this citation falls before Adamantius turns to the Marcionite text in this part of his treatise. Schmid thinks Tertullian, *Marc.* 5.14.4, alludes to vv. 5–9, but see the note on 8.9a. *Marc.* 5.10.11 cites v. 8, when commenting on 1 Cor 15.50: "[Paul's] custom in other places besides is to let a substance stand for the works of that substance, as when he says that those who are in the flesh cannot please God." Of course, we cannot be certain that he was careful to cite only from the Apostolikon in his own exegesis of Paul's meaning.
8.9a Tertullian, *Marc.* 5.14.4. Schmid considers all of vv. 5–9 encompassed in Tertullian's allusion; but I see only v. 9 reflected here, as does Harnack. The proposal of Refoulé, "Unité de l'Epître aux Romains et histoire du salut," that vv. 9–11 constitute an interpolation, is not supported by the evidence of the Apostolikon.
8.10–11 Tertullian, *Marc.* 5.14.4–5. Comparison with how Tertullian quotes v. 11 elsewhere is inconclusive in demonstrating any significant variant in the Apostolikon; see Schmid, *Marcion und sein Apostolos*, 103–4. One notes the apparent affirmation of physical resurrection in this verse, contrary to Marcion's reported views.
Rom 8.12–15a is unattested.
8.15b Adam* 2.19 (≠Harnack, Schmid). This verse is the most likely source of the quotation given by the Marcionite Markus in debate with Adamantius: "The good God is the father of those who believe, for Paul says, 'We have been received into adoption' (*eis huiothesian elēphthēmen*)." Although both Gal 4.5 and Laod (Eph) 1.5 have elements of this clause, the form in which Markus gives it fits best in the context of the surrounding clauses of Romans 8, and in its variations from the catholic text even resolves some tensions in the surrounding syntax ("we" in harmony with v. 15c and v. 16, instead of "you").
Rom 8.15c–18 is unattested.
8.19 Origen, *Hom. Ezech.* 1.7.2 (≠Harnack, Schmid). Harnack proposed the omission of 8.19–22, based on this passage of Origen:

> For "the expectation of creation awaits the revelation of the sons of God." And although those who have corrupted the apostolic scriptures are unwilling that words of this sort be found in their books by means of which Christ can be proved to be the creator, nevertheless therein all creation awaits the sons of God. (*Nam 'exspectatio creaturae revelationem filiorum Dei exspectat'. Et licet nolint hi, qui scripturas apostolicas interpolaverunt istiusmodi sermones inesse libris eorum, quibus possit creator Iesus Christus probari, exspectat ibi tamen omnis creatura filios Dei.*)

But Thomas Scheck, in his translation of this passage (*Origen: Homilies on Ezekiel 1–14*, 37), takes Origen to mean that "in those very books" of their own where the heretics insist no such identification of Christ with the creator is to be found, this passage stands to refute them. Everything rests on the referent of *ibi* ("there, therein"): either in "the apostolic scriptures" or in "their books." The grammar of Jerome's Latin translation would appear to support Scheck, presuming that it effectively rendered Origen's meaning in the original Greek. By this reading, then, Origen would actually be attesting the passage for the *Apostolikon*. Our sources had good reason to pass over the verses that follow in silence, since what it said about creation being subjected, enslaved, and in pain suited Marcionite views better than theirs.

Rom 8.20–9.3 is unattested. Adam 1.21 quotes 8.36, and if this testimony is credited for the Apostolikon, it goes some way toward delimiting the "immense chasm" Tertullian claims Marcion left in this part of the letter by an omission.

Omission: 9.4–10.1? Following a quotation of 8.11, Tertullian says,

> I overleap here an immense chasm left by scripture carved away (*salio et hic amplissimum abruptum intercisae scripturae*), though I take note of the apostle giving evidence for Israel that they have a zeal for God, their own God of course, though not by means of knowledge. (*Marc.* 5.14.6)

He proceeds to quote 10.2 at the other end of the "immense chasm." Schmid (*Marcion und sein Apostolos*, 110) notes the uncertainty over the extent of this gap. Harnack regarded as omitted the entirety of chapter 9, which is not attested for Marcion's text by any of our sources. Note, however, that the identification of those credited with zeal for God in 10.2 as "Israel" requires either the presence of some of the content of chapter 9 (references to "Israel" occur in 9.4, 6, 27, and 31) or, as Harnack notes (*Marcion*, 108*), 10.1 in a variant reading ("my supplication to God on behalf *of Israel*" instead of "on behalf of them") found in a large number of Greek manuscripts. Käsemann, *Commentary on Romans*, 258, notes an aporia of thought between 9.3. and 9.4: "Remarkably, Paul gives no reason for his sorrow, and the lament changes quietly into magnifying the advantages of Israel in salvation history." The lament of 9.1–3 picks up only with 10.1, and it seems most likely that the text of Romans in the Apostolikon lacked everything between.

10.2–4 Tertullian, *Marc.* 5.14.6; Epiphanius, *Scholion* 34 (v. 4 only). For v. 2, cf. Isa 1.3. In v. 3, Tertullian has "ignorant of God," while the catholic text has "ignorant of the rectitude of God." Necessarily, then, the following clause has an explicit "rectitude" ("and seeking to establish their own *rectitude*") as many Gk mss do.

Omission: 10.5–11.32? Tertullian says with regard to the words of 11.33:

> Whence that outburst? Out of his recollection of those scriptures to which he had already referred, out of his mediation upon those types and figures which he had previously expounded as bearing on the faith of Christ which was to emerge from the Law. If Marcion has of set purpose cut out these passages, what is this exclamation his apostle makes, when he has no riches of his god to look upon, a poor god and needy as

one must be who has created nothing, prophesied nothing, in fact possessed nothing, one who has come down to another's property? (5.14.9)

Harnack (*Marcion*, 108*) maintains that this remark indicates that the entirety of 10.5–11.32 was lacking in Marcion's text, and that 11.33 directly commented on 10.4. Schmid (*Marcion und sein Apostolos*, 111) expresses some doubt that the gap was so extensive. He points to a passage in Ireneaus, *Haer*. 1.27.3, which refers to a Marcionite belief in Christ's descent into Hades, and suggests that this belief is based on Rom 10.6–10. It is quite uncharacteristic of Schmid to credit anything outside of the more systematic sources, and to rely, as he does here, on an isolated comment about Marcionite teachings. I agree that explicit reports about Marcionite interpretation and application of biblical passages should be given tentative credit; but Irenaeus' remark scarcely rises to that standard, and Schmid's suggestion cannot be accepted.

11.33 Tertullian, *Marc*. 5.14.9. Marcion drew on the words of this verse for the opening lines of his *Antitheses*.

11.34–35 Tertullian, *Marc*. 5.14.10. Tertullian remarks of this quotation from Isa 40.13–14, "When you took away so much from the scriptures, why did you retain this, as though this too were not the creator's?" Note that it was quoted before by Paul (1 Cor 2.16) in a different form according to the catholic text, but in exactly this form in Marcion's text (as attested by Tertullian).

Rom 11.36–12.8 is unattested.

12.9–10 Tertullian, *Marc*. 5.14.11.

Rom 12.11 is unattested.

12.12 Tertullian, *Marc*. 5.14.11.

Rom 12.13 is unattested.

12.14 Tertullian, *Marc*. 5.14.11.

Rom 12.15 is unattested.

12.16–19 Tertullian, *Marc*. 5.14.12–13. In v. 17, Tertullian gives more of the quotation from Lev 19:18 than is found in most witnesses to the catholic version of this verse (but cf. Gk mss F and G), and gives no indication that he is making the addition himself; but Harnack does not credit the extended quote to the Apostolikon. Tertullian gives the wording of v. 18 after that from v. 19, and Harnack accepts this as the order in Marcion's text. The quote in v. 19 is from Deut 32.35 (Schmid does not count this quote as part of the Apostolikon, apparently assuming that Tertullian switches abruptly to his own text of Romans while discussing Marcion's).

Rom 12.20–13.8a is unattested. Several researchers have suggested that 13.1–7 is an interpolation, among them Barnikol, "Römer 13," and J. Kallas, "Romans xiii.1–7: An Interpolation."

13.8b Epiphanius, *Scholion* 35. Epiphanius has "neighbor" (*plēsion*; cf. Rom 13.9), in agreement with Gk ms 1735; other witnesses to the catholic text have "another" (*heteron*).

13.9–10 Tertullian, *Marc*. 5.14.13 (v. 9b); Adam 2.17 (Schmid does not credit the evidence of Adamantius, which may not be drawn from the Apostolikon). In v. 9 Adamantius has "adultery" and "murder" in reverse order relative to the standard catholic text, and omits "you will not lust" in agreement with Gk ms 1734 and Clement of Alexandria.

Rom 13.11–14.4 is unattested.

14.5a Adam* 2.5 (≠Harnack, Schmid). This quotation is omitted in Rufinus' Latin translation.

Rom 14.5b–9 is unattested.

14.10 Tertullian, *Marc.* 5.14.14. Tertullian gives "tribunal of Christos" instead of "tribunal of God," in agreement with a number of Greek manuscripts (but not those "Western" texts with which the Apostolikon typically agrees), and PolPhil 6.10; cf. 2 Cor 5.10. But Tertullian has this reading in his own text of Paul as well (*Praescr.* 44.1).

Rom 14.11–20 is unattested.

14.21 Eznik, *De Deo* 408 (≠Schmid).

Rom 14.22 is unattested.

14.23 Origen, *Comm. Rom.* 10.43.2, seems to state that this verse concluded the text of Romans in the Apostolikon (but see discussion of the omission below). That statement has not prevented modern researchers from proposing various additions here. D. De Bruyne has found an apparent closing salutation in four Latin manuscripts, "May favor be with all of the holy ones" (*Gratis cum omnibus sanctis*), which he suggests was Marcion's substitute ending after omitting chapter 15 ("Le deux derniers chapitres de la lettre aux Romains" and "La finale marcionite de la lettre aux Romains retrouvée"). This salutation is followed in these manuscripts by the doxology of 16.25–27.

Omission: 15.1–16.27 Origen, *Comm. Rom.* 10.43.2, says with reference to the doxology of 16.25–27 of canonical Romans:

> This section was completely cut from this epistle by Marcion, by whom the evangelical and apostolical writings have been falsified. And not only this, but he also cut out everything from the place where it is written, "anything which does not rise from trust is wrongdoing" (14.23) (*Caput hoc Marcion, a quo scripturae evangelicae atque apostolicae interpolatae sunt, de hac epistola penitus abstulit; et non solum hoc, sed et ab eo loco ubi scriptum est: omne autem quod non est ex fide peccatum est, usque ad finem cuncta dissecuit.*)

This statement has been taken by most to mean that Marcion's text of Romans ended at 14.23. In support of this, Tertullian, *Marc.* 5.14.14, alluding to the content of Rom 14.10, speaks of it as being *in clausula*, i.e., "in the closing" of the letter, and he mentions nothing else from the rest of the letter. In fact, his failure to mention the absence of chapters 15 and 16 from Marcion's version, or to cite anything from those chapters in any of his works, may suggest that he, too, only knew the fourteen-chapter version of the letter. On the other hand, Lagrange (*Saint Paul épitre aux Romains*, 381) and Scheck (*Origen, Commentary on the Epistle to the Romans*, vol. 2, 307 n. 350) contend that the verb *desecuit* means not "cut out" but "cut up," and some parts of chapters 15 to 16 may have been found in Marcion's text, whereas the doxology was "completely removed" (*penitus abstulit*). But, contrary to their reading of the verb, it ordinarily means "cut off, sever"; and why would Origen refer so precisely to 14.23 as the point where Marcion began to "cut up" the letter? Therefore, I have followed the consensus opinion that 14.23 marked the end of Marcion's text. There is clear evidence of a fourteen-chapter version of Romans in circulation in the Latin West (see Gamble, *The Textual History of the Letter to the Romans*), and the ninth-century Greek-Latin bilingual ms G separates chapters 15–16 from the end of chapter 14 by six blank lines. This sort of separation typically represents uncertainty about the unity of the preceding text with the following, as in cases where a copyist adds material found in another exemplar than the one primarily used as the basis for the copy; but the space is interpreted differently by Corssen ("Zur Überlieferungsgeschichte des Römerbriefes") and Dupont ("Pour l'histoire de la doxologie finale de l'épitre aux Romains"), who consider it to be a sign of the copyist's uncertainty about whether to place the doxology at this point, somewhere else, or, as the copyist ultimately decided, to omit it.

Several modern scholars have accepted the fourteen-chapter form of the letter as the probable original. Some of them consider chapters 15–16 to be non-Pauline (e.g., Baur, *Paul, the Apostle of Jesus Christ*, vol. 1, 352–65; Ryder, "The Authorship of Romans XV, XVI"), while others see them as constituted of a pastiche of Pauline passages from other letters (e.g., Rueckert, *Commentar über den Brief Pauli an die Römer*, 340–53; Lightfoot, *Biblical Essays*, 289–93). Alternatively, it has been suggested that Paul himself circulated the letter in two forms, with and without chapter 15 (e.g., Lake, *The Earlier Epistles of Saint Paul*, 361–70). Harry Gamble, while defending the originality of the full sixteen-chapter form of Romans, has made a compelling argument that the fourteen-chapter form was not the product of Marcion's editorial hand, but was an already circulating abridgement adopted by him (*The Textual History of the Letter to the Romans*). Despite the clear testimony of Origen that the Apostolikon did not contain the doxology that appears in various catholic manuscripts at 14.23, 15.33, or 16.25–27 ("Marcion . . . completely removed this section from this epistle"), it is persistently attributed to Marcion or to Marcionite editors in secondary literature (beginning with Corssen, "Zur Überlieferungsgeschichte des Römerbriefes"; for a review of this proposal, see Dupont, "Pour l'histoire de la doxologie finale de l'épitre aux Romains").

To Thessalonians 1

Prologue *Thessalonicenses sunt Macedones. Hi accepto verbo veritatis perstiterunt in fide etiam in persecutione civium suorum; praeterea nec receperunt ea quae a falsis apostolis dicebantur. Hos conlaudat apostolus scribens eis ab Athenis.* For the idea that the letter was written from Athens, see 1 Thess 3.1. Epiphanius says, "Since Marcion has everything from the fifth epistle, Thessalonians 1, in a distorted form. . . . I cite nothing from it. Since Thessalonians 2 . . . was similarly distorted by Marcion himself, again I cite nothing from it" (42.12.1). This appears to be nothing more than a gratuitous polemical way of excusing the absence of any citations from these letters in his argument.

1.1 Tertullian, *Marc.* 5.5.1–2 (≠Harnack, Schmid).

1 Thess 1.2–2.13 is unattested.

2.14–15a Tertullian, *Marc.* 5.15.1. Tertullian attests the reading "the Judeans killed *their own* prophets" (*occiderant Iudaei prophetas suos; interfecerunt . . . prophetas suos* > Gk *tous idious prophētas*), which he claims is Marcion's addition; but the reading is also found in Gk mss D^c, E*, K, L, Ψ, and many others, some versions and some patristic witnesses. Thus, the imaginable ideological motive for Marcion to make the change from "the prophets" to "their (i.e., Jewish) prophets" is beside the point, since the variant was already present in the textual tradition of Paul completely independently of Marcion (cf. Clabeaux, *A Lost Edition of the Letters of Paul*, 117 and n. 79). On the persecution of Christians in Judea mentioned here, cf. Gal 6.12. Tertullian omits "Jesus" following "the Master." Harnack also cites the verse from Adam 5.12, but Marcion's text is not involved here. Pearson, "1 Thessalonians 2:13–16: A Deutero-Pauline Interpolation," has made a case for an interpolation in this passage, to explain several oddities in the grammar and syntax, as well as inconsistencies with Paul's thought elsewhere (see also Eckart, "Der zweite echte Brief"). While the evidence of the Apostolikon does not confirm the entire passage as an interpolation, the most severe anomalies of the text are not attested for Marcion's text by our sources, in particular v. 15b–16. The Prologue's reference to the persecution of the Thessalonian Christians by their fellow countrymen comes from 2.14.

1 Thess 2.16–20 is unattested.

1 Thess 3.1–6 is unattested by our main sources. But the information in the Prologue that Paul wrote this letter from Athens depends upon these verses.

1 Thess 3.7–4.2 is unattested.

4.3–5 Tertullian, *Marc.* 5.15.3. In v. 4, Tertullian's use of *tractare* ("use," "control") instead of *possidere* or something similar for Greek *ktasthai* ("acquire") may be his own paraphrase or reflect a textual variant; but he has the same variant in his own text of Paul (*Res.* 16.11). He omits "sanctification" before "honor," and has simply "as the nations (do)" instead of "as also (do) those nations who do not know God." He seems to attest "not with lust" (*non in libidine*) instead of "not with an emotion of lust." Eckart, "Der zweite echte Brief," has proposed interpolations in 4.1–8, 10b–12, and 18; the first of these is not supported by the evidence of the Apostolikon.

1 Thess 4.6–15 is unattested.

4.16–17 Tertullian, *Marc.* 5.15.4; 5.20.7 (v. 17); Adam 1.25 (vv. 16–17; Schmid does not credit the evidence of Adamantius, who may not be using the Apostolikon here). Harnack and Schmid appear not to recognize that Tertullian has reordered the clauses of his quote, beginning with v. 17 and then returning to v. 16b, and not actually quoting v. 15 (and therefore not omitting v. 16a as Harnack supposes). Adamantius alone attests v. 16a, with several variants: "by a command *of God*"; "with the last trumpet" (cf. 1 Cor 15.52), rather than "with a trumpet of God"; "(*the*) *Master* will descend," in place of "he will descend." In v. 16b, Adamantius has "the dead will be awakened first (*egerthēsontai prōtoi*)" rather than "the dead in Christos will awaken first (*anastēsontai prōton*)"; but Tertullian attests the latter. In v. 17, Adamantius has "we *also* who remain for the presence" (*kai hēmeis hoi perileipomenoi eis tēn parousian*; Tertullian reads similarly, with the addition "of Christos") instead of "we the living who remain" (*hēmeis hoi zōntes hoi perileipomenoi*). Adamantius has "to a meeting with him" instead of "to a meeting with the Master in the air"; but Tertullian has the latter reading. Overall these verses provide a good example of how our sources can provide clear testimony to the presence of content while offering no consistent information on the exact wording of the passage in the Apostolikon.

1 Thess 4.18–5.18 is unattested. Friedrich, "1 Thessalonischer 5,1–11," has argued that the first eleven verses of chapter 5 constitute an interpolation.

5.19–20 Tertullian, *Marc.* 5.15.5. Eckart, "Der zweite echte Brief," has argued for interpolations in 5.12–22 and 5.27. The evidence of the Apostolikon shows that part of this material, at least, was already in the letter by the time of its adoption by Marcion.

1 Thess 5.21–22 is unattested.

5.23 Tertullian, *Marc.* 5.15.7–8. Tertullian gives the order "spirit, body, soul" rather than "spirit, soul, body"; whereas *Res.* 47.17–18 has "body, soul, spirit." He reads "be preserved without complaint" (*sine querela*) for "flawlessly" (*amemptōs*), a variant found also in the Vulgate tradition. He has "Master *and Rescuer*" and omits "Jesus" with "Christos." Schmid, *Marcion und sein Apostolos*, 104–5, discusses some of these variants.

1 Thess 5.24–28 is unattested. Harnack includes 5.26 based on the Pseudo-Pauline Laodiceans, which he believes to be a Marcionite compilation of passages from the Apostolikon.

To Thessalonians 2

2 Thess 1.1 is unattested, but some initial address must have been included.

1.2 Tertullian, *Marc.* 5.5.1–2 (≠Harnack, Schmid).

2 Thess 1.3–5 is unattested.

1.6–7 Tertullian, *Marc.* 5.16.1; Adam* 2.5–6 (Schmid does not credit the evidence of Adamantius). At first, when Adamantius reads the passage, he has "for (the) Master to repay (*apodounai*)" rather than "for

God to take vengeance on (*antapodounai*)," and Tertullian agrees on "Master" in place of "God," while the Vulgate tradition attests the two verbal alternatives. Yet when the Marcionite Megethius requotes the passage, his text agrees with the more common catholic text on both points (as does Rufinus' Latin translation in both places), almost certainly due to harmonization to the catholic text, given the support of Tertullian for the alternative text. Tertullian reads "*when he comes from (the) celestial sphere,*" in agreement with Ephrem Syrus against other witnesses to the catholic text, who do not have the italicized expression.

1.8 Tertullian, *Marc.* 5.16.1. Tertullian says, "But the heretic has extinguished the flame and fire by erasing them, lest, of course, he make God ours," suggesting the absence of "in a flaming fire" (*en puri phlogos*). Clabeaux, *A Lost Edition of the Letters of Paul*, 37, considers this a rare probable example of Marcion's own editorial hand, since it has no parallel in non-Marcionite witnesses to the catholic text.

1.9 Tertullian, *Marc.* 5.16.2.

2 Thess 1.10–12 is unattested.

2.1, 3–4 Tertullian, *Marc.* 5.16.4 (=Harnack and Schmid vv. 3–4 only, both apparently overlooking Tertullian's reference to v. 1: *domini adventum*). Tertullian has "person of fault" (*homo delicti*) instead of "man of lawlessness," in agreement with Gk mss A, D, F, G, Ψ, and indeed the majority, as well as some witnesses to the OL, and this is Tertullian's own wording elsewhere. This man "exalts himself" (*iactaturus*) rather than "shows himself," over everything that is "called a god *and* is an object of reverance" rather than "a god *or* an object of reverance" (in agreement with the Peshitta Syriac version). Tertullian refers further to "antichrist," but we cannot be sure that this term was in Marcion's text, or an added identification supplied by Tertullian.

2 Thess 2.2, 5–8 is unattested.

2.9 Tertullian, *Marc.* 5.16.4, 6. Notice that Tertullian can quote the verse at first (5.16.4) without the phrase "according to the operation of Satan," only to bring in that phrase, clearly quoted from Marcion's text, when it suits him (5.16.6).

2.10–12 Tertullian, *Marc.* 5.16.5. In v. 11 Tertullian gives a text at substantial divergence from most witnesses to the catholic version, representing a pious emendation of the text to avoid identifying God as the cause of error. Instead of "and because of this God sends into them an impulse of error, so that they believe the lie," he reads, "and because of this there will be for them an impulse of error" (*erit eis instinctum fallaciae*: Evans corrects this to *erit eis in instinctum fallaciae*, while Kroymann has *dabit eis instinctum*). The future tense is found also in several Greek and OL manuscripts; but we do not know if Tertullian's phrasing reflects Marcion's text or not.

2 Thess 2.13–3.9 is unattested.

3.10 Tertullian, *Marc.* 5.16.7.

2 Thess 3.11–18 is unattested.

To Laodiceans

Title See Tertullian, *Marc.* 5.11.12; 5.17.1; Epiphanius, *Pan.* 42 (Holl, *Panarion*, 105). This letter appears in several early manuscripts (e.g., P⁴⁶, ℵ*, B*, 6, 424ᶜ, 1739) with no specific addressee, while in most later manuscripts, it is addressed to Ephesians. The content of the letter clearly shows that it was composed in close relationship to the letter to the Colossians, and so its identification as, in fact, the letter to the Laodiceans that Paul mentions sending in his Colossian letter has been proposed completely apart from any evidence stemming from Marcion and the Apostolikon. The Marcionite prologue to Colossians says that the latter letter was written in Ephesus. If Laodiceans was written at the same time and in the same place as Colossians, this could explain its association with Ephesus in some lines of transmission.

Prologue Two possible texts have been proposed. The first proposal (e.g., Corssen; Harnack, *Marcion*, 129*) assumes that the "Ephesians" prologue is simply a lightly reworked version of the original Laodicean one, and that the latter read as follows: *Laodicenses sunt Asiani. Hi accepto verbo veritatis perstiterunt in fide. Hos conlaudet apostolus scribens eis a Roma de carcere per Tychicum diaconum* (Corssen, 38, notes that three manuscripts add to this prologue: *Sciendum sane quia haec epistola quam nos ad Ephesios habemus, haeretici et maxime Marcianistae ad Laudicenses adtitulant*). There are problems with this proposal, however. This prologue is a close copy of the one to Philippians, suggesting that it is a late substitute by an unoriginal hand. Its reference to incarceration at Rome violates the temporal sequence of the letters, and puts it out of order relative to Colossians that follows (Dahl, "The Origin of the Earliest Prologues," 249). One might expect rather that the original Laodicean prologue would resemble closely the prologue to Colossians, since the situation of the two communities and two letters had so much in common, and due to the presence in the Colossian prologue of several suggestions that it is repeating information given in the previous, Laodicean prologue: "Colossians are *also* of Asia, *also* reached beforehand by false apostles, Paul corrects them *also* by a letter." Schäfer, "Marcion und die ältesten Prologe," 148–9 and "Marius Victorinus und die marcionitischen Prologe," 12–14, argues that Marius Victorinus appears to have read such a prologue to "Ephesians," different from the one now found in biblical manuscripts, and more closely matching what the prologue to Colossians leads us to expect: the Ephesians were corrupted by false apostles to combine Judaism with the Christian discipline, the letter is written to correct and admonish them (see *Commentary on Ephesians* PL 8, 1235 B; 1237 A; 1239 A; 1252 D; 1267 D). The second proposal, then, reconstructs a prologue based upon the Colossian prologue (e.g., De Bruyne): *Laodicenses sunt Asiani. His praeventi erant a falsis apostolis. . . . Ad hos non accessit ipse apostolus . . . hos per epistulam recorrigit.*

Schäfer ("Marius Victorinus und die marcionitischen Prologe," 14–15) has made a good argument that it must also have included, as the Colossian prologue does, *scribit eis ab Epheso*. This clause had to be emended or suppressed when the letter was identified as one written *to* Ephesus, rather than *from* Ephesus (similarly Dahl, "The Origin of the Earliest Prologues," 250).

1.1 Adam* 2.12 (≠Harnack, Schmid). The Marcionite Markus merely quotes Paul's standard self-designation, "Paul, emissary of Jesus Christos" (reading "Jesus Christos" rather than "Christos Jesus"); cf. 1 Cor 1.1 vs. 2 Cor 1.1. None of our sources expressly quotes the second half of the verse, where Gk mss P^{46}, ℵ*, B*, 6, 424^c, 1739, as well as Origen read "the holy ones who exist" rather than "the holy ones who exist *in Ephesus*." It is hard to square this alternative reading with normal Greek grammar, and probably some place name originally appeared here, as in similar opening clauses of all of Paul's letters. Although the Apostolikon may have shared this reading, it cannot be ruled out that it actually read "in Laodicea," as the superscription of the letter in the Apostolikon would suggest.

1.2 Tertullian, *Marc.* 5.5.1-2 (≠Harnack, Schmid).

Eph 1.3–4 is unattested.

1.5 Possibly alluded to in Adam* 2.19, where the words *eis huiothesian elēphthēmen* are attributed to Paul; cf. Rom 8.15; Gal 4.5.

Eph 1.6–8 is unattested. Contrary to Harnack, we have no reason to think that Adam 5.12 is quoting vv. 6–7 from the Marcionite canon.

1.9–10 Tertullian, *Marc.* 5.17.1. Harnack indulges in a lot of speculative rewording and reordering based on Tertullian's paraphrase.

Eph 1.11 is unattested.

1.12 Tertullian, *Marc.* 5.17.3. Tertullian describes this clause as immediately following on v. 10 (*nam et sequentia quem renuntiant Christum, cum dicit*). He reads "praise of glory" rather than "praise of *his* glory," in agreement with Gk mss D*, F, and G, and some witnesses to the OL.

1.13 Tertullian, *Marc.* 5.17.4. Tertullian omits "of your rescue" following "the proclamation," and seems to read "the sacred spirit of *his* promise."

Eph 1.14–16 is unattested.

1.17–22a Tertullian, *Marc.* 5.17.5–6. On the possible interpolation of Eph 1.21 in Gal, see note to Gal 4.26 above. Tertullian does not quote it here, and it may have been absent from Laodiceans in the Apostolikon.

Eph 1.22b–23 is unattested.

2.1–2 Tertullian, *Marc.* 5.17.7. Schmid apparently overlooks Tertullian's reference to the last clause of v. 2 ("that now operates in the children of distrust").

2.3 Tertullian, *Marc.* 5.17.9–10. Tertullian initially reads "misdeeds" in place of "lusts of the flesh," but later lists both "misdeeds and the lusts of the flesh."

Eph 2.4–9 is unattested.

2.10 Tertullian, *Marc.* 5.17.11. Here as typically, Tertullian reads simply "Christos," omitting "Jesus."

2.11–14a Epiphanius, *Scholion* 36 (vv. 11–14a); Tertullian, *Marc.* 5.17.12–14; 5.11.13 (v. 12); Adam* 2.18 (vv. 11–13; Schmid does not credit the evidence of Adamantius). Epiphanius indicates that the passage continues to following verses, and Tertullian continues through v. 20. In v. 11, Epiphanius and Adamantius both omit "therefore" (*dio*, cf. Gk mss 104, 1311), and read *mnēmoneuontes* instead of *mnēmoneuete* (in agreement with Gk ms G and some witnesses to the OL). Epiphanius has a slightly different word order, and omits "that" (*hoti*, cf. Gk ms G). Epiphanius and Adamantius both omit "in flesh" (*en sarki*) following "nations"; but Tertullian has it. In v. 12, Adamantius has "in that time" (*en tōi kairōi ekeinōi*) instead of "at that time" (*tōi kairōi ekeinōi*), and Tertullian appears to concur, as do Gk ms P[46] and several others; but Epiphanius has the other reading. Tertullian has, without comment, "strangers to *their* contracts *and* promises" (*peregrini testamentorum et promissionis eorum*), while Epiphanius, Adamantius, and most witnesses to the catholic text read "strangers to the contracts of the promise"; Tertullian's reading is shared by Gk mss F and G and some witnesses to the OL. In v. 13, Adamantius reads "but now you," while Tertullian has "but now in Christos you" and Epiphanius has "but now in Christos Jesus you" (the latter is the most widely attested catholic text); Clabeaux, *A Lost Edition of the Letters of Paul*, 106, takes Tertullian's testimony as reliable (agreeing as it does with Gk ms L, some witnesses to the OL, Irenaeus and Origen), discounting without comment the contradictory evidence of the other two sources. Tertullian and Epiphanius both read "by his blood" (in agreement with Ephrem Syrus) rather than "by the blood of the Christos" found in Adamantius and most witnesses to the catholic text.

2.14b–16 Tertullian, *Marc.* 5.17.14–15. In v. 14b, Tertullian expressly notes the absence of "his" with "flesh" in Marcion's text (Schmid, *Marcion und sein Apostolos*, 112, shows that Clabeaux, *A Lost Edition of the Letters of Paul*, 120–21, is wrong to claim Ambrose, Jerome, and Quodvultdeus as supporting witnesses to this reading). Tertullian has three key agreements with Ephrem Syrus: "enmity" in a genitive form ("the intervening wall of enmity": *medio pariete inimicitiae*) in v. 14b; the omission of *tou phragmou* modifying the "intervening wall" in v. 14b; and "so that he might create the two in *himself* (*semetipso > heautōi*), rather than "in him" in v. 15 (also found in a number of Greek manuscripts, including D and G, the PSyr, Armenian, and some witnesses to the OL). On these parallel variants, see Bucher, "A Marcionite Reading in Ephrem's Commentary," 37–38.

2.17–20 Tertullian, *Marc.* 5.17.16; 4.39.6; Adam 2.19 (vv. 17–18; Schmid does not credit the evidence of Adamantius, who may not be using the Apostolikon here). In v. 17, Tertullian has simply "proclaimed" instead of "came and proclaimed," while Adamantius agrees with the latter. Tertullian and Adamantius agree on the omission of the second "peace." The same omission is found in the majority of Greek manuscripts and Ephrem Syrus, but not in P[46], D, F, G, etc. In v. 18, Tertullian omits both "through him" and "by one spirit," while

Adamantius attests the full catholic text. On v. 20, Tertullian comments on the omission of "and prophets," chiding Marcion for forgetting that Paul can refer to Christian prophets (as he does in 1 Cor 12.28). Harnack, *Marcion*, 150*, posits an ideological edit here. Clabeaux (*A Lost Edition of the Letters of Paul*, 2–3, 111, 121) demonstrates that the same words are lacking in Gk ms 112* and Lectionary 1, due to homoeoteleuton with the preceding *apostolōn* (Schmid, *Marcion und sein Apostolos*, 112, critiques Clabeaux's further patristic witnesses to this reading). Note that Tertullian says nothing about an omission of "and prophets" in the identical combination ("apostles and prophets") in 3.5 or 4.11.

Eph 2.21–3.7 is unattested.

3.8–9 Tertullian, *Marc.* 5.18.1; Adam 2.20; Schmid does not credit the evidence of Adamantius, who may not be using the Apostolikon here). In v. 8, Tertullian omits "sacred ones," but Adamantius has it. Only Adamantius quotes v. 8b, and he reads "*among* the nations" (*en tois ethnesin*), as does Ephrem Syrus, rather than "to the nations" (*tois ethnesin*). In v. 9, Adamantius and Tertullian agree in reading "illuminate somewhat *for all*" (*photisai pantas tis*), instead of "illuminate somewhat" (*photisai tis*), in agreement with P^{46}, $\aleph^c$, B, D, F, G, the majority of later manuscripts, witnesses to the OL, and the Syriac versions. Regarding v. 9, Tertullian says, "The heretic has removed the preposition 'in' and thus makes it read: hidden from ages past from the god who created everything." Yet Gk mss $\aleph^*$, 614, and 2412 similarly lack "in" (*en*), and although the verse could then be read as Tertullian reports or assumes the Marcionite interpretation, it is not necessarily so, and can also still be read in the same way as with *en* (see Clabeaux, *A Lost Edition of the Letters of Paul*, 121–22 and n. 89). Clabeaux (111) suggests that the omission can be explained mechanically by homoeoteleuton with *aiōnōn*. Adamantius, however, has the *en* in this clause (in the Greek text; Rufinus' Latin translation does not have an explicit *in*). Yet it is not certain that Adamantius is quoting from the Marcionite Apostolikon in this section.

3.10 Tertullian, *Marc.* 5.18.2. Tertullian omits "now," as do Gk mss F, G, 629, 2423*, the PSyr, several witnesses to the OL, and such church fathers as Origen and Ephrem Syrus. But this is also Tertullian's own text of Paul for the verse elsewhere; Clabeaux considers it the original reading of the verse (*A Lost Edition of the Letters of Paul*, 98–99).

Eph 3.11–4.4 is unattested.

4.5–6 Epiphanius, *Scholion* 40; Adam 2.19 (v. 6; Schmid does not credit the evidence of Adamantius, who may not be using the Apostolikon here). Epiphanius reports this passage from "Laodiceans" which he considers to be a separate letter from "Ephesians." He is not referring to the forged Pseudo-Pauline "Laodiceans" found in a number of Latin catholic biblical manuscripts, since these verses are not found in it. Probably Epiphanius derived the quotation from some intermediate source that used the original Marcionite designation of the letter. In v. 6, the Greek text of Adamantius omits "who is over all and through all"; but Rufinus' Latin translation retains it, as does Epiphanius. Both the Greek and Latin of Adamantius agree in reading "and in all *of us*"; but Epiphanius does not attest this variant, which is also found in Gk mss D, F, G and several others, as well as some of the versions of the catholic text.

Eph 4.7 is unattested.

4.8 Tertullian, *Marc.* 5.18.5

Eph 4.9–24 is unattested. Contrary to Harnack, we have no reason to think that Adam 5.7 quotes v. 10 from the Marcionite canon.

4.25–26 Tertullian, *Marc.* 5.18.6; Adam* 1.13 (v. 26b; Schmid does not credit the evidence of Adamantius). Tertullian jumps from here to 5.11 without interruption, as if presenting continuous text. In Adamantius, the Marcionite Megethius quotes v. 26 as a saying of Jesus. Actually, v. 26a quotes Ps 4.4.

Eph 4.27–5.1 is unattested.

5.2 Ephrem, *Hymns* 36.3 (≠Schmid). Ephrem notes the Marcionite use of this verse describing Christ as "an offering and a sacrifice to God."

Eph 5.3–10 is unattested.

5.11 Tertullian, *Marc.* 5.18.6.

Eph 5.12–13 is unattested.

5.14 Epiphanius, *Scholion* 37. The source of the quotation is not known.

Eph 5.15–17 is unattested.

5.18 Tertullian, *Marc.* 5.18.7. Tertullian gives a very loose paraphrase of the sentiment of this verse, saying merely that, "in drunkenness from wine (there is) shame" (*inebriari vino dedecori*).

5.19 Tertullian, *Marc.* 5.18.7.

Eph 5.20 is unattested.

5.21–23 Tertullian, *Marc.* 5.18.8. The implied verb of v. 22 is drawn from v. 21.

Eph 5.24–27 is unattested.

5.28–29 Tertullian, *Marc.* 5.18.8–9. A good cautionary example on using Tertullian's testimony. At first he seems to quote vv. 28–29 in an alternative, compressed and reordered form, lacking several parts of the verses (including v. 28a and 29a); Harnack, *Marcion*, 120*, falls prey to treating this phrasing as an exact quote, as does Schmid, *Marcion und sein Apostolos*, 340. But as Tertullian proceeds to make his point against Marcion, he quotes v. 29 in full more exactly, showing that v. 28b is not actually conflated with v. 29b. Nothing indicates that Tertullian is correcting the reading of Marcion's text by the reading of his own. Rather, he has delayed quoting part of the passage for rhetorical affect, choosing when to quote particular phrases as needed for his argument. The whole point of his polemical method, to use Marcion's own scripture against him, rules out the idea that he switches to his own biblical text here. Clabeaux, *A Lost Edition of the Letters of Paul*, 122–25, offers a heroic reconstruction of an elaborate textual history to account for what Tertullian at first seems to report, which at least serves to show how fluid this passage was in its transmission as various copyists tried to make sense of Paul's rather convoluted point (which is rather turgid without interpretive decisions of where punctuation should fall).

The only significant variant in which we can place confidence is "He loves his own *flesh* who loves his own wife" (v. 28b); cf. Ambrosiaster, with the sole difference of having "body" for "flesh" (on which, see Clabeaux, *A Lost Edition of the Letters of Paul*, 123 n. 92).
Eph 5.30 is unattested.
5.31–32 Epiphanius, *Scholion* 38 (v. 31); Tertullian, *Marc.* 5.18.9–10. Epiphanius reports the absence of "unto his wife" following "shall be joined" in v. 31 (the phrase is present when he quotes from his own text of Paul, *Pan.* 78.19.4), and the verb "joined" is in his reading *kollēthēsetai* rather than *proskollēthēsetai* found in many witnesses to the catholic text (and in Epiphanius' own text elsewhere, *Pan.* 78.19.4). Tertullian lacks both the verb and the object phrase. Clabeaux (*A Lost Edition of the Letters of Paul*, 112, 125–26) and Schmid (*Marcion und sein Apostolos*, 340) take Tertullian's report as the reliable one, given its agreement with Gk mss 6, 1739*, some witnesses to the OL, and Origen. Clabeaux explains this omission of the whole clause as a case of homoeoarcton from one *kai* to the next, jumping over an entire clause of the verse; Epiphanius' more limited omission, however, cannot be so explained. Clabeaux also points out the contradiction in supposing that Marcion removed a reference to being joined to a wife because of his ascetic ideology while retaining in the very same passage a reference to sexual union in the words "and the two will become one flesh." Epiphanius also has "his father" explicit, both when quoting Marcion's text and when quoting his own, whereas most witnesses to the catholic text have literally "the father" with the possessive implicit in the article. In v. 32, Tertullian attests "I am speaking regarding (*eis*) Christos and the assembly" rather than "I am speaking regarding (*eis*) Christos and regarding (*eis*) the assembly," in agreement with a variety of witnesses to the catholic text (Zuntz, *The Text of the Epistles*, 221, 237, regards this as the original text).
Eph 5.33 is unattested.
6.1–2 Tertullian, *Marc.* 5.18.11. Tertullian explicitly mentions the absence of v. 2b ("which is the first commandment with a promise"), while acknowledging that Marcion's text still retained the commandment itself (from Exod 20.12; see Schmid, *Marcion und sein Apostolos*, 94–95, 113).
Eph 6.3 is unattested.
6.4 Tertullian, *Marc.* 5.18.11.
Eph 6.5–10 is unattested.
6.11–12 Tertullian, *Marc.* 5.18.12–14. Tertullian appears to consistently omit "leaders," and have only the two remaining types of opponents, "authorities" and "world rulers."
6.13, 16 Adam* 1.19 (≠Harnack, Schmid). Adamantius conflates these two verses. He has "put on" (*endusasthe*) instead of "take up" (*analabete*) in both verses; and "in order to be able" (*pros to dunasthai*) instead of either "so that you may be able" (*hina dunēthēte*, v. 13) or "in which you will be able" (*en hōi dunēsesthe*, v. 16). He has "the flaming darts," instead of "all the flaming darts."
Eph 6.14–15, 17 is unattested (≠Harnack). Harnack includes the verses

on the basis of *Marc.* 3.14.4, but we cannot be sure that Tertullian was looking at Marcion's text in this part of his work.

6.18–20 Tertullian, *Marc.* 5.18.14 (≠Schmid; =Harnack vv. 19–20 only). Tertullian says of Paul, "He was already in bonds for the liberty of his preaching, and was in fact putting at the church's disposal that boldness in making known the mystery of the opening of his mouth, for which he now enjoined them to make supplication to God."

Eph 6.21–24 is unattested.

To Colossians

Prologue *Colossenses et hi sicut Laodicenses sunt Asiani. Et ipsi praeventi erant a pseudoapostolis nec ad hos accessit ipse apostolus, sed et hos per epistulam recorrigit. Audierant enim verbum ab Archippo, qui et ministerium in eos accepit. Ergo apostolus iam ligatus scribit eis ab Epheso* [*per Tychicum diaconum* C]. Note that this prologue only makes sense within a Pauline corpus that also included a preceding letter to Laodicea. The idea that Paul himself had not been to Colossae (or Laodicea) is found in 2.1, and that he was a prisoner comes from 4.18. The reference to Archippus derives from 4.17, that to Tychicus from 4.7.

1.1 Adam* 2.12 (≠Harnack, Schmid). Adamantius has "Jesus Christos" rather than "Christos Jesus"; this reading agrees with the catholic text of 1 Cor 1.1, but the order "Christos Jesus" is considered by modern text criticism to be more original for 2 Cor 1.1, Laod (Eph) 1.1, and Col 1.1.

1.2 Tertullian, *Marc.* 5.5.1–2 (≠Harnack, Schmid).

Col 1.3–4 is unattested.

1.5–6a Tertullian, *Marc.* 5.19.1. In v. 5, Tertullian appears to have "you heard" (*audistis* > Gk *ēkousate*) instead of "you heard before" (*proēkousate*), a reading found also in the Latin Vulgate, the SCopt, and Armenian.

Col 1.6b–14 is unattested. In v. 12, Gk mss D*, F, G, 33, etc., have "called" rather than "qualified" (and B has a text that conflates the two readings); D, F, G, and several others have "us," in harmony with v. 13, instead of "you."

1.15a Tertullian, *Marc.* 5.19.3; 5.20.4. Tertullian (5.20.4) quotes the words *Christum imaginem dei invisibilis*. From where does he get "Christos" in the preceding verses? Cf. 2 Cor 4.4.

Omission: 1.15b–16 Tertullian appears to say that Marcion's text lacked vv. 15b–16:

> If Christ is not "the firstborn of creation," as being that word of the creator "by whom all things were made and without whom nothing was made," if it is not true that "in him all things were created in heaven and on earth, things visible and things invisible, whether thrones or dominations or principalities or powers," if it is not true that "by him and in him all things were created"—for it was really necessary that Marcion would disapprove of this (*haec enim Marcioni displicere oportebat*)—then the

apostle would not have stated so plainly, "and he is before all (people)."
For how can he be before all (people) if he were not before all (things)?
And how before all (things) if he were not the firstborn of creation?
(*Marc.* 5.19.3–5)

While there have been a great many proposals for the original wording of the hymn used by Paul in this part of the letter, and the possibility of various interpolations, I have not been able to find one that exactly corresponds with the form found in the Apostolikon as reported by Tertullian (although suggestions of editorial expansions or interpolations in v. 16 are quite common). For those conditioned by the catholic form of the text, the redundancy of v. 17 with 15b–16 has passed unnoticed; one would expect, at least, a "therefore" (*oun*) rather than an "and" (*kai*) at the beginning of v. 17. Likewise, the perception of a supposed balance of the hymn in its catholic form rests upon the assumption that the hymn begins with v. 15; however, vv. 12–14 possess the same formal properties, and cannot be excluded from consideration for the overall structure and meaning of the hymn. It could be argued that the form of the passage attested for the Apostolikon possesses an equally clear structure and coherent meaning without vv. 15b–16 (and with or without v. 18).

1.17 Tertullian, *Marc.* 5.19.4 (=Harnack v. 17a only).

Col 1.18 is unattested.

1.19–20 Tertullian, *Marc.* 5.19.5. Tertullian gives the text as "in himself" (*semetipso* > Gk *heautōi*) instead of "in him" (*autōi*), and "to himself" (*semetipsum* > Gk *heauton*) instead of "to him" (*auton*). Harnack, *Marcion*, 122*, regards these as tendentious changes made by Marcion.

1.21–22 Tertullian, *Marc.* 5.19.6. In v. 21, Schmid (*Marcion und sein Apostolos*, 103) notes a minor difference in how Tertullian quotes the verse here, compared to *Res.* 23.1, which demonstrates that Marcion's text agreed with the majority of Greek manuscripts and versions (in reading *dianoia* in the dative case rather than the genitive) against Tertullian's own text of Paul and Gk mss D* and G. In v. 22 Tertullian quite clearly reads "in his body" (=Gk *en tōi sōmati . . . autou*) without "of the flesh" (*tēs sarkos*), because he himself must supply the argument that this body spoken of must be fleshly to have died; but he does not recognize anything wrong with the text. Harnack fails to include "through his death" at the end of v. 22, even though Tertullian clearly attests it (*reconciliari nos in corpore eius per mortem*).

Col 1.23 is unattested.

1.24 Tertullian, *Marc.* 5.19.6.

2.4 Tertullian, *Marc.* 5.19.7. Tertullian loosely paraphrases the gist of this verse.

Col 2.5–7 is unattested.

2.8 Tertullian, *Marc.* 5.19.7. Tertullian reverses the order of the phrases referring to the ordering forces and to tradition.

Col 2.9–12 is unattested.

2.13 Tertullian, *Marc.* 5.19.9. Tertullian's use of "with Christos" instead of "with him" is perhaps drawn from context, and not a reading of the exact text before him.

Col 2.14–15 is unattested. It is not at all surprising that our anti-Marcionite sources pass over in silence a passage such as this that played so well into Marcion's hands.

2.16–17 Epiphanius, *Scholion* 39; Tertullian, *Marc.* 5.19.9. Epiphanius reads "which is a shadow" in v. 17, agreeing with Gk mss B, F, G and a few others, instead of "which are" found in Tertullian and most witnesses to the catholic text.

2.18–22 Tertullian, *Marc.* 5.19.10–11. In v. 18, Tertullian refers to "visions of angels" (*ex visionibus angelicis*), rather than "cult of angels that one has observed." The referent of "that one has observed" is "servility and cult," not "angels," unless Tertullian was looking at a text with a different relative pronoun. But Harnack treats this as Tertullian's own paraphrase, and assumes the traditional catholic text. Tertullian may allude to the bulk of v. 19 when, following his quote "not holding firmly to the head" from that verse, he adds, "that is, him in whom all things are enumerated" (*id est ipsum in quo omnia recensentur*).

Col 2.23–3.8 is not directly attested. But Harnack (*Marcion*, 123*) points out that Tertullian, *Marc.* 5.19.11, implies the presence of the bulk of Colossians 3 when he says, "As the rest of his precepts are the same as elsewhere, let us be satisfied to have explained in other places how they have derived from the creator." Since he goes on to refer specifically to 3.9–10, we should at a minimum take him to be speaking of the presence of 3.5–8.

3.9–10 Tertullian, *Marc.* 5.19.11; *Carmen adv. Marc.* 5.20 (≠Schmid; =Harnack v. 9 only). Neither Harnack nor Schmid note that Tertullian refers to this passage with the words, "teaching them to put off the old man and put on the new" (*docebat exponere* [var. *deponere*] *veterem hominem et novum induere*). Harnack includes v. 9 based on the *Carmen adversus Marcionitas*.

Col 3.11–4.9 is unattested.

4.10–11 Adam* 1.5 (≠Schmid). The passage is explicitly read from the Apostolikon. In v. 10, Adamantius reads "so that (*hina*) he might come," instead of "if ever (*ean*) he might come," agreeing with some witnesses to the OL. He reads "you *therefore* (*oun*) welcome him." In v. 11, he has "are *my* coworkers," in agreement with Gk mss D*, F, G, 1898, the SCopt, Armenian, some Syriac versions, and some witnesses to the OL, and supplies the be-verb along with these witnesses and several others, which otherwise is left implied in most manuscripts and versions. He indicates that the passage continues following v. 11 ("and the rest"), probably meant to run to v. 14, which he again quotes explicitly.

Col 4.12–13 is not directly attested, but probably meant to be included by the remark in Adam* 1.5.

4.14 Adam* 1.5 (≠Schmid). Adamantius omits the epithet "the physician" following "Lukas."

Col 4.15–18 is unattested. Harnack includes v. 16 based on the Pseudo-

Pauline Laodiceans. The mention of Archippus in the Prologue depends on v. 17.

To Philippians

Prologue *Philippenses sunt Macedones. Hi accepto verbo veritatis perstiterunt in fide nec receperunt falsos apostolos. Hos apostolus conlaudat scribens eis a Roma de carcere per Epaphroditum.* Cf. Marius Victorinus, *Commentary on Philippians* (PL 8, 1235 A): *Qui ita sensit de Philippensibus, ut illos, non quomodo in ceteris epistolis, rectum sentire neque a pseudoapostolis seductos esse accepit, sed tantum exhortatoria epistola scripta et in prece: Gratia, inquit, Domini nostri Iesu Christi cum spiritu vestro.* The information that the letter was sent through Epaphroditus depends on 2.25. Harnack (*Marcion*, 124*–27*) reconstructs Marcion's text of this letter largely on the basis of the Latin Pseudo-Pauline Laodiceans, which is made up mostly of verses culled from Philippians. Harnack assumes it to be a Marcionite composition which can be relied upon to indicate what was present in the Apostolikon's text of Philippians. I do not follow him in these assumptions.

Phil 1.1 is not directly attested, but something like it must have begun the letter.

1.2 Tertullian, *Marc.* 5.5.1–2 (≠Schmid).

Phil 1.3–1.13 is unattested.

1.14–18 Tertullian, *Marc.* 5.20.1. Tertullian is quite paraphrastic, and some variants may be suggested. For example, at the beginning of v. 18, Tertullian quotes Paul as saying "It is nothing to me" (*nihil mea*).

Phil 1.19–22 is unattested.

1.23 Eznik, *De Deo* 420 (≠Schmid). Eznik provides quite paraphrastic wording: "I am desiring to go out from this flesh and to be with the Master."

Phil 1.24–2.4 is unattested.

2.5–8 Tertullian, *Marc.* 5.20.3–5; Eznik, *De Deo* 375 (vv. 5, 7; =Harnack vv. 6–8 only). In v. 7, Tertullian appears to attest the reading "of a human being (*anthrōpou*)" instead of "of human beings (*anthrōpōn*)," in agreement with Gk ms P[46], the Palestinian Syriac and Coptic versions, and Origen. Eznik is paraphrastic: "another thing which they say is . . . (that) the Good One . . . sent Jesus his own son to go and take the likeness of a slave and to come into being in the form of a human being." Barnikol, *Philipper 2*, has argued that vv. 6–7 constitute an interpolation introduced by Marcion into the text. The challenge to such a hypothesis lies in explaining how such a sectarian addition worked its way into every witness to the catholic text. To accept it, one must suppose that the catholic textual tradition of Paul depends on the Apostolikon, albeit with subsequent modifications.

Phil 2.9–3.3 is unattested. The Prologue's identification of the bearer of the letter as Epaphroditus depends upon 2.25.

3.4–5, 7–9 Tertullian, *Marc.* 5.20.6. In v. 9 Tertullian appears to read "through him" (. . . *per ipsum*), the reference of which he must explain as "Christ." Tertullian's anti-Marcionite argument even depends on this alternative reading, whereas most witnesses to the catholic version of this verse read "through *trust of Christ.*"

Phil 3.6, 10–19 is unattested.

3.20–21 Tertullian, *Marc.* 5.20.7. In v. 21 Tertullian adds "Christos, *when he comes from the celestial sphere*, will transform," perhaps drawn from the immediate context of v. 20.

To Philemon

Prologue *Philemoni familiares litteras facit pro Onesimo servo eius. Scribit autem ei a Roma de carcere.* Dahl, "The Origin of the Earliest Prologues," presents the argument for doubting that this prologue belonged to the original set. Stylistically it appears to belong to the secondary prologues.

Phlm 1–2 is unattested, but an equivalent of v. 1 must have been present.

3 Tertullian, *Marc.* 5.5.1–2 (≠Harnack, Schmid).

Phlm 4–25 is unattested, but Tertullian says, "This epistle alone has so profited by its brevity as to escape Marcion's falsifying hands" (*Marc.* 5.21.1).

Chapter Notes

Introduction

1. For example, Metzger, *The Canon of the New Testament*, 1: "The recognition of the canonical status of the several books of the New Testament was the result of a long and gradual process. . . . Although this was one of the most important developments in the thought and practice of the early Church, history is virtually silent as to how, when, and by whom it was brought about. Nothing is more amazing in the annals of the Christian Church than the absence of detailed accounts of so significant a process."

2. On the dates of Marcion, see the discussion in chapter 1.

3. Metzger, *The Canon of the New Testament*, 282.

4. With one partial exception: a reconstruction of the gospel portion of Marcion's collection was published as an appendix in C. Bradlaugh Bonner's English translation of P. L. Couchoud, *The Creation of Christ* in 1939. Couchoud's original French work, *Le mystère de Jésus* (1924), had been translated previously into Italian (1926) and Dutch (1933).

5. Streeter, *The Four Gospels*, 14–15.

6. This coalescence of events is pointed to by Shukster and Richardson, "Temple and *Bet Ha-midrash* in the Epistle of Barnabas."

7. John Knox states, "I find in the hypothesis of the continuance into the second century of distinctively Pauline communities (on a priori grounds surely a plausible hypothesis) the best explanation both of Marcion himself and of the amazingly quick and widespread response to him" (*Marcion and the New Testament*, 14–15).

8. See, e.g., the Scholars Press series *The New Testament in the Greek Fathers: Texts and Analyses*.

9. However, one may question the viability and relevance of establishing a definitive Greek text if, as I suggest later, we have reason to conclude that Marcion never created a single exemplar of his scriptures, but adopted existing texts in multiple copies, which already contained textual variants among them.

Chapter 1: Marcion

1. Until recently, the testimonies of Philastrius of Brescia and Epiphanius of Salamis (both from the second half of the fourth century), along with that of a catalog of heresies of uncertain date wrongly ascribed to Tertullian (and so referred to as Pseudo-Tertullian), were thought to share dependence on a common source dating to the first half of the

third century, a lost work of Hippolytus (See Lipsius, *Zur Quellenkritik des Epiphanios*; Harnack, Marcion: *Das Evangelium vom Fremden Gott*, 24*–28*). But recently Sebastian Moll ("Three against Tertullian") effectively demolished this source theory, showed the illegitimacy of forming the information in the three texts into a composite portrait, and in this way furthered an already widespread doubt that any of the material has historical merit.

2. *Marcion: Das Evangelium vom Fremden Gott* (English: *Marcion: The Gospel of the Alien God*).

3. May, "Marcion in Contemporary Views."

4. Moll, *The Arch-Heretic Marcion*, and "Marcion: A New Perspective on His Life, Theology, and Impact."

5. Irenaeus, *Haer.* 1.27.2; 3.4.3; Clement, *Strom.* 3.4.25; Rhodo *apud* Eusebius, *Hist. eccl.* 5.13; Tertullian, *Marc.* 1.1.4, etc.; Ps.-Tertullian, *Adv. haer.* 1.30.1. Epiphanius and Philastrius specify the city of Sinope, but this may be no more than supposition on their part, since it was the most important port and metropolis of Pontus.

6. Tertullian, *Marc.* 1.18.4; 3.6.3; 4.9.2; 5.1.2; Tertullian, *Praescr.* 30.1. At one point, Tertullian refers to Marcion's "ships," in the plural, although this may not be based on any specific information (*Marc.* 5.1.2). Tertullian's near contemporary Rhodon appears to independently confirm Marcion's occupation when he refers to him disparagingly as a "sailor" (ναύτης, reported in Eusebius, Hist. *eccl.* 5.13.3). That he was in fact a prosperous merchant is a conclusion supported by the contribution of 200,000 *sesterces* that Tertullian tells us he made to the Christian community of Rome when he first arrived (*Marc.* 4.4.3; *Praescr.* 30).

7. Clement, *Strom.* 7.17.106f.; Tertullian, *Marc.* 1.19; 5.19; *Praescr.* 30; Epiphanius, *Pan.* 42.1.7.

8. Tertullian, *Marc.* 1.19.2.

9. See Harnack, *Marcion*, 29/E19, 18*–20*. Doubts raised about Harnack's calculation are excessively pedantic. Anyone living in Tertullian's time would have understood the time reference as Harnack does, with Tiberius' fifteenth year commencing on 1 January 29 CE, and 6½ months indicating the Ides of July.

10. Moll, *The Arch-Heretic Marcion*, 34.

11. Tertullian does not inform us whether this date was commemorated by all Marcionites or was only kept by the local Marcionites of Tertullian's city, Carthage. It could refer to the date of Marcion's arrival in the latter city, or in Rome, or to the date on which he formally broke with the Roman community or formally declared the creation of his own Church. Ernst Barnikol's proposition that it refers to the date of Marcion's death (*Die Entstehung der Kirche*, 18–20) appears to be ruled out by the testimony of Justin Martyr.

12. That is, sometime after the death of bishop Hyginus, ca. 142 CE (Epiphanius, *Pan.* 42.1.7).

13. Irenaeus, *Haer.* 1.27.1–2: in the time of bishop Hyginus. But in *Haer.* 3.4.3 he seems to place his arrival in Rome more than a decade later, in the time of Anicetus. Irenaeus drew some of his information on Marcion

from Justin Martyr (see, e.g., *Haer.* 4.6.2) and Polycarp of Smyrna, both contemporaries of Marcion. Hippolytus, *Ref.* 7.29–31, follows Irenaeus on the earlier date. The *Chronicle of Edessa* reports that "Marcion left the Catholic church" in 449 of the Seleucid era, corresponding to 137/138 CE, the first year of the reign of Antoninus Pius. It is unclear from what source the *Chronicle* draws this information. But the Muslim bibliographer al-Nadim, writing in the ninth century, knows the same tradition, stating that Marcion "appeared" in the first year of Antoninus (Dodge, *The Fihrist of al-Nadim*, 775–76).

14. Clement places Marcion among those heretics who arose "in the time of the Emperor Hadrian . . . and they extended to the time of the elder Antoninus" (*Strom.* 7.17.106f). He states that Marcion "appeared at about the same time" as Basilides and Valentinus, but "associated with those younger people when he was already an old man." We cannot count on deriving a very exact chronology from Clement's broad remarks. Current scholarly opinion (based in part on this very passage) would put Basilides and Valentinus about a generation apart, with the former in the reign of Hadrian (117–38 CE) and the latter in that of Antoninus Pius (138–61 CE). Whether Clement had specific information that Marcion was already active in the time of Hadrian is unclear; equally uncertain is whether he means to convey just Marcion's earlier birth than the other two, or the fact that he came to public notice for his (in Clement's opinion) "heresy" later than the other two. Clement may be referring to the same collocation of "heretics" in Rome suggested by Irenaeus, *Haer.* 3.4.3, who reports Marcion coming (back?) to Rome in the time of Anicetus (when he would indeed have been an old man), after noting that Valentinus still remained in the city at that time, having arrived already in the time of Hyginus.

15. Harnack proposed the dates 85–155 CE for Marcion (*Marcion*, 21/E15) based primarily on two pieces of evidence: Justin Martyr, *1 Apol.* 26.5, attests him as still alive in the early 150s, and Clement of Alexandria, *Strom.* 7.17.107, remarks that Marcion "was already an old man" when he became associated in heresy with younger contemporaries such as Basilides and Valentinus in the reigns of Hadrian (117–38 CE) and Antoninus Pius (138–61 CE). Arguments to date Marcion earlier (Barnikol, *Die Entstehung der Kirche*; Couchoud, *The Creation of Christ*, 276; Hoffmann, *Marcion: On the Restitution of Christianity*) have not won acceptance. On the other hand, I agree with the qualifications of Harnack's estimate made by Sebastian Moll, *The Arch-Heretic Marcion*, 26 and 31–41), which would shift Marcion's birth about a decade later.

16. Tertullian, *Marc.* 1.1.6; 4.4.3; *Carn. Chr.* 2.4; *Praescr.* 30. Tertullian's comments about the letter have been taken by several researchers to indicate that Marcion spoke of that allegiance in the past tense in his letter, as a kind of reminiscence or account of his spiritual development. See Harnack, *Marcion*, 27/E18; Mahé, "Tertullien et l'epistula Marcionis"; Moll, *Marcion: A New Perspective*, 115–18. It seems more likely, however, that Tertullian is responsible for putting the allegiance reflected in the letter in the past tense, and that he is referring to a letter sent by Marcion in

advance of his arrival in Rome, and before his differences with the Roman community emerged. Such a formal letter of introduction, which also implies some sort of advance messenger, may be a clue in the question of Marcion's stature as a religious leader prior to coming to Rome. Two centuries later, Jerome reports that Marcion sent a woman ahead of him to Rome (*Romam praemisit mulierem, quae decipiendos sibi animos praepararet*, Letter 133.4). But, at such a far remove from Marcion's time, one must wonder where Jerome learned this detail, unreported in any surviving prior source, and so well suited to the polemical cliché that heretics gave men's proper roles to women.

17. Tertullian, *Marc.* 4.4.3; *Praescr.* 30. This significant sum amounted to the price of a nice house in Rome, or a good-sized farm in the countryside (Lampe, *From Paul to Valentinus*, 245).

18. *Pecuniam in primo calore fidei catholicae ecclesiae contulit* (*Marc.* 4.4.3).

19. E.g., May, "Marcion in Contemporary Views," 137.

20. Harnack cautioned that Tertullian's characterization of Marcion as making his sizable donation *in primo calore fidei* should not be pressed too far for historical value (Harnack, *Marcion*, 17* n. 2); cf. Blackman, *Marcion and His Influence*, 2 n. 4.

21. See Lüdemann, "The History of Earliest Christianity in Rome," for cautions about applying anachronistically the concept of "excommunication" to the decentralized and diverse set of Christian communities in Rome in the second century.

22. Tertullian, *Marc.* 1.2.1; Philastrius, *Div. her.* 45.

23. Tertullian, *Marc.* 3.16.5, 4.11.9; Philastrius, *Div. her.* 45.

24. Ps.-Tertullian, *Adv. haer.* 1.6.2; on this text, see n. 1 above.

25. Epiphanius, *Pan.* 42.2.1.

26. The historicity of some such debate is supported by the historically accurate detail preserved in Epiphanius' version of the story that Marcion confronts a body of presbyters and not, anachronistically, a bishop (Harnack, *Marcion*, 23*ff.; Lüdemann, "The History of Earliest Christianity in Rome," 122–23 n. 28).

27. Justin, *1 Apol.* 26.5; 58.1–2. Not all of this missionary work necessarily occurred in the decade since his impasse with the Roman Christian leadership, if Marcion already was a leader in east Mediterranean Christianity prior to coming to Rome.

28. Irenaeus, *Haer.* 3.4.3: in the time of bishop Anicetus. The *Carmen adversus Marcionitis* 3.296–97 likewise states that Marcion came to Rome in the time of bishop Anicetus, but this information may derive from Irenaeus. The notion that Marcion never left Rome, but remained settled there from his first arrival to the end of his life (see Moll, *The Arch-Heretic Marcion, passim*) is based on nothing in our sources, and is unlikely given the energetic missionary project attested by Justin Martyr. In *Praescr.* 30.2, Tertullian places Marcion in Rome in the time of the bishop Eleutherus (ca. 174–89 CE), but correlates this episcopacy with the reign of Antoninus Pius (138–61 CE). Clearly, Tertullian has made some sort of mistake here, and the reference to Eleutherus should be discounted, while placing

Marcion in the reign of Antoninus Pius is supported by every other source that dates Marcion's activities.

29. Ps.-Tertullian and Epiphanius (the latter probably dependent on the former) provide a highly suspect account of Marcion as the son of a Christian bishop, excommunicated by his own father for a sexual indiscretion. See the discussions of this story's credibility in Harnack, *Marcion*, 23/E16; May, "Marcion in Contemporary Views," 134–35; and Moll, "Three against Tertullian," 178–79.

30. Irenaeus, *Haer.* 3.3.4. Polycarp died between 156 and 166 CE.

31. Polycarp visited Rome in the time of Anicetus (reported by Irenaeus *apud* Eusebius, *Hist. eccl.* 5.24.16), and since some sources place Marcion there at roughly the same time, the encounter could have been a later one in both men's lives. Jerome assumed as much (*Vir. ill.* 17).

32. Irenaeus, *Haer.* 3.3.4 (cf. Eusebius, *Hist. eccl.* 14.7). This story is discussed in Harnack, *Marcion*, 24/E16–17 and 3*–5*. He is of the opinion that the encounter must have occurred in Asia prior to Polycarp's visit to Rome in 154 CE. Lüdemann likewise rejects placing the encounter in Rome, and more generally argues that Irenaeus is conflating several separate strands of tradition in this passage ("The History of Earliest Christianity in Rome," 115–17). It was Blackman who drew attention to the fact that the wording "recognize us" of Marcion's question suggests that more than simply an issue of personal familiarity with Marcion is involved (*Marcion and His Influence*, 2 n. 2); and, since the meaning of the exchange depends so much on Polycarp playing with the semantics of "recognize," it is unlikely that Irenaeus has built the story entirely on the basis of the expression "firstborn of Satan" in PolPhil 7.1, as has been suggested by Regul, *Die antimarcionitischen Evangelienprologe*, 189.

33. Philastrius says simply that Marcion was rejected in Ephesus by John (*Div. her.* 45.7, written ca. 388 CE). A fuller version of this story is contained in an anti-Marcionite prologue to the Gospel of John which has been found copied in ten Latin biblical manuscripts from the eighth through the eleventh centuries. Three were known to Harnack (*Marcion*, 11*); Donatien De Bruyne identified the rest ("Le plus anciens prologues latins des Evangiles"). This version of the story says that Marcion approached the aged apostle John somewhere, bearing certain books or letters from the Christians of Pontus (*is vero scripta vel epistulas ad eum, pertalerat a fratribus qui in Ponto fuerunt*), but John rejected him for unspecified reasons. Few have undertaken to defend the historical worth of this story as it stands. Regul concludes it to be a fourth-century invention (*Die antimarcionitischen Evangelienprologe*, 99–197); and Bacon, in "The Anti-Marcionite Prologue to John," has put forward reasons to think that the story is based almost entirely on a careless reading of remarks made by Tertullian in *Marc.* 3.8 and 4.3–4 (also *Carn. Chr.* 2; *Praescr.* 33, and *Prax.* 28) that John had rejected Marcion *by anticipation*, as it were, by writing against docetism, etc. One can easily agree with the assessment of Heard that the story "appears to stand at the end of a long chain of invention and misunderstanding" ("The Old Gospel Prologues," 15). Yet De Bruyne

has made a convincing case for the composition of all three surviving Latin gospel prologues (those for Mark, Luke, and John) as a set by the same author in a relatively early, anti-Marcionite context. Harnack hypothesized that the prologue corrupts an original story in which Papias—who is mentioned in connection with John in the prologue—met and rejected Marcion (*Marcion*, 12*–14*), while De Bruyne suggests that the statement about Marcion presenting a book or letters and being rejected refers to his activities in Rome ("Le plus anciens prologues latins des Evangiles," 208–9). But while Harnack accepts Irenaeus' testimony to a similar rejection of Marcion by Polycarp as historical, he does not explore the possibility that it is Polycarp who has been supplanted by John in the versions of the story supplied by Philastrius and the prologue. Could it not be that among the "combination at a late period of legendary material from different sources" referred to by Heard, the later story depends on Irenaeus' report of an encounter between Polycarp and Marcion, which immediately follows a story of the rejection of Cerinthus by John (*Haer.* 3.3.4)? The only distinctive and original material in the prologue is the reference to Marcion bringing certain books or letters with him from Pontus. A source for this element has so far not been identified (Bacon's proposal that it is a distortion of Marcion's letter referred to by Tertullian notwithstanding).

34. PolPhil 7.1. Trans. Ehrman, *The Apostolic Fathers*, 343.

35. Hoffmann, *Marcion: On the Restitution of Christianity*, 284, has suggested further correlating details, arguing that Polycarp shows he is in conflict with opponents who claim to be followers of Paul (3.2) and spread the idea that Christianity has been corrupted by false apostles (9.2). Meinhold, "Polykarpos," 1685–86, finds Marcionite subtext pervading the letter, but there is a danger here of reading too much into ordinary rhetorical tropes. Concurring on Marcion or an opponent of similar views as the target of Polycarp's letter is Harrison, *Polycarp's Two Epistles to the Philippians*, 197, and Knox, *Marcion and the New Testament*, 10–11; Harnack rejected the idea that Polycarp is alluding to Marcion (*Marcion*, 5* n. 4).

36. The current consensus would date Polycarp's criticisms in this letter to ca. 130–35 CE, contemporary with Marcion but before he went to Rome (Ehrman, *The Apostolic Fathers*, vol. 1, 328). Arguments to date the letter earlier, due to its seemingly contemporaneous reference to Ignatius of Antioch, have been met by the widely accepted hypothesis of Harrison (*Polycarp's Two Epistles to the Philippians*) that the letter is a composite of two letters, the first twelve chapters being a later document of ca. 130–35, at some point prefaced to a much earlier letter, given that Eusebius of Caesarea dates the martyrdom of Ignatius to the reign of Trajan. But recently Barnes, "The Date of Ignatius," has made a compelling argument for re-dating the martyrdom of Ignatius to the 140s, i.e., contemporaneously with Marcion. Campenhausen, while accepting Harrison's division of the letter, sees no reason why the later portion (containing the possible allusions to Marcion) could not have been written as late as the 150s (*The Formation of the Christian Bible*, 178 n.157). Indeed, Polycarp's admonition to "pray for the kings" (plural), if taken as more than generic, would ne-

cessitate dating the letter during a joint reign in the empire, perhaps that of Antoninus Pius and Marcus Aurelius beginning in 147 CE.

37. He mentions them only because, as slaves, they could be legally tortured to confirm the testimony of others.

38. Translation by Bettenson, *Documents of the Christian Church*, 3–4.

39. It perhaps is not wholly irrelevant to note here that the so-called Monarchian Prologue to Luke, which in some form may go back to the end of the second century, places Luke's death in Bithynia (whereas the alternative "anti-Marcionite" prologue places it in Boeotia). The historical basis of such information, of course, is at this point indeterminable, but could possibly reflect traditions about the initial circulation of the gospel.

40. For context see Vélissaropoulos, *Les nauclères grecs*, and Casson, *Ships and Seamanship in the Ancient World*.

41. See Lampe, *From Paul to Valentinus*, 247ff.; May, "Der 'Schiffsreeder' Markion." Lampe unduly stresses the burden of government contract work over its potential profits.

42. Balás, "Marcion Revisited," 99. On the ironies of Marcion's reputation in connection with Judaism, see Räisänen, "Marcion and the Origins of Christian Anti-Judaism."

43. See May, "Der 'Schiffsreeder' Markion," 151.

44. See May, "Marcion in Contemporary Views," 137; May, "Der 'Schiffsreeder' Markion," 151.

45. *Dig.* 50.6.5.6; 50.6.5.9.

46. The letter is addressed from the Christian community of Rome to that of Corinth. Dionysius of Corinth, writing in the 170s, is the first person to ascribe the letter in question to Clement, without specifying when he lived or wrote. For a thorough dismissal of the traditional arguments for dating Clement at the end of the first century, see Welborn, "On the Date of First Clement." Clement is referred to as a contemporary by Hermas who, according to the Muratorian Canon, was writing in the 150s. Clement cites over one hundred verses from Jewish scripture, and Lampe, *From Paul to Valentinus*, 75–76, provides a dozen examples of the letter's use of Jewish apocryphal tradition to expand on the biblical text.

47. "Christians from the sphere of influence of the synagogues, Jewish Christians as well as Gentile Christians, exercised an astonishing influence on the formation of theology in urban Roman Christianity in the first century" (Lampe, *From Paul to Valentinus*, 76).

48. Hermas and Justin do not directly quote or mention Paul at all in their extensive literary output. Clement gives him perfunctory recognition as the founder of the Corinthian church to which he addresses his letter. Hegesippus, a Jewish Christian with close ties to the leadership in Rome in the latter half of the second century (writing in the time of bishop Eleutheros, post-177 CE), appears to reject Paul's statement in 1 Cor 2.9 as a false understanding of the faith (Campenhausen, *The Formation of the Christian Bible*, 178). Cosgrove, "Justin Martyr and the Emerging Christian Canon," argues that the absence of Paul from Justin's writings is a consciously anti-Marcionite attitude on his part.

49. Rome was by no means unique in its neglect of Paul. Papias of

Hierapolis, a contemporary of Marcion and Polycarp, either did not know or deliberately ignored Paul in his collection of sayings of Jesus (even though Paul would have supplied valuable material for this purpose) and, interestingly, is equally silent on Luke (Grant, *The Formation of the New Testament*, 72). According to Robert Grant, Eusebius' negative view of Papias and his writings indicate that "they reflected a form of Christianity close to Judaism which did not later survive. It may be doubted that he had anything like a 'canon' of New Testament writings" (Grant, "The New Testament Canon," 291). Annand likewise sees Papias as representing an anti-Pauline, Judaizing minority in the largely Pauline environment of Asia Minor ("Papias and the Four Gospels," 49). "So long as Christianity stood close to Judaism, or was predominantly Jewish, scripture remained the Old Testament, and this situation can be seen persisting in such a document as 1 Clement, with its frequent and almost exclusive appeal to the Old Testament text" (Evans, "The New Testament in the Making," 234).

50. On the Gnostics as part of the catholic front against the literalist, Marcionite rejection of the Jewish scriptures, see the insightful discussion of Lüdemann, "The History of Earliest Christianity in Rome."

51. The letters exist in three recensions: short, middle, and long. The middle recension is the version accepted by most as the original, of which the shorter recension would be an abridgement and the longer recension an expansion. Some, e.g. Joly (*Le dossier d'Ignace d'Antioche*), regard even the middle recension as a forgery of the second half of the second century. The letter to the Smyrnaeans, in particular, is filled with echoes of the gospel of Luke, anachronistic language about "the gospel and apostle" as seemingly written sources of instruction, and uncharacteristic (for Ignatius) promotion of the prophets and patriarchs as the embodiment of God's chosen, all of which seem more at home in the post-Marcion situation of this later period than the traditional date of Ignatius. The short recension, surviving only in Syriac and having few of these problems of anachronism, still has its partisans. Given the late and limited manuscript basis of the Ignatian corpus, questions must remain about the integrity and original extent of the set of letters. Even the date to be ascribed to Ignatius cannot be regarded as well-established: while Eusebius of Caesarea places him in the time of Trajan, he may in fact have been active a couple of decades later, as argued by Barnes, "The Date of Ignatius."

52. E.g., IgnMag 9.1 and 10.3; IgnPhd 6.1.

53. This reading of the issue was proposed by Schoedel, "Ignatius and the Archives," and is embraced by Bruce, "Some Thoughts on the Beginning of the New Testament Canon," 41.

54. IgnPhd 8.2. Ignatius specifies that by "gospel" he means Christ's death, resurrection, and the faith he taught. Campenhausen notes that, "despite the strenuous theological controversy both parties agree in affirming the fundamental character of the biblical 'documents,' and neither knows of any canon other than the holy 'archives' of the past to put alongside of the oral preaching" (*The Formation of the Christian Bible*, 73).

55. "Thus," he continues, "the negative view of Judaism is more

emphatic in Ignatius than in the Pastorals and approaches the extreme position of *Barnabas*" (Schoedel, *Ignatius of Antioch*, 119).

56. It needs to be noted that only chap. 1–10 of what is often published as the Letter of Diognetus actually belongs to the treatise in question. The work survives in a single manuscript, with a break clearly indicated at the end of chap. 10. The additional material that follows, usually published as chap. 11 and 12, does not share the vocabulary and thought-world of the rest, and has been added from elsewhere as a supplement. Nielsen, "The Epistle to Diognetus," contends that the additional material represents an adaptation of the original to suit the catholic position after the appearance of Marcion. The "Law and Prophets" suddenly appear as scripture in this last section, along with repeated references to "the apostles" and one to "the gospels" in the plural (11.6) which, if dated as early as the rest of the treatise, would make it the earliest known such reference. This should be contrasted to the extensive arguments against the Jews in chap. 1–10, all made without a single quotation of the OT, that is, without any effort to make the usual appropriation of Jewish scriptures against their former possessors. See also Ehrman, *The Apostolic Fathers*, vol. 2, 124. But since the manuscript is late and still distinguishes the first ten chapters from the later, the combination is perhaps to be attributed to a scribe copying what he saw as related material from different sources, and not as a formal re-edition of the original work.

57. Diogn 1–2.
58. Diogn 8.1.
59. Diogn 8.10.
60. Diogn 5.3.
61. Diogn 7.1.
62. Diogn 9.1–2. This dramatic act of salvation evokes from the author of the letter the exclamation, "O unfathomable work of God! O blessings beyond all expectation!" which Nielsen notes is startlingly close to the opening lines of Marcion's *Antitheses* ("The Epistle to Diognetus," 87).
63. Diogn 5.17.
64. If Dahl is correct that the original set of seven *Prologues to the Letters of Paul* preserved in the Latin Vulgate are *not* Marcionite in origin, although of the second century, then they would be a further witness to a strand of Christianity at this time sharply separated from its Jewish roots and deeply concerned about maintaining too close an association with Jewish religious attitudes. The pre-Marcionite provenance of the prologues has been maintained also by Clabeaux, *A Lost Edition of the Letters of Paul*, 1–4, and Schmid, *Marcion und sein Apostolos*. I am not persuaded, however; see further below.
65. See Schmid, *Marcion und sein Apostolos*, 311: Marcion was merely a representative of a particularly Pauline branch of early Christianity, and it was among its followers that his teaching had his initial reception and rapid dissemination.
66. Nielsen, "The Epistle to Diognetus," 90–91. Similarly, Richard Pervo explains Acts' apparent anticipation of second-century tensions around the figure of Paul and the relationship of Christianity to Judaism,

while still dating Acts to a time before Marcion, by positing that "Marcion had predecessors in his radical Paulinism"(*Dating Acts*, 332–33).

67. Balás, "Marcion Revisited," 99. C.-B. Amphoux draws a similar connection between the Bar Kochba crisis and the emergence various alternative Christian schools in Rome, including Marcion's, in "Les premières editions de Luc," 83ff.

68. May, "Marcion in Contemporary Views," 148–49.

69. Knox, *Marcion and the New Testament*, 17.

70. McGiffert, *The Apostles' Creed*, proposed the crisis with Marcion as the occasion that produced the Old Roman Symbol. His arguments are reviewed by Blackman, who finds McGiffert's hypothesis plausible but unprovable. Knox prefers to see the Old Roman Symbol as a firming up of anti-Marcionite orthodoxy after the fact (*Marcion and His Influence*, 33–34).

71. Not including local gnostic groups, whose views of what constituted sacred scripture pose a complex historical issue.

72. And the list can almost certainly be expanded by the inclusion of several pseudepigraphical works that likely have an anti-Marcionite purpose. On this topic, see esp. Rist, "Pseudepigraphic Refutations." With respect to the Pastoral Epistles, Hoffmann effectively marshals the evidence of an anti-Marcionite sub-text (*Marcion: On the Restitution of Christianity*, 291–95).

73. E. Evans, "Tertullian's Commentary on the Marcionite Gospel," 699.

74. *Hist. eccl.* 4.24–25; Jerome's report of anti-Marcionite writings depends largely on Eusebius, and in most cases he probably had not personally read the treatise in question. We should probably add to this list of anti-Marcionite writers Ammonius of Alexandria, of whom Jerome reports a treatise "On the Harmony of Moses and Jesus" (*Vir. ill.* 55).

75. Irenaeus, *Haer.* 4.6.2, calls it Justin's "Syntagma against Marcion," and reports that Justin says in it "that he would not have believed the Lord himself had he preached a god other than the creator." Eusebius, *Hist. eccl.* 4.18, knows this passage from Irenaeus and refers elsewhere to Justin's work against Marcion (*Hist. eccl.* 4.11), but in seeming to quote from it in that instance, he in fact quotes from Justin's *First Apology*; cf. Jerome, *Vir. ill.* 23. Perhaps this work is the same as Justin's "Syntagma against all heresies," which, based upon Irenaeus' probable dependence upon it in *Haer.* 1.23–27, may have portrayed Marcion as the culmination of a demonic/heretical plot against Christianity (cf. *Haer.* 5.26.2). See Lüdemann, "The History of Earliest Christianity in Rome," 113–14 and n. 3.

76. Eusebius, *Hist. eccl.* 5.13 preserves a few quotes from it, where Marcion is referred to as "the sailor" (*ho nautēs*) and "the Pontic wolf" (*tōi pontikōi lukōi*); cf. Jerome, *Vir. ill.* 37.

77. "There is another extant letter of his to the Nicomedians in which he combats the heresy of Marcion and compares it with the rule of truth" (Eusebius, *Hist. eccl.* 4.23).

78. "A noble treatise . . . which has been preserved until now"

(Eusebius, *Hist. eccl.* 4.24); Jerome, *Vir. ill.* 25, appears to indicate direct knowledge of it.

79. Cf. Jerome, *Vir. ill.* 61.

80. "A most excellent treatise" (Eusebius, *Hist. eccl.* 4.25); cf. Jerome, *Vir. ill.* 30.

81. "Who excels beyond the rest in exposing to everyone the man's error" (Eusebius, *Hist. eccl.* 4.25); cf. Jerome, *Vir. ill.* 32.

82. Irenaeus, *Haer.* 1.27.4 and 3.12.12.

83. Eusebius, *Hist. eccl.* 5.8.

84. Justin, *1 Apol.* 26.5; 58.1. Justin says that Marcion's message had reached the whole human race; Tertullian confirms its remarkable success more than a half-century later (*Marc.* 5.19).

85. See Origen, *Cels.* 2.27; 5.62; 6.51ff.; 6.74; 7.25; 7.74.

86. May, "Marcion in Contemporary Views," 138–39.

87. These consist primarily of two closely related works, the so-called *Homilies* and *Recognitions*. The two heroes of this literary saga are Peter and, significantly, Clement of Rome. The Jewish Christian character of the material has been widely discussed and usually related to "Jewish Christian" cells in Syria. Few have taken up the issue of why the hero of these cells would be the distant figure of Clement. But this puzzle is resolved once one recognizes that Rome was a major center of "Jewish Christianity" in the first half of the second century. I leave to others better qualified than I a proper definition of the term in scare quotes, in all its own internal diversity; see most recently Broadhead, *Jewish Ways of Following Jesus*.

88. Grant, *Jesus after the Gospels*, 51.

89. Knox, *Marcion and the New Testament*, 2. Campenhausen rejects the idea of a deliberate imitation by Marcion of the bipartite structure of Law and Prophets (*The Formation of the Christian Bible*, 153, n. 23), but only by employing the same sort of psychological profiling of Marcion for which he elsewhere (148) criticizes Harnack.

90. Harnack speculates that Tatian's Diatessaron, written a generation after Marcion, was a response to Marcion's Evangelion, an attempt to match the advantage of a single, internally consistent account of Jesus (Harnack, *Marcion*, 72–73/E50). He goes on to say that Marcion invented the NT and the catholics responded within twenty years with one of their own (72–73/E50–51). May sees a similar role for Marcion: "It was through Marcion that the latent crisis of Christian foundations and norms became manifest. His straightforward assault, however, also aroused the forces of defense. In the discussion with Marcion, the process of theological clarification began almost convulsively, the results of which were the Catholic canon, the Rule of Faith, and the exhaustive presentations of ecclesiastical doctrines" ("Marcion in Contemporary Views," 149). Quispel argues that the "Western" text of the Gospels, Acts, and Pauline Epistles (used, e.g., by Irenaeus and Tertullian) was the first response of the Roman leadership to the challenge of Marcion, as part of a deliberate revision and canonization process. It is for this reason, he suggests, that the "Western" text preserves several readings shared with Marcion (because they were

close in time and locale to his activities) that were expunged in later revisions, such as the Alexandrian, and why there is no "Western" text of the Catholic Epistles or Revelation, since these were not included in the initial canon.

91. I am persuaded of its relative lateness by the arguments of Sundberg Jr., "Canon Muratori: A Fourth-Century List," and Hahneman, *The Muratorian Fragment and the Development of the Canon*.

Chapter 2: Marcion's New Testament

1. C. F. Evans, "The New Testament in the Making," 235.
2. McDonald, *The Formation of the Christian Biblical Canon*, 154–55.
3. F. F. Bruce, "Some Thoughts on the Beginning of the New Testament Canon," 43.
4. Campenhausen, *The Formation of the Christian Bible*, 148.
5. Metzger, *The Canon of the New Testament*, 40.
6. Petersen, "Textual Evidence of Tatian's Dependence."
7. "All speculations about the emergence of a Four-Gospel canon . . . prior to the time of Marcion, are without foundation, and rest simply on the arbitrary retrojection on to this period of an anachronistic idea" (Campenhausen, *The Formation of the Christian Bible*, 121). Such propositions are based in "a traditional prejudice, supported by great names, and, so it would seem, ineradicable by reason or evidence" (142–43).
8. Annand points out that Papias' remarks about the literary work of Mark and Matthew are critical, and serve to indicate the need for Papias' own exposition. This means that Papias does not regard their work as scripture, but something to be improved upon, and that he saw himself as belonging to an age where novel constructions of "the Gospel" had no onus attached to them ("Papias and the Four Gospels," 54, 57). Tatian clearly was still of the same frame of mind in the later second century, as were the authors of all of the apocryphal gospels that proliferated in that time.
9. Campenhausen, *The Formation of the Christian Bible*, 145ff. Moule speaks of a "slow, anonymous process" as the only alternative "if we abandon the idea that the collecting of the Pauline letters was the work of an individual, such as Onesimus or Marcion" (*The Birth of the New Testament*, 263).
10. Metzger, *The Canon of the New Testament*, 98.
11. Metzger, like several other biblical historians, sees the Montanist controversy of the second half of the second century as delivering a second shock to the Church's system, leading to the formation of a biblical canon. But the chief problem with such tidy causative models is that Christianity struggles on for another century and a half with nothing approximating a fixed NT canon. It is in large part a post-Reformation slant in our reading of the past that leads us to see the biblical canon as so central to early Church identity. In this respect, Harnack may be on to something in seeing Marcion as not just a generation or two ahead of his

time, but more than a thousand years ahead of his time—a kind of prototype of Martin Luther and the Protestant emphasis on the Bible.

12. Rougier, "La critique biblique dans l'antiquité," 4–5.

13. Werner, *Der Paulinismus des Irenaeus*, 21–46, argues that for Irenaeus the letters of Paul belonged to a secondary category, and did not have the full status of scripture he accorded the four gospels; not once in his 206 citations of Paul does Irenaeus use the expression *scriptura*.

14. William Farmer adopts as probable the suggestion of Alfred Loisy and Ernst Barnikol that the meeting of Polycarp of Smyrna with Anicetus of Rome ca. 154–55 CE was the moment when the four-gospel canon was agreed upon, with both sides accepting each other's preferred texts, despite certain reservations, as part of their organization of a united "catholic" front (Farmer et al., *The Formation of the New Testament*, 71–73; see Barnikol, *Die Entstehung der Kirche*, 25–300). Donatien De Bruyne proposes that the anti-Marcionite prologues to the gospels were composed for the four gospel edition issued in response to Marcion's single gospel ("Le plus anciens prologues latins des Evangiles," 211). Alternatively, one might propose that the prologues derive from a connected account of the gospel writers, written in an anti-Marcionite context and dismantled for their present use. Such a derivation would explain why Marcion appears explicitly only in the last prologue, that of John (a circumstance over which De Bruyne puzzles, 208–9), as a culmination. Might the absence of a prologue for Matthew be accounted for by such a scenario, namely that the original text was an account of the three gospels being put forward *in addition* to an already familiar and accepted Matthew?

15. Gamble, *The New Testament Canon*, 60.

16. Barton, "Marcion Revisited."

17. Barton, "Marcion Revisited," 343.

18. Barton attempts to argue otherwise: "The development of the New Testament followed its own logic, and Marcion did not influence it one way or the other" ("Marcion Revisited," 344). But to reach such a conclusion requires overlooking the presence of Marcion as a foil in some of our earliest "orthodox" discussions of the limits of scripture, such as Irenaeus' arguments for a four-fold gospel (*Haer.* 3.11.8–9) and the Muratorian Fragment's list. Barton's assessment depends on the traditional polemical view of Marcion as a rejecter of an existing larger proto-canon which in Barton's view carries on in this amorphous state for centuries more, following its own logic of development. He relies heavily on the conclusions of Franz Stuhlhofer, *Der Gebrauch der Bibel von Jesus bis Euseb*. But the latter's statistical methodology is crude and deeply flawed. Stuhlhofer arrives at the conclusion that material later included in the NT is already cited in the earliest Christian literature to a degree that suggests it already possessed the same status of sacred scripture afforded to the OT. But he arrives at this conclusion not by a direct statistical comparison of NT and OT citation, but by weighting NT citations relative to the total length of the NT in comparison to the total length of the OT. Thus, it is not the case that NT material is cited as much as OT material, or even anywhere near as much, but that it is cited *more than would be expected given the length of*

the NT relative to the OT. Among the factors that invalidate this procedure are the anachronism involved in relating the individual texts to the size of a later collection, and treating the whole OT as a point of statistical comparison, when Christians had very selective interest in only particular parts of it.

19. Harnack, *Marcion*, 206–15/E127–32.

20. "The chronological priority of Marcion's canon is . . . indisputable: nothing like this precedes him" (Gamble, *The New Testament Canon*, 60).

21. Campenhausen remarks, "A similar 'canonical' arrangement, despite all statements to the contrary, is nowhere attested and nowhere attempted before Marcion. We have become accustomed to this arrangement, and therefore easily overlook the fact that in itself there is nothing whatever obvious or inevitable about it" (153). He points to the popularity of apocalypses and church orders in early Christianity, as logical alternative text genres to combine with a gospel text, and concludes, "In fact the strange construction of Marcion's Bible is explicable solely in terms of his dogmatic Paulinism" (153).

22. Knox concurs with Harnack on this point: "One of the most convincing reasons for finding in Marcion the original occasion of the New Testament lies in the predominating position of Paul in the New Testament canon, a position apparently out of proportion to his influence on the church of the early second century" (*Marcion and the New Testament*, 159). The status of Paul in the canon is surprising against an early Christian background where Paul is almost entirely absent (Gamble, *New Testament Canon*, 43–44), except for Christian leaders writing to communities founded by Paul whom they wish to influence (namely, Clement writing to the Corinthians, and Ignatius and Polycarp writing to Aegean cities; see Lindemann, *Paulus im ältesten Christentum*).

23. Kinzig, "Καιη διαθήκη."

24. It is one of the weaknesses of Harnack's study that he follows Tertullian's presumptions, at least as far as a pre-Marcionite four-gospel canon is concerned. Campenhausen criticizes Harnack's mistake and notes that Knox had already effectively corrected it (*The Formation of the Christian Bible*, 149 n. 6; see also the extensive n. 40 on 156–59).

25. Tertullian reports (*Marc.* 4.3) that in the *Antitheses* Marcion "tries to destroy the status of those gospels that have been produced specially under the apostles' names."

26. Several pieces of evidence, including the Old Syriac canon known to Ephrem Syrus in the fourth century, and the prologues to Paul's letters preserved in Latin manuscripts, help to prove the existence of an older, ten-letter set of Paul's letters, lacking the very same letters that were missing from Marcion's NT. The Letter to the Hebrews was certainly in existence in Marcion's time, although its attribution to Paul was a later development. The same cannot be said with any assurance of the Pastorals, which are not quoted directly by any Christian writer until after Marcion's lifetime.

27. Tertullian, *Marc.* 4.2.4.

28. Noted already by Löffler, "Marcionem Pauli epistolas et Lucae

Evangelium adulterasse dubitaturi"; Schelling, *De Marcione paulinarum epistolarum Emendatore*; Eichhorn, *Einleitung in das Neue Testament*.

29. Denis Farkasfalvy remarks, "Marcion's Scripture suits his purpose so poorly that it is hardly believable that its origins are adequately explained by reference to this purpose," yet offers no clear alternative perspective on the question (Farmer et al., *The Formation of the New Testament*, 101).

30. David S. Williams, working with the twenty-three passages he identifies securely as part of Marcion's Evangelion, finds a quotation from the Jewish scriptures, references to Moses, the prophets, and David as an ancestor of Jesus, as well as a comment by Jesus that he desires to celebrate Passover ("Reconsidering Marcion's Gospel," 482). He remarks on these findings, "What little is known [of Marcion's Evangelion] seems in many instances to run counter to the traditional claims made concerning the document. In my view, the standard judgment that Marcion's Gospel was simply a bowdlerized version of Luke needs to be reassessed" (478).

31. This point was made already by Ritschl, *Das Evangelium Marcions*, 23ff., by Hilgenfeld, *Kritische Untersuchungen über die Evangelien Justins*, 446–47, and by Volckmar, "Über das Lukas-Evangelium," 120, all of whom sought to investigate the question solely on the basis of an analysis of Marcion's gospel text in comparison to Luke—and all of whom ultimately concluded that the evidence served to confirm in some way the polemical charge. The same point has been made in more recent times by Robbins, "A Socio-Rhetorical Look," 92; and Gregory, *The Reception of Luke and Acts*, who hypothesizes that "the tradition of Marcion as a mutilator of Scripture arose only later because Irenaeus and Tertullian assumed that Marcion must have received his copy of *Luke* in the same form that they received theirs and, consequently, that he had reduced his to suit his own purposes" (295; cf. his full discussion, 173–96). Tyson similarly has stressed the anachronistic and heresiological assumptions governing the viewpoint of our sources that makes their testimony on this question meritless (*Marcion and Luke-Acts*, 39).

32. As noted by Gregory, *The Reception of Luke and Acts*, 183–92, who astutely observes that "Irenaeus and Tertullian may in fact be unrepresentative" (185) in this regard, due to their particular interest in establishing the fourfold gospel—a concern not shared by earlier figures or by representatives of eastern Christianity where the fourfold gospel was not so closely identified as the hallmark of orthodoxy (185ff.).

33. A point made also by Gregory, *The Reception of Luke and Acts*, 175.

34. Harnack assumes that Marcion was familiar with all the material later incorporated into the orthodox NT—it was not yet collected and canonized, but was known and to varying degrees authoritative, and Marcion worked as a selector and redactor (Harnack, *Marcion*, 34/E23). This is only a tiny concession to modern biblical research against Tertullian's wholly anachronistic position.

35. This point is well made by Knox, *Marcion and the New Testament*, 5.

36. Harnack, *Marcion*, 64 n. 1/E150 n. 19 (English slightly corrected according to Harnack's original German).

37. It is therefore striking that Sebastian Moll, who otherwise calls into question almost everything said in our polemical sources about Marcion, accepts unquestioningly what they say about his editorial activity, "cutting out all passages . . . which show any positive reference to the Old Testament" and "all texts being completely freed from any positive reference to the Old Testament" ("Marcion: A New Perspective," 284 and 285, respectively). These statements could only be said by someone who has not made a close examination of the attested content of Marcion's Evangelion and Apostolikon, which contain multiple positive references to OT figures and their acts. The *relatively* lesser amount of such references in these texts compared to their catholic versions can be accounted for on non-ideological grounds, as was done already by Semler, who attributed the difference to the distinctive needs of the Gentile mission.

38. Tertullian, *Marc.* 4.4. The only specific remark that may reflect Marcionite knowledge of an alternative version of their gospel, i.e., Luke, is Tertullian's statement (4.3.4–5) that the Marcionites regarded the ascription of the Gospel to Luke as a falsification. This would relate to a superscription at the beginning, or subscription at the end, of the text, and not to the content of the text of the gospel itself. It is unclear whether Tertullian derived this information from Marcion's *Antitheses* or from statements made by contemporary Marcionites in North Africa. If the latter, it may only reflect a reaction to a subsequently circulating form of the gospel, and not necessarily to one known to Marcion.

39. An observation made already by Westcott, *A General Survey*, 315 n. 1.

40. Williams, "On Tertullian's Text of Luke," offers the most systematic recent attempt to explain Tertullian's remark in terms of this more narrow textual specificity that I characterize as a misunderstanding. In order to account for Tertullian citing passages from Matthew as material Marcion has excluded from "the gospel," Williams argues that Tertullian's own text of Luke must have had substantive harmonizations to Matthew missing from Marcion's Evangelion, as well as from any other currently known version of Luke. While his case for the existence of a text harmonizing Luke 6.35 with Matt 5.45 has merit, his broader argument has little to commend it. Volckmar, *Das Evangelium Marcions*, 4 n. 4, already suggested that Tertullian is using "gospel" to encompass the totality of narratives about Jesus, and not actually commenting on disparities between a single gospel text and Marcion's. Dieter Roth has recently made this argument anew ("Matthean Texts and Tertullian's Accusations").

41. The data substantiating these observations will be found in the text notes below. See also Pott, *Der Text des Neuen Testaments* and "De textu evangeliorum in saeculo secundo."

42. *Adversus Marcionem*, eds. E. Kroymann (Turnhout, 1954), E. Evans (Oxford, 1960), C. Moreschini (Milan, 1971), and R. Braun (Paris, 1990–94).

43. Consequently, he covers Romans in half the space he devotes to Galatians, even though the latter is two-thirds shorter than the former.

44. According to Schmid, *Marcion und sein Apostolos*, 105–14, Tertullian comments eighteen times on wording in the Apostolikon that differs

from the version of Paul's letters known to him: Gal 2.5 [*Marc.* 5.3.2], 3.7 [5.3.11], 3.15–16 and 4.3 [5.4.1–2], 4.22–26 [5.4.8]; 1 Cor 15.45 and 47 [5.10.7], 15.49 [5.10.10–11]; 2 Cor 4.4 [5.11.9]; Rom 2.2ff. [5.13.4], 8.11 and 10.1–2 [5.14.5–6], 11.33 [5.14.9–10]; 1 Thess 2.15 [5.15.1]; 2 Thess 1.8 [5.16.1]; Eph title [5.11.12], 2.14 [5.17.14], 2.20 [5.17.16], 3.9 [5.18.1], 6.2 [5.18.11]; Col 1.15–16 [5.19.3–4]. I do not agree that Tertullian is commenting on a textual difference in 1 Cor 15.49 [5.10.10–11] or 2 Cor 4.4 [5.11.9].

45. For analyses of the paraphrastic tendencies that limit the reliability of Tertullian's testimony, see Clabeaux, *A Lost Edition of the Letters of Paul*, 40–49; Schmid, *Marcion und sein Apostolos*, 60ff. Schmid, 98–105, finds only twelve passages that Tertullian quotes from the Apostolikon that he also quotes from his own biblical text elsewhere: Gal 2.9; 4.10; 1 Cor 1.20; 3.21–22; 10.6; 15.50; 15.55; 2 Cor 5.4; 5.10; Rom 8.11; 1 Thess 5.23; Col 1.21.

46. Quispel (*De bronnen van Tertullianus' Adversus Marcionem*), Clabeaux (*A Lost Edition of the Letters of Paul*), and Schmid (*Marcion und sein Apostolos*), believe that Tertullian worked from a Greek text of the Apostolikon. Harnack (*Marcion*), von Soden ("Der lateinische Paulustext bei Marcion und Tertullian"), and Higgins ("The Latin Text of Luke") contend he had a Latin text before him. See Balás, "Marcion Revisited," 103.

47. Holl and Dummer, *Panarion*.

48. Referring to both the Evangelion and the Apostolikon, Epiphanius contends that "I found that this compilation had been tampered with throughout, and had supplemental material added in certain passages" (*Pan.* 42.11.9), and, specifically on the Apostolikon, he refers to the letters contained within it as "mutilated as usual by Marcion's rascality" (42.11.8). Even so, he notes only a few minor textual variants in the Apostolikon, and reports no sizable omissions of the sort he identifies in the Evangelion.

49. For the main assessments, see Zahn, *Geschichte des Neutestamentlichen Kanons*; Harnack, *Marcion*. Clabeaux contends that "the text presented by Epiphanius as Marcionite contains significant disagreements with those presented in [Tertullian] *Adv. Marc.* 5 and *Dial. Adam.* 1 and 2," and that "his testimony cannot be relied upon when no other witnesses are extant to verify it" (*A Lost Edition of the Letters of Paul*, 14).

50. Clabeaux, *A Lost Edition of the Letters of Paul*, 65. "One gets the distinct impression that Epiphanius has compiled his list from citations made in other anti-Marcionite works," apparently because "his choice of verses is based more on theological concerns (i.e., what they say) than textual ones (how they say it)" (14). But, of course, Epiphanius is quite explicit that he sifted through Marcion's canon for passages whose content contradicted Marcion's own teachings, not out of any interest in recording textual variants. Clabeaux describes Tertullian's purpose in the same terms (40), but does not hold this against Tertullian's value as a witness.

51. Clabeaux, *A Lost Edition of the Letters of Paul*, 24–29.

52. Cf. Harnack, *Marcion*, 64*. Zahn, *Geschichte des Neutestamentlichen Kanons*, 409–19, interprets Epiphanius to say that he had used the Marcionite NT in composing a previous treatise, and later re-extracted

the quotations from that earlier treatise, in this way probably introducing some confusion and errors.

53. The date of this work is fixed by its dependence on Methodius on one side, and by its reference to conditions of persecution on the other, although the latter could be a dramatic conceit (See Bakhuyzen, *Der Dialog des Adamantius*, xvi).

54. Near the beginning of the imagined first debate, the Marcionite Megethius objects to any evidence being cited from the "spurious Apostolikon" of the catholic Christians, and Adamantius consents to taking evidence from the Marcionite Apostolikon, which he proceeds to quote (1.5). In 1.9 Megethius offers to prove his case from catholic scripture, but apparently only to identify problems with the catholic OT using the *Antitheses*. Quotations from "the gospel" are consistently from Luke, suggesting that the Evangelion is being used. An exception seems to prove the rule: when Adamantius quotes from John (1.17), Megethius notes that fact, and Adamantius accommodates him by returning to the Marcionite "gospel." But in 1.26–27 Adamantius lapses into quotations from John, and this time Megethius does not voice any objection. In the second debate, the Marcionite Markus begins to quote from the Evangelion (2.3), and when Adamantius seeks to make a point from scripture, Markus insists that it be taken from the Marcionite Apostolikon, with which Adamantius complies (2.4–5). In 2.10, the source of scripture is again brought up, and the Marcionite texts are specifically identified as the place from where argument will be drawn. A quote from John slips in at 2.14. Then, in 2.16, the Marcionite Markus begins to quote from John himself, intermixed with quotes from the Evangelion. In 2.18, in words highly reminiscent of Tertullian, Adamantius speaks of gathering up what Marcion has left behind in Paul's letters to use as evidence, proceeding to give a string of quotations. Afterwards, in 2.19, a lengthy discussion ensues about the correct reading of 1 Cor 15.45–47, with Adamantius commenting on how the wording he has just quoted from the Apostolikon differs from his own text of the passage.

55. In book 3, even though the Bardaisanite Marinus is the principal opponent, the Marcionite Megethius intrudes and quotes the Evangelion (3.7). Is Adamantius' quote of Rom 6.19 that follows taken from the same source?

56. Adamantius resumes citing from the Marcionite Evangelion in 5.14 under a contrived pretext reintroducing the Marcionite Megethius, but then relapses into using the catholic scriptures in 5.18–21. Then, in 5.22, he expressly states that he again is quoting from the Marcionite Apostolikon. Bakhuyzen, *Der Dialog des Adamantius*, 224, and Harnack, *Marcion*, 60*–62*, note that the string of Pauline citations that follow the latter statement (to the end of 5.27) are given in the order in which they would occur in the Apostolikon: Gal 2.20; 6.17; 1 Cor 6.15–16; 11.7; 15.29–53; 2 Cor 3.3; 3.11; 4.7; 4.11; 2 Cor 5.4; Rom 7.25; 8.1–2; Eph 2.17. Clabeaux is not persuaded by these features of the fifth debate, and does not consider it a reliable source (*A Lost Edition of the Letters of Paul*, 13,

169–74). While entertaining the possibility that the out-of-place references to Marcionites and the Marcionite Bible indicate that the author has turned to a distinct source (59), he observes that, among the supposed quotations of the Apostolikon given there, "no significant variants can be found which uncontestably appear" in either Tertullian or Epiphanius (61)—but see in this volume the text note to 1 Cor 15.50.

57. Harnack, *Marcion*, 58*–60*; Buchheit, *Tyrannii Rufini*, xii–xxxv; Clabeaux, *A Lost Edition of the Letters of Paul*; Schmid, *Marcion und sein Apostolos*, 207–9 and 236.

58. See Tsutsui, *Die Auseinandersetzung*, 148–49.

59. Harnack spells out his programmatic position on Adamantius in *Marcion*, 60*–63*, but in practice is somewhat less discerning, and makes final judgments based not on an analysis of Adamantius' use of sources, but on how well or poorly a particular quoted passage fits Marcion's ideology. Cf. Zahn, *Geschichte des Neutestamentlichen Kanons*, vol. 2, 419–25, and Zahn, "Die Dialoge des 'Adamantius' mit den Gnostikern." Zahn considered only the second debate with the Marcionite Markus, and a few isolated passages of the fifth debate, to have any value for reconstructing the Apostolikon.

60. This is true not only in multiple instances involving the Evangelion, which Schmid did not check before passing his sweeping judgment against Adamantius, but even in a number of verses in the Apostolikon that Schmid apparently overlooked.

61. Buchheit, *Tyrannii Rufini*, vii and xii-xxxv; cf. Bakhuyzen, *Der Dialog des Adamantius*, lxii-xliv.

62. Codex 452 ("Codex A") and Codex 312 ("Codex B") of the library of the Mechitarist Fathers of San Lazzaro, Venice. Both mss. were copied in 1195 CE, at Hagbat and Tarsus, respectively. An additional copy has since been identified, Escorial II.9.

63. Schäfers, *Eine altsyrische antimarkionistische Erklärung*; cf. Lyonnet, *Les Origines de la Version Arménienne et le Diatessaron*, 135–43; Preuschen, "Eine altkirchliche antimarionistische Schrift."

64. The work begins with a reference to Marcion's *Proevangelion* (i.e., his *Antitheses*) and an allusion to its opening lines: "O the exceeding greatness, the folly, the power, and the wonders, for there is nothing to say about it, nor to think concerning it, and there is nothing to render like unto it." Codex B has "the wisdom of the power" in place of "the folly, the power." The title preserved in Codex A, which may or may not reflect the original title of Ps.-Eph A, is "An Exposition of the Gospel." Codex B's title is "Against Marcion, who says nothing is like it, and an exposition concerning the parables of the evangelists." There is also a clear allusion to the opening verse of the Evangelion in Ps.-Eph A 1: "I have wondered how could there be a book of the Marcionites which they indeed named 'Before the Gospel,' when his disciples hopefully think [Codex B: read] that the beginning of the divinity in which they believe *appeared at those times, in the years of Pontius Pilate*."

65. Cf., e.g., Tertullian, *Marc.* 4.1.1, quoting the *Antitheses*: "It says in

the Law . . . but *the Lord says in his gospel* . . ." to Ps.-Eph A 2: "How much Marcion lied I will show, for he speaks not from the true foundation. *The Lord says in his gospel* . . ."

66. The text employed for this study is that of Egan, *Saint Ephrem*.

67. "I have looked at the Gospel quotations which are mentioned in the treatise and I never encountered readings which are *or could be* Marcionite (Harnack, *Marcion*, 183*, emphasis added; cf. 256*, 354*).

68. Egan, *An Analysis of the Biblical Quotations of Ephrem*.

69. Egan does not look at the presence or absence of whole passages, which is the most secure measure of determining a connection to the Evangelion and Apostolikon; instead, he draws all of his points of comparison from minor variants in reading reported for Marcion's text. Therefore, he fails to note that Ps.-Eph A never cites a passage from Luke known from other witnesses to have been absent from the Evangelion. He opts to set aside from consideration all quotations of passages where Marcion's text did not vary from other versions, which arguably skews his results. Most problematically, he arbitrarily selects the reading that differs from the Evangelion whenever the two recensions of Ps.-Eph A offer divergent readings, while offering no explanation of how one of the two recensions became "contaminated" by a Marcionite reading. In fact, it can be demonstrated that the recension in Codex A generally has biblical quotations harmonized to vulgate forms, while the recension in Codex B more often retains forms of the biblical text agreeing with the Evangelion. Egan offers no explanation as to why our author would select examples only from Luke if he was simply giving an exposition of his own community's gospel texts against the views of Marcion, nor is he able to propose a single consistent alternative to the Evangelion as the source of Pseudo-Ephrem's gospel quotations. The few points of variance he legitimately identifies between Ps.-Eph A and other witnesses to the text of the Evangelion are unremarkable, and fall within the familiar pattern of variances found among the other witnesses themselves due to occasional paraphrase or influence of forms of the text more familiar to the particular author.

70. BeDuhn, "Biblical Antitheses, Adda, and the Acts of Archelaus." A related source is the *Capitulam* of the Manichaean Faustus of Milevis, composed in the late fourth century and preserved in extensive quotes in Augustine of Hippo's *Contra Faustum*. In critiquing the gospel texts in use among non-Manichaean Christians, Faustus calls into question the material of the Synoptic account of Jesus exactly corresponding to Luke 1–3, known from other sources to have been lacking from the Evangelion.

71. First published by Lobel, Roberts, Turner, & Barns in 1957, in part 24 of *The Oxyrhynchus Papyri*, as item 2383. For the latest, improved transcription, see Wayment, "A New Transcription of P. Oxy 2383 (P^{69})."

72. The fragment stands far apart from other NT manuscripts in the number of variations from the norm. In twenty-seven lines, with an average of one word preserved per line, there are sixteen variations from the critical text, only two of which are attested in other manuscripts of Luke.

If this ratio is extended to the whole text, there would be nothing to compare to P⁶⁹ in degree of deviance.

73. The idea that P⁶⁹ may be a fragment of the Evangelion has been anticipated by Clivaz, "The Angel and the Sweat Like 'Drops of Blood,'" on the basis of a suggestion made to her by François Bovon (429 n. 80). Her arguments from Marcionite ideology, however, while valid in themselves, are unnecessary. See BeDuhn, "Is P⁶⁹ a fragment of Marcion's *Evangelion*?" (forthcoming).

74. Williams, "Reconsidering Marcion's Gospel."

75. The same conclusion of the Marcionite provenance of the prologues was arrived at independently by Peter Corssen, " Zur Überlieferungsgeschichte des Römerbriefes." Harnack defended the hypothesis in "Der marcionitische Ursprung"; cf. Harnack, *Marcion*, 127*–48*. For the best survey of the textual basis for these prologues, see Dahl, "The Origin of the Earliest Prologues."

76. "The main group of prologues constantly deals with false apostles and reactions to them, even in cases in which the text of the letters gives little reason for doing so" (Dahl, "The Origin of the Earliest Prologues," 248).

77. "The Prologues to Galatians, 1 Corinthians, Romans, 1 Thessalonians, (Ephesians), Colossians, and Philippians share a highly stereotyped phraseology and follow, with omissions and variations, a common pattern" (Dahl, "The Origin of the Earliest Prologues," 246–47). It can be demonstrated (e.g., Dahl, 248) that separate prologues for 2 Cor and 2 Thess were not originally envisioned, and that the prologues for 1 Cor and 1 Thess were meant to cover both letters to those churches.

78. See esp. Schäfer, "Marius Victorinus und die marcionitischen Prologe," who finds clear dependence of Marius Victorinus on the prologues, ca. 355–65 CE, already proposed by Corssen, "Zur Überlieferungsgeschichte des Römerbriefes," 40–41; Souter, *The Earliest Latin Commentaries*, 27; Frede, *Altlateinische Paulus-Handschriften*, 173–77.

79. Mindle, "Die Herkunft der 'marcionitischen' Prologe"; cf. Lagrange, "Les prologues prétendus marcionites"; Frede, *Altlateinische Paulus-Handschriften*; Dahl, "The Origin of the Earliest Prologues."

80. Schäfer, "Marius Victorinus und die marcionitischen Prologe," 32.

81. Dahl, "The Origin of the Earliest Prologues," concludes that a non-Marcionite origin has greater probability, finding no single characteristic that requires a Marcionite author, and weighing the fact of the prologues' adoption into the catholic textual tradition. But he disavows any certainty on the question, unlike many of those who have cited him as establishing their non-Marcionite origin.

82. See Schäfer, "Marius Victorinus und die marcionitischen Prologe," 11.

83. Origen, *Cels.* 7.18, which gives as the "laws" of Jesus: "a man cannot come forward to the Father if he is rich (cf. Luke 18.25), or loves power (cf. 22.24–26), or lays claim to any intelligence or reputation (cf. 10.21; 6.26), and that he must not pay attention to food (cf. 12.22–23) or to

his storehouse more than ravens (cf. 12.24) or to clothing any more than the lilies (cf. 12.27), and that to a man who has struck him once, he should offer himself to be struck again (cf. 6.29)."

84. See Zahn, *Geschichte des Neutestamentlichen Kanons*, vol. 2, 426–32.

85. The *Homilies* generally preserve more independent forms of biblical passages, while in the *Recognitions* they have been conformed to the standard text of later centuries. See Kline, *The Sayings of Jesus in the Pseudo-Clementine Homilies*.

86. See Zahn, *Geschichte des Neutestamentlichen Kanons*, vol. 2, 432–49.

87. See Blackman, *Marcion and His Influence*, 57–60, 128–71.

88. Clabeaux, *A Lost Edition of the Letters of Paul*.

89. Harnack, *Marcion*.

90. Tsutsui, "Das Evangelium Marcions."

91. E.g., Mühlenberg, "Marcion's Jealous God," 98: "We are not furnished with a list of omissions, so that the *argumentum e silentio* cannot be admitted."

92. The methodological objection is well summed up by Campenhausen, *The Formation of the Christian Bible*, 148: "If there is a fundamental objection to be made to Harnack's classic presentation it is this, that he all too quickly changes the dogmatic phenomenon that is Marcion into the picture of a particular man, and interprets it as a psychological expression of his personality and beliefs. . . . We constantly forget that we know absolutely nothing directly . . . about the personal assumptions, character, and development of the man himself."

93. Williams, "Reconsidering Marcion's Gospel."

94. Ulrich Schmid, *Marcion und sein Apostolos*.

95. Schmid, "How Can We Access Second-Century Texts?" 149.

96. For examples of variations in Tertullian's successive quotation of the same passage, see Williams 479 n. 7.

97. Williams also notes that the texts of Tertullian and Epiphanius are themselves edited on the basis of later copies in which biblical references might have been conformed to more familiar forms by copyists (479).

98. This characterization is an oversimplification, and a more detailed analysis of Schmid's methodology is offered in the introduction to the Apostolikon in chap. 4.

99. Schmid, "How Can We Access Second-Century Gospel Texts?," 142.

100. Dieter Roth has embraced Schmid's methodology, at least in principle, in his recent work on the Evangelion, whose final results in a reconstructed text has yet to appear. See "Towards a New Reconstruction" (*non vidi*) and "Marcion's Gospel," 291–92. Aware that Dr. Roth and myself were working in parallel on reconstructions of the Evangelion, I have avoided drawing upon his dissertation, which represents a segment of his larger project, and which it would be improper for me to appropriate before its author has had a chance to publish his full conclusions.

101. "In regard to allusions, the references are so vague that the *wording* of Marcion's text cannot be restored *at all*" (Williams, "Reconsidering Marcion's Gospel," 479–80, emphasis added). Williams is only interested

in what he identifies as direct quotations of the Evangelion. But his claim that allusions do not allow restoration of the text's wording "at all" is clearly an exaggeration. He cites the example of Tertullian, *Marc.* 4.32.1 ("Who is it that seeks for a lost sheep and a lost coin?"), and states that this quote "suggests that Marcion's Gospel contained something of these two pericopes, but [Tertullian] does not provide any further information as to specific wording." It is appropriate to Williams' argument that he has chosen one of the most minimal allusions in Tertullian's text. But, in fact, even in this extreme example, Tertullian provides first of all the wording *ovem . . . dragmam perditam* (lost sheep, lost coin), and if one follows his discussion of the passage, one encounters in addition the wording *perdidit* (lost) . . . *habuit* (possess) . . . *requisivit* (seek) . . . *invenit* (find) . . . *exultavit* (rejoice) . . . *paenitentia peccatoris* (repentence of a sinner). These elements correspond with wording in Luke, and the thrust of Tertullian's argument requires that they be present in Marcion's text, as well.

102. Schmid, *Marcion und sein Apostolos*, 26.

103. Tyson, *Marcion and Luke-Acts*, 43.

104. Cf. Clabeaux, "Abraham in Marcion's Gospel and Epistles," 71.

105. Indeed, Williams appears to have reached the same frustration with reconstructing the "original" text of Marcion's Evangelion, as have those who have sought to fix definitively the "original" text of any gospel. Williams goes so far as to treat differences in word order between Tertullian's Latin and Epiphanius' Greek as disagreements in their testimony to the passage ("Reconsidering Marcion's Gospel," 485), not allowing for ordinary differences in Latin and Greek grammar and syntax. He does not tolerate such correspondences as Latin *enim* for Greek *kai gar* in Luke 8.46 (488). He also counts as disagreements passages where one or the other witness terminates a quote earlier than the other (see, e.g., Luke 9.35 [486], Luke 16.16 [487], Luke 7.27 [490]).

106. "Marcion's Jealous God," 98.

107. E.g., the Temptation story in Luke 4.1–15, the synagogue reading in 4.16b–22, and the "casting lots" in 23.34, all noted as absent by Tertullian but not by Epiphanius.

108. As a result of these habits, the form of the text reconstructed from these sources appears streamlined, succinct, and to the point. In the case of the Evangelion, nearly every episode ends with a definitive remark or action of Jesus. In short, the text gives the impression of a cleaner, more focused text than that found in Luke, and we must be careful not to infer from that impression that Marcion's text must be earlier and more original than the relatively more cluttered and elaborated text of Luke. Similarly with respect to the Apostolikon, Tertullian's testimony in particular appears to present a tighter, more logically progressive argument than that found in the full text of the catholic version of Paul's letters. There are other reasons to consider the possibility that Marcion's texts have literary priority over their catholic counterparts, and we should not confuse matters by overlooking the distorting effect of the manner in which we have access to the former.

109. This is an important principle of Schmid's methodology (Schmid, *Marcion und sein Apostolos*, 26–29), as it is also of Roth's ("Marcion and the Early New Testament Text," 303 n. 6). Some resources for this task can be found, for the Evangelion, in Aalders, "Tertullian's Quotations from St. Luke"; Higgins, "The Latin Text of Luke in Marcion and Tertullian"; Eldridge, *The Gospel Text of Epiphanius of Salamis*; and for the Apostolikon, in von Soden, "Der lateinische Paulustext bei Marcion und Tertullian"; Osburn, *The Text of the Apostolos in Epiphanius of Salamis*. See also Blackman, *Marcion and His Influence*, 128–68.

110. Williams, "Reconsidering Marcion's Gospel," 480 n. 10 cites "for example" Epiphanius' statement (*Scholion* 31) that the Evangelion did not include the clause "God clothes the grass," whereas Tertullian discusses it as present (*Marc.* 4.29.1). But in fact this is the single instance where one source explicitly says something is missing that another attests as present. Williams' second example, 481 n. 11, does not hold up to close examination. At first, it appears that Tertullian says something is absent that Epiphanius quotes as present: *Vestitum plane eius a militibus divisum partim sorte concessum Marcion abstulit, respiciens psalmi prophetiam: Dispertiti sibi sunt vestimenta mea, et in vestitum meum sortem miserunt* (*Marc.* 4.42.4); cf. Epiphanius, *Scholion* 71: *kai diemerisanto ta himatia autou*. Williams quotes Tertullian as follows: "Evidently the statement that his [Jesus'] raiment was divided among the soldiers . . . has been excised by Marcion, because he had in mind the prophecy of the psalm, 'They parted my garments among them.'" Yet Epiphanius quotes the words "and they divided his garments." Tertullian's full statement is, in fact, "Evidently that his raiment was divided by the soldiers *partly by deference to lots* has been excised by Marcion, because he had in mind the prophecy of the psalm, 'They parted my vestments among them, *and upon my raimant did they cast lots'*" (notice Tertullian's terminological indication that he is talking about an omission regarding the *vestitum* [singular] over which lots are cast in the psalm, not to the *vestimenta* [plural] that the psalm says are divided). Epiphanius, while mentioning the division of garments, makes no reference to the casting of lots, and so does not contradict Tertullian's observation that that particular element of the passage was absent from the Evangelion. All other apparent divergences in testimony to the presence or absence of particular phrases or clauses rely on comparing quotations where one source or the other may be abbreviating, and so amount to arguments from silence.

111. Harnack, *Marcion*, 42–44, 173–74.

112. Zahn, *Geschichte des Neutestamentlichen Kanons*, vol.1, pt. 2, 613.

113. Clabeaux, *A Lost Edition of the Letters of Paul*, 14; Schmid, *Marcion und sein Apostolos*, 11, 29–31.

114. Clabeaux, *A Lost Edition of the Letters of Paul*, 34.

115. Cf. Schmid, *Marcion und sein Apostolos*, 15–16, who speaks in general terms of the possibility of textual variants, including even perhaps some of the significant omissions, in the manuscripts on which Marcion based his NT.

116. LaCapra, *History and Criticism*, 38.

117. Campenhausen, *The Formation of the Christian Bible*, 121.
118. Koester, *Ancient Christian Gospels*, 37.
119. See Becker and Reed, *The Ways that Never Parted*, and Fredriksen, *Augustine and the Jews*.
120. Gamble, "The New Testament Canon: Recent Research," 292.
121. Barton, *Holy Writings, Sacred Text*, 35–62.
122. Hahneman, "The Muratorian Fragment," 405.
123. Barton's suggestion that Marcion did not necessarily regard these texts as sacred scripture, but rather "abolished the category of 'Scripture' altogether" (*Holy Writings, Sacred Text*, 40) is poorly grounded on the assumption that Marcion felt free to edit them (which is unproven), and at the same time ignores the many historical examples of a religious leadership simultaneously redacting and sacralizing a text as authoritative. Nevertheless, his suggestion invites further investigation of what status exactly Marcion's canon had for his followers, and to which if any of the contemporary Christian views of scripture it approximates. Given the historical and cultural context in which this canon was originally promulgated, they may have viewed it more in terms of the Hellenic "classic" than in those associated with "revelation."
124. Brakke, "Canon Formation and Social Conflict," 419.
125. See Chapman, "How the Biblical Canon Began," 49.

Chapter 3: The Evangelion

1. Tertullian, *Marc.* 4.2; Epiphanius, *Pan.* 42.10; Adam 1.8.
2. Harnack, *Marcion*, E24, 149 n. 3.
3. Koester, "From Kerygma to Written Gospels"; cf. *Ancient Christian Gospels*, 37. Cf. Kelber, *The Oral and the Written Gospel*, 144–48.
4. Gregory, *The Reception of Luke and Acts*, 196.
5. Cosgrove, "Justin Martyr and the Emerging Christian Canon," 226.
6. In *Ref.* 7.18, Hippolytus alludes to Mark and Paul as Marcion's scriptural authorities. This statement shows that Hippolytus was unaware of the writings of Irenaeus and Tertullian on the subject, since both of them identify Marcion's Evangelion as a shorter version of Luke. Hippolytus seems to have viewed it as an expanded version of Mark, perhaps because it lacked the birth narratives that were distinctive to Luke, and instead began, like Mark, with Jesus' adult activities (the beginning of Marcion's Evangelion is cited in *Ref.* 7.19, showing that Hippolytus had in fact seen it).
7. Tertullian, *Marc.* 4.2.3; 4.3.4–5; Adam 1.5.
8. Irenaeus, *Haer.* 3.1.1 cf. Tertullian, *Marc.* 4.2. The Muratorian Canon says more specifically that Luke was Paul's *iuris studiosus*, or legal secretary.
9. Irenaeus, *Haer.* 1.27.2.
10. Tertullian, *Marc.* 4.2.1.
11. Tertullian, *Marc.* 4.2.4.
12. Even though Tertullian says, "I pass on next to show how this gospel . . . is in places adulterated: and this shall form the basis of my

order of approach" (*Marc.* 4.2.1), he does not in fact take this approach, and offers almost no comment throughout bk. 4 about differences between Marcion's gospel and catholic Luke. He opts instead to show how Marcion's ideas are contradicted by the text of his own gospel. Since Tertullian indicates that he rewrote his tract against Marcion several times, it is possible that the quoted statement is a relic of an earlier edition, before he decided to take the approach of disproving Marcion on the basis of what remained in Marcion's "adulterated" gospel.

13. *Marc.* 4.4.1–5 (Evans translation). The crucial passage in Latin is: *Si enim id evangelium quod Lucae refertur penes nos . . . ipsum est quod Marcion per Antitheses suas arguit ut interpolatum a protectoribus Iudaismi ad concorporationem legis et prophetarum.*

14. Sadly, Harnack provides the most egregious example. Harnack asserts, "Never and nowhere has M[arcion] asserted that he *discovered* anew the unfalsified gospel in an exemplar, but always only that he has *restored* it *again*" (Harnack 250*, with his original italics). This can only be characterized as a figment of Harnack's imagination. The use of "always" suggests a plurality of passages where Marcion asserts such a restoration; but in fact Harnack has in mind only this passage from Tertullian. Moreover, in quoting the passage, he leaves off the conditional "if" (*si*), and quotes Tertullian's words selectively as: "the Gospel, said to be Luke's which is current amongst us . . . , Marcion argues in his *Antitheses* was *interpolated by the defenders of Judaism*, for the purpose of a conglomeration with it of the law and the prophets" (Harnack, *Marcion*, 41 n. 4/E149 n. 6). This is scarcely a creditable way to use historical sources.

15. The only report Tertullian makes of Marcionite comment on or criticism of the Gospel of Luke he attributes not to Marcion himself, but to "they," that is, the Marcionites of his own time: "If that which Marcion has in use is not at once to be attributed to Luke, though it agrees with ours, since they allege ours is falsified in respect of its title, then it belongs to the apostles. And in that case ours too, which is in agreement with that other, no less belongs to the apostles, even if it is falsified in its title" (Tertullian, *Marc.* 4.3.4–5; Evans translation, slightly emended for clarity).

16. The Greek term daemon refers to a lower-level supernatural being of ambiguous identity and character; it does not necessarily have the sharply negative character associated with the English word demon.

17. On this subject, see Knox, *Marcion and the New Testament*, 78–81, and the important review and clarification of these debates in Roth, "Marcion's Gospel and Luke."

18. Baird, *History of New Testament Research*, vol. 1, 126.

19. Cf. Semler, *Neuer Versuch*, 162–63.

20. E.g., Corrodi, *Versuch einer Beleuchtung*, vol. 2, 158–69; Löffler, "Marcionem Pauli epistolas et Lucae Evangelium adulterasse dubitaturi"; Bolten, *Der Bericht des Lucas von Jesu dem Messia*; Griesbach, *Curae in historiam textus Graeci epistolarum Paulinarum*, 124ff.; Schmidt, *Historisch-Kritische Einleitung ins Neue Testament*; Eichhorn, *Einleitung in das Neue Testament*, vol. 1, 40–78; Bertholdt, *Historisch-kritische Einleitung in sämmtli-*

che kanonische und apokryphische Schriften, vol. 3, 1293ff.; Schleiermacher, *Einleitung ins neue Testament*, 64–65, 197–98, 214–15.

21. E.g., Storr, *Über den Zwek*, 254–65; Arneth, *Über die Bekanntschaft Marzions*; Neander, *Genetische Entwickelung*, 311ff.; Gratz, *Kritische Untersuchungen über Marcions Evangelium*; Hug, *Einleitung in die Schriften des Neuen Testaments*, 1847 ed., 64ff.; Hahn, *Das Evangelium Marcions in seiner ursprüngliche Gestalt*; Olshausen, *Die Echtheit der vier canonischen Evangelien*, 107–215. J. C. L. Gieseler, *Historisch-kritischer Versuch*, 24ff., originally agreed with Semler, but was won over by the contrary arguments of Hahn, and so stated in his review of Hahn in *Hall. Allg. Litt. Zeitung*, 225ff.

22. First in an extensive review of W. M. L. de Wette's *Lehrbuch der historisch-kritischen Einleitung* (4th ed.), 575–90, and then in his *Das nachapostolische Zeitalter*, vol. 1, 260–84.

23. *Das Evangelium Marcions*.

24. *Kritische Untersuchungen*, which reproduces verbatim his remarks in "Der Ursprung und Charakter des Lukas-Evangeliums."

25. They were actually anticipated in this position by the more tentative suggestions of Schmidt, "Über das ächte Evangelium des Lucas"; and by Eichhorn, *Einleitung in das Neue Testament*, 1820 ed., vol. 1, 43–84.

26. Baur, "Der Ursprung und Charakter des Lukas-Evangeliums," 595. Ritschl noted the difference in their views in "Das Verhältnis der Schriften."

27. "Über das Lukas-Evangelium," and *Das Evangelium Marcions*. In the latter, Volkmar reaches four conclusions: (1) Marcion edited Luke according to his own theological tendencies, primarily by omission, while variant readings in the common material are mostly to be explained by scribal alterations before Marcion (255–58); (2) Marcion used a range of editorial techniques, from removing whole passages for only the slightest divergence from his views to changing the meaning of a passage by changes to its literary context, to excision or slight alteration of individual words (258–60); (3) Marcion is our earliest witness to the existence of Luke, and to its text in those passages Marcion preserves intact (260–62); (4) Marcion's editorial work is not essentially different from that of the authors of the canonical gospels, all of whom combined and redacted source texts into new gospels, and Marcion belongs to the early age of such fluid gospel production, prior to the according of scriptural status to Christian literature (262–67). He did not rule out the possibility that some passages found in Luke but not in Marcion, for which no ideological motive for Marcionite omission could be identified, may be later additions to Luke not present in the exemplar used by Marcion (199–200).

28. *Kritische Untersuchungen über die Evangelien Justins*, 389–475, and "Das Marcionitische Evangelium."

29. Volckmar, "Über das Lukas-Evangelium," originally proposed as later additions to Luke lacking in Marcion's exemplar: 13.1–9, 12.6–7, and 21:18. But he later reversed himself in *Das Evangelium Marcions*, and reaffirmed the originality of all of these passages and their likely excision

by Marcion, while still maintaining that Marcion's text incidentally preserved more original readings in 10.21–22; 11.2; 12.38; 17.2; and 18.18. Hilgenfeld's list of later Lukan additions includes 5.39; 13.1–5; 21.18; and Marcion's text is to be preferred as more original than that of Luke at 10.21–22; 11.2; 12.38; 13.28; 16.17; 17.2; 18.19; 23.2; where it has further support from other mss. or witnesses to the biblical text. Hilgenfeld sustained these views in his subsequent work. For the important differences between Volckmar's and Hilgenfeld's ultimate positions, see Roth, "Marcion's Gospel and Luke."

30. "Über den gegenwärtigen Stand," esp. 528–33.

31. *Geschichte des neutestamentlichen Kanons*, vol. 1, 585–718; vol. 2, 409–529.

32. *Das Markusevangelium nach seinem Ursprung und Charakter*, 192–95, including 8.19; 10.21, 25; 12.8–9; 15.11–32; 18.31–34, 37; 19.9; 20.9–18, 37–38; 21.21–22; 22.16, 35–38; 24.25, 27, 32, 44–45.

33. Baur 1851, 212–25, noting among likely later additions Luke 1–2; 4.16–30; 5.39; 10.22; 12.6–7; 13.1–5; 16.17; 19.28–46; 21.18. He was undecided on whether Marcion had excised or Luke added 11.29–32, 49–52; 13.28–35; and 22.30.

34. "Is Marcion's Gospel One of the Synoptics?"

35. "The Date of Luke-Acts." Townsend positions himself as continuing the position of John Knox, but stresses anti-Marcionite motives in a mid-second–century redaction of Luke-Acts.

36. "Markion vs. Lukas." Similarly, with reference to the Pauline epistles, Raschke, "Der Römerbrief des Markion nach Epiphanius"; and Delafosse, *Le Ecrits de saint Paul*, vol. 1 (*L'épître aux romains*) and vol. 2 (*La Première épître aux Corinthiens*).

37. *Der Ursprung und die Komposition der synoptischen Evangelien*, 303ff. A similar position was taken by Usener, *Das Weihnachfest*, and in the 1911 ed., 83–101, he deals with the theological themes and pre-Lukan origin of the Evangelion independently of any association with Marcion.

38. *Marcion and the New Testament*.

39. *The Reception of Luke and Acts*, 193–96. "It is this middle view, I shall argue, that Marcion neither drew on canonical *Luke* as we would recognize it in a modern eclectic text, nor that *Luke* was derived from Marcion's Gospel, which best fits the evidence that we have for the relationship between Marcion's *Gospel* and that known to us as *Luke*" (193). Like Knox, Gregory still thinks that "Marcion did edit his text" (193), even though he rightly challenges the testimony of Irenaeus and Tertullian (and by implication Epiphanius) as mere supposition on their part based upon the observable differences between Marcion's Evangelion and their Luke (183–92). He retains the idea that Marcion edited his texts as part of a fairly circular scenario that "Marcion stood against the harmonizing tendency" of the second century (195), and sought to reduce harmonized Jesus material, such as Justin had, to an isolated gospel text. But this scenario in turn depends on a pervasive misunderstanding of remarks of Tertullian on Marcion cutting out from the gospel readings that do not, in fact, appear in Luke, and attributing these readings to a harmonized text

of Luke known to Tertullian. Dieter Roth has recently clarified the context of Tertullian's remarks, removing them from consideration in the reconstruction of either Tertullian's text of Luke or Marcion's editorial activities ("Matthean Texts and Tertullian's Accusations").

40. *Marcion and Luke-Acts.*

41. See Bellinzoni, "The Gospel of Luke in the Second Century CE"; and Gregory, *The Reception of Luke and Acts.*

42. See Schmid, "Marcions Evangelium und die neutestamentlichen Evangelien."

43. Williams, "Reconsidering Marcion's Gospel," lists among those holding this position Westcott & Hort, F. J. Foakes Jackson, B. H. Streeter, B. M. Metzger, F. F. Bruce, and D. L. Dungan (478). It should be pointed out that this position can withstand the growing consensus that Acts probably should be dated in the second century, particularly if it can be shown that the assumption of common authorship for Luke and Acts may be wrong. John Knox was the foremost proponent of a late date for Acts for much of the twentieth century, but consensus around this position has been building in recent decades, on which see Pervo, *Dating Acts.* That current consensus would put the composition in the first quarter of the second century, in the lifetime of Marcion, but not written in response to him, unless his activities started much earlier than our sources generally attest. Pervo states, "If Marcion was active early in the second century, it is possible that the canonical Luke and Acts do represent a revision of Marcion's Gospel, together with an additional volume placing Paul in the desired perspective" (Pervo, *Dating Acts,* 367), but adds, "Please note that I am not advocating that hypothesis here" (n. 20). For recent discussion of the possibility that Luke and Acts do not share a common author or date of composition, see Parsons and Pervo, *Rethinking the Unity of Luke and Acts;* Walters, *The Assumed Authorial Unity of Luke and Acts.*

44. Bellinzoni, "The Gospel of Luke in the Apostolic Fathers," 47.

45. Petersen, "Textual Traditions Examined," 45. Cf. Robbins, "A Socio-Rhetorical Look at the Work of John Knox on Luke-Acts," 93–94: "The weight of evidence for texts not considered to be sacred scripture ... lies on the side of substantive editorial rearrangement, addition, and omission as documents were copied and recopied during the last centuries BCE and the first two centuries CE. Put simply, the greatest likelihood is that the gospels and Acts were written and rewritten in various editions until ca. 150–220 CE, when they began to be considered part of the 'New Covenant' alongside the 'Old Covenant.'"

46. The earliest direct quotation of Acts is in the letter of the martyrs of Lugdunum, ca. 177–78 CE (Conzelmann, *Theology of St. Luke,* 299).

47. Sanday, *The Gospels in the Second Century,* 222–30.

48. Sanday stresses that in compiling his evidence for the stylistic unity of Luke, "care has been taken to put down nothing that was not verified by its preponding presence in the Lucan writings, and especially by its presence in that portion of the Gospel which Marcion undoubtedly received" (Sanday, 230). Yet his approach is undermined by the fact that

terms and stylistic features that stand out for their prepondering presence in canonical Luke do not necessarily do so in Marcion's text. In other words, they may become "characteristic" only by use multiple times in portions of Luke-Acts not found in the Evangelion, for which there may be only one instance of the same usage in the Evangelion—no more or even less than is found in other books of the NT. While Sanday stresses the presence of these features in the sections of Luke supposedly omitted by Marcion, he fails to demonstrate that they are indeed characteristic (that is, used often and distinctively) in the text common to Marcion and Luke. Knox has shown that Sanday further inflated his supporting evidence by assuming that any passage common to Luke and the Evangelion had exactly the same wording in the latter as it does in the former, even if the testimony to the presence of the passage is nothing more than the barest allusion (Knox, *Marcion and the New Testament*, 90–91). This assumption was based in a circular fashion on Sanday's acceptance of the patristic claim that Marcion had removed passages from Luke (without rewriting what remained), and did not take into account the opposite possibility that consistency of grammatical and stylistic features throughout Luke belong to the redactional gloss of a rewrite of the Evangelion.

49. "On the Vocabulary of Marcion's Gospel," further developed in Knox, *Marcion and the New Testament*, 86–96, and Appendix III.

50. *Marcion and the New Testament*, 93–94.

51. Knox, *Marcion and the New Testament*, 95–96.

52. The validity of Knox's objection to Sanday and Harnack's overconfidence in the identical wording of passages in the two gospels would seem to be supported by the evidence of P^{69}. Whether or not this leaf can be proved to be a fragment of Marcion's *Evangelion*, it shows the existence of a version of Luke divergent from the majority of manuscripts even in minor points of vocabulary and style.

53. See Cadbury, rev. of *Marcion and the New Testament*, 126–27, where he criticized Knox for not stopping at discrediting Sanday's arguments, but attempting the same sort of analysis to prove the opposite position. Knox accepted Cadbury's criticism, and later disavowed that part of his argument.

54. Cadbury, "Four Features of Lucan Style," 88. He adds that the significance of lexical arguments about peculiarities of an author's vocabulary "has been greatly overestimated."

55. See Harnack, "Über I. Kor. 14,32ff. und Rom. 16,25ff.," 527ff., and Harnack, *Neue Studien zu Marcion*, 32ff.

56. Harris, Bauer, and Lagrange made similar suggestions; von Soden and Zahn rejected the idea (see Wilson, *Marcion: A Study of a Second-Century Heretic*, 145–49). See Blackman, *Marcion and His Influence*, 50 n. 5, 51 n. 2, 60.

57. See BeDuhn, "The Myth of Marcion as Redactor," esp. 29–32.

58. This point has been made by Townsend, "The Date of Luke-Acts," 48; and by Williams, "Reconsidering Marcion's Gospel," 478 and 482.

59. Grant, *The Letter and the Spirit*, 117.

60. F. C. Grant, "Was the Author of John Dependent on the Gospel

of Luke?" esp. 303–6, argues that the text of Luke has been secondarily assimilated to John. Others have proposed that John was a source in the composition of Luke, as well as the reverse literary relationship. Regarding Luke's relationship to Matthew, a significant group of modern researchers argue that Luke had Matthew as a source. It would be interesting see if the evidence cited in this theory is present in the Evangelion, or whether it belongs to a secondary redactional layer.

61. See Streeter, *The Four Gospels*; Taylor, *Behind the Third Gospel*; Conzelmann, *Theology of St. Luke*, 172; Tyson, *Marcion and Luke-Acts*, 90–98.

62. "Is Marcion's Gospel One of the Synoptics?"

63. "The Date of Luke-Acts."

64. "Markion vs. Lukas."

65. On this subject, see Minear, "Luke's Use of the Birth Stories." While arguing for the unity of these chapters with the rest of Luke-Acts, Minear summarizes a great deal of the evidence that casts doubt on the likelihood of such unity; see especially the preponderance of "characteristic" Lukan style and vocabulary in chapters 1–2 rather than distributed evenly through Luke (114–16), and the contrasting attitudes towards Mary in the early and later parts of the gospel (128). Alfred Loisy, "Marcion's Gospel: A Reply," while highly critical of Couchoud's overall argument, acknowledges the validity of his observations regarding chapters 1–2 of Luke, and accepts the possibility of a proto-Luke lacking the birth and infancy stories; he considers Marcion's removal of them from an already expanded canonical Luke to be a lucky guess of amateur textual criticism on his part (381). Bruce, "Some Thoughts on the Beginning of the New Testament Canon," 44, similarly embraces an earlier form of Luke lacking the first two chapters, while cautioning against a simple identification of Marcion's Evangelion with this possible proto-Luke *Vorlage*.

66. "According to Marcion, Jesus began his ministry at Capernaum; according to Luke, at Nazareth; but by a curious oversight, Luke, who had hitherto made no mention of Capernaum, describes how Jesus imagines the men of Nazareth saying to Him, 'Whatsoever we have heard done in Capernaum, do also here in thy country' (iv.28). Now, up till then, nothing had happened in Capernaum. This negligence on the part of Luke clearly indicates that the order, Capernaum before Nazareth, as found in Marcion, is the original one" (Couchoud, "Is Marcion's Gospel One of the Synoptics?" 269). By the Schwegler Hypothesis, an anti-Marcionite motive to highlight Nazareth as Jesus' human, Jewish hometown prompted the rearrangement, inadvertently creating the awkward *aporia*. Loisy sought to account for the anomaly in Luke by the displacement of the Nazareth narrative to a much earlier place in the narrative than where it is found in Luke's source, Mark (Loisy, "Marcion's Gospel: A Reply," 381), failing to notice that the telltale reference to things "done in Capernaum" is not found in Mark, but is distinct to the Lukan version of the episode. His other suggested explanations (381–82) are even less persuasive.

67. Including such things as the Prologue's reference to many (*polloi*) previous gospel writers (with its critical tone, perhaps intended to

include the Evangelion itself), and signs of dependence on Matthew and perhaps John. While a number of modern scholars take the latter evidence as relevant for the initial composition of Luke, proponents of the Schwegler Hypothesis suggest that it was introduced at a secondary stage of redaction, since it is largely absent from the Evangelion. Couchoud, for instance, notes that two distinct kinds of literary relationship to Matthew can be identified in Luke. The first sort consists of loose parallelism with considerable grammatical independence, which Couchoud and Klinghardt ("The Marcionite Gospel and the Synoptic Problem") attribute to Matthew's dependence on the Evangelion (cf. West Jr., "A Primitive Version of Luke," and Sturdy, *Redrawing the Boundaries*, 42–48), but which could be explained also, and probably better, by common dependence on Q in accord with the two-source hypothesis. The second sort of material showing a literary relationship of Luke to Matthew consists of nearly verbatim duplication, which Couchoud attributes to direct use of Matthew by the later redactor who developed the Evangelion into Luke (273ff.). François Bovon, in his commentary on Luke, has identified a considerable number of what he regards as secondary harmonizations of the text to Matthew.

68. Knox, *Marcion and the New Testament*, 107–8. He points out that one could scarcely argue that Marcion deliberately removed passages not confirmed by parallels in the other Synoptic gospels, since Marcion did not accept the authority of any other gospel (110). Of course, another pre-Marcionite editor might have been so motivated, but the absence from the Evangelion of some synoptic passages found in Luke prompts Knox to suggest that Marcion did remove some material from his source, and that an original proto-gospel stands behind both the expansion into Luke and the reduction into the Evangelion.

69. See Talbert, *Luke and the Gnostics*, 109; Hays, "Marcion vs. Luke: A Response," 228–30.

70. Volckmar, *Das Evangelium Marcions*, 256–57.

71. Harnack enumerated thirty-four harmonizations to Matthew and Mark in the Evangelion not found in witnesses to Luke. Leland Edward Wilshire lists thirty-two ("Was Canonical Luke Written in the Second Century?" 252–53).

72. This problem is highlighted in Wilshire, "Was Canonical Luke Written in the Second Century?"

73. To be clear, in some passages Luke has unharmonized readings while the Evangelion shows secondary harmonization, while in other passages it is the Evangelion that shows a more independent, unharmonized text compared to that of Luke. The evidence does not consistently support priority either way, and so appears to point to the Semler Hypothesis.

74. Knox, *Marcion and the New Testament*, 156. Yet Knox suggests that the Evangelion's apparent harmonizations to Matthew and Mark might not be harmonizations at all, but might reflect an original text more closely dependent on the common Synoptic tradition, while Luke repre-

sents a text worked over literarily, polished and rephrased in a way that de-harmonized it, so to speak (156 n. 42).

75. It should not go unremarked that such comparative assessments of harmonization are problematic when they employ a modern eclectic critical text to stand for Luke, since the dominant principles of modern text scholarship favor readings that are more divergent from parallels in other gospels. We may therefore risk intruding into the issue a text that may be artificially disharmonized in a way no single manuscript of Luke ever was at any given time.

76. Williams, "Reconsidering Marcion's Gospel," 481–82 n. 14, notes as examples of this phenomenon: 12.31 (Tertullian, *Marc.* 3.24.8, *primum* ["first"]=Matt 6.33, absent from Epiphanius, *Scholion* 33; but cf. Tertullian, *Marc.* 4.29.5, with *enim* for *primum*); 18.19 (Epiphanius, *Scholion* 50, *eis estin* ["one is (good)"]=Matt 19.17, while Tertullian, *Marc.* 4.36.3, has *sed quis* ["but who is (good)"], and Luke reads *oudeis* ["no one is (good)"] in agreement with Mark 10.18); 9.41 (Tertullian, *Marc.* 4.23.1–2, and Epiphanius, *Scholion* 19 repeat "how long" a second time=Matt 17.17 and Mark 9.19 against Luke). Williams fails to note that Adam 1.1 and 2.17 attest 18.19 for the Evangelion, and Hippolytus, *Ref.* 7.31.6, supports Epiphanius.

77. This understanding of the evidence has been based on the scenario imagined in the Patristic Hypothesis, in which Marcion produced a single redacted exemplar whose subsequent copies should not show any variation in harmonizations to other gospels, since they would be transmitted in isolation from other gospels within the Marcionite NT and community. This assumed scenario, then, has dictated the conclusion that where Tertullian and Epiphanius report different readings involving harmonizations, they must be the ones introducing them.

78. The research of Williams, "Reconsidering Marcion's Gospel," also supports the independent development of the Marcionite and catholic versions of the gospel. Within the twenty-three passages that he regards as reconstructable for Marcion's text, one can detect no pattern of editorial principle that might have been followed by Marcion if he was editing canonical Luke. There is no consistent principle of ideological inclusion or exclusion. Moreover, the evidence of divergent harmonization to one of the other Synoptics between the Evangelion and witnesses to Luke effectively rules out the dependence of either on the other, that is, both the Patristic and Schwegler hypotheses. For these reasons, Williams calls for reopening the question of the relationship of the Evangelion to Luke in a way that moves in particular beyond the accepted traditional account of Marcion's presumed editorial actions and motives (478).

79. *Marcion and the New Testament.*

80. *Marcion and Luke-Acts.*

81. Among the evidence bearing on the question, Knox cites the likely dependence of Luke on Josephus (e.g., cf. Luke 3.1–2 to *Ant.* 20.7.1 and Acts 5.34ff. to *Ant.* 20.5.1f.), a dependence which would put the composition (or final edition) of Luke-Acts in the last years of the first century

at the earliest (i.e., into Marcion's lifetime; Knox, *Marcion and the New Testament*, 128), and which also is entirely lacking from Marcion's form of the gospel (137). Knox further notes that several characteristic interests of Luke as identified by Cadbury (local color, historical references, soldiers, cities, Jerusalem, lodging and dining, signs and wonders, angels, visions, holy spirit), while making little appearance in Marcion's text (Knox, *Marcion and the New Testament*, 100–103), are even more dominant in Acts, suggesting that they are features of a final, expanded edition of Luke-Acts.

82. Tyson, *Marcion and Luke-Acts*, 45–48, 98–109.

83. Yet Marcion apparently referenced Jesus' baptism by John and did not deny that it happened, only questioned its worth (Epiphanius, *Pan.* 42.3.10). This testimony raises doubts that he would have been ideologically motivated to remove the baptism story from the gospel he wished to canonize, had it been present there.

84. Knox, *Marcion and the New Testament*, 110. Tyson rejects the full Schwegler Hypothesis mostly on the grounds of the implausibility that an orthodox writer would base a gospel on the work of a heretic; rather, Tyson imagines, the redactor of Luke-Acts went back to the source text from which Marcion had edited out material, retained what Marcion had omitted, and added new material to strengthen it against a Marcionite interpretation (*Marcion and Luke-Acts*, 83-120).

85. Is it possible that Marcion innocently adopted a version of the gospel that had been cut down or mutilated prior to him, and that the longer version found in canonical Luke is still closer to the original composition? That possibility cannot be ruled out, but requires such a large degree of speculation as to be almost pointless. In effect, it merely shifts the presumed motives typically ascribed to Marcion back one generation. If we can determine no consistent, coherent motives at work in the presumed omissions of Marcion, we will do no better ascribing them to some unknown predecessor.

86. In the same terms, if we eventually find clear evidence that Marcion *did* edit the text ideologically, we may be forced to reconsider precisely what his ideology was. Given what appears to have been contained in the Evangelion, it might be necessary to reject most polemical accounts of his positions as gross distortions, and move him much closer to what would become the Christian mainstream.

87. Farmer, "The Present State of the Synoptic Problem," 34, states categorically, "the two-source hypothesis is not technically possible. The main reason for this assertion is the extensive amount of agreement between Matthew and Luke against Mark."

88. Of the fifty-two "significant" minor agreements listed by McLoughlin, "Les accords mineurs Mt-Lc contre Mc et le problem synoptique," thirty-one can be checked against the Evangelion's text in some way. Of these thirty-one, twenty do not occur, while eleven do. Only six can be checked against Greek witnesses to the Evangelion (Epiphanius and Adamantius): *epiballei* in 5.36 (absent from Epiphanius,

present in Adamantius); *ekchuthēsetai* in 5.37 (absent from both); *didaskontos* in 20.1 (present in Epiphanius); *tis estin ho paisas se* in 22.64 (present in Epiphanius); *enetulixen* in 23.53 (present in both); *astraptousē* in 24.4 (absent from Epiphanius). Of these six, then, three are absent in at least one witness, and four present in at least one witness, with one showing variation between them. Unfortunately, Epiphanius does not quote these same verses anywhere else from his own biblical text for comparison.

89. See Friedrichsen, "The Matthew-Luke Agreements against Mark," for a persuasive argument that such agreements should be attributed to an ongoing oral tradition that tended towards harmonization of the distinctive gospel accounts.

90. The original proponents of this theory were Streeter, *The Four Gospels*, esp. 199–222, and Taylor, *Behind the Third Gospel*. They were able to demonstrate convincingly that Mark does not form the narrative base of Luke's gospel, but is only a source of extracts incorporated into a more substantial narrative outline.

91. See West Jr., "A Primitive Version of Luke."

92. This would explain the "Minor Agreements" between Matthew and Luke that have plagued the two-source hypothesis since its inception (although the evidence of the Evangelion points to a different solution). On this proto-Luke hypothesis, Peter Richardson has commented, "It would seem that the hypothesis came at exactly the wrong moment to be considered seriously. Frequently alluded to, it has not been thoroughly examined, for it came at the tail end of the concern for source critical questions, when that approach had been exhausted, and in the midst of the excitement over form criticism. Perhaps it is time to return to some of the source critical questions, for fresh attention to these might change significantly the way in which some of the redaction critical studies are being pursued. Specifically, consideration of the Proto-Luke hypothesis might call for a fundamental revision of Lukan redactional studies" ("The Thunderbolt in Q," 93 n. 10).

93. John the Baptist appears only three times in the Evangelion: (1) the episode about fasting that features the practices of John's disciples, found in Luke 5 and Matthew 9, deriving from Mark; (2) the question sent to Jesus by John and Jesus' teaching on John found in Matthew 11 and Luke 7, deriving from Q; (3) the identification of John as the end of the Law and Prophets found in Matthew 11 and Luke 16, likewise deriving from Q.

94. Lührmann has suggested that the Temptation episode should not be included in reconstructions of Q, and that Matthew and Luke derive this material independently from some other source (*Die Redaktion der Logienquelle*, 56). He notes among other anomalous features the direct quotation of the OT, otherwise seen very rarely in Q (98).

95. The Gospel of Thomas likewise attests no material included in current reconstruction of Q before the Sermon on the Mount/Plain (Q 6.20/ Thomas 54).

96. Thomas 3 (Luke 17.21b), 5 (8.17), 10 (12.49), 14 (10.8–9), 16 (12.49,

51–53), 21 (12.35, 37), 45 (6.44–45), 47 (5.39), 61 (17.34), 63 (12.16–21), 64 (14.16–24), 72 (12.13–14), 79 (11.27–28; 23.29), 91 (12.56), 95 (6.34–35), 96 (13.21), 102 (11.42–43), 103 (12.35), 113 (17.20–21).

97. Luke 6.44 in Thomas 45; 5.39 in 47; 17.34 in 61; and 23.29 in 79.

Chapter 4: The Apostolikon

1. Williams, "Eznik's Résumé of Marcionite Doctrine," 73. See the full text, section 358 of Eznik's treatise, in Blanchard and Young, *Eznik of Kolb*, 181–85. For a discussion of this theme in Marcionite thought, see Vinzent, "Christ's Resurrection."

2. Among those arguing for early and sustained attention to Paul: Lindemann, *Paulus im ältesten Christentum*; Dassmann, *Der Stachel im Fleisch*; Rensberger, "As the Apostle Teaches."

3. See W. Schneemelcher, "Paulus in der griechischen Kirche."

4. It must be noted that none of these three writings can be definitively dated to the time before Marcion, and a number of modern researchers have argued that they at least belong to the second century, perhaps even to the time when Marcion was forcing a response on the authority of Paul.

5. Uncertainty over the date and integrity of the letters of Ignatius makes it inadvisable to use them for evidence of the status of Paul before Marcion. Even the date of Clement remains controversial, although most would place him before Marcion.

6. See Gamble, "The New Testament Canon: Recent Research," 283.

7. E.g., Couchoud, "La première édition de S. Paul"; in a slightly more qualified form, Hoffmann, *Marcion: On the Restitution of Christianity*.

8. Including the Pastoral letters, which are first clearly referenced by Irenaeus and, it has been suggested, were either composed or at least added to the smaller corpus of Paul for the express purpose of countering Marcion and "domesticating" Paul from radical interpretation (see, e.g., Carroll, "The Expansion of the Pauline Corpus").

9. Similarly Clabeaux, *A Lost Edition of the Letters of Paul*, 148: "The false trail that many textual critics have been following has been the attempt to explain how the Marcionite text infiltrated the O[ld] L[atin]—especially at a time when Marcion and the Marcionites were on the wane. The various hypotheses about a Latin Marcionite Pauline Corpus as the first OL Pauline Corpus are prime examples of the following of this false trail."

10. On various theories about the development of the Pauline corpus, see Gamble, *The New Testament Canon*, 36–41; Price, "The Evolution of the Pauline Canon"; Lovering, "The Collection, Redaction, and Early Circulation of the Corpus Paulinum."

11. Gamble Jr., *The Textual History of the Letter to the Romans*, 11.

12. Gamble, "The New Testament Canon: Recent Research," 283.

13. Gamble, "The New Testament Canon: Recent Research," 284. Clabeaux, *A Lost Edition of the Letters of Paul*, 147, notes a correspondence between the textual traditions that show the closest connection to the variant readings in Marcion's text (the "I-type" Old Latin witnesses,

and the witnesses to the older Syriac versions) and the places where the "Marcionite"—actually, chronological—order of the letters is attested (in the Latin Prologues and in the commentary of Ephrem Syrus). He follows Frede (*Altlateinische Paulus-Handschriften*, 167 and 178) in suggesting that the Old Latin version was based on a Greek text from Antioch in Syria, thus drawing together the two regions where we find the closest connection to Marcion's text, at least in the minor textual variants (see Clabeaux, 147–48). He casts appropriate doubt on the idea that Marcion got his NT texts in Rome.

14. Gamble, "The New Testament Canon: Recent Research," 284.
15. Clabeaux, *A Lost Edition of the Letters of Paul*, 148.
16. Gamble, "The New Testament Canon: Recent Research," 284; cf. Quispel, "Marcion and the Text of the New Testament," 351. On the date of P^{46}, see Pickering, "The Dating of the Chester Beatty-Michigan Codex."
17. This positive assessment of Marcion's testimony to an early text of Paul's letters appears already in Molitor, *Der Paulustext des hl. Ephräm*, 38*, and in Zuntz, *The Text of the Epistles*.
18. Clabeaux, *A Lost Edition of the Letters of Paul*, 5. His reconstruction of eighty-two passages of a pre-Marcion "lost edition" of Paul, based upon a systematic comparison of Apostolikon readings with parallels preserved in the catholic textual tradition, goes well beyond "a few pages," and correspondingly heightens the significance of the Apostolikon.
19. Dahl, "The Origin of the Earliest Prologues," 252. Cf. Clabeaux, *A Lost Edition of the Letters of Paul*, 4: "The text of Marcion's Pauline Corpus which can be constructed from the quotations made by Tertullian, Epiphanius, and Adamantius is the only sizable witness to the state of the Pauline Corpus in the first half of the second century"; similarly Zuntz, *The Text of the Epistles*, 265: "The two main streams of the [textual] tradition [of Paul's letters] emerge from that great common reservoir, the popular text of the second century. Marcion is its fullest extant witness."
20. In fact, nearly all of the different sequences of Paul's letters other than that found in the Apostolikon appear to be intended as ordered by length, from longest to shortest, with differences arising out of alternative systems of calculating length (Finegan, "The Original Form of the Pauline Collection"), or by breaking the collection into smaller subsets (such as multiple letters to the same community) arranged by the same principle (as in modern NTs, where letters to communities are listed separately from the letters to individuals, with each section arranged by length and Hebrews placed afterward due to its uncertain association with Paul). Like P^{46}, the Apostolikon did not include the Pastoral letters; unlike P^{46}, it also lacked the letter to the Hebrews, a non-Pauline addition to the catholic Pauline corpus.
21. Harnack maintained this view despite his knowledge of the same order appearing in some non-Marcionite collections, attributing such parallels to Marcionite influence on the Pauline corpus generally, perhaps even introducing Paul to the Syrian Christian environment where the parallel order is attested.

22. Lewis, *Studia Sinaitica*, 13–14. This ninth-century miscellany includes a (defective) stichometry of the Bible, and lists Paul's letters in the following order: Galatians, 1 Corinthians, 2 Corinthians, Romans, Hebrews, Colossians, Ephesians, Philippians, 1 Thessalonians, 2 Thessalonians, [1 Timothy], 2 Timothy, Titus, Philemon. The order through Romans matches that of the Apostolikon.

23. Ephrem Syrus, *Commentarii in Epistolas d. Pauli*. The original order was detected by Harris, *Four Lectures*, 21–22, and accepted by Zahn, "Das Neue Testament Theodors von Mopsuestia," 798–99. Harris noted a reference at the beginning of the commentary on Romans to previous discussions of Galatians and Corinthians (in that order), and at the beginning of that on Hebrews to prior discussion of Galatians, Corinthians, Romans, etc. (*quum nec in epistolis scriptis ad Galatos, ad Corinthios, et ad proximos quos viderat, id fecerit, neque in epistolis ad Romanos datis, et ad caeteros quos non viderat, tale quoddam egerit*; note that Ephrem's commentary includes Hebrews and the Pastorals, as well as 3 Corinthians, but not Philemon). The possibility that Ephrem's commentary was actually written on the Apostolikon was disproven by Frede, *Altlateinische Paulus-Handschriften*, 167–68, who found none of the identifying omissions of the Apostolikon in Ephrem's commentary, even though the latter does contain several unique readings in common with the text of the Apostolikon.

24. The Marcionite provenance of the prologues was arrived at independently by Donatien De Bruyne, "Prologues biblique," and Peter Corssen, "Zur Überlieferungsgeschichte des Römerbriefes." Harnack defended their Marcionite origin in "Der marcionitische Ursprung"; cf. Harnack, *Marcion*, 127*–48*. For the best survey of the textual basis for these prologues, see Dahl, "The Origin of the Earliest Prologues," and the discussion in Frede, *Altlateinische Paulus-Handschriften*, 165–78.

25. Frede, *Altlateinische Paulus-Handschriften*, 165–66, 295–97; Frede, "Die Ordnung der Paulusbriefe"; Schäfer, "Marius Victorinus und die marcionitischen Prologe," 11; Clabeaux, *A Lost Edition of the Letters of Paul*; Schmid, *Marcion und sein Apostolos*, 294–96.

26. Gamble, "The New Testament Canon: Recent Research," 283–84, discusses Dahl's arguments regarding the non-Marcionite provenance of the Prologues as the definitive piece of evidence.

27. Hilgenfeld, "Das Apostolikon Marcions."

28. Zahn, *Geschichte des Neutestamentlichen Kanons*, vol. 2, pt. 2, 409–529; see also vol. 1, pt. 2, 585–718.

29. Harnack, *Marcion*, 40*–254*.

30. Hilgenfeld, "Append. 2. Marcion's Text des Galaterbrief," 223ff.

31. Van Manen, "Marcion's brief van Paulus aan de Galatiërs."

32. K. Schäfer, "Die Überlieferung des altlateinische Galaterbriefes."

33. H. Raschke, "Der Römerbrief des Markion nach Epiphanius."

34. Schmid, *Marcion und sein Apostolos*.

35. See Clabeaux, *A Lost Edition of the Letters of Paul*, 36.

36. Schmid finds twelve passages of the Apostolikon quoted by Tertullian that differ from his quotations of the same passage in other works (Gal 2.9; 4.10;1 Cor 1.20; 3.21–22; 10.6; 15.50; 15.55; 2 Cor 5.4; 5.10;

Rom 8.11; 1 Thess 5.23; Col 1.21). He identifies a further eighteen passages explicitly identified by Tertullian as quotations (Gal 2.5; 3.7; 3.15–16 with 4.3; 4.22–26; 1 Cor 15.45 and 47; 15.49; 2 Cor 4.4; Rom 2.2ff.; 8.11 with 10.1–2; 11.33; 1 Thess 2.15; 2 Thess 1.8; the title of Ephesians; Eph 2.14; 2.20; 3.9; 6.2; Col 1.15–16). In another eleven passages, Tertullian either comments directly on the wording or repeats wording exactly. A further thirty-seven passages appear to be direct quotations without some sort of confirmation that the wording is exact (Schmid, *Marcion und sein Apostolos*, 98-149). Epiphanius presents more exact quotation practices, through his collection of excerpted, often abbreviated passages as *scholia*. Schmid finds fourteen cases where Epiphanius quotes the same passage twice with slightly different wording (161–67). He identifies eight instances where it is possible to compare a quotation of the Apostolikon with the corresponding passage in Epiphanius' own text of Paul, in three of which he surmises influence of the latter on the former (Schmid, *Marcion und sein Apostolos*, 176–81).

37. Gamble, *The Textual History of the Letter to the Romans*, 12.
38. Gamble, *The Textual History of the Letter to the Romans*, 12.
39. Such omissions were already known to Origen; see Bauernfeind, *Der Römerbrieftext des Origenes*.
40. On this phenomenon, see Dahl, "The Particularity of the Pauline Epistles." To explain why only three of the letters were generalized by removing specific addressees, Trobisch, *Paul's Letter Collection*, has proposed that the three must have circulated as an independent set (along with Hebrews) as an ecumenical or "catholic" text, alongside of the more familiar full set whose specific addressees were left in place. He suggests that Paul himself edited the two sets.
41. E.g., Dupont "Pour l'histoire de la doxologie," 7–8.
42. Gamble, "The New Testament Canon: Recent Research," 283, 286.
43. Richards, "The Codex and the Early Collection of Paul's Letters," has proposed that Paul kept a personal copy of his letters in a notebook (note the reference to the *membranas* in 2 Tim 4.13), and that the Pauline corpus derives from this notebook. This practice would have facilitated the incorporation of additional material prior to the formation of a circulating set.
44. Van Manen, "Marcion's brief van Paulus aan de Galatiërs," argued that the shorter text was the original form of the letter, and that the canonical version offers a post-Marcion catholic recension. But there are other alternatives, especially when we consider that Paul's letter to the Galatians *must have* been sent in multiple copies, since it presumably went to more than one city in the province of Galatia. Did he send out not just multiple copies, but slightly different versions, based on some knowledge of his audience?
45. Gaston, *Paul and the Torah*, 65.
46. Betz, *Galatians*, 137.
47. See Betz, *Galatians*, 138–39.
48. "It is Christ as the 'Son of God' [See Gal 1.16; 2.20; 4.4, 6] who makes adoption as 'sons' [See Gal 4.4–6; Rom 8.3f., 14–17, 29] available

through the gift of the Spirit [See Gal 3.1–5; 4.6; Rom 8.2–29; etc.]" (Betz, *Galatians*, 186).

49. Betz, *Galatians*, 156–57.

50. See Hurd Jr., *The Origin of I Corinthians*, 43–47; Jewett, "The Redaction of I Corinthians."

51. Furnish, *II Corinthians*, 29–30. Clement of Rome, writing to the Christians of Corinth in the late first or early second century, appears to know of only 1 Cor.

52. For a comprehensive survey of such theories, see Betz, *2 Corinthians 8 and 9: A Commentary*. See also Furnish, *II Corinthians*, 371–83, 429–33, and the literature cited there.

53. Betz, *2 Corinthians 8 and 9: A Commentary*, 141.

54. (1) in its current form, (2) without chapter 16, (3) without chapters 15–16, (4) Marcion's text. Our earliest papyri of Paul's letters are fragmentary in Romans, limiting their usefulness for comparison to the text of the Apostolikon. P^{46} preserves only 5.17–6.14, 8.15ff. The only other early manuscript is a student's writing exercise, P^{10}, which partially preserves 1.1–7.

55. See Gamble Jr., *The Textual History of the Letter to the Romans*, esp. 16–29, 96–124. After a review of the evidence and arguments for attributing the fourteen-chapter version of Romans to Marcion's editorial hand, Gamble concludes: "Summarily, the widely held view that the origin of the fourteen-chapter text of Romans is to be traced to Marcion, a view occasioned primarily by the testimony of Origen, has no firm foundation in the available evidence and must be set aside in favor of some other explanation. At best the evidence indicates that Marcion employed the short form of the text, and, given the wide use of this text during the same period, it must be assumed that Marcion took over a text of Romans which was already in circulation" (113).

56. *Biblical Essays*, 315–19. Gamble, *The Textual History of the Letter to the Romans*, 97, notes the problem with this scenario, that a removal of the specifically Roman content would entail cutting 15.14ff., not making a cut at 15.1.

57. Gamble, *The Textual History of the Letter to the Romans*, 36.

58. Smith, "Address and Destination of St. Paul's Epistle to the Romans"; "Unto Romans XV and XVI" (1901); "Unto Romans XV and XVI" (1902). Smith was reviving an observation made previously by Ernst Renan. Despite an irritatingly bombastic style, Smith raises serious issues about the ideological and rhetorical tensions between chapters 15 and 16 and the rest of Romans, and indeed between those chapters and Paul's letters generally. Smith demonstrated that the first half of chapter 15 is made up of an artificial string of isolated remarks, in some ways redundant to chapter 14, in other ways moving toward a very different perspective than found anywhere else in Paul's writings. W. H. Ryder had made a similar, less developed argument a few years earlier in "The Authorship of Romans XV, XVI."

59. Lake, *The Earlier Epistles of Saint Paul*, 362–65.

60. Knox, "A Note on the Text of Romans"; Knox, "Romans 15:14–33 and Paul's Apostolic Mission."

61. Knox, "A Note on the Text of Romans," 192. M. Jack Suggs, "'The Word is Near You,'" similarly suggested that Paul circulated this general letter as a formal statement in anticipation of his impending Jerusalem trip, addressing the sort of issues he would face there.

62. The words are *Gratis cum omnibus sanctis*; De Bruyne, "Le deux derniers chapitres de la lettre aux Romains"; De Bruyne, "La finale marcionite de la lettre aux Romains retrouvée."

63. Dodd, *The Epistle of Paul to the Romans*, 23.

64. Dodd, *The Epistle of Paul to the Romans*, 161ff.

65. Dodd, *The Epistle of Paul to the Romans*, 164, 163.

66. Refoulé, "Unité de l'Épitre aux Romains et Histoire du Salut"; Refoulé, "Cohérence ou Incohérence de Paul en Romains 9–11?"

67. See the succinct summary of this problem in Jewett, *The Thessalonian Correspondence*, 3–18. His analysis is vitiated by a misplaced certitude that a forgery could not occur close in time to an authentic letter. On the contrary, as his own argument for authenticity acknowledges, the rhetoric of 2 Thess 3.17 presupposes proximity in time, and even contemporaneity of rival "Pauline" letters.

68. Harnack, "Das Problem des zweiten Thessalonicherbriefes." A similar idea had been aired earlier by Hugo Grotius.

69. Ellis, "Paul and His Co-Workers."

70. On this subject, see esp. Collins, "A propos the Integrity of I Thes."

71. Pearson, "1 Thessalonians 2.13–16: A Deutero-Pauline Interpolation."

72. But see 1 Clem 36.2, 59.3. I leave aside the evidence of Ignatius here, due to the uncertainty that he predates Marcion.

73. Among those listed by Barth, *Ephesians*, 38, are some of the leading NT scholars of the twentieth century.

74. Barth, *Ephesians*, 10; cf. Ewald, *Die Briefe des Paulus*, 13–14.

75. In fact, Tertullian defends its identity as Ephesians not from Paul's words of address in the letter, but on the basis of its *titulus* (*Marc.* 5.17) or *praescriptam* (5.11) in his copy, as does Origen a generation later (Ewald, *Die Briefe des Paulus*, 14).

76. Lightfoot, *St. Paul's Epistles*; Abbott, *Critical and Exegetical Commentary*; Ewald, *Die Briefe des Paulus*, 13–20; Rutherford, "St. Paul's Epistle to the Laodiceans."

77. Ewald, *Die Briefe des Paulus*, 14.

78. Moule, *Ephesians*, 25; J. Rutherford, "St. Paul's Epistle to the Laodiceans," *Expository Times* 19 (1907/8) 311–14.

79. See Barth and Blanke, *Colossians*, 122–25.

Bibliography

Aalders, G. J. D. "Tertullian's Quotations from St. Luke." *Mnemosyne* 5 (1937) 241–82.
Abbott, T. K. *Critical and Exegetical Commentary on the Epistles to the Ephesians and to the Colossians.* Edinburgh: Clark, 1897/1974.
Adversus Marcionem. Eds. E. Kroymann, *CCSL* I, vol. 1 (Turnhout, 1954); E. Evans (Oxford, 1960); C. Moreschini (Milan, 1971); and R. Braun (Paris, 1990–94).
Amphoux, Christian-Bernard. "La révision marcionite du 'Notre Père' de Luc (11,2-4) et sa place dans l'histoire du texte." Pp. 105–21 in *Recherches sur l'histoire de la Bible latine.* Eds. R. Gryson and P.-M. Bogaert. Louvain-la-Neuve: Faculté de Théologie, 1987.
_____. "Les premières editions de Luc, I. Le texte de Luc 5." *Ephemerides theologicae Lovanienses* 67 (1991) 312–27.
Annand, Rupert. "Papias and the Four Gospels." *Scottish Journal of Theology* 9,1 (1956) 46–62.
Arneth, M. *Über die Bekanntschaft Marzions mit unserem Canon des neuen Bundes, insbesondere über das Evangelium desselben.* Linz, 1809.
Baarda, T. "Marcion's Text of Gal 1:1. Concerning the Reconstruction of the First Verse of the Marcionite Corpus Paulinum." *Vigiliae Christianae* 42 (1988) 236-56.
Bacon, B. W. "The Anti-Marcionite Prologue to John." *Journal of Biblical Literature* 49 (1930) 43–54.
Baird, William. *History of New Testament Research, I: From Deism to Tübingen.* Minneapolis: Fortress, 1992.
Bakhuyzen, W. H. van de Sande. *Der Dialog des Adamantius. ΠΕΡΙ ΤΗΣ ΕΙΣ ΘΕΟΝ ΟΡΘΗΣ ΠΙΣΤΕΩΣ.* Leipzig: J. C. Hinrichs, 1901.
Balás, David L. "Marcion Revisited: A 'Post-Harnack' Perspective." Pp. 95–108 in *Texts and Testaments: Critical Essays on the Bible and Early Church Fathers.* Ed. W. Eugene March. San Antonio: Trinity University Press, 1980.
Barnes, Timothy D. "The Date of Ignatius." *Expository Times* 120 (2008) 119–30.
Barnikol, Ernst. *Die Entstehung der Kirche im zweiten Jahrhundert und die Zeit Marcions.* 2d ed. Kiel: Walter Mühlau Verlag, 1933.
_____. "The Non-Pauline Origin of the Parallelism of the Apostles Peter and Paul. Galatians 2:7–8." *Journal of Higher Criticism* 5 (1998) 285–300.

———. *Philipper 2. Der marcionitische Ursprung des Mythos-Satzes Phil. 2,6–7*. Kiel: Mühlau, 1932.

———. "Römer 13. Der nichtpaulinische Ursprung der absoluten Obrigkeitsbejahrung von Römer 13,1–7." Pp. 65–133 in *Studien zum Neuen Testament und zur Patristik. Erich Klostermann zum 90. Geburtstag dargebracht*. Berlin: Akademie Verlag, 1961.

Barth, Markus. *Ephesians: Introduction, Translation, and Commentary on Chapters 1–3*. Garden City: Doubleday, 1974.

Barth, Markus, and Helmut Blanke. *Colossians*. New York: Doubleday, 1994.

Barton, John. *Holy Writings, Sacred Text: The Canon in Early Christianity*. Louisville: Westminster John Knox Press, 1997.

———. "Marcion Revisited." Pp. 341–54 in *The Canon Debate*. Ed. Lee McDonald and James Sanders. Peabody: Hendrickson, 2002.

Bauernfeind, O. *Der Römerbrieftext des Origenes nach dem Codex von der Goltz*. T. U. 44.3. Leipzig: 1923.

Baur, Ferdinand Christian. *Das Markusevangelium nach seinem Ursprung und Charakter, nebst einem Anhang über das Evangelium Marcion's*. Tübingen: 1851.

———. "Der Ursprung und Charakter des Lukas-Evangeliums." *Theologische Jahrbücher* 5 (1846) 413–615.

———. *Kritische Untersuchungen über die kanonischen Evangelien*. Tübingen: 1847.

———. *Paul, the Apostle of Jesus Christ*. Vol. 1. London: Williams and Norgate, 1876.

Becker, Adam H., and Annette Yoshiko Reed, eds. *The Ways that Never Parted: Jews and Christians in Late Antiquity and the Early Middle Ages*. Minneapolis: Fortress, 2007.

BeDuhn, Jason. "Biblical Antitheses, Adda, and the Acts of Archelaus." Pp. 131–47 in *Frontiers of Faith: The Christian Encounter with Manichaeism in the Acts of Archelaus*. Ed. J. BeDuhn and P. Mirecki. Leiden: Brill, 2007.

———. "The Myth of Marcion as Redactor: The Evidence of 'Marcion's' Gospel against an Assumed Marcionite Redaction." *Annali di storia dell'esegesi* 29 (2012) 21–48.

Beeson, Charles Henry. *Hegemonius: Acta Archelai*. Leipzig: J. C. Hinrichs, 1906.

Bellinzoni, Arthur J. "The Gospel of Luke in the Apostolic Fathers: An Overview." Pp. 45–66 in *Trajectories through the New Testament and the Apostolic Fathers*. Ed. Andrew Gregory and Christopher Tuckett. Oxford University Press, 2005.

———. "The Gospel of Luke in the Second Century CE." Pp. 59–76 in *Literary Studies in Luke-Acts: Essays in Honor of Joseph B. Tyson*. Ed. Richard P. Thompson and Thomas E. Phillips. Atlanta: Mercer University Press, 1998.

Bertholdt, L. *Historisch-kritische Einleitung in sämmtliche kanonische und apokryphische Schriften des alten und neuen Testaments.* Vol 3. Erlangen: 1813.
Bettenson, Henry. *Documents of the Christian Church.* 2d ed. Oxford: Oxford University Press, 1963.
Betz, Hans Dieter. *2 Corinthians 8 and 9: A Commentary on Two Administrative Letters of the Apostle Paul.* Philadelphia: Fortress, 1985.
———. *Galatians.* Philadelphia: Fortress Press, 1979.
Birdsall, J. N. Review of Clabeaux, *A Lost Edition of the Letters of Paul. Journal of Theological Studies* 41 (1990) 631–34.
Blackman, E. C. *Marcion and His Influence.* London: SPCK, 1948.
Blanchard, Monica J., and Robin Darling Young. *Eznik of Kolb: On God.* Leuven: Peeters, 1998.
Blass, F. *Philology of the Gospels.* London: MacMillan, 1898.
Bolten, J. A. *Der Bericht des Lucas von Jesu dem Messia.* Altona: 1796.
Bovon, François. *Luke.* Minneapolis: Fortress Press, 2002-2012.
Brakke, David. "Canon Formation and Social Conflict in Fourth-Century Egypt: Athanasius of Alexandria's Thirty-Ninth *Festal Letter.*" *Harvard Theological Review* 87 (1994) 395–419.
Broadhead, Edwin K. *Jewish Ways of Following Jesus.* Tübingen: Mohr Siebeck, 2010.
Bruce, F. F. "Some Thoughts on the Beginning of the New Testament Canon." *Bulletin of the John Rylands University Library of Manchester* 65,2 (1983) 37–60.
Bucher, V. F. "A Marcionite Reading in Ephrem's Commentary on the Pauline Epistles." *Bulletin of the Bezan Club* 5 (1928) 37–38.
Buchheit, Vinzenz. *Tyrannii Rufini Librorum Adamntii Origenis Adversus Haereticos Interpretatio.* München: Wilhelm Fink Verlag, 1966.
Bultmann, Rudolf. "Glossen im Römerbrief." *TLZ* 7 (1947) 197–202.
Bundy, David. "Marcion and the Marcionites in Early Syriac Apologetics." *Le Muséon* 101 (1988) 21–32.
———. "The Anti-Marcionite Commentary on the Lucan Parables (Pseudo Ephrem A): Images in Tension." *Le Muséon* 103 (1990) 111–23.
Burkitt, F. C. "The Exordium of Marcion's Antitheses." *Journal of Theological Studies* 30 (1929) 279–80.
Cadbury, Henry J. "Four Features of Lucan Style." Pp. 87–102 in *Studies in Luke-Acts: Essays presented in honor of Paul Schubert.* Ed. Keck and Martyn. London: SPCK, 1968.
———. "A Possible Case of Lukan Authorship (John 7:53–8:11)." *Harvard Theological Review* 10 [1917] 237–44.
———. Review of *Marcion and the New Testament* by John Knox. *Journal of Biblical Literature* 62 (1943) 126–27.
Carroll, Kenneth L. "The Expansion of the Pauline Corpus." *Journal of Biblical Literature* 72 (1953) 230–37.

Carruth, S., and A. Garsky. "The Database of the International Q Project: Q 11:2b–4." Pp. 4–18 in *Documenta Q*. Ed. S. D. Anderson. Leuven: 1996.

Casey, Robert P. "The Armenian Marcionites and the Diatessaron." *Journal of Biblical Literature* 57 (1938) 185–94.

Casson, Lionel. *Ships and Seamanship in the Ancient World*. 2d ed. Baltimore: The Johns Hopkins University Press, 1995.

Chapman, Stephen. "How the Biblical Canon Began: Working Models and Open Questions." Pp. 29–51 in M. Finkelberg and G. G. Stroumsa, *Homer, the Bible, and Beyond: Literary and Religious Canons in the Ancient World*. Leiden: Brill, 2003.

Clabeaux, John J. "Abraham in Marcion's Gospel and Epistles: Marcion and the Jews." Pp. 69–92 in *When Judaism and Christianity Began: Essays in Memory of Anthony J. Saldarini*. Ed. Alan J. Avery-Peck et al. Leiden: Brill, 2004.

———. *A Lost Edition of the Letters of Paul: A Reassessment of the Text of the Pauline Corpus Attested by Marcion*. Washington: Catholic Biblical Association of America, 1989.

Clivaz, Claire. "The Angel and the Sweat Like 'Drops of Blood' (Lk 22:43–44): P69 and *f*13." *Harvard Theological Studies* 98 (2005) 419–40.

Collins, Raymond F. "A propos the Integrity of I Thes." *Ephemerides theologicae lovanienses* 55 (1979) 67–106.

Conybeare, F. C. "Ein Zeugnis Ephräms über das Fehlen von c. 1 und 2 im Texte des Lucas." *Zeitschrift für die neutestamentliche Wissenschaft und die Kunde des Urchristentums* 3 (1902) 192–97.

Conzelmann, Hans. *Theology of St. Luke*. New York: Harper, 1960.

Cope, L. "1 Cor 11:2–16: One Step Further." *Journal of Biblical Literature* 97 (1978) 435–36.

———. "First Corinthians 8–10: Continuity or Contradiction?" *Anglican Theological Review Supplements* 11 (1990) 114–23.

Corrodi, H. *Versuch einer Beleuchtung der Geschichte des jüdischen und christlichen Bibel-kanons*. Vol. 2. Halle: 1792.

Corssen, Peter. "Zur Überlieferungsgeschichte des Römerbriefes." *Zeitschrift für die neutestamentliche Wissenschaft* 10 (1909) 1–45, 97–102.

Cosgrove, C. H. "Justin Martyr and the Emerging Christian Canon: Observations on the Purpose and Destination of the Dialogue with Trypho." *Vigiliae Christianae* 36 (1982) 209–32.

Couchoud, Paul-Louis. *The Creation of Christ: An Outline of the Beginnings of Christianity*. Vol. 2. Trans. C. Bradlaugh Bonner. London: Watts & Co., 1939 [*Le mystère de Jésus*. Paris: Rieder, 1924].

———. "Is Marcion's Gospel One of the Synoptics?" Trans. Joan Ferro. *Hibbert Journal* 1936: 265–77.

———. "La première édition de S. Paul." *Revue de l'Histoire des Religions* 83 (1926) 242–63.

Cramer, John Anthony. *Catenae in Sancti Pauli Epistolas ad Galatas, Ephesios, Philippenses, Colessenses, Thessalonicenses.* Oxford. 1842.

Dahl, Nils A. "The Origin of the Earliest Prologues to the Pauline Letters." *Semeia* 12 (1978) 233–77.

———. "The Particularity of the Pauline Epistles as a Problem in the Ancient Church." Pp. 261–71 in *Neotestamentica et Patristica: Freundesgabe O. Cullmann.* Leiden: Brill, 1962.

Dassmann, E. *Der Stachel im Fleisch: Paulus in frühchristlichen Literatur bis Irenaeus.* Munster: Aschendorff, 1979.

De Bruyne, Donatien. "Prologues bibliques d'origin Marcionite." *Revue Bénédictine* 24 (1907) 1–14.

———. "Le deux derniers chapitres de la lettre aux Romains." *Revue bénédictine* 25 (1908) 423–30.

———. "La finale marcionite de la lettre aux Romains retrouvée." *Revue bénédictine* 28 (1911) 133–42.

———. "Le plus anciens prologues latins des Evangiles." *Revue Bénèdictine* 40 (1928) 193–214.

Delobel, Joël. "Extra-Canonical Sayings of Jesus: Marcion and Some 'Non-received' Logia." Pp. 105–16 in *Gospel Traditions in the Second Century.* Ed. W. Petersen. Notre Dame: University of Notre Dame Press, 1989.

———. "The Lord's Prayer in the Textual Tradition: A Critique of Recent Theories and Their Views on Marcion's Role." Pp. 293–309 in *The New Testament in Early Christianity.* Ed. Jean-Marie Sevrin, Leuven: Peeters, 1989.

Delafosse, Henri. *Le Ecrits de saint Paul 1, L'épître aux romains.* Paris: Rieder et Cie, 1926.

———. *Le Ecrits de saint Paul 2, La Première épître aux Corinthiens.* Paris: Rieder et Cie, 1926.

Dinkler, E. *Signum Crucis: Aufsätze zum Neuen testament und zur christlichen Archäologie.* Tübingen: Mohr Siebeck, 1967.

Dodd, C. H. *The Epistle of Paul to the Romans.* Rev. ed. London: Collins, 1959.

Dodge, Bayard. *The Fihrist of al-Nadim.* New York: Columbia University Press, 1970.

Drijvers, Hans. "Christ as Warrior and Merchant: Aspects of Marcion's Christology." *Studia Patristica* 21 (1989) 73–85.

———. "Marcion's Reading of Gal. 4,8: Philosophical Background and Influence on Manichaeism." Pp. 339–48 in *A Green Leaf: Papers in Honour of Professor Jes P. Asmussen.* Ed. J. Duchesne-Guillemin et al. Leiden: Brill, 1988.

Dupont, Jacques. "Pour l'histoire de la doxologie finale de l'épître aux Romains." *Revue Bénédictine* 58 (1948) 3–22.

Eckart, K.-G. "Der zweite echte Brief des Apostels Paulus an die Thessalonischer." *Zeitschrift für Theologie und Kirche* 58 (1961) 30–44.

Egan, George. *Saint Ephrem: An Exposition of the Gospel.* CSCO 291–92. Louvain: Peeters, 1968.

———. *An Analysis of the Biblical Quotations of Ephrem in 'An Exposition of the Gospel' (Armenian Version).* Louvain: Peeters, 1983.

Ehrman, Bart. *The Apostolic Fathers.* 2 vols. Loeb Classical Library 24 & 25. Cambridge: Harvard University Press, 2003.

———. "Jesus and the Adultress." *New Testament Studies* 34 (1988) 24–44.

———. *Orthodox Corruption of Scripture: The Effect of Early Christological Controversies on the Text of the New Testament.* New York: Oxford University Press, 1993.

Eichhorn, Johann Gottfried. *Einleitung in das Neue Testament.* Vol. 1. Leipzig: Weidmann, 1804, 1820.

Eldridge, Lawrence A. *The Gospel Text of Epiphanius of Salamis.* Salt Lake City: University of Utah Press, 1969.

Ellis, E. Earle. "Paul and His Co-Workers." *New Testament Studies* 17 (1970–71) 437–52.

Ephrem Syrus. *Commentarii in Epistolas d. Pauli.* Venice: Sanctus Lazarus, 1893.

Evans, C. F. "The New Testament in the Making." Pp. 232–83 in *Cambridge History of the Bible. Volume 1: From the Beginning to Jerome.* Cambridge: Cambridge University Press 1970.

Evans, E. "Tertullian's Commentary on the Marcionite Gospel." Pp. 699–707 in *Studia Evangelica: Papers presented to the International Congress on "The Four Gospels in 1957" held at Christ Church, Oxford, 1957.* Ed. Kurt Aland, et al. Berlin: Akademie Verlag, 1959.

Ewald, P. *Die Briefe des Paulus an die Epheser, Kolosser und Philemon.* Leipzig: Deichert, 1905.

Farmer, William. "The Present State of the Synoptic Problem." Pp. 11–36 in Richard P. Thompson and Thomas E. Phillips, *Literary Studies in Luke-Acts: Essays in Honor of Joseph B. Tyson.* Macon: Mercer University Press, 1998.

Farmer, William, Denis Farkasfalvy, and Harold W. Attridge. *The Formation of the New Testament: An Ecumenical Approach.* New York: Paulist Press, 1983.

Fee, G. D. *The First Epistle to the Corinthians.* Grand Rapids: Eerdmans, 1987.

Finegan, J. "The Original Form of the Pauline Collection." *Harvard Theological Review* 49 (1956) 85–104.

———. *Hidden Records of the Life of Jesus.* Philadelphia: Pilgrim Press, 1969.

Fitzmyer, Joseph. *The Gospel according to Luke.* Garden City: Doubleday, 1981–85.

Frede, Hermann J. *Altlateinische Paulus-Handschriften.* Freiburg: Herder, 1964.

———. "Die Ordnung der Paulusbriefe." Pp. 290–303 in H. J. Frede, *Vetus Latina. Die Reste der Altlateinischen Bibel 24.2: Epistulae ad Philippenses et ad Colossenses.* Freiburg: Herder, 1969.

Fredriksen, Paula. *Augustine and the Jews*. New Haven: Yale University Press, 2008.
Freudenberger, R. "Zum Text der zweiten Vaterunserbitte." *New Testament Studies* 15 (1968–69) 419–32.
Friedrich, G. "1 Thessalonischer 5,1–11, der apologetische Einschub eines Späteren." *Zeitschrift für Theologie und Kirche* 70 (1973) 288–315.
Friedrichsen, Timothy A. "The Matthew-Luke Agreements against Mark." Pp. 335–91 in *L'Évangile du Luc. The Gospel of Luke*. Ed. F. Neirynck. 2d ed. Leuven: Leuven University Press/Peeters, 1989.
Furnish, V. P. *II Corinthians*. Garden City: Doubleday, 1984.
Gamble, Harry Y. *The New Testament Canon: Its Making and Meaning*. Philidelphia: Fortress Press, 1985.
———. "The New Testament Canon: Recent Research and the Status Quaestionis." Pp. 267–94 in *The Canon Debate*. Ed. L. M. McDonald and J. A. Sanders. Peabody: Hendrickson, 2002.
———. *The Textual History of the Letter to the Romans: A Study in Textual and Literary Criticism*. Grand Rapids: Eerdmans, 1977.
Gaston, Lloyd. *Paul and the Torah*. Vancouver: University of British Columbia Press, 1987.
Gieseler, J. C. L. Review of *Das Evangelium Marcions* by A. Hahn. In *Hallische Allgemeine Literatur-Zeitung*, 1823, 225ff.
———. *Historisch-kritischer Versuch über die Entstehung und die frühesten Schicksale der schriftlichen Evangelien*. Leipzig: 1818.
Graef, H. C. *St. Gregory of Nyssa: The Lord's Prayer, The Beatitudes*. ACW 18. New York: Newman, 1954.
Grant, F. C. "Was the Author of John Dependent on the Gospel of Luke?" *Journal of Biblical Literature* 56 (1937) 285–307.
Grant, Robert M. *The Formation of the New Testament*. New York: Harper & Row, 1965.
———. *Jesus after the Gospels: The Christ of the Second Century*. Louisville: Westminster-John Knox, 1990.
———. *The Letter and the Spirit*. London: SPCK, 1957.
———. "The New Testament Canon." Pp. 284–308 in *Cambridge History of the Bible. Volume 1: From the Beginnings to Jerome*. Cambridge: Cambridge University Press, 1970.
Gratz, P. A. *Kritische Untersuchungen über Marcions Evangelium*. Tübingen: 1818.
Green, H. B. "Matthew, Clement and Luke." *Journal of Theological Studies* 40 (1989) 1–25.
Gregory, Andrew. *The Reception of Luke and Acts in the Period before Irenaeus*. Tübingen: Mohr Siebeck, 2003.
Gressmann, H. *Vom Reichen Mann und armen Lazarus. Eine literargeschichtliche Studie*. Berlin: 1918.
Griesbach, J. J. *Curae in historiam textus Graeci epistolarum Paulinarum*. Jena: 1799.

Gundry, R. H. "Matthean Foreign Bodies in Agreements of Luke with Matthew against Mark: Evidence that Luke used Matthew." Pp. 1467–95 in *The Four Gospels 1992: Festschrift F. Nierynck*. Vol. 2. Ed. F. Van Segbroeck et al. Leuven, 1992.

Hagen, W. H. "Two Deutero-Pauline Glosses in Romans 6." *Expository Times* 92 (1981) 364–67.

Hahn, A. *Das Evangelium Marcions in seiner ursprüngliche Gestalt*. Königsberg: 1823.

Hahneman, Geoffrey Mark. *The Muratorian Fragment and the Development of the Canon*. Oxford: Clarendon Press, 1992.

———. "The Muratorian Fragment and the Origins of the New Testament Canon." Pp. 405–15 in *The Canon Debate*. Ed. Lee McDonald and James Sanders. Peabody: Hendrickson, 2002.

Harnack, Adolf von. "Das Problem des zweiten Thessalonicherbriefes." *Sitzungsbericht der Preussischen Akademie der Wissenschaft zu Berlin, phil.-hist. Klasse* 31 (1910) 560–78.

———. "Der marcionitische Ursprung der ältesten Vulgata-Prologe zu den Paulus-briefen." *Zeitschrift für die neutestamentliche Wissenschaft* 24 (1925) 204–18.

———. *Marcion: Das Evangelium vom Fremden Gott*. 2d ed. Leipzig: J. C. Hinrichs, 1924 [English: *Marcion: The Gospel of the Alien God*. Tran. John E. Steely and Lyle D. Bierm. Durham: Labyrinth Press, 1990].

———. *Neue Studien zu Marcion*. Leipzig: Hinrichs, 1923.

———. "Über I. Kor. 14,32ff. und Rom. 16,25ff. nach der ältesten Überlieferung und der Marcionitischen Bibel." Sitzungsberichte der Preussischen Akademie des Wissenschaft, 1919.

Harris, J. R. *Four Lectures on the Western Text of the New Testament*. London: C. J. Clay, 1894.

———. "New Points of View in Textual Criticism." *Expositor* 7 (1914) 318–20.

Harrison, P. N. *Paulines and Pastorals*. London: Villiers, 1964.

———. *Polycarp's Two Epistles to the Philippians*. Cambridge: Cambridge University Press, 1936.

Hays, Christopher M. "Marcion vs. Luke: A Response to the *Plädoyer* of Matthias Klinghardt." *Zeitschrift für die Neutestamentliche Wissenschaft* 99 (2008) 213–32.

Heard, R. G. "The Old Gospel Prologues." *Journal of Theological Studies* n.s. 6 (1955) 1–16.

Higgins, A. J. B. "The Latin Text of Luke in Marcion and Tertullian." *Vigilae Christianae* 5 (1951) 1–42.

Hilgenfeld, Adolf. "Append. 2. Marcion's Text des Galaterbrief." *Der Galaterbrief* (Leipzig 1852) 223ff.

———. "Das Apostolikon Marcions." *Zeitschrift für die historische Theologie* 25 (1855) 426–84.

_____. "Das Marcionitische Evangelium und seine neueste Bearbeitung," *Theologische Jahrbücher* 12 (1853) 192–244.

_____. *Kritische Untersuchungen über die Evangelien Justins, der Klementinischen Homilien und Marcions*. Halle: 1850.

Hoffmann, R. Joseph. *Marcion: On the Restitution of Christianity*. Chico: Scholars Press, 1984.

Holl, K., and J. Dummer, eds. *Panarion*. GCS 31. Berlin: Akademie Verlag, 1980.

Horn, F. W. "1 Korinther 15,56—Ein exegetischer Stachel." *Zeitschrift für die neutestamentliche Wissenschaft* 82 (1991) 88–105.

Hug, J. L. *Einleitung in die Schriften des Neuen Testaments*. Stuttgart: 1821, 1847.

Hurd Jr., John C. *The Origin of I Corinthians*. Macon: Mercer University Press, 1983.

Jackson, Howard. "The Setting and Sectarian Provenance of the Fragment of the 'Celestial Dialogue' Preserved by Origen from Celsus's Ἀληθὴς Λόγος." *Harvard Theological Review* 85 (1992) 273–305.

Jewett, Robert. "The Redaction of I Corinthians and the Trajectory of the Pauline School." *Journal of the American Academy of Religion*. Supplement 44.4 (1978) 389–444.

_____. *The Thessalonian Correspondence: Pauline Rhetoric and Millenarian Piety*. Philadelphia: Fortress, 1986.

Joly, R. *Le dossier d'Ignace d'Antioche*. Brussels: Editions de l'Université de Bruxelles, 1979.

Kallas, J. "Romans xiii.1–7: An Interpolation." *New Testament Studies* 11 (1965) 365–74.

Käsemann, Ernst. *Commentary on Romans*. Grand Rapids: Eerdmanns, 1980.

Kelber, *The Oral and the Written Gospel*. Philadelphia: Fortress Press, 1983.

Keck, L. E. "The Post-Pauline Interpretation of Jesus' Death in Rom 5,6–7." Pp. 237–48 in *Theologia Crucis—Signum Crucis: Festschrift für Erich Dinkler*. Ed. C. Andresen and G. Klein. Tübingen: Mohr Siebeck, 1979.

Kinzig, Wolfram. "Καινη διαθήκη: The Title of the New Testament in the Second and Third Centuries." *Journal of Theological Studies* 45 (1994) 519–44.

Kittel, G. and G. Friedrich. *Theological Dictionary of the New Testament*. Grand Rapids: Eerdmans Publishing, 1971.

Klijn, A. F. J. "Matthew 11:25/Luke 10:21." Pp. 3–14 in *New Testament Textual Criticism: Its Significance for Exegesis*. Eds. E. J. Epp and G. D. Fee. Oxford: Clarendon Press, 1981.

Kline, L. L. *The Sayings of Jesus in the Pseudo-Clementine Homilies*. Missoula: Scholars Press, 1975.

Klinghardt, Matthias. "The Marcionite Gospel and the Synoptic Problem: A New Suggestion." *Novum Testamentum* 50 (2008) 1–27.

———. "Markion vs. Lukas: Plädoyer für die Wiederaufnahme eines alten Falles." *NTS* (52 (2006) 484–513.

Koester, Helmut. "From Kerygma to Written Gospels." *New Testament Studies* 35 (1989) 361–81.

———. *Ancient Christian Gospels*. Philadelphia: Trinity Press International, 1990.

Köstlin, Karl Reinhold. *Der Ursprung und die Komposition der synoptischen Evangelien*. Stuttgart: 1853.

Knox, John. *Marcion and the New Testament: An Essay in the Early History of the Canon*. Chicago: University of Chicago Press, 1942 [reprinted by AMS, 1980].

———. "A Note on the Text of Romans." *New Testament Studies* 2 (1955/56) 191–93.

———. "On the Vocabulary of Marcion's Gospel." *Journal of Biblical Literature* 58 (1939) 193–201.

———. "Romans 15:14–33 and Paul's Apostolic Mission." *Journal of Biblical Literature* 83 (1964) 1–11.

LaCapra, Dominick. *History and Criticism*. Ithaca, NY: Cornell University Press, 1985.

Lake, Kirsopp. *The Earlier Epistles of Saint Paul*. London: 1911.

Lagrange, Marie-Joseph. "Les prologues prétendus marcionites." *Revue biblique* 35 (1926) 161–73.

———. *Saint Paul épitre aux Romains*. Paris: Librairie Victor Lecoffre, 1916.

Lampe, Peter. *From Paul to Valentinus: Christians at Rome in the First Two Centuries*. Minneapolis: Fortress Press, 2003.

Leaney, R. "The Lucan Text of the Lord's Prayer (Lk XI,2–4)." *Novum Testamentum* 1 (1956) 103–11.

Lefort, L. "Fragments bibliques en dialecte akhmimique." *Le Museon* 66 (1953) 1–30.

———. "Fragments de S. Luc en akhmimique." *Le Museon* 62 (1949) 199–205.

Lewis, A. S. *Studia Sinaitica 1, Catalogue of the Syriac MSS*. London: 1894.

Lietzmann, H. *Zeitschrift der Neutestamentliche Wissenschaft* 33 (1934).

Lightfoot, J. B., et al. *Apostolic Fathers*. 2d ed. Grand Rapids: Baker Book House, 1992.

———. *Biblical Essays*. London: Macmillan, 1893 [Eugene: Wipf & Stock 2005].

———. *St. Paul's Epistles to the Colossians and to Philemon*. London: Macmillan, 1875.

Lindemann, A. *Paulus im ältesten Christentum: Das Bild des Apostels und die Rezeption der paulinischen Theologie in der frühchristlichen Literatur bis Markion*. Tübingen: Mohr-Siebeck, 1979.

Lipsius, R. A. *Zur Quellenkritik des Epiphanios.* Vienna: Braumüller, 1865.
Löffler, J. F. C. "Marcionem Pauli epistolas et Lucae Evangelium adulterasse dubitaturi." *Commentationes Theologicae* 1 (1794) 180–218.
Loisy, Alfred. "Marcion's Gospel: A Reply." *Hibbert Journal* 34 (1936) 378–87.
Lovering, E. H. "The Collection, Redaction, and Early Circulation of the Corpus Paulinum." Ph.D. diss., Southern Methodist University, 1988.
Lüdemann, Gerd. "The History of Earliest Christianity in Rome." *Journal of Higher Criticism* 2 (1995) 112–41.
Lührmann, Dieter. *Die Redaktion der Logienquelle.* Neukirchen-Vluyn: Neukirchener Verlag, 1969.
Lyonnet, S. *Les Origines de la Version Arménienne et le Diatessaron.* Rome: Pontificio istituto biblico, 1950.
MacDonald, Dennis R. "A Conjectural Emendation of 1 Cor 15:31–32: Or the Case of the Misplaced Lion Fight," *Harvard Theological Review* 73 (1980) 265–76.
Magne, J. "La réception de la variante 'Vienne ton Esprit Saint sur nous et qu'il nous purifie' (Lc 11,2) et l'origine des épiclèses du baptême et du 'Notre Père.'" *Ephemerides Liturgicae* 102 (1988) 81–106.

———. "Les paroles sur la coupe." Pp. 485–90 in *Logia: Les paroles de Jésus: Mémorial Joseph Coppens.* Ed. Joël Delobel. Leuven: Peeters, 1982.
Mahé, Jean-Pierre. "Tertullien et l'epistula Marcionis." *RSR* 45 (1971) 358–71.
Mai, Angelo. *Novae Patrum Bibliothecae.* Vol. 4. Roma, 1847.
Manson, T. W. "St. Paul's Letter to the Romans—and Others" (1962). Pp. 3–15 reprinted in *The Romans Debate.* Rev. ed. Ed. K. P. Donfried. Peabody: Hendrickson, 1991.
Matson, M. A. *In Dialogue with Another Gospel? The Influence of the Fourth Gospel on the Passion Narrative of the Gospel of Luke.* Atlanta: Scholars Press, 2001.
May, Gerhard. "Der 'Schiffsreeder' Markion." *Studia Patristica* 21 (1989) 142–53.

———. "Marcion in Contemporary Views: Results and Open Questions." *Second Century* 6 (1987/88) 129–51.
McDonald, Lee M. *The Formation of the Christian Biblical Canon.* Peabody: Hendrickson, 1995.
McGiffert, Arthur Cushman. *The Apostles' Creed.* New York: C. Scribner's, 1902.
McLachlan, H. *St. Luke Evangelist and Historian.* London: Sherratt and Hughes, 1912.
McLoughlin, S. "Les accords mineurs Mt-Lc contre Mc et le problem synoptique. Vers la théorie des deuz sources." *Ephemerides Theologicae Lovanienses* 43 (1967) 17–40.

Meinhold, Peter. "Polykarpos." *Paulys Realencyclopädie der classischen Altertumswissenchaften* 42 (1952) 1685–86.

Metzger, Bruce. *The Canon of the New Testament: Its Origin, Development, and Significance*. Oxford: Clarendon Press, 1987.

———. *A Textual Commentary on the Greek New Testament*. London: United Bible Societies, 1975.

Mindle, Wilhelm. "Die Herkunft der 'marcionitischen' Prologe zu den paulinischen Briefen," *Zeitschrift für die neutestamentliche Wissenschaft* 24 (1925) 56–77.

Minear, Paul S. "Luke's Use of the Birth Stories." Pp. 111–30 in *Studies in Luke-Acts: Essays presented in honor of Paul Schubert*. Ed. Keck & Martyn. London: SPCK, 1968.

Mitchell, C. W., S. *Ephraim's Prose Refutations of Mani, Marcion and Bardaisan*. London: Williams and Norgate, 1921.

Molitor, Joseph. *Der Paulustext des hl. Ephräm*. Rome: Papstliches Bibelinstitut, 1938.

Moll, Sebastian. *The Arch-Heretic Marcion*. Tübingen: Mohr-Siebeck, 2010.

———. "Three against Tertullian: The Second Tradition about Marcion's Life." *Journal of Theological Studies* n.s. 59 (2008) 169–80.

———. "Marcion: A New Perspective on his Life, Theology, and Impact." *Expository Times* 121 (2010) 281–86.

Moule, C. F. D. *The Birth of the New Testament*. 3d ed. San Francisco: Harper & Row, 1982.

Mühlenberg, Ekkehard. "Marcion's Jealous God." Pp. 93-113 in *Disciplina Nostra. Essays in Memory of Robert F. Evans*. Ed. D. F. Winslow. Philadelphia: Fortress, 1979.

Murphy-O'Connor, J. "Interpolations in 1 Corinthians." *Catholic Biblical Quarterly* 48 (1986) 81–94.

Neander, A. *Genetische Entwickelung der vornehmsten gnostischen Systeme*. Berlin: 1818.

Nielsen, Charles. "The Epistle to Diognetus: Its Date and Relationship to Marcion." *Anglican Theological Review* 52 (1970) 77–91.

Nock, A. D. "The Gild of Zeus Hypsistos." *Harvard Theological Review* 29 (1936) 39–88.

Olshausen, H. *Die Echtheit der vier canonischen Evangelien aus der Geschichte der zwei Jahrhunderte erwiesen: ein Versuch*. Königsberg: 1823.

Osburn, Caroll D. *The Text of the Apostolos in Epiphanius of Salamis*. Atlanta: Society of Biblical Literature, 2004.

Parker, D. C. *The Living Text of the Gospels*. Cambridge: Cambridge University Press, 1997.

Parsons, M. C., and Richard I. Pervo, ed. *Rethinking the Unity of Luke and Acts*. Minneapolis: Fortress Press, 1993.

Pearson, Birger. "1 Thessalonians 2.13–16: A Deutero-Pauline Interpolation." *Harvard Theological Review* 64 (1971) 79–94.

Pervo, Richard. *Dating Acts: Between the Evangelists and the Apologists*. Santa Rosa: Polebridge, 2006.

Petersen, William. "Textual Evidence of Tatian's Dependence upon Justin's 'ΑΠΟΜΝΗΜΟΝΕΥΜΑΤΑ.'" *New Testament Studies* 36 (1990) 512–34.

———. "Textual Traditions Examined: What the Text of the Apostolic Fathers tells us about the Text of the New Testament in the Second Century." Pp. 29–46 in *The Reception of the New Testament in the Apostolic Fathers*. Ed. Andrew Gregory and Christopher Tuckett. Oxford: Oxford University Press, 2005.

———. "What Text Can New Testament Textual Criticism Ultimately Reach?" Pp. 136–52 in *New Testament Textual Criticism, Exegesis and Church History*. Ed. B. Aland and J. Delobel. Kampen: Kok Pharos, 1994.

Pickering, S. R. "The Dating of the Chester Beatty-Michigan Codex of the Pauline Epistles (P^{46})." Pp. 216–27 in *Early Christianity, Late Antiquity and Beyond*. Vol. 2. Ed. T. W. Hilliard et al. Grand Rapids: Eerdmans, 1998.

Pott, August. *Der Text des Neuen Testaments nach seiner geschichtlichen Entwicklung*. 2d ed. Leipzig: Teubner, 1919.

———. "De textu evangeliorum in saeculo secundo." *Mnemosyne* 48 (1920) 267–309, 338–65.

Pretty, Robert A. *Adamantius, Dialogue on the True Faith in God*. Leuven: Peeters, 1997.

Preuschen, E. "Eine altkirchliche antimarcionistische Schrift unter dem Namen Ephräms." *Zeitschrift für die neutestamentliche Wissenschaft* 12 (1911) 243–69.

Price, R. M. "Apocryphal Apparitions: 1 Corinthians 15:3–11 as a Post-Pauline Interpolation." *Journal of Higher Criticism* 2 (1995) 69–99.

———. "The Evolution of the Pauline Canon." *Hervormde teologiese studies* 53 (1997) 36–67.

Quispel, Gilles. *De bronnen van Tertullianus' Adversus Marcionem*. Leiden: Burgersdijk & Niermans, 1943.

———. "Marcion and the Text of the New Testament." *Vigiliae Christianae* 52 (1998) 349–60.

Räisänen, Heikki. "Marcion and the Origins of Christian Anti-Judaism." *Temenos* 33 (1997) 121–35.

Raschke, Harmann. "Der Römerbrief des Markion nach Epiphanius." *Schriften der Bremer Wissenschaftlichen Gesellschaft. Reihe D: Abhandlungen und Vorträge*. Jahrg. 1. Hft. 2/3 (1926) 128–201.

Rauer, Max et al., ed. *Homélies sur S. Luc : texte latin et fragments grecs*. Paris: Éditions du Cerf, 1998.

Refoulé, François. "Cohérence ou Incohérence de Paul en Romains 9–11?" *Revue Biblique* 98 (1991) 51–79.

———. "Unité de l'Épitre aux Romains et Histoire du Salut." *Revue des sciences philosophiques et theologiques* 71 (1987) 219–42.
Regul, Jürgen. *Die antimarcionitischen Evangelienprologe*. Freiburg: Herder, 1969.
Rensberger, D. "As the Apostle Teaches: The Development of the Use of Paul's Letters in Second Century Christianity." Ph.D. diss., Yale University Press, 1981.
Richards, E. Randolph. "The Codex and the Early Collection of Paul's Letters." *Bulletin for Biblical Research* 8 (1998) 151–66.
Richardson, Peter. "The Thunderbolt in Q and the Wise Man in Corinth." Pp. 91–111 in *From Jesus to Paul: Studies in Honour of Francis Wright Beare*. Ed. Peter Richardson and John C. Hurd. Waterloo: Wilfrid Laurier, 1984.
Rist, Martin. "Pseudepigraphic Refutations of Marcionism." *Journal of Religion* 22 (1942) 39-62.
Ritschl, Albrecht. *Das Evangelium Marcions und das kanonische Evangelium des Lucas*. Tübingen: 1846.
———. "Das Verhältnis der Schriften des Lukas zu der Zeit ihrer Entstehung." *Theologische Jahrbücher* 6 (1847) 293–304.
———. "Über den gegenwärtigen Stand der Kritik der synoptischen Evangelien," *Theologische Jahrbücher* 10 (1851), 480–538.
Robbins, Vernon. "A Socio-Rhetorical Look at the Work of John Knox on Luke-Acts." Pp. 91–105 in *Cadbury, Knox, and Talbert: American Contributions to the Study of Acts*. Ed. Mikeal C. Parsons and Joseph B. Tyson. Atlanta: Scholars Press, 1992.
Roth, Dieter. "Marcion and the Early New Testament Text." Pp. 302–12 in *The Early Text of the New Testament*. Ed. Charles E. Hill and Michaeal J. Kruger. Oxford: Clarendon, 2012.
———. "Marcion's Gospel and Luke: The History of Research in Current Debate." *Journal of Biblical Literature* 127 (2008) 513–27.
———. "Marcion's Gospel: Relevance, Contested Issues, and Reconstruction." *Expository Times* 121 (2010) 287–94.
———. "Matthean Texts and Tertullian's Accusations in *Adversus Marcionem*." *Journal of Theological Studies* 59 (2008) 580–97.
———. "Towards a New Reconstruction of the Text of Marcion's Gospel: History of Research, Sources, Methodology, and the Testimony of Tertullian." Ph.D. diss., University of Edinburgh, 2009 (*non vidi*).
Rougier, P. "La critique biblique dans l'antiquité: Marcion et Fauste de Milève." *Cahiers du Cercle Ernest Renan* 18 (1958) 1–16.
Rueckert, J. *Commentar über den Brief Pauli an die Römer*. 2d ed. Vol. 2. Leipzig: 1839.
Rutherford, J. "St. Paul's Epistle to the Laodiceans." *Expository Times* 19 (1907/8) 311–14.

Ryder, W. H. "The Authorship of Romans XV, XVI." *Journal of Biblical Literature* 17 (1898) 184–98.
Salvoni, Fausto. "Textual Authority for John 7:53–8:11." *Restoration Quarterly* 4 (1960) 11–15.
Sanday, William. *The Gospels in the Second Century*. London: 1876.
Schäfer, K. T. "Die Überlieferung des altlateinische Galaterbriefes." Pp. 1–40 in *Staatliche Akademie zur Braunsberg Personal- und Vorlesungs-Verzeichnis*. 1939.
———. "Marcion und die ältesten Prologe zu den Paulusbriefen." Pp. 135–50 in *Kyriakon. Festschrift Johannes Quasten*. Ed. P. Granfield and J. A. Jungmann. Münster: Aschendorff, 1970.
———. "Marius Victorinus und die marcionitischen Prologe zu den Paulusbriefen." *Revue Bénédictine* 80 (1970) 7–16.
Schäfers, Joseph. *Eine altsyrische antimarkionistische Erklärung von Parabeln des Herrn und zwei andere altsyrische Abhandlungen zu Texten des Evangeliums*. Münster: Aschendorff, 1917.
Scheck, Thomas, trans. *Origen: Homilies on Ezekiel 1–14*. New York: Newman Press, 2010.
———. *Origen, Commentary on the Epistle to the Romans*. Vol. 2. Washington: Catholic University of America Press, 2002.
Schelling, F. W. J. *De Marcione paulinarum epistolarum Emendatore*. Tübingen: 1795.
Schleiermacher, F. *Einleitung ins Neue Testament*. Berlin: 1845.
Schmid, Ulrich. "How Can We Access Second-Century Gospel Texts? The Cases of Marcion and Tatian." Pp. 139–50 in *The New Testament Text in Early Christianity: Proceedings of the Lille colloquium, July 2000*. Ed. Ch.-B. Amphoux and J. K. Elliott. Lausanne: Éditions du Zèbre, 2003.
———. "Marcions Evangelium und die neutestamentlichen Evangelien: Rückfragen zur Geschichte und Kanonisierung der Evangelienüberlieferung." Pp. 67–77 in *Marcion und seine kirchengeschichtliche Wirkung/Marcion and His Impact on Church History*. Ed. G. May and K. Greschat. Berlin: Walter de Gruyter, 2002.
———. *Marcion und sein Apostolos: Rekonstruktion und historische Einordnung der marcionitischen Paulusbriefausgabe*. Berlin: W. de Gruyter, 1995.
Schmidt, J. E. C. *Historisch-Kritische Einleitung ins Neue Testament*. Vol. 1. Giesen: 1804.
———. "Über das ächte Evangelium des Lucas, eine Vermuthung." *Magazin für Religionsphilosophie, Exegese und Kirchengeschichte* 5 (1796) 468–520.
Schneemelcher, W. "Paulus in der griechischen Kirche des zweiten Jahrhunderts." *Zeitschrift für Kirchengeschichte* 75 (1964) 1–20.

Schneider, G. "Die Bitte um das Kommen des Geistes im lukanischen Vaterunser (Lk 11,2 v. 1)." Pp. 344–73 in *Studien zum Text und zur Ethik des Neuen Testaments. Festschrift H. Greeven.* Ed. W. Schrage. Berlin: 1986.

Schnelle, U. "1 Kor 6:14 — Eine nachpaulinische Glosse." *NovTest* 25 (1983) 217–19.

Schoedel, William R. "Ignatius and the Archives." *Harvard Theological Review* 71 (1978) 97–106.

———. *Ignatius of Antioch.* Philadelphia: Fortress Press, 1985.

Schürmann, H. *Das Lukasevangelium.* Vol. 1. Freiburg: Herder, 1969.

Schwegler, Albert. *Das nachapostolische Zeitalter in den Hauptmomenten seiner Entwicklung.* Vol. 1. Tübingen: 1846.

———. Review of *Lehrbuch der historisch-kritischen Einleitung in die kanonischen Bücher des Neuen Testaments* (4th ed.) by W. M. L. de Wette. *Theologische Jahrbücher* 2 (1843) 544–90.

Semler, Johann Salomo. *Neuer Versuch, die gemeinüzige Auslegung und Anwendung des Neun Testament zu befördern.* Halle: 1786.

———. *Vorrede zu Townson's Abhandlung über die vier Evangelien.* Leipzig: 1783.

Shukster, Martin B., and Peter Richardson. "Temple and *Bet Ha-midrash* in the Epistle of Barnabas." Pp. 17–31 in *Anti-Judaism in Early Christianity. Volume 2: Separation and Polemic.* Ed. Stephen G. Wilson. Waterloo: Wilfred Laurier University Press, 1986.

Smith, William Benjamin. "Address and Destination of St. Paul's Epistle to the Romans." *Journal of Biblical Literature* 20 (1901) 1–21.

———. "Unto Romans XV and XVI." *Journal of Biblical Literature* 20 (1901) 129–57.

———. "Unto Romans XV and XVI." *Journal of Biblical Literature* 21 (1902) 117–69.

Souter, Alexander. *The Earliest Latin Commentaries on the Epistles of St. Paul.* Oxford: Clarendon, 1927.

Speigl, J. *Der römische Staat und die Christen: Staat und Kirche von Domitian bis Commodus.* Amsterdam: Hakkert, 1970.

Storr, G. C. *Über den Zwek der evangelischen Geschichte un der Briefe Johannis.* Tübingen: 1786.

Strack, H. L. and P. Billerbeck. *Kommentar zum Neuen Testament aus Talmud und Midrasch.* München: Beck, 1922.

Streeter, B. H. *The Four Gospels: A Study of Origins.* 5th ed. London: Macmillan, 1956.

Stuhlhofer, Franz. *Der Gebrauch der Bibel von Jesus bis Euseb: Eine statistische Untersuchung zur Kanongeschichte.* Wuppertal: Brockhaus, 1988.

Sturdy, J. V. M. *Redrawing the Boundaries: The Date of Early Christian Literature.* London: Equinox, 2007.

Suggs, M. Jack. "'The Word is Near You': Romans 10:6–10 within the Purpose of the Letter." Pp. 289–97 in *Christian History and Interpretation: Studies Presented to John Knox*. W. R. Farmer et al. Cambridge: Cambridge University Press, 1967.
Sundberg Jr., Albert C. "Canon Muratori: A Fourth-Century List." *Harvard Theological Review* 66 (1973) 1–41.
Talbert, Charles H. *Luke and the Gnostics*. Nashville: Abingdon, 1966.
———. "A Non-Pauline Fragment at Romans 3:24–26?" *Journal of Biblical Literature* 85 (1966) 287–95.
Taylor, Vincent. *Behind the Third Gospel*. Oxford: Clarendon Press, 1926.
———. "Narrative of the Crucifixion." *New Testament Studies* 8 (1961/2) 333–34.
Titus, E. L. "Did Paul Write I Corinthians 13?" *Journal of Biblical Research* 27 (1959) 299–302.
Townsend, John. "The Date of Luke-Acts." Pp. 47–62 in Charles H. Talbert, *Luke-Acts: New Perspectives from the Society of Biblical Literature Seminar*. New York: Crossroad, 1984.
Trobisch, D. *Paul's Letter Collection*. Minneapolis: Fortress, 1994.
Trompf, G. W. "On Attitudes toward Women in Paul and Paulinist Literature: 1 Corinthians 11.3–16 and Its Context." *Catholic Biblical Quarterly* 42 (1980) 196–215.
Tsutsui, K. "Das Evangelium Marcions. Ein neuer Versuch der Textrekonstruction." *Annual of the Japanese Biblical Institute* 18 (1992) 67–132.
———. *Die Auseinandersetzung mit dem Markioniten im Adamantios-Dialog*. Berlin: de Gruyter, 2004.
Tyson, Joseph. *Marcion and Luke-Acts: A Defining Struggle*. Columbia, SC: University of South Carolina Press, 2006.
Usener, Hermann. *Das Weihnachfest*. Bonn: 1889, 1911.
van Manen, W. C. "Marcion's brief van Paulus aan de Galatiërs." *Theologisch Tijdschrift* 21 (1887) 382–404, 451–533 (*non vidi*).
Vélissaropoulos, Julie. *Les nauclères grecs. Recherches sur les institutions maritimes en Grèce et dans l'Orient hellénnisé*. Genève-Paris: Droz, 1980.
Vinzent, Markus. "Christ's Resurrection: the Pauline Basis of Marcion's Teaching." *Studia Patristica* 31 (1997) 225–33.
———. "Der Schluß des Lukasevangeliums bei Marcion." Pp. 79–94 in *Marcion and His Impact on Church History*. Ed. Gerhard May and Katharina Greschat. Berlin: Walter de Gruyter, 2002.
Vogels, H. *Evangelium Palatinum*. NTA no. 12.3. Münster: Aschendorff, 1926.
Volckmar, Gustav. *Das Evangelium Marcions, mit Rücksicht auf die Evangelien des Märtyrers Justin, der Klementinen und der apostolischen Väter*. Leipzig: Weidmann, 1852.

---. "Über das Lukas-Evangelium nach seinem Verhältniss zu Marcion und seinem dogmatischen Charakter." *Theologische Jahrbücher* 9 (1850) 110–38, 185–235.

von Campenhausen, Hans. *The Formation of the Christian Bible*. Minneapolis: Augsburg Fortress, 1972.

von Soden, Hans. "Der lateinische Paulustext bei Marcion und Tertullian." Pp. 229–81 in *Festgabe für Adolf Jülicher*. Ed. R. Bultmann. Tübingen: Mohr-Siebeck, 1927.

Walker Jr., William O. "1 Corinthians 2.6–16: A Non-Pauline Interpolation?" *Journal for the Study of the New Testament* 47 (1992) 75–94.

---. "1 Corinthians 11:2–16 and Paul's Views regarding Women." *Journal of Biblical Literature* 94 (1975) 94–110.

---. "Is First Corinthians 13 a Non-Pauline Interpolation?" *Catholic Biblical Quarterly* 60 (1998) 484–99.

---. "'Nazareth': A Clue to Synoptic Relationships?" Pp. 105–18 in *Jesus, the Gospels, and the Church: Essays in Honor of William R. Farmer*. Ed. E. P. Sanders. Macon: Mercer University Press, 1987.

---. "Romans 1.18–2.29: A Non-Pauline Interpolation?" *New Testament Studies* 45 (1999) 533–52.

---. "The Vocabulary of 1 Corinthians 11:3–16: Pauline or Non-Pauline?" *Journal for the Study of the New Testament* 35 (1989) 75–88.

Walters, Patricia. *The Assumed Authorial Unity of Luke and Acts: A Reassessment of the Evidence*. Cambridge: Cambridge University Press, 2009.

Wayment, Thomas A. "A New Transcription of P. Oxy 2383 (P[69])." *Novum Testamentum* 50 (2008) 351–57.

Welborn, L. L. "On the Date of First Clement." *Biblical Research* 29 (1984) 35–54.

Werner, Johannes. *Der Paulinismus des Irenaeus*. Leipzig: J. C. Hinrichs, 1889.

West Jr., H. Philip. "A Primitive Version of Luke in the Composition of Matthew." *New Testament Studies* 14 (1967) 75–95.

Westcott, B. F. *A General Survey of the History of the Canon of the New Testament*. 6th ed. Cambridge: MacMillan, 1889 [Grand Rapids: Eerdmans, 1980].

Westcott, B. F. and F. J. A. Hort, *The New Testament in the Original Greek, vol. 2. Introduction and Appendix*. 2d ed. Cambridge: Cambridge University Press, 1896.

Williams, C. S. C. "Eznik's Résumé of Marcionite Doctrine." *Journal of Theological Studies* 45 (1944) 65–73.

Williams, David Salter. "On Tertullian's Text of Luke." *Second Century* 8 (1991) 193–99.

_____. "Reconsidering Marcion's Gospel." *Journal of Biblical Literature* 108 (1989), 477–96.
Williams, Frank. *The Panarion of Epiphanius of Salamis, Book I (Sects 1–46)*. Leiden: Brill, 1987.
Wilshire, Leland Edward. "Was Canonical Luke Written in the Second Century?—A Continuing Discussion." *New Testament Studies* 20 (1974) 246–53.
Wilson, Robert Smith. *Marcion: A Study of a Second-Century Heretic*. London: Clarke, 1933.
Zahn, Theodor. "Das Neue Testament Theodors von Mopsuestia und der ursprüngliche Kanon der Syrer." *Neue kirkliche Zeitschrift* 11 (1900) 788–806.
_____. "Die Dialoge des 'Adamantius' mit den Gnostikern." *Zeitschrift f. Kirchengeschichte* 9 (1888) 193–239.
_____. *Geschichte des neutestamentlichen Kanons*. 2 vols. Erlangen: 1888–92.
Zuntz, G. *The Text of the Epistles: A Disquisition upon the Corpus Paulinum*. London: British Academy, 1953.

Index

[to substantive comments only, not mere citation]

Acts of Archelaus 41, 133, 171, 288, 300
addition to Marcion's text 136, 184
Amphoux, C.-B. 158–59, 330 n67
Annand, R. 128, 327–28 n49, 332 n8
Antitheses 29, 35–36, 39–41, 44–45,
  68–69, 71, 133, 139, 152, 167, 169,
  177, 276, 303, 329 n62, 334 n25, 336
  n38, 338 n54, 339 n64, 339–40 n65,
  346 n13
Aphraates 138–39

Baarda, T. 261
Bacon, B. W. 325–26 n33
Bakhuyzen, W. H. S. 288, 299, 338 n56
Balas, D. 17, 20
Barnabas, Letter of 18–19, 66, 328–29
  n57
Barnes, T. D. 326 n36, 328 n51
Barnikol, E. 263, 303, 318, 322 n11, 323
  n15, 333 n14
Barrabas 125, 190–91
Barth, M. 224, 361
Barton, J. 27, 60–61, 333 n18, 345 n123
Baur, F. C. 78–79, 305, 348 n33
Bellinzoni, A. J. 80, 140
Betz, H. D. 219, 359–60 n48
Birdsall, J. N. 284–85
Blackman, E. C. 135, 284, 325 n32, 330
  n70
Blass, F. 152
Bovon, F. 341, 351–52 n67
Brakke, D. 61
Bruce, F. F. 25, 328 n53, 351 n65
Bucher, V. F. 311
Buchheit, V. 40
Bultmann, R. 297, 300
Bundy, D. 180
Burkitt, F. C. 133, 142–43, 169

Cadbury, H. J. 82, 184, 350 n53, n54,
  353–54 n81

Campenhausen, H. von 25, 26, 326 n36,
  328 n54, 331 n89, 332 n7, 334 n21,
  n24, 342 n92
canon, 6–7, 23, 25–9, 31, 59–62, 89–90,
  203, 213, 227, 327–28 n49, 328 n54,
  331 n90, 332 n7, n11, 333 n14, n18,
  334 n21, n22, n24, 345 n123
  defined 4, 26
Carmen adversus Marcionitis 324 n28
Carruth, S. and A. Garsky 158
Casey, R. P. 192
Catalogus Sinaiticus 207, 260, 358 n22
Celsus 22, 44, 177, 186, 341–42 n83
Chronicle of Edessa 322–23 n13
Clabeaux, J. J. 37–38, 46, 51, 57, 204–6,
  208, 261–64, 270–71, 273, 275, 279–
  80, 282, 284–86, 306, 308, 311–14, 329
  n64, 337 n45, n49, n50, 338–39 n56,
  356 n9, 357 n18, n19
Clement, 1st 18, 66, 139, 140, 161, 174,
  203–4, 327 n46, n48, 327–28 n49, 334
  n22, 356 n5, n13, 360 n51
Clement of Alexandria 5, 8, 12, 31, 67,
  142, 152–53, 157, 163, 323 n14, n15
Clementine *Homilies* and *Recognitions*
  23, 45, 155, 163, 175–76, 331 n87,
  342 n85
Clivaz, C. 341 n73
Colossians Hymn 315–16
Conybeare, F. C. 128
Cope, L. 280–81
Corssen, P. 305, 309, 341 n75, 358 n24
Cosgrove, C. H. 66, 327 n48
Couchoud, P.-L. 79, 84, 321 n4, 323 n15,
  351 n65, n66, 351–52 n67

Dahl, N. A. 272, 294–95, 309–10, 319,
  329 n64, 341 n75, n76, n77, n81, 358
  n24, n26
De Bruyne, D. 42, 222, 304, 309, 325–26
  n33, 333 n14, 358 n24

383

Delobel, J. 152, 157
Dialogue of the Savior 141
Diatessaron 44–47, 62, 134, 155, 157, 168, 170, 172, 175, 177–78, 180, 182, 191–95, 198, 331 n90
Didache 139
Dinkler, E. 263
Diognetus, Letter to 19, 329 n56, n62
Dodd, C. H. 222
Drijvers, H. 150, 268
Dupont, J. 305

Ebionites, Gospel of 146
Eckart, K.-G. 306–7
Egan, G. 40, 340 n69
Ehrman, B. 184, 185, 198–99, 326 n36
Ellis, E. E. 223
ending of Evangelion 198–200
Ephesians as Laodiceans 4, 37, 224, 309
Ephrem Syrus 31, 44, 47, 67, 128, 151, 192, 197–98, 207, 260, 269, 334 n26
Epiphanius 36–38, 51, 52, 57, 67, 69, 87, 89–90, *et passim*
Eusebius 330 n76, n77, 330–31 n78, 331 n80, n81
Evans, C. F. 25, 327–28 n49
Evans, E. 22
Eznik of Kolb 44–45, 192, 197–98, 203, 277, 286, 294

Farkasfalvy, D. 335 n29
Farmer, W. 333 n14, 354 n87
Faustus of Milevis 128–29, 340 n70
Fayum Fragment 187
Fee, G. D. 284
Fitzmyer, J. 188
Frede, H. J. 358 n23, n24
Freudenberger, R. 158
Friedrich, G. 307
Friedrichsen, T. A. 355 n89

Gamble, H. Y. 27, 60, 205–6, 213-215, 221, 305, 334 n20, 358 n26, 360 n55, n56
Gieseler, J. C. L. 347 n21
Grant, F. C. 350–51 n60
Grant, R. M. 84, 327–28 n49
Green, H. B. 174
Gregory, A. 66, 79, 335 n31, n32, n33, 348 n39
Gundry, R. H. 149

Hagen, W. H. 300
Hahneman, G. M. 60, 332 n91

harmonization 58, 86, 88–90, 93, 130, 134–35, 138–39, 141, 151, 156–57, 159–60, 162–64, 166, 168–69, 172, 182, 184, 188–89, 192–94, 215, 280–81, 308, 336 n40, 340 n69, 348 n39, 352 n71, n73, n74, 353 n75, n77, n78, 355 n89
Harnack, A. von 27, 31–32, 39–41, 47–49, 52, 57, 65, 79–83, 86, 134–43, 147–66, 169–82, 189–91, 198, 204, 208, 223, 228, 261–77, 280–85, 288, 293–303, 307, 309–13, 316–18, 322 n9, 323 n14, 324 n20, 325 n29, n32, 325–26 n33, 326 n35, 331 n89, n90, 332–33 n11, 334 n24, 335 n34, 337 n46, 338 n56, 339 n59, 340 n67, 341 n75, 342 n92, 346 n14, 352 n71, 357 n21, 358 n24
Harris, J. R. 269, 350 n56, 358 n23
Harrison, P. N. 296, 326 n35, n36
Heard, R. G. 325–26 n33
Hegesippus 327 n48
Heracleon 164
Hermas 327 n46, n48
Higgins, A. J. B. 337 n46
Hilgenfeld, A. 78–79, 168, 183, 208, 347–48 n29
Hippolytus 43, 66, 321–22 n1, 322–23 n13, 345 n6
Hoffmann, R. J. 323 n15, 326 n35, 330 n72, 356 n7

Ignatius of Antioch 19, 197, 326 n36, 328 n51, n54, 356 n5
interpolations 88, 130, 214, 217, 219–20, 222–23, 226, 228, 263, 274, 280, 282–86, 289, 296–303, 306–7, 310, 316, 318
Irenaeus 26, 43, 62, 67, 69, 203, 303, 322–23 n13, 323 n14, 325 n32, 330 n75, 333 n13, n18

Jackson, H. 136, 160
Jerome 44, 261, 264–65, 267, 269, 270, 302, 323–24 n16, 325 n31, 330 n74
Jewett, R. 361 n67
John, Gospel of 70, 74, 77, 84, 128, 132, 144, 179, 184–98, 350–51 n60, 351–52 n67
John the Baptist/Washer 69, 72, 76, 85, 91, 94–5, 100, 103–4, 106, 109, 116, 121, 128–9, 134, 142–43, 167, 172, 354 n83, 355 n93

Joly, R. 328 n51
Josephus 168, 178–79, 183, 353–54 n81
Judas Iscariot 123–24, 137, 184, 188
Justin Martyr 13, 18, 22, 26, 31, 66–67, 199, 322–23 n13, n15, 327 n48, 330 n75, 331 n84

Kallas, J. 303
Käsemann, E. 302
Keck, L. E. 298
Kinzig, W. 28
Klijn, A. F. J. 155
Klinghardt, M. 79, 84, 351–52 n67
Knox, J. 21, 79, 81–82, 85–86, 90–91, 143, 147, 150, 174, 221–22, 321 n7, 326 n35, 330 n70, 334 n22, n24, 348 n35, 349 n43, 349–50 n48, 350 n52, n53, 352 n68, n74, 353–54 n81
Koester, H. 59, 65
Köstlin, K. R. 79

LaCapra, D. 58
Lagrange, M.-J. 304, 350 n56
Lake, K. 221, 305
Lampe, P. 327 n41, n46, n47
Leaney, R. 158
Lefort, L. 175
Lightfoot, J. B. 221, 305
Loisy, A. 333 n14, 351 n65, n66
Lüdemann, G. 324 n21, n26, 325 n32, 328 n50
Lührmann, D. 355 n94
Luke, priority vis-à-vis Evangelion 78–92, 336 n38, 343 n108, 351 n65, n66, 351–52 n67, 352 n73, n74, 353 n75, n78, 353–54 n81, 354 n84, n85

MacDonald, D. R. 286
Magne, J. 158, 282
Manen, W. C. van 208, 359 n44
Manson, T. W. 296
Marcion
　life 12
　profession 12, 16–18
　theology 14, 19, 83, 212
　Christology 83–84, 295
　conflict with Roman Christians 12–13, 21–22
　compiler of first NT 4, 6–7, 23, 25, 27
　role as redactor 9, 28–30, 32, 58, 67–69, 77–92, 143, 157, 204–6, 211–14, 226, 269, 278, 296, 312, 316, 336 n37, 347 n27, 347–48 n29, 348 n39, 352 n68, 353 n77, n78, 354 n83, n84, n86
　Paulinism of 6, 7, 21, 28, 203, 228, 334 n21
　relation to Judaism 6, 13, 17, 18, 20–21, 59–60, 185, 213, 226, 306, 327 n42
　view of OT 6, 20, 21, 23, 27, 29, 83, 143, 211–12, 278, 280, 335 n30
Marius Victorinus 309
Mark, Longer Ending of 45–46, 195, 199–200
Matson, M. A. 188
May, G. 11, 20, 22–23, 325 n29, 331 n90
McDonald, L. M. 25
McGiffert, A. C. 330 n70
McLachlan, H. 184
Meinhold, P. 326 n35
Menander 286
Metzger, B. 4, 25–26, 135, 162, 265, 321 n1, 332 n11
Minear, P. S. 351 n65
Minor Agreements 84, 88–89, 93, 96, 135, 137, 143, 147, 149, 151, 189, 354 n87, 354–55 n88, 355 n89, n92
Molitor, J. 357 n17
Moll, S. 11, 12, 321–22 n1, 323 n15, 324 n28, 325 n29, 336 n37
Moule, C. F. D. 332 n9
Mühlenberg, E. 52, 342 n91
Muratonian Canon 23, 327 n46, 332 n91, 333 n18, 345 n8
Murphy-O'Connor, J. 284

Nadim, Ibn al- 322–23 n13
Nazarenes, Gospel of 155
Nielsen, C. 20, 329 n56
Nock, A. D. 140

omissions from Marcion's text 37, 49, 52, 54–55, 83–84, 87–88, 128–31, 135, 137, 145–46, 155, 161–63, 166, 168, 170, 172, 174, 177–88, 191–92, 204, 208, 214, 219–20, 222, 224–26, 262–66, 268–69, 271, 279–80, 282, 284–85, 295–96, 298, 301–4, 312, 314–16, 337, 342 n91, 344 n115, 354 n85, 358 n23
orality 58–59, 65–66
order of Marcion's text 43, 129, 134, 136, 143, 172, 207, 260, 351 n66
Origen 43–44, 157, 181, 222, 261, 267,

295, 296, 297–99, 301–2, 304–5, 310, 359 n39

P^{69} (P. Oxy 2383) 41–42, 50, 53, 187–89, 340 n71, n72, 341 n73, 350 n52
Papyrus Egerton 2 180
POxy 1224 134, 152
Papias 26, 154, 327–28 n49, 332 n8
Parker, D. C. 158, 184
Paul
  authorship of letters 4, 7, 213–14, 223–25, 227, 334 n26
  multiple versions of letters 213–18, 293, 305, 359 n40, n44, 360 n54, n55
  neglect in 2nd c. 18, 203–4, 327 n48, 327–28 n49, 333 n13, 334 n22, 356 n2
Pearson B. 306
Pervo, R. 329–30 n66, 349 n43
Peter, Gospel of 191–93
Petersen, W. 80, 197
Philastrius of Brescia 13–14, 321–22 n1, 322 n5, 325–26 n33
Pliny (the Younger) 15–16
Polycarp 14, 140, 159, 322–23 n13, 325 n30, n31, n32, 325–26 n33, 326 n35, n36, 333 n14
Pontius Pilate 75–76, 99, 125–26, 128, 168, 190–91, 193, 339
Price, R. M. 285
Prologues (Marcionite) 42–43, 207, 260, 294–95, 309–10, 315, 319, 329 n64, 334 n26, 341 n75, 76, 77, 81, 356–57 n13, 358 n24, n26
Protevangelium of James 192
Proto-Luke 78, 93–94, 96, 351 n65, 355 n90, n92
Pseudo-Ephrem A 34, 40–41, 200, 339 n62, n64, 339–40 n65, 340 n66, n67, n69

Q 92–96, 351–52 n67, 355 n93, n94, n95
Quispel, G. 331 n90, 337 n46

Räisänen, H. 327 n42
Raschke, H. 208
reconstruction
  principles 33, 46–55
  sources 34–46
Refoulé, F. 222, 301
Regul, J. 325 n32, n33
Richards, E. R. 359 n43

Richardson, P. 355 n92
Rist, M. 330 n72
Ritschl, A. 78–79
Robbins, V. 335 n31, 349 n45
Roth, D. 336 n40, 342 n100, 344 n109, 346 n17, 347–48 n29, 348–49 n39
Rougier, P. 26
Rueckert, J. 305
Ryder, W. H. 305, 360 n58

Salvoni, F. 184
Sanday, W. 81–82, 349–50 n48
Satan 74, 110, 114, 184, 245, 252, 275–76, 308
Schäfer, K. T. 208, 309–10
Schäfers, J. 180
Scheck, T. 301–2, 304
Schmid, U. 39, 48–50, 52–53, 57, 135, 159, 205, 208, 261–64, 266–69, 271, 273, 277, 279, 282, 287, 293, 296, 301, 303, 307, 311–14, 316–17, 329 n64, n65, 336–37 n44, 337 n45, n46, 339 n60, 342 n98, 344 n109, n115, 358–59 n36
Schmidt, J. E. C. 347 n25
Schneider, G. 158
Schnelle, U. 276
Schoedel, W. R. 19, 328 n53, 328–29 n55
Schürmann, H. 129
Schwegler, A. 78
Schwegler hypothesis 79, 81, 84–86, 351 n66, 351–52 n67, 354 n84
Semler, J. S. 78
Semler hypothesis 79, 81, 86–92, 336 n37, 352 n73, 353 n78
Shepherd of Hermas 164
Shukster, M. B. and P. Richardson 321 n6
Smith, W. B. 221, 360 n58
Soden, H. von 337 n46, 350 n56
Sophia of Jesus Christ 200
Streeter, B. H. 5, 355 n90
Stulhofer, F. 333 n18
stylistic analysis 81–82, 349–50 n48, 351 n65
Suggs, M. J. 361 n61
Sundberg, A. C. 60, 332 n91

Talbert, C. H. 298
Taylor, V. 191, 355 n90
Tertullian 34–36, 51, 52, 57, 67–69, 87, 89–90, *et passim*

Theophilus of Antioch 156
Thomas, Gospel of 45–46, 96, 134, 135, 138, 141, 143, 146, 153, 161, 162, 164 167, 169, 355 n95, 355–56 n96, 356 n97
Thomas the Contender 138
Titus, E. L. 283
Townsend, J. 79, 84, 348 n35, 350 n58
Trobisch, D. 359 n40
Trompf, G. W. 281
Tsutsui, K. 138, 141–57, 160–62, 165–78, 181, 185–86, 190–91
Tyson, J. 51, 79, 90–91, 194, 335 n31, 354 n84

Usener, H. 348 n37

Vinzent, M. 198, 356 n1
Vogels, H. 136
Volckmar, G. 78–79, 86, 146, 163, 168, 174, 176, 183, 336 n40, 347 n27, 347–48 n29

Walker, W. O. 130, 274, 281, 283, 296
Werner, J. 333 n13
Westcott and Hort, "Western non-interpolation" 135, 164, 189, 193–98
Williams, D. S. 42, 48–52, 147, 151, 155, 163, 165, 176, 186, 335 n30, 336 n40, 342 n96, n97, 342–43 n101, 343 n105, 344 n110, 349 n43, 350 n58, 353 n76, n78
Williams, F. 283
Wilshire, L. E. 352 n71, n72
Wilson, R. S. 158, 191

Zahn, T. 57, 79–80, 208, 337–38 n52, 339 n59, 350 n56, 358 n23
Zuntz, G. 273, 279–80, 282–84, 314, 357 n17, n19

About the Author

Jason BeDuhn is Professor of the Comparative Study of Religions at Northern Arizona University, a Guggenheim and National Humanities Center Fellow, and author of *The Manichaean Body* (2000, winner of the American Academy of Religion Best First Book Award), *Truth in Translation* (2003), *Augustine's Manichaean Dilemma* (vol. 1 2010, vol. 2 2013), and *The First New Testament* (2013).

www.ingramcontent.com/pod-product-compliance
Lightning Source LLC
Chambersburg PA
CBHW051047200426
43507CB00004B/103